JOHN WILLIS'

THEATRE WORLD

1979–1980 SEASON

VOLUME 36

CROWN PUBLISHERS, INC.
ONE PARK AVENUE
NEW YORK, N.Y. 10016

with Charlton Heston in "The Tumbler" (1960); with George Grizzard in "School for Scandal" (1962); with Ellis Rabb, Nancy Marchand, Clayton Corzatte in "Man and Superman" (1964); with George Grizzard in "The Tavern" (1964); Top: with Lee Montague in "The Climate of Eden" (1952); with Aubrey Morris, Paul Rogers in "Troilus and Cressida" (1956); "The Disenchanted" (1958); with Maximilian Schell in "Interlock" (1958)

with Donald Moffat in "War and Peace" (1967); with Clayton Corzatte in "You Can't Take It With You" (1967); with Robert Shaw, Mary Ure in "Old Times" (1971); "The Merchant of Venice" (1973); Above: "Judith" (1965); with Robert Preston in "The Lion in Winter" (1966); with Helen Hayes, Ellis Rabb in "School for Scandal" (1966)

with James Farentino
in "A Streetcar Named
Desire" (1973)

"The Royal Family"
(1975)

"The Three Sisters"
(1977)

"The Seagull"
(1980)

T O
R O S E M A R Y   H A R R I S

*. . . .a truly consummate actress whose beauty and talent leave
indelible memories of her brilliant performances*

Photos by Friedman-Abeles, Bob Goldby, Henry Grossman, Martha Swope, Vandamm, Van Williams

Martha Swope Pho

MANDY PATINKIN and PATTI LuPONE
in "Evita"
1980 winner of Drama Critics Circle Award for Best Musical, and 7 "Tonys" (page 17)

CONTENTS

EDITOR: JOHN WILLIS

Assistant Editor: Stanley Reeves

Staff: Curtis Campagna, Maltier Hagan, William Schelble

Staff Photographers: Joseph Abeles, Bert Andrews, J. M. Viade, Van Williams

Once again the theatre enjoyed an economically successful season. According to *Variety,* boxoffice receipts topped all available records, as did playing weeks on Broadway. Touring companies topped Broadway grosses as well as touring records of previous years. Ticket prices rose again ($30 top) as did production and operating costs. There was less activity than usual during the early part of the season, but by its closing there had been more productions than last year: 38 plays, 17 musicals, 2 revues, 4 special attractions, 12 revivals, and 11 continuing productions from other seasons.

Creatively, it was a poor season, except for performances, sets, and costumes. Most of the best productions were revivals, including the musicals "Peter Pan" starring Sandy Duncan in a record-breaking "flight," "Oklahoma!" with Mary Wickes, Christine Andreas, Laurence Guittard, Harry Groener, and Martin Vidnovic winning applause, "West Side Story" with Jossie de Guzman, Hector Jaime Mercado, and Debbie Allen (Drama Desk Award winner), and "The Most Happy Fella" with its memorable score sung by Giorgio Tozzi, Sharon Daniels, and Richard Muenz. The outstanding revival of a play was the 1939–40 failure "Morning's at Seven." In its perfect setting it had the most beautiful ensemble work that Broadway has seen in several years. It was rewarded with 3 "Tonys": for Outstanding Revival, Direction, and Featured Actor (David Rounds), and 4 Drama Desk Awards. Other interesting revivals were "Watch on the Rhine," "Major Barbara," and Al Pacino's "Richard III" that received little critical approval.

New plays worth noting are "Loose Ends," "On Golden Pond," "Romantic Comedy" with Anthony Perkins baring all to Mia Farrow, "Hide and Seek" with Elizabeth Ashley, "Past Tense," NEC's transplanted "Home," "Nuts" with Anne Twomey in a critically praised Broadway debut, "Billy Bishop Goes to War," and "Bent" with impressive performances by Richard Gere and David Dukes. Enjoyable musicals were "1940's Radio Hour" that deserved a longer run, "Black Broadway," and "Sugar Babies" with those delightfully indefatigable performers Ann Miller and Mickey Rooney—the latter in his long-delayed Broadway debut.

Among the award-winning productions this season are "Talley's Folly," transferred from Circle Repertory Theatre, and recipient of the Pulitzer Prize as well as NY Drama Critics Circle citation for Best Play. It received a well-deserved "Tony" for Outstanding Scenic Design—a tie with the musical "Barnum." The latter was awarded other "Tonys" for outstanding Actor in a Musical (Jim Dale), and Costume Design. It received the Outer Critics Circle Award for Best Musical. The most honored musical was "Evita." In addition to being chosen Best Musical by NY Drama Critics Circle, it was voted 7 "Tonys": Outstanding Musical, Direction, Actress (Patti LuPone), Featured Actor (Mandy Patinkin), Book, Score, and Lighting. It was also the recipient of 6 Drama Desk Awards. The delightful "A Day in Hollywood/A Night in the Ukraine" was awarded "Tonys" for Choreography and Outstanding Featured Actress in a Musical (Priscilla Lopez). The compelling "Children of a Lesser God" was voted "Tonys" for Outstanding Play, Actor (John Rubinstein), Actress (Phyllis Frelich), 2 Drama Desk Awards, and Outer Critics Circle Award for Most Distinguished Production. The "Tony" for Outstanding Featured Actress in a Play went to Dinah Manoff for her Broadway debut in "I Ought to Be in Pictures." It should be noted that there was an unusual number of newcomers among the "Tony" nominations. The Special Theatre '80 Awards were presented to Hobe Morrison (*Variety*'s Theatre Editor), Actors Theatre of Louisville, Ky., Goodspeed Opera House (East Haddam, Ct.), and Richard Fitzgerald of Sound Associates, not, it is hoped, for the increased reliance on "mikes." Helen Hayes received the Lawrence Langner Award. NY Drama Critics Circle cited the English import "Betrayal" as the Best Foreign Play. Gerald Hiken was honored with Best Actor Award by Outer Critics Circle.

In addition to those already mentioned, the roster of outstanding performers on Broadway includes Maureen Anderman, Jane Alexander, Charles Brown, Pamela Burrell, John Cullum, Glenn Close, Blythe Danner, Leslie Denniston, Patricia Elliott, Ed Flanders, David Garrison, Bob Gunton, Janet Gaynor, Judd

Hirsch, Gregory Hines, George Hearn, Earle Hyman, Stephen James, Ann Jillian, Susan Kellermann, Dorothy Loudon, Joseph Maher, James Naughton, Geraldine Page, Eric Peterson, Joan Plowright, Roy Scheider, Maggie Smith, Marianne Tatum, Crissy Wilzak, and Irene Worth.

Off Broadway did not provide a very impressive season. However, it presented several noteworthy productions, including the plays "Goodnight, Gracie," "The Price," "Father's Day," "Ladyhouse Blues," "Modigliani," "Class Enemy," "Table Settings," Tom Taylor's excellent "Woody Guthrie," "Come Back to the 5 & Dime, Jimmy Dean," "A Coupla White Chicks Sitting Around Talking" with entertaining performances by Eileen Brennan and Susan Sarandon, and Pat Carroll's superb one-woman show "Gertrude Stein." Enjoyable musicals were "Scrambled Feet," "King of Schnorrers," "Tintypes," and "One Mo' Time" with engaging performances by Vernel Bagneris, Topsy Chapman, Thais Clark, and Sylvia Williams. Circle Repertory Theatre's exceptional season included "Innocent Thoughts, Harmless Intentions," "The Woolgatherer," and, in repertory, "Hamlet" with William Hurt, and "Mary Stuart." Equity Library Theatre's always worthwhile season had its "Canterbury Tales" transferred to Broadway's reclaimed Rialto Theatre, but without its hoped-for success. Manhattan Theatre Club had interesting productions of "Losing Time" with Jane Alexander and Shirley Knight, and the highly praised "Mass Appeal" with Milo O'Shea and Eric Roberts. "Chinchilla" was the Phoenix Theatre's most admired production. The hive of activity in the Public Theater produced exemplary viewings of "Happy Days" with Irene Worth, "The Art of Dining," "Sorrows of Stephen," and a new version of "Mother Courage" with Gloria Foster. Roundabout Theatre had successful revivals of "A Month in the Country," "The Dark at the Top of the Stairs," and "Fallen Angels." Brooklyn Academy of Music presented a new and talented repertory company, giving hopes for a bright future.

Other Off-Broadway performers deserving recognition are Catherine Burns, Powers Boothe, Evalyn Baron, Joseph Buloff, Pamela Blair, Richard Backus, Jacqueline Brookes, Maxwell Caulfield, Shami Chaikin, Lindsay Crouse, Michael Cristofer, John Driver, Craig Dudley, Alix Elias, Valerie French, Fannie Flagg, Boyd Gaines, Tammy Grimes, June Gable, Fred Gwynne, John Heard, Jonathan Hogan, Laurie Kenneth, Perry King, Piper Laurie, Joe Morton, Larry Marshall, Lonny Price, Estelle Parsons, Bo Rucker, Jess Richards, Danton Stone, Janie Sell, Isao Sato, John Shea, Don Scardino, Kristoffer Tabori, Fritz Weaver, Dianne Wiest, Jane White, Peter Weller, and Jerry Zaks.

Notations during the season worth recording: Disagreements between Actors Equity Association and Off-Off-Broadway theatres continued. After AEA set new rules, 54 OOB theatres broke with AEA on June 18, 1979, and began working under their own payment plan. AEA also engaged in a struggle with playwrights over a new Off-Broadway code.... For the first time, theatres were permitted to collect money for other than the Actors Fund in order to help Cambodian refugees.... This marked the initial season of the British-American Repertory Co. in a limited engagement of Tom Stoppard's "Dogg's Hamlet, Cahoot's Macbeth."... Pulitzer Prize-winner Walter Kerr succeeded Richard Eder as full-time critic on the *New York Times* and was warmly welcomed back.... The Rialto Theatre, built in 1935 as a film house on the site of Hammerstein's Victoria Theatre, was converted and reopened as a legitimate house on February 12, 1980.... The 17 Schubert theatres were in the process of renovation and redecoration.... "Grease," with 3388 performances, broke the long-run record of "Fiddler on the Roof," but was forced to close April 13, 1980, a victim of the transit strike. For 11 days, neither buses nor subways were in operation, and there was a dire effect on the boxoffice.... On January 5, 1980, for the fourth time in history, Broadway's lights were dimmed for one minute in tribute to the genius of Richard Rodgers who composed 39 musicals for theatergoers. His death leaves a void, but his beautiful melodies will be a constant reminder of his great talent.... Once again, Alexander H. Cohen, with his accustomed expertise, produced the exemplary "Tony" Awards TV Special.

Patti LuPone
in "Evita"

Trish Hawkins,
Judd Hirsch in
"Talley's Folly"

BROADWAY CALENDAR
June 1, 1979, through May 31, 1980

Ann Miller, Mickey Rooney
in "Sugar Babies"
Left: Phyllis Frelich, John
Rubinstein in "Children of
a Lesser God"

Jim Dale
in "Barnum"

Mia Farrow, Anthony Perkins
in "Romantic Comedy"

7

RADIO CITY MUSIC HALL

Opened Friday, June 1, 1979.*
Radio City Music Hall Entertainment Center presents:

A NEW YORK SUMMER

Producer-Director, Robert F. Jani; Creative Director, Tom Bahler; Production Executive, John Jay Moore, Executive Musical Director, Donald Pippin; Art Director, John William Keck; Costumes, Frank Spencer; Lighting, Billy B. Walker; Dialogue and Narration, Stanley Hart; Choreography and Staging, Dru Davis, Violet Holmes, Louis Johnson, Linda Lemac, Howard Parker; Production Coordinators, Charles Gillette, Anthony Salerno; Organists, Lance Luce, Chad Weirick

CAST

Karen Anders, Tim Cassidy, Anthony Falco, John Hallow, John J. Martin, Christina Saffran

ROCKETTS: Pauline Achillas, Carol Beatty, Catherine Beatty, Dottie Belle, Susan Boron, Katie Braff, Deniene Bruck, Barbara Ann Cittadino, Eileen Collins, Susanne Doris, Joyce Dwyer, Jody Erickson, Jacqueline Fancy, Deniene Fenn, Phyllis Frew, Prudence Gray, Carol Harbich, Ginny Hounsell, Cynthia Hughes, Holly Jones, Pan Kelleher, Dee Dee Knapp, Judy Little, Leslie Gryszko-McCarthy, Geraldine McDonough, Barbara Moore, Ann Murphy, Joan Peer, Cindy Peiffer, Sheila Phillips, Lorraine Salerno, Jereme Sheehan, Terry Spano, Pam Stacey, June Taylor, Susan Theobald, Carol Toman, Rose Ann Woolsey, Phyllis Wujko

THE APPLES: Steve (Ace) Williams, Stanley Dalton, Rodney Green, Carl Hardy, Mercie J. Hinton, Jr., Ivson (Scooter) Polk

THE NEW YORKERS: Steve Baumann, Nancy Byne, Lou Ann Csaszar, Scott Dainton, Marcia-Anne Dobres, Christine Doelger, Cecily Douglas, Jeffrey Dreisbach, Barry Eric, Sharon Ferrol, Neal Gold, Lisa Grant, Bill Hedge, Deirdre Kane, Dirk Lombard, Michelle Marshall, Tony Moore, Alan Nicholson, Andy Parker, Lorraine Person, Teresa Puente, Joel Rosina, Tina Sherman, Robin Stone, Chris Wheeler, Curtis Worthy

PRODUCTION DANCERS: Phillip Bond, John Cashman, Jerry James, Mic Kozyra, Tony Lillo, James Parker, Malcolm Perry, Ken Prescott, Robert Raimondo, David Roman, Randy Skinner, J. Thomas Smith

PROGRAM

Overture, New York New York, Manhattan Street Scene, A Visit to the United Nations, Central Park in Summertime/in Wintertime, Folk Art of New York, Streets of Harlem, Coney Island, New York at Night, Broadway 1979, Our Salute to Mr. Broadway, (George M. Cohan), Disco, Street Scene at Night, Shopping on the Avenue, A Visit to St. Patrick's Cathedral, On Our Way through Rockefeller Center, Radio City Music Hall Movie Memories, The Music and Glamour of the Nation's Showplace, 50 years of America's Rockettes, Where in the World but in America.

Press: Gifford/Wallace
Stage Managers: Jeff Hamlin, George Cort, Peter I. Elencove, Linda Harris, Frank Hawkins, Neil Jay Miller

* Closed Sept. 26, 1979 after 203 performances.

Rockettes (also top right)

John J. Martin, Karen Anders

CIRCLE IN THE SQUARE
Opened Thursday, June 7, 1979.*
Circle in the Square (Theodore Mann, Artistic Director; Paul
Libin, Managing Director) presents:

LOOSE ENDS

By Michael Weller; Director, Alan Schneider; Scenery, Zack Brown;
Costumes, Kristina Watson; Lighting, David F. Segal; Hairstyles,
Michael Wasula; Wardrobe, Virginia Merkel; Production Assistant,
Rand Mitchell

CAST

Paul	Kevin Kline
Susan	Roxanne Hart†1
Janice	Patricia Richardson
Balinese Fisherman	Ernest Abuba
Doug	Jay O. Sanders
Maraya	Celia Weston
Ben	Steve Vinovich†2
Selina	Jodi Long
Russell	Michael Kell
Lawrence	Michael Lipton
Phil	Jeff Brooks

A drama in 2 acts and 8 scenes. The action takes place from 1970
to 1979 in Bali, Boston, New York and New Hampshire.

Company Manager: William Conn
Press: Merle Debuskey, Tom Trenkle, Leo Stern
Stage Managers: Randall Brooks, James Bernardi

* Closed Jan. 27, 1980 after 270 performances and 19 previews.
† Succeeded by: 1. Christine Lahti, 2. David Rasche

Cecilia Vettraino Photos

**Right: Roxanne Hart, Kevin Kline, Jay O. Sanders,
Celia Weston Top: Roxanne Hart, Kevin Kline**

Roxanne Hart, Kevin Kline

WINTER GARDEN THEATRE
Opened Tuesday, June 12, 1979.*
Lee Guber and Shelly Gross present:

BRUCE FORSYTH ON BROADWAY!

A one-man show presented by Music Fair Concerts; Production Supervisor, Peter Mavoides; Musical Director, Don Hunt; Lighting, Richard Nelson; Assistant to Producers, Connie Simmons; Drummer, Freddie Adamson; Production Assistants, Victor Irving, Joanna Gerngross

General Manager: Stephen H. Arnold
Press: Solters & Roskin, Milly Schoenbaum, Rima Corben
Stage Manager: Ian Wilson

* Closed June 16, 1979 after limited engagement of 5 performances and 1 preview.

Right: Bruce Forsyth

22 STEPS THEATRE
Opened Wednesday, June 13, 1979.*
Gladys Rackmil, Fritz Holt, Barry M. Brown present:

THE MADWOMAN OF CENTRAL PARK WEST

By Phyllis Newman and Arthur Laurents; Music and Lyrics, Peter Allen, Leonard Bernstein, Jerry Bock, Martin Charnin, John Clifton, Betty Comden, Fred Ebb, Jack Feldman, Adolph Green, Sheldon Harnick, John Kander, Ed Kleban, Barry Manilow, Phyllis Newman, Joe Raposo, Mary Rodgers, Carole Bayer Sager, Stephen Sondheim, Bruce Sussman; Director, Arthur Laurents; Scenery, Phillip Jung; Costumes, Theoni V. Aldredge; Lighting, Ken Billington; Sound, Abe Jacob; Orchestrations, John Clifton; Musical Direction, Herbert Kaplan; Special Orchestrations, Kirk Nurock; Producers' Associate, Amos Abrams; Wardrobe, Sydney Smith; Hairstylist, Dan Smutz; Music Coordinator, Earl Shendell

CAST
Phyllis Newman

MUSICAL NUMBERS: Up Up Up, My Mother Was a Fortune Teller, Cheerleader, What Makes Me Love Him, Don't Laugh, No One's Toy, Better, Don't Wish, Copacabana, My New Friends, List Song

A musical one-woman show in two acts.

General Manager: Marvin A. Krauss
Company Manager: Gary Gunas
Press: Shirley Herz
Stage Managers: James Pentecost, Rick Ralston

* Closed Aug. 25, 1979 after 86 performances.

Phyllis Newman

CORT THEATRE
Opened Thursday, June 14, 1979.*
The Shubert Organization, Victor Potamkin and Moe Septee present:

RICHARD III

By William Shakespeare; Director, David Wheeler; Associate Producer-Production Supervisor, Porter Van Zandt; Scenery, Tony Straiges; Lighting, Thomas Skelton; Costumes, Jeanne Button; Music, Charles Gross; Hairstylist, Steve Atha; Wardrobe, Clarence Sims; Fight Coordinator, Jake Turner; Production Assistant, Elisa Septee

CAST

King Edward IV/Earl of Surrey/Friar Penker	Bill Moor
Richard, Duke of Gloucester/Richard III	Al Pacino
George, Duke of Clarence	Richard Jamieson
Lord Hastings	Ronald Hunter†
Sir Robert Brakenbury	J. T. Walsh
Elizabeth, Queen to Edward IV	Linda Selman
Anthony Woodville/Duke of Norfolk	John Mahon
Lord Grey/Captain	Judson Earney
Marquis of Dorset/Messenger	Daniel Zippi
Sir Thomas Vaughan/Sir William Lovel	Frederick C. Neumann
Duke of Buckingham	Rex Robbins
Earl of Derby	Larry Bryggman
First Murderer	Richard Bright
Second Murderer	Max Wright
Lady Anne	Penelope Allen
Sir Richard Ratcliffe	Jaime Sanchez
Duchess of York	Harriet Rogers
Lady Margaret Plantagenet/ Mistress Jane Shore	Laura Harrington
Archbishop of York/Sir James Tyrrel/ Sir William Brandon	Dominic Chianese
Duke of York	Glenn Scarpelli
Prince of Wales	Keith Gordon
Lord Mayor of London/Bishop of Ely	Frederic Kimball
Sir James Blunt	Bruce Waite
Page	Don Monahan
Henry Tudor, Earl of Richmond	Gary Bayer

A drama in three acts.

General Manager: Marvin A. Krauss
Company Manager: Mary Ellyn Devery
Press: Max Eisen, Robert Ganshaw
Stage Managers: Bigelow Green

* Closed July 15, 1979 after limited engagement of 81 performances.
† Succeeded by Barry Snyder

Penelope Allen, Al Pacino Top Right: Paul Guilfoyle, Jaime Sanchez, Al Pacino Right Center: Keith Gordon, Glenn Scarpelli, Al Pacino, Paul Guilfoyle, Jaime Sanchez

MINSKOFF THEATRE
Opened Monday, June 25, 1979.*
Jerry Brandt presents:

GOT TU GO DISCO

Book, John Zodrow; Music and Lyrics, Kenny Lehman, John Davis, Ray Chew, Nat Adderley, Jr., Thomas Jones, Wayne Morrison, Steve Boston, Eugene Narmore, Betty Rowland, Jerry Powell; Director, Larry Forde; Choreographers, Jo Jo Smith, Troy Garza; Scenery, James Hamilton; Lighting, S. A. Cohen; Costumes, Joe Eula; Musical Direction, Kenny Lehman; Vocal Direction, Kenny Lehman, Mitch Kerper; Film Sequences, Robert Rabinowitz; Sound, Lenny Will; Associate Artistic Director, Ron Ferri; Produced in association with Roy Rifkind, Julie Rifkind, Bill Spitalsky, WKTU Radio 92; Assistant Director, Donnis Honeycutt, Jr.; Wardrobe, Mark Immens; Special Effects, Chris Langhart; Cast Album by Casablanca Records

CAST

Narrator	Joe Masiell
Cassette	Irene Cara
Billy	Patrick Jude
Minnie	Lisa Raggio
Contact	Laurie Dawn Skinner
Antwerp	Patti Karr
Lila	Jane Holzer
Cubby	Charlie Serrano
Snap-Flash	Rhetta Hughes
Pete	Justin Ross
Marc	Marc Benecke
Spinner	Bob Pettie

SINGERS: Robin Lynn Beck, Gloria Covington, Gerry Griffin, Jack Magradey, Billy Newton-Davis
DANCERS: Connie Marie Brazelton, Prudence Darby, Ronald Dunham, Miguel Gonz, Christien Jacobsen, Peter Kapetan, Patrick Kinser-Lau, Julia Lema, Bronna Lipton, Mark Manley, Jodi Moccia, Jamie Patterson, Dee Ranzweiler, Adrian Rosario, Willie Rosario, Sue Samuels, Tony Constantie (Swing)
MUSICAL NUMBERS: Puttin' It On, Disco Shuffle, All I Need, It Won't Work, Trust Me, In and Out, Got Tu Go Disco, Pleasure Pusher, If That Didn't Do It It Can't Be Done, Inter-mish-un, Hanging Over and Out, Chic to Cheap, Bad Glad Good and Had, Cassie, Takin' the Light, Gettin' to the Top
UNDERSTUDIES: Julia Lema (Cassette), Billy Newton-Davis (Billy), Connie Marie Brazelton (Snap-Flash), Dee Ranzweiler (Minnie), Jamie Patterson (Cubby), Sue Samuels (Lila), Patrick Kinser-Lau (Vitus), Bronna Lipton (Contact), Ronald Dunham (Pete), Peter Kapetan (Marc), Miguel Gonz (Spinner)

An "entertainment" in 2 acts and 14 scenes.

General Manager: Theatre Now, Inc.
Company Manager: Robb Lady
Press: Owen Levy, Valerie Warner, Connie DeNave
Stage Managers: Michael Turque, Arlene Grayson, John Fennessy, Les Magerman

* Closed June 30, 1980 after 8 performances and 9 previews.

Bert Andrews Photos

Justin Ross, Rhetta Hughes

Irene Cara, Patrick Jude
Top Left: Patti Karr, Jane Holzer

Tanya Tucker

ST. JAMES THEATRE
Opened Friday, July 27, 1979.*
Family Affair Enterprizes, Inc., presents:

BROADWAY OPRY '79
A Little Country in the Big City

Executive Producers, David S. Fitzpatrick, Edward J. Lynch, Jr.; Associate Producers, Spyros Venduras, Joseph D'Alesandro; Creative Director, Jonas McCord; Talent Coordination, Niles Siegel; Scenery and Lighting, Michael J. Hotopp, Paul dePass; Sound, Sound Associates; Production Assistant, Kathleen Kirshner; Technical Adviser, Don Smith

CAST

Tanya Tucker
Floyd Cramer
Don Gibson
Mickey Newbury
Waylon Jennings
The Crickets
The Waylors

A series of country music concerts.

General Manager: Frank Scardino
Company Manager: Sam Pagliaro
Press: The Merlin Group, Becky Flora, Glen Gary, Marguerite Wolfe
Stage Managers: Ed Aldridge, Bruce Laffey

* Closed Aug. 2, 1979 after 6 performances.

WINTER GARDEN THEATRE
Opened Thursday, August 2, 1979.*
Ron Delsener presents:

GILDA RADNER
LIVE FROM NEW YORK

Producer-Director, Lorne Michaels; Written by Anne Beatts, Lorne Michaels, Marilyn Suzanne Miller, Don Novello, Michael O'Donoghue, Gildna Radner, Paul Shaffer, Rosie Shuster, Alan Zweibel; Choreography, Patricia Birch; Musical Consultation, Paul Shaffer; Music Director, Howard Shore; Production Design, Eugene Lee, Akira Yoshimura; Costumes, Franne Lee, Karen Roston; Lighting, Roger Morgan; Sound, Abe Jacob; Associate Producer, Barbara Burns; Associate to the Producer, Stan Feig; Wardrobe, Margaret Karolyi; Hairstylist, Lyn Quiyou; Assistant to Producer, Cherie Fortis; Production Assistants, Joe Forristal, Stacy Sandler

CAST

Gilda Radner
Bob Christianson
Don Novello
Paul Shaffer
Nils Nichols
The Rouge: Diana Grasselli, Myriam Valle, Maria Vidal
The Candy Slice Group: John Caruso, Paul Shaffer, Howard Shore, G. E. Smith

An entertainment in two acts.

General Manager: Marvin A. Krauss
Associate Manager: Gary Gunas
Press: Solters & Roskin, Milly Schoenbaum, David LeShay, Kevin Patterson
Stage Manager: Alisa Adler

* Closed Sept. 22, 1979 after limited engagement of 51 performances and 5 previews.

Edie Baskin Photos

Gilda Radner, also above

LONGACRE THEATRE
Opened Tuesday, July 31, 1979.*
Arch Nadler, Anita MacShane and the Urban Arts Theatre
present:

BUT NEVER JAM TODAY

Book, Vinnette Carroll, Bob Larimer; Adapted from the works of
Lewis Carroll; Lyrics, Bob Larimer; Music, Bert Keyes, Bob
Larimer; Devised and Directed by Vinnette Carroll; Choreography,
Talley Beatty; Music Director-Incidental Music, Donald Johnston;
Scenery and Costumes, William Schroder; Lighting, Ken Billington;
Choral Arrangements, Cleavant Derricks; Production Supervisor,
Robert L. Borod; Sound, T. Richard Fitzgerald; Orchestration, Bert
Keyes; Dance Music, H. B. Barnum; Special Orchestration, H. B.
Barnum, Larry Blank; Associate Producers, Herb Hugel, Gene
Messinger; Assistant to Miss Carroll, Ralph Farrington; Wardrobe,
Josephin Zampedri

CAST

Alice	Marilynn Winbush
Caterpillar/Cook/Tweedledee/7 of Spades	Cleavant Derricks
Persona Non Grata	Lynne Thigpen
Black Queen	Lynne Clifton-Allen
White Rabbit/Cheshire Cat/ Mock Turtle	Jeffrey Anderson-Gunter
Duchess/Humpty-Dumpty/King of Hearts	Reginald Vel Johnson
Mad Hatter/Tweedledum/2 of Spades	Jai Oscar St. John
March Hare/Cook/5 of Spades	Sheila Ellis
Dormouse/Cook	Celestine DeSaussure
White Queen/Queen of Hearts	Charlene Harris
Guards	Clayton Strange, Garry Q. Lewis
Mushrooms	Brenda Braxton, Clayton Strange, Sharon K. Brooks, Gary Q. Lewis, Celestine DeSaussure, Jeffrey Anderson-Gunter

MUSICAL NUMBERS: Curiouser and Curiouser, Twinkle Twin-
kle Little Star, Long Live the Queen, A Real Life Lullaby, The More
I See People, My Little Room, But Never Jam Today, Riding for a
Fall, All the Same to Me, I've Got My Orders, God Could Give Me
Anything, I Like to Win, And They All Call the Hatter Mad,
Jumping from Rock to Rock, They

A musical in 2 acts and 16 scenes.

General Manager: McCann & Nugent
Company Manager: James Kimo Gerald
Press: Alpert & LeVine, Mark Goldstaub
Stage Managers: Robert L. Borod, Robert Charles, Gerard
Campbell

* Closed Aug. 5, 1979 after 7 performances and 9 previews.

Martha Swope Photos

Marilynn Winbush and company
Top Right: Charlene Harris

Cleavant Derricks Above: Derricks, Celestine
DeSaussure, Sheila Ellis, Jai Oscar St. John

LUNT-FONTANNE THEATRE

Opened Thursday, September 6, 1979.*
Zev Bufman and James M. Nederlander in association with
Jack Molthen, Spencer Tandy and J. Ronald Horowitz present:

PETER PAN

Book from the play by Sir James M. Barrie; Lyrics, Carolyn Leigh;
Music, Mark Charlap; Additional Lyrics, Betty Comden, Adolph
Green; Additional Music, Jule Styne; Original production, con-
ceived, directed and choreographed by Jerome Robbins; Entire pro-
duction directed and choreographed by Rob Iscove; Musical and
Vocal Direction, Jack Lee; Scenery, Peter Wolf; Costumes, Bill
Hargste; Lighting, Thomas Skelton; Production Manager, Barbara-
Mae Phillips; Hairstylist, Werner Sherer; Sound, Richard Fitz-
gerald; Special Laser Effects, Laser Media; Flying by Foy; Technical
Supervisor, Mitch Miller; Wardrobe, Jennifer Bryan, Patricia Eiben;
Associate Conductor, Jean Marie Browne; Assistant to Director,
Penny Peters McGuire; Production Assistant, Mary Welch

CAST

Michael	Jonathan Ward
Nana	James Cook
Liza/Ostrich	Maggy Gorrill†1
Wendy/Jane	Marsha Kramer
John	Alexander Winter
Mrs. Darling	Beth Fowler
Mr. Darling/Captain Hook	George Rose†2
Peter Pan	Sandy Duncan
Lion	Jim Wolfe
Turtle	Cleve Asbury†3
Kangaroo	Reed Jones†4
Slightly	Chris Farr†5
Curly	Michael Estes
First Twin	Rusty Jacobs†6
Second Twin	Joey Abbott†7
Tootles	Carl Tramon†8
Nibs	Dennis Courtney
Noodler	Guy Stroman
Smee	Arnold Soboloff†9
Crocodile	Kevin McCready
Tiger Lily	Maria Pogee†10
Starkey	Jon Vandertholen
Cecco	Trey Wilson†11
Mullins	Steven Yuhasz
Jukes	Gary Daniel†12
Wendy, grown up	Neva Rae Powers
Trees	C. J. McCaffrey, Kevin McCready, David Storey

PIRATES: William Carmichael, James Cook, Gary Daniel,
Dianna Hughes, Guy Stroman, Jon Vandertholen, Trey Wilson,
Steven Yuhasz
INDIANS: Cleve Asbury, Maggy Gorrill, Sharon-Ann Hill, Reed
Jones, C. J. McCaffrey, Kevin McCready, David Storey, Jim Wolfe
UNDERSTUDIES: Maggy Gorrill (Peter/Tiger Lily), Arnold
Soboloff (Darling/Hook), Trey Wilson (Smee), Dianna Hughes
(Wendy Jane), Neva Rae Powers (Mrs. Darling), Chris Farr (John),
Carl Tramon (Michael), Dance Alternates: Penny Peters McGuire,
Jack Magradey
MUSICAL NUMBERS: Tender Shepherd, I've Got to Crow,
Neverland, I'm Flying, Morning in Neverland, Pirate Song, A
Princely Scheme, Indians!, Wendy, Another Princely Scheme, I
Won't Grow Up, Mysterious Lady, Ugg-a Wugg, Distant Melody,
Hook's Waltz, The Battle

A musical in 3 acts and 9 scenes. The action takes place in the
nursery of the Darling home, in Neverland, on the Jolly Roger.

General Manager: Theatre Now, Inc.
Assistant General Manager: Charlotte Wilcox
Company Manager: Camille Ranson
Press: Solters & Roskin, Joshua Ellis, Rima Corben, David
LeShay
Stage Managers: Barbara-Mae Phillips, David Rubinstein,
Nelson K. Wilson

* Still playing May 31, 1980. For original musical production, see
THEATRE WORLD Vol. 11. It opened Oct. 20, 1954 with Mary
Martin and Cyril Ritchard and ran for 149 performances at the
Winter Garden Theatre.
† Succeeded by: 1. Spence Ford, 2. Christopher Hewett, 3. Richard
Loreto, 4. Robert Brubach, 5. Matthew McGrath, 6. Robert
McGuire, 7. Johnny Morgal, 8. Demetrius Pena, 9. Ronn Carroll,
10. Marybeth Kurdock, 11. Gibby Brand, Anthony Hoylen

Martha Swope Photos

**Top Right: Jonathan Ward, Marsha Kramer,
Sandy Duncan Below: George Rose, Sandy Duncan**

**Sandy Duncan and the Lost Boys
Above: The Pirates**

15

CENTURY THEATRE
Opened Wednesday, September 12, 1979.*
Frank Gero, Frederick Zollo and Mark Gero in association
with Budd Block present:

ON GOLDEN POND

By Ernest Thompson; Director, Craig Anderson; Set and Costumes,
Steven Rubin; Lighting, Craig Miller; Assistant to Director, Stacia
Smales; Production Coordinator, Louis D. Pietig; Sound, David S.
Rapkin; Wardrobe, Bonnie Dudovitz

CAST

Norman Thayer, Jr.	Tom Aldredge
Ethel Thayer	Frances Sternhagen
Charlie Martin	Ronn Carroll†1
Chelsea Thayer Wayne	Barbara Andres
Billy Ray	Mark Bendo†2
Bill Ray	Stan Lachow

A comedy in 2 acts and 5 scenes. The action takes place at the
present time in the living room of the Thayer's summer home on
Golden Pond in Maine.

General Managers: Leonard Soloway, Allan Francis
Company Manager: Keith Waggoner
Press: Shirley Herz, Jan Greenberg, Sam Rudy
Stage Managers: Daniel Morris, Judith Elizabeth Lowry

* Closed March 14, 1980 after 212 performances.
† Succeeded by: 1. Ben Slack, 2. Rickey Paul Golden

Left: Frances Sternhagen, Tom Aldredge

Tom Aldredge, Mark Bendo

Frances Sternhagen, Tom Aldredge
Above: Ronn Carroll, Barbara Andres

BROADWAY THEATRE
Opened Tuesday, September 25, 1979.*
Robert Stigwood in association with David Land presents:

EVITA

Lyrics, Tim Rice; Music, Andrew Lloyd Webber; Director, Harold Prince; Sets, Costumes, Projections by Timothy O'Brien, Tazeena Firth; Lighting, David Hersey; Sound, Abe Jacob; Choreography, Larry Fuller; Musical Director, Rene Wiegert; Orchestrations, Hershy Kay, Andrew Lloyd Webber; Executive Producers, R. Tyler Gatchell, Jr., Peter Neufeld; Wardrobe, Adelaide Laurino, John Laurino; Hairstylist, Richard Allen; Production Assistant, Wiley Hausam; Original Cast Album by MCA Records.

CAST

Eva . . . . Patti LuPone, Terri Klausner (matinees)
Che . . . . Mandy Patinkin
Peron . . . . Bob Gunton
Peron's Mistress . . . . Jan Ohringer
Magaldi . . . . Mark Syers
Children . . . . Megan Forste, Bridget Francis, Nicole Francis,
Michael Pastryk, Christopher Wooten

PEOPLE OF ARGENTINA: Seda Azarian, Dennis Birchall, Peppi Borza, Tom Carder, Robin Cleaver, Andy De Gange, Mark East, Teri Gill, Carlos Gorbea, Pat Gorman, Rex David Hays, Terri Klausner, Michael Lichtefeld, Carol Lugenbeal, Paula Lynn, Morgan MacKay, Peter Marinos, Sal Mistretta, Jack Neubeck, Marcia O'Brien, Nancy Opel, Davis Sacks, James Sbano, David Staller, Michele Stubbs, Robert Tanna, Clarence Teeters, Susan Terry, Phillip Tracy, David Vosburgh, Mark Waldrop, Sandra Wheeler, Brad Witsger, John Leslie Wolfe, Nancy Wood, John Yost

UNDERSTUDIES: Nancy Opel (Eva), Tom Carder (Che), Rex David Hays (Peron), Sal Mistretta (Magaldi), Nancy Wood (Mistress)

MUSICAL NUMBERS: A Cinema in Buenos Aires, Requiem for Evita, Oh What a Circus, On This Night of a Thousand Stars, Eva Beware of the City, Buenos Aires, Goodnight and Thank You, The Art of the Possible, Charity Concert, I'd Be Surprisingly Good for You, Another Suitcase in Another Hall, Peron's Latest Flame, A New Argentina, On the Balcony of the Casa Rosada, Don't Cry for Me Argentina, High Flying Adored, Rainbow High, Rainbow Tour, The Actress Hasn't Learned, And the Money Kept Rolling In, Santa Evita, Waltz for Eva and Che, She Is a Diamond, Dice Are Rolling, Eva's Final Broadcast, Montage, Lament

A musical in two acts based on the life of Eva Peron, the Second wife of Argentine dictator Juan Peron.

General Manager: Howard Haines
Company Manager: John Caruso
Press: Mary Bryant, Patt Dale, Philip Rinaldi
Stage Managers: George Martin, John Grigas, Andy Cadiff, Carlos Gorbes

P* Still playing May 31, 1980. Winner of 1980 NY Drama Critics Circle Award for Best Musical, and 7 "Tony's" for Best Musical, Director, Actress (Patti LuPone), Score, Book, Featured Actor (Mandy Patinkin), and Lighting.

Martha Swope Photos

Right Center: Bob Gunton, Patti LuPone (C)
Above: LuPone (LC), Mandy Patinkin (RC)
Top: Patti LuPone (C)

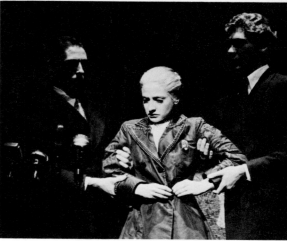

Bob Gunton, Terri Klausner

Patti LuPone

22 STEPS THEATRE
Opened Wednesday, October 3, 1979.[3]
Inter-Action's British American Repertory Company presents:

DOGG'S HAMLET, CAHOOT'S MACBETH

By Tom Stoppard; Director, ED Berman; Designer, Norman Coates; Lighting, Howard Eaton; Wardrobe, Mhairi McKechnie; Associate Producer, James Ware

CAST

"Dogg's Hamlet"
Abel/Bernardo/Marcellus/Laertes . . . . Peter Grayer
Baker/Francisco/Horatio/Osric . . . . Stephen D. Newman
Charlie/Ophelia. . . . . Davis Hall
Dogg/Shakespeare/Claudius . . . . Louis Haslar
Easy . . . . John Challis
Lady. . . . . Ruth Hunt
Mrs. Dogg/Gertrude . . . . Sarah Venable
Fox/Hamlet. . . . . Ben Gotlieb
Ghost/Gravedigger. . . . . John Straub
Polonius . . . . Alan Thompson
"Cahoot's Macbeth"
Witch1/Duncan/Lennox/Morris. . . . . John Straub
Witch 2/Malcolm/Murderer 1 . . . . Ben Gotlieb
Witch 3/Hostess . . . . Sarah Venable
Macbeth . . . . Stephen D. Newman
Banquo/Cahoot. . . . . Alan Thompson
Ross/Murderer 2/Messenger 2/Boris. . . . . Louis Haslar
Lady Macbeth . . . . Ruth Hunt
Messenger 1/Macduff . . . . Davis Hall
Inspector . . . . Peter Woodthorpe
Easy . . . . John Challis

A comedy in two parts.

Company Manager: Johanna Pool
Press: Seymour Krawitz, Patricia McLean Krawitz
Stage Managers: George Elmer, Jennifer Smith, Richard Delahanty, David Millard

* Closed Oct. 28, 1979 after limited engagement of 32 performances to tour.

Above: Grayer, Stephen D. Newman, Hall
Davis Hall, Peter Grayer, Louis Haslar

Top: (L) Ruth Hunt, Stephen D. Newman
(R) Alan Thompson, Peter Woodthorpe

ST. JAMES THEATRE

Opened Sunday, October 7, 1979.*
Jujamcyn Productions, Joseph P. Harris, Ira Bernstein and
Roger Berlind present:

THE 1940'S RADIO HOUR

By Walton Jones; Based on an idea by Walton Jones and Carol Lees;
Director, Walton Jones; Musical Numbers Staged by Thommie
Walsh; Musical Supervision and Direction, Stanley Lebowsky; Sce-
nery, David Gropman; Lighting, Tharon Musser; Costumes, Wil-
liam Ivey Long; Sound, Otts Munderloh; Orchestrations, Gary S.
Fagin; Assistant Conductor-Vocal Arrangements, Paul Schierhorn;
Furs, Michael Forrest; Technical Supervisor, Jeremiah Harris;
Wardrobe, Deborah Cheretun; Hairstylist, Angela Gari; Assistant to
Mr. Jones, David Rotenberg; Production Assistant, Howard P. Lev;
Wigs, Paul Huntley

CAST

Pops Bailey	Arny Freeman
Stanley	John Sloman
Clifton A. Feddington	Josef Sommer
Zoot Doubleman	Stanley Lebowsky
Wally Fergusson	Jack Hallett
Lou Cohn	Merwin Goldsmith
Johnny Cantone	Jeff Keller
Ginger Brooks	Crissy Wilzak
Connie Miller	Kathy Andrini
B. J. Gibson	Stephen James
Neal Tilden	Joe Grifasi
Ann Collier	Mary-Cleere Haran
Geneva Lee Browne	Dee Dee Bridgewater
Biff Baker	John Doolittle

STANDBYS AND UNDERSTUDIES: Susan Elizabeth Scott
(Ann/Ginger), Etta Green (Geneva), Bob Freschi (Johnny/Neal),
Lynn Stafford (Biff/Wally/Stanley), James Lockhart (Pops/Lou/-
Clifton) Jo Speros (Connie), John Sloman (B. J.)

A musical performed without intermission. The action takes place
in the WOV Broadcast Studios, Algonquin Room on the ground
floor of the Hotel Astor in NYC on Dec. 21, 1942 about 8 P.M.

General Manager: Frank Scardino
Company Manager: Susan Bell
Press: Merlin Group, Cheryl Sue Dolby, Glen Gary, Sandy
Manley, Becky Flora, Marguerite Wolfe
Stage Managers: Edwin Aldridge, Craig Jacobs, James Lockhart

* Closed Jan. 6, 1980 after 105 performances and 14 previews.

Martha Swope Photos

**Right: Stephen James, Kathy Andrini, Joe Grifasi,
Crissy Wilzak, Josef Sommer**

**Jack Hallet, Stephen James, Kathy Andrini, Josef Sommer, Crissy Wilzak,
Jeff Keller, Dee Dee Bridgewater, Joe Grifasi, Mary-Cleere Haran**

MARK HELLINGER THEATRE
Opened Monday, October 8, 1979.*
Terry Allen Kramer and Harry Rigby in association with Columbia Pictures present:

SUGAR BABIES

Conceived by Ralph G. Allen, Harry Rigby; Sketches, Ralph G. Allen based on traditional material; Music, Jimmy McHugh; Lyrics, Dorothy Fields, Al Dubin; Additional Music and Lyrics, Arthur Malvin; "Sugar Baby Bounce" by Jay Livingston and Ray Evans; Staged and Choreographed by Ernest Flatt; Sketches directed by Rudy Tronto; Entire Production Supervised by Ernest Flatt; Associate Producer, Jack Schlissel; Scenery and Costumes, Raoul Pene du Bois; Lighting, Gilbert V. Hemsley, Jr.; Vocal Arrangements, Arthur Malvin; Additional Arrangements, Hugh Martin, Ralph Blane; Musical Director, Glen Roven; Orchestrations, Dick Hyman; Dance Music Arrangements, Arnold Gross; Associate Producers, Thomas Walton Associates, Frank Montalvo; Hairstylist, Joseph Dal Corso; Associate Conductor, Patrick Holland; Assistant to Producers, Hank Flacks; Wardrobe, Florence Aubert, Irene Ferrari

CAST

Mickey	Mickey Rooney
Scot	Scot Stewart
Jillian	Ann Jillian†1
Tom	Tom Boyd
Peter	Peter Leeds
Jack	Jack Fletcher
Jimmy	Jimmy Mathews
Ann	Ann Miller
Sid	Sid Stone
Gaiety Quartet	Jonathan Aronson, Eddie Pruett,

Michael Radigan, Jeff Veazey, Hank Brunjes (alternate)

THE SUGAR BABIES: Laura Booth,†2, Christine Busini, Diane Duncan†3, Chris Elia, Debbie Gornay†4, Barbara Hanks†5, Jeri Kansas†6, Barbara Mandra†7, Robin Manus, Faye Fujisaki Mar, Linda Ravinsky, Michele Rogers, Rose Scudder, Patti Watson, Alternates: Laurie Sloan, Terpsie Toon†8
UNDERSTUDIES: Rudy Tronto (Mickey Rooney), Rose Scudder, Toni Kaye (Ann Miller), Diane Duncan, Michele Rogers (Ann Jillian), Tom Boyd (Mickey/Jack/Peter/Sid/Jimmy), Michael Radigan (Scot), Hank Brunjes (Tom)
SONGS AND SKETCHES: A Memory of Burlesque, A Good Old Burlesque Show, Welcome to the Gaiety, Let Me Be Your Sugar Baby, Meet Me 'Round the Corner, Travelin', In Louisiana, I Feel a Song Comin' On, Goin' Back to New Orleans, The Broken Arms Hotel, Feathered Fantasy, Sally, The Pitchman, Ellis Island Lament, Immigration Rose, Scenes from Domestic Life, Don't Blame Me, Torch Song, Orientale, The Little Red Schoolhouse, The New Candy-Coated Craze, The Sugar Baby Bounce, Special Added Attraction, Down at the Gaiety Burlesque, Mr. Banjo Man, Candy Butcher, Girls and Garters, I'm Keeping Myself Available for You, Exactly Like You, Justice Will Out, In a Greek Garden, Warm and Willing, Presenting Madame Alla Gazaza, Tropical Madness, Cuban Love Song, Cautionary Tales, McHugh Medley, Presenting Bob Williams, Old Glory, You Can't Blame Your Uncle Sammy

A "burlesque musical" in two acts.

General Management: Jack Schlissel, Jay Kingwill
Company Manager: Alan Wasser
Press: Henry Luhrman, Terry M. Lilly, Kevin P. McAnarney
Stage Managers: Thomas Kelly, Bob Burland, Jay B. Jacobson, David Campbell, Kay Vance

* Still playing May 31, 1980.
† Succeeded by: 1. Anita Morris, 2. Kaylyn Dillehay, 3. Phyllis Frew, 4. Lesley Kingley, 5. Clare Leach, 6. Dana Moore, 7. Dorothy Stanley, 8. Carole Cotter
Martha Swope Photos

Top Left: Mickey Rooney and the Sugar Babies
Below: Mickey Rooney, Ann Miller

Ann Miller, Mickey Rooney
(also above center)

HELEN HAYES THEATRE
Opened Wednesday, October 10, 1979.*
Doris Cole Abrahams and Eddie Kulukundis in association
with Leon Becker present:

ONCE A CATHOLIC

By Mary O'Malley; Director, Mike Ockrent; Scenery, William Ritman; Costumes, Patricia Adshead; Lighting, Marc B. Weiss; Assistant to Producers, Phil Leach; Wardrobe, Gene Wilson

CAST

The Teachers
Mother Peter............................Rachel Roberts
Mother Basil................................Peggy Cass
Mother Thomas Aquinas...................Pat Falkenhain
Mr. Emanuelli..............................Joseph Leon
The Priest
Father Mullarkey.............................Roy Poole
The Girls
Mary Mooney...........................Mia Dillon
Mary McGinty..........................Terry Calloway
Mary Gallagher.........................Virginia Hut
Mary Hennessey.........................Bonnie Hellman
Mary Flanagan............................Joyce Cohen
Mary O'Grady........................Christine Mitchell
Mary Murphy.............................Loretta Scott
The Boyfriends
Derek..Bill Buell
Cuthbert..................................Charley Lang

STANDBYS AND UNDERSTUDIES: Liz Sheridan (Mothers
Peter, Basil, Thomas), Patrick Farrelly (Mullarkey/Emanuelli),
Maxwell Caulfield (Cuthbert/Derek), Christine Mitchell (Mooney/-
Gallagher) Joyce Cohen (McGinty), Linda Beckett (Hennessey/-
Flanagan/O'Grady/Murphy)

A comedy in two acts. The action takes place in Harlesden, London, 1956–57.

General Management: Gatchell & Neufeld
Company Manager: Douglas C. Baker
Press: Alpert/LeVine, Mark Goldstaub
Stage Managers: Robert Vandergriff, Audrey Koran, Linda
Beckett
* Closed Oct. 14, 1979 after 6 performances and 9 previews.

Martha Swope Photos

**Left: Joseph Leon, Mia Dillon
Top: Bonnie Hellman, Mia Dillon,
Rachel Roberts**

**Terry Calloway (standing), Virginia Hut, Joyce Cohen, Mia Dillon, Peggy Cass,
Christine Mitchell, Bonnie Hellman, Loretta Scott**

MAJESTIC THEATRE
Opened Thursday, October 11, 1979.*
Sherwin M. Goldman presents:

THE MOST HAPPY FELLA

Music, Lyrics and Book by Frank Loesser; Based on Sidney Howard's play "They Knew What They Wanted"; Director, Jack O'-Brien; Choreographer, Graciela Daniele; Musical Director, Andrew Meltzer; Scenery, Douglas W. Schmidt; Costumes, Nancy Potts; Lighting, Gilbert V. Hemsley, Jr.; Orchestrations, Don Walker; Presented in association with Michigan Opera Theatre, David DiChiera, General Director, and Emhan, Inc.; Assistant Producer, Virginia Hymes; Assistant to Producer, Joey Parnes; Wardrobe, Elonzo Dann, Mary P. Eno; Production Assistant, John Roccosalva; Associate Conductor, Alfonso Cavaliere; Conductor, Eric Stern

CAST

Cashier/Brakeman .... Bill Hastings
Cleo .... Louisa Flaningam
Rosabella .... Sharon Daniels, Linda Michele (matinees)
Waitresses .... Karen Giombetti, Tina Paul, D'Arcy Phifer,
Smith Wordes
Busboy .... Tim Flavin
Postman .... Dan O'Sullivan
Tony .... Giorgio Tozzi, Frederick Burchinal (matinees)
Marie .... Adrienne Leonetti
Max .... Steven Alex-Cole
Herman .... Dennis Warning
Clem .... Dean Badolato
Jake .... David Miles
Al .... Kevin Wilson
Sheriff .... Stephen Dubov
Joe .... Richard Muenz
Giuseppe .... Gene Varrone
Pasquale .... Darren Nimnicht
Ciccio .... Franco Spoto
Doctor .... Joe McGrath
Priest .... Lawrence Asher
Bus Driver .... Michael Capes
Neighbor Ladies .... Melanie Helton, Dee Etta Rowe,
Jane Warsaw, Sally Williams

NEIGHBORS: Steven Alex-Cole, Lawrence Asher, Dean Badolato, Michael Capes, Richard Croft, Stephen Dubov, Tim Flavin, Karen Giombetti, Bill Hastings, D. Michael Heath, Melanie Helton, David Miles, Tina Paul, D'Arcy Phifer, Patrice Pickering, Candace Rogers, Dee Etta Rowe, Bonnie Simmons, Jane Warsaw, Richard White, Carla Wilkins, Sally Williams, Kevin Wilson, Smith Wordes
UNDERSTUDIES: Dee Etta Row (Cleo), Richard White (Cashier), David Miles (Herman), Carla Wilkins (Marie), Dan O'Sullivan (Pasquale), Franco Spoto (Doctor/Giuseppe), Richard Croft (Ciccio), Lawrence Asher (Postman), Stephen Dubov (Al), D. Michael Heath (Jake), Michael Capes (Clem), Swings: Phillip Jerry, Laurie Scandurra
MUSICAL NUMBERS: Ooh! My Feet, I Know How It Is, 7 Million Crumbs, I Don't Know, Maybe He's Kind of Crazy, Somebody Somewhere, The Most Happy Fella, A Long Time Ago, Standing on the Corner, Joey, Soon You Gonna Leave Me Joe, Rosabella, Abbondanza, Plenty Bambini, Sposalizio, Special Delivery, Benevenuta, Aren't You Glad?, No Home No Job, Eyes Like a Stranger, Don't Cry, Fresno Beauties, Cold and Dead, Love and Kindness, Happy to Make Your Acquaintance, I Don't Like This Dame, Big D, How Beautiful the Days, Young People, Warm All Over, Old People Gotta, I Like Everybody, I Love Him, Like A Woman Loves a Man, My Heart Is So Full of You, Hoedown, Mamma, Goodbye Darlin', Song of a Summer Night, Please Let Me Tell You, Tell Tony and Rosabella Goodbye for Me, She Gonna Come Home With Me, Nobody's Ever Gonna Love You, I Made a Fist!

A musical in 2 acts and 10 scenes. The action takes place in San Francisco and Napa, California in the mid 1930's.

General Manager: Mario De Maria
Press: Merlin Group, Becky Flora
Stage Managers: Herb Vogler, Ben Janney, Phillip Jerry

* Closed Nov. 25, 1979 after 53 performances. The original production opened at the Imperial Theatre on May 3, 1956 and ran for 678 performances with Robert Weede, Jo Sullivan, and Art Lund. See THEATRE WORLD, Vol. 12.

Dirk Bakker Photos

Top Right: Giorgio Tozzi, Sharon Daniels
Below: Bonnie Simmons, Dean Badolato, Kevin
Wilson, David Miles, Dennis Warning

Giorgio Tozzi, Sharon Daniels Above: Darren
Nimnicht, Gene Varrone, Franco Spoto

RADIO CITY MUSIC HALL
Opened Thursday, October 18, 1979.*
Radio City Music Hall Productions presents:

SNOW WHITE
and the Seven Dwarfs

Adapted from Walt Disney's film; Book, Joe Cook; Producer, Robert F. Jani; Director-Choreographer, Frank Wagner; Production Executive, John J. Moore; Executive Musical Director, Donald Pippin; Conductor, Don Smith; Orchestrations, Philip J. Lang; Scenery, John William Keck; Costumes, Frank Spencer; Mask and Animal Costumes, Joe Stephen; Lighting, Ken Billington; For Stage Production: Lyrics by Joe Cook, Music by Jay Blackton; For Film: Lyrics by Larry Morey, Music by Frank Churchill; Associate Conductor, Elman Anderson; Assistant to Director, Marsha Wagner; Wardrobe, Randy Beth

CAST

David Pursley (Chamberlain), Thomas Ruisinger (King), Anne Francine (Queen), Mary Jo Salerno (Snow White), Charles Hall (Mirror/Witch), Yolande Bavan (Luna), Heidi Coe (Greta), Richard Bowne (Prince Charming), Laura Lipson (Mother), Bruce Sherman (Huntsman), Don Potter (Doc), Richard Day (Happy), Benny Freigh (Grumpy), Louis Carry (Sneezy), Jay Edward Allen (Bashful), Jerry Riley (Sleepy), Michael E. King (Dopey)

SINGERS: Ronald Brown, Kenneth Cantor, Peter Costanza, David Dusing, Clifford Fearl, G. Jan Jones, Patricia Landi, Lauren Lipson, Linda Motshami, Dawn Parrish, Caryl Tenney, Swing: Tony Gilbert, Marsha Miller
DANCERS: Connie Brazelton, Beth Baker, Mary-Pat Carey, John Cashman, Danny Clark, Heidi Coe, Joan Cooper, Jay Coronel, Christopher Daniels, Ron Dunham, Alfred Gonzales, Martha Goodman, Jennifer Hammond, Norb Joerder, Janet Marie Jones, David Lee, Kim Leslie, Malcolm Perry, Michael Ragan, Patricia Register, Roger Rouillier, Jerry Sarnat, Hope Sogawa, Reisa Sperling, Thomas J. Stanton, Cassie Stein, Lynn Williford, Kim Wollen, Swing: James Paolelli, Jane Wilson
UNDERSTUDIES: Dawn Parrish (Snow White), Ronald Brown (Prince), Michael Lee Berman (Dwarfs), Peter Costanza (King), Kenneth Kantor (Huntsman), Lauren Lipson (Queen), Linda Motashami (Luna), Clifford Fearl (Chamberlain)
MUSICAL NUMBERS: Welcome to the Kingdom, Queen's Presentation, I'm Wishing, One Song, With a Smile and a Song, Whistle While You Work, Heigh-Ho, Bluddle-Uddle-Um-Dum, Will I Ever See Her Again, Dwarf's Yodel Song, Someday My Prince Will Come, Here's the Happy Ending

A musical presented without intermission

Company Manager: Michael Lonegan
Press: Gifford/Wallace, Deborah Morgenthal, Linda Friberg
Stage Managers: Jeff Hamlin, Neil Miller, Thomas Stanton

* Closed Nov. 18, 1979 after 33 performances, and after touring, returned Friday, Jan 11, 1980 for 70 additional performances through Mar. 9, 1980.

Mary Jo Salerno and the seven dwarfs Top: Mary Jo Salerno
Right Center: Mary Jo Salerno, Richard Bowne

BIJOU THEATRE
Monday, November 5–25, 1979 (12 performances)*
Arthur Shafman International presents:

A KURT WEILL CABARET

His Broadway and Berlin Songs; Production Supervisor, Billie McBride; Production Adviser, Richard G. Miller; Production Associates, Evelyn Gross, Eileen Jaffe, Susan Balsam; General Manager, Christopher Dunlop; Company Manager, John Scott; Press, Henry Luhrman, Robert Pontarelli; At the Piano, Steven Blier

CAST

Martha Schlamme
Alvin Epstein †
SONGS: Moritat, Barbara Song, Alabama Song, Duet Herr Jakob Schmidt, Ballad of Sexual Slavery, Ballad of the Pimp and the Whore, Pirate Jenny, Kanonensong, Soldatenweib, Eating, That's Him, September Song, Saga of Jenny, Bilboa Song, Sailor's Tango, Surabaya Johnny, The Life That We Lead

* Returned Wednesday, December 26–31, 1979 for 6 additional performances, Friday, Jan. 4, 1980–March 8, 1980 for 34 performances, Tuesday, May 6,–June 1, 1980 for 32 performances.
† Succeeded by Leonard Frey (Feb. 11–Mar. 8, 1980).

Martha Swope Photo

Martha Schlamme, Alvin Epstein

Engelbert Humperdinck

MINSKOFF THEATRE
Opened Friday, November 9, 1979.*
Lee Guber and Shelly Gross present:

ENGLEBERT ON BROADWAY

Musical Director, Jeff Sturges; Set, Richard Williams; Lighting, Kyle Shew; Adapted by Richard Nelson; Sound, Jim Anderson; Personal Management, Harold Davison; Production Coordinators, Donna Dees, Larry Richard; Assistant to Producers, Laurie Kaufman; Production Assistant, Michele Jacobson; A Music Fair Concerts Presentation

CAST

Englebert Humperdinck
Dick Capri
The Engle-ettes:
Anna Pagan
Anita Sherman
Carol Stallings

An entertainment in two parts.

General Manager: Marvin A. Krauss
Associate Manager: Gary Gunas
Company Manager: Stephen H. Arnold
Press: Solters & Roskin, Bud Westman, Milly Schoenbaum

* Closed Nov. 18, 1979 after limited engagement of 14 performances.

JOHN GOLDEN THEATRE

Opened Wednesday, November 7, 1979.*
Emanuel Azenberg, the Shubert Organization, Craig Anderson
and Dasha Epstein present:

DEVOUR THE SNOW

By Abe Polsky; Director, Terry Schreiber; Scenery, Steven Rubin;
Costumes, David Murin; Lighting, Dennis Parichy; Technical Coordinator, Arthur Siccardi; Wardrobe, Kate Gaudio; Hairstylist, Michael Wasula; Dialect Consultant, Nora Dunfee

CAST

Sheriff George McKinstry	Eddie Jones
John A. Sutter	Paul David Richards
James Reed	Stephen Joyce
Lewis Keseberg	Jon DeVries
William Eddy	James Ray Weeks
Bill Foster	Edward Seamon
Phillipine Keseberg	Jill Andre
Margaret Reed	Gloria Maddox
Georgia Donner	Sarah Inglis
Fallon	Kevin O'Connor

UNDERSTUDIES AND STANDBYS: Edward Seamon (Lewis),
Berkeley Harris (Reed/Foster), Joanne Dorian (Philippine/Margaret), Patrick Farrelly (McKinstry/Sutter/Eddy), Eddie Jones (Fallon), Laura Cullen (Georgia)

A drama in 2 acts and 3 scenes. The action takes place in a
common hall serving as a courtroom at Sutter's Fort in northern
California during May of 1847.

General Manager: Max Allentuck
Associate Manager: Harold Sogard
Press: Bill Evans/Howard Atlee, Jim Baldassare, Claudia
McAllister
Stage Managers: Frank Marino, Joanne Dorian

* Closed Nov. 10, 1979 after 5 performances and 8 previews. Originally presented at the Hudson Guild Theatre May 2, 1979. See
THEATRE WORLD, Vol. 35.

Martha Swope Photos

Top Right: Jon DeVries
Below: Eddie Jones, Gloria Maddox

Jon DeVries, Eddie Jones, Stephen Joyce, James Ray Weeks

ETHEL BARRYMORE THEATRE
Opened Thursday, November 8, 1979.*
Morton Gottlieb presents:

ROMANTIC COMEDY

By Bernard Slade; Director, Joseph Hardy; Scenery, Douglas W. Schmidt; Costumes, Jane Greenwood; Lighting, Tharon Musser; Associate Producers, Ben Rosenberg, Warren Crane; Produced in association with Thornhill Productions Inc.; Wardrobe, Penny Davis; Hairstylist, Ray Iagnocco; Production Assistant, Jeff Martin

CAST

Jason Carmichael	Anthony Perkins
Blanche Dailey	Carole Cook†1
Phoebe Craddock	Mia Farrow
Allison St. James	Holly Palance
Leo Janowitz	Greg Mullavey
Kate Mallory	Deborah May†2

STANDBYS: Wayne Carson (Jason/Leo), Ellen Tobie (Phoebe)

A comedy in 3 acts and 7 scenes. The action takes place in the study of Jason Carmichael's New York townhouse in the mid-1960's.

General Manager: Ben Rosenberg
Company Manager: Martin Cohen
Press: Solters & Roskin, Milly Schoenbaum, Kevin Patterson
Stage Managers: Warren Crane, Wayne Carson

* Still playing May 31, 1980.
† Succeeded by: 1. Neva Patterson, 2. Marilyn Clark

Martha Swope Photos

**Left: Holly Palance, Mia Farrow,
Anthony Perkins**

**Mia Farrow, Carole Cook, Anthony Perkins
Above: Farrow, Greg Mullavey, Perkins**

**Anthony Perkins, Mia Farrow
Above: Perkins, Carole Cook, Deborah
May, Farrow**

HELEN HAYES THEATRE

Opened Wednesday, November 14, 1979.*
Arthur Whitelaw and Miriam Bienstock in associaiton with
Lita Starr present the Chelsea Theatre Production of:

STRIDER

By Mark Rozovsky; Adapted from a story by Leo Tolstoy; English
Version, Robert Kalfin, Steve Brown; Based on a translation by
Tamara Bering Sunguroff; Directed and Staged by Robert Kalfin,
Lynne Gannaway; Music originally composed by M. Rozovsky, S.
Vetkin; Original Russian Lyrics, Uri Riashentsev; Adapter, Com-
poser of new additional music, vocal and instrumental arrange-
ments, and Musical Director, Norman L. Berman; New English
Lyrics, Steve Brown; Scenery, Wolfgang Roth; Costumes, Andrew
B. Marlay; Lighting, Robby Monk; Sound, Gary Harris; Wardrobe,
Sylvia Myrvoid; Technical Director, Sander Gossard

CAST

Vaska/Mr. Willingstone	Roger DeKoven
Prince Serpuhofsky	Gordon Gould
General/Announcer	Ronnie Newman
Viazapurikha/Mathieu/Marie	Pamela Burrell†
Strider	Gerald Hiken
Actors	Katherine-Mary Brown, Jeannine Khoutieff, Vicki Van Grack, John Brownlee, Nancy Kawalek, Tad Ingram
Groom	Skip Lawing
Gypsies	Nina Dova, Karen Trott, Steven Blane
Count Bobrinsky/Darling/Lieutenant	Benjamin Hendrickson
Feofan/Fritz	Igors Gavon
Bet Taker	Vincent A. Feraudo
Vendor	Charles Walker

UNDERSTUDIES: Ted Ingram (Strider/Serpuhofsky/General-
/Announcer/Vaska), Katherine-Mary Brown (Viazapirikha/Math-
ieu/Marie), Skip Lawing (Bobrinsky/Darling/Lt.), John Brownlee
(Groom), Charles Walker (Feofan)

A play with music in 2 acts.

General Manager: Arthur Whitelaw
Company Manager: Sam Pagliaro
Press: Shirley Herz, Jan Greenberg, Sam Rudy
Stage Managers: Zoya Wyeth, Laurie F. Stone, Vincent A.
Feraudo

* Closed May 18, 1980 after 214 performances. Moved from the
Chelsea Westside Theatre where it played 187 performances. See
THEATRE WORLD Vol. 35.
† Succeeded by Taina Elg.

**Top: Gerald Hiken, Benjamin Hendrickson
Pamela Burrell Right Center: Hiken, John
Brownlee, Skip Lawing, Igors Gavon, Gordon Gould**

**Igors Gavon, Gordon Gould,
Gerald Hiken, Roger DeKoven**

LONGACRE THEATRE

Opened Tuesday, November 20, 1979.*

The Shubert Organization, Eugene V. Wolsk, Emanuel Aze
berg and Dasha Epstein present:

LAST LICKS

By Frank D. Gilroy; Director, Tom Conti; Setting, William Ritma
Costumes, Pearl Somner; Lighting, Tharon Musser; Production S
pervisor, Jerry Adler; Wardrobe, Josephine Zampedri; Productic
Assistants, Jerry Glick, Charles Johnson; Hairstylist, Patrik
Moreton

CAST

Matt Quinlan	Ed Flande
Dennis Quinlan	J. T. Wal
Fiona Raymond	Susan Kellerma

STANDBYS: Vince O'Brien (Matt), Peter McRobbie (Denni
Marie Wallace (Fiona), Jonathan Weiss (Dennis)

A play in two acts. The action takes place at the present time
Brooklyn, NY in early September.

General Manager: Jose Vega
Company Manager: Manny Kladitis
Press: Bill Evans/Howard Atlee, Claudia McAllister, Jim
Baldassare
Stage Manager: Jonathan Weiss

* Closed Dec. 2, 1979 after 15 performances and 10 previews.

Martha Swope Photos

Susan Kellermann, Ed Flanders

**Top: Susan Kellermann, J. T. Walsh,
Ed Flanders**

RADIO CITY MUSIC HALL

Opened Sunday, November 25, 1979.*
Radio City Music Hall Productions Presents:

THE MAGNIFICENT CHRISTMAS SPECTACULAR

Conceived and Produced by Robert F. Jani; Executive Musical Director-Conductor, Donald Pippin; Direction and Choreography by Dru Davis, Howard Parker; Rockettes Choreography, Violet Holmes; Production Executive, John J. Moore; Associate Production Executive, Jeff Hamlin; Scenic Design, Charles Lisanby; Costumes, Frank Spencer; Lighting, Ken Billington; Associate Conductors, Elman Anderson, Fernando Pasqualone; Narration Material, James Englehart; Hairstylists, Steve Atha, James Ameral; Wardrobe, Randy Beth, Barbara Van Zandt.

CAST

Pauline Achillas, Robert Amirantĕ, Tim Barber, Carol Beatty, Kathy Beatty, Dottie Bell, Karen Berman, Nina Berman, Phillip Bond, Susan Boron, Katy Braff, Edy Bryce, David Cahn, John Caleb, John Cashman, Cindy Chevrefils, Ron Chisholm, Barbara Ann Cittadino, Nora Cole, Eileen Collins, Buddy Crutchfield, Caroline Daly, Scott Dainton, Brie Daniels, Alvin Davis, Marica Anne Dobres, Susanne Doris, Jeff Dreisbach, Joyce Dwyer, Jody Erickson, Jacqueline Fancy, Sharon Ferrol, Deniene Fenn, Phyllis Frew, Prudie Gray, Leslie Gryszko, Lisa Grant, Carol Harbich, Edward Henkel, Nina Hennessey, Ginny Hounsell, Cindy Hughes, Holly Jones, Deirdre Kane, Pamela Kelleher, Dee Dee Knap, Jane Krakowski, Dale Kristien, Beverly Lambert, Judy Little, Andrea L. Lyman, Barbara Moore, Tony Moore, Ann Murphy, Robert Mullis, Alan Nicholson, Sylvia Nolan, Denise O'Neill, James Parker, Joan Peer, Cindy Pfeiffer, Susan Powers, Gerri Presky, Cleo Price, Jeffory Robinson, Sheila Rodriguez, David Roman, Thomas Ruisinger, John Salvatore, Marie Santell, Michael Shaffer, Sam Singhaus, Jody Smith, Theresa Spano, Pamela Stacey, Laurie Stephenson, Michael Stuart-Andrews, Jeff Suter, Susan Theobald, Carol Toman, Jayne Turner, Kay Walbye, Paula Ward, Geoffrey Webb, Scott Whiteleather, Rose Ann Woolsey, Bob Wrenn, Phyllis Wujko.

PROGRAM

Christmas Caroling, Deck the Halls, A Christmas Carol, O Tannenbaum, Highlights from the Nutcracker Suite, Fum Fum Fum, My First Real Christmas, The Night Before Christmas, International Holiday Traditions, 'Twas Like a Dream, If Our God Had Not Befriended, Blessings for the Chanukah Lights, The Twelve Days of Christmas, A Holiday Medley, Sing a Little Song of Christmas, Toyland, Parade of the Wooden Soldiers (Rockettes), The Living Nativity

Presented without intermission.

Press: Gifford/Wallace, Keith Sherman
Stage Managers: Neil Miller, Les Cockayne, Peter Rosenberg

* Closed Jan. 6, 1980 after limited engagement of 93 performances.

Jayne Turner, Jeff Suter, Jody Smith

**Scott Dainton, Dierdre Kane,
Scott Whitelather**

**Brie Daniels, Tony Moore,
Cathy Beatty**

ANTA THEATRE

Opened Tuesday, November 27, 1979.*
James M. Nederlander, Kennedy Center and Michael Codron present:

NIGHT AND DAY

By Tom Stoppard; Director, Peter Wood; Scenery and Costumes, Carl Toms; Lighting, Neil Peter Jampolis; Executive Producers, Elizabeth I. McCann, Nelle Nugent; Wardrobe, Rosalie Lahm; Production Assistant, Jean doPico; Hairstylist, Hiram Ortiz.

CAST

George Guthrie . . . . Dwight Schultz
Francis . . . . Larry Riley
Ruth Carson . . . . Maggie Smith
Alastair Carson . . . . T. J. Scott
Dick Wagner . . . . Paul Hecht
Jacob Milne . . . . Peter Evans
Geoffrey Carson . . . . Joseph Maher
President Mageeba . . . . Clarence Williams III

STANDBYS AND UNDERSTUDIES: Dennis Lipscomb (George/Jacob), Jonathan Farwell (Dick/Geoffrey), Milledge Mosley (Mageeba/Francis), Peter James (Alastair)

A play in two acts. The action takes place in Kambawe, a former British colony in Africa, at the present time.

Company Manager: Susan Gustafson
Press: Solters & Roskin, Joshua Ellis, Tom Trenkle, David LeShay
Stage Managers: William Dodds, Jay Adler, Leslie Lyles

* Closed Feb. 17, 1980 after 95 performances and 7 previews.

Zoe Dominic Photos

Right: Joseph Maher, Larry Riley, Dwight Schultz Top: Maggie Smith, Peter Evans

T. J. Scott, Maggie Smith

Maggie Smith, Joseph Maher

NEW APOLLO THEATRE
Opened Sunday, December 2, 1979.*
Jack Schlissel and Steven Steinlauf present:

BENT

By Martin Sherman; Director, Robert Allan Ackerman; Settings, Santo Loquasto; Lighting, Arden Fingerhut; Costumes, Robert Wojewodski; Music, Stanley Silverman; Co-Producers, Lee Minskoff, Patty Grubman; Special Effects, Randy McAndrews; Production Associate, Gilbert A. Wang; Wardrobe, Clarence Sims; Production Assistants, Karen Gromis, Marjorie Ornston

CAST

Max	Richard Gere†1
Rudy	David Marshall Grant†2
Wolf	James Remar
Guard	Kai Wulff
Guard	Philip Kraus†3
Greta	Michael Gross
Uncle Freddie	George Hall
Officer	Bryan E. Clark†4
Guard	John Snyder
Horst	David Dukes†5
Captain	Ron Randell

UNDERSTUDIES: David Davies (Max/Officer/Capt./Uncle Freddie), Gregory Salata (Horst), James Remar (Rudy), John Snyder (Greta), Kai Wulff (Wolf), Michael Morrows (Guards)

A drama in two acts.

General Management: Jay Kingwill
Company Manager: Al Isaac
Press: Jeffrey Richards, Warren Knowlton, Alan Eichler, Marjorie Ornston, Robert Ganshaw, Helen Stern, Karen Gromis
Stage Managers: Robert Bennett, Donald Walters

* Closed June 28, 1980 after 241 performances and 15 previews.
† Succeeded by: 1. Michael York, 2. Dennis Boutsikaris, 3. David Davies, Sam Stoneburner, 4. David Davies, 5. Jeffrey DeMunn

James Hamilton Photos

Right: Michael Gross, David Marshall Grant, Richard Gere Top: James Remar, Richard Gere, David Marshall Grant

Michael York, Jeffery DeMunn Above: Gregory Salata, Dennis Boutsikaris, Michael York

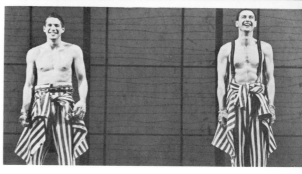

Richard Gere, David Dukes Above: George Hall, Richard Gere 31

BROOKS ATKINSON THEATRE
Opened Sunday, December 16, 1979.*
Joseph Kipness, Jule Styne, Marvin A. Krauss present the
Guthrie Theatre production of:

TEIBELE AND HER DEMON

By Isaac Bashevis Singer and Eve Friedman; Director, Stephen
Kanee; Sets and Costumes, Desmond Heeley; Lighting, Duane
Schuler; Music, Richard Peaslee; Associate Producers, Charlotte
Dicker, Dorothy Dicker; Production Supervisor, Fritz Holt; Assis-
tant to Producers, Richard Vos; Wardrobe, Peter FitzGerald; Hair-
stylist, Claudia Kaneb; Production Assistants, Jamie Haskins, Jim
Rupp, Michael Petro; Assistant to Director, Herschel Fox

CAST

Alchonon	F. Murray Abraham
Teibele	Laura Esterman
Menasha	Barry Primus
Genendel	Lee Lawson
Rabbi	Stefan Schnabel
Beadle Treitel	Ron Perlman
Beadle Leib	Stephan Weyte

STANDBYS AND UNDERSTUDIES: Steven Gilborn (Alcho-
non), Mimi Turque (Teibele/Genendel), Ron Perlman (Rabbi), Stephan Weyte (Menasha)

A drama in two acts. The action takes place in Frampol, Poland,
in the 1800's.

General Management: Marvin A. Krauss Associates
Associate Manager: Gary Gunas
Press: Seymour Krawitz, Patricia McLean Krawitz, Scott Mauro
Stage Manager: Mimi Turque

* Closed Jan. 6, 1980 after 25 performances.

Sy Friedman Photos

**Laura Esterman, F. Murray Abraham, and at top
with Stefan Schnabel, Lee Lawson, Ron Perlman,
Stephan Weyte, Barry Primus**

WINTER GARDEN THEATRE
Opened Thursday, December 20, 1979.*
Ridgely Bullock and Albert W. Selden in association with Columbia Pictures present:

COMIN' UPTOWN

Book, Philip Rose, Peter Udell; Based on Charles Dickens' "A Christmas Carol"; Music, Garry Sherman; Lyrics, Peter Udell; Director, Philip Rose; Choreography, Michael Peters; Scenery, Robin Wagner; Costumes, Ann Emonts; Lighting, Gilbert V. Hemsley, Jr.; Sound, Jack Shearing; Musical Director, Howard Roberts; Orchestrations and Vocal Arrangements, Garry Sherman; Dance Music Arrangements, Timothy Graphenreed; Associate Choreographer, Frances Lee Morgan; Hairstylists, Breelun Daniels, Michael Craig Robinson; Associate Producer, Leslie K. Bullock; Associate Producers, Anthony Weymouth, Kimako; Wardrobe, Ellen Lee; Assistant Conductor, Lloyd Mayers; Assistant to Producers, Howard P. Lev

CAST

Salvation Army Trio	Deborah Lynn Bridges, Deborah Burrell, Jenifer Lewis
Scrooge	Gregory Hines
Bob Cratchit	John Russell
Tenant's Representative	Larry Marshall
Mary, Director Recreation Center	Saundra McClain
Minister	Robert Jackson
Marley	Tiger Haynes
Christmas Past	Larry Marshall
Time	Frances Lee Morgan
Mary (Younger)	Loretta Devine
Young Scrooge	Duane Davis
His Assistant	Vernal Polson
Reverend Byrd	Ned Wright
Gospel Singer	Esther Marrow
Bob Cratchit, Deacon	John Russell
Mrs. Cratchit, Deacon's Wife	Virginia McKinzie
Christmas Present	Saundra McClain
Cratchit Daughters	Shirley Black-Brown, Allison R. Manson
Martha Cratchit	Carol Lynn Maillard
Tiny Tim	Kevin Babb
Christmas Future	Robert Jackson

HARLEM RESIDENTS: Kevin Babb, Shirley Black-Brown, Roslyn Burrough, Barbara Christopher, Duane Davis, Ronald Dunham, Milton Grayson, Linda James, Kevin Jeff, Carol Lynn Maillard, Allison R. Manson, Esther Marrow, Frances Lee Morgan, Raymond Patterson, Vernal Polson, Gloria Sauve, Eric Sawyer, Kiki Shepard, Faruma Williams, Ned Wright
UNDERSTUDIES: Larry Marshall (Scrooge), Ned Wright (Marley), Otis Sallid (Christmas Past), Gloria Sauve (Christmas Present/Mrs. Cratchit), Kevin Jeff (Christmas Future), Carol Lynn Maillard (Young Mary), Swing: Prudence Darby, Otis Sallid
MUSICAL NUMBERS: Christmas Is Comin' Uptown, Now I Lay Me Down to Sleep, Get Your Act Together, Lifeline, What Better Time for Love, It Won't Be Long, Get Down Brother Get Down, Sing a Christmas Song, Have I Finally Found My Heart?, Nobody Really Do, Goin' Gone, One Way Ticket to Hell, Born Again

A musical in 2 acts and 13 scenes. The action takes place in Harlem at the present time.

General Manager: Jay Kingwill
Company Manager: Louise M. Bayer
Press: Merle Debuskey, Leo Stern
Stage Managers: Mortimer Halpern, Nate Barnett, Lisa Blackwell

* Closed Jan. 27, 1980 after 45 performances and 19 previews.

Martha Swope Photos

**Top Right: Larry Marshall, Gregory Hines, Deborah Lynn Bridges, Jenifer Lewis, Deborah Burrell
Below: Gregory Hines, Tiger Haynes
Right Center: Loretta Devine, Gregory Hines**

Duane Davis, Gregory Hines

JOHN GOLDEN THEATRE
Opened Thursday, January 3, 1980.*
Lester Osterman, Marc Howard, The Kennedy Center in association with Spencer H. Berlin present the Long Wharf Theatre production of:

WATCH ON THE RHINE

By Lillian Hellman; Director, Arvin Brown; Setting, John Jensen; Costumes, Bill Walker; Lighting, Ronald Wallace; Production Supervisor, Anne Keefe; Dialect Consultant, Elizabeth Smith; Wigs and Hairstyles, Paul Huntley; "Soldier's Song" by Thomas Fay

CAST

Anise, the housekeeper	Mary Fogarty
Fanny Farrelly	Jan Miner
Joseph, the butler	Robert Judd
David Farrelly, Fanny's son	Joel Stedman
Marthe de Brancovis, a countess	Jill Eikenberry
Teck de Brancovis, her husband	Harris Yulin
Sara Muller, Fanny's daughter	Joyce Ebert
Kurt Muller, her husband	George Hearn
Joshua Muller, their elder son	Mark McLaughlin
Babette Muller, their daughter	Monica Snowden
Bodo Muller, their younger son	Bobby Scott

A drama in three acts. The action takes place in the living room of the Farrelly country house, about twenty miles from Washington, D.C., in the late spring of 1940.

General Managers: Leonard Soloway, Allan Francis
Press: Jeffrey Richards Associates, Warren Knowlton, Robert Ganshaw, Alan Eichler, Helen Stern, Karen Gromis, Ted Killmer
Stage Manager: Leon Gagiardi

* Closed Feb. 3, 1980 after 36 performances and 13 previews. Original production opened at the Martin Beck Theatre Apr. 1, 1941 and ran for 378 performances with Lucile Watson, Paul Lukas, Mady Christians and Anne Blythe.

Joel Stedman, George Hearn, Jan Miner, Joyce Ebert
Top Left: Bobby Scott, Monica Snowden, Mark McLaughlin, Joyce Ebert

TRAFALGAR THEATRE
Opened Saturday, January 5, 1980.*
Roger L. Stevens, Robert Whitehead, James M. Nederlander present:

BETRAYAL

By Harold Pinter; Director, Peter Hall; Designed by John Bury; Production Assistant, Bill Becker; Wardrobe, Gene Wilson, Kathleen Foster

CAST

Jerry	Raul Julia
Emma	Blythe Danner†
Barman	Ian Thomson
Robert	Roy Scheider
Waiter	Ernesto Gasco

STANDBYS AND UNDERSTUDIES: Caroline Lagerfelt (Emma), James Hurdle (Jerry/Robert), Ian Thomson (Waiter)

A drama in 2 acts and 9 scenes. The action takes place from 1977 regressing to 1968 in a pub, Jerry's house, a flat, Robert and Emma's house, hotel room in Venice, and a restaurant.

General Manager: Oscar E. Olesen
Press: Seymour Krawitz, Patricia Krawitz, Scott Mauro
Stage Managers: Marnel Sumner, Ian Thomson

* Closed May 31, 1980 after 170 performances and 14 previews. Cited by NY Drama Critics Circle as Best Foreign Play of the season.
† Succeeded by Caroline Lagerfelt

Sy Friedman Photos

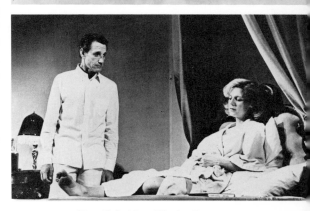

Top: Blythe Danner, Roy Scheider, Raul Julia

Roy Scheider, Blythe Danner
Above: Raul Julia, Roy Scheider

MOROSCO THEATRE

Opened Thursday, January 31, 1980.*
Richard Barr, Lester Osterman, Roger Berlind, Marc Howard,
Spencer H. Berlin and Hale Matthews present:

THE LADY FROM DUBUQUE

By Edward Albee; Director, Alan Schneider; Setting, Rouben Ter-Arutunian; Costumes, John Falabella; Lighting, Richard Nelson; Miss Worth's Costume, Pauline Trigere; Associate Producer, Leslie Strager; Wardrobe, Margot Moore; Assistant to Director, Walter Schoen; Production Assistant, Adam Dales

CAST

Lucinda	Celia Weston
Sam	Tony Musante
Jo	Frances Conroy
Fred	Baxter Harris
Edgar	David Leary
Carol	Maureen Anderman
Oscar	Earle Hyman
Elizabeth	Irene Worth

STANDBYS: M'el Dowd (Elizabeth), Paul Vincent (Sam/Fred/Edgar), Carol Potter (Jo/Carol/Lucinda)

A drama in two acts. The action takes place at the present time in Sam and Jo's home.

General Management: Leonard Soloway, Allan Francis
Company Manager: Michael Kasdan
Press: Shirley Herz, Jan Greenberg, Bruce Cohen, Sam Rudy
Stage Managers: Julia Gillett, Dan Hild

* Closed Feb. 9, 1980 after 12 performances and 8 previews.

David Leary, Maureen Anderman, Frances Conroy

**Top: (L) Irene Worth, Earle Hyman
(R) Frances Conroy, Tony Musante**

MARTIN BECK THEATRE
Opened Thursday, February 7, 1980.*
Frank Milton and Weitzenhoffer in association with Courtney
Burr and Nancy Rosenthal present:

HAROLD AND MAUDE

By Colin Higgins; Director, Robert Lewis; Music, Lyrics and
Sounds, David Amram; Scenery, Tony Straiges; Costumes, Florence
Klotz; Lighting, Neil Peter Jampolis; Sound, Otts Munderloh; Spe-
cial Effects, Chic Silber; Wardrobe, Josephine Zampedri; Assistant
to Director, Judd Mathison; Hairstylist, James Nelson; Production
Assistant, Elizabeth Shepherd

CAST

Harold	Keith McDermott
Mrs. Chasen	Ruth Ford
Marie	Berit Lagerwall
Dr. Matthews	Chet Doherty
Maude	Janet Gaynor
Priest	Jack Bittner
Gardener	Frank Ammirati
Sylvie Gazel	Denny Dillon
Inspector Bernard	Jay Barney
Sergeant Doppel	Marc Jordan
Nancy Mersch	Nonnie Weaver
Sunshine Dore	Nita Novy
Removal Men	Valentine Mayer, Doug Bergman
Mourners	Doug Bergman, Brian Brownlee, Catherine Bruno

STANDBYS AND UNDERSTUDIES: Paula Trueman (Maude),
Brian Brownlee (Harold), Lynne Rogers (Mrs. Chasen), Frank Am-
mirati (Priest), Douglas Bergman (Sergeant/Gardener), Marc Jordan (Inspector), Catherine Bruno (Sylvie/Nancy/Marie)

A comedy in two acts. The action takes place at the present time.

General Management: Richard Horner Associates
Manager: Malcolm Allen
Press: Solters & Roskin, Joshua Ellis, Tom Trenkle, David
LeShay, Cindy Valk
Stage Managers: Ben Strobach, Valentine Mayer, Douglas
Bergman

* Closed Feb. 9, 1980 after 4 performances and 21 previews.

Martha Swope Photos

Top Right: Keith McDermott, Janet Gaynor

**Nonnie Weaver, Nita Novy, Keith
McDermott, Denny Dillon**

**Keith McDermott, Ruth Ford,
Berit Lagerwall**

ST. JAMES THEATRE

Opened Sunday, February 10, 1980.*

Danny O'Donovan and Helen Montagu in association with
Mecca Productions present:

FILUMENA

By Eduardo DeFilippo; English version by Wallis Hall, Keith Waterhouse; Director, Laurence Olivier; Settings and Costumes, Raimonda Gaetani; Lighting, Thomas Skeleton; Assistant Director, Larry Forde; An original Franco Zeffirelli production; Wardrobe, Peta Ullmann; Hairstylist, J. Alexander Scafa; Production Assistants, Julie Hoffman, Lee Merrill; Speech Consultant, Edith Skinner; A re-write of "The Best House in Naples."

CAST

Filumena Marturano	Joan Plowright
Domenico Soriano	Frank Finlay
Alfredo Amoroso	Ernest Sarracino
Rosalia Solimene	Miriam Phillips
First Waiter	Gabor Morea
Second Waiter	Bill Karnovsky
Diana	Donna Davis
Lucia, the maid	Lisa Passero
Pasquale Nocella, attorney	Pierre Epstein
Umberto	Dennis Boutsikaris
Riccardo	Stephen Schnetzer
Michele	Peter Iacangelo

STANDBYS AND UNDERSTUDIES: Bernice Massi (Filumena), Lou Bedford (Domenico), Gabor Morea (Alfredo/Nocella), Nina Dova (Rosalia), Bill Karnovsky (Michele/Riccardo), Dorie DonVito (Lucia/Diana), Robert Rigamonti (Umberto/Waiters)

A comedy in three acts. The action takes place in Domenico Soriano's house in Naples, Italy, in 1946.

General Manager: Theatre Now, Inc.
Associate General Manager: Charlotte W. Wilcox
Company Manager: Terence Erkkila
Press: Seymour Krawitz, Patricia Krawitz, Scott Mauro
Stage Managers: Larry Forde, Robert Rigamonti, Dorie DonVito

* Closed March 9, 1980 after 32 performances and 7 previews.

Martha Swope Photos

Lisa Passero, Miriam Phillips, Frank Finlay, Joan Plowright, Ernest Sarracino, Peter Iancangelo, Stephen Schnetzer, Dennis Boutsikaris Top Right: Frank Finlay, Joan Plowright

RIALTO THEATRE
Opened Tuesday, February 12, 1980.*
Burry Fredrik and Bruce Schwartz present the Equity Library
Theatre production of:

CANTERBURY TALES

By Martin Starkie and Nevill Coghill; Based on translation of Geoffrey Chaucer by Nevill Coghill; Music, Richard Hill, John Hawkins; Lyrics, Nevill Coghill; Director, Robert Johanson; Choreography, Randy Hugill; Musical Direction and Vocal Arrangements, John Kroner; Costumes, Sigrid Insull; Setting, Michael Anaia; Lighting, Gregg Marriner; Production Assistant, Gina Barnett

CAST

Chaucer (January)	Earl McCarroll
Knight	Robert Stoeckle
Squire (Nicholas/Damian/Horse)	Robert Tetirick
Yeoman (John/King Arthur)	Andy Ferrell
Prioress	Mimi Sherwin
Nun (Prosperina)	K. K. Preece
Molly (Guenevere)	Kaylyn Dillehay
May	Tricia Witham
Alison (Sweetheart)	Krista Neumann
Friar (Justinus)	Andrew Traines
Merchant (Gervase)	Vance Mizelle
Clerk (Robin/Page/Horse)	Richard Stillman
Cook (Miller's Wife/Duenna)	Polly Pen
Miller	Win Atkins
Steward (Carpenter/Placebo)	Ted Houck, Jr.
Wife of Bath (Old Woman)	Maureen Sadusk
Summoner (Absalon/Alan)	Kelly Walters
Pardonner (Executioner)	Martin Walsh
Host (Pluto)	George Maguire

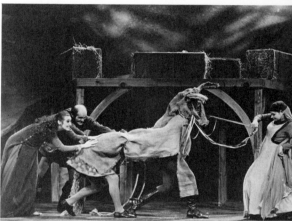

UNDERSTUDIES: David Asher (Host/Knight/Squire/Pardonner/Friar), Andy Ferrell (Clerk), George Maguire (Chaucer), Kim Morgan (Molly/Allison/May/Cook), Polly Pen (Nun/Prioress), K. K. Preece (Wife of Bath), Richard Stillman (Yeoman/Summoner), Andrew Traines (Merchant/Miller), Martin Walsh (Steward)
MUSICAL NUMBERS: Prologue, Welcome Song, Goodnight Hymn, Canterbury Day, Horse Ride, I Have a Noble Cock, There's the Moon, Darling Let Me Teach You How To Kiss, It Depends on What You're At, Beer Is Best, Love Will Conquer All, Come On and Marry Me Honey, Where Are the Girls of Yesterday, April Song, If She Has Never Loved Before, I'll Give My Love a Ring, Pear Tree Sextet, What Do Women Most Desire, I Am All Ablaze

A musical in 2 acts and 10 scenes with a prologue. The action takes place in the late 1300's during a four-day pilgrimage to Canterbury Cathedral.

General Manager: David Lawlor
Press: Shirley Herz, Jan Greenberg, Sam Rudy
Stage Managers: M. R. Jacobs, Jim R. Sprague, David Asher

* Closed Feb. 24, 1980 after 16 performances and 4 previews. Original production opened at the O'Neill Theatre on Feb. 3, 1969 and played 122 performances with Sandy Duncan, Martyn Green, George Rose, Hermione Baddeley and Ed Evanko. See THEATRE WORLD Vol. 25.

Gary Wheeler Photos

Top Right: Andy Ferrell, Andrew Traines, Maureen Sadusk, Robert Tetirick, Richard Stillman, Ted Houck, Jr. Below: Kaylyn Dillehay, Win Atkins, Polly Pen (Horse: Richard Stillman, Kelly Walters)

Entire Cast

MINSKOFF THEATRE
Opened Thursday, February 14, 1980.*
Gladys Rackmil, John F. Kennedy Center and James M. Nederlander in association with Zev Bufman present:

WEST SIDE STORY

Book, Arthur Laurents; Based on a Jerome Robbins Conception; Music, Leonard Bernstein; Lyrics, Stephen Sondheim; Entire production directed and choreographed by Jerome Robbins; Book co-directed by Gerald Freedman; Scenery, Oliver Smith; Costumes, Irene Sharaff; Lighting, Jean Rosenthal; Co-Choreographer, Peter Gennaro; Musical Direction, John DeMain, Donald Jennings; Choregraphy reproduced with the assistance of Tom Abbott, Lee Becker Theodore; Orchestrations, Leonard Bernstein, Sid Ramin, Irwin Kostal; Associate Producers, Alan Tessler, Steven Jacobson, Stewart F. Lane; Executive Producer, Ruth Mitchell; Sound, Jack Mann; Assistant Musical Director, Jim Stenborg; Wardrobe, Patricia Britton; Production Associate, Marion Kinsella; Production Assistant, Lee Merrill

CAST

"The Jets"
Riff, the leader	James J. Mellon
Tony, his friend	Ken Marshall
Action	Mark Bove
A-Rab	Todd Lester
Baby John	Brian Kaman
Snowboy	Cleve Asbury
Big Deal	Reed Jones†1
Diesel	Brent Barrett
Gee-Tar	G. Russell Weilandich
Mouthpiece	Stephen Bogardus†2
Tiger	Mark Fotopoulos
Graziella	Georganna Mills
Velma	Heather Lea Gerdes
Minnie	Frankie Wade
Clarice	Charlene Gehm
Pauline	Nancy Louise Chismar
Anybodys	Missy Whitchurch

"The Sharks"
Bernardo, the leader	Hector Jaime Mercado
Maria, his sister	Jossie De Guzman
Anita, his girl	Debbie Allen
Chino, his friend	Ray Contreras
Pepe	Michael Rivera
Indio	Darryl Tribble
Luis	Adrian Rosario
Anxious	Michael DeLorenzo
Nibbles	Willie Rosario†3
Juano	Michael Franks†4
Toro	Mark Morales
Moose	Gary-Michael Davies
Rosalia	Yamil Borges
Consuelo	Nancy Ticotin
Francisca	Harolyn Blackwell
Teresita	Stephanie E. Williams
Estella	Marlene Danielle
Marguerita	Amy Lester

The Adults
Doc	Sammy Smith
Schrank	Arch Johnson
Krupke	John Bentley
Gladhand	Jake Turner

UNDERSTUDIES: Chris Wheeler, Harolyn Blackwell (Maria), Stephen Bogardus (Tony), Marlene Danielle (Anita/Rosalia), Michael Rivera (Bernardo), Cleve Asbury (Riff), John Bentley (Doc/Schrank), Mark Morales (Gladhand/Action), Mark Fotopoulos (A-Rab), Tim O'Keefe (Baby John/Mouthpiece), Jake Turner (Krupke), Nancy Louise Chismar (Anybodys), Frankie Wade (Graziella), Richard Caceres (Snowboy), Will Mead (Riff/Action), Swing Dancers: Nancy Butchko, Richard Caceres, Tim O'Keefe

MUSICAL NUMBERS: Prologue, Jet Song, Something's Coming, The Dance at the Gym, Maria, Tonight, America, Cool, One Hand One Heart, The Rumble, I Feel Pretty, Somewhere, Gee Officer Krupke, A Boy Like That, I Have a Love, Taunting, Finale

A musical in 2 acts and 15 scenes. The action takes place on the West Side of New York City during the last days of the summer of 1957.

General Management: Theatre Now, Inc.
Company Manager: Michael Lonergan
Press: Betty Lee Hunt, Maria Cristina Pucci, Clarence Allsopp, James Sapp
Stage Managers: Patrick Horrigan, Brenna Krupa, Arlene Grayson

* Still playing May 31, 1980. Original production opened at the Winter Garden Sept. 26, 1957 with Larry Kert, Ken LeRoy, Carol Lawrence and Chita Rivera and played 732 performances. See THEATRE WORLD Vol. 14.
† Succeeded by: 1. Jeffrey Reynolds, 2. Brent Barrett, 3. Herman W. Sebek, 4. Tony Constantine

Roger Greenawalt, Martha Swope Photos

Top Right: Ray Contreras, Debbie Allen, Hector Jaime Mercado, Jossie DeGuzman
Below: DeGuzman, Ken Marshall

Above: Hector Jaime Mercado and "The Sharks" (L), James J. Mellon and "The Jets" (R)

BROOKS ATKINSON THEATRE
Opened Wednesday, February 20, 1980.*
Nancy Cooperstein, Porter Van Zandt and Marc Howard
present the Circle Repertory Company's production of:

TALLEY'S FOLLY

By Lanford Wilson; Director, Marshall W. Mason; Setting, John Lee
Beatty; Costumes, Jennifer von Mayrhauser; Lighting, Dennis Pa-
richy; Sound, Chuck London; Assistant Director, John Bard Manu-
lis; Production Assistants, Steven Burnett, Peter Janis; Technical
Coordinator, Arthur Siccardi; Wardrobe/Hairstylist, Donald
Draper

CAST

Matt Friedman .... Judd Hirsch†1
Sally Talley .... Trish Hawkins†2

STANDBYS: Jordan Charney, Mary Hamill

A play without intermission. The action takes place in an old
boat-house on the Talley Place, a farm near Lebanon, Missouri, on
a July evening in 1944.

General Management: Gatchell & Neufeld Ltd.
General Management Associate: Douglas C. Baker
Company Manager: Mark Andrews
Press: Jeffrey Richards, Bill Miller, Warren Knowlton, Robert
Ganshaw, Helen Stern, Joseph M. Santi, Karem Gromis,
Theodore Killmer
Stage Managers: Fred Reinglas, John Weeks

* Still playing May 31, 1980. Recipient of Pulitzer Prize, NY
Drama Critics Circle Award for Best Play of the 1979–1980 season, and 1980 "Tony" for Best Scenic Design. For original production, see THEATRE WORLD Vol. 35.
† Succeeded by: 1. Jordan Charney, 2. Debra Mooney

Gerry Goodstein Photos

Top Right: Judd Hirsch, Trish Hawkins

Jordan Charney, Debra Mooney

Trish Hawkins, Judd Hirsch

43

BELASCO THEATRE
Opened Wednesday, February 27, 1980.*
Eugene V. Wolsk and Marc Howard in association with Marlene Mancini present:

CHARLOTTE

By Peter Hacks; Director, Herbert Berghof; Setting, Lester Polakov; Costumes, Patricia Zipprodt; Lighting, Pat Collins; Wardrobe, Angelo Quilici; Production Assistants, John Saltonstall, Ruth Ann Nelson; Hairstylist, Patrik D. Moreton; Translated and adapted from the German by Uta and Herbert Berghof

CAST

Charlotte von Stein........................... Uta Hagen
Josias von Stein....................... Charles Nelson Reilly

A play in two acts. The action takes place in October of 1786 in the green salon of the von Stein's country estate near Weimar.

General Manager: GRQ Productions, Ltd., Manny Kladitis
Company Manager: Barbara Laney
Press: Merle Debuskey, William Schelble
Stage Managers: Mitch Erickson, Timothy Farmer

* Closed March 1, 1980 after 5 performances and 18 previews.

Martha Swope Photos

Uta Hagen, Charles Nelson Reilly

Roy Dotrice

MOROSCO THEATRE
Opened Monday, February 25, 1980.*
David Susskind presents:

ROY DOTRICE
as
MISTER LINCOLN

By Herbert Mitgang; Director, Peter Coe; Designed by David L. Lovett; Lighting, Allan Stichbury; Supervised by Richard Winkler; Producer, Isobel Robins; A Citadel (Edmonton) Production

Company Manager: Louise M. Bayer
Press: Arlene Goodman, Frank Goodman
Stage Manager: John Wilbur

* Closed March 9, 1980 after 16 performances and 5 previews.

44

ROYALE THEATRE

Opened Sunday, February 24, 1980.*
Emanuel Azenberg, James M. Nederlander and Ray Cooney present:

WHOSE LIFE IS IT ANYWAY?

By Brian Clark; Director, Michael Lindsay-Hogg; Scenery, Alan Tagg; Costumes, Pearl Somner; Lighting, Tharon Musser; Wardrobe, Reet Pell; Hairstylist, John Quaglia

CAST

Claire Harrison	Mary Tyler Moore
Nurse Anderson	Beverly May
Mary Jo Sadler	Suzanna Hay
John	Northern J. Calloway
Dr. David Scott	James Naughton†
Dr. Michael Emerson	Josef Sommer
Mrs. Boyle	Johanna Leister
Margaret Hill	Susan Kellermann
Dr. Paul Jacobs	Edmond Genest
Peter Kershaw	John Straub
Dr. Robert Barr	Joseph McCaren
Andrew Eden	Eric Booth
Judge Wyler	James Higgins

STANDBYS AND UNDERSTUDIES: Catherine Gaffigan (Anderson/Hill/Boyle), Eric Booth (Jacobs/Kershaw/Barr), Edmond Genest (Scott), James Higgins (Emerson), Joseph McCaren (Jacobs), John Straub (Wyler/Emerson), Dianne Trulock (Saddler), David Harris (John)

A drama in two acts. The action takes place at the present time in a hospital in the United States.

General Manager: Jose Vega
Company Managers: Max Allentuck, Louise Bendall
Press: Bill Evans, Howard Atlee, Leslie Anderson, Jim Baldassare
Stage Managers: Martin Herzer, Cathy B. Blaser, Dianne Trulock

* Closed May 18, 1980 after 96 performances. For original Broadway production with Tom Conti, see THEATRE WORLD Vol. 35.
† Succeeded by Everett McGill

Martha Swope Photos

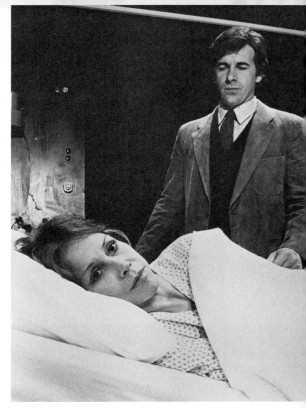

Mary Tyler Moore, James Naughton

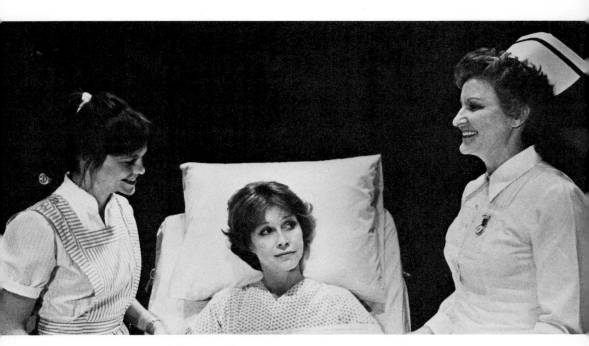

Suzanna Hay, Mary Tyler Moore, Beverly May

CIRCLE IN THE SQUARE THEATRE
Opened Tuesday, February 26, 1980.*
Circle in the Square (Theodore Mann, Artistic Director; Paul Libin, Managing Director) present:

MAJOR BARBARA

By George Bernard Shaw; Director, Stephen Porter; Scenery and Costumes, Zack Brown; Lighting, John McLain; Wigs and Hairstyles, Paul Huntley; Wardrobe, Millicent Hacker; Production Assistant, James White

CAST

Lady Britomart	Rachel Gurney
Stephen Undershaft	Nicholas Walker
Morrison	Donald Buka
Barbara Undershaft	Laurie Kennedy
Sarah Undershaft	Gina Franz
Adolphus Cusins	Nicholas Surovy
Charles Lomax	Rand Bridges
Andrew Undershaft	Philip Bosco
Rummy Mitchens	Paddy Croft
Snobby Price	Norman Allen
Jenny Hill	Amanda Carlin
Peter Shirley	Frank Hamilton
Bill Walker	Jon DeVries
Mrs. Baines	Joan Croydon
Bilton	Jamey Sheridan

UNDERSTUDIES: Dalton Cathey (Adolphus/Stephen), Jamey Sheridan (Charles/Snobby/Bill), Donald Buka (Peter), Sarah-Jane Gwillim (Rummy/Jenny/Mrs. Baines)

A comedy in three acts. The action takes place in the library of Lady Britomart Undershaft's house in Wilton Crescent, the yard of the West Ham Shelter of the Salvation Army, and the Foundry-Perival St. Andrews.

Company Manager: William Conn
Press: Merle Debuskey, Leo Stern
Stage Managers: Nicholas Russiyan, Robert O'Rourke

* Closed March 30, 1980 after limited engagement of 40 performances and 28 previews.

Martha Swope Photos

Laurie Kennedy, Joan Croydon, Frank Hamilton, Amanda Carlin, Philip Bosco Nicolas Surovy Top Left: Laurie Kennedy, Rachel Gurney, Nicolas Surovy Below: Surovy, Kennedy, Bosco, Gurney

PRINCESS THEATRE
Opened Thursday, March 6, 1980.*
Michael White and Eddie Kulukundis present:

CENSORED SCENES FROM KING KONG

By Howard Schuman; Music, Andy Roberts; Director, Colin Bucksey; Choreography, David Toguri; Scenery, Mike Porter; Lighting, Richard Nelson; Costumes, Jennifer von Mayrhauser; Sound, Robert Kerzman; Wigs, Charles LoPresto; Associate Producer, Robert S. Fishko; Hairstylist, Esther Teller; Musical Supervisor, Keith Herrmann; Assistant to Producers, Susan Dorsey; Production Assistants, Sherry Cohen, Angela Manno; Dialect Coach, Elizabeth Smith

CAST

Stephen	Stephen Collins
Voice of the Producer	Nicky Mieholes
Voice of the Author	Pete Flasher
Vogels/Sagar/Chiaruggi	Peter Reigert
Iris	Carrie Fisher
Deborah	Alma Cuervo
Benchgelter	Chris Sarandon
Walter Wilma	Edward Love

UNDERSTUDIES: Candy Darling (Iris/Deborah), Ron Fassler (Stephen/Benchgelter/Vogels/Sagar/Chiaruggi), Kenny Brawner (Walter)
MUSICAL NUMBERS: Ha-Cha, Banana Oil, He Ain't Scared of Nothing, Number One, Soft Shoe Freak, The Other Side of the Wall

A "comic extravaganza" with music in two acts. The action takes place at the present time in London, England.

General Manager: Harris Goldman
Press: Front Page Enterprises/Elizabeth Rodman
Stage Managers: Steven Zweigbaum, Candy Darling

* Closed March 9, 1980 after 5 performances and 11 previews.

Ken Howard Photos

**Top: Edward Love, Chris Sarandon,
Carrie Fisher, Alma Cuervo**

Stephen Collins, Peter Riegert

RADIO CITY MUSIC HALL
Opened Friday, March 14, 1980.*
Radio City Music Hall Productions Inc. presents:

IT'S SPRING
The Glory of Easter

Conceived and Produced by Robert F. Jani; Executive Musical Director, Donald Pippin; Directed and Choreographed by Dru Davis, Howard Parker; Rockettes Choreography, Violet Holmes; Production Executive, John J. Moore; Associate Production Executive, Jeff Hamlin; Scenic Design, John William Keck; Lighting, Ken Billington; Costumes, Frank Spencer: Bud Santora; Conductor, Elman Anderson; Vocals devised by Ronald Melrose; New Yorkers Medly arranged by Elman Anderson; Orchestrations, Philip J. Lang, Michael Gibson, Elman Anderson, Gary Anderson; Original Music, Sammy Cahn, Donald Pippin.

CAST
The Vienna Choir Boys
The Rockettes
The New Yorkers
The Famous People Players

An entertainment performed without intermission.
General Manager: Robert A. Buckley
Press: Gifford/Wallace, Robin Gellman, Ellen Seh, Keith Sherman
Stage Managers: Neil Miller, Peter Rosenberg, Ray Chandler

⁺ Closed April 13, 1980 after 56 performances.

The Vienna Choir Boys

Top: The New Yorkers
Below: The Rockettes

ANTA THEATRE

Opened Wednesday, March 19, 1980.*
Kim D'Estainville presents The Group TSE in:

HEARTACHES OF A PUSSYCAT

By Genevieve Serrau and James Lord; Based on story by Balzac;
Director, Alfredo Rodriguez Arias; Masks, Rostislav Douboujinsky;
Costumes, Claudie Gastine; Sets, Emilio Carcano; Lighting, Beverly
Emmons; Original Designs, Andre Diot; Cheoreography, Marilu
Marini; Musical Direction, Michael Sanvoisin; Associate Producer,
Jack Schlissel; Wardrobe, Josephine Zampedri

CAST

Christy/Tomcat/Doctor/Altolaguirre	Jacques Jolivet
Pussycat/Lulu/Cactus	Amelie Berg
Old Maid/Risque/Puss-in-Boots	Facundo Bo
Minister/Tomcat/Beggar	Larry Hager
Mother of Beauty/Rhoda/Rose	Raquel Iruzubieta
Beauty	Marilu Marini
Mother of Lulu/Sir Midas Asset	Horacio Pedrazzini
Captain Pack/Tomcat	Alain Salomon
Arabella/Butterfly	Jerome Nicolin
Rabbit/Guitarist	Joachin Riano
Dog/Viola Player	Jean-Jacques Gueroult

A "spectacle" in two acts inspired by the drawings of French
illustrator, J. J. Grandville, in "Scenes de la vie privee et publique
des animaux" (1840). The action takes place circa 1840 in Ireland,
London and the English countryside.

General Managers: Jack Schlissel, Jay Kingwill
Company Manager: Larry Goosen
Press: Jeffrey Richards, Robert Ganshaw, Warren Knowlton, Bill
Miller, Ben Morse, Helen Stern, Ted Killmer, Karen Gromis,
Joseph Santi
Stage Manager: Jane E. Neufeld

* Closed March 23, 1980 after 5 performances and 18 previews.

CORT THEATRE
Opened Wednesday, March 26, 1980.*
Elliot Martin in association with Donald Cecil and Columbia
Pictures presents:

CLOTHES FOR A SUMMER HOTEL

By Tennessee Williams; Director, Jose Quintero; Scenery, Oliver
Smith; Costumes, Theoni V. Aldredge; Lighting, Marilyn Rennagel;
Original Music, Michael Valenti; Dance Consultant, Anna Sokolow;
Dance Coordinator, Weyman Thompson; Hairstylist, Alan Schu-
bert, Michael Heller; Assistant to Producers, Joanne F. Benson;
Wardrobe, Karen Mae Lloyd; Assistant to Director, John Handy

CAST

German Sisters	Madeleine le Roux, Josephine Nichols
Ghosts	Marilyn Rockafellow, Tanny McDonald, Garrison Phillips, Scott Palmer, Weyman Thompson, Audree Rae
F. Scott Fitzgerald	Kenneth Haigh
Gerald Murphy	Michael Connolly
Becky	Mary Doyle
Zelda Fitzgerald	Geraldine Page
Journalist	Robert Bays
Photographer	Scott Palmer
Nurses	Madeleine le Roux, Tanny McDonald
Intern/Edouard	David Canary
Sara Murphy	Marilyn Rockafellow
Madame Egorova	Audree Rae
Mrs. Patrick Campbell	Josephine Nichols
Dr. Zeller/Dr. Baum	Michael Granger
Hemingway	Robert Black
Hadley Hemingway	Tanny McDonald
Singer	Weyman Thompson
Dancer	Madeleine le Roux

UNDERSTUDIES: Tanny McDonald, Madeleine le Roux (Zelda),
Michael Connolly (Scott), Scott Palmer (Edouard/Intern), Robert
Bays (Hemingway), Garrison Phillips (Gerald/Journalist), Audree
Rae (Becky), Mary Doyle (Sara), Madeleine le Roux (Hadley), Jose-
phine Nichols (Mme. Egorova).

A "ghost play" in two acts. The action takes place at Highland
Hospital on a windy hilltop near Asheville, N.C., Zelda's final asylum.

General Manager: Victor Samrock
Company Manager: John Larson
Press: Betty Lee Hunt, Maria Cristina Pucci, Robert W. Larkin,
James Sapp
Stage Managers: John Handy, Scott Palmer

* Closed Apr. 6, 1980 after 15 performances and 6 previews.

Jack Buxbaum Photos

Geraldine Page, David Canary
Top Right: Kenneth Haigh, Geraldine Page

BILTMORE THEATRE

Opened Thursday, March 27, 1980.*
Michael Butler and Eric Nazhad with David Cogan present:

REGGAE

Concept and Production, Michael Butler; Story, Kendrew Lascelles; Book, Melvin Van Peebles, Kendrew Lascelles, Stafford Harrison; Music and Lyrics, Ras Karbi, Michael Kamen, Kendrew Lascelles, Stafford Harrison, Max Romeo, Randy Bishop, Jackie Mittoo; Director, Glenda Dickerson; Additional Direction, Gui Andrisano; Choreographer, Mike Malone; Executive Producer, Woodie King, Jr.; Musical Director, Michael Kamen; Cultural Consultant, Rex Nettleford; Set, Ed Burbridge; Costumes, Raoul Pene DuBois; Lighting, Beverly Emmonds; Sound, Lou Gonzalez; Associate Music Director, Michael Tschudin; Hair and Wig Designer, Eric Turner; Assistant to Producers, Sally Shafer; Conductor, Jackie Mittoo; Wardrobe, Ellen Lee; Production Assistants, Julio Mario Santo Domingo, Michael Goodman, Mark Fitzgibbons, Bob Phillips

CAST

Anancy, The Spider	Alvin McDuffie
Faith	Sheryl Lee Ralph
Esau	Philip Michael Thomas
Rockets	Obba Babatunde
Mrs. Brown	Fran Salisbury
Louise	Louise Robinson
Ras Joseph	Calvin Lockhart
Natty	Ras Karbi
Gorson	Charles Wisnet
Binghi Maytal	Sam Harkness

UNDERSTUDIES: Obba Babatunde (Esau), Constance Thomas (Faith), Thomas Pinnock (Ras Joseph), Paul Cook'tartt (Rockets/-Binghi), Ras-Jawara Tesfa (Natty), Louise Robinson (Mrs. Brown), Alternates: Brenda Braxton, Andy Torres

MUSICAL NUMBERS: Jamaica Is Waiting, Rise Tafari, Farmer, Hey Man, Mash Em Up, Mrs. Brown, Everything That Touches You, Mash Ethiopia, Star of Zion, Reggae Music Got Soul, Talkin' 'Bout Reggae, Rise Up Jah-Jah Children, No Sinners in Jah Yard, Banana Banana Banana, Promised Land, Rasta Roll Call, Ethiopian Pageant, Rastafari, Roots of the Tree, I and I, Gotta Take a Chance, Chase the Devil, Now I See It

A musical in 2 acts and 11 scenes. The action takes place in one day in Jamaica, BWI.

General Manager: Ken Myers
Company Manager: Dennis Purcell
Press: Merlin Group, Cheryl Sue Dolby, Sandra Manley, Marguerite Wolfe
Stage Managers: Robert D. Currie, Lee Murray, Breena Clarke

* Closed Apr. 13, 1980 after 21 performances and 11 previews.

Philip Michael Thomas, Obba Babatunde

Philip Michael Thomas, Obba Babatunde (L) and chorus

LONGACRE THEATRE
Opened Sunday, March 30, 1980.*
Emanuel Azenberg, The Shubert Organization, Dasha Epstein,
Ron Dante present the Mark Taper Forum production of:

CHILDREN OF A LESSER GOD

By Mark Medoff; Director, Gordon Davidson; Set, Thomas A.
Walsh; Costumes, Nancy Potts; Lighting, Tharon Musser; Associate
Producers, William P. Wingate, Kenneth Brecher; Wardrobe, Jim
Hodson; Assistant to Producers, Leslie Butler; Production Assistants,
Eric Fitzgerald, Neila Ruben; Sign Language Consultant, Lou
Fant; Interpreter, Jean Worth

CAST

Sarah Norman	Phyllis Frelich
James Leeds	John Rubinstein
Orin Dennis	Lewis Merkin
Mr. Franklin	William Frankfather
Mrs. Norman	Scotty Bloch
Lydia	Julianne Gold
Edna Klein	Lucy Martin

UNDERSTUDIES: A. Linda Bove (Sarah), Robert Steinberg
(James), Nanci Jagielski (Lydia), Richard Kendall (Orin), Howard
Brunner (Mr. Franklin), Jill Andre (Edna/Mrs. Norman)

A drama in two acts.

General Manager: Jose Vega
Company Manager: Lilli Afan
Press: Bill Evans, Howard Atlee, Bruce Cohen, Leslie Anderson,
Jim Baldassare
Stage Managers: Mark Wright, Jonathan Barlow Lee, Richard
Kendall

* Still playing May 31, 1980. Received 1980 "Tony's" for Best Play,
Best Actress (Phyllis Frelich), and Best Actor (John Rubinstein)

Martha Swope Photos

**Phyllis Frelich, John Rubinstein, and top with
Julianne Gold, Lewis Merkin, William Frankfather,
Lucy Martin, Scotty Bloch**

JOHN GOLDEN THEATRE
Opened Wednesday, April 2, 1980.*
Joel W. Schenker, Jay J. Cohen, Richard Press, Chester Gore
with Alan Silverman and Bernard Schwartz present:

HOROWITZ AND MRS. WASHINGTON

By Henry Denker; Director, Joshua Logan; Setting, Steven Rubin;
Costumes, William Schroder; Lighting, Marc B. Weiss; Associate
Producer, Theodore Ravinett; Wardrobe, Toni Baer; Assistant to
Director, Joseph C. Curtis; Production Assistant, Claudia Anderson

CAST

Samuel Horowitz	Sam Levene
Marvin Hammond	Theodore Sorel
Mrs. Harriet Washington	Esther Rolle
Conrad Bruton	Christopher Blount
Mona Fields	Patricia Roe
Dr. Tannenbaum	Joe DeSantis

STANDBYS AND UNDERSTUDIES: Joe DeSantis (Samuel),
Rosanna Carter (Harriet), Skipp Lynch (Marvin/Tannenbaum),
Pegge Winslow (Mona)

A comedy in two acts. The action takes place at the present time
in an apartment on Central Park West in New York City during the
month of July.

General Manager: Victor Samrock
Company Manager: David Payne
Press: Max Eisen, Sol Jacobson, Francine L. Trevens
Stage Managers: Howard Whitfield, Skipp Lynch

* Closed April 6, 1980 after 6 performances and 10 previews.

Martha Swope Photos

**Top: Patricia Roe, Sam Levene,
Esther Rolle**

**Christopher Blount, Esther Rolle,
Sam Levene**

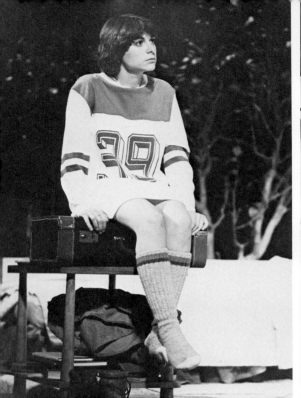

EUGENE O'NEILL THEATRE
  Opened Thursday, April 3, 1980.*
Emanuel Azenberg presents:

I OUGHT TO BE IN PICTURES

By Neil Simon; Director, Herbert Ross; Set, David Jenkins; Costumes, Nancy Potts; Lighting, Tharon Musser; Assistant to Director, Carol Patella; Wardrobe, Frank Green; Assistant to Producer, Leslie Butler

CAST

Libby	Dinah Manoff
Steffy	Joyce Van Patten
Herb	Ron Leibman

STANDBYS: Mimi Cozzens (Steffy), Valerie Landsburg (Libby)

A comedy in two acts. The action takes place at the present time in Herb's home in West Hollywood, California.

Manager: Jose Vega
Press: Bill Evans, Howard Atlee, Leslie Anderson, Jim Baldassare
Stage Managers: Frank Marino, Arlene Grayson

* Still playing May 31, 1980. Dinah Manoff received a 1980 "Tony" for Best Featured Actress in a play.

Martha Swope Photos

**Top: Dinah Manoff (L)
Ron Leibman (R)**

**Ron Leibman, Dinah Manoff,
Joyce Van Patten**

LYCEUM THEATRE
Opened Thursday, April 10, 1980.*
Elizabeth I. McCann, Nelle Nugent, Ray Larsen present:

MORNING'S AT SEVEN

By Paul Osborn; Director, Vivian Matalon; Setting, William Ritman; Costumes, Linda Fisher; Lighting, Richard Nelson; Wardrobe, Rosalie Lahm; Hairstylist, Karol Coeyman, Paul Huntley

CAST

Theodore Swanson	Maurice Copeland
Cora Swanson	Teresa Wright
Aaronetta Gibbs	Elizabeth Wilson
Ida Bolton	Nancy Marchand
Carl Bolton	Richard Hamilton
Homer Bolton	David Rounds
Myrtle Brown	Lois de Banzie
Esther Crampton	Maureen O'Sullivan
David Crampton	Gary Merrill

UNDERSTUDIES: Harriet Rogers (Ida/Esther/Aaronetta/Cora), Jonathan Farwell (David/Theodore/Carl), Martha Miller (Myrtle), Daniel Ziske (Homer)

A play in three acts. The action takes place in two backyards in a small midwestern town during 1922.

Company Manager: Barbara Darwall
Press: Solters/Roskin/Friedman, Joshua Ellis, David LeShay, Cindy Valk
Stage Managers: Marnel Sumner, Ellen Raphael

* Still playing May 31, 1980. Recipient of 1980 "Tony's" for Best Revival, Best Direction, and Best Featured Actor (David Rounds). Original production opened at the Longacre Theatre on Nov. 30, 1939 with Dorothy Gish, Jean Adair, Kate McComb, Enid Markey and Effie Shannon and ran for 44 performances.

Martha Swope Photos

Standing: Nancy Marchand, Richard Hamilton, Lois de Banzie, Elizabeth Wilson, Gary Merrill Seated: David Rounds, Teresa Wright, Maurice Copeland, Maureen O'Sullivan

Nancy Marchand, Maureen O'Sullivan, Richard Hamilton, David Rounds, Lois de Banzie Gary Merrill, Elizabeth Wilson, Teresa Wright, Maurice Copeland

Florence Anglin, Gale Sondergaard,
Jane Alexander

NEW AMBASSADOR THEATRE
Opened Wednesday, April 23, 1980.*
The Producer Circle Company (Martin Richards, Mary Lea Johnson, Bill Barnes) in association with Sam Crothers and Allen Litke presents:

GOODBYE FIDEL

By Howard Sackler; Director, Edwin Sherin; Settings, Rouben Ter-Arutunian; Costumes, Florence Klotz; Lighting, Toshiro Ogawa; Sound, Jack Shearing; Technical Adviser, Arthur Siccardi; Wardrobe, Adelaide Laurino; Hairstylists, Steve Atha, Peg Schierholz, Angela Gari; Assistant to Director, Julie Forsmith; Production Assistants, Steven Burnett, Maris Clement; Wigs, Paul Huntley, Bob Kelly; Production Associate, Joel Brykman

CAST

D./Prison Commandante	Ralph Byers
Natalia	Jane Alexander
Alvaro	Lee Richardson
Elena	Concetta Tomei
Miguelito	David Schramm
Billy	Curt Karibalis
Carmen/1st Woman	Stephanie Cotsirilos
Isabel	Kathy Bates
Bobby	Tony Diaz
Leon	Guy Sorel
Prudencia	Gale Sondergaard
Eufemia/Mrs. Berman	Florence Anglin
James Sinclair	Christopher Cazenove
Peggy Sinclair	Pamela Brook
Captain/Jose	Raymundo Hidalgo-Gato
Corporal	Arnaldo Santana
Rosita	Vera Lockwood
Second Woman/Joanne	Suzanne Toren
Mr. Scharf	Bernie Passeltiner
Chantal	Ivonne Coll

STANDBYS AND UNDERSTUDIES: Ruth Nelson (Prudencia), Stephanie Cotsirilos (Natalia), Ivonne Coll (Euphemia/Elena), Suzanne Toren (Isabel/Peggy/Carmen/Rosita), Arnaldo Santana (Bobby/Captain/Billy/D.), David Schramm (Scharf), Raymundo Hidalgo-Gato (Alvaro/Miguelito), Ralph Byers (James/Jose), Curt Karibalis (Corporal), Vera Lockwood (Prudencia/Mrs. Berman), Bernie Passeltiner (Leon/Commandante), Tony Diaz (Soldier)

A drama in 2 acts and 7 scenes. The action takes place from 1958 to 1962 in Natalia's house, Alvaro's farm outside Havana, Campamento de Columbia, Hotel Windsor in Miami, Airport Motel in San Juan, and Alvaro's apartment in Madrid.

General Management: Gatchell & Neufeld
Associate: Douglas C. Baker
Company Manager: Leo K. Cohen
Press: Betty Lee Hunt, Maria Cristina Pucci, Robert W. Larkin, James Sapp
Stage Managers: Steve Zweigbaum, Jonathan Penzner, Tony Diaz, Suzanne Toren

* Closed April 26, 1980 after 6 performances and 23 previews.

Roger Greenwalt Photos

**Top Left: Christopher Cazenove, Jane Alexander
Below: Christopher Cazenove, Lee Richardson, Concetta Tomei**

CIRCLE IN THE SQUARE THEATRE
Opened Thursday, April 24, 1980.*
Circle in the Square (Theodore Mann, Artistic Director; Paul Libin, Managing Director) presents:

PAST TENSE

By Jack Zeman; Director, Theodore Mann; Scenery, Zack Brown; Costumes, Kristina Watson; Lighting, John McLain; Wardrobe, Millicent Hacker; Hair and Wig Supervisor, Michael Wasula; Assistant to Director, Garrison Fishgall

CAST

Emily Michaelson . . . . Barbara Feldon
Ralph Michaelson . . . . Laurence Luckinbill†

A play in two scenes, performed without intermission. The action takes place at the present time during late fall in Emily and Ralph Michaelson's living room.

Company Manager: William Conn
Press: Merle Debuskey, Leo Stern
Stage Managers: Nicholas Russiyan, Robert O'Rourke

* Closed June 1, 1980 after 45 performances and 23 previews.
† Succeeded by Michael Miller

Martha Swope Photos

Top: Laurence Luckinbill, Barbara Feldon

Barbara Feldon, Laurence Luckinbill

57

MOROSCO THEATRE
Opened Sunday, April 27, 1980*
Leonard Soloway, Allan Francis, Hale Matthews in association
with Marble Arch Productions present:

HAPPY NEW YEAR

Book, Burt Shevelove; Based on play "Holiday" by Philip Barry;
Songs by Cole Porter; Edited by Buster Davis; Director, Burt Sheve-
love; Choreography, Donald Saddler; Associate Producer, Dorothy
Cherry; Musical Direction-Vocal Arrangements, Buster Davis; Or-
chestrations, Luther Henderson; Additional Orchestrations, Daniel
Troob; Dance Music Arrangements, Charles Coleman; Designed by
Michael Eagan; Costumes, Pierre Balmain; Lighting, Ken Billing-
ton; Sound, Tom Morse; Assistant Choreographer, Mercedes Elling-
ton; Costume Supervision, John Falabella; Assistants to Producers,
Cassia Farkas, Cathy Lesser; Hairstylist, Gerry Leddy; Speech Con-
sultant, Robert Williams; Production Assistant, Robin Walker;
Wardrobe, Joe Busheme; Associate Conductor, Charles H. Coleman.

CAST

The Narrator	John McMartin
Edward Seton	William Roerick
Edward Seton, Jr.	Richard Bekins
Julia Seton	Kimberly Farr
Linda Seton	Leslie Denniston
Johnny Case	Michael Scott
Frazer	Roger Hamilton
Charles/Anderson	Morgan Ensminger
Patrick	J. Thomas Smith
George/Thompson	Tim Flavin
Steven/Harrison	Richard Christopher
Victor/Dixon	Lara Teeter
Rose/Nancy	Lauren Goler
Maude/Miss Madden/Mary	Mary Sue Finnerty
Annie/Gloria	Bobbie Nord
Bridget/Joan	Michele Marshall

STANDBYS: Michele Marshall (Julia), Lara Teeter (Ned), Roger
Hamilton (Narrator/Mr. Seton), Ken Mitchell (Frazer/Charles),
Terry Rieser, Ken Mitchell (Staff/Stork Club Set)
MUSICAL NUMBERS: At Long Last Love, Ridin' High, Let's Be
Buddies, Boy Oh Boy, Easy to Love, You Do Something to Me, Red
Hot and Blue, Once Upon a Time, Night and Day, Let's Make It
a Night, Ours, After You Who?, I Am Loved, When Your Troubles
Have Started

A musical in two acts. The action takes place on the five floors in
the Fifth Avenue townhouse of Edward Seton in New York City in
December 1933 and January 1934.

General Management: Soloway & Francis
Company Manager: Michael Kasdan
Press: Shirley Herz, Jan Greenberg, Sam Rudy
Stage Managers: Nina Seely, Zane Weiner, Alan Mann

* Closed May 10, 1980 after 17 performances and 27 previews.

Roger Greenawalt Photos

**Right: John McMartin, Leslie Denniston
Top: Leslie Denniston, Richard Bekins
Below: Denniston, Kimberly Farr**

Leslie Denniston (L)

**Leslie Denniston, Richard Bekins, William Roerick,
Kimberly Farr, John McMartin**

BILTMORE THEATRE
Opened Monday, April 28, 1980.*
Stevie Phillips in association with Universal Pictures presents
the WPA Theatre Production of:

NUTS

By Tom Topor; Director, Stephen Zuckerman; Setting, Tom Schwinn; Lighting, Roger Morgan; Costumes, Christina Weppner; Associate Producers, Bonnie Champion, Danny Kreitzberg; Wardrobe, Terence Kotch; Hairstylist and Makeup, Steve Atha; Assistant to Director, Darlene Kaplan

CAST

Officer Harry Haggerty	Dave Florek
Aaron Levinsky	Richard Zobel
Franklin MacMillan	Gregory Abels
The Recorder	Linda Howes
Rose Kirk	Lenka Peterson
Arthur Kirk	Hansford Rowe
Dr. Herbert Rosenthal	Paul Stolarsky
Judge Murdoch	Ed VanNuys
Claudia Faith Draper	Anne Twomey

UNDERSTUDIES: Erika Peterson (Claudia), Philip Polito (Rosenthal/Levinsky), Dave Florek (MacMillan), Georgine Hall (Rose/Recorder)

A drama in three acts. The action takes place during February of 1979 in the courtroom of the psychiatric wing of Bellevue Hospital, New York City.

General Management: Jack Schlissel, Jay Kingwell
Company Manager: Larry Goossen
Press: Jeffrey Richards, C. George Willard, Warren Knowlton, Robert Ganshaw, Bill Miller, Ted Killmer, Karen Gromis
Stage Managers: Lola Shumlin, Kathy Arit

* Closed July 19, 1980 after 96 performances and 8 previews.

Chip Goebert Photos

**Linda Howes, Ed VanNuys, Paul Stolarsky, Anne Twomey
Top Right: Anne Twomey, Richard Zobel Below: Hansford Rowe, Lenka Peterson, Anne Twomey**

ST. JAMES THEATRE
Opened Wednesday, April 30, 1980.*
Judy Gordon, Cy Coleman, Maurice Rosenfield, Lois F. Rosenfield in association with Irvin Feld and Kenneth Feld present:

BARNUM

Book, Mark Bramble; Music, Cy Coleman; Lyrics, Michael Stewart; Directed and Staged by Joe Layton; Scenery, David Mitchell; Costumes, Theoni V. Aldredge; Lighting, Craig Miller; Sound, Otts Munderloh; Orchestrations, Hershy Kay; Vocal Arrangement, Cy Coleman, Jeremy Stone; Music Director, Peter Howard; Circus Training by The Big Apple Circus/NY School for Circus Arts; Associate Producers, Steven A. Greenberg, Michael Scharf; Hairstylist, Ted Azar; Technical Supervisor, Peter Feller; Assistant to Producers, Erik P. Sletteland; Wardrobe, Mary P. Eno; Production Assistants, Michael Der Manuelian, Deborah Birch, Joanna Chapin; Assistant to Director, John Mineo; Assistant Conductor, Peter Phillips; Original Cast Album by CBS Masterworks Records

CAST

Phineas Taylor Barnum	Jim Dale
Chairy Barnum	Glenn Close
Ringmaster/Julius Goldschmidt/ James A. Bailey	William C. Witter
Chester Lyman/Humber Morrissey	Terrence V. Mann
Joice Heth	Terri White
Amos Scudder/Edgar Templeton	Kelly Walters
Lady Plate Balancer	Catherine Carr
Lady Juggler	Barbara Nadel
Chief Bricklayer	Edward T. Jacobs
White-faced Clown	Andy Teirstein
Sherwood Stratton	Dirk Lumbard
Mrs. Sherwood Stratton	Sophie Schwab
Tom Thumb	Leonard John Crofoot
Susan B. Anthony	Karen Trott
Jenny Lind	Marianne Tatum
One-Man Band	Steven Michael Wilton
	Bruce Robertson
Lady Aerialist	Robbi Morgan
Pre-curtain Entertainers	Bradley Steven-Fields, Catherine Carr, Andy Teirstein, Bruce Robertson
Pianists	Karen Gustafson, Peter Phillips

STANDBYS AND UNDERSTUDIES: Harvey Evans (Barnum), Suellen Estey (Chairy/Jenny), Bruce Robertson (Lyman), Dirk Lumbard (Goldschmidt/Templeton/Morrissey), Terrence V. Mann (Bailey/Stratton), Mary Testa (Joice), Leonard John Crofoot (Scudder), Barbara Nadel (Mrs. Stratton/Susan Anthony), Edward T. Jacobs (Tom Thumb), Kelly Walters (Wilton), Bradley Steven-Fields (Ensemble)

MUSICAL NUMBERS: There's a Sucker Born Ev'ry Minute, Thank God I'm Old, The Colors of My Life, One Brick at a Time, Museum Song, I Like Your Style, Bigger Isn't Better, Love Makes Such Fools of Us All, Out There, Come Follow the Band, Black and White, The Prince of Humbug, Join the Circus

A musical in two acts. The action takes place all over America and the major capitals of the world from 1835 through 1880.

General Management: James Walsh
Company Manager: Susan Bell
Press: David Powers, Barbara Carroll
Stage Managers: Mary Porter Hall, Marc Schlackman, Michael Mann

* Still playing May 31, 1980. Recipient of 1980 "Tony's" for Best Actor in a Musical (Jim Dale), Best Scenic Design, and Best Costumes.

Martha Swope Photos

Top Left: Jim Dale, Marianne Tatum
Below: Jim Dale (C)

Glenn Close, Jim Dale

JOHN GOLDEN THEATRE
Opened Thursday, May 1, 1980.*
Alexander H. Cohen and Hildy Parks present:

A DAY IN HOLLYWOOD
A NIGHT IN THE UKRAINE

Book and Lyrics, Dick Vosburgh; Music, Frank Lazarus; Directed and Choreographed by Tommy Tune; Co-Choreographer, Thommie Walsh; Scenery, Tony Walton; Lighting, Beverly Emmons; Costumes, Michel Stuart; Sound, Otts Munderloh; Musical Direction-Vocal and Dance Arrangements, Wally Harper; Hairstylist, Joseph Dal Corso; Co-Producer, Roy A. Somlyo; Associate Producer, Philip M. Getter; Production Associate, Seymour Herscher; Production Assistant, Margaret Barrett; Wardrobe, Elonzo Dann; Original Cast Album by DRG Records

CAST

"A Day in Hollywood"

Priscilla Lopez	David Garrison
Stephen James	Peggy Hewett
Niki Harris	Frank Lazarus
Albert Stephenson	Kate Draper

MUSICAL NUMBERS: Just Go to the Movies, Famous Feet, I Love a Film Cliché, Nelson, The Best in the World, It All Comes out of the Piano, Richard Whiting Medley, Thanks for the Memory, Another Memory, Doin' the Production Code, A Night in the Ukraine

INTERMISSION

"A Night in the Ukraine"—loosely based on Chekhov's "The Bear"
Mrs. Pavlenko, a rich widow.................. Peggy Hewett
Carlo, her Italian footman.................... Frank Lazarus
Gino, her gardener .... Priscilla Lopez
Serge B. Samovar, a Moscow lawyer .... David Garrison
Nina, Mrs. Pavlenko's daughter .... Kate Draper
Constantine, a coachman..................... Stephen James
Masha, a maid............................. Niki Harris
Sascha, a manservant .... Albert Stephenson

STANDBYS AND UNDERSTUDIES: Mitchell Greenberg (Garrison/Lazarus), Trudi Roach (Lopez/Draper), Celia Tackaberry (Hewett), Karen Harvey (Harris), Jack Magradey (James/Stephenson)
MUSICAL NUMBERS: Samovar the Lawyer, Just Like That, Again, A Duel! A Duel!, Natasha, A Night in the Ukraine

The action takes place in the morning room of the Pavlenko residence in the Ukraine before the revolution.

General Manager: Roy A. Somlyo
Company Managers: Charles Willard, Jodi Moss
Press: Alpert/LeVine, Mark Goldstaub
Stage Managers: Thomas Kelly, Christopher A. Cohen

* Still playing May 31, 1980. Recipient of 1980 "Tony's" for Best Featured Actress in a Musical (Priscilla Lopez), and Best Choreography.

Martha Swope Photos

Top Left: Priscilla Lopez, David Garrison, Kate Draper, Stephen James Below: Priscilla Lopez, David Garrison, Frank Lazarus

Stephen James, Priscilla Lopez, David Garrison

Carol Lawrence

RADIO CITY MUSIC HALL
Opened Friday, May 2, 1980.*
Radio City Music Hall Productions presents:

A ROCKETTE SPECTACULAR
with
Ginger Rogers[†]

Producer-Director, Robert F. Jani; Executive Musical Director, Donald Pippin; Scenery, John W. Keck; Dialogue, Stan Hart; Rockettes Choreography, Violet Holmes; Costumes, Frank Spencer; Miss Rogers Choreography, Howard Parker; Lighting, Ken Billington; Conductor, Elman Anderson

CAST

Ginger Rogers, Gail Nelson, Jack Blackton, and Dancers: David Brownlee, John Cashman, Ron Crofoot, David Fredericks, Michael Lang, Bobby Longbottom, Daryl Murphy, Scott Plank, Patrick Roddy, David Roman, Brent Saunders, David Scala, Lyn Schaal, and *The Rockettes*

PROGRAM

Overture, The March, In Their Dressing Room, Rockette Rehearsal, In the Star's Dressing Room, My Big Moment, Alike Alike, Dance Dance Dance, Fifty Years of the Rockettes, Stage-Struck, Five Minutes 'Til Showtime, Hoedown, On Her Own, Finale

Press: Gifford/Wallace, Keith Sherman
Stage Managers: Neil Miller, Peter Rosenberg, Ray Chandler

* Closed June 22, 1980 after 96 performances.
† Succeeded by Carol Lawrence

Martha Swope Photos

Top: Ginger Rogers and Rockettes

BELASCO THEATRE
Opened Sunday, May 4, 1980.*
Michael Frazier and Bill McCutcheon in association with Susan
Madden Samson present:

HIDE AND SEEK

By Lezley Havard; Director, Melvin Bernhardt; Set, John Lee
Beatty; Lighting, Arden Fingerhut; Costumes, Jennifer von Mayr-
hauser; Sound, Gary Harris; Wardrobe, Mark Immens; Assistant to
Director, Greg Johnson; Assistant to Producers, Charles M. Mirotz-
nik; Production Assistant, Kristin Johnson; Fight Choreography, J.
Allen Suddeth

CAST

Jennifer Crawford	Elizabeth Ashley
Matt Erskine	Peter Crombie
Martha Turner	Sylvia Short
Richard Crawford	David Ackroyd
Elly Bart	Christine Baranski
John Bart	Tom Klunis
Vicki Bennett	Alexandra Borrie
Tony Crawford	Michael Ayr
Dr. Hugh McKenna	Robert Gerringer

UNDERSTUDIES: Kelly Ellen Collins, Herbert Duval, Tom Klu-
nis, Leslie Lyles, Leslie Ann Ray, Robert Townsend
  A mystery thriller in 2 acts and 6 scenes. The action takes place
at the present time in an old farmhouse.
General Management: Theatre Now Inc.
Company Manager: Peter H. Russell
Press: Betty Lee Hunt, Maria Cristina Pucci, Robert W. Larkin,
James Sapp
Stage Managers: Frank Hartenstein, Robert Townsend

* Closed May 11, 1980 after 9 performances and 5 previews.

Theo Westenberger Photos

**David Ackroyd, Elizabeth Ashley Top Right: Elizabeth Ashley, Tom Klunis,
Christine Baranski Below: Peter Crombie, Sylvia Short**

TOWN HALL
Opened Sunday, May 4, 1980*
George Wein in association with Honi Coles, Robert Kimball
and Bobby Short presents the Newport Jazz Festival production of:

BLACK BROADWAY

Designer, Leo Gambacorta; Orchestrations and Musical Arrangements: Dick Hyman; Musical Direction, Frank Owens; Associate
Producer, John P. Fleming; Sound, Paul Blank-Omnisound; Assistants to the Producers, Marilyn Posnick, Sylvia Pancotti, Elizabeth
Spahr

CAST

John W. Bubbles	Gregory Hines
Nell Carter	Bobby Short
Honi Coles	Elisabeth Welch
Adelaide Hall	Edith Wilson

and Charles "Cookie" Cook, Leslie "Bubba" Gaines, Mercedes Ell-
ington, Carla Earle, Terri Griffin, Wyetta Turner
MUSICAL NUMBERS: Runnin' Wild, Under the Bamboo Tree,
Oh Say Wouldn't It Be a Dream, Broadway in Dahomey, The
Unbeliever, Doin' the New Low-Down, When Lights Are Low,
Solomon, Love for Sale, Creole Love Song, I Must Have That Man,
Digga Digga Do, I Can't Give You Anything But Love, Ill Wind,
Between the Devil and the Deep Blue Sea, As Long As I Live,
Brownskin Gal in the Calico Gown, Jump for Joy, Cotton Club
Stomp, There's a Boat That's Leavin' Soon for New York, It Ain't
Necessarily So, Black and Blue, He May Be Your Man, Tan Man-
hattan, Charleston Rag, Silver Rose, I'm a Little Blackbird, Charles-
ton, I've Got a Feeling I'm Falling, Legalize My Name, Taking a
Chance on Love, Heat Wave, You're Lucky to Me, Suppertime,
Honey in the Honeycomb, Stormy Weather, Dinah, Sweet Georgia
Brown, Memories of You

A musical entertainment in two parts, featuring musical numbers
introduced by black performers from 1899 to 1946.
Press: Henry Luhrman, Terry M. Lilly, Robert Pontarelli, Kevin
P. McAnarney
Stage Managers: Victor Caamano, Sandy Musloff

* Closed May 24, 1980 after limited engagement of 24 performances
and 3 previews.

Martha Swope Photos

**Leslie "Bubba" Gaines, Gregory Hines, Honi Coles, Charles "Cookie" Cook, Bobby Short,
Elizabeth Welch, Adelaide Hall, Edith Wilson, (seated) Nell Carter, John W. Bubbles
Top Left: Bobby Short and chorus**

CORT THEATRE

Opened Wednesday, May 7, 1980.*

Elizabeth I. McCann, Nelle Nugent, Gerald S. Krone and Ray Larsen present the Negro Ensemble Company production of:

HOME

By Samm-Art Williams; Director, Douglas Turner Ward, originated by Dean Irby; Scenery, Felix E. Cochren; Costumes, Alvin B. Perry; Lighting, Martin Aronstein; Scenery Supervision, Lynn Pecktal; Costume Supervision, Jeanne Button; Associate Producer, Tommy DeMaio; Wardrobe, Veneda Truesdale; Production Assistant, William H. Grant III

CAST

Cephus Miles	Charles Brown
Woman One/Pattie Mae Wells	L. Scott Caldwell
Woman Two	Michele Shay
Understudies:	Chuck Patterson, Lorey Hayes

A drama performed without intermission. The action takes place from the late 1950's to the present in Cross Roads, N.C., a prison in Raleigh, N.C., and a very large American city.

Company Manager: Susan Gustafson
Press: Solters/Roskin/Friedman, Joshua Ellis, Becky Flora, David LeShay, Cindy Valk
Stage Managers: Horacena J. Taylor, Ron Nguvu

* Still playing May 31, 1980.

Martha Swope Photos

Top: (L) L. Scott Caldwell, Michele Shay, Charles Brown (R) Brown, Shay

Michele Shay, Charles Brown, L. Scott Caldwell

WINTER GARDEN THEATRE
Opened Thursday, May 8, 1980.*
Paramount Pictures Corporation presents:

THE ROAST

By Jerry Belson and Garry Marshall; Director, Carl Reiner; Scenery, William Ritman; Costumes, Alvin Colt; Lighting, Tharon Musser; Sound, Otts Munderloh; Producers, Joseph P. Harris, Ira Bernstein; Wardrobe, Bill Campbell; Assistant to Director, Marva Miny; Production Assistant, Howard P. Lev; Hairstylist, Steven A. M. Jefairjian

CAST

Gus Mizzy	Bill Macy
Tambi Rothman	Larry Gelman
Sid Ball	Barney Martin
Delores	Becky Gonzalez
Hal St. Denis	John Arch-Carter
Charles Browning	Doug McClure
Denver Cody	David Huddleston
B. B. Gunn	Antonio Fargas
Danny	Rob Reiner
Mr. Lang	Reynaldo Rey
Sonny Silver	Arny Freeman
Elaine	Crissy Wilzak
Garry Allen	Joe Silver
Phil Alexander	Peter Boyle

STANDBYS: Jeff Keller (Danny/Charles), Mickey Deems (Gus/-Denver/Sid/Sonny), James Lockhart (Phil/Garry/Tambi/Hal/-Lang), Reynaldo Rey (Gunn), Melodie Somers (Elaine/Delores)

A comedy in two acts. The action takes place in the Century Park Banquet Room in Beverly Hills, California, at the present time on a Sunday morning before the roast and that evening during the roast.

Business Manager: Peter T. Kulok
Press: Solters/Roskin/Friedman, Milly Schoenbaum, Kevin Patterson, Lisa Kasteler, Merrill Gaskin
Stage Managers: Ed Aldridge, Victoria Merrill, James Lockhart

* Closed May 10, 1980 after 4 performances and 9 previews.

Top: Bill Macy, David Huddleston, Larry Gelman, Antonio Fargas, Joe Silver, Barney Martin

Arny Freeman, Becky Gonzalez, Rob Reiner Above: Rob Reiner, Peter Boyle

RIALTO THEATRE
Opened Wednesday, May 14, 1980.*
Lesley Savage and Bert Stratford present the Equity Library
Theatre production of:

MUSICAL CHAIRS

Book, Barry Berg, Ken Donnelly, Tom Savage; Based on an original
story concept by Larry J. Pontillo; Music and Lyrics, Tom Savage;
Direction and Choreography, Rudy Tronto; Scenery, Ernest Allen
Smith; Lighting, Peggy Clark; Costumes, Michael J. Cesario; Direc-
tor-Assistant Choreographer, Susan Stroman; Musical Direction,
Barry H. Gordon; Arrangements and Orchestrations, Ada Janik,
Dick Leib; Wardrobe, Pamela Ellsworth; Production Assistant,
George Wabey

CAST

Joe Preston	Ron Holgate†1
Matty	Eileen McCabe
Stage Manager	Douglas Walker
Sally's Boyfriend	Scott Ellis
Millie	Enid Blaymore
Roberta	Grace Keagy†2
Brad	Randall Easterbrook
Miranda	Leslie-Anne Wolfe
Lillian	Patti Karr
Harold	Brandon Maggart
Gary	Jess Richards
Janet	Joy Franz
Brown Suit	Edward Earle
Blue Suit	Tom Breslin
Tuxedo	Rick Emery
Valerie Brooks	Lee Meredith

MUSICAL NUMBERS: Overture, Tonight's the Night, My Time,
Who's Who, If I Could Be Beautiful, What I Could Have Done
Tonight, There You Are, Sally, Other People, Hit the Ladies, Musi-
cal Chairs, Suddenly Love, Better Than Broadway, Every Time the
Music Starts
   A musical in two acts. The action takes place at the present time
at an Off-Broadway theatre on opening night in a section of the
audience.

General Manager: Leonard A. Mulhern
Company Manager: Malcolm Allen
Press: Jeffrey Richards, Warren Knowlton, C. George Willard,
Ben Morse
Stage Managers: Douglas F. Goodman, Douglas Walker

* Closed May 25, 1980 after 15 performances and 6 previews.
† Succeeded by: 1. Tom Urich, 2. Helon Blount

Peter Cunningham Photos

Brandon Maggart, Patti Karr

**Enid Blaymore, Grace Keagy, Tom Breslin, Randall Easterbrook,
Lee Meredith, Scott Ellis**

MAJESTIC THEATRE
Opened Monday, May 19, 1980.*
Columbia Artists Theatrical Corporation and Blackstone Magik Enterprises present:

BLACKSTONE!

Directed and Choreographed by Kevin Carlisle; Assistant to Mr. Carlisle, Betty Brawley; Scenery, Peter Wolf; Costumes, Winn Morton; Lighting, Martin Aronstein; Magic Production Designer, Jack Hart; Musical Supervisor-Conductor, Milton Setzer; Orchestrations, Richard Bellis; Magic Direction, Charles Reynolds; Production Supervisor, Jackie Schrock; Illusion Supervisor, Bill Smith; Wardrobe, Kathleen Gallagher

CAST

Harry Blackstone

Gay Blackstone	Becky Garrett
Elaine Barnes	Richard Ruth
Lynn Castles	Bill Smith
Karen Curlee	Nikki Summerford
Ann McLean	Jim Thompson
Robbin McDowell	John Traub
Mary McNamara	Michal Weir
Reenie Moore	

PROGRAM

ACT I: Overture, The Vanishing Birdcage, A Salute to Our Heritage, The Wizard, Cassadaga Propaganda, Mysteries of the Orient, Hare, The Incredible Buzzsaw
ACT II: The Enchanted Garden, Roses for Your Lady, The Wizard Returns, The Extraordinary Floating Lightbulb, Moorish Fantasies, So You Want to Be a Magician, Circus of Mysteries

General Management: Theatre Now, Inc.
Company Manager: Hans Hortig
Press: Alpert/LeVine, Marilynn LeVine, Michael Alpert, Mark Goldstaub, Alan Hale
Stage Managers: Sam Clester, Stephen Nimmer

* Closed Aug. 17, 1980 after 104 performances.

Ken Howard Photos

Harry Blackstone and company
Top Left: Harry Blackstone

CENTURY THEATRE

Opened Tuesday, May 27, 1980.*

Patricia Flynn Peate presents the Theatre Off Park production of:

OF THE FIELDS, LATELY

By David French; Director, Jamie Brown; Set, J. Robin Modereger; Supervised by James Tilton; Costumes, Dolores Gamba; Lighting, Richard Dorfman; Props/Wardrobe, Tamara Block; Assistants to Producer, Jeff Solis, Emily Segal

CAST

Ben Mercer	Christopher W. Cooper
Jacob Mercer	William Cain
Mary Mercer	Mary Fogarty
Wiff Roach	John Leighton

A drama in 2 acts and 4 scenes. The action takes place during January 1961 in the Toronto, Canada, home of Mary and Jacob Mercer who were originally from Newfoundland.

General Management: Berenice Weiler, Marilyn S. Miller
Manager: Barbara Carrellas
Press: Jeffrey Richards, Warren Knowlton, Robert Ganshaw, C. George Willard, Ben Morse, Helen Stern, Ted Killmer
Stage Managers: Brooke Allen, Larry Rosler

* Closed June 1, 1980 after 8 performances and 4 previews.

Top: Christopher W. Cooper, William Cain, Mary Fogarty, John Leighton

William Cain, Mary Fogarty, John Leighton

MOROSCO THEATRE
Opened Thursday, May 29, 1980.*
Mike Nichols and Lewis Allen present:

BILLY BISHOP GOES TO WAR

Written, Composed and Directed by John Gray, in collaboration with Eric Peterson; Scenery, David Gropman; Lighting, Jennifer Tipton; Sound, Robert Kerzman; Co-Produced by Vancouver East Cultural Centre; Executive Director, Christopher Wootten; Associate Producers, Stephen Graham and Ventures West Capital, Inc.; Wardrobe, Dolores Gamba

CAST

Billy Bishop, Upperclassman, Adjutant Perrault, Officer, Sir Hugh Cecil, Lady St. Helier, Cedric, Doctor, General John Higgins, Tommy, Lovely Helene, Albert Ball, Walter Bourne, General Hugh M. Trenchard, Servant, King George V . . . .
. . . . Eric Peterson†1, Cedric Smith (matinees)
Narrator and Pianist. . . . . John Gray†2, Ross Douglas (matinees)

Performed with one intermission. All characters and incidents are based on actual facts. ,

General Manager: Robert S. Fishko
Company Manager: Harris Goldman
Press: David Powers, Barbara Carroll
Stage Managers: George Gracey, T. Schuyler Smith

* Closed June 7, 1980 after 12 performances and 7 previews.
† Succeeded by: 1. Cedric Smith, 2. Ross Douglas

Joe B. Mann Photos

Top Right: Eric Peterson, John Gray
Below: Cedric Smith (L), Ross Douglas (R)

BROADWAY PRODUCTIONS FROM PAST SEASONS THAT CLOSED THIS SEASON

Title	Opened	Closed	Performances
Grease	2/14/72	4/13/80	3388
Mummenschanz	3/30/77	4/20/80	1326
Dracula	10/20/77	1/6/80	925
Chapter Two	12/4/77	12/9/79	857
Da	5/1/78	1/1/80	697
Eubie!	9/20/78	10/7/79	439
Bedroom Farce	3/29/79	11/24/79	278
Whose Life Is It Anyway?	4/17/79	10/27/79	223
Whoopee!	2/14/79	8/12/79	204
Knockout	5/6/79	9/16/79	154
I Remember Mama	5/31/79	9/2/79	108

LONGACRE THEATRE
Opened Tuesday, May 8, 1978.*
(Moved January 29, 1979 to Plymouth Theatre)
Emanuel Azenberg, Dasha Epstein, the Shubert Organization,
Jane Gaynor and Ron Dante present:

AIN'T MISBEHAVIN'

Conceived and Directed by Richard Maltby, Jr.; Based on an idea
by Murray Horwitz, and Richard Maltby, Jr.; Musical Numbers
Staged by Arthur Faria; Associate Director, Murray Horwitz; Mu-
sic Supervision, Orchestrations and Arrangements, Luther Hender-
son; Vocal Arrangements, William Elliott, Jeffrey Gutcheon; Sets,
John Lee Beatty; Costumes, Randy Barcelo; Lighting, Pat Collins;
Sounds, Otts Munderloh; Hairstylist, Michael Weeks, Paul Lopez;
Wardrobe, Max Hager, Warren S. Morrill; Technical Coordinator,
Arthur Siccardi; Assistant to Producers, Leslie Butler; Production
Assistant, Jane Robison; Production Supervisor, Clint Spencer

CAST

Nell Carter†1	Ken Page†4
Andre De Shields†2	Charlaine Woodard†5
Armelia McQueen†3	Luther Henderson (Pianist)†6

STANDBYS: Shezwae Powell, Ellia English, Gail Boggs, George
Merritt, Eric Riley
MUSICAL NUMBERS: Ain't Misbehavin', Lookin' Good but Fee-
lin' Bad, Tain't Nobody's Bizness If I Do, Honeysuckle Rose,
Squeeze Men, Handful of Keys, I've Got a Feelin' I'm Fallin', How
Ya Baby, Jitterbug Waltz, The Ladies Who Sing with the Band,
Yacht Club Swing, When the Nylons Bloom Again, Cash for Your
Trash, Off-Time, The Joint Is Jumpin', Spreadin' Rhythm Around,
Lounging at the Waldorf, Viper's Drag, Mean to Me, Your Feet's
Too Big, That Ain't Right, Keepin' Out of Mischief, Find Out What
They Like, Fat and Greazy, Black and Blue, Finale

A musical entertainment based on the music of Thomas "Fats"
Waller, performed in two parts.

Manager: Jose Vega
Company Manager: John M. Kirby
Press: Bill Evans, Howard Atlee, Leslie Anderson, Jim
Baldassare
Stage Managers: Lani Ball, Bruce Birkenhead, Linda Cohen

* Still playing May 31, 1980. For original production see THE-
ATRE WORLD Vol. 34. Received 1978 "Tonys" for Best Musi-
cal, Featured Actress (Nell Carter), Director, voted Best Musical
by NY Drama Critics, Drama Desk, and Outer Critics Circle.
† Succeeded by: 1. Avery Sommers, Zoe Walker, Yvette Freeman,
Roz Ryan, 2. Alan Weeks, 3. Yvette Freeman, Teresa Bowers,
Loretta Bowers; 4. Ken Prymus, Jason Booker, 5. Debbie Allen,
Adriane Lenox, 6. Frank Owens, Hank Jones

Martha Swope Photos

Teresa Bowers, Ken Prymus, Adriane
Lenox, Alan Weeks, Yvette Freeman
(also Top Right)

Teresa Bowers, Ken Prymus
Above: Adriane Lenox, Alan Weeks

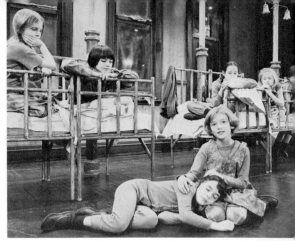

ALVIN THEATRE

Opened Thursday, April 21, 1977.*
Mike Nichols presents:

ANNIE

Book, Thomas Meehan; Based on "Little Orphan Annie" comic strip; Music, Charles Strouse; Lyrics, Martin Charnin; Choreography, Peter Gennaro; Director, Martin Charnin; Producers, Irwin Meyer, Stephen R. Friedman, Lewis Allen; Settings, David Mitchell; Costumes, Theoni V. Aldredge; Lighting, Judy Rasmuson; Musical Direction-Dance Music Arrangements, Peter Howard; Orchestrations, Philip J. Lang; Produced by Alvin Nederlander Associates-Icarus Productions; Produced in association with Peter Crane; Assistant Conductor, Robert Billig, Paul Cianci; Wardrobe, Adelaide Laurino, Joy Ortiz; Production Assistants, Sylvia Pancotti, Stephen Graham; Assistant Choreographer, Mary Jane Houdina; Hairstylist, Ted Azar, Sonia Rivera, Hector Garcia; Original Cast Album by Columbia Records.

CAST

Molly	Jennine Babo
Pepper	Jenn Thompson†1
Duffy	Randall Ann Brooks†2
July	Jodi Ford†3
Tessie	Kim Fedena†4
Kate	Karen Schleifer†5
Annie	Sarah Jessica Parker†6
Miss Hannigan	Dolores Wilson†7
Bundles McCloskey/Ickes/Sound Effects Man	James Hosbein†8
Apple Seller/Jimmy Johnson/Howe	David Brummel
Dog Catcher/Fred McCracken/Honor Guard	Gary Gendell†9
Dog Catcher/Hull	Donald Craig†10
Sandy	Himself
Lt. Ward/Bert Healy/Morgantheau	Richard Ensslen
Sophie/Annette/Ronnie Boylan	Chris Jamison†11
Grace Farrell	Mary Bracken Phillips
Drake	Edwin Bordo
Mrs. Pugh/NBC Page/Perkins	Edie Cowan†12
Miss Greer/Bonnie Boylan	Ann Ungar†13
Cecille/Connie Boylan	Edie Cowan†14
Oliver Warbucks	John Schuck
Rooster Hannigan	Robert Fitch†15
Lily	Annie McGreevey†16
Justice Brandeis	Richard Ensslen

UNDERSTUDIES: Tiffany Blake (Annie), Raymond Thorne (Warbucks), Roy Meachum (FDR), Henrietta Valor (Miss Hannigan), Donna Thomason (Grace), Laura Kerr (Pepper/Duffy/July/Tessie/Kate), Tara Kennedy (Molly), Larry Ross (Rooster), Jane Robertson (Lily), David Brummel (Drake), Richard Walker (Healy), Ensemble: Don Bonnell, Jane Robertson, Roy Meachum, Barrie Moss

MUSICAL NUMBERS: Maybe, It's the Hard-Knock Life, Tomorrow, We'd Like to Thank You, Little Girls, I Think I'm Gonna Like It Here, N. Y. C., Easy Street, You Won't Be an Orphan for Long, You're Never Fully Dressed without a Smile, Something Was Missing, I Don't Need Anything But You, Annie, A New Deal for Christmas

A musical in 2 acts and 13 scenes. The action takes place December 11–25, 1933 in New York City.

General Management: Gatchell & Neufeld Ltd.
Company Manager: Douglas C. Baker
Press: David Powers, Barbara Carroll
Stage Managers: Brooks Fountain, Patrick O'Leary, Roy Meachum, Barrie Moss, Steven David

* Still playing May 31, 1980. For original production see THEATRE WORLD Vol. 33. Received 1977 NY Drama Critics Circle, and "Tony" Awards for Best Musical.
† Succeeded by: 1. Caroline Daly, 2. Stacey Lynn Brass, 3. Martha Byrne, 4. Tiffany Blake, 5. Tara Kennedy, 6. Allison Smith, 7. Alice Ghostley, 8. R. Martin Klein, 9. Larry Ross, 10. Richard Walker, 11. Shelly Burch, 12. Henrietta Valor, 13. Donna Thomason, 14. Marianne Sanazaro, 15. Gary Beach, 16. Rita Rudner

Martha Swope Photos

**Top Right: (C) Jennine Babo, Allison Smith
Below: Rita Rudner, Gary Beach, Alice Ghostley**

**Finale with full company
Above: John Schuck, Allison Smith**

FORTY-SIXTH STREET THEATRE
Opened Monday, June 19, 1978.*
Universal Pictures presents:

THE BEST LITTLE WHOREHOUSE IN TEXAS

Book, Larry L. King, Peter Masterson; Music and Lyrics, Carol Hall; Direction, Peter Masterson, Tommy Tune; Musical Numbers Staged by Tommy Tune; Sets, Marjorie Kellogg; Costumes, Ann Roth; Lighting, Dennis Parichy; Musical Supervision, Direction and Vocal Arrangements, Robert Billig; Hairstylist, Michael Gottfried; Associate Choreographer, Thommie Walsh; Wardrobe, Karen L. Eifert, Lancey Saunders Clough; Conductor, Peter Blue; Assistant to Director, Janie Rosenthal; Original Cast Albums by MCA Records

CAST

Rio Grande Band	Craig Chambers, Racine Romaguera, Harvey Shapiro, Pete Blue, Michael Holleman, Ernie Reed
Girls	Monica Tiller, Karen Sutherland, Donna King, Nancy Lynch, Becky Gelke
Cowboys.	Beau Allen, Stephen Bray, Beau Gravitte
Farmer/Melvin P. Thorpe	Clint Allmon
Shy Kid	Gerry Burkhardt
Miss Wulla Jean	Debra Zalkind
Traveling Salesman/C. J. Scruggs/Chip Brewster/ Governor	Jay Garner†1
Slick Dude/Soundman	K. C. Kelly†2
Choir	Jay Bursky, Diana Broderick, Candace Tovar, Edwina Lewis, Jan Merchant, Peter Heuchling
Angel	Gena Ramsel†3
Shy	Cheryl Ebarb
Jewel	Delores Hall
Mona Stangley.	Carlin Glynn†4
Her Girls:	
Linda Lou	Donna King
Dawn	Monica Tiller
Ginger	Louise Quick-Bowen†5
Beatrice	Jan Merchant
Taddy Jo	Jill Cook†6
Ruby Rae.	Becky Gelke†7
Eloise	Diana Broderick
Durla	Debra Zalkind
Leroy Sliney.	Gene O'Neill†8
The Dogettes	Gerry Burkhardt, Jay Bursky, Peter Heuchling, Beau Gravitte
Stage Manager/Cameraman/Specialty Dancer	Tom Cashin
Mayor Poindexter/Senator Wingwoah	J. Frank Lucas
Sheriff Ed Earl Dodd	Henderson Forsythe†1 1
Melvin Thorpe Singers	Candace Tovar, Karen Sutherland, Beau Allen, Jan Merchant, Stephen Bray, Diana Broderick
Edsel Mackey	Don Crabtree†9
Doatsey Mae	Susan Mansur†10
T.V. Announcer	Larry L. King
Angelette Imogene Charlene	Monica Tiller
Aggies.	Peter Heuchling, Beau Allen, Jay Bursky, Gene O'Neill, Stephen Bray, Gerry Burkhardt, Tom Cashin, Beau Gravitte
Reporters	Bobbi Jo Lathan, Peter Heuchling, Beau Gravitte
Governor's Aide	Jay Bursky

STANDBYS AND UNDERSTUDIES: Gil Rogers (Sheriff), Bobbi Jo Lathan (Miss Mona), Diana Broderick (Ginger), Jan Merchant (Doatsey Mae), John Newton (Sheriff/Mayor/Senator/Scruggs), Monica Tiller (Angel), Edwina Lewis (Jewel), Ernie Reed (Edsel/- Narrator), Gerry Burkhardt (Governor/Thorpe), Laura Ackerman (Dawn), Candace Tovar (Shy), Alternate Dancers: Jerry Yoder, Laura Ackerman

MUSICAL NUMBERS: Prologue, 20 Fans, A Lil Ole Bitty Pissant Country Place, Girl You're a Woman, Watch Dog Theme, Texas Has a Whorehouse in It, 24 Hours of Lovin', Doatsey Mae, Angelette March, The Aggie Song, Bus from Amarillo, The Sidestep, No Lies, Good Old Girl, Hard Candy Christmas, Finale

A musical in two acts. The action takes place in the State of Texas.

General Management: Jack Schlissel, Jay Kingwell
Company Manager: Leonard A. Mulhern
Press: Jeffrey Richards, Warren Knowlton, C. George Willard, Ben Morse, Robert Ganshaw, Helen Stern
Stage Managers: Paul J. Phillips, Jay Schlossberg-Cohen, Nancy Lynch

J. Frank Lucas, Fannie Flagg
Top: Fannie Flagg Below: The Aggies

* Still playing May 31, 1980. Miss Glynn and Mr. Forsythe received 1979 "Tonys" for Best Performances in a Musical. For original production see THEATRE WORLD Vol. 34.
† Succeeded by: 1. Patrick Hamilton, 2. Gene O'Neill, 3. Tina Johnson, 4. Fannie Flagg, 5. Becky Gelke, 6. Karen Sutherland, 7. Candace Tovar, 8. Stephen Bray, 9. John Newton, 10. Bobbi Jo Lathan, 11. Gil Rogers

SHUBERT THEATRE

Opened Sunday, October 19, 1975.*

Joseph Papp presents a New York Shakespeare Festival production in association with Plum Productions:

A CHORUS LINE

Conceived, Choreographed and Directed by Michael Bennett; Book, James Kirkwood, Nicholas Dante; Music, Marvin Hamlisch; Lyrics, Edward Kleban; Co-Choreographer, Bob Avian; Musical Direction-Vocal Arrangements, Don Pippin; Associate Producer, Bernard Gersten; Setting, Robin Wagner; Costumes, Theoni V. Aldredge; Lighting, Tharon Musser; Sound, Abe Jacob; Music Coordinator, Robert Thomas; Orchestrations, Bill Byers, Hershy Kay, Jonathan Tunick; Assistant to Choreographers, Baayork Lee; Music Coordinator, Robert Thomas; Musical Direction, Robert Rogers; Wardrobe, Alyce Gilbert; Production Supervisor, Jason Steven Cohen; Original Cast Album by Columbia Records

CAST

Roy	Dean Badolato†1
Kristine	Christine Barker
Sheila	Kathrynann Wright†2
Val	Lois Englund†3
Mike	Don Correia†4
Butch	Kevin Chinn
Larry	R. J. Peters†5
Maggie	Marcia Lynn Watkins
Richie	Larry G. Bailey†6
Tricia	Diane Fratantoni
Tom	Jon Michael Richardson†7
Zach	Scott Pearson
Mark	Timothy Wahrer
Cassie	Cheryl Clark
Judy	Joanna Zercher†8
Lois	Gail Mae Ferguson†9
Don	Dennis Edenfield
Bebe	Karen Meister
Connie	Janet Wong
Diana	Chris Bocchino
Al	Jim Corti†10
Frank	Claude Tessier†11
Greg	Danny Weathers
Bobby	Ronald Stafford
Paul	Rene Clemente
Vicki	Angelique Ilo†12
Ed	Jon Michael Richardson
Sam	James Beaumont
Jenny	Jannet Horsley
Jarad	T. Michael Reed
Ralph	Dennis Parlato
Linda	Diane Duncan
Agnes	Betty Lynd

UNDERSTUDIES: James Beaumont (Paul/Mark/Larry), Kevin Chinn (Richie), Dennis Daniels (Al/Mike), Diane Duncan (Judy/Kristine), Dennis Edenfield (Mike), Diane Frantantoni (Diana/Val/Connie/Maggie/Bebe), Troy Garza (Mike/Mark/Paul Larry/Al), Deborah Henry (Cassie), Janet Horsley (Sheila/Kristine/Judy), Angelique Ilo (Cassie), Betty Lynd (Val/Kristine/Maggie/Connie), Tim Millett (Zach/Don/Larry), Bebe Neuwirth (Cassie), Dennis Parlato (Zach/Al/Don), Michael-Day Pitts (Greg), Jon Michael Richardson (Bobby/Greg), Tracy Shayne (Bebe/Diana/Maggie), James Warren (Zach), Marcia Lynn Watkins (Sheila), Joanna Zercher (Judy/Kristine/Sheila/Val)

MUSICAL NUMBERS: I Hope I Get It, I Can Do That, And . . ., At the Ballet, Sing!, Hello Twelve Hello Thirteen Hello Love, Nothing, Dance: 10 Looks: 3, Music and the Mirror, One, The Tap Combination, What I Did for Love, Finale

A musical performed without intermission. The action takes place at the present time during an audition in the theatre.

General Manager: Robert Kamlot
Company Manager: Bob MacDonald
Press: Merle Debuskey, Bob Ullman, Richard Kornberg, William Schelble
Stage Managers: Tom Porter, Wendy Mansfield, Jon Michael Richardson, James Beaumont

* Still playing May 31, 1980. Cited as Best Musical by NY Drama Critics Circle, Winner of Pulitzer Prize, 1976 "Tonys" for Best Musical, Best Book, Best Score, Best Director, Best Lighting, Best Choreography. A Special Theatre World Award was presented to every member of the creative staff and original cast. See THEATRE WORLD Vol. 31 for original production.

Deborah Henry, Cheryl Clark, Rene Clemente, Scott Pearson, Chris Bocchino, Kathrynann Wright Top: Ralph Glenmore

† Succeeded by: 1. Dennis Daniels, 2. Bebe Neuwirth, 3. Deborah Henry, Mitzi Hamilton, Deborah Henry, 4. Buddy Balou, 5. T. Michael Reed, Michael-Day Pitts, 6. Carleton T. Jones, Ralph Glenmore, 7. Claude Tessier, Tim Millett, 8. Angelique Ilo, 9. Bebe Neuwirth, Tracy Shayne, 10. James Warren, 11. Michael-Day Pitts, Troy Garza, 12. Joanna Zercher

Martha Swope Photos

BROADHURST THEATRE
Opened Monday, March 27, 1978.*
Jules Fisher, The Shubert Organization (Gerald Schoenfeld, Chairman; Bernard B. Jacobs, President), and Columbia Pictures present:

DANCIN'

Conceived, Directed and Choreographed by Bob Fosse; Scenery, Peter Larkin; Costumes, Willa Kim; Lighting, Jules Fisher; Music and Lyrics, Johann Sebastian Bach, Ralph Burns, George M. Cohan, Neil Diamond, Bob Haggart, Ray Bauduc, Gil Rodin, Bob Crosby, Jerry Leiber, Mike Stoller, Johnny Mercer, Harry Warren, Louis Prima, John Philip Sousa, Carole Bayer Sager, Melissa Manchester, Barry Mann, Cynthia Weil, Felix Powell, George Asaf, Sigmund Romberg, Oscar Hammerstein 2nd, Cat Stevens, Edgar Varese, Jerry Jeff Walker; Associate Producer, Patty Grubman; Music Conducted and Arranged by Gordon Lowry Harrell; Orchestrations, Ralph Burns; Hairstylist, Romaine Greene; Sound, Abe Jacob; Wardrobe, Joseph Busheme; Production Assistant, Vicki Stein; Assistants to Mr. Fosse, Kathryn Doby, Christopher Chadman, Gwen Verdon; Associate Conductor, Michael Camilo

CAST

Gail Benedict†1	Vicki Frederick†9
Sandahl Bergman†2	Linda Haberman†10
Karen G. Burke†3	Richard Korthaze
Rene Ceballos†4	Edward Love†11
Christopher Chadman†5	John Mineo†12
Wayne Cilento†6	Ann Reinking†13
Jill Cook†7	Blane Savage†14
Gregory B. Drotar†8	Charles Ward†15

ALTERNATES: Valerie-Jean Miller, David Warren-Gibson, Gregory B. Drotar, James Dunne, Eileen Casey, Deborah Phalen, Bryan Nicholas, Laurent Giroux, Katherine Meloche, Beth Shorter, James Horvath, Bill Hastings

MUSICAL NUMBERS: Prologue (Hot August Night), Crunchy Granola Suite, Mr. Bojangles, Chaconne, Percussion, Ionisation, I Wanna Be a Dancin' Man, Big Noise from Winnetka, If It Feels Good Let It Ride, Easy, I've Got Them Feelin' Too Good Today Blues, Was Dog a Doughnut, Sing Sing Sing, Here You Come Again, Yankee Doodle Dandy, Gary Owen, Stouthearted Men, Under the Double Eagle, Dixie, When Johnny Comes Marching Home, Rally Round the Flag, Pack Up Your Troubles in Your Old Kit Bag, Stars and Stripes Forever, Yankee Doodle Disco, Dancin'

A "musical entertainment" in 3 acts and 13 scenes.

General Manager: Marvin A. Krauss
Associate General Manager: Gary Gunas
Company Manager: G. Warren McClane
Press: Merle Debuskey, William Schelble
Stage Managers: Peter von Mayrhauser, Patrick Ballard, Richard Korthaze

* Still playing May 31, 1980. Recipient of 1978 "Tonys" for Best Choreography and Best Lighting. For original production, see THEATRE WORLD Vol. 34.
† Succeeded by: 1. Janet Eilber, 2. P. J. Mann, 3. Wendy Edmead, 4. Barbara Yeager, 5. Gary Flannery, Christopher Chadman, Michael Kubala, 6. Michael Ricardo, Timothy Scott, Chet Walker, 7. Eileen Casey, 8. Ross Miles, Gregory B. Drotar, Clif de Raita, 9. Christine Colby, 10. Terri Treas, 11. Bruce Anthony Davis, 12. Michael Ricardo, 13. Vicki Frederick, Ann Reinking, Gail Mae Ferguson, 14. David Warren-Gibson, Robert Warners, 15. James Dunne, Robert LaFosse, James Dunne, Gary Chryst, Hinton Battle

Martha Swope Photos

Top Right: Gail Benedict, Clif de Raita, Gail Mae Ferguson Below: Gary Chryst

Eileen Casey, Michael Kubala, Gail Benedict

Elizabeth Parrish, William LeMassena

THE MUSIC BOX
Opened Sunday, February 26, 1978.*
Alfred de Liagre, Jr. and Roger L. Stevens present:

DEATHTRAP

By Ira Levin; Director, Robert Moore; Set, William Ritman; Costumes, Ruth Morley; Lighting, Marc B. Weiss; Wardrobe, Mariana Torres; Assistant to Director, George Rondo; Assistant to Producers, Dorothy Spellman, Jean Bankier

CAST

Sidney Bruhl	John Wood†1
Myra Bruhl	Marian Seldes
Clifford Anderson	Victor Garber†2
Helga ten Dorp	Marian Winters†3
Porter Milgrim	Richard Woods†4

STANDBYS: William Kiehl (Sidney Bruhl/Porter Milgrim), Jan Farrand (Myra Bruhl/Helga ten Dorp), Ernest Townsend (Clifford Anderson)

A "thriller" in 2 acts and 6 scenes. The action takes place at the present time in Sidney Bruhl's study in the Bruhl home in Westport, Connecticut.

General Manager: C. Edwin Knill
Company Manager: Constance Coble
Press: Jeffrey Richards, Warren Knowlton, Robert Ganshaw, Helen Stern, C. George Willard, Karen Gromis
Stage Managers: Ben Strobach, Robert St. Clair

* Still playing May 31, 1980. For original production see THEATRE WORLD Vol. 34.
† Succeeded by: 1. Patrick Horgan, Stacy Keach, John Cullum, 2. Daren Kelly, Steve Bassett, 3. Elizabeth Parrish, 4. William LeMassena

Sy Friedman Photos

Top: John Cullum, Marian Seldes, Steve Bassett

BOOTH THEATRE
Opened Thursday, April 19, 1979.*
Richmond Crinkley, Elizabeth I. McCann, Nelle Nugent present the American National Theatre and Academy production of:

THE ELEPHANT MAN

By Bernard Pomerance; Director, Jack Hofsiss; Setting, David Jenkins; Costumes, Julie Weiss; Lighting, Beverly Emmons; Associate Producers, Ray Larsen, Ted Snowdon; Production Supervisor, Brent Peek; Wardrobe, Lillias Norel; Hairstylist, Frank A. Melon, Hiram Ortiz; Wigs, Paul Huntley; Production Coordinator, Scott Steele; Assistant to Director, Eugene Draper; Projections, Wendall Harrington; Music, Bach, Sammartini, Saint-Saens, Faure, Elgar, Heiss; Musical Arrangments, David Heiss

CAST

Belgian Policeman/Dr. Frederick Treves	Kevin Conway†1
Carr Gomm/Conductor	Richard Clarke
Ross/Bishop/Snork	I. M. Hobson
John Merrick	Philip Anglim†2
Pinhead Manager/Policeman/Will/Earl/ Lord John	John Neville-Andrews†3
Pinhead/Miss Sandwich/Countess/ Princess Alexandra	Cordis Heard†4
Pinhead/Mrs. Kendal	Carole Shelley†5
Orderly	Dennis Creaghan†6
Cellist	David Heiss†7

UNDERSTUDIES: Peter Webster (John Merrick), John C. Vennema (Treves/Policeman), Dennis Creaghan (Pinhead Manager/-Policeman/Will/Lord John), Judith Barcroft (Mrs. Kendal), JoAnne Belanger (Pinhead/Miss Sandwich/Princess Alexandra), Peter Vogt (Gomm/Conductor/Ross/Bishop/Snork/Orderly), Laurence Lenske (Cellist).

A drama in 2 acts and 21 scenes. John Merrick was a real person who spent the years 1886 to his death in 1890 in the London Hospital, Whitechapel.

Company Managers: Susan Gustafson, James Kimo Gerald
Press: Solters/Roskin/Friedman, Joshua Ellis, Becky Flora, David LeShay, Tom Trenkle, Cindy Valk, Craig Macdonald
Stage Manager: Pat De Rousie

* Still playing May 31, 1980. Recipient of the NY Drama Critics Circle Award, and 1979 "Tonys" for Best Play, Best Direction, and Carole Shelley for Best Actress.
† Succeeded by: 1. Donal Donnelly, 2. Jack Wetherall, Bruce Davison, Jeff Hayenga, 3. John C. Vennema, 4. Concetta Tomei, Judith Barcroft, 5. Patricia Elliott, 6. Munson Hicks, Dennis Creaghan, 7. Michael Goldschlager.

Top Right: Bruce Davison, Donal Donnelly, Patricia Elliott

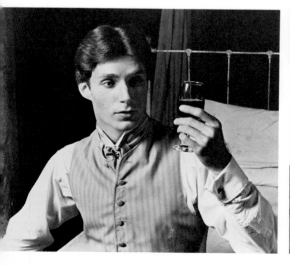

Jeff Hayenga

Bruce Davison, Patricia Elliott

THE LITTLE THEATRE
Opened Saturday, May 21, 1977.*
Jerry Arrow by arrangement with Circle Repertory Company
and PAF Playhouse presents:

GEMINI

By Albert Innaurato; Director, Peter March Schifter; Supervised by
Marshall W. Mason; Setting, Christopher Nowak; Costumes, Ernest
Allen Smith; Lighting, Larry Crimmins; Sound, Leslie A. De-
Weerdt, Jr.; Production Assistant, Richard Groff, Thomas Bain;
Production Supervisor, Fred Reinglas; Wardrobe, Arthur Curtis,
Paula Iasella; Hairstylist, Peter Brett

CAST

Francis Geminiani	Dennis Bailey†1
Bunny Weinberger	Jessica James
Randy Hastings	Reed Birney†2
Judith Hastings	Stephanie Musnick†3
Herschel Weinberger	Warren Pincus†4
Fran Geminiani	Danny Aiello†5
Lucille Pompi	Anne DeSalvo†6

UNDERSTUDIES: Jennie Ventriss (Lucille/Bunny), Michael
Klingher (Francis/Herschel/Randy), Stephanie Musnick (Judith)

A comedy in 2 acts and 4 scenes. The action takes place June 1
& 2, 1973 in the Geminiani-Weinberger backyard in South Philadelphia, Pa.

General Manager: R. Robert Lussier
Company Manager: Thom Shovestull
Press: Max Eisen, Francine L. Trevens
Stage Managers: James Arnemann, Michael K. Klingher

* Still playing May 31, 1980. For original production, see THE-
ATRE WORLD Vol. 33.
† Succeeded by: 1. Philip Cates, S. Edward Singer, 2. Bill Randolph,
3. Lisa Sloan, Marilyn McIntyre, 4. Wayne Knight, 5. Dick Boccelli, Frank Biancamano, 6. Barbara Coggin

**Frank Biancamano, Barbara Coggin, Lisa Sloan, Bill Randolph,
(standing) S. Edward Singer, Wayne Knight Top Left: Wayne
Knight, Bill Randolph, Jessica James**

EDISON THEATRE
Opened Friday, September 24, 1976.*
Hillard Elkins, Norman Kean, Robert S. Fishko present:

OH! CALCUTTA!

Devised by Kenneth Tynan; Contributors, Jules Feiffer, Dan Greenburg, Lenore Kandel, John Lennon, Jacques Levy, Leonard Melfi, David Newman and Robert Benton, Sam Shepard, Clovis Trouille, Kenneth Tynan, Sherman Yellen; Music and Lyrics, Robert Dennis, Peter Schickele, Stanley Walden; Additional Music and Lyrics, Stanley Walden, Jacques Levy; Choreography, Margo Sappington; Musical Director, Stanley Walden; Conceived and Directed by Jacques Levy; Scenery, James Tilton; Lighting, Harry Silverglat; Costumes, Kenneth M. Yount, supervised by James Tilton; Musical Conductor, Norman Bergen; Sound, Sander Hacker; Assistant to Director, Nancy Tribush; Assistant Musical Conductor, Dan Carter; Technical Directors, Thomas Healy, Charles Moran; Wardrobe, Gordon Needham

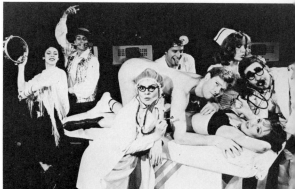

CAST

Jacqueline Carol†	Tom Lantzy
Cheryl Hartley	Katherine Liepe
Mary Hendrickson	Gary Meitrott
Barra Kahn	Jerry Clark
William Mesnick	September Thorp

ACT I: Taking Off the Robe, Will Answer All Sincere Replies, Rock Garden: Delicious Indignities, The Paintings of Clovis Trouille, Suite for Five Letters, One on One
ACT II: Jack and Jill, Spread Your Love Around, Was It Good for You Too?, Coming Together Going Together

An erotic musical in two acts.

Company Managers: Maria DiDia, Doris J. Buberl
Press: Les Schecter, Barbara Schwei
Stage Managers: Ron Nash, Maria DiDia

* Still playing May 31, 1980. For original production, see THEATRE WORLD Vol. 33.
† During the season, the following were replacements in the production: Scott Baker, Richert Easley, Norman Weiler, William Wright

Martha Swope Photos

Top: William Wright, Cheryl Hartley, Richard Easley, Barra Kahn, Norman Weiler, Jacqueline Carol, Gary Meitrott, Scott Baker, September Thorp

URIS THEATRE
Opened Thursday, March 1, 1979.*
Richard Barr, Charles Woodward, Robert Fryer, Mary Lea Johnson, Martin Richards in association with Dean Manos and Judy Manos present:

SWEENEY TODD
The Demon Barber of Fleet Street

Music and Lyrics, Stephen Sondheim; Book, Hugh Wheeler; Based on a version of "Sweeney Todd" by Christopher Bond; Director, Harold Prince; Dance and Movement, Larry Fuller; Production Design, Eugene Lee; Costumes, Franne Lee; Lighting, Ken Billington; Orchestrations, Jonathan Tunick; Musical Director, Paul Gemignani; Associate Producer, Marc Howard; Assistant to Director, Ruth Mitchell; Assistants to Producers, Jerry Sirchia, Sam Crothers; Sound, Jack Mann; Wigs, Lynn Quiyou; Makeup, Barbara Kelly; Technical Director, Arthur Siccardi; Wardrobe, Adelaide Laurino; Hairstylist, Vincenzo Prestia; Production Assistants, Fran Soeder, Toby Beckwith; Original Cast Album by RCA Records

CAST

Anthony Hope	Victor Garbert†1
Sweeney Todd	Len Cariou†2
Beggar Woman	Merle Louise
Mrs. Lovett	Angela Lansbury†3
Judge Turpin	Edmund Lyndeck
The Beadle	Jack Eric Williams
Johanna	Sarah Rice†4
Tobias Ragg	Ken Jennings
Pirelli	Joaquin Romaguera
Jonas Fogg	Robert Ousley

THE COMPANY: Duane Bodin, Walter Charles, Carole Doscher, Nancy Eaton, Mary-Pat Green, Cris Groenendaal, Skip Harris, Marthe Ihde, Betsy Joslyn, Nancy Killmer, Frank Kopyc, Spain Logue, Robert Ousley, Richard Warren Pugh, Maggie Task
UNDERSTUDIES: Maggie Task (Mrs. Lovett), Walter Charles (Sweeney), Robert Hendersen (Anthony), Candace Rogers (Johanna), Michael Kalinyen (Beadle), Robert Ousley (Turpin), Skip Harris (Tobias), Frank Kopyc (Pirelli), Pamela McLernon (Beggar Woman), Denise Lor (Mrs. Lovett), Swings: Heather B. Withers, Robert Hendersen

MUSICAL NUMBERS: The Ballad of Sweeney Todd, No Place Like London, The Barber and His Wife, The Worst Pies in London, Poor Thing, My Friends, Green Finch and Linnet Bird, Ah Miss, Johanna, Pirelli's Miracle Elixir, The Contest, Wait, Kiss Me, Ladies in Their Sensitivities, Quartet, Pretty Women, Epiphany, A Little Priest, God! That's Good!, By the Sea, Not While I'm Around, Parlor Songs, City on Fire!, Finale

A musical in two acts. The action takes place during the 19th Century in London on Fleet Street and environs.

General Management: Gatchell & Neufeld Ltd.
Company Managers: Drew Murphy, James G. Mennen
Press: Mary Bryant, Patt Dale, Philip Rinaldi
Stage Managers: Alan Hall, Larry Mengden, Ruth E. Rinklin

* Closed June 29, 1980 after 557 performances and 19 previews. Winner of 1979 "Tonys" for Best Book, Best Score, Best Scenic Design, Best Costume Designs, Best Actress (Angela Lansbury), Best Actor (Len Cariou), Best Direction, and Best Musical. It also received the NY Drama Critics Circle Award. See THEATRE WORLD Vol. 35.
† Succeeded by: 1. Cris Groenendaal, 2. George Hearn, 3. Dorothy Loudon, 4. Betsy Joslyn

Top Left: Dorothy Loudon, George Hearn
Below: Cris Groenendaal, Betsy Joslyn,
Edmund Lyndeck, Jack Eric Williams
Left Center: Edmund Lyndeck, George Hearn

Ken Jennings, Craig Lucas, Martha Ihde,
Mary-Pat Green, Walter Charles, Dorothy Loudon

IMPERIAL THEATRE
Opened Sunday, February 11, 1979.*
Emanuel Azenberg presents:

THEY'RE PLAYING OUR SONG

Book, Neil Simon; Music, Marvin Hamlisch; Lyrics, Carole Bayer Sager; Director, Robert Moore; Musical Numbers Staged by Patricia Birch; Scenery and Projections, Douglas W. Schmidt; Costumes, Ann Roth; Lighting, Tharon Musser; Music Direction, Larry Blank; Orchestrations, Ralph Burns, Richard Hazard, Gene Page; Assistant to Director, George Rondo; Sound, Tom Morse; Associate Conductor, Fran Liebergall; Wardrobe, Michael Dennison, Mary Beth Regan; Hairstylist, John Quaglia; Assistant to Producer, Leslie Butler; Hair and Wig Designs, Kathryn Blondell; Production Supervisor, Philip Cusack; Original Cast Album by Casablanca Records

CAST

Vernon	Robert Klein†1
Sonia Walsk	Lucie Arnaz†2
Voices of Vernon Gersch	Wayne Mattson, Andy Roth, Greg Zadikov†3
Voices of Sonia Walsk	Helen Castillo, Celia Celnik Matthau, Debbie Shapiro†4
Voice of Phil, the engineer	Philip Cusack†5

STANDBYS AND UNDERSTUDIES: John Hammil (Vernon), Pat Gorman (Sonia), and Andy Roth, Hal Shane, Dorothy Kiara, Max Stone, Lani Sundsten
MUSICAL NUMBERS: Fallin', Workin' It Out, If He Really Knew Me, They're Playing Our Song, Right, Just for Tonight, When You're In My Arms, I Still Believe in Love (reprise sung by Johnny Mathis), Fill in the Words

A comedy in 2 acts and 13 scenes. The action takes place at the present time in Vernon's New York City apartment, in Le Club, Sonia's apartment, on the street, on the road, in a beach house in Quogue, Long Island, in a recording studio, in a Los Angeles hospital room.

General Manager: Jose Vega
Company Managers: Susan Bell, Maria Anderson, Maurice Schaded, Louise Bendall, Linda Cohen
Press: Bill Evans, Howard Atlee, Leslie Anderson, Jim Baldassare
Stage Managers: Robert D. Currie, David Taylor, Bernard Pollock, Pat Trott

* Still playing May 31, 1980. For original production, see THEATRE WORLD Vol. 35.
† Succeeded by: 1. John Hammil, Tony Roberts, 2. Rhonda Farer, Stockard Channing, Rhonda Farer, 3. John Hillner, 4. Donna Murphy, 5. Hal Shane

Jay Thompson Photos

Left and Top: Stockard Channing, Tony Roberts

Tony Roberts, Rhonda Farer

Tony Roberts, Rhonda Farer

PLAYERS THEATRE
Thursday, June 28, - July 29, 1979 (38 performances and 27 previews)
Hibiscus Productioms presents:

SKY HIGH

Written and Directed by Brian O'Hara; Producer, E. David Rosen; Music and Lyrics, Ann Harris; Sets and Costumes, Angel Jack; Lighting, Johnny Dodd; Choreography, The Harris Sisters; Additional Music and Arrangements, Frederic Harris; Associate Producer, Gene Hodge; General Manager, Don Joslyn; Assistant to Producer, James Hellman; Press, Bruce Cohen, Richard Cohen

CAST

Donna Lee Betz (Sadie/Mother Nature), Richard DePasquale (Dirty Bird), Ginger Grace (Miss America/Cute Birdie), Ann Harris (Starina), Eloise Harris (Mermaid Queen/Jayne Champagne), Jayne Anne Harris (Shiekstress/Princess Slit dagger), Lulu Belle Harris (Nuit/Queen Cobra), Angel Jack (Devil), Sandt Litchfield (Rigmaster), Tom Matthews (Mrs. Gottrocks), Brian O'Hara (Jour), Janet Sala (Little Girl/Pretty Kitty), Musicians: Frederick Harris, Walter Michael Harris
MUSICAL NUMBERS: Rainbow, Walk Thru That Golden Gate, I'm Mother Nature of You All, She'll Get the Business in the End, Behold the Coming of the Sun, I'm Betting on You, One Cell, Singing Mermaids, South American Way, Queen Cobra, Fly Away, When He Calls Half-Hour, Birdie Follies, Ringmaster Song, Broadway New York, Clown Song, Let's Go to the Dogs, Kitty Kat Song, Toast of the Town, Gut Rocks, Au Revoir, Sheik Song, Opium Song, I'm Lazy, Do It Yourself, Giddyup, Miss America, Hot as Hades, Devil Man, Champagne Song

Carol Rosegg Photo

APOLLO THEATRE
Tuesday, June 5,-17, 1979 (16 performances)
Apollo Theatre presents:

MISS TRUTH

Book, Music and Lyrics, Glory Van Scott; Musical Concept, Scenery, Direction and Choreography, Louis Johnson; Musical Director-Conductor, Thom Bridwell; Lighting, Gary Harris; Costumes, Alice E. Carter, Judy Dearing; Additional Music and Arrangements, Thom Bridwell, Louis Johnson; General Manager, David E. McCarthy; Stage and Company Manager, Clinton Jackson; Stage Manager, David M. Cooper; Wardrobe, Alice Carter

CAST

Glory Van Scott (Sojourner Truth), Christopher Pierre (Narrator), Phoebe Redmond (Cleaning Lady), Loretta Abbott (Dancer), Lloyd McNeill (Flutist), Syrena Irvin (Slave Dancer), Charles LaVont Williams (Slave Dancer/Charles/Butler), Pat Lundy (Pat), Herbert Lee Rawlings, Jr. (Slave), Loretta Devine (Loretta), Candice Graig (Little Girl)
MUSICAL NUMBERS: Disco, Miss Truth, Children Are for Loving, I Sing the Rainbow, Self-Made Woman, My Religion, Do Your Thing Miss Truth, Shame, This Is a Very Special Day, Freedom Diet, Lift Every Voice and Sing

A musical in 11 scenes.

James Lott photos

**Tom Matthews, Angel Jack, Brian O'Hara,
Lulu Belle Harris in "Sky High"**

CARTER THEATRE
Opened Tuesday, June 5, 1979.
Virgil Engeran and Jim Payne present:

NOT TONIGHT, BENVENUTO!

Director, Jim Payne; Musical Numbers Staged by Robin Reseen; Instrumental and Vocal Arrangements, Larry Hochman; Musical Direction, Steven Freeman; Costumes, Sherri Buchs; Sets, James Morgan, Peter A. Schue; Lighting, Jessie Ira Berger; General Manager, Jim Payne; Stage Managers, Richard Switaski, Roger Noonan; Press, Herb Striesfield

CAST

Paul Alessi (Officer/Giovanni/Caruso), Nelia Bacmeister (Statue/-Wench), Ada Berry (Aida), Daniel Fortier (Beggar/Poodidicci/-Judge), Christopher Hensel (Benvenuto Cellini), Shelly Herrington (Statue/Madeline), Cynde Lauren (Statue/Mother), Jonathan Luks (Willie/Sailor), Marion Markham (Statue/Bounty Hunter), Michael Mitorotondo (Leonardo/Monk/Sentry), Sharon Murray (Madonna/Mother Superior), Roger Noonan (Federico), Gene Stilwell (Bobo,) Paula Ward (Diana), Ron Wyche (Suitor/Narrator)
MUSICAL NUMBERS: How Do You Do, Can't Make Love Without You, Why Do I Love Bennie?, Who Can Control the Human Heart, Diana, Lullaby, Funeral Procession, Poppin', This Is Our World, Now I Lay Me Down to Sleep, Search for Diana, Gonna Get Right Some Day, Together, Wedding Ball

A musical in 2 acts and 14 scenes. The action takes place in 1524 in Florence, Italy.

Closed June 6, 1979 after 2 performances and 34 previews.

Above: "Not Tonight, Benvenuto!"

**Christophe Pierre, Glory Van Scott
in "Miss Truth"**

PARK ROYAL THEATER
Wednesday, June 6,–24, 1979 (24 performances)
Playhouse Repertory Company (Kent Paul, Artistic Director;
Karl Allison, Managing Director) presents the New York premiere of:

THE DAYS BETWEEN

By Robert Anderson; Director, Kent Paul; Sets and Lighting, T.
Winberry; Costumes, Linda Fisher; Assistant to Director, Robert
Scott; Technical Director, Gary Olson; Production Consultant,
Barry Kearsley; Stage Managers, Penny Stegenga, Douglas Clark;
Press, Susan Bloch, Bill Rudman, Sally Christiansen

CAST

Douglas Clark (George Hawkins), Judith Elder (Mrs. Walker), Dan
Hamilton (David Ives), Jansen Lambie (Roger Ives), Richard Morse
(Ted Sears), Kathleen Nolan (Barbara Ives)

A drama in 2 acts and 5 scenes. The action takes place near a New
England college town in the early 1960's.

Martha Swope Photos

**Richard Morse, Jansen Lambie
in "The Days Between"**

CENTURY THEATRE
Opened Thursday, June 7, 1979.
Michael Harvey and Peter A. Bobley in association with Columbia Pictures present:

LONE STAR/PVT. WARS

By James McLure; Directors, Stuart White (Lone Star), Garland
Wright (Pvt. Wars); Scenery, John Arnone; Costumes, Giva Taylor;
Lighting, Frances Aronson; Associate Producers, Stewart F. Lane,
Jack Tantleff; General Manager, Albert Poland; Associate Producer,
Jonathan Pelzer; Production Assistant, Amy Koblenzer; Stage Managers, Susie Cordon, Gregory Grove; Press, Betty Lee Hunt, Maria
Cristina Pucci, Fred Hoot, James Sapp

CAST

LONE STAR: Powers Boothe (Roy), Leo Burmester (Ray), Clifford Fetters (Cletis), Understudies: Gregory Grove, Tony Campisi.
The action takes place one night in Maynard, Texas, just behind
Angel's Bar at 1 A.M. on a summer night at the present time.
PVT. WARS: Gregory Grove (Woodruff Gately), Tony Campisi
(Silvio), Clifford Fetters (Natwick), Understudies: Leo Burmester
(Gately/Silvio), Powers Boothe (Natwick). The action takes place
on an outdoor terrace of an army veterans hospital at the present
time.

Closed Aug. 5, 1979 after 69 performances and 8 previews.

Roger Greenawalt Photos

**Above: Clifford Fetters, Gregory
Grove, Tony Campisi in "Pvt.
Wars"**

**Powers Boothe, Leo Burmester
in "Lone Star"**

THE ARK ON PARK
Friday, June 8,–24, 1979 (12 performances)
Revelations, The Parish of Calvary, Holy Communion and St. George's, and John Amato Petale present:

CHEERS!

By Richard E. Castagna; Music, Bill Bly; Director, James R. Shaffer; Set, Richard C. Hankins; Costumes, Ann Lloyd; Lighting, Juliet O. Campbell; Musical Director, Bill Bly; Hairstylist, Harriet Brown; Assistant Director, Bryan Burdick; Artistic Director, James R. Shaffer; General Manager, John Amato Petale; Stage Managers, Nansi Lee Charles, Tom Fontana, Linda Sheean

CAST

Henry Butler (Herb), Richard M. Davidson (Walsh), David Ellis (Grandpa), Ray Horvath (Teddy), Brian Muehl (Narrator), Ron Piretti (Martin), Barbara Rubenstein (Cheerleader), Nancy Sears (Beatrice), Lucy Winner (Connie), Chris DeBlasio (Pianist)

**Brian Muehl, Henry Butler, Barbara
Rubenstein in "Cheers!"**

NO SMOKING PLAYHOUSE
Monday, June 11–17, 1979 (13 performances)
Dove Productions presents:

THE VOICE OF THE TURTLE

By John Van Druten; Director, Edward Morehouse; Set adapted by Mr. Morehouse from Stewart Chaney's original; Costumes, John Lee, Douglas James; Lighting, Wayne Schrengohst, Dennis Murphy; Sound, Jay Bond; Stage Managers, Kathryn Callaghan, Binnie Ravitch; Press, Judy Jacksina, Glenna Freedman

CAST

Monica Merryman (Olive Lashbrooke), Jacalyn O'Shaughnessy (Sally Middleton), James Umphlett (Bill Page)

A comedy in 3 acts and 6 scenes. The action takes place over a weekend in early April in an apartment in the East Sixties, near Third Avenue, in New York City.

Left Center: Jacalyn O'Shaughnessy

HAROLD CLURMAN THEATRE
Monday, June 18–28, 1979 (19 performances)
Rene Savich presents:

WINE UNTOUCHED

By Bjorg Vik; Translated by Erle Bjornstad; Director, Lynne Guerra; Set, Marjorie Kellogg; Lighting, Elizabeth Holloway; Costumes, Albert Wolsky; General Manager, Weiler/Miller; Company Manager, Barbara Carrellas; Stage Managers, Alisa Jill Adler, Paul Brasuell; Press, Judy Jacksina, Glenna Freedman

CAST

Susan Slavin (Gry), Swoosie Kurtz (Evelyn), Donna McKechnie (Lillian), Glenn Close (Helen), Patricia Elliott (Ann)

A drama in two acts. The action takes place at the present time in Helen's apartment.

Len Kaltman Photo

**Donna McKechnie, Patricia Elliott, Swoozie
Kurtz, Susan Slavin, Glenn Close**

VILLAGE GATE
Opened Monday, June 11, 1979.*
James Adams Vaccaro and Jimmy Wisner is association with Ciro A. Gamboni present:

SCRAMBLED FEET

By John Driver and Jeffrey Haddow; Musical Direction and Arrangements, Jimmy Wisner; Director, John Driver; Sets, Ernest Allen Smith; Costumes, Kenneth M. Yount; Lighting, Robert F. Strohmeier; Assistant Musical Director and Additional Arrangements, Roger Neil; Wardrobe, Paula Davis

CAST

Evalyn Baron †
John Driver
Jeffrey Haddow
Roger Neil
Hermione

ACT I: Going to the Theatre, P. T. Playwrighting Kit, Makin' the Rounds, Answering Machine, Agent, Composer Tango, No Small Roles, Stanislaw, Only One Dance, Good Connections, Olympics, Theatre-Party-Ladies
ACT II: Guru, Party Doll, Love in the Wings, Huns/British, Could Have Been, Sham Dancing, Improv/EDT, Have You Ever Been on Stage?, Advice to Producers, Happy Family

General Manager: Leonard A. Mulhern
Press: Bruce Cohen, Richard Cohen, Jeffrey Richards Associates
Stage Manager: Sari E. Weisman

* Still playing May 31, 1980.
† Original cast succeeded by Jonathan Hadary, Steve Liebman, Susan Edwards, Jim Walton

Peter Cunningham, Carol Rosegg Photos

Jim Walton, Susan Edwards
Top: Roger Neil, Jeffrey Haddow,
John Driver, Evalyn Baron, Hermione

PLAYHOUSE THEATRE
Opened Tuesday, June 19, 1979.*
Jack Garfein in association with Jack Clark presents the Harold Clurman Theatre production of:

THE PRICE

By Arthur Miller; Director, John Stix; Setting, David Mitchell; Costumes, Bob Wojewodski; Lighting, Richard Nelson; Assistant to Director, Katherine Perry; Hairstylist, Keith Benedict

CAST

Victor Franz	Mitchell Ryan
Esther Franz	Scotty Bloch
Gregory Solomon	Joseph Buloff
Walter Franz	Fritz Weaver

Standbys: Tom Brennan, Susan Lang
A drama in two acts. The action takes place on the attic floor of a Manhattan, NYC, brownstone in 1958.

General Manager: Albert Poland
Company Manager: Louise M. Bayer
Press: Joe Wolhandler, C. George Willard, Marilyn White
Stage Managers: David S. Rosenak, Daniel Pollack

Closed Oct. 21, 1979 after 144 performances and 7 previews.

Carol Rosegg Photos

Fritz Weaver, Joseph Buloff,
Mitchell Ryan, Scotty Bloch

AMERICAN PLACE THEATRE
Opened Thursday, June 21, 1979.*
James Cresson, Christopher Ohman, Sam Crothers present:

FATHER'S DAY

By Oliver Hailey; Director, Rae Allen; Scenery, Christina Weppner; Costumes, Jane Greenwood; Lighting, John Gisondi; Associate Producer, Edward Merkow; General Management, Dorothy Olim Associates; Management Associate, Thelma Cooper; Production Associate, Mark Gillespie; Production Assistant, Bonnie Monte; Company Manager, Gail Bell; Stage Managers, Herb Vogler, Elisabeth Von Benken; Press, The Merlin Group, Becky Flora, Robert Pontarelli, Marguerite Wolfe, Glen Gary

CAST

Louise	Susan Tyrrell
Estelle	Mary Beth Hurt
Marian	Tammy Grimes
Richard	Lee Richardson
Harold	Graham Beckel
Tom	John Cunningham

Understudies: Judy Jurgaitis, Elisabeth Von Benken, Larry Pine

A comedy in two acts. The action takes place on late Sunday morning of Father's Day, on the terrace of an apartment in New York City.

* Closed Sept. 16, 1979 after 101 performances.

Martha Swope Photos

(standing) John Cunningham, Susan Tyrrell, Lee Richardson, (front) Mary Beth Hurt, Graham Beckel, Tammy Grimes

ACTORS PLAYHOUSE
Opened Friday, July 6, 1979.*
Wayne Adams with Douglas Urbanski presents:

SAY GOODNIGHT, GRACIE

By Ralph Pape; Director, Austin Pendleton; Set, Jack Chandler; Lighting, Cheryl Thacker; Costumes, Patricia A. Wiegleb; Associate Producer, Willard Morgan; Wardrobe, Agnes Burke

CAST

Jerry	Tom McKitterick †1
Steve	Mark Blum †2
Ginny	Molly Regan
Bobby	Danton Stone †3
Catherine	Carolyn Groves

Understudies: Paul Perri, Lynnie Green

A comedy performed without intermission. The action takes place during 1976 in an apartment in the East Village in New York City.

General Management: Douglas Management
Company Manager: Kevin Dowling
Press: The Press Department, Clarence Allsopp, Joe Wolhandler, C. George Willard
Stage Managers: Amy Whitman, Norman Katz

* Closed March 23, 1980 after 300 performances. It had previously played 117 performances at the 78th street Playhouse.
† Succeeded by: 1. Eric Tull, Austin Pendleton, Robert Dorfman, 2. Eric Tull, Scott Wentworth, 3. Paul Perri, Steven Fromewick, Alan Safier

Marbeth, Carol Rosegg Photos

Molly Regan, Mark Blum, Carolyn Groves, Danton Stone, Tom McKitterick

Left Center: Eric Tull, Mark Blum, Molly Regan

SOUTH STREET THEATRE

Opened Tuesday, June 26,–July 8, 1979 (18 performances)
South Street Theatre Company (Jean Sullivan, Michael Fischetti, Producers) presents:

CONFESSIONS OF A REFORMED ROMANTIC

Conceived and Performed by Ellen Gould; Director, Alan Fox; Music Arranged by Michael Roth; Choreography, Harry Streep III; Costumes, Patricia McGourty; Lighting, Richard Winkler; Piano, Carl Bellante; Bass, Joseph Barone; Production Consultant, Holly Gewandter; Production Assistant, Liz Martin; Sound, Jeff Margolis; Stage Manager David Reinhardsen; Press, Richard Kornberg

CAST

Ellen Gould

Performed without intermission.

Carol Rosegg Photo

Ellen Gould

JONES BEACH THEATRE

Opened Thursday, June 28, 1979.*
Richard Horner in association with Long Island State Parks and Recreation Commission presents:

THE MUSIC MAN

Book, Music and Lyrics, Meredith Willson; Story, Meredith Willson, Franklin Lacey; Director, John Fearnley; Scenery, Lynn Pecktal; Costumes, Robert Fletcher; Lighting, Jeremy Johnson; Musical Director, Sande Campbell; Choreography, Frank Wagner; Assistant Choreographer, Jack Kauflin; Managing Director, Alvin Dorfmann; Production Associate, Lynne Stuart; General Manager, Malcolm Allen; Stage Managers, Bryan Young, Leanna Lenhart, Consuelo Mira, Debra Lyman; Hairstylist, Alvin Beam; Associate Conductor, Alyce Billington; Press, Henry Luhrman Associates, Bill Miller, Terry M. Lilly, Kevin P. McAnarney

CAST

Jack Fletcher, Andrew Gale, G. Jan Jones, Bruce Sherman (Traveling Salesmen), Ralph Vucci (Charlie Cowell), William Bush (Conductor), Don Stewart (Harold Hill), Alan North (Mayor), Edward A. Price (Ewart Dunlop), Edward Penn (Oliver Hix), William James (Jacey Squires), Clifford F. Fearl (Olin Britt), Gibby Brand (Marcellus Washburn), George Pesaturo (Tommy), Mary D'Arcy (Marian), Toni Darnay (Mrs. Paroo), Danielle Susan Carter (Amaryllis), Scott Perrin (Winthrop Paroo), Joan Shea (Eulalie), Mary-Pat Carey (Zaneeta), Laura Condon (Gracie), Florence I. Fox (Alma), Marcia Brushingham (Maud), Mary Leigh Stahl (Ethel), Dixie Stewart (Mrs. Squires), William Bush (Constable), and Phylis Bash, Kim Leslie Beasom, Mary Lou Belli, Heidi Coe, Joni Fritz, Linda Griffin, Elisa Lenhart, Debra Lyman, Marsha Miller, Elyssa Paternoster, Tina Paul, Pat Register, Mary Leigh Stahl, Ann Tell, Phyllis Van Houten, Kimberly Woollen, Jennifer Hammond, Mark Bove, Eugene Edwards, Timothy Flavin, David Fredericks, Andrew Gale, Ramon Galindo, Norb Joerder, Michael David Krisch, Michael Lane, Rich McElhiney, Morgan Richardson, Jimmy Rivers, Thomas Stanton, Larry Ross
MUSICAL NUMBERS: Rock, Iowa Stubborn, Trouble, Piano Lesson, Goodnight My Someone, 76 Trombones, Sincere, The Sadderbut-Wiser Girl, Pickalittle, Goodnight Ladies, Marian the Librarian, My White Knight, Wells Fargo Wagon, It's You, Shipoopi, Lida Rose, Will I Ever Tell You, Gary Indiana, Till There Was You, Finale

A musical in two acts. The action takes place in 1912 in River City, Iowa.

* Closed September 2, 1979 after limited engagement of 67 performances.

Sy Friedman Photos

Mary D'Arcy, Don Stewart
(also above)   **87**

VILLAGE GATE
Tuesday, July 17–29, 1979 (12 performances)
Charles Kandel presents:

TWO GROWN MEN

Written, Conceived and Performed by Paul Kandel and Mitchell Greenberg; Technical Director, Carl Seltzer; Sound, John Rohlehr; Props, Bruce Evans; Stage Manager, Jeanne Boyle; Press, Susan L. Schulman

Susan Cook Photo

Right: Paul Kandel, Mitchell Greenberg

PARK ROYAL THEATRE
Saturday, July 21,–28, 1979 (12 performances)
ABM Associates in conjunction with T.O.M.I. presents:

SHORTAGES

By Ruth Pearl; Director, Anthony B. Doren; Scenery and Costumes, Ursula Belden; Lighting, Victor En Yu Tan; Administrative Director, Jean C. Dotterweich; Sound, Regina Mullen; Technical Director, Frank Herbert; Stage Managers, Alicia Quintano, Tony Batelle, Caren Ryer; Press, Mark Arnold

CAST

Herbert Cooper . . . . Herbert Rubens
Beatrice Cooper . . . . Mary Sharmat

A play in 2 acts and 5 scenes. The action takes place in the country home of Herbert and Beatrice Cooper during the winter of 1979.

Charles Hettinger Photos

Left Center: Herbert Rubens, Mary Sharmat in "Shortages"

METROPOLITAN OPERA HOUSE
Monday, July 30,–August 4, 1979. (8 performances)
The Kennedy Center and the Metropolitan Opera present:

EVERY GOOD BOY DESERVES FAVOUR

By Tom Stoppard and Andre Previn; From an original concept by Trevor Nunn; Director, Tom Stoppard; Sets and Costumes, Eldon Elder; Lighting, Thomas Skelton; Producer, Roger L. Stevens; Orchestra conducted by David Gilbert; Sound, Dennis Roe; Wardrobe, Deborah Cheretun; Company Manager, John H. Wilson; Stage Managers, Mitchell Erickson, Pat DeRousie, Stephen Nasuta; Press, Alpert/LeVine, Marilynn LeVine, Mark Goldstaub

CAST

Rene Auberjonois (Ivanov), Eli Wallach (Alexander), Carol Teitel (Teacher), Bobby Scott (Sacha), Remak Ramsay (Doctor), Carl Low (Colonel Rozinsky)

A play for actors and orchestra performed without intermission.

Jack Buxbaum Photo

Remak Ramsay, Carl Low, Eli Wallach

ORPHEUM THEATRE

Opened Tuesday, August 14, 1979.*

David Richmond in association with Alan Schuster presents:

BIG BAD BURLESQUE!

Musical Numbers Conceived and Staged by Don Brockett; Director, Celeste Hall; Sets, Charles Vanderpool, Laurel Douglas; Production Consultant, Scott Robbe; Musical Director, Jim Walton; Technical Director, Paul Shetter; Administrative Assistant, Shari Teitelbaum; Wardrobe, Karen Brown

CAST

Tamara Brandy†	Susan Orem
Nina David	Eva Parmelee
Roy Doliner	Deborah Pollack
Danny Herman	Donna Sontag
Tina Kay	Mitchell Steven Tebo
Steve Liebman	Jim Walton

Understudies: Scott Ross, Pat Tallman

MUSICAL NUMBERS: Big Bad Burlesque, Glamour Girls, Patriotic Finale, School Days, Flora and Fauna, Wonderful Burlesque Days

SKITS: Meet Me Round the Corner, The Westfall Murder, The Bullfight, Schoolroom, Crazy House, Man on the Street

* Closed Nov. 18, 1979 after 112 performances and 16 previews.
† Members of the cast were succeeded by Sharon Tillotson, Chris James, Pat Tallman, Claude Mathis, Joe Elic

Gary Hill Photos

Entire cast of "Big Bad Burlesque!"

CARNEGIE HALL

Tuesday, September 4,–15, 1979 (11 performances)

LIZA MINNELLI IN CONCERT
with Roger Minami and Obba Babatunde

Produced, Written and Directed by Fred Ebb; Choreography, Ron Lewis, Wayne Cilento; Musical Coordinator, Larry Grossman; Costumes, Halston; Set, Lawrence Miller; Lighting, Deanna Wenble, Don Stearn; Associate Producer, Deanna Wenble; Arrangements, Ralph Burns, Michael Abene, Billy Byers; Musical Director, Bill LaVorgna; Hairstylist, Carol Shurley; Wardrobe, Helen Tarr; Technical Director, Lawrence Brashaw; Production Manager, Mark Gero

Left Center: Liza Minnelli

SOUTH STREET THEATRE

September 6–23, 1979 (12 performances)
American Theater Experiment presents:

THE COUNTRY GIRL

By Clifford Odets; Director, Sandra Hastie; Sets, Michael Charles Smith; Lighting, William Plachy; Costumes, Darcy Casteleiro; Stage Manager, Amelia Haywood

CAST

John Carroll, Bruce Carr, Jim de Marse, Michael Galloway, Margo McKee, Harvey Pierce, Cindy Rosenthal, Donald Smith

Ricardo Albert Photo

Michael Galloway, Margo McKee, John Carroll

**Wyman Pendleton, Tom Everett,
Sudie Bond in "Dance for Me Simeon"**

**Left Center: Mark Soper, Brian Watson,
George J. Peters**

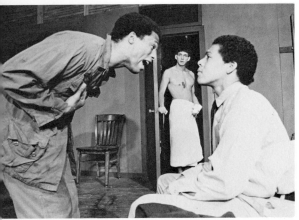

**Bo Rucker, John Martinuzzi,
Jay Fernandez**

ASTOR PLACE THEATRE
September 10,–16, 1979 (8 performances and 12 previews)
Newplays Inc. presents:

AFTER THE RISE
An Illustrated Interview

Written and Directed by Gerhard Borris; Scenery and Costumes, Don Jensen; Film, Gunter Glinka; Lighting, T. Winberry; Assistant to Director, Andrew Parton; Production Assistant, Muriel Johnstone; General Manager, Lily Turner; Stage Manager, Harold Apter; Press, Alpert/LeVine, Mark Goldstaub

CAST

Gigi Deckter (Jackie), Peter DeMaio (Dave), Herb Aronson (Oscar), Catherine Wolf (Helen), Robert Payson (Cecil B. Dryer), Roy Steinberg (Jack Roots), Ward Asquith (Lee Brown), Jeannie Leigh Allison (Mary-Ann), Nicholas Saunders (John O'Connor), Alexandra Isles (Irene), Lucinda Johnson (Billie)

Presented in two acts.

(No photos available)

THE ANNEX
Wednesday, September 12–29, 1979 (12 performances)
The American Theater of Actors (Jim Jennings, Artistic Director) presents:

DANCE FOR ME SIMEON

By Joseph Maher; Director, Stephan Maro; Setting, Debbie Schectre; Lighting, Tony Castrigno; Costumes, Patricia Lucenti; Stage Manager, Frank Skokan

CAST

Tom Everett	Simeon
Sudie Bond	Roseanna
Wyman Pendleton	Wilkie

Anita Feldman Photo

AMDA STUDIO ONE THEATRE
September 13–30, 1979 (12 performances)
Peter M. Paulino presents the friends repertory company production of:

STREAMERS

By David Rabe; Director, Mitchell Weiss; Scenery, Sally Friedman; Costumes, Amanda J. Klein, Jeffrey Mazor; Lighting, Technical Direction, Kenneth Evans; Assistant Director, Josh Blum; Stage Managers, Douglas Whitt, Kathryn Bonomi, Dean Hill, Patricia Catalano; Press, Richard Kornberg

CAST

John Amplas (Martin), Jay Fernandez (Roger), Dean Hill (M.P.), Richard Kusyk (M.P./LT.), John Martinuzzi (Richie), Don Paul (M.P.), George J. Peters (Sgt. Cokes), Bo Rucker (Carlyle), Mark Soper (Billy), Brian Watson (Sgt. Rooney), Douglas Whitt (M.P.)

A drama in two acts. The action takes place in an army barracks in Virginia in 1965.

Carol Rosegg Photo

SYMPHONY SPACE

Wednesday, September 19–30, 1979 (12 performances)
Symphony Space (Allan Miller, Isaiah Sheffer, Artistic Directors) presents:

THE SHADOW OF A GUNMAN

By Sean O'Casey; Director, Isaiah Sheffer; Scenery, Robert Ellsworth; Costumes, Denise R. Hewes; Lighting, Albert Bergeret; Music, Robert Rogers; Administrative Assistant, Kathie Irving; Sound, John Morton; Stage Manager, Gina Leonetti; Press, Kay Catarulla'

CAST

Stephen Lang (Donal Davoren), Malachy McCourt (Seamus Shields), Brian Early (Maguire), John Leighton (Mulligan), Christine Baranski (Minnie Powell), Roger Hendricks Simon (Tommy), Yvonne Vincic (Mrs. Henderson), Peter Van Norden (Gallogher), Virginia Downing (Mrs. Grigson), Steven Gilborn (Grigson), Geral Graham Brown (An Auxiliary)

A tragic comedy in two acts. The action takes place during May 1920 in a tenement room in Dublin, Ireland.

Robert Ellsworth Photo

**Stephen Lang, Malachy McCourt (in bed)
in "The Shadow of a Gunman"**

PLAYHOUSE 46

Tuesday, September 25–October 21, 1979 (28 performances)
Michael Shepley presents:

DELI'S FABLE

By Susan Dworkin; Director, Leonard Peters; Scenery, Raymond C. Recht; Sound, Sam Agar; Costumes, Bruce Harrow; Lighting, Richard Winkler; General Manager, Susan Bell; Assistant to Director, William Wesbrooks; Stage Managers, Gloria Yetter, Trey Hunt; Press, Kate MacIntyre, Linda Ford

CAST

Bryce Holman (Frank), Ben Kapen (Solomon Geduldig), Elisa Morgan (Anita DeJesus), Michael M. Ryan (Alex), Peter Wetzel (Sing Sing), Olivia Williams (Delia Swinburne)

A play in 2 acts and 9 scenes. The action takes place at the present time in New York City.

John Rosenthal Photo

Left Center: Cast of "Deli's Folly"

78th STREET THEATRE LAB

Thursday, September 27,–October 14, 1979 (16 performances)
BMC Production Company (Bruce Waite, Producer-Artistic Director) presents:

THE SUN ALWAYS SHINES FOR THE COOL

By Miguel Pinero; Director, Jaime Sanchez; Original Music, Galt MacDermot; Musical Staging, Julie Arenal; Sets, David Potts; Lighting, Ruth Roberts; Costumes, Ticia Blackburn, Carrie Robbins; Associate Producer, Susan Mackin; General Manager, Leonard Mulhern; Business Manager, Michael Strauss; Technical Director, David Stuart Thalenberg; Wardrobe, Ally Sheedy; Stage Managers, Mark Elliott Field; Press, Owen Levy, Valerie Warner, Judith Shahn; Title Song sung by Carl Hall; Pianist, Kevin Di Simone

CAST

Haru Aki (Hooker), Cydney Cort (Phebe), Alan Eisenman (A John), Ramon Franco (Bam Bam Boy), Hugh Hurd (Justice), Carol Katz (Hooker), Susan Liebman (Hooker), Juanita Mahone (Satisfaction), Jose Maldonado (Jr. Baloon), Raul Martinez (A John), Chino Melao (A John), Santos Morales (Viejo), Faith Peter (Hooker), Ramiro Ray Ramirez (Diamond Ring), Sandra Rivera (Kahlu), Ivette Rodriguez (Rosa), Izzy Sanabria (Lefty "G"), Laura Summer (Hooker,) Rachel Ticotin (Chile Girl), Jaime Tirelli (Cat Eyes), Bridge Travis (Hooker), Jeff Travis (A John), Bruce Waite (Willie "B")

A drama performed without intermission. The action takes place at the present time during Indian Summer in Justice's Bar and in a small hotel room.

Bert Andrews Photo

**Bruce Waite, Chino Melao,
Ramon Franco**

THEATRE FOUR
Thursday, October 4–7, 1979 (6 performances and 7 previews)
Karen Kantor, Philip Swaebe, Stanley A. Glickman, Ashton
Springer present:

THE ALL NIGHT STRUT!

Conceived, Directed and Choreographed by Fran Charnas; Musical
Direction and Orchestrations, Michael Dansicker; Lighting, Glenn
Heinmiller; Production Coordinator, Susan Greenbaum; Vocal Ar-
rangements, Tom Fitt, Gil Lieb, Dick Schermesser; Costumes, Celia
Eller; Hairstylist, Michael Kriston; Sound, Louis Erskine; General
Manager, Karen Kantor; Assistant to Producers, Bruce Allardyce;
Set Decoration, Tom Smith; Press, Susan L. Schulman, Barbara
Carroll

CAST

Andrea Danford	Tony Rich
Jess Richards	Jana Robbins

MUSICAL NUMBERS: Chattanooga Choo Choo, Minnie the
Moocher, Brother Can You Spare a Dime?, In the Mood, Gimme
a Pigfoot and a Bottle of Beer, A Nightingale Sang in Berkeley
Square, Fascinating Rhythm, Java Jive, WW2 Medley, I Get Ideas,
Ain't Misbehavin', Operator, Dream, Beat Me Daddy Eight to the
Bar, A Fine Romance, Tuxedo Junction, Juke Box Saturday Night,
As Time Goes By, Hit That Jive Jack, Billie's Bounce, It Don't Mean
a Thing, Lullaby of Broadway

A musical entertainment in two acts.

Martha Swope Photo

**Andrea Danford, Jess Richards,
Tony Rich, Jana Robbins
in "The All Night Strut!"**

Lloyd Battista, Philip Casnoff

HAROLD CLURMAN THEATRE
Opened Thursday, October 4, 1979.*
Eric Krebs and Sam Landis present:

KING OF SCHNORRERS

Book, Music and Lyrics by Judd Woldin; Freely based on Israel
Zangwill's novella; Developed by The Moving Company; Directed
and Choreographed by Grover Dale; Sets, Adrianne Lobel; Light-
ing, Richard Nelson; Costumes, Patricia Adshead; Instrumental and
Vocal Arrangements, Norman L. Berman; Musical Director, Hank
Ross; Conductor Keyboards, Robert Billig; General Manager, Linda
Canavan; Props, Gayle Palmieri; Production Associates, Bill Fitz-
gerald, Nathan Hurwitz, Peter Taylor; Stage Managers, Jay Fox,
Christopher Adler, Jesse Garnee; Press, Shirley Herz, Jan Grenberg,
Sam Rudy

CAST

Lloyd Battista (DaCosta), Paul Binotto (Aaron/Wilkinson/Cos-
metician), Ralph Bruneau (Harry Tinker), Philip Casnoff (David)
succeeded by John Dossett, Ed Dixon (Isaac/Belasco/Chancellor),
Jerry Mayer (Mendel/Butler/Furtado), Rick McElhiney (Green-
baum/Councillor), Angelina Reaux (Sadie/Mrs. Grobstock/-
Housekeeper), Thomas Lee Sinclair (Grobstock/President), Sophie
Schwab (Deborah)
MUSICAL NUMBERS: Hail to the King, Chutzpah, I'm Only a
Woman, Just for Me, I Have Not Lived in Vain, The Fine Art of
Schnorring, Tell Me, What Do You Do?, It's Over, Murder, Dead,
Guided by Love, Sephardic Lullaby, Each of Us, Finale

A musical comedy in 2 acts and 16 scenes. The action takes place
during 1791 in the East End of London.

* Closed Nov. 18, 1979 after 54 performances and moved Nov. 21
to the Playhouse Theatre where it gave 63 additional performances, closing Jan. 13, 1980.

Suzanne Krebs Photos

**Left Center: Ralph Bruneau, Ed Dixon,
Angelina Reaux, Rick McElhinay,
Thomas Lee Sinclair, Paul Binotto, Jerry Mayer**

CHERRY LANE THEATRE
Tuesday, October 9–21, 1979 (15 performances)
Rodger Hess presents:

POTHOLES

Book and Lyrics, Elinor Guggenheimer; Music, Ted Simons; Choreography, Wayne Cilento; Director, Sue Lawless; Sets, Kenneth Foy; Costumes, Ann Emonts; Lighting, Robby Monk; Musical Director, Steven Oirich; Lighting Consultant, Patrika Brown; Associate Producer, Sheila Tronn Cooper; Company Manager, Sue McIntosh; Production Assistant, Nancy Rassiga-Tripp; Wardrobe, Nancy Thompson; Production Associates, Michael Julie Thomas, Dawn Litwak, Florence Wozar; Assistant to Director, Ruth O'Donnell; Stage Managers, Marcia McIntosh, Joe Romagnoli; Sound, Vern Carlson; Press, Gifford/Wallace, Linda Friberg

CAST

Jill Cook, Brandon Maggart, Carol Morley, Cynthia Parva, Lee Roy Reams, Joe Romagnoli, J. Keith Ryan, Samuel E. Wright
MUSICAL NUMBERS: Lost New York, Welcome, Back in the Street, Mad About, Can You Type?, Madison Avenue, Ropin' Dogies, Just Sit Back, Giant, Yoga and Yoghurt, Politicians' Song, Tickets' Song, St. Patrick's Day Parade, Starved, Fast Food, Network, Sound and Light, Looking for Someone, Suddenly She Was There, Dog Walker, Typical New Yorkers, Finale

A musical in two acts. The action takes place at the present time in New York City.

Fedora Photo

J. Keith Ryan, Cynthia Parva, Lee Roy Reams in "Potholes"

PORTOBELLO THEATRE
Friday, October 12–28, 1979 (12 performances)

BEES

Written and Directed by Dan Bredemann; Setting, Tim Holcomb; Costumes, Debbie Ann Gioello; Press, Alpert/LeVine, Mark Goldstaub. No other details available.

CAST

Irene Frances Kling
Shelia Russell
Sheri Myers

A romantic comedy. The action takes place at the present time in a Park Avenue apartment in New York City.

Right Center: Irene Frances Kline, Sheri Myers, Shelia Russell

Frederick Coffin, Alan David-Little, David Christmas, Elizabeth Moore, Anne DeSalvo, Peter J. Saputo, Holly Villaire

ENTERMEDIA THEATRE
Sunday, October 14–November 25, 1979 (49 performances)
Edith Vonnegut in association with Warner Theatre Productions and Mark Gasarch presents:

GOD BLESS YOU, MR. ROSEWATER

By Kurt Vonnegut; Book and Lyrics, Howard Ashman; Music, Alan Menken; Additional Lyrics, Dennis Green; Director, Howard Ashman; Musical Staging, Mary Kyte; Scenery, Edward T. Gianfrancesco; Costumes, David Graden; Lighting, Craig Evans; Musical Direction-Vocal Arrangements, David Friedman; Orchestrations, Daniel Troob; Dance Arrangements, Jimmy Roberts; Associate Producer, Laurie Tisch; General Managers, Leonard Soloway, Allan Francis; Company Manager, Steven Suskin; Sound, Barry Reed; Wardrobe, Sylvia Myrvold; Assistant Director, Nancy Parent; Musical Supervisor, Earl Shendell; Press, Betty Lee Hunt, Maria Cristina Pucci, James Sapp

CAST

Frederick Coffin (Eliot Rosewater), Janie Sell (Sylvia Rosewater), Jonathan Hadary (Norman Mushari), Pierre Epstein (Kilgore Trout), David Christmas (Warmergran/Ulm), Anne DeSalvo (Mary Moody/Blanche), Will Hussung (Senator Rosewater), Alan David-Little (Jerome/Sgt. Boyle), Elizabeth Moore (Diana Moon Glampers), Peter J. Saputo (Noyes/Fred), John Towey (Psychiatrist/Fireman), Ed VanNuys (Thurmond McAllister), Holly Villaire (Dawn/Caroline), Charles C. Welch (Delbert Peach)
MUSICAL NUMBERS: The Rosewater Foundation, Dear Ophelia, Thank God for the Volunteer Fire Brigade, Mushari's Waltz, 30 Miles from the Banks of the Ohio, Look Who's Here, Cheese Nips, Since You Came to This Town, A Poem by William Blake, Rhode Island Tango, Eliot, Sylvia, Plain Clean Average Americans, A Firestorm Consuming Indianapolis, I Eliot Rosewater

A musical in two acts.

Roger Greenawalt Photo

93

THEATER OF ST. PETER'S CHURCH
Opened Friday, October 5, 1979.*
ANTA presents:

LADYHOUSE BLUES

By Kevin O'Morrison; Director, Tony Giordano; Setting, Hugh Landwehr; Costumes, David Murin; Lighting, Frances Aronson; Sound, Phillip Campanella; Producer, Richmond Crinkley; Hairstylist, Michael Kriston; Technical Directors, Bruce Porter, Bruce Rayvid; Production Associates, Alison Clarkson, Toby Simpkins; Wardrobe, Glenn Gress; Props, Leslie Johnson; General Manager, Scott Steele; Stage Managers, David N. Feight, Johnna Murray; Press, Craig Macdonald

CAST

Helen .... Laurie Kennedy
Eylie .... Christine Estabrook
Dot .... Jobeth Williams
Liz .... Jo Henderson
Terry .... Wendy Fulton
Understudy: Johnna Murray

A drama in two acts. The action takes place during late August of 1919 in the Madden kitchen in South St. Louis, Missouri.

* Closed Dec. 16, 1979 after 85 performances.

Susan Cook Photos

Jobeth Williams, Wendy Fulton, Jo Henderson, Laurie Kennedy, Christine Estabrook (front) in "Ladyhouse Blues"

Herman Arbeit, James Rosin, Everett Ensley, Lois Diane Hicks, Donald G. Creech, Karen Sederholm, Marvin Chatinover, Beth Darwick, John Pinero, Charles Randall, Dick Boccelli

AMDA STUDIO ONE
Sunday, October 14,–November 4, 1979 (12 performances)
The Chelden Theater Group presents:

A YANK IN BEVERLY HILLS

By James Rosin; Director, Milton Moss; Set, Richard Singer; Lighting, Larry Zinn; Sound, Vito Perri, Lew Harrison; Assistant to Director, Alan Willig; Production Assistants, Barry Barnes, Michael Stewart; Stage Manager, Carol Baer; Press, Herb Striesfield

CAST

James Rosin (Michael Meridith), Marvin Chatinover (Hersh), Dick Boccelli (Giardano), John Pinero (Emilio), Charles Randall (Father), Herman O. Arbeit (Botnick/Movie Man/Producer), Lois Diane Hicks (Hooker/Blind Lady), Everett Ensley (Alphonso), Donald G. Creech (Driver 63), Beth Darwick (Claire), Karen Sederholm (Maria)

Ken Howard Photo

PROVINCETOWN PLAYHOUSE
Opened Tuesday, October 23, 1979.*
Mary Ellyn Devery presents the SEA-Ker production of:

GERTRUDE STEIN GERTRUDE STEIN GERTRUDE STEIN

By Marty Martin; Director, Milton Moss; Set, Tony Straiges; Costume, Garland Riddle; Lighting, Ruth Roberts; Production Consultant, Porter Van Zandt; Research Consultant, Alan Willig; Production Assistant, Helen Moss; Stage Managers, Jim Fauvell, Diana Banks; Press, Jan Morgan

CAST

Pat Carroll as Gertrude Stein

A solo performance in two acts. The action takes place during 1938 in Miss Stein's apartment at 27 Rue de Fleuris in Paris, France.

* Closed August 3, 1980 after 309 performances.

Gerry Goodstein Photo

Pat Carroll as Gertrude Stein

VILLAGE GATE/DOWNSTAIRS

Opened Monday, October 22, 1979.*
Art D'Lugoff, Burt D'Lugoff, Jerry Wexler in association with
Shari Upbin present:

ONE MO' TIME

Conceived and Directed by Vernel Bagneris; Additional Staging,
Dean Irby; Production Consultant, Pepsi Bethel; Musical Arrangements, Lars Edegran, Orange Kellin; Costumes, Joann Clevenger;
Settings, Elwin Charles Terrel II; Lighting, Joanne Schielke; Wardrobe, Morgan Clevenger

CAST

Bertha Williams .... Sylvia "Kuumba" Williams
Ma Reed .... Thais Clark
Thelma .... Topsy Chapman
Papa Du.............................. Vernel Bagneris †
Theatre Owner .... John Stell

The New Orleans Blue Serenaders: Lars Edegran (Piano/Co-Direc-
tor), Orange Kellin (Clarinet/Co-Director), John Robichaux
(Drums), William Davis (Tuba), Jabbo Smith (Trumpet)
UNDERSTUDIES: Nora Cole for Ms. Chapman, Carol Wood for
Ms. Clark, Bruce Stickland for Mr. Bagneris, Denise Rogers for Ms.
Williams

Bertha Williams and her touring company are in the Lyric Theatre in New Orleans, La., to perform "One Mo' Time." The time is
1926. Performed with one intermission.

General Manager: Albert Poland
Company Manager: Pamela Hare
Press: Solters & Roskin, Milly Schoenbaum, Kevin Patterson
Stage Manager: Sharj Upbin

* Still playing May 31, 1980.
† Succeeded by Bruce Strickland

Bert Andrews Photos

**Top Right: Sylvia "Kuumba" Williams,
Vernel Bagneris, Thais Clark Below:
Clark, Bagneris, Topsy Chapman**

TOWN HALL

Opened Sunday, November 4, 1979.*
Shalom Yiddish Musical Comedy Theatre, Raymond Ariel,
David Carey, Theo Roller present:

REBECCA, THE RABBI'S DAUGHTER

Book, William Siegel; Director, Michal Greenstein; Musical Director-Conductor, Renee Solomon; Original Score, Abraham Ellstein;
Choreography, Felix Fibich; Scenery, Adina Reich; Additional Music, Alexander Lustig; Wardrobe, Joni Rudesill; Photographer,
Gerry Goodstein; Press, Max Eisen, Francine L. Trevens

CAST

David Ellin (Gabbai), David Carey (Yosele), Fay Nicoll (Julia),
Mary Soreanu (Rivkele/Rebecca), Reizl Bozyk (Dvoyreh), Shifra
Lerer (Sossl), Yankele Alperin (Zelig), Eleanor Reissa (Soorele),
Solo Moise (Yukl), Karol Latowicz (Lawyer Butch), and Fibich
Dancers: Shamus Murphy, Shelly Pappas, Jim Sayger, Dafna Soltes
MUSICAL NUMBERS: Prologue, My Dreams, Everyone Has a
Right to Love, Rivkele Dem Rebns, Forget Me Not, Once It Was
Different, When a Jew Sings, How Good It Is, Chassene, I Want to
Be a Bride, You Are My Solace, Hollywood, Potpourri, Couplet,
Charleston

A musical in 2 acts and 5 scenes with a prologue.

* Closed Jan. 6, 1980 after 84 performances.

Gerry Goodstein Photos

Yankele Alperin, Mary Soreanu

ASTOR PLACE THEATRE
Opened Tuesday, November 6, 1979.*
Albert Poland, Seymour Morgenstern and Arthur Bartow
present:

MODIGLIANI

By Dennis McIntyre; Director, Allen R. Belknap; Setting, Paul
Eads; Costumes, Ruth Morley; Lighting, Joanna Schielke; Music,
Gary Levinson; Wardrobe, Teresa Lynnette Snider, Wendy L.
Stuart; Music Consultant, William A. Graham

CAST

Chaim Soutine............................. George Gerdes
Maurice Utrillo............................. Ethan Phillips
Amedeo Modigliani .... Jeffrey DeMunn
Leopold Zborowski........................ Michael Tucker
Beatrice Hastings .... Mary-Joan Negro
Guillaume Cheron........................... Richard Seff
Waiter .... Michael Coerver
UNDERSTUDIES: Tony Campisi (Modigliani), Peggy Schoditsch
(Beatrice), Michael Coever (Cheron), Steven Memel (Utrillo/-
Soutine/Zborowski/Waiter)

The action takes place during the late fall of 1916 in the Montparnasse section of Paris, from Wednesday through Friday.

General Manager: Albert Poland
Company Manager: Margay Whitlock
Press: Betty Lee Hunt, Maria Cristina Pucci, James Sapp
Stage Managers: Brian Meister, Michael Coerver

* Closed Feb. 24, 1980 after 119 performances.

Ian Anderson Photos

Right: Richard Seff, Jeffrey DeMunn
Above: George Gerdes, Ethan Phillips
Top: Jeffrey DeMunn, Mary-Joan Negro

Peter Burnell, Daniel Goldfeld

HAROLD CLURMAN THEATRE
Thursday, November 15–December 2, 1979 (21 performances)
The Harold Clurman Theatre (Jack Garfein, Artistic Director)
presents:

FLYING BLIND

By Bill Morrison; Director, Christopher Bond; Setting, James Tilton; Costumes, Bob Wojewodski; Lighting, Todd Elmer; Production
Supervisor, David S. Resenak; Assistant to Director, Judy Andersen; Technical Director, Jeffrey L. Glave; Stage Managers, Harold
Apter, Dean Tulipane, Josef Quirinale; Press, C. George Willard

CAST

Lynne MacLaren (Liz Poots), Raymond Hardie (Smyth), Dean
Tulipane (Tully), Daniel Goldfeld (Michael), Dan Strickler (Dan
Poots), Nonnie Weaver (Carol), Peter Burnell (Boyd), Caroline Sid-
ney Abady (Bertha), Todd Michael Lewis (Mac), Tom Lacy
(Magoo), Dennis Bacigalupi (Shorty/Sean), Bairbre Dowling (Una)

A play in two acts. The action takes place in a house in Belfast
at the present time.

Nathaniel Tileston Photo

THEATRE FOUR
Opened Sunday, November 18, 1979 (1 performance and 12 previews)
Donal H. Rothey presents:

ALTAR BOYS

By Stephen Magowan; Director, Elaine Shore; Setting and Lighting, John Wright Stevens; Costumes, William Ivey Long; Sound, Torrie Smith; Wardrobe, Bob Graham; Assistant to Producer, Maureen Fremont; General Management, Weiler/Miller; Stage Managers, Rick Ralston, Mark Rubinsky; Press, Shirley Herz, Jan Greenberg, Sam Rudy

CAST

Vere . . . . David Reinhardsen
Rudi . . . . Octavio Ciano
Understudy: Joel Marks

A drama in two acts. The action takes place in West Hollywood, California, on the evening of November 5, 1979, and the following morning.

Patrick Dougherty Photo

Octavio Ciano, David Reinhardsen

PLAYERS THEATRE
Opened Thursday, November 15, 1979.*
Howard J. Burnett in association with Reade Nimick presents:

CLASS ENEMY

By Nigel Williams; Director, Tony Tanner; Set, Edward Burbridge; Lighting, Marshall S. Spiller; Costumes, Clifford Capone; Associate Producer, Paul B. Berkowsky; Assistant to Producer, Maggi Burnett

CAST

Iron (Herron) . . . . Maxwell Caulfield †1
Skylight (Skellet) . . . . Bruce Wall
Nipper (Napier) . . . . Lance Davis †2
Racks (Rakes) . . . . Lonny Price †3
Sweetheart (Sowerthwaite) . . . . Jay Lowman †4
Snatch (Cameron) . . . . Alvin Alexis
Master . . . . Daniel DeRaey
Understudies: Ahvi Spindell, Alan Silver

A drama in two acts. The action takes place in a schoolroom in Ballsache High, a state comprehensive school in one of the poorest parts of South London, England, at the present time.

General Manager: Paul B. Berkowsky
Company Manager: Paul P. Matwiow
Press: Jeffrey Richards, Warren Knowlton, Robert Ganshaw, Alan Eichler, Lisa Lipsky, Karen Gromis, Ted Killmer, Marjorie Ornston
Stage Managers: Robert I. Cohen, Ahvi Spindell

* Closed April 27, 1980 after 184 performances and 5 previews.
† Succeeded by: 1. Tom Wiggin, Keith Szarabajka, 2. Alan Silver, 3. Peter Hagen, 4. Jay Lowman

Bruce Rasmussen Photos

(standing) Bruce Wall, Maxwell Caulfield, Charles Bloom, (seated) Troy Nicholson, Lonny Price, Lance Davis

**Above: Tom Wiggin, Daniel DeRaey
Left: Maxwell Caulfield,
Lance Davis**

97

THEATER FOR THE NEW CITY
Opened Wednesday, November 11, 1979.*
Theater for the New City (Bartenieff/Field) presents:

BAG LADY

By Jean-Claude van Itallie; Director, Elinor Renfield; Environment Design, Barbara Sonneborn; Costume, Mary Brecht; Sound, Paul E. Garrity; Lighting, Pat Stern; Composer, Peter Golub; Stage Managers, Matthew Waterman, Hal Panchansky; Press, Howard Atlee, Jim Baldassare

CAST

Shami Chaikin

Performed without intermission. The action takes place at the present time in New York City.
* Closed March 17, 1980 after 89 performances.

Nathaniel Tileston Photo

Shami Chaikin

**Scott Robertson, Suellen Estey (top),
Josie O'Donnell, Jess Richards**

BOLTAX
Opened Tuesday, November 20, 1979.*
Leonard M. Landau presents:

THE LULLABY OF BROADWAY
or Harry Who?

The Music of Harry Warren; Director, Judith Haskell; Choreographer, Eleanore Treiber; Musical Director, Jeremy Harris; Costumes, Kevin Reid; Script, Judith Haskell, Mark O'Donnell; Lighting, Rick Belzer; Stage Manager, Charlotte Brown; Press, David Powers, Tony Origlio

CAST

Suellen Estey
Josie O'Donnell
Jess Richards
Scott Robertson
* Closed Dec. 16, 1979 after limited engagement of 36 performances.

Roy Blakey Photo

CHELSEA THEATER CENTER
November 23–December 29, 1979 (8 performances)
New York Theatre Studio (Richard V. Romagnoli, Artistic Director; Cheryl Faraone, Managing Director) presents:

GOTHAM AGONISTES

An original revue created and performed by Megan Bagot, Tom Carder, Mary Cunniff, Philip DiBelardino, Ellen Greenfield; Director, Cheryl Faraone; Costumes, Walker Hicklin; Press, Ellen Schaplowsky

Gotham Agonistes

STAGE 15
November 23–December 23, 1979 (19 performances)
Alan A. Gabor presents:

GREAT CATHERINE

By George Bernard Shaw; Director, Alan A. Gabor; Sets, Esteban Fernandez; Costumes, Fern Mehler, A. Gabor; Lighting, Paul Merwin; Artwork, Joe Turetski; Stage Manager, Fern Mehler; Press, Howard Atlee, Jim Baldassare

CAST

Elizabeth DeCharay (Catherine II), Patrick Chicalese (Prince Patiomkin), Deborah Gabinetti (Varinka), Jeffry Burchfield (Maryshkin), Donna Gilbert (Claire), Terry Brown (Sergeant), Katya Colman (Princess Dashoff), Allison James Burnett (Capt. Edstaston)

Right: Elizabeth DeCharay, Allison James Burnett

CHERRY LANE THEATRE
November 26, 1979–January 6, 1980 (47 performances)
Harold Leventhal/Michael Diamond in association with Alison H. Clarkson present:

TOM TAYLOR
as
WOODY GUTHRIE

Developed by Tom Taylor; Adapted by George Boyd, Michael Diamond, Tom Taylor from the writings and songs of Woody Guthrie; Director, George Boyd; Set and Costume, Robert Blackman; Lighting, Daniel Adams; Assistant to Producers, Irene Allong; General Manager, Harris Goldman; Stage Manager, Scott Allen; Press, Judy Jacksina, Glenna Freedman

Performed in two acts. The action takes place in the United States from the 1920's to the 1960's.

Paul Appleby Photo

Left: Tom Taylor as Woody Guthrie

THREE MUSES THEATRE
November 29–December 16, 1979 (12 performances)
Virgo Productions presents;

THE LOVES OF CASS McGUIRE

By Brian Friel; Director, Carol Sica; Scenic Consultant, Bil Mikulewicz; Lighting, Sara Schrager; Costumes, Sydney Brooks; Stage Manager, Janet Friedman

CAST

Irene Dailey (Cass), Nancy Franklin (Alice), Richard Kuss (Harry), David Saint (Dom), Patrizia Norcia (Tessa), Roger Fawcett (Pat Quinn), Leora Dana (Trilbe Costello), William Duell (Ingram), Margaret Barker (Mother/Mrs. Butcher)

A comedy in three acts. The action takes place in Ireland just before Christmas.

(No photos available)

Irene Dailey

PARK ROYAL THEATRE
November 29–December 22, 1979 (20 performances)
The New Princess Theatre Company (Gerald Bordman, Berthe Schuchat, Ethel Watt) presents:

OH, BOY!

Book and Lyrics, Guy Bolton, P. G. Wodehouse; Music, Jerome Kern; Director, Donnis Honeycutt; Choreography, Daniel Levans; Musical Direction, Vocal and Dance Arrangements David Krane; Sets and Lighting, Paul C. McGuire; Costumes, Carol H. Beule; Technical Director, Robert L. Anderson; Production Assistant, Joy Levien; Hairstylist, Richard Ferrera; Stage Managers, Carol Horne, Bruce Turner; Wardrobe, Katherine Landro; Press, Craig Macdonald

CAST

Peter Blaxill (Briggs), Judith Blazer (Lou Ellen Carter), Catherine Campbell (Sheila Ryve), Larro Chelsi (Judge Carter), Lydia Edwards (Mrs. Carter), Jim Fitzpatrick (Sims), Kelby Fries (Phil Ossify), Lauren Goler (Billie Dew), Andrea Lee (Jane Packard), Greg Minahan (Jim Marvin), Brian Quinn (Club Waiter), Gene Paul Rickard (George Budd), Tim Salce (Phelan Fyne), Gary Smiley (Hugo Chaseit), Elaine Swann (Penelope Budd), Gillian Walke (Polly Andrus), Julie Wilder (Jacky Sampson)
MUSICAL NUMBERS: Let's Make a Night of It, You Never Knew about Me, A Package of Seeds, Be a Little Sunbeam, An Old Fashioned Wife, A Pal Like You, Letter Song, Till the Clouds Roll By, Little Bit of Ribbon, First Day of May, Ain't It a Grand and Glorious Feeling, Rolled into One, Oh Daddy Please, Nesting Time in Flatbush, Words Are Not Needed, Flubby-Dub, Finale

A musical comedy in 2 acts and 3 scenes. The action takes place in the bachelor apartment of George Budd, in Meadowsides, Long Island, New York, and at the country club.

Morgan Reese Photo

Julie Wilder, Greg Minahan in "Oh, Boy!"

Catherine Burns

Al Pacino

PROCESS STUDIO THEATRE
December 3–17, 1979 (21 performances)
Dana Matthow presents:

METROPOLITAN MADNESS

By Sidney Morris; Director, John Camera; Scenery and Lighting, Mickey Elias; Music Coordinated by Eric Diamond; Technical Directors, David Little, James Vincent Miraglia; Dialect Coach, Robert Fleet; Producer's Assistants, Deborah Dane, Michelle Matthow, Florence Flanger, Natalie Strauss; Stage Manager, Jim Wilson; Press, Bruce Cohen

CAST

Ira Lee Collings (David Miller), Richard Hoyt-Miller (Anchorperson 1), Bonnie Loren (Anchorperson 2), Eric McGill (Herbert Smith), Frank Nastasi (Max Dubinsky), Paula Parker (Judith Sanderson), Bernie Rachelle (Simon Grey), Mona Sands (Lola Eastman), Kay Williams (Rita O'Shay)

A "theatre piece" in two acts.

COLONNADES THEATRE
December 1–7, 1979 (limited run of 6 performances)
Circle in the Square presents:

JUNGLE OF CITIES

By Bertolt Brecht; Translated by Anselm Hollo; Director, Liviu Ciulei; Scenery, Nancy Winters; Costumes, Vel Riberto; Lighting, Betsy Adams; Sound, Andy Bloor; Production Assistant Randall Etheredge; Stage Managers, James Pentecost, Gloria Yetter

CAST

Al Pacino (George Garga), Roy Brocksmith (The Worm), Ivar Brogger (Salvation Army Officer), Catherine Burns (Jane Larry), Sam J. Coppola (Baboon), Ron Faber (John Garga), Sharon Goldman (Mary Garga), Donald Madden (Shlink), Carol Morley (Mae Garga), James Tolkan (Skinny), Peter Van Norden (Pat Manky), Gerry Vichi (C. Maynes)

(No photos available)

Paula Parker, Ira Lee Collings

78th STREET THEATRE LAB

December 4, 1979–January 2, 1980 (26 performances)
Rose Productions presents:

SHARON SHASHANOVAH

Written and Directed by Alexander Francis Horn; Music and Lyrics, Judy Castelli; Lights, Jeff Davis; Puppets, Nicholas Cortes; Set and Costumes, Sharon Horn; General Manager, Sam Hochman; Stage Managers, Michael Aitchison, Tina Turturro; Press, Howard Atlee, Barbara Atlee, Jim Baldassure

CAST

Morton Banks (Producer Joseph Ravensky), Susan Carr (Script Girl Elene), Judy Castelli (Singer Andrea), Marc Fortunato (Actor Billy Brenner), Sharon Gans (Actress Sharon Shashanovah), Rita Karin (Teacher Mme. Natasha Ravenskaya), Norberto Kerner (Critic Otto Schechler), Emanuel Yesckas (Playwright Castillo)

A play in three acts. The action takes place at the present time in Hollywood and New York.

Martha Swope Photo

**Sharon Gans, Marc Fortunato
and cast of "Sharon Shashanovah"**

**Bay Baynes, Brian Kale
in "Benya the King"**

EMANU-EL MIDTOWN YM-YWHA

December 13, 1979–January 6, 1980 (18 performances)
Jewish Repertory Theatre (Ran Avni, Artistic Director; Betsy Imershein, Managing Director) presents:

BENYA THE KING

By Richard Schotter; Inspired by Isaac Babel's "Tales of Odessa"; Director, Roger Hendricks Simon; Music, Ken Collins; Sets and Costumes, John Scheffler; Lighting, Jeffrey Beecroft; Stage Manager, Lynn Gutter; Assistant Director, Steve Robert Bloom
CAST: Michael Marcus, Brian Kale, Jeffrey Lorber, Gay Baynes, Willy Switkes, Hope Arthur, Jerry Rockwood, Harold Herbstman, John Martello, Ellen Newman, Mary Beidler, Libby Richman, Andy Stein

AMDA STUDIO ONE

December 18, 1979–February 10, 1980 (32 performances)
Amrow Productions presents:

LILIOM

By Ferenc Molnar; Director, Franz Harland; No other details available.

CAST

Ronald Guttman (Liliom), Charles Gordone (Ficsur), Gretchen Whitman (Julie), Anita Lobel (Mrs. Muskat), Florence Anglin (Mother Hollander), Gail Simmons (Marie), Richard Spore (Wolf Beifeld), William McKinney Randall, Eric Trules, Bruce Waite

Ronald Guttman as Liliom

HAROLD CLURMAN THEATRE
December 19, 1979–January 20, 1980 (31 performances)
The Harold Clurman Theatre (Jack Garfein, Artistic Director) presents:

PARIS WAS YESTERDAY
with
CELESTE HOLM

By Janet Flanner; Adapted and Directed by Paul Shyre; Designed by Eldon Elder; Lighting, William M. Barclay; Sound, Robert L. Etter; Production Supervisor, David S. Rosenak; Technical Director, Jeffrey L. Glave; Stage Manager, Lois J. Kier; Press, Joe Wolhandler, C. George Willard

A solo performance based on the works of Janet Flanner (Genet) that appeared originally in the New York Magazine from 1925 to 1975.

Celeste Holm as Janet Flanner

Michael Calkins, Mark Holleran, Roger Lawson, Ed Jacobs in "Babes in Toyland"

FELT FORUM
December 21, 1979–January 1, 1980 (16 performances)
American Entertainment Enterprises presents:

BABES IN TOYLAND

Based on Victor Herbert's "Babes in Toyland" from an original idea by Barry Weissler; Producers, Barry Weissler, Fran Weissler; New Music and Lyrics, Shelly Markham, Annette Leisten; Book Adaptation, Ellis Weiner; Director, Munson Hicks; Choreography, Tony Stevens; Scenery and Costumes, Michael J. Hotopp, Paul de Pass; Lighting, Associated Theatrical Designers; Musical Direction-Rock Orchestration, Bob Christianson; Orchestral Arrangements, Kirk Nurock; Dance Arrangements, Bob Stecko; Company Manager, Jay Humphry; Stage Manager, Naomi Wexler; Press, The Merlin Group

CAST

Mark Holleran (Tom/Vendor), Roger Lawson (Sugarbear/Vendor), Michael Calkins (Horace/Vendor), Dan Kruger (Promoter Old King Cole), Edward T. Jacobs (Haystack), Ken Bonafons (Grandfather), Alan F. Seiffert (Jack Be Nimble/Drummer Boy/Humpty Dumpty), Debbie McLeod (Mary), S. Barkley Murray (Mother Goose/Shroud), C. A. Hutton (Barnaby), Lynn Hippen (Old Woman in the Shoe/Toy Soldier), Mona Finston, Steve Mathews (Children in the Shoe), Robert Hancock (The Wall/Computer Bob), Shari Watson (Little Bo Peep)

Peter Cunningham Photo

LINCOLN CENTER LIBRARY THEATRE
December 26, 27, 28, 1979 (4 performances)
Stage Directors and Choreographers Workshop Foundation presents:

SAY IT WITH MUSIC

A salute to Irving Berlin and his music; Created and Staged by Jeffery K. Neill; Musical Adaptation and Direction, Wendell Kindberg; Costumes and Props, Charles W. Roeder; Millinery, Sy Robin; Assistant Choreographer, Suzanne Kaszynski; Stage Manager, Ruth E. Kramer

CAST

Richard P. Bennett, Sean McNickle, Mimi Moyer, Ken Seiter, Rima Starr, Karen Stefko

Cast of "Say It with Music"

ALICE TULLY HALL
December 26–30, 1979 (10 performances; returned to Town Hall February 22–March 7, 1980 for 10 additional performances)
The Paper Bag Players (Judith Martin, Director) presents:

MAMA'S GOT A JOB

Conceived, written and directed by Judith Martin; Music and Lyrics, Donald Ashwander; with Irving Burton, Pat Brodhead, James Lally, Judith Martin; Press, Judy Jacksina, Glenna Freedman

Right: Judith Martin, James Lally, Irving Burton

TOWN HALL
January 16–March 2, 1980 (55 performances)
Shalom Yiddish Musical Comedy Theatre presents:

A MILLIONAIRE IN TROUBLE

Book, Moshe Tamir; Music, Alexander Lustig; Adapted by Michael Greenstein; Lyrics, Yankele Alperin; Director, Yankele Alperin; Musical Direction, Renee Solomon; Musical Numbers Staged by Felix Fibich; Wardrobe, Joni Rudesill; Technical Adviser, Kirk Dehling; Properties and Costumes, Equity Library Theatre; Suits, Adolpho; Sound, George Jacobs; Press, Max Eisen, Francine L. Trevens

CAST

Chaim Levin (Philip), Diane Cypkin (Goldele), Bernardo Hiller (Teddy), Yakov Bodo (Simon Oppenheim), Solo Moise (Harry Fishbein), Moishe Rosenfeld (Attorney Green), Raquel Yossifon (Emma Shayn), Paul Czolczynski (Yukel Kishke), Chayele Ash (Esther Shayn)
MUSICAL NUMBERS: Promises and Love, How Do You Do, A Happy Life, Many Trades, Mother Son, Drunkeness, Longing, Mazel Tov, Hard To Be a Pauper

A musical in two acts.

Right Center: Raquel Yossifon, Solo Moise

RICHARD ALLEN CENTER
January 24–February 10, 1980 (12 performances)
THE SIGN IN SIDNEY BRUSTEIN'S WINDOW by Lorraine Hansberry; Director, Helaine Head; Set, John Scheffler; Lighting, Victor En Yu Tan; Costumes, Jesse Harris; Technical Director-Stage Manager, Ron McIntyre; Producer, Hazel J. Bryant.
CAST: Victor Arnold (Sidney Brustein), Thommie Blackwell (Alton Scales), Edna Dix (Iris Parodus Brustein), Robert Carnegie (Wally O'Hara), Jim Aucoin (Max), Jill Tomarken (Mavis Parodus Bryson), Robert Ground (David Ragin), Ann Convery (Gloria Parodus)

Larry Neilson Photo

Right Center: Thommie Blackwell, Victor Arnold

NEW VIC THEATRE
January 29–February 17, 1980 (16 performances)
Soho Artists Theatre (Dino Narizzano, Producer) presents:

VIADUCT

By Aleen Malcolm; Director, C. K. Alexander; Set, Bob Phillips; Lighting, Victor En Yu Tan; Costumes, Patricia Alexander; Sound, James Nisbet Clark; Associate Producer, John Corey; Stage Managers, Matt Dolph, Lourana Howard, Debbie Bessen; Press, Kathy Dunn

CAST

John Clarkson (BBC Announcer), George Taylor (George Biggins), Eric Schurenberg (David Biggins), Aleen Malcolm (Dora Biggins), David Cantor (Brian)

A melodrama in two acts. The action takes place during the spring of 1959 in North Paddington, London, England.

Aleen Malcolm, George Taylor in "Viaduct"

Jane White

ONE SHERIDAN SQUARE
January 29–March 28, 1980 (51 performances)
Saffron Ltd. presents:

JANE WHITE, WHO? . . .

By Jane White and Joe Masteroff; Musical Direction, Roger Leonard; Lighting and Technical Director, Ian McKay; Musical Arrangements, Stan Freeman, Lloyd Mayers, Roy Glover; Ms. White's Wardrobe, Halston, Chor Bazaar; Wigs, Tony Loscinto; Set Pieces, Second Hand Rose; Stage Manager, Charles Murdoch; Press Ellen Levene

CAST

Jane White

An autobiographical musical in two acts.

Nathaniel Tileston Photo

PLAYWRIGHTS HORIZONS
Opened Monday, January 14, 1980.*
(Moved Tuesday, May 6, 1980 to Chelsea Theatre Center)
Stephen Graham, Luis Sanjurjo, and Joan Stein present:

TABLE SETTINGS

Written and Directed by James Lapine; Settings, Heidi Landesman; Costumes, Bob Wojewodski; Lighting, Beverly Emmons; Assistant to Director, Lynda Lee Burks; Production Assistant, Nancy Kohlbeck

CAST

Younger Son.	Mark Blum
Older Son	Brent Spiner†1
Wife	Chris Weatherhead
Granddaughter	Marta Kober
Mother	Frances Chaney
Grandson	Eric Curry†2
Girlfriend	Carolyn Hurlburt
Voice Over	Paul Sparer

A comedy performed without intermission. The action takes place at the present time around or near a table stage center.

General Manager: Albert Poland
Company Manager: Erik Murkoff
Press: David Powers, Barbara Carroll
Stage Managers: Michael Spellman, Brooke Allen

* Closed Aug. 31, 1980 after 264 performances.
† Succeeded by: 1. Dan Desmond, 2 Matthew Kolmes

Martha Swope Photos

Top Right: Mark Blum, Frances Chaney

Chris Weatherhead, Mark Blum, Frances Chaney, Marta Kober, Carolyn Hurlburt, Brent Spiner, Eric Gurry (under table)

ANNEX THEATRE
January 30–February 2, 1980 (4 performances)
American Theatre of Actors (James Jennings, Artistic Director) presents:

DUNE ROAD

By Joseph Gath Gottfried; Director, Anthony DeVito; Set and Costumes, Katrina Blumenstock, Edward W. Seltzer; Stage Manager, Stephen Bonnell; Press, David Lipsky

CAST

Marjorie Austrian (Mag), Robert Kasel (Lark), Richard Voights (Fred), Donna Ritchie (Betsy)

A play in three acts. The action takes place at the present time in the living room and deck of Mag and Fred Lustgarden's beach house at the end of summer.

Left: Marjorie Austrian, Robert Kasel, Richard Voigts *(Anita Feldman Photo)*

SOUTH STREET THEATRE
January 31–March 9, 1980 (24 performances)
Encompass The Music Theater (Roger Cunningham, Producer; Nancy Rhodes, Artistic Director) presents:

ELIZABETH AND ESSEX

Book, Michael Stewart, Mark Bramble; Based on Maxwell Anderson's play "Elizabeth the Queen"; Music, Orchestrations and Vocal Arrangements, Doug Katsaros; Lyrics, Richard Engquist; Director, Nancy Rhodes; Musical Direction, Jack Gaughan; Choreography, Sharon Halley; Sets, Michael C. Smith; Lighting, Carol B. Sealey; Costumes, A. Christina Giannini; General Manager, Jerry J. Thomas; Technical Director, David Gscheidle; Production Assistant, Vicki Kahn; Wigs, Ray Iagnucco; Stage Managers, Richard Switaski, Peter Jablonski; Press, Richard Kornberg

CAST

Estelle Parsons (Elizabeth), Richard White (Essex), Florence Lacey (Penelope Gray), Brian Wolfe (Fool), Lisa Ann Cunningham (Tressa/Old Woman), Paul Farin (Marvel), Fran Ferrone (Martha), Randy Hansen (Guard/Soldier/Courier), Wade L. Hardy III (Lord Herbert), Ted Kowal (Capt. Armin/Man-at-arms/Courier), Patricia Ludd (Lady Ann), Court Miller (Bacon), William Ryall (Walter Raleigh), Gordon Stanley (Cecil), Molly Stark (Lady Charlotte/Irish Woman)
MUSICAL NUMBERS: Fa La, As You Are, Cheers, I'll Be Different, Gloriana, Gossip, The First to Know Ireland, Love Knots, Not Now, She's a Woman, It Takes a Man, The Lady Lies, All I Remember Is You, Finale

A musical in two acts. The action takes place during the second half of the 16th Century in Whitehall Palace, Ireland, Essex' house on the Strand, and The Queen's apartment in the Tower.

Martha Swope Photo

Florence Lacey, Richard White, Estelle Parsons in "Elizabeth and Essex"

HAROLD CLURMAN THEATRE
February 14–March 16, 1980 (37 performances)
The Harold Clurman Theatre presens:

THESE MEN

By Mayo Simon; Director, Zoe Caldwell; Setting, David Potts; Costumes, Jane Greenwood; Lighting, Todd Elmer; Sound, Robert L. Etter; Production Supervisor, David S. Rosenak; Technical Director, Jeffrey L. Glave; Assistant to Director, Victoria Sanders; Production Assistant, Toby Simpkins; Stage Managers, Kimberly Francis Kearsley, Joan Ungaro; Press, Joe Wolhandler, C. George Willard

CAST

Cloris .... Jill Larson
Shelly .... Alix Elias
Understudy: Janice Lathen

A comedy in two acts. The action takes place at the present time in Laurel Canyon, a mile from the main streets of Los Angeles, California.

Carol Rosegg Photo

Jill Larson, Alix Elias

SYMPHONY SPACE

February 14–27, 1980 (8 performances)
Rick Hobard with the sponsorship of Goethe House, Piscator Foundation, New School for Social Research, State University of New York at Stony Brook presents:

WAR AND PEACE

By Erwin Piscator and Alfred Neumann from the novel by Leo Tolstoy; Associate Producer-Director, Alfred G. Brooks; Setting, Douglas Kraner; Lighting, Steven Pollock; Costumes, Timothy Miles; Sound, Brian Byrnes; Assistant to Producer, George Gitto; Wardrobe, Karen Sugihara; Stage Managers, Rosemary McMullan, Susan Hochtman; Press, Solters & Roskin, Milly Schoenbaum, Kevin Patterson

CAST

Lewis Arlt (Narrator), Michael Auclair (Kusmich), James Bartz (Dolokhof), Peter Basch (Nicolai), Denise Bessette (Natasha), Craig Dudley (Napoleon), Elizabeth Hubbard (Countess Rostova), Scott Klavan (Alpatich/Kutusov), Michael Kovaka (Kuragin), Timothy Landfield (Pierre), Carl Low (Old Prince), James Lyons (Karatayev), Anne Hamilton Martin (Maria), Kurt Schlesinger (Andrei)

A drama in three acts. The action takes place in Europe between the Rhine and Mitischi from 1805–1812.

Kurt Schlesinger, Timothy Landfield, Denise Bessette in "War and Peace"

THEATRE FOUR

February 17–March 9, 1980 (24 performances)
Cheryl Crawford and Eryk Spektor present:

THE HOUSEWIVES' CANTATA

Music, Mira J. Spektor; Lyrics, June Siegel; Book, Willy Holtzman; Direction and Choreography, Rina Elisha; Musical Direction, Richard A. Schacher; Vocal Arrangements, Richard A. Schacher, Mira J. Spektor; Orchestrations, Musicworks, Inc.; Scenery, Raymond C. Recht; Lighting, Marshall S. Spiller; Costumes, Judy Dearing; Wardrobe, James Kabel; Management Associate, Sheala N. Berkowsky; General Manager, Paul B. Berkowsky; Company Manager, Paul P. Matwiow; Stage Managers, Roger Shea, Michael Hartman; Press, Jeffrey Richards, Warren Knowlton, Robert Ganshaw, Bill Miller, Lisa Lipsky, Karen Gromis, Ted Killmer, Joseph Santi

CAST

Patti Karr (Flora), Sharon Talbot (Lily), Forbesy Russell (Heather), William Perley (Everyman/Harvey/Freddie/Sheldon/Allen/Judge/Rod/etc), Michael Hartman (Understudy)
MUSICAL NUMBERS: Dirty Dish Rag, Sex, Song of the Bourgeois, Early Morning Rain, Little Women, Adultery Waltz, Divorce Lament, Suburban Rose, Song of the Open Road, Legs, M.C.P., Daughter's Lullaby, Guinever among the Grapefruit Peels, Apartment Lament, Middle Aged, Mr. Fixer, White House Resident, A New Song

A musical in three parts: 1962, 1972, and the present.

Peter Cunningham Photo

Sharon Talbot, Patti Karr, Forbesy Russell in "Housewives' Cantata"

LION THEATRE

February 20–March 30, 1980 (40 performances)
Lion Theatre Company (Gene Nye, Artistic Director; Eleanor Meglio, Producing Director) presents:

STAR TREATMENT

By Jack Heifner; Director, Garland Wright; Music and Lyrics, Janis Ian; Musical Director, David Lewis; Scenic Design, John Arnone; Lighting, Frances Aronson; Sound, Regge Life; Wardrobe, Frances Miksits; Stage Managers, Susana Meyer, Mark Schorr; Press, Betty Lee Hunt, Maria Cristina Pucci

CAST

June Gable (Elaine), David Lewis (Frank), Allan Carlsen (Bill), Conan McCarty (Michael), Olana (Thomas)

A play with music in two acts. The action takes place at the present time in an apartment and a nightclub in New York City.

Roderick Robinson Photo

June Gable, David Lewis in "Star Treatment"

THEATRE DeLYS
February 19–24, 1980 (7 performances)
Dorothy Love and John Britton present:

CHANGES

Conceived and Directed by Dorothy Love; Musical Staging, Ronn Forella; Lyrics, Danny Apolinar; Music, Addy Fieger; Scenery, Don Jensen; Costumes, Miles White; Lighting, Richard Nelson; Arrangements and Orchestrations, Larry Fallon; Musical Director, Hal Serra; Sound, Bill Merrill; Original Dance Music and Vocal Arrangements, Larry Fallon; Wardrobe, Lisa Gardner; Production Assistant, Risa Steinberg; Assistant to Producers, Keith Sherman; General Management, Dorothy Olim Associates; Company Manager, Gail Bell; Stage Managers, William Hare, Frank Cruz; Press, David Powers, Barbara Carroll

CAST

Kelly Bishop   Larry Kert
Irving Allen Lee   Trina Parks

MUSICAL NUMBERS: Changes, Have I Got A Girl for You, Have I Got a Guy for You, So Much for Me, Happy New Year, Isn't This Fun, Three Beats Too Late, Sunday, Is This the Way, Keep Love Away, All of a Sudden It's Spring, Man about Town, All Because of You, Do You Want to Go, Summer Ain't So Hot, Is This the Way, Running Out of Time, Love Is A Whole Other Scene, The Ideal Deal, Love Like Ours, Merry Christmas to Me

A musical without intermission. The action takes place in a city at the present time, and spans the course of one year, beginning and ending on New Year's Eve.

Martha Swope Photo

**Irving Allen Lee, Kelly Bishop,
Larry Kert, Trina Parks
in "Changes"**

CAVALRY EPISCOPAL CHURCH
February 22–March 9, 1980 (12 performances)
LDP Productions (L.D. Pietig, Producer) presents:

LENZ

By Michael Stott; Director, Geraldine Court; Scenery and Costumes, David Loveless; Lighting, Toni Goldin; Stage Managers, Shari Genser, Nick Calderazzo; Press, Howard Atlee, Jim Baldassare

CAST

Yolanda Childress (Magda Schonefeld), Richard Dow (Rev. Johann Oberlin), Ronald M. Johnson (Sebastian Scheidecker), Roger Grunwald (Jacob Lenz), William Van Hunter (Christoph Kaufman)

A play in two acts. The action takes place during 1775 in the Oberlin household outside Strasbourg.

Ewig-Sandoval Photo

**Yolanda Childress, Roger Grunwald, Margaret
Warncke, Richard Dow in "Lenz"**

WONDERHOUSE THEATRE
February 28–March 16, 1980 (14 performances)
New World Theatre (Jane Stanton, Producer-Artistic Director) presents:

UNCLE MONEY

By Owen S. Rachleff; Director, Bob Bosco; Set, Cornelius Conboy; Lighting, John Walker; Costumes, Kim Walker; Stage Managers, Dan Zittel, Bob Doxsey; Press, Max Eisen, Francine L. Trevens

CAST

Chevi Colton (Dottie Rusko), Brian Watson (Herbie Rusko), Roy Miller (Joey Rusko), Diane Ciesla (Larraine Dutton), Roger Hendricks Simon (Marty Geiger)

A play in 3 acts and 5 scenes. The action takes place during September of this year in the living room of the Rusko house in New Jersey.

Esther Bubley Photo

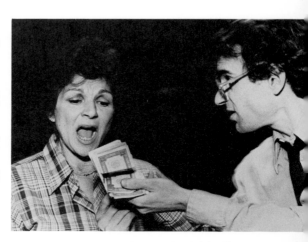

**Chevi Colton, Roger Hendricks Simon
in "Uncle Money"**

CHERRY LANE THEATRE
February 28–March 30, 1980 (27 performances)
Garrick Productions Inc. presents:

AN EVENING WITH W. S. GILBERT
with
Lloyd Harris

By John Wolfson; Music Director, Alfred Heller; Songs, poems, lyrics and letters, W. S. Gilbert; Music, Arthur Sullivan, Osmond Carr, Edward German; Set, Douglas McKeown; Costumes, Linda Sampson; Lighting, Joanna Schielke; General Manager, Albert Poland; Assistant General Manager, Margay Whitlock; Production Assistant, Sam Sexton; Stage Manager, Christine Lawton; Press, Betty Lee Hunt, Maria Cristina Pucci, Robert W. Larkin, James Sapp

A musical biography in 2 acts and 10 scenes. The setting is designed after the drawing room in Gilbert's country estate, Grim's Dyke, Harrow, England.

Marbeth Photo

Left: Lloyd Harris as W. S. Gilbert

THEATER OF ST. PETER'S CHURCH
March 3–18, 1980 (9 performances)
The Common presents:

AFFECTIONATELY YOURS, FANNY KEMBLE
with
Eugenia Rawls

A solo performance by Miss Rawls who collected her material from the diary and letters of the celebrated 19th Century actress and advocate of women's rights.

Eugenia Rawls

**Adam Philipson, Vera Johnson
in "Show Me a Hero"**

ST. MALACHY'S THEATRESPACE
March 11–29, 1980 (16 performances)
St. Malachy's Theatrespace (Gregory Abels, Artistic Director; Mike Houlihan, Producing Director) presents:

SHOW ME A HERO

By Sally Dixon Wiener; Music and Lyrics, Miss Wiener; Director, Gregory Abels; Scenery, Mark Haack; Lighting, Robert Griffin; Costumes, Margo LaZaro; Technical Director, Tom Robinson; Production Assistant, Gemma Kallaugher; Stage Manager, Barbara Sussman; Press, David Roggensack

CAST

Adam Philipson (Ben Roy Harlow), Don Reeves (Roy Harlow), JoAnn Beckson (Lacy Harlow), Vera Johnson (Vida Harlow), Eric Uhler (Gil Cutler), Shyrl Ryanharrt (Winona Waddell), Hal Blankenship (T. J. Flag)

A play in 2 acts and 5 scenes. The action takes place during July 1973 in the Harlow farmhouse in northern Colorado.

Gregory Abels Photo

AMDA STUDIO ONE
March 14–29, 1980 (12 performances)
New Theatre Associates in association with AMDA Studio One presents:

THE CHAMELEON

Written and Directed by G. Warren Steele; Set, George Morison; Lighting, Paul Henle; Costumes, Suzanne Laroche; Stage Manager, Carol Baer; Press, Judy Jacksina, Glenna Freedman

CAST

Michael Cullen (Evan Spencer), Judy Nazemetz (Jennifer Irwin), Michael Tylo (David Irwin), Frank J. Ragazzo (Super and Family), Deborah Stern (Policewoman), Anita Lento (Sheila Kleven), L B Williams (Gerald Porter)

A play in 2 acts and 12 scenes. The action takes place at the present time during February and March in Evan Spencer's New York City apartment.

Robert Willis Photo

Right Center: Judy Nazemetz, Michael Tylo

Judy Nazemetz, Michael Cullen

HORACE MANN THEATRE

March 25–April 6, 1980 (16 performances)
Columbia University Center for Theatre Studies in association with the Center for United States-China Arts Exchange presents:

PEKING MAN

By Cao Yu; Translated by Leslie Lo with Don Cohn, Michelle Vosper; Director, Kent Paul; Designed by Quentin Thomas; Technical Director-Production Supervisor, Gary R. Hotvedt; Assistant to Director, Joshua Worby; Assistant Producer, Michele Rudnick; Stage Managers, Robert Owens, Marci Stoeven; Press, Susan Bloch, Bill Rudman, Adrian Bryan-Brown

CAST

Kitty Mei-Mei Chen (Su Fang), Lori Tan Chinn (Zeng Siyi), Willy Corpus (Xiao Zhuer), Addison Lau (Collector), Jae Woo Lee (Zhang Shun), Freddy Mao (Jiang Tai), Kim Miyori (Zeng Wencai), Isao Sato (Zeng Wenqing), Keenan Kei Shimizu (Zeng Ting), David So (Collector), Philip Soo Hoo (Collector/Policeman), Mary Mon Toy (Chen Naima), Marcia Uriu (Yuan Yuan), Ginny Yang (Ruizhen), Peter Yoshida (Zeng Hao), Henry Yuk (Yuan Rengan)

A drama in 3 acts. The action takes place in the late 1920's in the parlor of the Zeng family in Peking China.

Peter Krupenye Photo

Top Right: Peter Yoshida, Isao Sato

Ginny Yang, Keenan Kei Shimizu, Isao Sato, Lori Tan Chinn, Peter Yoshida, Henry Yuk

William Clausson, Alexandra O'Karma, Kelly Fitzpatrick, Evan Thompson

WONDERHORSE THEATRE

March 24–April 13, 1980 (18 performances)
New World Theatre (Jane Stanton, Artistic Director) presents:

KNITTERS IN THE SUN

By George Bemberg; Director, Jane Stanton, Set, Bob Phillips; Lighting, Alan Blacher; Costumes, Kim Walker; Stage Managers, Mark Keller, Mary O'Leary; Press, Max Eisen, Francine Trevens

CAST

Alexandra O'Karma (Harriet), William Clauson (Eric North), Basia McCoy (Mrs. Riley), Evan Thompson (Bayard Carsters), Kelly Fitzpatrick (Andrew)

A drama in 2 acts and 4 scenes. The action takes place at the present time during spring in the Carsters' ancestral home in Wilmot, a small university town in rural New England.

Esther Bubley Photo

CITY CENTER THEATRE
March 26–April 13, 1980 (20 performances)
Columbia Artists presents:

SHANGHAI ACROBATIC THEATER

Artistic Director, Wang Feng; Deputy Director, Zhang Lihui; Tour Director, Li Taicheng; Administrative Director, Guo Gensong; Stage Managers, Xu Zhiyuan, Allison D. Liddicoat; Press, Gloria Lynne Friedman, Jeffrey Richards, Warren Knowlton

PROGRAM

Foot Juggling, Jolly Cooks, Teeterboard, Handstand, Wrestling, Celestial Mural, Jar Juggling, Springboard, Spinning Plates, Contortionist, Pantomine, Nose Balancing, Pagoda of Bowls, Hoops, Cycling, Finale

THE SECOND STAGE
April 4–20, 1980 (14 performances)
The Second Stage (Robyn Goodman, Carole Rothman, Artistic Directors) presents:

SPLIT

By Michael Weller; Director, Carole Rothman; Set, Heidi Landesman; Costumes, Irene Nolan; Lighting, Victor En Yu Tan; Sound, Gary Harris; Technical Director, Robert L. Anderson; Stage Managers, Loretta Robertson, David Caine, Erol Tammerman; Press, Judy Jacksina, Glenna Freedman

CAST

Brooke Adams (Carol), Pamela Blair (Marge), Polly Draper (Jean), John Heard (Paul), Rick Lieberman (Jay), Paul McCrane (Jeff), Chip Zien (Bob)

A play in two acts. The action takes place at the present time in New York City and abroad.

Stephanie Saia Photo

**Brooke Adams, John Heard
in "Split"**

111

Rosita Londner, Henry Gerro,
Molly Picon

TOWN HALL
April 6–13, 1980 (6 performances)
Shalom Yiddish Musical Comedy Theatre presents:

ABI GEZUNT

with

Molly Picon
Henry Gerro
Rosita Londner

A "musical entertainment rich in Yiddish-English humor and nostalgia," presented in two acts.

WESTBETH THEATRE
April 7
American Theatre Alliance under the direction of Jerold Barnard and Aaron Levin presents:

OLD FLAMES

By Ted Whitehead; Director, Aaron Levin; Set, John Kasarda; Lighting, Robby Monk; Assistant Director, Paul Shetter; Technical Director, Steve Aberg; Stage Managers, Paul Shetter, Kenneth Elliott; Press, Richard Kornberg

CAST

Lisa Sutton (Sally), Leon Russom (Edward), Wrenn Goodrum (Julie), Lin Kosy (Diana), Jacqueline Brookes (Muriel), Standby: Terese Hayden

A play in two acts. The action takes place on a houseboat.

Susan Cook Photo

Jacqueline Brookes, Leon Russom

Entire company of "Irma La Douce"

ALL SOULS CHURCH
April 12–28, 1980 (11 performances)
The All Souls Players present:

IRMA LA DOUCE

Book and Lyrics, Julian More, David Heneker, Monte Norman; Music, Marguerite Monnot; Staged by Jeffery K. Neill; Musical Director, Wendell Kindberg; Associate Musical Director, Joyce Hitchcock; Scenery, Thomas Newby; Costumes, Hank Laurencelle; Lighting, Tran William Rhodes; Assistant to Director, Suzanne Kaszynski; Producers, Henry Levinson, Tran William Rhodes, Howard Van der Meulen; Stage Managers, Lisa Harbach, John Vought; Pianos, Wendell Kindberg, Joyce Hitchcock; Percussion, James Erwin

CAST

Coleman Cohen (Bob Le Hotu), Kathee Kendall (Irma La Douce), Jeffrey Calder (Nester Le Fripe), Richard Renzaneth (Jojo Les Yeux Sales), Barry Brunetti (Roberto Les Dians), Tony Powell (Persil Le Noir), Clayton Berry (Frangipane), Robert Alpaugh (Polyte Le Mou), Thomas Brooks (Police Inspector), and Andrew Alloy, Charles Ewing, Stephen Joseph, James A. L'Ecuyer, Len Rella

Geoff Rosengarten Photo

ANNEX THEATRE
April 14–16, 1980 (3 performances)
T. L. Boston and Jenny Deyo present:

TWO

Two one-act plays by Fredricka Weber; Music by Misha Segal; Choreography, Reggie Israel; Costumes, Aunt Jimmy Anderson; Pianist, John Jacobson; Manager, T. L. Boston; Production Assistants, Steve Wittig, Pat MacDonnell

CAST

Philip Bruns (Father/Uncle Bud), Liz Otto (Mother), Peter Simpson (Dickie), Fredricka Weber (Frannie)
MUSICAL NUMBERS: Illinois, Gonna Be Good, I've Got a Secret, The Answer to Life Is Death, Frannie, I Lost Something, My God Laughs, Don't Lose that Spark

The action takes place in Illinois in the 1940's, in the small town of Dwight, and the smaller town of Beardstown.

Above: Peter Simpson, Liz Otto, Philip Bruns

Fredricka Weber

THEATRE DeLYS
April 15–May 4, 1980 (24 performances)
Stuart Oken and Jason Brett present:

THE MAN IN 605

By Alan Gross; Director, Sheldon Patinkin; Settings and Costumes, David Emmons; Leighting, Geoffrey Bushor; An Apollo Group Production; Associate Producer, Eve Lettvin; General Management, Sylrich Management; Stage Manager, Mary Fran Loftus; Press, Seymour Krawitz, Patricia McLean Krawitz

CAST

W. H. Macy (Jerry Green), Dick Cusack (Mr. Grabish), Byrne Piven (Eldon Schweig)

A play in two acts. The action takes place at the present time and in 1966 in Greenwich Village, New York City.

Right: Dick Cusack, W. H. Macy, Byrne Piven

Paul Sorvino, Janet Sarno

BOLTAX THEATRE
April 16–May 31, 1980 (45 performances)
Alan Cohen presents:

MARLON BRANDO SAT RIGHT HERE

By Louis LaRusso II; Director, Paul Sorvino; Set, Dick Young; Lighting, Maureen Strutton; Costumes and Hairstylist, Phyllis Della; Managers, Dennis LaRusso, Fonda St. Paul; Wardrobe, Jerry Wetzel; Press, Max Eisen, Francine L. Trevens

CAST

Paul Sorvino (Beep-ity-Beep), Janet Sarno (Gracie), Jay Acovone (Larry), Hy Anzell (Fat the Miser), Michael J. Aronin (Sonny Swag), Frank Bongiorno (Sibby), Leonard D'John (Nunzie Clark Gable), Martin Donegan (E.B.), Ross Fenton (Richie), Andrew Gerado (Trucky), Dan Lauria (Nick the Cripple), Frank Megna (Gomp), Rose Roffman (Momma Pollynose)

A play in 2 acts and 4 scenes. The action takes place during the spring of 1955 in Gracie's Place, a waterfront restaurant in Hoboken, N.J.

Jimmy Demetropoulos Photo

Left Center: Rose Roffman, Janet Sarno

THEATER OF ST. PETER'S CHURCH
Opened Thursday, April 17, 1980.*
The Common (Cathryn J. Mattson, Executive Director) and
ANTA present:

TINTYPES

Conceived by Mary Kyte with Mel Marvin and Gary Pearle; Director, Gary Pearle; Musical Staging, Mary Kyte; Setting, Tom Lynch; Costumes, Jess Goldstein; Lighting, Paul Gallo; Musical Direction and Arrangements, Mel Marvin, John McKinney; Producer, Richmond Crinkley; General Manager, Scott Steele; Company Manager, John Parsons; Production Assistant, Esther Beth Cohen; Props, Alice Maguire; Wardrobe, Karyl Anne Leigh; Hairstylist, Peg Schierholz; General Assistant, Jack Lines; Stage Managers, Bonnie Panson, Pauletta Pearson; Press, Craig Macdonald

CAST

Carolyn Mignini	Mary Catherine Wright
Lynne Thigpen	Jerry Zaks†
Trey Wilson	Mel Marvin (Pianist)

UNDERSTUDIES: Pauletta Pearson, S. Epatha Merkerson, Jeff Brooks†, Marie King

A musical revue with selected songs from 1876 to 1920.

* Closed Aug. 10, 1980 after 137 performances.
† Succeeded by Wayne Bryan

Susan Cook Photos

Right: Mary Catherine Wright, Jerry Zaks, Trey Wilson

Lynne Thigpen

WESTBETH THEATRE
April 17–May 11, 1980 (16 performances)
Westbeth Theatre Center presents:

OVER THE WALL

Written and Directed by Jan Cohen; Lighting, Eric Cornwell; Costumes, Suzi Tucker Friedman; Music, Dennis Cruz; Slides, Roberta Cantow; Stage Manager, Lisa Miller; Press, Howard Atlee, Jim Baldassare

CAST

Deborah Whitcomb (Imagist/Female Guard), Ellen Maddow (Molly Samuels), Owen Wilson (Roger Wade), George Santana (Officer Chumley), Frank Cardo (Willi Williams), Arthur Strimling (Terry Dugan), James Pickens, Jr. (Inmate/Cat), Ahmad Sharbaan (Jonesie), John Morris (Zak), Mark Anthony Simone Butler (Mandoomi/Card Player/Heroin Man), Dennis Cruz (Quinto)

A play in two acts. The action takes place during the fall of 1972 through the spring of 1973.

Peter Hamburger Photo

Left: Frank Cardo, Arthur Strimling
Below: Arthur Strimling, Ellen Maddow

JAYCEE STUDIO
April 18–May 4, 1980 (12 performances)

THE RELICS

By Sal Coppola; Director, Marc Field; Set, David Harnish; Costumes, Claudia Brown; Lighting, Beth Plane; Music, Chris Pondish; Stage Manager, Ellen Sontag; Press, Nansi Charles, Delia Perez

CAST

Sal Anthony, Bob Bella, R. Nolan Carley, James Carrol, John Edwards, John Homa, Bruce Kronenberg, Sam Locante, Renata Majer, Mike Vega

A drama in two acts. The action takes place in the Little Italy section of New York City.

Joseph Marisola Photo

Jim Carroll, Renata Majer,
John Edwards, Bob Bella

SYMPHONY SPACE
April 23–May 3, 1980 (10 performances)
Symphony Space (Allan Miller, Isaiah Sheffer, Artistic Directors) presents:

DIALOGUE FOR LOVERS

Sonnets of William Shakespeare arranged for the theatre by Eve Merriam; Staged by Isaiah Sheffer; Design, Daniel Michaelson; Lighting, Albert Bergeret; Musical Supervision, Sheila Schonbrun; Managing Director, Linda P. Rogers; Press, Kay Cattarulla, Richard Kornberg

CAST

Estelle Parsons (Woman, Fritz Weaver (Man), Sheila Schonbrun (Singer), Wendy Gillespie, Mary Springfels (Viola da Gamba)

Performed without intermission.

Martha Swope Photo

**Left: Fritz Weaver, Estelle Parsons,
and below with Eve Merriam**

AMDA STUDIO ONE
April 24–May 10, 1980 (15 performances)
Peter M. Paulino and Tom Taldone present the friends repertory company production of:

LES BLANCS

By Lorraine Hansberry; Director, Mitchell Weiss; Choreography, Pearl Primus; Scenery, Frank J. Boros; Costumes, Jeffrey N. Mazor, Richard Schurkamp; Lighting and Technical Direction, Kenneth Evans; Sound, Bill Dreisbach; Sound Score, Onwin Babajide Borde; Stage Manager, Jesse Wooden, Jr.; Press, Richard Kornberg; Special Adviser and Consultant, Robert Nemiroff

CAST

Paul Anderson (Maj. Rice), Virginia Downing (Mme. Neilsen), William Duff-Griffin (DeKoven), Keith Esau (Eric), Robert Jason (Tshembe), DelRoy Lind (Abioseh), David Little (Charlie Morris), Gary Newman (Soldier), Patricia Patton (Villager), Nathaniel Robinson (Ngago), Joe Seneca (Peter), Melin Threadgill (African Child), Dona D. Vaughn (Marta Gotterling), Kahlil Wheaton (Villager), Mary Waithe (Dancer)

A drama in two acts. The action takes place during 1959 in and about a mission compound in Africa, and the hut of a tribal leader.

Carol Rosegg Photo

Virginia Downing, Robert Jason

ACTORS PLAYHOUSE
Opened Sunday, April 27, 1980.*
Jonathan Scharer presents:

FOURTUNE

Book and Lyrics, Bill Russell; Music, Ronald Melrose; Director, Ron Troutman; Choreography, Troy Garza; Musical Direction and Arrangements, Janet Hood; Sets, Harry Silverglat; Lighting, Michael Newton-Brown; Costumes, Joan Culkin; Associate Producer, Carol Jackson; Sound, Bob Casey; General Manager, David Musselman; Assistant to Producer, Michael Stulberg; Assistant Choreographer, Cynthia Onrubia; Hairstylist, Don Oster; Stage Managers, Peter William Valentine, Ken Arthur; Press, Fred Hoot, Judy Jacksina, Glenna Freedman

CAST

Ken Arthur   Barbara Richardson
Gail Hebert   Justin Ross

MUSICAL NUMBERS: Prologue, Four Part Harmony, Rich and Famous, Women in Love, Fantasy, Funky Love, No One Ever Told Me Love Would Be So Hard, I'd Rather Be a Fairy Than a Troll, Complications, On the Road, What Do I Do Now?, Making It, I'll Try It Your Way, Fortune

A musical in two acts.

* Still playing May 31, 1980.

Ken Howard Photo

Top Right: (front) Gail Hebert, Barbara Richardson, (back) Ken Arthur, Justin Ross

HAROLD CLURMAN THEATRE
April 29–May 17, 1980 (21 performances)

THE AMERICAN CLOCK

By Arthur Miller; Inspired by Stud Terkel's "Hard Times"; Director, Daniel Sullivan; Setting, Douglas W. Schmidt; Costumes, Robert Wojewodski; Lighting, Pat Collins; Composer, Robert Dennis; Sound, Robert L. Etter; Production Supervisor, David S. Rosenak; Stage Manager, Naomi Wexler; Assistant to Producer, Nick James; Assistant to Director, Heather Ganzer; Production Assistants, Cindy Keiter, Robert Pena; Hairstylist, Marlies Terwine-Vallant; Press, Joe Wolhandler Associates, Steve Wolhandler

CAST

Francine Beers (Fanny/Mrs. Margolies), Joan Copeland (Rose Baum), Andrew Davis (Speakeasy Waiter/Howard/Joe/Bush), George Ede (Livermore/Frank/Judge/Graham/Alfred Ramsey/Benny), Peter Evans (Lee/Deputy), Hank Frazier (Clarence/Banks/Isaac), Robert Harper (Rosman/Clayton/Charlie Sidney/Ralph), Laurie Heineman (Diana/Mrs. Taylor/ Miss Fowler/Grace/Edie/Lucille), Salem Ludwig (Grandpa/Tony/Kapush), David Margulies (Moe/Farmer) succeeded by John Randolph, Bernie McInerney (Quinn/Durant/Taylor/Toland), Jess Osuna (Robertson/Eowa Bidder/Dugan), Lisa Pelikan (Harriet/Doris/Isabel/Lucy/Frieda), Louise Stubbs (Irene), J. T. Walsh (Brewster/Rudy/Ryan/Stanislaus/Sheriff)

A play in two acts.

Roger Greenawalt Photos

Lisa Pelikan, Laurie Heineman,
   Francine Beers, Joan Copeland

ASTOR PLACE THEATRE
Opened Monday, April 28, 1980.*
Sweet Olive Inc., Maryellen Flynn, Bonnie Weeks present:

A COUPLA WHITE CHICKS SITTING AROUND TALKING

By John Ford Noonan; Director, Dorothy Lyman; Scenery, Charles Cosler; Costumes, Gary Lisz; Lighting, F. Mitchell Dana; Original Songs, Loudon Wainwright III; General Management, Marilyn S. Miller, Berenice Weiler; Manager, Barbara Carrellas; Wardrobe, Benjamin Wilson; Stage Managers, Sherry Cohen, Donna Daley; Press, Judy Jacksina, Glenna Freedman, Angela Wilson, Dolph Browning

CAST

Eileen Brennan[1]
Susan Sarandon[2]

A comedy in two acts. The action takes place at the present time, in early June at 19 Charlemagne Lane in the town of Fox Hollow in a secluded corner of northern Westchester County, N.Y.

Still playing May 31, 1980.
† Succeeded by: 1. Dixie Carter. 2. Dorothy Lyman

Stephanie Saia Photo

Right: Eileen Brennan, Susan Sarandon

Eileen Brennan, Susan Sarandon

Dorothy Lyman, Dixie Carter

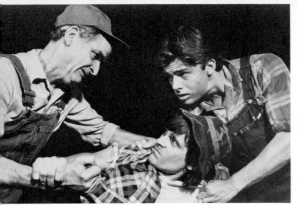

Conrad McLaren, Dustin Evans,
Maxwell Caulfield in "Crimes and Dreams"

THEATRE FOUR
May 15–16, 1980 (2 performances and 8 previews)
Fisher Theatre Foundation, Inc. presents:

CRIMES AND DREAMS

By LaVonne Mueller; Director, Chris Silva; Scenery, Karen Schulz; Lighting, Peter Anderson; Costumes, Denise Romano; Sound, Terry Alan Smith; Guitar Music Composed by Dennis Bacigalupi; Wardrobe, Nancy Kubale; Assistant to Director, Jim Graebner; General Management, Dorothy Olim Associates; Company Manager, Gail Bell; Stage Managers, William Hare, John Ingle; Press, Jeffrey Richards, Warren Knowlton, Robert Ganshaw, C. George Willard, Ben Morse, Helen Stern, Ted Killmer, Elizabeth Shepherd

CAST

Maxwell Caulfield (Frazer), Dustin Evans (R. C.), Graham Frazier (Casey Rainwater), Conrad McLaren (Cy Imboden), Tony Pasqualini (Justin), Myra Stennett (Lucy Imboden), Deborah Taylor (Betty Krambuel), Richard Woods (Shelt Taylor)

A drama in two acts. The action takes place at the present time during August in Mendota, Illinois.

Bert Andrews Photo

Peter Toran, Ross Petty, Betsy
Jamison, Carol Cass, Allan Stevens
in "It's Wilde!"

THEATRE EAST
May 21–25, 1980 (7 performances)
Stages Theatrical Productions, Ltd. (Herbert Acevedo, Executive Producer) presents:

IT'S WILDE!

Book, Lyrics, and Direction, Burton Wolfe; Music, Orchestrations and Arrangements, Randy Klein; Scenery, John Falabella; Costumes, James Corry; Lighting, Frances Aronson; Choreography, Buck Heller; Stage Managers, Paula Ellen Cohen, Sidney J. Burgoyne; Press, Shirley Herz, Jan Greenberg, Sam Rudy

CAST

Ross Petty (Wilde), Allan Stevens (Carson), Betsy Jamison (Constance), Peter Toran (Bosie), Carol Cass (Spectator), Sidney J. Burgoyne (Understudy)
MUSICAL NUMBERS: Times Divine, Two Should Be Harmonious, I Need One Man, Masses of Masses, Exquisite Passions, Jail-House Blues, It's Wilde!, Our Special Love, Society Means Propriety, Poor Teddy Bear, Medley, All the Flowers Turn to Snow, We're Back, Reach for the Sky, Get Thee to Bed, Hot Chocolate and Marshmallow, Rape Me, Love Please Stay, What Do I Believe In, Our Special Love, You Are My Gold, Finale

A musical in 2 acts and 6 scenes.

Garry Wheeler Photo

SECOND STAGE
May 23–June 15, 1980 (21 performances)
Second Stage (Robyn Goodman, Carole Rothman, Artistic Directors) presents:

BITS AND PIECES

By Corinne Jacker; Director, Caymichael Patten; Set, Michael Smith; Lighting, Victor En Yu Tan; Costumes, Denise Romano; Sound, Gary Harris; Stage Manager, Jonathan Silver; Press, Judy Jacksina, Glenna Freedman

CAST

Robyn Goodman (Iris), Verna Bloom (Helen), Robert Fields (Philip), Vic Polizos (Doctor/Farley/Dr. Bernard/Antonio/Monk), Lynn Milgrim (Technician/Alice Langley/Mrs. Eberly)

A comedy in two acts. The action takes place in the present and past.

Vic Polizos, Robyn Goodman
in "Bits and Pieces"

AMERICAN PLACE THEATRE

Wynn Handman, Director
Julia Miles, Associate Director
Sixteenth Season

Business Manager, Joanna Vedder; Literary Adviser, Bonnie Marranca; Assistant to Miss Miles, Elaine DeLeon; Administrative Assistant, Martha Fischer; Women's Project, Susan Lehman, Amy Ober; Technical Director, Russell L. Fredericks; Press, Jeffrey Richards Associates, Louis Sica, Alan Eichler, Ted Killmer, Karen Gromis, Marge Ornston

AMERICAN PLACE THEATRE
Sunday, June 17,–July 16, 1979 (9 performances)
The American Place Theatre presents in its American Humorist series:

THE IMPOSSIBLE H. L. MENCKEN

Adapted from the works of H. L. Mencken by John Rothman; Director, Scott Redman; Scenic Design, Michael Molly; Costumes, William Ivey Long; Lighting, Ira Mark Lichtman; Musical Director, John Forster; Choreography, Harry Streep, Myrna Packer; Technical Director, Russell Stevens; Stage Manager, Nancy Harrington; Wardrobe, K. L. Fredericks; Press, Jeffrey Richards Associates

CAST

John Rothman (H. L. Mencken), Edward Kearney (Bartender), John Forster (Pianist)

**John Rothman
as H. L. Mencken**

**Peter Boyden
as Alexander Woollcott**

AMERICAN PLACE THEATRE
Wednesday, October 17,–December 30, 1979 (71 performances)
American Place Theatre Humorists Series presents:

SMART ALECK
Alexander Woollcott at 8:40

Written and Directed by Howard Teichmann; Scenic and Lighting Design, Charles Cosler; Costume, David Toser; Stage Manager, Nancy Harrington; Technical Director, Russell Stevens

CAST

Peter Boyden
as
Alexander Woollcott

Performed without intermission.

AMERICAN PLACE THEATRE
Saturday, October 20,–November 11, 1979 (35 performances)
The American Place Theatre presents:

LETTERS HOME

By Rose Leiman Goldemberg; Based on Sylvia Plath's "Letters Home"; Edited by Aurelia Plath; Director, Dorothy Silver; Set, Henry Millman; Lighting, Roger Morgan; Costumes, Susan Denison; Production Assistant, William Sevedge, Jr.; Stage Managers, Mary R. Lockhart, W. Scott Allison

CAST

Mrs. Plath . . . . Doris Belack
Sylvia . . . . Mary McDonnell

Performed with one intermission.

Martha Holmes Photo

Doris Belack, Mary McDonnell

AMERICAN PLACE THEATRE
Thursday, December 6–16, 1979 (12 performances)

HOLY PLACES

By Gail Kriegel Mallin; Director, Victoria Rue; Sets and Costumes, Kate Edmunds; Lighting, Annie Wrightson; Production Assistant, John Connole; Wardrobe, Rebecca Kreinin; Technical Director, Russell Stevens; Stage Manager, Mary R. Lockhart

CAST

Joyce Aaron (Rona), Clifford David (Mickey), Tresa Hughes (Helen), Bill Randolph (Shane)

A drama in three acts. The action takes place during the winter in Brooklyn.

Left Center: Tresa Hughes, Clifford David

AMERICAN PLACE THEATRE
January 13–February 3, 1980 (24 performances)

PARIS LIGHTS

Based on an idea by William Russo; Developed by Michael Zettler, George Ferencz; Music, William Russo; Book, Michael Zettler; Director, George Ferencz; Scenery, Bill Stabile; Lighting, Laura Rambaldi; Costumes, Kathleen Smith, Sally Lesser; Musical Direction, Michael Ward; Orchestrations and Incidental Music, William Russo, Micheal Ward; Dances, Jane Summerhays; Literary Material Compiled by Bonnie Marranca

CAST

Margery Cohen (Alice B. Toklas/Edna St. Vincent Millay), Rhetta Hughes (Josephine Baker/Kiki), Trisha Long (Gertrude Stein), Stephen Mellor (John "Buffy" Glassco/Harry Crosby), Christopher Murray (Charles Lindbergh), Jane Summerhays (Sylvia Beach/Zelda Fitzgerald), John David Westfall (Robert McAlmon/Jimmy Charters), Nicholas Wyman (James Joyce/F. Scott Fitzgerald)
MUSICAL NUMBERS: Haschich Fudge, First Fig, Thursday, Mariposa, I Blow My Nose, mr. youse, Lifting Belly, Oh Your Mother Is in Bed, who knows if the moon's a balloon, you shall above all things, Jam, The Jewel Stairs Grievance, Let Her Be, I Have Been Heavy, If I Could Tell You

A "musical celebration in their own words" in two acts. The spoken words and lyrics are by the characters portrayed who were in Paris in the 1920's.

Martha Holmes Photo

James York, Trisha Long

AMERICAN PLACE THEATRE
March 21–April 27, 1980 (45 performances)
The American Place Theatre presents the Wooster Group production of:

RUMSTICK ROAD

Composed by Spalding Gray, Elizabeth LeCompte in collaboration with Libby Howes, Bruce Porter, Ron Vawter; Director, Elizabeth LeCompte; Designed by Jim Clayburgh, Elizabeth LeCompte; Technical Assistant, Michael French; Stage Manager, Kate Valk; Press, Jeffrey Richards Associates, Helen Stern, Ben Morse, Ted Killmer, Karen Gromis

CAST

Spalding Gray (Spud), Libby Howes (Woman), Jim Clayburgh (Operator), Ron Vawter (Man), Willem Dafoe (Operator's Assistant), and the voices of Margaret Horton, Dorothy Spalding Gray, Rockwell Gray, Sr., Dr. Henry Bradford

Performed without intermission.

Martha Holmes Photo

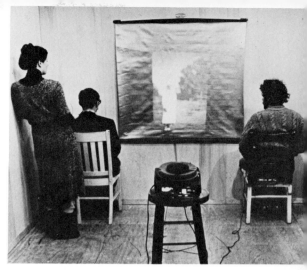

Libby Howes, Ron Vawter, Spalding Gray

AMERICAN PLACE THEATRE
April 30–May 3, 1980 (6 performances)
The Acting Company (John Houseman, Producing Artistic Director; Michael Kahn, Alan Schneider, Artistic Directors; Margot Harley, Executive Producer) presents:

ELIZABETH I

By Paul Foster; Directed and Designed by Liviu Ciulei; Costumes, Dunya Ramicova; Musical Direction, Dennis Deal; Choreography, Kathryn Posin; Lighting, Gregory C. MacPherson; Incidental Music, Steven Zor-Zor; Songs, Dan Aldea; Wigs, Bob Kelly, Paul Huntley; Company Manager, Joseph W. Thomas, Jr.; Technical Director, Gavin J. Smith; Wardrobe, Kathleen B. Boyette; Stage Managers, Douglas Gray, Christopher J. Markle; Press, Fred Nathan

CAST

Lisa Banes (Player Queen Elizabeth), Suzanne Costallos (Pata Sola the Witch), Janet DeMay (Real Queen Elizabeth), Harriet Harris (Mary of Scotland/Tilly Boom), Laura Hicks (Queen Catherine), J. Michael Butler (Paulet/Mous/Clown), John Greenleaf (Philip/Tamburlaine), Matthew Kimbrough (Lord Mayor/Pope Pius/Adelantado), Robert Lovitz (Francis Bacon/Whitgift/Archbishop), William McGlinn (Hatton/Lord), Randle Mell (Killer/Robert Cecil/Martin), Richard Ooms (Lord Burghley/Nostradamus/Inquisitor), Tom Robbins (Killer/Spanish Ambassador/Lazarus Tucker), Charles Shaw-Robinson (Bowyer/Earl of Leicester), Scott Walters (Walsingham/Pope Gregory)

A play in two acts.

Sunday, May 4, 1980 (1 performance)

Left Center: "Elizabeth I"

THE WHITE DEVIL

By John Webster; Director, Michael Kahn; Settings, Andrew Jackness; Costumes, Jane Greenwood; Lighting, Dennis Parichy; Fights Staged by Alex Stevens

CAST

Lisa Banes (Isabella), Suzanne Costallos (Zanche), Janet DeMay (A Medium), Harriet Harris (Vittoria), Laura Hicks (Giovanni), J. Michael Butler (Marcello), John Greenleaf (Dr. Julio), Matthew Kimbrough (Camillo), Robert Lovitz (Gasparo), William McGlinn (Author/Horatio), Randle Mell (Flamineo), Richard Ooms (Cardinal Monticelso), Tom Robbins (Duke of Florence), Charles Shaw-Robinson (Duke of Brachiano), Scott Walters (Lodovico)

A play in two acts.

Martha Swope Photo

Charles Shaw-Robinson, Laura Hicks, Richard Ooms in "Elizabeth I"

ACTORS' COLLECTIVE

Founders: Michael Bofshever, Celia Lee

RAY GORDON THEATRE

June 25–July 12, 1979 (12 performances)
MOONCHILDREN by Michael Weller; Director, Bruce Gray; Designer, Whitney Quesenbery; Stage Manager, Bernadette Yeager. CAST: Michael Bofshever (Mike), Celia Lee (Ruth), Allan Wasserman (Cootie), John Jellison (Norman), Mark Hofmaier (Dick), Jayne Bentzen (Kathy), Donald Silva (Bob), Joan Montgomery (Shelly), Richard Borg (Ralph), Joe McCabe (Willis), Thomas Blum (Lucky), Todd Lewis (Bream), John McGuire (Effing), J. D. Clark (Uncle Murray), Sol Frieder (Cootie's Father).

July 23–August 9, 1979 (12 performances)
FISHING by Michael Weller; Director, Jonathan Alper; Set, Ellen-Marie Jervey; Lighting, Jeffrey McRoberts; Stage Manager, Bernadette Yeager. CAST: Michael Bofshever (Rob), Donald Silva (Bill), Celia Lee (Shelly), Joan Montgomery (Mary-Ellen), Allan Wasserman (Dane), James Selby (Rory), Joe McCabe (Reilly).

April 3–May 4, 1980 (16 performances)
BILLY IRISH by Thomas Babe; Director, Nyla Lyon; Co-Produced with Out-Law Productions; Set, Reagan Cook; Lighting, Jeffrey McRoberts. CAST: Donald Silva (Billy Irish), James King Lawrence (Joe Witness), Mercedes Ruehl (Girl), Paul Greco (Boy).

May 20–June 13, 1980 (16 performances)
MISALLIANCE by George Bernard Shaw; Director, David William Kitchen; Set, J. Patrick Mann; Costumes, Bob Graham; Stage Manager, Ellen Sontag. CAST: James Selby (Johnny), Reed Birney (Bentley) Celia Lee (Hypatia), Tom McGreevey (Summerhays), June Hunt (Mrs. Tarleton), Stratton Walling (Tarleton), David McCarver (Joey), Joan Montgomery (Lina), Michael Bofshever (Gunner), Leonie Fletcher (Maid)

Allan Wasserman, Donald Silva, Michael Bofshever, Joan Montgomery, Celia Lee in "Fishing"

AMERICAN FOLK THEATER

Dick Gaffield, Artistic Director
Program Coordinator, Donald Griffith; Associate Directors, Jewelle Gomez, Esteban Ferre; Resident Playwright, Felton Perry; Resident Composer, Oscar Brown, Jr.; Press, Howard Atlee, Jim Baldassare

THEATER AT HOLY NAME HOUSE

Thursday, June 28,–July 23, 1979 (16 performances)
American Folk Theater presents:

BLUES FOR MISTER CHARLIE

By James Baldwin; Director, Dick Gaffield; Sets, Sandi Marks; Lighting, Leonard Buggs; Production Assistant, Audrey Walton; Administrative Coordinator, Judy Barnett; Stage Managers, Gwen Gilliam, Daniel Snow

CAST

Kevin Brady (State), Mike Brennan (Rev. Phelps), Dameon Carot (Counsel), Maryce Carter (Mother Henry), Christine Devereaux (Lillian), John R. Evans (Papa D), Gene Harvey (Lorenzo), Julius V. Hollingsworth, Jr. (Pete), Robert Johansen (George), Jacquelyn Lynch (Student), Peter Manzione (Ralph), Jeanne Nicolosi (Susan), Shirley Peacock (Juanita), Steve Reicher (Parnell), Bo Rucker (Richard Henry), Raynor Scheine (Lyle), Erika Smith (Student), Evelyn Smith (Hazel), Harold Smith (Tom), Jonathan Smith (Arthur), Kathleen Stephans (Jo), Del Willard (Ellis), Elwoodson Williams (Meridian)

A drama in two acts. The action takes place in the present and past in a small Southern town.

November 13–December 20, 1799 (16 performances)
RICHARD II by William Shakespeare; Director, Dick Gaffield; Lighting, Tony Giovannetti; Costumes, Samuel Barton; Stage Manager, Christie Gesler; Production Assistants, Judith Elaine, Steven Rivera; Press, Howard Atlee, James Baldassare. CAST: Gylan Kain (Richard II), Joseph S. King (Gaunt), Rodney Hudson (Bolingbroke), Al Rodriguez (Mowbray), Petie Seale (Duchess of Gloucester), Will Rose (Fitzwater), Daniel Snow (Aumerle), Gordon Kupperstein (Green), Lionel Pina, Jr. (Bushy), Mel Gionson (Herald), Dwight R. B. Cook (Baggot), Warrington Winters (Duke of York), Gwynn Press (Queen), Judith Barnett (Lady), Andrea Hunt (Lady), John A. Bakos (Nurthumberland), Vit Horejs (Sir Pierce), Judy Kelley (Percy), Patrick Flanagan (Salisbury), Derek Williams (Bishop of Carlisle), George Norman (Scroop), Robert Johansen (Gardener), Carol London (Duchess of York), Musicians: Julio Hernandez, John Rivera, John Robinson

January 16–February 4, 1980 (12 Performances)
DARKNESS, FIERCE WINDS by James Childs; Director, Leslie Lee; Lighting, Mark Collmer; Costumes, Florence Rutherford; Production Assistants, Jim Cavett, Jerome Perkins; Stage Managers, Linda Beckett, Duane Brodnick. CAST: Tony Noll (Author), Nancy Kandal (Jeanne), Diane Spiro (Ann), Ben Dukes (Charlie), Frank Sixt (Pete)

February 21–March 9, 1980 (12 performances)
WHO WANTS TO BE THE LONE RANGER? Written and Directed by Lee Kalcheim; Lighting, William J. Plachy; Set and Costumes, Sara Denning; Stage Manager, F. Laun Maurer; Press, Howard Atlee, James Baldassare. CAST: Peter Stelzer (Ben), Chrissy Penza (Gilian), Gavin Moses (Jerry), Dulce Mann (Evelyn), Marcia McBroom (Louise), Spence Adams (Mrs. Jensen), Michael Burke (Jensen)

March 27–April 20, 1980 (16 (performances)
MULATTO by Langston Hughes; Director, Samuel Barton; Choreographer, Otis A. Sallid; Music, Cornelia Post; Lighting, William Plachy; Costumes, Neil Cooper; Sound, Valeria Ferrand; Stage Managers, Elizabeth F. Wallace, Adrian Turner; Technical Director, Erik Ruff. CAST: John A. Bakos (Norwood), Betty Vaughn (Cora), Christopher Moore (William), Sharon Dennis (Sallie), Keith F. Williams (Robert), Garwood Perkins (Sam), Neil S. Napolitan (Fred), Dwight R. B. Cook (Mose), Erika Vaughn (Marybell), Terrance Turner (Billy), Robert D. Moseley (Talbot), Richard Rochester (Storekeeper), Richard Mooney (Undertaker), Luis A. Berrios, Jr., Pat Flanagan (Undertaker's Helpers), Cornelia Post (Livonia), Sharon K. Brooks (Young Cora), Judy Kelley (Mrs. Norwood), Field Hands: Anthony Scott, Harold Smith, Adrian Turner

Harold Smith, Raynor Scheine, Jacquelyn Lynch, Bo Rucker, Shirley Peacock in "Blues for Mr. Charlie"

THEATRE AT HOLY NAME HOUSE

May 8–June 9, 1980 (12 performances)
A LONG WAY BACK TO ME by Shirley Peacock; Director, Jennifer Vermont; Set, Abdul Sumchai; Lighting, Marty Goldenberg; Costumes, Neil Cooper; Sound, Garland Wright, Jr.; Stage Manager, Leigh Abernathy. CAST: Lucy Holland (Shirley), March Sanders (Clarence), Joyce Sylvester (Jackie), Harold Smith (Robert), Erma Campbell (Mrs. Waters), Lamont Clark (Fred), Learie Callender (Anthony), William Williams (Det. Dawson)

May 20–June 12, 1980 (12 performances)
LOVE ME, LOVE ME DADDY, OR I SWEAR I'M GONNA KILL YOU by William Wellington Mackey; Director, Dick Gaffield; Music, Cornelia Post; Lighting, Tony Giovanetti; Costumes, Marcia Smith, Diane Cleare; Assistant Director, Rebecca Holderness; Production Coordinator Guy Sherman; Stage Manager, Christobel Carambo; Press, Owen Levy, Valerie Warner. CAST: Cheryl Lynn Bruce or Edythe Davis (Angel/Selina/Mama), Deryck Smyth (Danny, Jr.), Reggie Bailey (Marcus, Jr.), Michael Manigault (Norman, Jr.), Charles Harley (Marcus), Paul Knowles (Danny), Lamont Clark (Norman), Carol London (Laura Anne), Judy Barnett (Doreen), Gavin Moses (Bobby), Choir: Eleanor London, Cornelia Post, Jon Ruppert, Harold Smith

**Mark Sanders, Lucy Holland
in "A Long Way Back to Me"**

AMERICAN RENAISSANCE THEATER

Robert Elston, Artistic Director
September 27–October 14, 1979 (12 performances)
RUBY RUBY SAM SAM by Stan Edelman; Director, Anita Khanzadian; Set, Terry Noble; Costumes, Marla R. Kaye; Lighting, Dale Jordan; Producer, Robert Elston; Stage Manager, Mimi Hordan Sherin. CAST: Elizabeth Perry (Ruby), Berkeley Harris (Sam), Jack Davidson (Joe), Catherine Wolf(Rosalie)

October 25–November 11, 1979 (12 performances)
EQUALS, SILENCES, CURSES by Patricia Ryan; Director, Robert Elston; Music, Robert Mitchell; Lighting, Tony Quintavala; Costumes, Veneda Truesdale. CAST: "Equals": Bob Keiber (Man), Vanya Cassell (Woman), "Silences": Michael Shaffer, Peter Aitken, Shirley Bodtke, Rhoda Fairman, Scott Jarvis, Bob Keiber, Vicky Rutkowski, Candy Wolfson, "Curses": Etain O'Malley (Mary), Molly Adams (Jane), Scott Jarvis (Dick), Jered Holmes (Tom/Harry)

November 29–December 16, 1979 (12 performances)
WOMEN OF IRELAND compiled and arranged by Susan Reed; Produced and Directed by Robert Elston; Lighting, Tony Quintavala; Stage Manager, Alex Simmons. CAST: Susan Reed, Bambi Linn

January 10–13, 1980 (4 performances)
JERED HOLMES—UP FRONT! Jered Holmes in concert. Producer, Robert Elston; Director, Sylvia Harman; Lighting/Stage Manager, Alex Simmons; Musical Director, Phyllis Grandee

February 7–March 2, 1980 (16 performances)
ARCHY AND MEHITABEL with Book by Joe Darion and Mel Brooks; Music, George Kleinsinger; Lyrics, Joe Darion; Based on stories by Don Marquis; Director, Robert Elston; Choreography, Kathy-Jo Hubner; Musical Director, Jim Ferrario; Set, Terry Noble, Susan Reed; Lighting, Dale Jordan; Costumes, Marla R. Kaye; Stage Managers, David Simpson, Paul Jensen. CAST: Marvin A. Chatinover (Newspaperman), Ed Clein (Archy), Barbara Gilbert (Mehitabel), Roy Barry (Big Bill), Robert Elston (Tyrone T. Tattersall), Mehitabel's Cohorts/Ladybugs: Mary Rocco, Del Green, Jon Kent, Judith Lesley

May 1–25, 1980 (16 performances)
CHARRED PAPER by Walter Leyden Brown; Music, Lou Rodgers; Set, Christopher Nolan; Lighting, Steve Aberg; Stage Managers, Alex Simmons, David Simpson; Producer, Robert Elston; Director, Terry Gregory. CAST: Merriman Gatch, Walter Leyden

May 19–24, 1980 (4 performances)
NOTES FROM UNDERGROUND at Lincoln Center Library and Donnell Library; Thoreau's "Walden" adapted by Elizabeth Perry; Dostoevsky's "Notes from Underground" adapted by Robert Elston, Elizabeth Perry; Kafka's "Report to an Academy" adapted by Robert Elston; Director, Russell Treyz. Performed by Robert Elston.

**Robert Elston in "Notes from Underground"
Above: Marvin Chatinover in "Archy and
Mehitabel"**

**Top Left: Bambi Linn, Susan Reed
in "Women of Ireland"**

BROOKLYN ACADEMY OF MUSIC

BAM/ATTIC THEATRE
October 23,—November 11, 1979 (24 performances)
Dodger Theater presents:

EMIGRES

By Slawomir Mrozek; Translated by Maciej Wrona, Teresa Wrona, Robert Holman; Director, Andre Ernotte; Scenery, Andrew Jackness; Costumes, Jennifer von Mayrhauser; Lighting, John McLain; Sound, Pril Smiley; Stage Manager, Bonnie Panson

CAST

XX . . . . Jon Polito
AA . . . . Brent Spiner
Understudy, Stephen Rowe

Performed without intermission.

Tom Caravaglia Photo

BROOKLYN ACADEMY OF MUSIC/ATTIC THEATRE
November 27–December 16, 1979 (24 performances)
Dodger Theater (Michael David, Des McAnuff, Edward Strong, Sherman Warner, Associate Directors) presents:

HOLEVILLE

By Jeff Wanshel; Songs and Direction by Des McAnuff; Scenery, Heidi Landesman; Costumes, Carol Oditz; Lighting, Richard Nelson; Sound-Electronic Music, Pril Smiley; Fight Choreography, B. H. Barry; Musical Director, Curt Neishloss; Technical Director, Steven Greer; Stage Managers, Suzanne Egan, James Furlong

CAST

Don Scardino (Rich Forrester), John Bottoms (Sal Video), Philip Casnoff (Front Man of the Band), Saul Rubinek (Gus Quid), Deborah Rush (Mother Quid), Christopher Murney (Frisks/McDo)

A musical in two acts.

Ken Howard Photo

John Bottoms, Saul Rubinek, Don Scardino in "Holeville" Above: Brent Spiner, Jon Polito in "Emigres"

BAM THEATER COMPANY
David Jones, Artistic Director
Arthur Penn, Associate Director
Managing Director, Charles Dillingham; Associate Manager, Suzanne Sato; Production Supervisor, Richard Elkow; Production Assistant, Nina Lannan; Wardrobe, Robert Sniecinski; Wigs, Leon Gagliardi, Paul Huntley; Stage Managers, Stephen McCorkle, Susie Cordon, Ron Durbian, Peter Glazer; Press, Rima Corben

**BROOKLYN ACADEMY OF MUSIC
HELEN OWEN CAREY PLAYHOUSE**
Opened Tuesday, February 12, 1980.*

THE WINTER'S TALE

By William Shakespeare; Director, David Jones; Set, David Gropman, Costumes, Julie Weiss; Lighting, William Mintzer; Composer, Bruce Coughlin; Choreographer, Cheryl McFadden

CAST

Sheila Allen (Paulina), C. B. Anderson (Gaoler/Shepherd), Gerry Bamman (Officer of Justice), Gary Bayer (Archidamus), Christine Estabrook (Perdita), Boyd Gaines (Florizel), Avril Gentles (Emilia), Michael Hammond (1st Lord/Shepherd), Roxanne Hart (1st Lady/Shepherdess), John Heffernan (Antigonus), Patrick Hines (Old Shepherd), Richard Jamieson (Dion), Cherry Jones (Dorcas), Stephen Lang (Young Shepherd), Anna Kluger Levine (Mopsa), Frank Maraden (3rd Lord/Time/Shepherd), Marti Maraden (Hermione), Kevin McClarnon (Attendant Lord/Mariner), Michael John McGann (5th Lord/Shepherd), Guy Michaels (Mamillius), Bill Moor (Cleomenes), Keith Moore (Servant/Shepherd), Joe Morton (Autolycus), Brian Murray (Leontes), Peter Phillips (4th Lord/Shepherd), Jon Polito (Rogero/Shepherd), John Seitz (Camillo), Norman Snow (Polixenes), Sherry Steiner (2nd Lady/Shepherdess)

Performed in two acts. The action takes place in Sicilia and Bohemia.

* Closed April 6, 1980 after 34 performances in repertory.

Ken Howard Photo

Norman Snow, Guy Michaels, Marti Maraden, Brian Murray in "Winter's Tale"

Left Center: Joe Morton, Patrick Hines, Stephen Lang in "Winter's Tale"

BAM THEATER COMPANY
Opened Wednesday, February 27-May 5, 1980 (37 performances)

JOHNNY ON A SPOT

By Charles MacArthur; Director, Edward Cornell; Set, John Lee Beatty; Costumes, William Ivey Long; Lighting, William Mintzer; Stage Managers, Susie Cordon, Ron Durbian

CAST

C. B. Anderson (Bert/Sims), Gerry Bamman (Ben Kusick), Gary Bayer (Nicky Allen), Jerome Dempsey (Doc Blossom), Boyd Gaines (Radio Announcer/Bailiff), Avril Gentles (Pearl LaMonte), Michael Hammond (Fred/Trooper/Flanagan), John Jeffernan (Judge Webster), Patrick Hines (Mayor Lovett), Richard Jamieson (Camerman), Stephen Lang (Reporter), Anna Kluger Levine (Barbara Webster), Frank Maraden (Dapper), Kevin McClarnon (Creeper), MichaelJohn McGann (Reporter/Policeman), Bill Moor (Col. Wigmore), Keith Moore (Reporter), Joe Morton (Lucius), Peter Phillips (Sgt./Salesman), Jon Polito (Pepi Pisano), John Seitz (Gov. Upjohn/Chief of Police), Norman Snow (McClure/Policeman)

A comedy in three acts. The action takes place in the early 1940's on election eve and election day in the outer office of the Governor of a Southern state.

Ken Howard Photo

BAM/PLAYHOUSE
April 16–May 18, 1980 (27 performances in repertory)

BARBARIANS

By Maxim Gorky; Translated by Kitty Hunter Blair, Jeremy Brooks and Michael Weller; Director, David Jones; Set, Andrew Jackness; Costumes, Dunya Ramicova; Lighting, William Mintzer; Composer, Bill Vanaver; Stage Managers, Stephen McCorkle, Ron Durbian, Peter Glazer; Press, Rima Corben

CAST

Sheila Allen (Nadezhda), Gary Bayer (Pritykin), Jerome Dempsey (Ivakin), Christine Eastabrook (Katya), Boyd Gaines (Stepan), Avril Gentles (Tatyana Nikolayevna), Michael Hammond (Drobyazgin), John Heffernan (Pavlin), Patrick Hines (Redozubov), Richard Jamieson (Chief of Police), Stephen Lang (Matvey), Anna Kluger Levine (Styopa), Frank Maraden (Dunka's Husband), MichaelJohn McGann (Grisha), Bill Moor (Dr. Makarov), Brian Murray (Monakhov), Joan Pape (Pelageya), Peter Phillips (Yefim), Jon Polito (Cherkoon), John Seitz (Tsyganov), Sherry Steiner (Maria Ivanovna)

A comedy in 3 acts and 4 scenes. The action takes place during the early 1900's in a small, provincial Russian town, in the garden and sitting room of Tatyana Nikolayevna's house.

Ken Howard Photo

BAM/LEPERCQ SPACE
May 27–June 15, 1980 (24 performances)
BAM Theater Company presents:

THE MARRIAGE DANCE

Two one-act plays; Director, Andre Ernotte; Sets, Heidi Landesman; Costumes, John David Ridge; Lighting, F. Mitchell Dana; Music, Jim Ragland; Stage Managers, Stephen McCorkle, Ron Durbian; Press, Rima Corben

CAST

THE WEDDING by Bertolt Brecht; Translated by Richard Nelson assisted by Helga Ciulei from the original German; with Sheila Allen (The Wife), Christine Estabrook (The Bride), Avril Gentles (Mother of the Groom), Patrick Hines (Father of the Bride), Anna Kluger Levine (Bride's Sister), Frank Maraden (The Groom), Kevin McClarnon (Young Man), Jon Polito (The Husband), Norman Snow (Groom's Friend)

The action takes place in the living room of the bride and groom's apartment in Germany during 1919.

THE PURGING by Georges Feydeau; Adapted by Peter Barnes; with Brian Murray (Follavoine), Roxanne Hart (His Wife Julie), Guy Michaels (Their Son), Michele Seyler (Their Maid Rose), Bill Moor (Chouilloux), Sherry Steiner (Mme. Chouilloux), Michael Hammond (Her Cousin Truchet)

The action takes place in the study of Follavoine and Julie's apartment in Paris during 1910.

**Gary Bayer, Patrick Hines (C)
in "Johnny on a Spot"**

**Roxanne Hart, John Seitz, Jon Polito,
Patrick Hines in "Barbarians"**

BAM/PLAYHOUSE
May 28–June 15, 1980 (28 performances in repertory)
BAM Theater Company presents:

HE AND SHE

By Rachel Crothers; Director, Emily Mann; Set, John Jensen; Costumes, Jennifer von Mayrhauser; Lighting, William Mintzer; Stage Managers, Susie Cordon, Peter Glazer; Press, Rima Corben

CAST

Gerry Bamman (Tom Herford), Jerome Dempsey (Dr. Remington), Helen Harrelson (Maid), Richard Jamieson (Keith McKenzie), Cherry Jones (Millicent), Laurie Kennedy (Ann Herford), Marti Maraden (Ruth Creel), Joan Pape (Daisy Herford)

A comedy in three acts. The action takes place in 1911 in a studio on the basement floor and in the living room of the Herford home in Lower New York City.

Ken Howard Photo

**Above: Jerome Dempsey, Laurie Kennedy (C)
in "He and She"**

CHELSEA THEATER CENTER

Robert Kalfin, Producing Director

Managing Director, A. Harrison Cromer; Production Manager, Peter Elencovf; Assistant to Producing Director/Cabaret Director, James Kramer; Design Consultant, Wolfgang Roth; Assistant to Managing Director, Brian Wyatt; Technical Director, Robert Baldwin; Press, Edward T. Callaghan, Lynda C. Kinney, Celayne Hill, Elizabeth Royte

CHELSEA THEATRE CENTER
January 10–February 16, 1980 (24 performances)

DAS LUSITANIA SONGSPIEL

with

Sigourney Weaver   Christopher Durang
Bob Goldstone at the piano

Producers, Milton Justice, Jack Heifner; Written by Christopher Durang, Sigourney Weaver; Production Supervisor, Garland Wright; General Manager, Albert Poland; Company Manager, Erik Murkoff; Wardrobe, Barbara Perkins; Press, Betty Lee Hunt, Maria Cristina Pucci, James Sapp
MUSICAL NUMBERS: Overture from The Rise and Fall of the City of Mahagonny, The Frogs, The Young Sailor's Lesson, The Bouillabaisse Song, The Song of Economic Reality, Medley

The theatre songs of Bertolt Brecht, a parody of a Bertolt Brecht-/Kurt Weill cabaret, performed without intermission.

**Sigourney Weaver, Christopher Durang
in "Das Lusitania Songspiel"**

CHELSEA THEATER UPSTAIRS
January 24–February 17, 1980 (30 performances)

MONSIEUR AMILCAR

Adapted by George Gonneau and Norman Rose from the play by Yves Jamiaque; Director, Robert Kalfin; Set, Michael Sharp; Costumes, Elizabeth P. Palmer; Lighting, Robby Monk; Composer, John McKinney; Assistant to Director, Catherine Breeze; Production Assistants, Allison Sommers, Lenny Pass, Betsy Aidem; Stage Managers, Don Judge, Kathleen M. Tosco

CAST

Larry Keith (Alexander Amilcar), K. Lype O'Dell (Machou), Sheila K. Adams (Virginia), Judith Barcroft (Eleanor), Mark Keyloun (Nicky), Patricia Falkenhain (Melie)

A play in two acts. The action takes place at the present time in Paris.

Carol Rosegg Photo

**Larry Keith, Patricia Falkenhain,
Judith Barcroft in "M. Amilcar"**

March 20–April 13, 1980 (30 performances)

DONA ROSITA: WHILE SHE WAITS

or "The Language of Flowers" by Federico Garcia Lorca; English version by John Olon; Director, Mr. Olon; Design, Wolfgang Roth; Music, John Olon on a theme by Dominick Argento; Musical Direction, Lee Goldstein; Costumes, Holly Lei Cole; Dances and Musical Staging, Dennis J. Grimaldi; Sound, Sam Agar; Stage Managers, Don Judge, Marvin Peisner; Assistant to Director, Tom Herman; Production Assistant, Melanie Sutherland

CAST

June Ballinger (Spinster), Donald F. Berman (Workman/Boy), Joel Colodner (Nephew), Curt Dawson (Uncle), Jan Downing (Manola/-Miss Ayola), Mary Hara (Aunt), Peggy Harmon (Manola), Prudence Wright Holmes (Spinster), Annette Hunt (Rosita), Joyce Krempel (Nanny) succeeded by Sylvia O'Brien, Marvin Peisner (Don Martin), Marian Primont (Mother), Steve Pudenz (Workman), Walter Rhodes (Mr. X), Myra Stennett (Spinster), Annie Szamosi (Manola/Miss Ayola)

A play in three acts. The action takes place in 1885, 1900 and 1910 in Granada.

Carol Rosegg Photo

**Annette Hunt, Mary Hara
in "Dona Rosita"**

CIRCLE REPERTORY THEATRE

Marshall W. Mason, Artistic Director
Eleventh Season

Managing Director, Lindsay Gambini; Artistic Coordinator, Daniel Irvine; Business Manager, William Waters; Assistant to Mr. Mason, John Manulis; Administrative Assistant, Jeanna Gallo; Production Manager, Penny Gebhard; Stage Manager, Fred Reinglas; Technical Director, Robert Yanez; Props-Wardrobe, Liz Watson; Press, Richard Frankel, Glenna Clay

CIRCLE REPERTORY THEATRE

Tuesday, June 5, - October 21, 1979 (76 performances)
(Moved Oct. 23, 1979 to Provincetown Playhouse)
Circle Repertory Theatre presents the Sea-Ker production of:

GERTRUDE STEIN GERTRUDE STEIN GERTRUDE STEIN

By Marty Martin; Director, Milton Moss; Producer, Mary Ellen Devery; Set, Tony Straiges; Costume, Garland Riddle; Lighting, Ruth Roberts; Production Consultant, Porter Van Zandt; Research Consultant, Alan Willig; Production Assistant, Helen Moss; Stage Managers, Jim Fauvell, Diana Banks; Press, Jan Morgan

Cast

Pat Carroll

A solo performance in two acts. The action takes place at 27 Rue de Fleuris in Paris during 1938 in Miss Stein's apartment.

Gerry Goodstein Photo

Pat Carroll as Gertrude Stein

CIRCLE REPERTORY THEATRE

Opened Wednesday, June 20, 1979.*
Circle Repertory presents the 1979 Pulitzer Prize play:

BURIED CHILD

By Sam Shepard; Director, Robert Woodruff; Set, David Gropman; Lighting, John P. Dodd; Ms. Brookes costumes, Joan E. Weiss; Production Manager, Penny Gebhard; Technical Director, Robert Yanez; Stage Managers, Fred Reinglas, Peter Bogyo; Press, Richard Frankel, Glenna Clay

CAST

Dodge	Edward Seamon
Halie	Jacqueline Brookes
Tilden	Tom Noonan
Bradley	William M. Carr
Shelly	Mary McDonnell
Vince	Christopher McCann
Father Lewis	Bill Wiley

A drama in three acts. The action takes place at the present time in the home of Dodge and Halie.

* Closed Sept. 29, 1979 after 90 performances.

Edward Seamon, Mary McDonnell, William M. Carr in "Buried Child"

CIRCLE REPERTORY THEATRE

Wednesday, October 10–November 15, 1979 (42 performances)

REUNION

Three one-act plays Written and Directed by David Mamet; Set, John Lee Beatty; Costumes, Clifford Capone; Lighting, Dennis Parichy; Stage Manager, Jody Boese

CAST

Lindsay Crouse
Michael Higgins

THE SANCTITY OF MARRIAGE: A husband and wife in their home; DARK PONY: A father and daughter in an automobile at night; REUNION: A daughter and her father in his apartment on an afternoon in March. Performed with one intermission following "Dark Pony."

Gerry Goodstein Photo

Lindsay Crouse, Michael Higgins in "Reunion"

CIRCLE REPERTORY THEATRE
Opened Wednesday, December 12, 1979.*

HAMLET

By William Shakespeare; Director, Marshall W. Mason; Sets, David Jenkins; Costumes, Laura Crow; Lighting, Dennis Parichy; Original Music, Norman L. Berman; Sound, Chuck London; Duels staged by B. H. Barry; Assistant Director, John Bard Manulis; Stage Manager, Fred Reinglas

CAST

Michael Ayr (Laertes), Gary Berner (Francisco/Luciano), William M. Carr (Bernardo/Norwegian Captain/Sailor), Roger Chapman (Rosencrantz), Lindsay Crouse (Ophelia), Jack Davidson (Player King/Gravedigger), Lindsey Ginter(Voltemand/English Ambassador), Bruce Gray (Osric), Charles T. Harper (Reynaldo), William Hurt (Hamlet), Ken Kliban (Guildenstern), Burke Pearson (Polonius), Timothy Shelton (Horatio), Beatrice Straight (Gertrude) succeeded by Jacqueline Brookes, Elizabeth Sturges (Player Queen), Robert Tenuta (Marcellus/Priest), Rob Thirkield (Ghost/Fortinbras), Douglass Watson (Claudius), Mollie Collison (Lady-in-Waiting), Pages: Greg Germann, Bruce McCarty

Performed with two intermissions.

* Closed Feb. 10, 1980 after 37 performances and 8 previews in repertory with "Mary Stuart."

Opened Thursday, December 13, 1979.*

MARY STUART

By Friedrich von Schiller; Director, Marshall W. Mason; Assistant Director, Amy Schecter; Sets, David Jenkins; Costumes, Laura Crow; Lighting, Dennis Parichy; Stage Manager, Fred Reinglas

CAST

Michael Ayr (Mortimer), Gary Berner (O'Kelly), Tanya Berezin (Elizabeth), Mollie Collison (Margaret), Jack Davidson (Melvil), Lindsey Ginter (Bellievre), Stephanie Gordon (Mary Stuart), Charles T. Harper (Kent), William Hurt (Davison), Ken Kliban (Burleigh), Burke Pearson (Paulet), Timothy Shelton (Leicester), Elizabeth Sturges (Hanna), Robert Tenuta (Aubespine), Rob Thirkield (Earl of Shrewsbury)

Performed with one intermission

* Closed Feb. 17, 1980 after 40 performances and 7 previews in repertory with "Hamlet."

Gerry Goodstein Photos

**Lindsay Crouse, William Hurt
in "Hamlet"**

**Stephanie Gordon, Tanya Berezin
in "Mary Stuart"**

CIRCLE REPERTORY THEATRE
February 27–March 30, 1980 (39 performances)

INNOCENT THOUGHTS, HARMLESS INTENTIONS

By John Heuer; Director, B. Rodney Marriott; Set, Tom Lynch; Lighting, Dennis Parichy; Costumes, Joan E. Weiss; Stage Manager, Pamela Singer; Richard Frankel, Glenna Clay

CAST

Roger Chapman (Robert "Smitty" Smith), John Dossett (Walter "Fishfoot" Fitzbout), Jonathan Hogan (Ernie Blagg), Kiya Ann Joyce (Inganoatuk), Zane Lasky (Paul Johnson), Christopher North (James "Duke" Wade), Timothy Shelton (Frank "Walky" Walcheim), Ben Siegler (John "Gunts" Gunzel), Brian Tarantina (Enzio "Spats" Spadatini), James Ray Weeks (Sgt. Steidle), Patricia Wettig (The Girl)

A drama in three acts. The action takes place in the attic of a Minnesota country house in the winter of 1931-32, and in the barrack quarters of a U. S. Army outpost in Alaska during the winter of 1951–52.

Gerry Goodstein Photo

**Roger Chapman, Brian Tarantina, Jonathan
Hogan, Zane Lasky in "Innocent Thoughts . . ."**

CIRCLE REPERTORY THEATRE
April 17–May 11, 1980 (39 performances)

BACK IN THE RACE
A Family Album

By Milan Stitt; Director, Leonard Peters; Set, Bil Mikulewicz; Costumes, James Berton Harris; Lighting, John Gisondi; Sound, David Rapkin; Production Manager, Alice Galloway; Technical Director, Robert Yanez; Stage Managers, Jody Boese, Mollie Collison, Fred Reinglas; Wardrobe, Joan E. Weiss; Press, Richard Frankel, Glenna Clay

CAST

William Carden (Jonathan), Joyce Reehling (Zabrina), John Randolph (Cliff)

A play in two acts. The action takes place at the present time at various locations around Lake Tawas, Michigan.

Gerry Goodstein Photo

**William Carden, John Randolph
in "Back in the Race"**

CIRCLE REPERTORY THEATRE
Opened Wednesday, May 28, 1980.*
Circle Repertory Company presents:

THE WOOLGATHERER

By William Mastrosimone; Director, John Bettenbender; Set, Karl Eigsti: Costumes, Joan E. Weiss; Lighting, Dennis Parichy; Stage Manager, Jody Boese; Press, Richard Frankel, Glenna Clay

CAST

Rose .... Patricia Wettig
Cliff .... Peter Weller

A play in two acts. The action takes place at the present time in an efficiency apartment in South Philadelphia, Pennsylvania.

* Still playing May 31, 1980.

**Peter Weller, Patricia Wettig
in "The Woolgatherer"**

CSC/CLASSIC STAGE COMPANY
Christopher Martin, Artistic Director
Twelfth Season
Executive Director, Dennis Turner; General Manager, Alberto Torre; Resident Designer, Terry A. Bennett; Technical Director, Seth Price; Stage Manager, Steve Adler; Composer/Music Director, Noble Shropshire; Choreographer, Carol Flemming

COMPANY

Cal Bedford, Alan Brooks, Arthur Hanket, Phillip Kerr, Vivienne Lenk, Howard Lucas, Christopher Martin, Mary Eileen O'Donnell, Jack Powell, Catherine Rust, Robert Stattel, Karen Sunde, Martin Treat, William Verderber

PRODUCTIONS

"Cuchulain the Warrior King" by William Butler Yeats, "The Cavern" by Jean Anouilh, "Doctor Faustus" by Christopher Marlowe, "Don Juan" by Moliere, "The Merchant of Venice" by William Shakespeare

Gerry Goodstein Photos

**Left Center: Phillip Kerr, Robert Stattel
in "Cuchulain"**

**Phillip Kerr, Robert Stattel
in "Dr. Faustus"**

THE CLASSIC THEATRE
Maurice Edwards, Artistic Director
Nicholas John Stathis, Executive Director

THE CLASSIC THEATRE
November 16, 1979–March 16, 1980 (43 performances)

NOTES FROM UNDERGROUND, PART I
with
Norman Sample

By Fyodor Dostoyevsky; Translated by Mirra Ginsburg; Director, Maurice Edwards; Set, Tracy Sherman; Lighting, Lisa Grossman; Costumes, Ruth Thomason; Production Director, Ron Daley; Stage Manager, Randy Norton. Performed with one intermission.

Roy Schatt Photo

January 11–April 6, 1980 (32 performances)
JOURNEY'S END by R. C. Sherriff; Director, Ron Daley; Producer, Nicholas John Stathis; Set, Bob Phillips; Costumes, Mary Rindfleisch; Lighting, Lisa Grossman; Sound, Jim Duvoli; Assistant Director, Randy Norton; Stage Manager, Kevin Cuba; Press, Betty Lee Hunt, Maria Cristina Pucci
CAST: Charles S. Averill (Hardy), Andrew MacMillan (Osborne), Todd Waring (Mason), Courtney Tucker (Raleigh), David Purdham (Stanhope), Stephen Root (Trotter), Craig Harvey (Hibbert), Dennis L. Smith (Sergeant Major), Craig Purinton (Colonel), John E. C. Doyle (Bert/German Soldier), Richard Abernethy (Colonel)

A drama in 3 acts and 6 scenes. The action takes place in a dugout near St. Quentin, France, in the spring of 1918.

May 8–25, 1980 (12 performances)
THE BACHELOR by Turgenev; Director, Jonathan Amacker; Producer, Nicholas John Stathis; Set, Tracy Sherman; Costumes, Charlotte Howell; Lighting, Terri Lucas; Assistant to Director, Sonia Dressner; Stage Managers, Laurie Rae Waugh, Andrea Weinstein; Production Assistant, Mike Forman; Press, Margaret Underwood
CAST: Richard Klessig (Stratilat), Maurice Edwards (Mikhail Ivanych Moshkin), Ellen Feldman (Malania), Murray Moston (Filippe Egorovich Shpundik), Antoinette Terry (Maria Vasilevna), Florence Rupert (Ekaterina), Joel Lefert (Rodion Karylch von Fonk), Mark Johannes (Pyotr Ilych Vilitski), Lawrence S. Hofmann (Alkiviad Martynych Sozemenos)

A play in three acts. The action takes place in St. Petersburg, Russia, during the winter of 1850.

Antoinette Perry, Joel Leffert, Florence Rupert, Maurice Edwards, Murray Moston in "The Bachelor"
Above: Norman Sample in "Notes from. . . ."

COLONNADES THEATRE LAB
Michael Lessac, Artistic Director
Executive Producer, Robert N. Lear; General Manager, Mary T. Nealon; Assistant to Producer, Lisbeth Roman; Production Manager, Randy Becker; Stage Manager, R. T. Schwartz; Associate Artistic Director, Tom V. V. Tammi; Associate Producer, Val Bisoglio; Wardrobe, Kim E. Weiss

COLONNADES THEATRE
February 1–March 16, 1980 (40 performances)
SHAKESPEARE'S CABARET developed and directed by Michael Lessac; Lyrics, William Shakespeare; Music, Lance Mulcahy; Musical Direction and Arrangements, Donald G. Jones; Musical Direction and Arrangements, Donald G. Jones; Musical Direction and Arrangements, Donald G. Jones;
CAST: Alan Brasington, Maureen Brennan, Mel Johnson, Jr., Patti Perkins, Roxanne Reese, Keith R. Rice, Peter Van Norden
MUSICAL NUMBERS: If Music and Sweet Poetry Agree, How Should I Your True Love Know?, Come Live with Me and Be My Love, If I Profane, Tell Me Where Is Fancy Bred?, What Thou See'st When Thou Dost Awake, Come Away Death, How Should This a Desert Be?, All That Glisters Is Not Gold, Crabbed Age and Youth, If Music Be the Food of Love, Fathers That Wear Rags, Epitaph for Marina, Will You Buy Any Tape?, The Willow Song, Pyramus Arise, Shepherd's Song, Shall I Compare Thee to a Summer's Day?, Come unto These Yellow Sands, Lawn as White as Driven Snow, The Phoenix and the Turtle, I Am St. Jacques' Pilgrim, Tomorrow Is St. Valentine's Day, Rosalinde, Then Let Me the Canakin Clink, Epitaph and Celebration

Performed in two acts.

Elizabeth Adams Photos

February 22–May 18, 1980 (88 performances)
THE IRISH HEBREW LESSON by Wolf Mankowitz; Director, Michael Lessac; Scenery, Johneine Papandreas; Lighting, Betsy Adams
CAST: Nicholas Kepros (The Man), Curtis Armstrong (The Boy), Charlie Stavola (Black and Tan), Nesbitt Blaisdell (Black and Tan)
GUESTS OF THE NATION by Neil McKenzie; Adapted from a short story by Frank O'Connor; Directors, Tom V. V. Tammi, Michael Lessac; Costumes, Hilary A. Sherred; Sound, Scott Lehrer
CAST: Marty Vale (Barney/Narrator), Richard Cottrell (Joseph Noble), Charlie Stravola ('Awkins), Nesbitt Blaisdell (Belcher), Curtis Armstrong (Cooney), Robert Mason (Doody), Brian O Mallon (Jeremiah), Carmel O'Brien (Kate O'Connell)

Patti Perkins, Peter Van Norden, Keith Price, Maureen Brennan, Mel Johnson, Roxanne Reese, Alan Brasington in "Shakespeare's Cabaret"

Left Center: Marty Vale, Charlie Stavola, Richard Cottrell, Nesbitt Blaisdell in "Guests of the Nation"

COUNTERPOINT THEATRE COMPANY

Howard Green, Artistic Director
Paulene Reynolds, Managing Director
Terry Walker, Associate Artistic Director
Sixth Season

COUNTERPOINT THEATRE

January 11–February 4, 1980 (16 performances)
THE LOVER and LANDSCAPE by Harold Pinter; Scenery, Milad Ishak; Lighting, Jesse Ira Berger; Costumes, Deborah Shaw; Stage Managers, Bill Thorne, Mary Ann Hilary
THE LOVER: Director, Terry Walker. CAST: Howard Green (Richard), Paulene Reynolds (Sarah), David Karpell (John) LANDSCAPE: Director, Howard Green. CAST: Frank Hamilton (Duff) succeeded by Sam Gray, Hope Cameron (Beth)

February 29–March 24, 1980 (16 performances)
MIRANDOLINA by Carlo Goldoni; Translated by Lady Gregory; Director, June Rovenger; Scenery and Lights, Howard Paul Beals, Jr.; Costumes, Patricia Adshead; Stage Managers, Kehaulani Haydon, Lawrence Berrick, Frances Smith; Original Music, Lee Calhoun. CAST: Ted Sod (Marquis), Elek Hartman (Count), Carolyn Mignini (Mirandolina), John Jellison (Captain), Michael Albert Mantel (Fabrizio), Thomas Blum (Servant)

April 18, May 12, 1980 (16 performances)
CORNERS *(World Premiere)* by Brooke Breslow; Director, Howard Green; Scenery, Milad Ishak; Lights, Natasha Katz; Costumes, Karen Barbano; Stage Manager, Gary Marks; Assistant to Director, Valerie Brown; Technical Adviser, Jeremy Benton. CAST: Sam Gray (Manny Postman), Katherine Cortez (Nurse), Jonathan Margulies (Boy), Hope Cameron (Sookie Postman), Thomas Blum (Young Man), Barry Johnson (Policeman), Michael Albert Mantel (Howard Postman), Harris Shore (Businessman), Deborah Holt (Wife), Lynn Polan (Susan Postman Meredith), Carol Grant (Leslie Murphy Postman), Ann Freeman (Doctor)

Sam Gray, Hope Cameron in "Landscape"

**John Jellison, Carolyn Mignini
in "Mirandolina"**

DIRECT THEATRE

Allen R. Belknap, Artistic Director
Judy Horne, Executive Director

NAT HORNE THEATRE

February 15–March 23, 1980 (39 performances)
INTERNATIONAL DIRECTORS' FESTIVAL presented 54 one-act plays, and the five best were given an extended one-week run: STARTUP by Margaret Ann Spiers; Director, Taylor Brooks; Stage Manager, Christopher Rogers. CAST: Jackie Bellamy (Ruth), Jan Buttram (Orpha), Betty Pelzer (Naomi) SECOND VERSE by Sharon Tipsword; Director, Lynn Green; Stage Manager, Beth Andrisevic; Assistant Director, Alissa Begell. CAST: Martha Horstman (Viv), Debra Jo Rupp (Helen). AND OTHER SONGS with Music and Lyrics by Keith Levenson; Director, Jack Romano; Musical Direction, Ronald Botting, CAST: Ronald Botting, Susan Davis, Robin Curtis, David Margolis CAVEAT EMPTOR by Betta Shafran; Director, Elowyn Castle; Stage Manager, Richard Ross. CAST: Michael M. Ryan (Franky), T. A. Taylor (Charlie) NOT I by Samuel Beckett; Director, John Kazanjian; Assistants, Nina Moser, Maura Robinson. CAST: Mary Ewald (Mouth), Buddy Hardin (Auditor)

April 13–May 17, 1980 (35 performances)
INTERVIEW by Thom Thomas; Director, Allen R. Belknap; Set, Paul Kelly; Lighting, Joanna Schielke; Costumes, Giva Taylor; Sound, Rick Ross; Stage Manager, John R. Weatherford. CAST: Louis Edmonds (The Very Famous Man), Lewis Arlt (The Young Man), Samurai (Aki Aleong)

**Louis Edmonds, Lewis Arlt
in "Interview"** *(Janus Purins Photo)*

**Left Center: Debra Jo Rupp, Martha Horstman
in "Second Verse"** *(Ian Anderson Photo)*

EQUITY LIBRARY THEATRE

George Wojtasik, Managing Director
Lynn Montgomery, Production Director
Thirty-seventh Season

Business Manager, Ann B. Grassilli; Technical Director, John Patterson Reed; Assistant Technical Director, Bruce Farnworth; Costumiere, Kate Rogers; Assistant Musical Director, Stephen R. Milbank; Sound, Hal Schuler; Photographer, Gary Wheeler; Press, Lewis Harmon, Sol Jacobson

MASTER THEATRE

September 20–October 14, 1979 (32 performances)
Equity Library Theatre presents:

THE SOUND OF MUSIC

Book, Howard Lindsay, Russel Crouse; Suggested by "The Trapp Family Singers" by Maria A. Trapp; Music, Richard Rodgers; Lyrics, Oscar Hammerstein II; Direction and Musical Numbers Staged by Syprienne Gabel; Musical Direction, Richard C. Wall; Assistant to Director, Marcia Milgrom; Scenery, Linda Skipper; Costumes, Patrice Alexander; Lighting, Toni Goldin; Stage Managers, Nidal Mahayni, Ellen Holt, Kayla Evans, Connie Cloyed McDonnell; Production Assistant, Allison Sommers; Wardrobe, Barbara Sariego; Press, Sol Jacobson, Lewis Harmon

Michael David Krisch, Janine Geary, Andrew Owen Forste, Marianne Tatum, Wendy Ann Finnegan, Robbi Smith, Tristine Schmukler in "The Sound of Music"

CAST

Marianne Tatum (Maria), Mimi Kelly (Sister Berthe), Rose Lischner (Sister Margaretta), Jane Judge (Mother Abbess) succeeded by Marilyn Hudgins, Carol Peden (Sister Sophia), David Barron (Trapp), Edwin Karp (Franz), Lee Sanders (Frau Schmidt), Alys Clemmitt (Liesl), Michael David Krisch (Friedrich), Robbi Smith (Louisa), Andrew Owen Forste (Kurt), Janine Geary (Grigitta), Tristine Schmukler (Marta), Wendy Ann Finnegan (Gretl), Bill Johnson (Rolf), Kris Karlin (Elsa), Terry Baughan (Ursula), Don Woodman (Max), Jay Pierce (Zeller), Henry J. Quinn (Baron Elberfeld), Kate Owen (Baroness), Barbara Surosky (Frau Zeller), Michele Mundell (Postulant), Henry J. Quinn (Adm. von Schreiber), Kate Owen (Fraulein Schweiger), John C. Introcaso, Jack Kyrieleison (Gestapo)

MUSICAL NUMBERS: Preludium, The Sound of Music, Maria, My Favorite Things, Do-Re-Mi, 16 Going on 17, Lonely Goatherd, How Can Love Survive, The Laendler, So Long Farewell, Morning Hymn, Climb Every Mountain, No Way to Stop It, Ordinary Couple, Processional, Edelweiss, Finale

A musical in 2 acts and 20 scenes.

MASTER THEATRE

October 25–November 11, 1979 (22 performances)

ALL THE WAY HOME

By Tad Mosel; Adapted from James Agee's novel "A Death in the Family"; Director, Jamie Brown; Scenery, Paul Eads, John Davis; Lighting, Richard Dorfman; Costumes, Dolores Gamba; Incidental Music, Leon Odenz; Production Assistant, Everett Fine; Stage Managers, Beverly Ann Hand, Brooke Allen, Arthur Pinkus

CAST

Scott Schwartz (Rufus Follet), Andrew Owen Forste, Adam Smith (Boys), Michael Hartman (Jay Follet), Nicola Sheara (Mary Follet), Mark Simon (Ralph Follet), Cathryn Ann Fleuchaus (Sally Follet), Frederick Beals (John Henry Follet), Anne Barclay (Jessie Follet), Wade Raley (Jim-Wilson), Mary Mims (Aunt Sadie), Leila Danette (Great-Great-Granmaw), B. Constance Barry (Catherine Lynch), Virginia Downing (Aunt Hannah), John Armstrong (Joel Lynch), Larry Rosler (Andrew Lynch), William Walsh (Father Jackson)

A drama in three acts. The action takes place in and around Knoxville, Tennessee, in May of 1915.

Gary Wheeler Photo

Michael Hartman, Scott Schwartz
134   in "All the Way Home"

MASTER THEATRE
November 29–December 23, 1979 (30 performances)*

CANTERBURY TALES

Book, Martin Starkie, Nevill Coghill; Based on Nevill Coghill's translation of Geoffrey Chaucer; Music, Richard Hill, John Hawkins; Lyrics, Nevill Coghill; Director, Robert Johanson; Choreography, Randy Hugill; Musical Direction, John Kroner; Scenery, Michael Anania; Costumes, Sigrid Insull; Lighting, Gregg Marriner; Assistant to Director, Sydnie Grosberg; Stage Managers, M. R. Jacobs, Sarah Hayden, Betsy Nicholson

CAST

David Asher (Knight), Win Atkins (Miller), Kaylyn Dillehay (Molly), Andy Ferrell (Yeoman), Ted Houck, Jr. (Steward), George Maguire (Host), Earl McCarroll (Chaucer), Vance Mizelle (Merchant), Krista Neumann (Alison), Polly Pen (Cook), Mimi Sherwin (Prioress), William Ryall (Pardonner), Maureen Sadusk (Wife of Bath), Richard Stillman (Clerk), Robert Tetirick (Squire), Andrew Traines (Friar), Melanie Vaughan (Nun) succeeded by K. K. Preece, Kelly Walters (Summoner), Tricia Witham (May)

* Re-opened on Broadway Feb. 12, 1980. See Broadway Calendar.

Top Right: Krista Neumann, Robert Tetirick, Earl McCarroll in "Canterbury Tales"

MASTER THEATRE
January 10–27, 1980 (23 performances)

ROMEO AND JULIET

By William Shakespeare; Director, Dan Held; Fight Choreography, Al Borer; Scenery, Michael Anania, Karen Beth Eliot; Lighting, Helen Anne Gatling; Costumes, Karen Hummel; Incidental Music, Patrick Cook; Choreography, Beth Kurtz; Stage Manager, Doug Laidlaw

CAST

Joseph Adams (Balthasar) succeeded by Jay Fruchtman, Leslie Barrett (Friar Laurence), Hoban Blake (Lady Capulet), Edward Cannan (Lord Capulet), Mark Capri (Chorus/Escalus/Apothecary), Elowyn Castle (Lady Montague), George Cavey (Lord Montague/Friar John) succeeded by Garrison Phillips, Deborah Charney (Lady/Musician), Ralph Elias (Tybalt), Jonathan Emerson (Paris), Mary Leonard Held (Rosaline), Curtis Hostetter (Romeo), James Leach (Peter/Abram), Lydia Leeds (Juliet), Jack Milo (Sampson/2nd Watch), Dennis Prister (Gregory/Chief Watch), Sherill Price (Nurse), Peter Toran (Benvolio), Scott Wentworth (Mercutio)

Right Center: Curtis Hostetter, Lydia Leeds in "Romeo and Juliet"

MASTER THEATRE
February 7–24, 1980 (22 performances)

THE TIME OF THE CUCKOO

By Arthur Laurents; Director, James Pentecost; Scenery, Ken Holamon; Lighting, David H. Murdock; Costumes, Robin S. Becker; Music, Andy Bloor; Production Assistants, Sandra Sochngen, Maria R. McNamara; Dialect Coach, Ernesto Gasco; Wardrobe, Alin Millo; Stage Managers, Mark Rubinsky, Dianna M. Paradis, Loretta Robertson; Press, Lewis Harmon, Sol Jacoboson

CAST

Ned Eisenberg (Vito), Amy Gootenberg (Giovanna), Lee Kheel (Mrs. McIlhenny), Stan Lachow (Renato Di Rossi), Diane Martella (Signora Fioria), Judith McIntyre (June Yeager), David Medina (Mauro), Harvey Pierce (McIlhenny), Anita Sorel (Leona Samish), Bill Tatum (Eddie Yeager)

A play in two acts and six scenes. The action occurs in the garden of the Pensione Fioria, Venice, Italy, in the summer of 1953.

Stan Lachow, Anita Sorel in "The Time of the Cuckoo"

MASTER THEATRE

March 6–30, 1980 (31 performances)
Equity Library Theatre presents:

PLAIN AND FANCY

Book, Joseph Stein, Will Glickman; Music, Albert Hague; Lyrics, Arnold B. Horwitt; Director, Bill Herndon; Musical Director, Kristen Blodgette; Choreography, Diana Baffa-Brill; Scenery, Carl A. Baldasso; Lighting, Nat Cohen; Costumes, Charlotte Sorre; Stage Managers, William Gregg, John N. Concannon, Tony Berk, Rita Rack; Production Assistant, Kathleen Marsters; Wardrobe, Bea Bevis; Press, Sol Jacobson, Lewis Harmon

CAST

Jon-Alan Adams (Isaac) succeeded by Erick Devine, Ellyn Arons (Rachel), Sheri Barron (Rebecca), Donna Bullock (Katie), C. J. Critt (Ruth), Michael Howell Deane (Abner Zook #2), Cecil Fulfer (Amishman), David Greenan (Dan), Jacob Mark Hopkin (Papa Yoder), Melinda Koblick (Sarah), Beverly Lambert (Hilda), Sandy Lundwall (Bessie), Brian McAnally (Samuel/Dance Captain), Tom McBride (Jacob), Paul McGoldrick (Moses), Chip Mitchell (Ezra), Alison Morgan (Esther), Michael Schilke (Abner Zook #1), Larry Small (Peter), Vernon Steele (Ike), Mary Stout (Emma), Lee Trink (Miller Boy), Elizabeth Ward (Miller Girl)
MUSICAL NUMBERS: It Wonders Me, Plenty of Pennsylvania, Young and Foolish, Why Not Katie?, Lantern Dance, It's a Helluva Way to Run a Love Affair, This Is All Very New to Me, Plain We Live, How Do You Raise a Barn?, City Mouse Country Mouse, I'll Show Him!, Take Your Time and Take Your Pick, Finale

A musical in 2 acts and 15 scenes. The action takes place in and around Bird-in-Hand, a town in the Amish country of Pennsylvania.

MASTER THEATRE

April 10–27, 1980 (22 performances)

MERTON OF THE MOVIES

By George S. Kaufman, Marc Connelly; Director, Ted Weiant; Set, Tom Cariello, Lighting, Ned Hallick; Costumes, Deborah Shaw; Original Score, David McHugh; Movement Consultant, Mindy Landow; Stage Managers, Gerard J. Campbell, Connie Cloyed McDonnell, Ada H. Citron, Philip Fries, Jon Secor; Production Assistants, Kelley Jackson, Lisa Salomon; Wardrobe, Nilaja Waters

CAST

Robert Boyle (Elmer Huff), Kathleen Conry (Tessie/Montague Girl), Leslie Feagan (M. Fingertoe), Jim Fitzpatrick (Sigmond Rosenblatt), Philip Fried (Key Grip), Chris Grabenstein (Cameraman), Richard Hayes (Merton), Bryce Holman (Harold Parmalee), Kelley Jackson (Soundman), Ron Johnston (Walberg), Christiane McKenna (Casting Director), Bruce Mohat (Gaffer), John Pankow (Cameraman), Mike Paradine (Weller), Wende Pollock (Muriel), Richard Portnow (Jeff Baird), Laura Summer (Beulah Baxter), John Turetzky (Mrs. Patterson), Bill Wiley (Gashwiler/Montague)

A comedy in 2 acts and 6 scenes. The action takes place during 1920-1921 in Simsbury, Illinois, and Hollywood, California.

Kathleen Conry, Jim Fitzpatrick, Richard Hayes in "Merton of the Movies"
Above: C. J. Critt, Beverly Lambert, David Greenan in "Plain and Fancy"

MASTER THEATRE

May 8–June 1, 1980 (30 performances)
Equity Library Theatre presents:

ANNIE GET YOUR GUN

Book, Herbert Fields, Dorothy Fields; Music and Lyrics, Irving Berlin; Director, Susan Schulman; Choreographer, Steven Gelfer; Musical Director, Phil Hall; Scenery, Rob Hamilton; Costumes, Martha Hally; Lighting, Ruth Roberts; Hair and Wigs, Tim Coppins; Assistant to Director, Margaret Denithorne; Wardrobe, Ali Davis, Mary Lou Rios; Stage Managers, Barbara Schneider, Allison Sommers, Bruce Conner

CAST

Paul Ames (Charlie Davenport), Pamela Bierly (Mrs. Sylvia Potter-Porter), Nancy Burke (Mrs. Adams), Mauricio Bustamante (Sitting Bull), Cheryl Lynn Crabtree (Mrs. Henderson), Keith Curran (Foster Wilson), Ann-Maxine Dawson (Dolly Tate), Ralph Farnworth (Buffalo Bill), Kristie Hannum (Young Lady), Joseph Hukills (Moonshine Quartet/Cowboy), Michael Irwin (Cowboy/Quartet), Gary Kirsch (Cowboy/Messenger), Alexandra Korey (Annie Oakley), Paul Mack (Mac), Patrick McCaffrey (Little Jake), Mara Mellin (Nellie), Bud Nease (Frank Butler), Ann Neville (Mrs. Little Horse), Lisa Peters (Young Girl), Donna Ramundo (Cowgirl), Maggie Ranone (Jessie), Cissy Rebich (Mrs. Black Tooth), Ken Seiter (Waiter/Quartet), Guy Waid (Pawnee Bill), Rene Alexander (Quartet)
MUSICAL NUMBERS: Colonel Buffalo Bill, I'm a Bad Bad Man, Doin' What Comes Natu'lly, The Girl That I Marry, You Can't Get a Man with a Gun, There's No Business Like Show Business, They Say It's Wonderful, Moonshine Lullaby, Wild West Pitch Dance, My Defenses Are Down, Indian Ceremonial Dance, I'm an Indian Too, Lost in His Arms, I Got the Sun in the Morning, Old Fashioned Wedding, Anything You Can Do, Finale

A musical in 2 acts and 8 scenes.

Ann-Maxine Dawson, Bud Neae, Alexandra Korey in "Annie Get Your Gun"

EQUITY LIBRARY THEATRE
INFORMALS SERIES

George Wojtasik, Managing Director
Debra Waxman, Producer

LINCOLN CENTER LIBRARY & MUSEUM

September 17, 18, 19, 1979 (3 performances)
AN OPEN STAGE with Music and Lyrics by Hank Fellows; Musical Direction, Zelman Mlotek; Staged by Howard Rossen; Technical Director, Bruce Farnworth; Stage Manager, Andrea Naier; Lighting, Frederick MacGowan. CAST: Scott Campbell, Christopher Councill, Nazig Edwards, Valerie Piacenti, Ruth Redland, Zalmen Mlotek (at the piano)

October 15, 16, 17, 1979 (3 performances)
INTERMISSION and BELLE FEMME by Tony Salerno; Director, Jerry Rockwood; Set, Marianne Terrell; Lighting and Sound, Mary Lou Graulau; Stage Managers, Sandy Borcum, Paula Bozzone. CAST: "Intermission" with Shelly Rogers (Judy), Jeffrey Kilgore (Butch), Annie Korzen (Stage Manager), Win Atkins (Sir Jonathan Barrister), David St. James (Lord Twills), Norma Frances (Lady Barrister), Linda Nenno (Marguerite), Yvonne Rossetti (Woman), "Belle Femme" with Charlotte Jones (Ida Komiczewski), Chris Weatherhead (Karen Clooney)

November 19, 20, 21, 1979 (3 performances)
FORGET THE ALAMO by Michael Glenn-Smith; Director, Taylor Brooks; Setting and Lights, Tom Deschenes; Costumes, Robert Horek; Production Co-Ordinator, Ada H. Citron; Stage Manager, Connie McDonnell. CAST: Mona Stiles (Verda), Catherine Foster (Nancy), Cindie Lovelace (Sarazanne), Steven Stahl (Wayne), and LITTLE TIPS by Timothy Meyers, with Gabrielle Sinclair (Amanda), Paula De Caro (Marlene) Gray Basnight (Landry), Eleanor Tauber (Thelma), Celia Barrett (Bishop)

December 10, 11, 12, 1979 (3 performances)
THE ELECTRA MYTH with Music Composed and Performed by Allan Greene; Director, Cyprienne Gabel; Assistant Director, Nancy Nutter; Set and Lights, Alix Martin; Stage Managers, Kayla Evans, Mark Spina. CAST: Richard Costabile (Chorus/Tutor), Essene R (Clytemnestra), Anthony Heald (Orestes), Patricia Reilly (Electra), Petie Seale (Clytemnestra), Victor Slezak (Orin/Orestes), Sona Vogel (Electra)

January 21, 22, 23, 1980 (3 performances)
PATERSON by William Carlos Williams; Director, Warren Kliewer; Setting and Light, Phillip Leppel; Stage Manager, Nidal Mahayni. CAST: Lee Billington, Robert Chamberlain, Seymour Penzner, Richard Riner.
NOT LIKE HIM by Marcia Savin; Director, John Wolf; Stage Manager, Ada H. Citron; Technical Director, Bruce Farnworth. CAST: William DaPrato (Michael Rivers), Ruth Miller (Sally McGuire)

March 3, 4, 5, 1980 (3 performances)
WINTERVILLE adapted for the stage by William Koch from poetry by George Cherry; Director, William Koch; Musical Director, Bill Mearns; Set and Lights, John Wolf; Stage Managers, Arthur Karpfe, Jack Carlson; Original words and music, George Cherry, Bill Mearns. CAST: Ed Allman, Barbara Colton, Toni Dorfman, Karl Heist, Norman Jacob, Robert Lydiard, Ruthe Staples, Kay Walbye, Richard Patrick-Warner

April 28, 29, 30, 1980 (3 performances)
. . . . AND PETE with Book, Lyrics and Music by Vince Rhomberg and Jerry Radloff; Direction and Choreography, Vince Rhomberg; Musical Director, Eileen LaGrange; Costumes, Bonnie Miller; Lighting, Vivien Leone; Production Assistant, David Cantor; Assistant Director, Murray Changer; Stage Managers, George Kinney, Matt Dolth; Assistant Choreographer, Joni Masella. CAST: Joel Blum, Callan White, Teresa Parente, Annie Willette, Sandy Laufer, Christine Anderson, Mary Ann Reitman, Maryellen Landon, Nina Paragher

May 12, 13, 14, 1980 (3 performances)
THE CHRONICLE OF QUEEN ANNE by Florence Stevenson; Director, Elowyn Castle; Costumes, Claudia Brown; Lighting, Robin McAllister; Stage Manager, Wendy Orshan. CAST: Jayne Chamberlin (Lady Dudley), Deborah Charney (Bess Tylney), John Fanning (Guildford Dudley), John Flynn (Dudley), Gael Hammer (Henry Grey), Suzanne Heitmann (Mary Tudor), Louisa Huntington (Nanny), Lorna Johnson (Frances Grey), David Schall (Pembrook), Jeanette Topar (Jane Grey), Russ Weatherford (Lord Arundel)

(No photos available)

FANTASY FACTORY

Bill Vitale, Artistic Director

NEWFOUNDLAND THEATRE

December 15, 1979–January 13, 1980 (19 performances)
MY CHILD with Book, Music and Lyrics by Ben Finn; Based on the life of Phillis Wheatley; Director, Bill Vitale; Musical Direction and Arrangements, James Abruzzo; Choreography and Musical Staging, Robert Speller; Lighting, Alex Palacios; Assistant Musical Director, Michael Collins; Scenery, Richard George; Stage Managers, Tom Tippett, Myra Oney, Robert Lebovic, Patrick Rameau; Press, Jim Wilson; Costumes, Angeline Thomas. CAST: Jan Maxwell (Susannah Wheatley), Tavia Day, Lisa Lovely (Younger Phillis), Ray Atherton (John Wheatley), Donna Lisa Hunte, Beverley Mickins (Older Phillis), Nathylin Flowers (Sukey), David Jonathan Vaughn (Prince), Gabrielle Sinclair (Mary Wheatley), Mark Lebowitz, Robert Lebovic (Nat Wheatley), Cary Burkett (auctioneer/-Marsdale), Michael Collins (Rev. Mather/Coarse Man), Steve Pastor (Rev. Lathrop/Gentleman), Louis Zippin (Rutherford/Angry Man), Joan Neuman (Lady/Wedding Guest), Timothy Craig (John Hancock/Minister/Dock Worker), Deeann Devnie, Liza-Grace Vachon-Coco (Young Girls), Richard Fillyaw (Slave/Slave Catcher), Vincent Gangi (Little Boy)

December 29, 1979–January 13, 1980 (12 performances)
ATTACHMENTS by Ed Kuczewski; Music and Direction, Richard Foltz; Pianist, Richard Foltz. CAST: Marc Castle, Richard Foltz, Ed Kuczewski, Ted Sod, Roger Williams, Joe Zogby, Maurice James, Pat Klees

Marian Kelner Photo

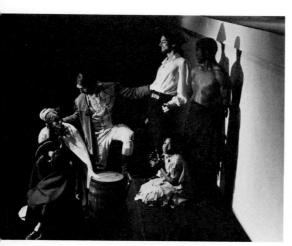

Vincent Gangi, Jan Maxwell, Ray Atherton, Cary Burkett, Lisa Lovely, Patrick Rameau in "My Child"

HUDSON GUILD THEATRE

David Kerry Heefner, Producing Director
Judson Barteaux, Managing Director

HUDSON GUILD THEATRE
Wednesday, September 19–October 21, 1979 (30 performances)
Hudson Guild Theatre presents the American premiere of:

THE BANANA BOX

By Eric Chappell; Director, Geoffrey Sherman; Set, Phillip Jung; Costumes, David Murin; Lighting, Patricia Moeser; Wardrobe, Bob Graham; Production Manager, Peter Meleck; Stage Managers, Thomas J. Rees, Buzz Cohen; Press, Becky Flora

CAST

Edward Zang (Rooksby), Brad O'Hare (Noel Parker), Howard E. Rollins, Jr. (Phillip Smith), Veronica Castang (Ruth Jones), Janet League (Lucy)

A play in 2 acts and 6 scenes. The action takes place at the present time in the bedroom and sitting-room of a flat on the top floor of a gloomy Victorian house.

Ken Howard Photo

Janet League, Howard E. Rollins, Jr., Brad O'Hare in "The Banana Box"

HUDSON GUILD THEATRE
November 23,–December 23, 1979

MY SISTER'S KEEPER

A Drama in 2 acts and 5 scenes by Ted Allan; Director, David Kerry Heefner; Set, Steven Rubin; Costumes, Pamela Scofield; Lighting, Dennis Parichy

CAST

Robert Waller . . . . Richard Jamieson
Sarah Lawson . . . . Gale Garnett

The action takes place at the present time in Robert Waller's apartment in New York City over a period of a month.

Left: Richard Jamieson, Gale Garnett

HUDSON GUILD THEATRE
January 9–February 10, 1980 (30 performances)

SNAPSHOT

Music, Herbert Kaplan; Lyrics, Mitchell Bernard; Director, Thomas Gruenewald; Set, James Leonard Joy; Costumes, Kenneth M. Yount; Lighting, Pat Collins; Musical Direction, Bruce Coyle; Stage Managers, Thomas J. Rees, Buzz Cohen; Press, Becky Flora

CAST

John Cunningham (Russell), Patti Karr (Janet), Helon Blount (Frances), Kathy Morath (Denise), Robert Polenz (Philip), Elissa Wolfe (Kathie)

MUSICAL NUMBERS: Snapshot, Someday, Siblings, Normal, Forty-three, Watching the News, Cemetery Plot, What If, Creation, Ballad of Sheldon Roth, Point of View, Trio, My Son, If You Run into Bruno, Breakfast, Queen of Hollywood, Tell Me I'm Good, Another Love Song, Divorce, Temporary Thing, Post Card, Coffee, Russell's Song, Janet's Ballad, Little Girl, Ordering the Pizza, Voices, Dear Death, Soon, What Marriage Is, Something in a Birth, Snapshot II

Patti Karr, John Cunningham in "Snapshot"

HUDSON GUILD THEATRE
January 14–February 5, 1980 (8 performances)

HUGHIE

By Eugene O'Neill; Director, Mary B. Robinson; Performed by J.
R. Horne and Frank Girardeau

Right: Frank Girardeau

HUDSON GUILD THEATRE
February 27–March 30, 1980 (30 performances)

COME BACK TO THE 5 & DIME, JIMMY DEAN, JIMMY DEAN

By Ed Graczyk; Directors, Barbara Loden, David Kerry Heefner;
Set, John Falabella; Costumes, David Murin; Lighting, Dennis Pa-
richy; Hairstylist, Michael Kriston; Stage Managers, Thomas J.
Rees, Buzz Cohen; Press, Becky Flora

CAST

Gregory Berdger (Joe) succeeded by Daniel Watkins, Peggy Cos-
grave (Stella May), Mary Donnet (Monathen), Fannie Flagg (Sissy),
Margaret Hilton (Juanita), Linda Kampley (Edna Louise), Barbara
Loden (Mona) who succeeded Sandy Dennis in previews, Maida
Meyers (Sissy then), Judith Roberts (Joanne).

A play in three acts. The action takes place on Sept. 30, 1975 and
Sept. 30, 1955, in a 5 & Dime store in McCarthy, a small town in
west Texas.

Right: Fannie Flagg, Judith Roberts, Barbara Loden in "Come Back, Jimmy Dean"

March 3–25, 1980 (8 performances)

CACCIATORE

A Comedy in two acts by Joseph Pintauro; Director, Randal Hoey;
Set, Robert McBroom; Production Manager, Peter Meleck; Stage
Managers, Thomas Rees, Karin Young, Buzz Cohen, Iris Bond;
Press, Becky Flora

CAST

CACCIATORE I: VITO AND CHARLIE: Thomas De Franco
(Vito), Victor Arnold (Charlie). The action takes place in 1973 in
Vito's room in the DiGiovanni house in Astoria, Queens, New York.
CACCIATORE II: FLYWHEEL AND ANNA: Carol Morley
(Anna), Victor Arnold (Flywheel). The action takes place in August
of 1973 in a house on Shelter Island, N.Y.

May 7,–June 8,1980 (30 performances)

Right: Victor Arnold

THE PENULTIMATE PROBLEM OF SHERLOCK HOLMES

A Drama in 2 acts and 5 scenes by John Nassivera; Director, David
Kerry Heefner; Setting, Frank J. Boros; Costumes, Christina
Weppner; Lighting, Robby Monk; Assistant to Director, Tom Jarus

CAST

Munson Hicks (A Gentleman), Curt Dawson (Dr. Watson), Keith
Baxter (Sherlock Holmes), Sasha von Scherler (Mrs. Hudson),
Lowry Miller (Inspector Lestrade), Dorothy Lancaster (Mrs. Piper),
Yusef Bulos (M. Dupin), Marion Lines (Irene Adler), Edward Zang
(Prof. James Moriarty)

**Curt Dawson, Dorothy Lancaster, Keith Baxter
in "The Penultimate Problem . . ."**

IMPOSSIBLE RAGTIME THEATRE

Ted Story, Artistic Director/Co-Producer
Laurice Firenze, Executive Producer
Sixth Season
Co-Producer, Cynthia Crane; Production Manager, Michael S.
Mantel; Technical Director, John Aulbach; Assistant to Executive
Director, Bruce K. Macaulay

IMPOSSIBLE RAGTIME THEATRE
October 12–29, 1979 (18 performances)
THE CAT AND THE CANARY by John Willard; Director, Ted
Story; Set, Larry Fulton; Lighting, Candice Dunn; Costumes,
Amanda J. Klein; Sound, Robert and Takeko Lepre. CAST: Freder-
ick Rein (Roger), Joy Lindsay (Mamba), David Hyatt (Harry),
Caroline Sidney Abady (Susan), Judy Goldner (Cicely), Otis Stuart
(Charles), Pat McCord (Paul), Barbara Michalak (Annabelle), Dick
Sollenberger (Hendricks), Kilian Ganly (Patterson)

November 16–December 9, 1979 (18 performances)
THE SHEM PLAYS by Samuel Shem; Director, Ted Story; Cos-
tumes, Rebecca Cunningham; Lighting, Charles S. Bullock. "Napo-
leon's Dinner" with Peter Waldren (Denis), Hugh Byrnes (Rawls),
John Mawson (Sammy), "Room for One Woman" with Jennifer
Sternberg (Lil), Virginia Stevens (Pedley), Estelle Kemler (Beesley)

January 4–28, 1980 (18 performances)
DARK AGES by Kevin O'Morrison; Director, Stephen Zucker-
man; Set, Ursula Belden; Costumes, Mimi Maxmen; Lighting, Curt
Ostermann; Sound, Robert Lepre; Assistant to Director, Eiko Le-
vitch; Stage Manager, J. Rudolph Abate. CAST: Thomas Barbour
(Pring/Mick), Dann Florek (Zack/Jerval), Georgine Hall (Connie/-
Mel), Michael Kaufman (Joe), Larry Kelly (Willis/Carl), Johanna
Leister (Flo/Judith), Arthur McFarland (Professor/Roger), Ennis
Smith (Eddie), Colby Willis (Dorcas)

February 8–March 3, 1980 (18 performances)
JESSE AND THE BANDIT QUEEN by David Freeman; Director,
John Pynchon Holmes; Set and Lights, Richard Harmon; Costumes,
Steven L. Birnbaum. CAST: Gale Garnett (Belle), Jay Ingram
(Jesse)

March 14–April 14, 1980 (18 performances)
WHEN THE WAR WAS OVER by Max Frisch; Translated by
James L. Rosenberg; Director, Jude Schanzer; Set, Loy Arcenas;
Lighting, Jo Mayer; Costumes, Mimi Maxmen; Sound, Michael
Schanzer, CAST: Danielle Baum (Marthe), Jack L. Davis (Ossip),
Fred Einhorn (Mihail), David Forsyth (Horst), Michael Garin (Pi-
otr), Susan Lang (Gitta), Robert McFarland (Halske), Armin Shim-
erman (Stepan), Jennifer Sternberg (Agnes), Peter Waldren (Jehuda)

April 25–May 19, 1980 (18 performances)
THE SEAGULL by Anton Chekhov; Translated by Robert W.
Corrigan; Edited by Nicholas Saunders; Director, Ted Story; Set-
tings, Bob Phillips; Lighting, Mark Diquinzio; Costumes, Amanda
J. Klein; Sound, Michael Schanzer; Stage Managers, Judy Baldwin,
Althea Miller; Production Assistant, Nora Ryan. CAST: Pat
McCord (Medvedenko), Sara Venable (Masha), Arthur Anderson
(Sorin), James Farkas (Treplev), Michael Phelps (Yakov), Lucinda
Hitchcock Cone (Nina), Brian Hartigan (Dorn), Norma Fire
(Polina), Barbara Andres (Irina), Steve Carlisle (Shamraev), Dan
Ziskie (Trigorin), Nora Ryan (Maid)

Peter Waldren, John Mawson in "Shem Plays"
Below: Jay Ingram, Gale Garnett in "Jesse
and the Bandit Queen" *(Ken Howard Photo)*

INTERNATIONAL ARTS
RELATIONS/INTAR

Max Ferra, Artistic Director
General Manager, Frank Hibrandt; Press, Clarence Allsopp, Ilka
Tania; Assistant to Director, Robert Morgen; Designer, Randy Bar-
celo; Lighting, Dennis Dugan; Music Director/Sound, Tania Leon;
Stage Manager, Joseph Carroll

INTAR THEATRE
October 4–November 11, 1979 (24 performances)
RICE AND BEANS by Hector Quintero; Translated by Luis
Avalos; Director, Max Ferra; Sets and Costumes, Randy Barcelo;
Lights, Dennis Dugan; Stage Manager, Joseph Carroll. CAST: Ilka
Tanya (Lala), Miriam Cruz (Fefa), Elizabeth Pena (Lalita), Pedro
Santaliz (Anselmo), David Crumet (Anselmito), Clara Hernandez
(Angelita), Victor Martin (Pepe), Ernesto Fuentes (Alfredo)

March 6–20, 1980 (28 performances)
SWALLOWS by Manuel Martin, Jr.; Music, Paul Radelat; Lyrics,
Mr. Martin; Choreographed Movement, Walter Raines; Director,
Manuel Martin, Jr.; Scenery, Donald Eastman; Costumes, Karen
Barbano; Lighting, Larry Steckman; Musical Director, Tania Leon;
Pianist, Mary Rodgers; Stage Manager, Raul Sentenat; Technical
Director, Tom Carroll. CAST: Richard Adan, Magaly Alabau, Vir-
ginia Arrea, Christofer De Oni, Felipe Corostiza, Gil Pacheco, Car-
men Rosario, Gloria Zelaya

May 15–June 22, 1980 (24 performances)
BLOOD WEDDING by Federico Garcia Lorca; Director, Max
Ferra; Music, Francisco Zumaque; Design, Randy Barcelo; Light-
ing, Dennis Dugan; Associate Designer, David Dangle; Movement,
Adolfo Vazquez; Stage Manager, Eiko Levitch. CAST: Antonia Rey
(Mother), Felipe Gorostiza (Groom), Carmen Rosario (Neighbor),
Dina Paisner (Mother-in-Law), Barbara Quintero (Wife), Emil
Herrera (Leonardo), Dean Hill (Woodcutter), Barbara Goldman
(Young Girl), Anita Lobel (Servant), Norberto Kerner (Father),
Brenda Feliciano (Bride), Nereida (Young Girl), Lenny Foglia
(Woodcutter), Michael Stevens (Young Man), Gunter Stern (Wood-
cutter), Daniel Oreskes (Woodcutter), Michael Kemmerling (Young
Man), John Hilburn Wells (Moon)

Rafael Llerena Photos

**Norberto Kerner, Antonia Rey, Felipe Gorostiza,
Brenda Feliciano in "Bloodwedding"**

LIGHT OPERA OF MANHATTAN

William Mount Burke, Producer-Director
Eleventh Year
Associate Director, Raymond Allen; Choreographer, Jerry Gotham;
Assistant Musical Director-Pianist, Brian Molloy; Assistant Conductor-Organist, J. Michael Bart; Costumes, James Nadeaux,
George Stinson, William Schroder; Sets, Elouise Meyer, William
Schroder; Stage Manager, Jerry Gotham

COMPANY

Raymond Allen, Dennis English, James Nadeaux, Tom Olmstead,
Gary Pitts, Gary Ridley, Julio Rosario, James Weber, Elizabeth
Burgess-Harr, Karen Hartman, Joan Lader, Ethel Mae Mason,
Georgia McEver, Mary Lee Rubens, Nancy Temple
GUEST ARTISTS: John Bonk, Lloyd Harris, Michael Harvey, Ron
Mandelbaum, Terry McNulty, Richard Ploch, Tony Tamburello,
Jeanne Beauvais, Marilyn Florez, Betsy Harris, Karen-Johanna Johannsen, Jean Stroup Miller, Sherrie Overholt, Cheryl Savitt, Sharlie
Stuart, Martha Wright
ENSEMBLE: Don Adkins, Sal Basile, Brian Bonnar, Gregory Colan, Clem Egan, Joseph Emma, Jonathan Fluck, Ed Harrison, Jonathan Levy, Bruce McKillip, Steven O'Mara, Craig Schulman, Tom
Stone, Ron Thomas, Ron Wiseman, Steve Wusinich, Joyce Bolton,
Cathy Cosgrove, Julia Davidson, Ellie Davis, Luann Davis, Hallie
Frazer, Pat Genser, Joanne Jamieson, Lucille Mascia, Claudia
O'Neill, Donna Shanklin, Rhanda Spotton

PRODUCTIONS

Ten Nights in a Bar Room, H.M.S. Pinafore, The Mikado, Mlle.
Modiste, Iolanthe, The Merry Widow, Ruddigore, Princess Ida,
Pirates of Penzance, Babes in Toyland, Yeoman of the Guard, The
Fortune Teller, Savoyard Masque, The Sorcerer, Trial by Jury,
Naughty Marietta, The Gondoliers

**Right: Raymond Allen, Georgia McEver
in "Yeoman of the Guard" Top: James
Nadeaux, James Weber, Raymond Allen
in "The Fortune Teller"**

Kathy Rossiter in "Mrs. Moses"

LYRIC THEATER OF NEW YORK

Neal Newman, Artistic Director

18th STREET PLAYHOUSE
September 6–23, 1979 (12 performances)
THE BEGGAR'S OPERA by John Gay; Direction, Musical Realization, Adaptation Neal Newman; Costumes, Susan Cox; Scenery,
George T. Barron; Lighting, Richard Clausen; Assistant Director,
Douglas Cox; Associate Producer, Margo Price; Stage Manager,
Sally Hopkinson; Production Assistant, Debra Legge. CAST: John
Dennehy, Jr. (Beggar), William J. Brooke (Peachum), Philip Schultz
(Filch), Lynne Greene-Brooke (Mrs. Peachum), Paula Bailey
(Polly), John Schmedes (Macheath), Neal Newman (Matt), David
Sloan (Ben Budge), G. Michael Trupiano (Twitcher), Tom DiGiovanni (Paddington), Sally Hopkinson (Servant), Karen Siegel
(Jenny Diver), Colleen Heffernan (Mrs. Coaxer), Karen DeMauro
(Suky Tawdry), Fenton Crawford-Barnes (Molly), Thomas Brooks
(Lockit), Dominic Adinolfi (Turnkey), Vivian Paszamant (Mrs.
Trapes), Jane Milne (Lucy)

April 18–May 4, 1980 (11 performances)
MRS. MOSES with Book by Bill Solly, Donald Ward; Music and
Lyrics, Bill Solly; Director, Neal Newman; Choreography, Jennifer
Howard; Set, Terrence Byrne; Costumes, Susan Cox; Lighting,
Richard Clausen; Pianist and Arrangements, Glen Kelly; Musical
Direction-Vocal Arrangements, John Forchelli; Assistant to Producer, G. Michael Trupiano; Stage Manger, Ava Fradkin. CAST:
Larro Chelsi (Jethro), Fenton Crawford (Anshar), Susi Grace (Bersippah), Jean Hendrickson (Oomah), Jackie Karasek (Nipsi), Debra
Legge (Kish), Susan Bell Van Zant (Nuff), Kathy Rossetter (Zipporah), Joseph Garaventa (The Aynak), Lawrence Raiken (Moses),
Bronwen Brown (Miriam), Edward Lynch (Aaron)

Beryl Vosburgh Photos

MANHATTAN THEATRE CLUB

Lynne Meadow, Artistic Director
Barry Grove, Managing Director
Eighth Season

Associate Artistic Director, Stephen Pascal; Business Manager, Connie L. Alexis; Press, Robert Pontarelli, David Balsom; Assistant to Artistic Director, Michael Bush; Assistant to Managing Director, Molly Scoville; Production Manager, Paul Fitzmaurice; Technical Director, Robert Buckler

MANHATTAN THEATRE CLUB

Tuesday, September 11–October 21, 1979 (48 performances)
LOSING TIME by John Hopkins; Director, Edwin Sherin; Set, Karl Eigsti; Costumes, Jess Goldstein; Lighting, Frances Aronson; Assistant to Director, Julie Forsmith; Production Assistant, Stephen Helper; Stage Managers, Amy Pell, P'nenah Goldstein. CAST: Jane Alexander (Joanne), Shirley Knight (Ruth), Tom Mardirosian (Mike), Bernie McInerney (Wally), Tony Roberts (Tod)

A drama in two acts. The action takes place at the present time in Joanne's NYC apartment.

MANHATTAN THEATRE CLUB

October 9–November 4, 1979 (28 performances)
ICE by Michael Cristofer; Director, Robert Woodruff; Set and Costumes, Sally Jacobs; Lighting, Marc B. Weiss; Assistant to Director, Karen Ryker; Sound, Skip LaPlante; Production Assistant, Esther Beth Cohen; Stage Managers, William Chance, Barbara Abel. CAST: William Russ (Murph), J. T. Walsh (Ray), Susan Sharkey (Sunshine). A drama performed without intermission. The action takes place in an isolated cabin in the Alaskan wilderness.

November 6–December 16, 1979 (48 performances)
THE JAIL DIARY OF ALBIE SACHS by David Edgar; Director, Lynne Meadow; Set, John Lee Beatty; Costumes, Jess Goldstein; Lighting, Jennifer Tipton; Assistant to Director, Douglas Hughes; Production Assistants, Ed Bevan, Madeline Murray, Kim Powers; Stage Managers, Jason LaPadura, Rita Calabro, Katharine Peyton; Dialect Coach, Elizabeth Smith. CAST: Brian Murray (Albie Sachs), John Clarkson (Sgt./McIntyre/Dr. Samols/Constable/-Cameraman), Michael Burg (Constable/Warrant Officer Volk/Sgt.), Vic Polizos (Lt. Wagenaar), Paul Collins (Phil Freeman/Sgt./Dr. Kraal), Count Stovall (Danny Young/Constable), Humbert Allen Astredo (Capt. Rossouw), Peter Michael Goetz (Warrant Officer Snyman/Capt. Swanepoel). A drama in two acts. The action takes place in the early 1960's in Cape Town, South Africa.

November 20–December 16, 1979 (32 performances)
NACHA GUEVARA with Alberto Favero; Lighting, Tony Tucci; Stage Manager, Bonnie Panson.

December 18–23, 1979 (8 performances)
A CHRISTMAS GARLAND devised by Eileen Atkins and Helen Dawson; Director, John Tillinger; Stage Manager, Toby Simpkins; Production Assistant, Amy L. Richards. CAST: Eileen Atkins, Richard Dunne, Edward Herrmann, John McMartin, Joan Moore, Don Scardino, John Tillinger

MANHATTAN THEATRE CLUB

January 1–February 10, 1980 (46 performances)
ENDGAME by Samuel Beckett; Director, Joseph Chaikin; Set, Sally Jacobs; Costumes, Mary Brecht; Lighting, Beverly Emmons; Associate Director, Steven Gomer; Production Assistant, James Stern; Stage Managers, Phillip Price, Virginia Hunter. CAST: Daniel Seltzer (Hamm), Michael Gross (Clov), James Barbosa (Nagg), Joan MacIntosh (Nell). Performed without intermission.

Top Right: Shirley Knight, Jane Alexander in "Losing Time" Below: J. T. Walsh, Susan Sharkey, William Russ in "Ice" Right Center: Brian Murray, Michael Burg in "The Jail Diary of Albie Sachs"

Daniel Seltzer, Michael Gross in "Endgame"

MANHATTAN THEATRE CLUB

January 8–February 3, 1980 (32 performances)
ONE WEDDING, TWO ROOMS, THREE FRIENDS by John
Gwilym Jones; Director, Thomas Bullard; Set, Barry Robison; Costumes, Jess Goldstein; Lighting, Dennis Parichy; Stage Managers,
Kevin Mangan, Bill McGraw; Assistant to Director, Michael
Bloom. CAST: Stephen Burleigh (Dick), Catherine Burns (Meg),
Miles Chapin (Huw), Kristin Griffith (Lis/Sian), Dale Helward
(Tom), Bernie McInerney (Em), Jamey Sheridan (Mike), Marueen
Silliman (Nel), Neil Vipond (Dan)

February 19–March 16, 1980 (32 performances)
DUSA, FISH, STAS & VI by Pam Gems; Director, Nancy Meckler;
Scenic Consultant, Kate Edmunds; Based on an original set design
by Tanya McCallin; Costumes, Calista Hendrickson; Lighting,
Roger Morgan; Stage Managers, Barbara Abel, Esther Beth Cohen;
Production Assistant, Renee Dykas. CAST: Kathryn Grody (Vi),
Laura Esterman (DUSA), Ellen Parker (Stas), Judith Ivey (Fish). A
play in two acts. The action takes place at the present time in a
London apartment.

February 26–April 6, 1980 (48 performances)

BIOGRAPHY

By S. N. Behrman; Director, Lynne Meadow; Set, John Lee Beatty;
Costumes, Jess Goldstein; Lighting, Pat Collins; Original Music,
Robert Dennis; Assistant to Director, Theodore Pappas; Production
Assistant, Nora Peck; Hairstylist, Peg Schierholz; Wardrobe, Karyl
Ann Leigh; Stage Managers, William Chance, Katharine Peyton;
Press, Robert Pontarelli, David Balsom; Dialect Coach, Robert Williams

CAST

P. L. Carling (Orrin Kinnicott), George Guidall (Leander Nolan),
Piper Laurie (Marion Froude), Barbara Lester (Minnie), Theodore
May (Warwick Wilson), Alan Rosenberg (Richard Kurt), Stefan
Schnabel (Melchio Feydak), Diane Warren (Slade Kinnicott),
Standbys: Diana Kirkwood, Peter Crombie.

A comedy in three acts. The action takes place during 1932 in
Marion Froude's studio in New York City.

Gerry Goodstein Photo

February 28–March 8, 1980 (6 performances)
AN EVENING WITH MARGERY COHEN AND JONATHAN
HADARY: Stage Manager, Mary Ann Hilary

March 11–23, 1980 (16 performances)
AN EVENING WITH VIVECA LINDFORS AND KRIST-
OFFER TABORI: director, Paul Austin; Movement, Gui Andrisano; Stage Manager, K. Anna Moore; Arranged by Ms. Lindfors
and Messrs. Austin and Tabori

April 22–July 20, 1980 (104 performances)
MASS APPEAL by Bill C. Davis; Director, Geraldine Fitzgerald;
Set, David Gropman; Costumes, William Ivey Long; Lighting, F.
Mitchell Dana; Stage Managers, Bethe Ward, Virginia Hunter.
CAST: Milo O'Shea (Father Tim Farley), Eric Roberts (Mark Dolson) succeeded by Bill C. Davis; Standbys: Robert Emmet, Geoff
Garland. A play in two acts. The action takes place at the present-
time in Father Farley's office and in St. Francis Church.

**Top Right: Stephen Burleigh, Catherine Burns
in "One Wedding" Below: Kathryn Grody, Laura
Esterman in "Dusa, Fish, Stas, Vi" Right
Center: Barbara Lester, Piper Laurie
in "Biography"**
Gerry Goodstein Photos

Eric Roberts, Milo O'Shea
in "Mass Appeal"

MANHATTAN PUNCH LINE

Faith Catlin, Mitch McGuire, Founding Directors
Steve Kaplan, Artistic Director
Managing Director, Bruce Pachtman; Press, Reva Cooper; Musical Consultant, Kathrin King Segal; Design Consultant, Tony Castrigno; Theatre Designer, William Otterson

MANHATTAN PUNCH LINE

October 17–November 5, 1979 (13 performances)
THE VEGETABLE by F. Scott Fitzgerald; Director, Steve Kaplan; Set, Reagan Cook; Costumes, Francis L. Sabino; Stage Manager, Janet Friedman; Lighting, Tony Castrigno; Props, Reed Bergen; Set, Nanette Ferreri; Sound, Bill Dreisbach. CAST: Patrick Husted (Narrator), Tom Cuff (Jerry), Katherin King Segal (Charlotte), Bill Wiley (Dada), Marcia Hepps (Doris), Mitch McGuire (Snooks), Brad Bellamy (Fish), Doug Baldwin (Jones), Brian Rose (Maj.-Gen. Pushing), Barry Ford (Chief Justice Fossiel), Stephen Ahern (Stutz-Mozart), Brendan Conway, John Griesemer (Detectives).

October 24–November 3, 1979 (8 performances)
THE BROADWAY LOCAL with Domenick Irrera, Michael King, Lisa Mende, Mary Thompson, George Wilson. An improvisational comedy directed by Olga Holub; Musical Director-Pianist, Sue Anderson

November 14–December 3, 1979 (12 performances)
THE CUEL by David Gild; Director, Alex Dmitriev; Set and Lights, Whitney Quesenbery; Costumes, Elaine Mason; Stage Manager, Cathy Harte. CAST: Nickolas Saunders (Samoylenko), Marvin Pearl (Kerbalay), Peter Brouwer (Ivan), James Selby (Von Koren), John Foley (Pobyedov), Jacqueline Schultz (Nadyezhda), Richard Stack (Kirilin), Joel Bernstein (Atchimianov), Brad Bellamy (Clerk), Arva Holt (Marya), Betsy Reilly (Katya), Barry Ford (Ustimovich), Cindy Schneidal (Lady)

November 23–December 29, 1979 (12 performances)
BORN TO WARP Written, Composed and Performed by Trans-Verse Industries; Director, Nicola Sheara; Stage Manager, Vicki Giamanco; Lights, Chris Noyes. CAST: David Jenness (Jet Pepper), Judson Mitsock (Billy Byle), Thomas Singer (Fran Garson)

December 13, 1979–January 13, 1980 (24 performances; returned for 28 additional performances from February 16 through March 14, 1980)
ROOM SERVICE by John Murray and Allen Boretz; Director, Dan Held; Assistant Director, Reed Bergen; Stage Manager, Gene Smith; Set, Tony Castrigno; Lights, Karen Singleton; Costumes, Karen Hummel.
CAST: Bill Britten (Sasha Smirnoff), Brian Rose (Gordon Miller), David Berry (Joseph Gribble), Doug Baldwin (Harry Binion), Royce Rich (Faker Englund), Kathleen Wiggins (Christine Marlowe), Terry Layman (Leo Davis), Karen Kleeger (Hilda Manney), Regis Bowman (Gregory Wagner), Gordon Gene Jones (Simon Jenkins), Timothy Jenkins (Timothy Hogarth), Jerry Tullos (Dr. Glass), Brendan Conway (Bank Messenger), Bill Wiley (Senator Blake)

January 18–February 23, 1980 (12 performances)
A MANHATTAN PUNCH LINE, improvisational comedy with Alice Barrett, Jeffrey Essmann, JoAnne Gellman, Steve Kaplan, Karen Keeger, Deborah Klose, Mark Moritz, Tony Noll, Steve Shaffer, Tom Shelton, Lois Tibbetts

February 29–April 5, 1980 (11 performances)
SONGWRIGHT: The story songs of Jim Friedman; Conceived by Steve Kaplan, Rick Cummins; Director, Steve Kaplan; Choreographer, Cathryn Williams; Stage Manager, Jennifer Borge. CAST: Ellen Gould, Kenny Morris, Ralph Penner, Kathrin King Segal, John Spalla, Jim Friedman, Rick Cummins

April 24–May 18, 1980 (16 performances)
THE MAN WHO SHOT THE MAN WHO SHOT JESSE JAMES conceived and created by Thornebrake Theatre; Director, Christopher Coddington; Set, Tony Castrigno; Lighting, Gregory Chabay; Costumes, Karen Hummel; Choreographer, Janet Watson; Props, Anne Sawyer; Stage Manager, John Kingsbury. CAST: Andy Lerner (Dell/LeSinge/Tom Drayson), Jane Unger (Ma/Mormon Queen), Doug Baldwin (Soapy Siddons/Bill Saul Turtland), Brad Bellamy (Robert Ford), Evelyn Seubert (Dottie Evans Ford), Marcia Hepps (Virginia Marlotte/Dog/Stranger/Lola Montez), Maggie Low (Lulu Slain/Emma Evans), Tom Shelton (J. Benjamin Tuthill/Charley Ford/Desmond), Lucy Lee (Mary/Darla Deulappe)

May 2–June 28, 1980 (15 performances)
THE BROADWAY LOCAL'S BACK, an improvisational comedy with Domenick Irrera, Michael King, Lisa Mende, Mary Thompson, George Wilson

John Griesemer, Kathrin King Segal, Mitch McGuire, Tom Cuff in "The Vegetable"

Brian Rose, Timothy Jenkins, Doug Baldwin in "Room Service" Below: Ellen Gould, John Spalla, Kathrin King Segal in "Songwright"

June 12–July 6, 1980 (16 performances)
THE INCOMPARABLE MAX by Jerome Lawrence and Robert E. Lee; Director, Steve Kaplan; Stage Manager, Jim McGivney; Sets, Geoffrey Hall; Lights, Helen Anne Gatling; Costumes, Francis L. Sabino.
CAST: Glen Agrin (William Rothenstein/Frenchman), Brad Bellamy (Enoch Soames), Regis Bowman (Col. Elbourne/Portly Man), Faith Catlin (Mrs. Blake/Library Clerk), Michael Champagne (A. V. Laider), Michael Eliot Cooke (Max Beerbohm), Joan Grant (Mrs. Elbourne/Wife), Gregory Johnson (Blake/Clerk/Young Man/Lewis), Ray Lloyd (The Man/Uncle Sydney), Elizabeth Logun (Girl/Library Attendant/Maid), Gretchen Pasanen (Usher)

THE MEAT & POTATOES COMPANY

Neal Weaver, Artistic Director

Production Manager, Ann Folke; Administrative Director, Jane Dwyer; Technical Consultant, Terry H. Wells; General Manager, Bonnie Arquilla

September 13–October 6, 1979 (16 performances)
THE ROVER by Mrs. Aphra Behn; Designed and Directed by Neal Weaver; Assistant Director, David Rosett; Stage Managers, Bradley Damien, Michael Moloney, George Thompson. CAST: Cynthia Bock (Valeria), Richard Bourg (Don Pedro), Toni Brown (Callis/-Moretta), Bradley Damien (Stephano/Composer), Paul DeBoy (Belvile), Donna Della Femina (Lucetta), Sara Eldridge (Angellica Bianca), Barbara Knowles (Florinda), Barbara Leto (Hellena), Michael Moloney (Phillipo/Biskey), Geof Prysirr (The Rover), David Rosett (Sebastian/Captain), Lou Spirito (Don Antonio), Spike Steingasser (Frederick), Charles Sweigart (Blunt), Theoge Thompson (Dancer/Diego/Sancho), Mary Wright (Masquer/Dancer) succeeded by Lizzy Townsend

October 18–November 11, 1979 (16 performances)
THE HEIR written and directed by Neal Weaver; Stage Manager, Jim Burleson; Lighting, Ann Folke. CAST: Vyvyan Pinches (Charles Finlay Arden), Barbara Knowles (Nan Arden), Joey Ginza (Ahito), John Daggan (Jerry Collins)

November 23–December 16, 1979 (16 performances)
MONEY by Edward Bulwer-Lytton; Director, Neal Weaver; Assistant Director, Larry Hough; Choreographer, Jane Dwyer; Stage Managers, Evan Senreich, Tom Starace, Michael Michik, Alexander Peck, Tony Zada. CAST: John Daggan (Blount), Richard Fay (Smooth), Jenny Gault (Clara), Larry Hough (James/MacFinch), Jack Kyrieleison (Alfred), Scott Leva (MacStucco/Tom), Michael Michik (Tabouret/Tom), Sarah Nall (Lady Franklin), Joel Parsons (Vesey), Alexander Peck (Toke/Flat/Grab), Dennis Pfister (Frantz-/Waiter), Mark Sarro (Stout), Tom Starace (Old Member/Patent), David Schmitt (Graves), Evan Senreich (Sharp), Richard Spore (Glossmore), Lizzy Townsend (Georgina), Tony Zada (Crimson/-Harris/Policeman)

January 10–February 10, 1980 (20 performances)
DUBLIN DUET by Sean O'Casey; Director, James E. Dwyer; Set, M. Cabot McMullen; Stage Managers, Michael Michik, Tom Starace. CAST: "A Pound on Demand" with Sara Nall (Post Office Girl), Donald Pace (Jerry), Evan Thompson (Sammy), Jeanne Schlegel (Woman), Tom Starace (Policeman) "Bedtime Story" with Gene Borio (John Jo Mulligan), Elissa Napolin (Angela Nightingale), Dan Brown (Daniel Halibut), Tom Starace (Policeman), Jeanne Schlegel (Miss Mossie), Michael Michik (Doctor), Sarah Nall (Nurse)

February 21–March 16, 1980 (16 performances)
HAMLET by William Shakespeare; Director, Neal Weaver; Stage Managers, Larry Hough, Michael Michik, Michael Decker. CAST: Dan Brown (Osric), Peter Bogyo (Horatio) succeeded by Richard Hayes, Richard Bourg (Ghost/Gravedigger/Ambassador), Steve Cassidy (Bernardo/Player Queen), Rodney W. Clark (Claudius), Anne Deauville (Lady-in-waiting), Michael Decker (Francisco/Lucianus/Fortinbras), Larry Hough (Reynaldo/Lord), K. C. Kizziah (Hamlet), Barbara Knowles (Gertrude), Ben Lemon (Laertes) succeeded by Paul DeBoy, Barbara Leto (Ophelia), Scott Leva (Rosencrantz) succeeded by Don Taylor, Michael Michik (Cornelius/Player Prologue/Priest), Kevin O'Malley (Guildenstern), Joel Parsons (Polonius), Christopher Reilly (Marcellus), Penny Weinberger (Lady-in-waiting), Harvey Wilson (Voltimand/Player King/-Gravedigger)

March 27–April 10, 1980 (16 performances)
GREEN FIELDS by Peretz Hirshbein; Director, Neal Weaver; Translation by Joseph C. Landis; Design, Neal Weaver; Stage Managers, Michael Michik, Dustyn Taylor, CAST: Jeanne Kaplan (Rokhel), Leslie Lewis, Henry J. Quinn (Elkone), Joan Conrad (Gittl), Sally Mercer (Tsine), Donna Della Femina (Stere), David Rosett (Avrom-Yankev), K. C. Kizziah (Levi-Yitskhok), Christopher Karczmar (HershBer)

May 1–25, 1980 (16 performances)
VERDICT by Agatha Christie; Design and Direction, Neal Weaver; Stage Managers, Larry Hough, Penny Weinberger. CAST: Franklin Brown (Det. Ins. Ogden), Joan Conrad (Anya Hendryk), Dan Deitch (Prof. Karl Hendryk), Victoria Ezer (Lisa Koletzky), Larry Hough (Sgt. Pearce), Barbara Leto (Helen Rollander), Donald Nardini (Lester Cole), Vyvyan Pinches (Sir William Rollander), Henry J. Quinn (Dr. Stoner), Jeanne Schlegel (Mrs. Roper)

Top Right: K. C. Kizziah, Barbara Leto in "Hamlet" Below: Graham Brown, Barbara Montgomery, Leon Morenzie, Adolph Caesar in "Lagrima del Diablo"

NEGRO ENSEMBLE COMPANY

Douglas Turner Ward, Artistic Director
Twelfth Season

Managing Director, Gerald S. Krone; Assistant to Artistic Director, Horacena J. Taylor; General Manager, Leon B. Denmark; Assistant General Manager, Asante Scott; Administrative Assistant, Brenda Freeman; Executive Assistant, Deborah McGee; Press, Howard Atlee, James Baldassare

ST. MARKS PLAYHOUSE

November 16–December 9, 1979 (22 performances)
THE MICHIGAN by Dan Owens; Director, Dean Irby; Scenery, Wynn Thomas; Costumes, Alvin B. Perry; Lighting, William H. Grant III; Stage Managers, Ron Nguvu, Femi Sarah Heggie; Technical Director, Sylvester N. Weaver, Jr.; Wardrobe, Ali Davis; Production Assistant, Twawanda Jones; Sound, Otis Davis. CAST: Hattie Winston (Pilar Murray), Douglas Turner Ward (Fletcher "Flick" Lacey). A play in two acts. The action takes place at the present time in Roxbury, Massachusetts.

December 14, 1979–January 6, 1980 (28 performances; returned February 28–April 13, 1980 for 54 additional performances. Moved to Broadway May 7, 1980. See Broadway Calendar)
HOME by Samm-Art Williams; Director, Dean Irby; Scenery, Felix Cochran; Costumes, Alvin B. Perry; Lighting, William H. Grant III; Stage Managers, Ron Nguvu. CAST: Charles Brown (Cephus Miles), L. Scott Caldwell (Woman One/Pattie Mae Wells), Michele Shay (Woman Two). Performed without intermission. The action takes place from the late 1950's to the present.

January 10–February 3, 1980 (30 performances)
LAGRIMA DEL DIABLO (The Devil's Tear) by Dan Owens; Director, Richard Gant; Scenery, Wynn Thomas; Costumes, Quay Barnes Truitt; Lighting, Kathy A. Perkins; Stage Manager, Femi Sarah Heggie. CAST: Leon Morenzie (Dacius Soulimare), Graham Brown (Pontiflax), Adolph Caesar (Aquilo), Barbara Montgomery (Belin), Chuck Patterson (Captain), Charles Brown (Soldier One), Zackie Taylor (Soldier Two)

February 7–24, 1980 (22 performances)
COMPANIONS OF THE FIRE by Ali Wadud; Director, Horacena J. Taylor; Scenery, Wynn Thomas; Costumes, Judy Dearing; Lighting, William H. Grant III; Stage Manager, Ron Nguvu. CAST: Charles Brown (Man), Barbara Montgomery (Woman). The action takes place in Harlem during autumn of the present year.
BIG CITY BLUES by Roy R. Kuljian; A Trilogy. CAST: Samm-Art Williams (Jackhammer Man), Chuck Patterson (Revival), Frances Foster (Goodbye, Mrs. Potts). The action takes place at the present time in Los Angeles, California.

NEW YORK SHAKESPEARE FESTIVAL PUBLIC THEATER

Joseph Papp, Producer

General Manager, Robert Kamlot; Company Manager, Roger Gindi; Assistant General Manager, Richard Berg; Press, Merle Debuskey, Bob Ullman, Richard Kornberg; Executive Assistant to Mr. Papp, Louise Edmondson; Production Manager, Andrew Mihok; Technical Director, Mervyn Haines, Jr.; Production Supervisor, Jason Steven Cohen

PUBLIC/NEWMAN THEATER

Tuesday, June 5,–August 26, 1979 (100 performances)
Joseph Papp presents:

HAPPY DAYS

By Samuel Beckett; Director, Andrei Serban; Scenery, Michael Yeargan, Lawrence King; Costumes, Jane Greenwood; Lighting, Jennifer Tipton; Hairstylist-Makeup, Marlies Vallant; Wardrobe, Martha Dye; Stage Managers, Julia Gillett, Dan Hild

CAST

Winnie . . . . Irene Worth
Willie . . . . George Voskovec

Performed without intermission

**George Voskovec, Irene Worth
in "Happy Days"** *(Martha Swope Photo)*

PUBLIC/OTHER STAGE

Thursday, June 28,–July 1, 1979 (6 performances)
Joseph Papp presents:

POETS FROM THE INSIDE

Conceived, and material collected by Jeremy Blahnik and Barbara Allison Penn; Director, Jeremy Blahnik; Assistant Director, Carolyn Baxter; Lighting, Victor En Yu Tan; Production Associate, Barbara Allison Penn; Production Supervisor, Jason Steven Cohen; Wardrobe, Sally Thomas; Stage Manager, Evan Canary; Press, Bob Ullman, Richard Kornberg

CAST

Susan Batson, Carl Craig, Tandy Cronyn, Nancy Cushman, Katherine Diamond, Dortha Duckworth, Phyllis Frelich, Rita Karin, Deborah Offner, Antonia Rey, Socorro Santiago, Madge Sinclair, DeeDee Smith, Jeanne Worth, Melissa Zollo

A presentation of works collected from the deaf, aged, mental patients, prisoners and school children.

Carol Rosegg Photo

"Poets from the Inside"

PUBLIC/ANSPACHER THEATER

Opened Sunday, July 15, 1979.*
Joseph Papp presents:

SPELL #7

By Ntozake Shange; Director, Oz Scott; Music, Butch Morris, David Murray; Choreography, Dianne McIntyre; Costumes, Grace Williams; Scenery, Robert Yodice; Lighting, Victor En Yu Tan; Production Supervisor, Jason Steven Cohen; Assistant to Director, Bernadine Jennings; Wardrobe, Anita Ellis

CAST

Larry Marshall	Beth Shorter
Avery Brooks	LaTanya Richardson
Ellis Williams	Reyno
Dyane Harvey	Mary Alice
Laurie Carlos	

Understudies: S. Epatha Merkerson, Akin Babatunde

A choreopoem performed in two acts.

Press: Bob Ullman, Richard Kornberg
Stage Managers: Jacqueline Yancey, Dinah Crosland

* Closed Dec. 9, 1979 after 175 performances.

Martha Swope Photos

"Spell #7"

PUBLIC/LuESTHER HALL
Wednesday, October 17–November 25, 1979 (39 performances)
Joseph Papp presents:

MERCIER & CAMIER

A novel by Samuel Beckett; Adapted, Directed, and Setting Concept By Frederick Neumann; Music, Philip Glass; Photographic Illustrations, Bill Longcore; Sound, Charles Cowing; Lighting, Michael Kuhling, B. St. John Schofield; Technical Director, Burt Dallas; Stage Managers, B. St. John Schofield, Linda Justice; A NY Shakespeare Festival/Mabou Mines Production.

CAST

Frederick Neumann (Mercier), Bill Raymond (Camier), Terry O'Reilly (Waiter/Officer of the Law/Madden/Old Man), Harvey Spevak (Musician/Quinn), Honora Fergusson (Helen), David Warrilow (Storyteller/Watt), Children: David Neumann, Chris Neumann

A drama in three acts with a prologue and epilogue.

Martha Swope Photo

Bill Raymond, Honora Fergusson, Frederick Neumann in "Mercier & Camier"

PUBLIC/OTHER STAGE
Opened Sunday, October 21, 1979.*
Joseph Papp presents:

SORROWS OF STEPHEN

By Peter Parnell; Director, Sheldon Larry; Scenery, Stuart Wurtzel; Costumes, John Helgerson; Lighting, Dennis Parichy; Production Supervisor, Jason Steven Cohen; Taxi Cab, Perry McLamb; Sound, Valeria Ferrand; Wardrobe, Mark Niedzolkowski; Stage Managers, Michael Chambers, Susan Green.

CAST

Bum/Howard Fishbein	John Del Regno
Stephen Hurt	John Shea †1
Liz	Sherry Steiner
Taxi Driver/Ginny Tremaine	Kathy McKenna
Man at the opera	William Duff-Griffin
Woman at the opera	Barbara Williams
William	Richard Backus
Waitress/Sophia Pickle	Ellen Green †2
Christine	Pamela Reed †3

A comedy in two acts. The action takes place at the present time in Stephen Hurt's apartment and in various places in and around New York City.

* Closed Oct. 27, 1979 after 24 performances. Re-opened Tuesday, December 11, 1979 in the Public Theater Cabaret, and closed April 13, 1980 after 168 additional performances.
† Succeeded by: 1. Don Scardino, 2. Anne DeSalvo, 3. Frances Conroy

Martha Swope Photos

John Shea, Pamela Reed in "Sorrows of Stephen"

PUBLIC/OTHER STAGE
November 12, 1979–January 21, 1980 (44 performances)
Joseph Papp presents:

TONGUES
with
Savage/Love

performed by Joseph Chaikin

A Collaboration by Sam Shepard and Joseph Chaikin; Director, Robert Woodruff; Costumes, Mary Brecht; Lighting, Beverly Emmons; Production Supervisor, Jason Steven Cohen; Assistant Director, Dan Moran; Movement, Phoebe Neville; Wardrobe, Tim Buckley; Stage Manager, Ruth Kreshka
SAVAGE/LOVE: Music by Skip LaPlante, Harry Mann, Sam Shepard; performed by Skip LaPlante and Harry Mann
TONGUES: Music by Sam Shepard; performed by Skip LaPlante

Richard Backus, Pamela Reed in "Sorrows of Stephen"

PUBLIC/NEWMAN THEATRE

Opened Thursday, December 6, 1979.*

Joseph Papp in association with John F. Kennedy Center for the Performing Arts presents:

THE ART OF DINING

By Tina Howe; Director, A. J. Antoon; Scenery, David Jenkins; Costumes, Hilary Rosenfeld; Lighting, Ian Calderon; Hairstylist and Makeup, J. Roy Helland; Production Supervisor, Jason Steven Cohen; Production Assistant, Madeleine Rudin

CAST

Suzanne Collins (Ellen), Ron Rifkin (Cal), Jane Hoffman (Hannah Galt), Robert Gerringer (Paul Galt), Dianne Wiest (Elizabeth Barrow Colt) or Brenda Currin, Kathy Bates (Herrick Simmons), Margaret Whitton (Nessa Vox), Jacklyn Maddux (Tony Stassio), George Guidall (David Osslow)

A comedy in two acts performed without an intermission but with a pause to denote the passing of an hour. The action takes place at the present time, early in the evening, at the Golden Carousel Restaurant in New Jersey.

* Closed December 9, 1979 after 6 performances and 65 previews.

Sy Friedman Photo

Dianne Wiest, George Guidall
in "The Art of Dining"

PUBLIC/OTHER STAGE

January 11–27, 1980 (11 performances)

Joseph Papp presents:

HARD SELL

Conceived and Directed by Murray Horwitz; Written by Roger Director and Murray Horwitz; Music Composed and Directed by John Lewis; Additional Material, Mimi Kennedy, Ted Mann, Herb Sargent, Wendy Wasserstein; Musical Staging, Sammy Dallas Bayes; Scenery Coordinated by Barry Robison; Costumes, Pegi Goodman; Lighting, Gail Dahl; Production Supervisor, Jason Steven Cohen; Production Assistant, Jeri Lynn Cohen; Stage Manager, Bonnie Panson

CAST

Seth Allen, Murray Horwitz, Andrea Martin, Carolyn Mignini, Steve Vinovich

Right Center: Carolyn Mignini, Seth Allen, Steve Vinovich in "Hard Sell"

PUBLIC/ANSPACHER THEATER

January 23–February 17, 1980 (53 performances)

Joseph Papp presents:

SALT LAKE CITY SKYLINE

By Thomas Babe; Director, Robert Allan Ackerman; Scenery, Marjorie Kellogg; Costumes, Robert Wojewodski; Lighting, Arden Fingerhut; Hairstylist/Makeup, J. Roy Helland; Musical Direction, Eddie Rabin; Production Supervisor, Jason Steven Cohen; John's Theme by John Lithgow; Assistant to Director, Mary-Ann Monforton; Stage Managers, Zane Weiner, Sally Greenhut; Press, Bob Ullman, Richard Kornberg

CAST

Peter Bosche (Bailiff), James Carruthers (Clerk), Richard Frank (Guard), James Greene (The Prosecution), Fred Gwynne (The Judge), John Lithgow (Joe Hill), Tom McKitterick (John Dawson), Mark Metcalf (The Defense), Hariet Miller (Mrs. Seeley), Frank Muller (Guard), Will Patton (Gruber), Don Plumley (Mr. Jefferson), J. C. Quinn (Jerusalem Slim), Raynor Scheine (Mr. Smith), Gail Strickland (Elizabeth Dawson)

A drama in two acts. The action takes place in a courtroom in Salt Lake City, Utah.

Martha Swope Photo

Fred Gwynne (top), John Lithgow
in "Salt Lake City Skyline"

PUBLIC/NEWMAN THEATER

February 3–March 15, 1980 (47 performances)
Joseph Papp presents:

MARIE AND BRUCE

By Wallace Shawn; Director, Wilford Leach; Scenery, Jim Clayburgh, Wilford Leach; Costumes, Patricia McGourty; Lighting, Martin Tudor; Assistant to Director, Jack Chandler; Wardrobe, Daniel Lomax; Stage Managers, Peter Dowling, Jacqueline Yancey; Production Supervisor, Jason Steven Cohen;

CAST

Bob Balaban (Bruce), Tom Costello (Antoine/Waiter), Griffin Dunne (Henry/Tim), John Ferraro (Fred/Bert), Sakina Jaffrey (Bettina), Louise Lasser (Marie), Parker McCormick (Jean), Frank Modell (Herb/Max), Angela Pietropinto (Enid/Ilse).

A play performed without intermission. The action takes place at the present time.

Martha Swope Photo

Bob Balaban, Louise Lasser, and entire
cast in "Marie and Bruce"

PUBLIC/LuESTHER HALL

March 31–May 25, 1980 (64 performances)
Joseph Papp presents:

THE HAGGADAH
A Passover Cantata

By Elizabeth Swados; Adapted and Directed by Miss Swados; Narration Adapted from texts by Elie Wiesel; Scenery, Costumes, Masks and Puppetry, Julie Taymor; Lighting, Arden Fingerhut; Production Supervisor, Jason Steven Cohen; Wardrobe, Kathy Roberson; Stage Managers, Gregory Meeh, Andy Lopata

CAST

Roger Babb, Suzanne Baxtresser, Shami Chaikin, Craig Chang, Victor Cook, Keith David, Patrick Jude, Aisha Kahlil, Esther Levy, John S. Lewandowski, Martha Plimpton, Martin Robinson, Wes Sanders, David Schechter, Kate Schmitt, Svee Scooler, Ira Siff, Kerry Stubbs, Deborah Anne Wise
MUSICAL NUMBERS: Four Questions, Prelude, Pesach Has Come to the Ghetto, Slave Chant, God of Faithful, By the Waters of Babylon, Shepherd Song, Burning Bush, Pharoah's Chant, Why Hast Thou Done Evil to These People?, The Plagues, Death of the Firstborn, Look at the Children, We Are All Dead Men, Puppet Rebbe, Dayenu Chant, Crossing the Red Sea, Who Is Like Unto Thee, Three Midrash, Country That Is Missing, Golden Calf, God of Mercy, Ten Commandments, Hebrew Benediction, Death of Moses, A Blessing, Elijah, Song of Songs

Performed without intermission.

Martha Swope Photo

PUBLIC/MARTINSON THEATER

April 30–May 18, 1980 (23 performances)
Joseph Papp presents:

THE MUSIC LESSONS

By Wakako Yamauchi; Director, Mako; Scenery, James E. Mayo; Associate, Akira Yoshimura; Costumes, Susan Hum; Lighting, Victor En Yu Tan; Assistant Director, David Oyama; Production Assistant, Peter Chiang; Stage Managers, Greg Fauss, Ruth Kreshka; Production Supervisor, Jason Steven Cohen

CAST

Dana Lee (Nakamura), Jane Mandy (Waitress), Haunani Minn (Chizuko Sakata), Kestutis Nakas (Billy Kane), Keenan Shimizu (Ichiro Sakata), Sab Shimono (Kaoru Kawaguchi), Lauren Tom (Aki Sakata), Gedde Watanabe (Tomu Sakata).

A play in 2 acts and 10 scenes. The action takes place during September 1935 in Imperial Valley, California.

(No Photos available)

Craig Chang, Martin Robinson
in "The Haggadah"

149

PUBLIC/ANSPACHER THEATER
May 3–4, 1980 (4 performances and 17 previews)
Joseph Papp presents:

SUNDAY RUNNERS IN THE RAIN

By Israel Horovitz; Director, Sheldon Larry; Scenery and Costumes, Paul Steinberg, Lighting, Roger Morgan; Production Supervisor, Jason Steven Cohen; Dialect Coach, Gordon Jacoby; Assistant to Director, Nora Peck; Stage Managers, Susan Green, Barbara Abel

CAST

Maureen Anderman (Amy McClennon), John Aquino (Farnie Sears), Robert Fields (Gus Swaddle), Keith Gordon (Sean Coon), William Hickey (Macintosh Squires), Jonathan Hogan (Tom O'Malley), Judith Ivey (Kathleen Herlihy), Larry Joshua (Zeke Sears), Carol Kane (Midgie Swaddle), Steven Keats (Eli Linsky), Michael Kell (Porker Martino), Peter Riegert (Pasta Gonzaga), Ebbe Roe Smith (Morgie Coffin), Mark Soper (Harvey/Dave McGrath), Neil Vipond (Fred Folger)

A play in two acts. The action takes place at the present time on a Sunday in late September at the interior and exterior of a doughnut shop on a vast parking lot in Gloucester, Massachusetts.

Frederic Ohringer Photo

Maureen Anderman, Jonathan Hogan, William Hickey in "Sunday Runners in the Rain"

NO SMOKING PLAYHOUSE

Norman Thomas Marshall, Artistic Director
Associate Directors, George Wolf Reily, John von Hartz; Administrative Director, Fay Bright; Press, Anne Einhorn, Adam Redfield; General Manager, Lily Turner

NO SMOKING PLAYHOUSE
November 29–December 23, 1979 (20 performances)
REFLECTED GLORY by George Kelly; Director, Marvin D. Einhorn; Set, Leon Munier; Costumes, Mimi Maxmen; Lighting, Natasha Katz; Technical Director, Warren Jorgenson; Hairstylist, Lee Pola; Props, Carolyn Dixon; Stage Managers, Ann Mathews, Rita Robbins. CAST: Peter Jolly (Howard), Allen Lane (Charlie), Maggie Miller (Florence), Edward Penn (Hanlon), Adam Redfield (Waiter/Bruno), George Wolf Reily (Omansetter), Peter Reznikoff (Wall), Shelley Rogers (Miss Flood), Cathy Roskam (Miss Sloane), J. B. Waters (Hattie). A comedy in 3 acts and 4 scenes. The action takes place during the early 1930's.

February 24–March 16, 1980 (10 performances)
ONLY WHEN I LAUGH written and performed by Sally-Jane Heit; Musical Direction, Donald Sosin; Additional Material, Doris Adler; Technical Director, George Elmer; Stage Managers, D. C. Rosenberg, Rickie Grosberg. Performed with one intermission.

February 21–March 17, 1980 (20 performances)
MOTHERS AND DAUGHTERS by John von Hartz; Director, Norman Thomas Marshall; Set, Don Jensen; Lighting, George Allison Elmer; Costumes, J. B. Waters; Assistant Designer, Gordon Brown; Stage Manager, Robert Ulrich; Sound, Philip Armstrong; Props, Christian Cockerton; Original Music Composed and Performed by William Schimmel. CAST: Fran Carlon (Mae), Anne O'Sullivan (Meredith), Cathy Roskam (Frankie), Peter Jolly (Mac), George Wolf Reily (Wally)

William Garner Photos

PUBLIC/NEWMAN THEATER
May 13–June 15, 1980 (40 performances and 22 previews)
Joseph Papp presents:

MOTHER COURAGE AND HER CHILDREN

By Bertolt Brecht; Adaptation by Ntozake Shange; Lyrics adapted by Louisa Rose; Music, William Elliott; Directed and Designed by Wilford Leach; Costumes, Patricia McGourty; Lighting, Jennifer Tipton; Associate Set Designer, Jack Chandler; Production Supervisor, Jason Steven Cohen; Production Assistant, Jeff Marcus; Assistant to Director, Jack Chandler; Hair, Wigs and Make up, Marlies Valiant; Wardrobe, Mark Niedzolkowski; Stage Managers, Louis Rackoff, Jacqueline Yancey

CAST

Thomas Martell Brimm (Old Cowhand/Farmer/Soldier/Klansman), Robert Christian (Cook), C. David Colson (General/Rancher/Klansman), Jose Luis Espinosa (Young Cowhand/Mestizo Son/Soldier/Klansman), Gloria Foster (Mother Courage), Morgan Freeman (Chaplain), Ruthanna Graves (Katie), Samuel L. Jackson (Sgt./Kiowa Man/Soldier/Klansman), Jerriese Daniel Johnson (Yvette's Servant/Farm Child/Soldier/Klansman), Jack Landron (Enoch), Carol-Jean Lewis (Mestizo Woman/Farm Woman), Jerry Mayer (Officer/Deputy/Ranger/Klansman/Soldier), Peter Oliver-Norman (Clerk/Soldier/Klansman), Reyno (Smoked Cheese/Soldier/Klansman), Raynor Scheine (Rebel with Patch/Ranger/Klansman/Soldier), Anna Deavere Smith (Kiowa Woman/Farm Child), Ellis Williams (Officer/Soldier/Klansman), Hattie Winston (Yvette), Trazana Beverley (Standby)

A drama in two acts.

Martha Swope Photo

Left Center: Robert Christian, Gloria Foster in "Mother Courage. . . ."

Peter Jolly, Edward Penn, Shelley Rogers in "Reflected Glory"

THE PHOENIX THEATRE

T. Edward Hambleton, Managing Director
Daniel Freudenberger, Artistic Director
Founders: T. Edward Hambleton, Norris Houghton
Twenty-seventh Season

MARYMOUNT MANHATTAN THEATRE
Monday, June 4, 1979–June 17, 1979 (22 performances)
The Phoenix Theatre by arrangement with Lewis and Jay Allen
and Stephen Graham presents:

CHINCHILLA

"Figures in a Classical Landscape with Ruins" by Robert David
MacDonald; Direction and Design, Philip Prowse; Scenery Supervision, Hugh Landwehr; Costumes, David Murin; Lighting, Dennis
Parichy; Production Coordinator, Donna Lieberman; Production
Assistants, Brooke Allen, Gina Lansford; Stage Managers, Barbara
Mae Phillips, William Chance; Wardrobe, Deborah Van Wetering;
Press, Susan Bloch & Co., Bill Rudman, Adrian Bryan-Brown

CAST

James Vincent Albanese (Clorindo), David Berman (Vatza), Philip
Casnoff (Fedya), Michael Cristofer (Chinchilla), Laura Esterman
(Mimi), June Gable (Tamara), John Goffredo (Tancredi), Merwin
Goldsmith (Gabriel), Joseph Pugliese (Maxim), William Robertson
(Socrate), Laurence Senelick (Levka), Kevin Sessums (Konstantin),
Wallace Shawn (Ilya), Margaret Whitton (Nina)

A drama in two acts. The action takes place mainly on the Lido,
Venice, Italy, in July 1914.

Martha Swope Photos

Michael Cristofer, William Robertson, Merwin
Goldsmith, Joseph Pugliese (foreground), Philip
Casnoff (seated), James Albanese, Wallace Shawn,
Laura Esterman in "Chinchilla"

MARYMOUNT MANHATTAN THEATRE
Monday, October 22–November 11, 1979 (22 performances)
The Phoenix Theatre presents:

THE WINTER DANCERS

By David Lan; Director, Keith Hack; Scenery, Karen Schulz; Lighting, Paul Gallo; Sound, David Rapkin; Consulting Ethno-Musicologist, Ida Halpern; Copper and Sun, Guy Neuve; General Manager,
Mitchell Kurtz; Assistant, Lynne Kemen; Production Coordinator,
Donna Lieberman; Stage Managers, Tom Aberger, John Kazanjian;
Press, Susan L. Schulman, Barbara Carroll

CAST

Jacqueline Brookes (Betsy Hunt), Larry Bryggman (Fool), Glenn
Close (Kettle), Richard Council (Sparrow), Randy Danson (One
Foot), Alex Diakun (Bloodlip), Clarence Felder (Whale), Tom Klunis (Sky), Stephen McHattie (Carver), Bill Moor (Life Owner),
Barry Snider (Mountain Peak), Thomas A. Stewart (Dancer)

A drama in 2 acts and 11 scenes. The action takes place on
Vancouver Island, off the coast of British Columbia from 1876 to
1896.

Martha Swope Photos

Stephen McHattie, Larry Bryggman
in "The Winter Dancers"

MARYMOUNT MANHATTAN THEATRE
Thursday, December 27, 1979–January 20, 1980 (22 performances)
The Phoenix Theatre presents:

SHOUT ACROSS THE RIVER

By Stephen Poliakoff; Director, Robert Woodruff; Scenery, Hugh
Landwehr; Costumes, Linda Fisher; Lighting, Stephen Ross; Sound,
David Rapkin; Dialect Consultant, Timothy Monich; Production
Manager, Donna Lieberman; Wardrobe, TerriLynne Brown; Stage
Managers, Tom Aberger, Connie Cloyed McDonnell; Press, Susan
L. Schulman

CAST

Barbara eda-Young (Mrs. Forsythe), Ed Setrakian (Lawson), Ellen
Barkin (Christine), Ebbe Roe Smith (Mike), David Saint (Martin)

A drama in 2 acts and 10 scenes. The action takes place in South
London, England.

Martha Swope Photo

Ellen Barkin, Barbara eda-Young
in "Shout Across the River"   **151**

MARYMOUNT MANHATTAN THEATRE
Monday, January 28–February 17, 1980 (30 performances)
The Phoenix Theatre presents:

THE TROUBLE WITH EUROPE

By Paul D'Andrea; Director, Daniel Freudenberger; Scenery and Costumes, Manuel Lutgenhorst; Lighting, Dennis Parichy; Movement, Ara Fitzgerald; Fight Director, Peter Nels; Sound, David Rapkin; General Manager, Lynne M. Kemen; Production Manager, Donna Lieberman; Wardrobe, Ronn Tombaugh; Assistant to Director, Vilma Vaccaro; Stage Managers, Alan Fox, Roger Kent Brechner; Press, Susan L. Schulman

CAST

Christine Baranski (Amanda/Mme. Igrec/2nd Underworld Figure), Yusef Bulos (Pres. Raymond/Henri Hubert/3rd Underworld Figure), James Cahill (Henry Townley/Lavender Peagrim/Milgrom Dengel), Perry King (Wilbur Tilbury), James Rebhorn (Pres. Lehman/Ben Bragge/1st Underworld Figure), Kristoffer Tabori (Inspector Jogot)

A play in 2 acts and 6 scenes "designed to put a stop to the 20th Century."

Martha Swope Photos

**Perry King, Kristoffer Tabori
in "The Trouble with Europe"**

**Michael Ayr, Jill Eikenberry, Evelyn
Mercado, Luis Avalos, Linda Atkinson,
Remak Ramsay in "Save Grand Central"**

MARYMOUNT MANHATTAN THEATRE
Monday, March 3–16, 1980 (22 performances)
The Phoenix Theatre presents:

SAVE GRAND CENTRAL

By William Hamilton; Director, Gene Saks; Scenery, Lawrence King; Costumes, Jane Greenwood; Lighting, Robby Monk; Wardrobe, Jacqueline Watts; Hairstylist, Jean Louis David; General Manager, Lynne M. Kemen; Assistant, Sherri Kotimsky; Production Manager, Donna Liebman; Stage Managers, Tom Aberger, Connie Cloyed McDonnell; Press, Susan L. Schulman

CAST

Linda Atkinson (Lucy Maynard), Luis Avalos (Luis Apaka), Michael Ayr (Charles Malcolm), Jill Eikenberry (Cristina Malcolm), Evelyn Mercado (Maria Perez), Remak Ramsay (Roger Maynard)

A comedy in 2 acts and 9 scenes. The action takes place at the present time.

Martha Swope Photos

MARYMOUNT MANHATTAN THEATRE
Thursday, April 3–20, 1980 (22 performances)
The Phoenix Theatre presents:

SECOND AVENUE RAG

By Allan Knee; Director, Gerald Freedman; Scenery, Marjorie Kellogg; Costumes, Jeanne Button; Lighting, Christine Wopat; Sound, David Rapkin; Assistant to Director, Mitchell Ivers; Production Manager, Donna Lieberman; Wardrobe, Sheila A. Andersen; Stage Managers, Alan Fox, Kathleen Marsters; Press, Susan L. Schulman, Kate McIntyre

CAST

Herman O. Arbeit (Morris/Husband), Richard Bey (Shlomo), Leslie Goldstein (New Man/Manager), Harold Guskin (Elias), Cynthia Harris (Bertha), Jane Hoffman (Mrs. Weinblatt), Allen Joseph (Simon), Joseph Leon (Moshkovitch), Mark Margolis (Moish), Marcell Rosenblatt (Fanny)

A comedy in 2 acts and 8 scenes. The action takes place in a NY tenement, Engelman's Clothing Store, a Hudson Dayliner, Bertha's apartment, Dressing room at the Thalia Theatre.

Martha Swope Photos

**Richard Bey, Marcell Rosenblatt
in "Second Avenue Rag"**

PLAYWRIGHTS HORIZONS

Manhattan/Queens
Robert Moss, Producing Director
Andre Bishop, Artistic Director
Ninth Season
Managing Director, Jane Moss; Business Manager, Ira Schlosser;
Press, David Izakowitz, Lucy Stille; Production Manager, Dorothy
J. Maffei; Photographer, Susan Cook

MANHATTAN MAINSTAGE

October 24–November 18, 1979
JUSTICE by Terry Curtis Fox; Director, Thomas Babe; Set, Andrew Jackness; Costumes, Bob Wojewodski; Lighting, Jennifer Tipton; Stage Manager, Michael Spellman. CAST: Rick Lieberman, Richard Hoxie, Andrew Davis, Barney Laverty, Andrea Masters, Neil Harris, Ellen Parker

April 17–May 4, 1980
SURVIVAL KITSCH written and performed by Bill Weeden, David Finkle, Sally Fay; Director, Jerry Adler; Choreography, Cathy Rice; Set, Barry Robison; Costumes, Steven Birnbaum; Lighting, Annie Wrightson; Stage Manager, Lynda Ann Martin

May 16–June 15, 1980
PASSIONE written and directed by Albert Innaurato; Set, David Gropman; Costumes, William Ivey Long; Lighting, Paul Gallo; Fight, B. H. Barry; Sound, Alex McIntyre; Special Effects, Scott Glenn; Stage Manager, Jay Adler. CAST: Jerry Stiller, Sloane Shelton, Dick Latessa, Angela Paton, Tom Mardirosian, Dominic Chianese, Laurel Cronin

May 31–June 28, 1980
FABLES FOR FRIENDS by Mark O'Donnell; Director, Douglas Hughes; Set, Joe Mobilia; Costumes, Steven Birnbaum; Lighting, Frederick Buchholz; Stage Manager, Barbara Abel. CAST: Jay O. Sanders, Anthony Heald, Robert Joy, Patricia Richardson, Ann McDonough, Mia Dillon

PLAYWRIGHTS HORIZONS QUEENS

October 13–November 4, 1979
OH, COWARD! conceived and directed by Roderick Cook from the works of Noel Coward; Set, Dean Reiter; Costumes, Jan Morrison; Lighting, Annie Wrightson; Stage Manager, Richard S. Viola. CAST: Roderick Cook, Jennifer Bassey, Larry Conroy

November 10–December 2, 1979
TWO SMALL BODIES by Neal Bell; Director, Harold DeFelice; Set, Bil Mikulewicz; Costumes, Linda Fisher; Lighting, Robby Monk; Stage Manager, Peter Glazer. CAST: Ron McLarty, Anita Morris

March 8–30, 1980
COMPANY by Georg Furth and Stephen Sondheim; Director, Andre Ernotte; Musical Staging, Theodore Pappas; Musical Direction-Conductor, Michael Starobin; Set, Raymond C. Recht; Costumes, Molly Maginnis; Lighting, William D. Anderson; Stage Manager, Bonnie Panson. CAST: Peter Evans, Cynthia Crumlish, Walter Bobbie, Sheilah Rae, Tony Blake, Patricia Richardson, James Seymour, Jane Galloway, Randall Easterbrook, Diane Findlay, Conrad McLaren, Mary Testa, Christine Baranski, Sonja Stuart

April 5–27, 1980
TIME STEPS by Gus Kaikkonen; Director, Edward Cornell; Set, Leo Gambacorta; Costumes, Elizabeth P. Palmer; Lighting, David F. Segal; Stage Manager, Fredric H. Orner. CAST: Bill Sadler, Kate Kelly, Michael O'Neil, Philip Casnoff, Randy Danson, Leora Dana, Conrad McLaren, Stephen Mendillo, Parker McCormick, Sarah Chodoff, David Rakower

May 3–25, 1980
ARMS AND THE MAN by George Bernard Shaw; Director, Harold Scott; Set, David Potts; Costumes, Carrie Robbins, Margarita Delgado, Roberta Favant; Lighting, Annie Wrightson; Sound, Richmond Hoxie; Stage Manager, Mimi Jordan Sherin. CAST: Ann McDonough, Margaret Hall, Liz McDonald, Brad O'Hare, Ken Cazan, Christopher Loomis, Gil Rogers, Dana Mills

Top Right: Angela Paton, Dick Latessa, Jerry Stiller, Sloane Shelton in "Passione" Below: Margaret Hall, Ann McDonough, Gil Rogers in "Arms and the Man" Right Center: Leora Dana, Philip Casnoff in "Time Steps"
Susan Cook Photos

Peter Evans in "Company"

POTTER'S FIELD THEATRE COMPANY

Michael Moriarty, Actor Manager
Lisa Baker, General Manager
Directors, Ronald Hufham, Michael Moriarty, Edwin Sherrin; Designers, Paul Gallo (Lighting), Robert Wagner (Scenery), William James Wall (Scenery/Costumes); Composer, Lee Hoiby; Stage Manager, Lisa Baker; Press, Shellie Mulrad

COMPANY

Peter Alzado, Mark Arnott, Frank Askin, Scott Baker, Kim Beaty, JoAnne Belanger, Susan Charette, Jonathan Clifford, Mark Cohen, Lee Cotterell, Sara Croft, Gail d'Addario, Edna Dix, Mary Dooley, Star Droner, Sarah Fairfax, Nina Faragher, Garald Lee Farnham, Michael A. Farris, Mary Feeney, Bryant Fraser, Colin Garrey, Carolyn Geer, Barbara Gilbert, John Griesemer, Tammy Grimes, Dianne Hammarth, Leslie Haydn, Louis F. Homyak, Jeffrey Horowitz, Sharita Hunt, Lee Jines, Timothy Jude, Nancy-Elizabeth Kammer, Gail Kerbel, Bruce Kronenberg, George J. Kunze, Beth Kurtz, John Anthony Lack, Vicki LaViscount, Thomas Lenz, Paul McCarren, Jay McCormack, Anne Hamilton Martin, James Maxson, Vance Mizelle, Abbie Morris, Patsy Moss, Michael Moriarty, Frank Mullaney, Joyce O'Conner, Amy Plummer, Nina Rivera, Alison Robertson, Carol Saltus, Jose Santana, Catherine Schultz, M. Tulis Sessions, Evelyn Mary Seubert, Andrea Skolnick, Gary Stine, Otis Stuart, Eric Tull, Margaret Warncke, Anthony Watts
Margaret Avery, Susan Carr, Scott Crawford, Charles Duval, Roberta D. Espanoza, David W. Evans, Anna Galiena, Lynne Gentile, Patricia A. Gill, Karen Goldfarb, Tira Harpaz, Jason Howard, Johanna Jensen, Suzannah Knight, Joanne Lehmann, Laura Levya, Julia A. McLaughlin, Muriel Mason, Arnie Mazer, Kim Miyori, Christopher Moore, Sherry Nadine, Anthony Newfield, Robin Norton, George Patelis, Andrea Pines, Margrit Polak, Dolly Reisman, Nick Salamone, Noel Stilphen, Charles Sullivan, Barry Theiler, Leslie Thompson, Peter Von Berg, Charles Whiteside, Kelly Yaegermann, Diego Zuniga

PRODUCTIONS

Street Players at the Cloisters, Love's Labour's Lost, The Mischief You Foresee, Macy's Shakespearathon '80, The Seagull, An Evening of Renaissance Songs and Sonnets

Peter Alzado, Anne Hamilton Martin in "Love's Labour's Lost"

THE PRODUCTION COMPANY

Norman Rene, Artistic Director
Third Season
Executive Director, Samuel Platt; Associate Artistic Director, Sheldon Epps; Business Manager, Carol Graebner; Press, Clarence Allsopp

PLAYHOUSE 46

November 7–December 16, 1979 (42 performances)
HOSANNA by Michel Tremblay; Translated by John Van Burek and Bill Glassco; Director, Norman Rene; Set, John Shaffner; Costumes, Jeanette Oleksa; Lighting, Debra J. Kletter; Stage Manager, Patricia Saphier; Technical Director, Random Gott; Production Assistants, Sharon Harris, Russell Parker. CAST: Kenneth Norris (Hosanna), Kevin Wade (Cuirette), Clayton Berry (Standby). A play in two acts. The action takes place in Montreal, Quebec, late Halloween night.

January 2–February 10, 1980 (42 performances)
THE GUARDSMAN by Ferenc Molnar; Translated by Frank Marcus; Director, John Roach; Set, Jack Stewart; Costumes, John Carver Sullivan; Lighting, Debra J. Kletter; Stage Managers, David L. Nathans, Susi Mara; Technical Director, Random Gott. CAST: Judith Drake (Usherette), Diane Heles (Liza), Lillie Robertson (Ilona), Noble Shropshire (Creditor), Eric Tavaris (Nandor), Sy Travers (Bela), Susan Willis (Mother)

February 20–March 30, 1980 (42 performances)
MY GREAT DEAD SISTER by Arthur Bicknell; Director, Norman Rene; Set, June DeCamp; Costumes, Jeanette Oleksa; Lighting, Debra J. Kletter; Technical Director, David Gscheidle; Stage Managers, David L. Nathans, Charles Michael Wright. CAST: Robert Carnegie (Glen Johnson), Marc Castle (Elliot Whitmocker), Judith Drake (Charlene Metcalf), Georgine Hall (Aunt Zoe), Rica Martens (Margaret Metcalf), Nicholas Saunders (Curtis Metcalf), Charles Michael Wright (Gerald Metcalf). A play in two acts. The action takes place during late October of the mid-1960's in the kitchen of the Metcalf home in upstate New York.

March 26–May 11, 1980 (51 performances)
BLUES IN THE NIGHT conceived and directed by Sheldon Epps; Choreography, Gregory Hines; Vocal and Musical Arrangements, Chapman Roberts, Sy Johnson; Set, June DeCamp; Costumes, Jeanette Oleksa; Lighting, Debra J. Kletter; Stage Manager, Consuelo Mira; Production Associate, Linda Beckett. CAST: David Brunetti, Rise Collins, Suzanne M. Henry, Gwen Shepherd. A musical in two acts. The action takes place in Chicago in the late 1930's in a cheap hotel.

Chip Goebert Photos

Suzanne M. Henry, David Brunetti, Gwen Shepherd, Rise Collins in "Blues in the Night"

Left Center: Robert Carnegie, Nicholas Saunders, Judith Drake, Rica Martens, Michael Wright in "My Great Dead Sister"

QUAIGH THEATRE

Will Lieberson, Artistic Director
Managing Director, Paul Matwiow; Executive Director, Irene Klein; Production Coordinator, Richard Young; Press, Max Eisen, Francine L. Trevens

QUAIGH THEATRE

Tuesday, July 10,–29, 1979 (18 performances)
MEN IN WHITE by Sidney Kingsley; Director, Will Lieberson; Set, Bob Phillips; Lighting, Linda McNeilly; Costumes, Elisabeth Lynch; Production Coordinator, Irene Klein; Sound, George Jacobs; Stage Managers, Karin Clauson, Theresa Speita, Kevin G. Cuba, Darcy Heller.
CAST: Spence Adams (Mrs. D'Andrea), Glen Alterman (Pete), Stephen Berenson (Shorty), Jeremy Brooks (Dr. Cunningham), Eva Charney (Barbara), Kevin G. Cuba (Orderly), Leslie Goldstein (Dr. Levine), Judy Grebelsky (Nurse Jamison), Bonita Griffin (Nurse Maureen), Robert W. Holliday (Orderly), Jeannie Hudak (Nurse Sandy), Tony Jarosz (Mooney), Peter Johl (Hochberg), Michael Kimak (Rummond), Fred Lazarus (Houghton), John MacKane (Michaelson), Susan Kay Monts (Laura), Gene Morra (Vitale/Smith), John A. Murray (Spencer), Patty O'Brien (Nurse Ryan), Harvey Pierce (McCabe), Carol Poppenger (Mrs. Smith), Henry J. Quinn (Hudson), Jeff Rubin (Ferguson), Don Sharton (Gordon), Stanley Taub (Dr. Wren), Melissa Thea (Dorothy)

Bert Bach Photo

THE BOOR by Anton Chekhov; Adapted by Louise Henry; Director, Will Lieberson. CAST: Therese Letendre (Mrs. Popov), John Cloke (Luka), Jeffrey Spolan (Smirnov), Charles Gonzalez (Fyodor)
BEDTIME STORY by Sean O'Casey; Director, Carole Warwick. CAST: Gisli Jonsson (John Jo Mulligan), Maureen Tilyou (Angela Nightingale), Don Smith (Dan Halibut), Ruby Payne (Miss Mossie), Charles Gonzalez (Policeman), John Cloke (Doctor), Diane Hammarth (Nurse)

QUAIGH THEATRE

Tuesday, September 18,–October 7, 1979 (18 performances)*
THE OFFICE MURDERS by Martin Fox; Director, Kimothy Cruse; Set, Bob Phillips; Costumes, Amanda J. Klein; Sound, George Jacobs; Lighting, Mal Sturchio; Technical Director, Derald Plumer; Stage Managers, Irene Klein, Alan Preston, Doug Sheppard; Press, Max Eisen, Francine L. Trevens; Presented by Will Lieberson, Albert Brower
CAST: Austin Pendleton (Jack), Bob McDonald (Maury), Joel Crothers (Howard), Laura Gardner (Barbara).

A comedy-drama performed without intermission. The action takes place at the present time on a hot weekend afternoon.

* Re-opened Friday, Nov. 9, 1979 at Theatre East with Harry Reems as Jack, and presented by Jeffrey Altshuler.

Ken Howard Photo

QUAIGH THEATRE

January 30–March 1, 1980 (24 performances)*
Will Lieberson presents:

MECCA

By E. A. Whitehead; Director, Kevin Conway; Set, Bob Phillips; Lighting, Marie Barrett; Costumes, Sam Fleming; Sound, Gary Massey; Assistant Director, Marjorie Horne; Dialect Coach, Robert Williams; Technical Director, Derald Plummer; Assistants to Director, Nancy Panzarella, Gillian Marshall; Stage Managers, Rita Calabro, Tracy Cohen; Press, Max Eisen, Francine L. Trevens

CAST

Shelby Brammer (Sandy), Gil Rogers (Andrew), Holly Barron (Jill), Mila Burnette (Eunice), Christopher Curry (Ian), Stephen D. Newman (Martin), Larin Yalkowsky (Boy), Arnaldo Santana (Ahmed)

A drama in 2 acts and 4 scenes. The action takes place in the recent past in the suntrap of a hotel located on the outskirts of a small Moroccan town.

* Re-opened Friday, May 2, 1980 and played 32 additional performances. Gil Rogers was succeeded by Joseph Daly.

Ken Howard Photo

Top right: Eva Charney, Jeff Rubin in "Men in White" Below: Joel Crothers, Bob McDonald, Laura Gardner, Harry Reems in "Office Murders"

QUAIGH THEATRE
LUNCHTIME SERIES

December 11, 1979–January 18, 1980: KRAPP'S LAST TAPE by Samuel Beckett; Directed by Mary Tierney; Performed by William Hickey. February 25–March 7, 1980: SANDCASTLE by Barbara Allan Hite; Director, R. C. Lawson; Performed by Michael Norman, Jan Dorn, Buzz Witherell, Joel Weiss, Sara Jackson, Caroline Abady, Julianne Ross. March 10–21, 1980: WHITMAN SONATA: II SPECIMEN DAYS by Paul Hilderbrand, Jr. and Thom Wagner; Director, Robert Graham Small; Performed by Patty O'Brien, Lloyd Davis, Thomas Simpson, Susan Waring, Jerry Whiddon. April 14–25, 1980: PAINTING A WALL by David Lan. May 12–23, 1980: GERANIUM by Knox Turner; Director, Tri Garraty; Performed by Elaine Eldridge, Christopher Marcantel, George Mead. May 27–June 6, 1980: DRUMS by Margot Welch; Director, Carole Warwick; performed by Mel Barnard, Robert O'Gorman, Sallyanne Tackus, Margot Welch.

Above: Stephen D. Newman, Christopher Curry, Mila Burnette in "Mecca"

155

ROUNDABOUT THEATRE

Gene Feist   Michael Fried
Producing Directors
Fourteenth Season

Assistant to Producing Directors, Arthur Pearson; Technical Director, Philip Giller; Composer-Musical Director, Philip Campanella; Costume Supervisor, Shelly Friedman; Stage Managers, Morton Milder, Rita Ribbins, Holley Jack Horner; Production Assistants, Ray Kornfeld, Mitch Silver; Wardrobe, Wendy Garson; Business Manager, Patricia Yost; Press, Susan Bloch & Co., Ted Goldsmith

ROUNDABOUT STAGE TWO

Tuesday, June 26,–July 8, 1979 (81 performances)
Roundabout Theatre Company presents:

LITTLE EYOLF

By Henrik Ibsen; Adapted and Directed by Gene Feist; Scenery, Reagan Cook; Lighting, Robert Strohmeier; Costumes, Debra Stein; Original Score, Philip Campanella; Stage Manager, Holly Jack Horner

CAST

Asta . . . . Julia MacKenzie
Rita. . . . . Concetta Tomei
Alfred. . . . . Ross Petty
Little Eyolf . . . . Jacob Tanenbaum
The Ratwife. . . . . Elizabeth Owens
Borghejm . . . . John Blazo

A drama in 2 acts and 3 scenes. The action takes place in Alfred and Rita Allmer's home, near a fjord, 12 or so kilometers outside of Christiania, Norway, in late summer of 1894.

Peter Krupenye Photos

John Blazo, Julia MacKenzie, Ross Petty, Concetta Tomei, Elizabeth Owens, Jacob Tanenbaum in "Little Eyolf"

ROUNDABOUT STAGE ONE

Opened Tuesday, September 11, 1979.*
Roundabout Theatre Company presents:

DIVERSIONS AND DELIGHTS

By John Gay; Director, Joseph Hardy; Scenery, Reagan Cook; Lighting, Norman Coates; Costumes, Noel Taylor

CAST
Vincent Price as Oscar Wilde

The setting is a concert hall on the Rue de la Pepinier, Paris, France, in 1899.

*Closed Oct. 14, 1979 after 40 performances, and returned for 6 additional performances from Oct. 31 through Nov. 4, 1979.

Left: Vincent Price

ROUNDABOUT STAGE ONE

Opened Tuesday, October 16, 1979.*

LETTERS OF LOVE AND AFFECTION
with
IRENE WORTH

Letters selected by Miss Worth include those of Queen Elizabeth I, Jonathan, Theon II, Alexander Pope, Franz Joseph Hayden, Abraham Lincoln, Victor Hugo, Zelda Fitzgerald, James Joyce, Napoleon I, Benjamin Franklin, Jean Anthelme Brillat-Savarin, Sarah Bernhardt, Groucho Marx, Lord Byron, Allegra Byron, From a Friend's Family Papers, Anonymous Captain, John Newton, Maria Perkins, Spicer to Laura Spicer, Elsie Leslie, Mark Twain, Helen Keller, Wolfgang Amadeus Mozart, Johannes Brahms, Beatrix Potter, Oscar Wilde, Anton Chekhov, Louisa May Alcott, Albert Einstein, Giorgio Vasari

Presented in two parts. Lighting by Jason Kantrowitz.

* Closed October 28, 1979 after limited engagement of 16 performances. Returned for 8 additional performances Nov. 6–11, 1979.

Irene Worth

ROUNDABOUT STAGE TWO
Opened Tuesday, November 6, 1979.*

THE DARK AT THE TOP OF THE STAIRS

By William Inge; Director, John Stix; Set, Philipp Jung; Costumes, Jim Lowe; Lighting, Todd Elmer; Sound, Vernon Trapp; Technical Coordinator, Steven Boyle; Stage Manager, Lewis Rosen

CAST

Rubin Flood	Earl Hindman
Cora Flood	Dorothy Tristan †
Sonny Flood	Adrian Curran or Shepherd Frankel
Reenie Flood	Lory Nurenberg
Flirt Conroy	Katherine Cortez
Morris Lacey	Joe Ponazecki
Lottie Lacey	Patricia Sales
Sammy Goldenbaum	Gilbert Cole
Punky Givens	Peter Burch

A drama in three acts. The action takes place during early spring of the 1920's in the home of Rubin Flood in a small Oklahoma town.

* Closed January 20, 1980 after 92 performances.
† Succeeded by. Gloria Hoye

Peter Krupenye Photos

Top Right: Earl Hindman, Lory Nurenberg, Shepherd Frankel, Dorothy Tristan in "The Dark at the Top of the Stairs"

ROUNDABOUT STAGE ONE
Opened Friday November 23, 1979.*

A MONTH IN THE COUNTRY

By Ivan Turgenev; Translated by Ariadne Nicolaeff; Director, Michael Kahn; Scenery, Lawrence King, Michael H. Yeargan; Costumes, Jane Greenwood; Lighting, Todd Elmer; Stage Manager, Morton Milder

CAST

Natalya, Arkady's wife	Tammy Grimes
Mikhail Rakitin, friend of the family	Farley Granger
Herr Shaaf, German tutor	Clement Fowler
Anna, Arkady's mother	Bette Henritze
Liza, Anna's companion	Jane Cronin
Kolya, Arkady's son	Thor Fields
Aleksei Belyayev, Russian tutor	Boyd Gaines †1
Matvey, a servant	Paul Walker
Shpigelsky, the doctor	Philip Bosco †2
Vera, Natalya's ward	Amanda Plummer †3
Arkady Islayev, a wealthy landowner	Jerome Kilty †4
Katya, a servant	Katie Grant
Bolshintsov, a neighbor	Haskell Gordon

A comedy in 2 acts and 6 scenes. The action takes place during the early 1840's on Arkady Islayev's estate.

* Closed April 5, 1980 after 155 performances.
† Succeeded by: 1. Kelsey Grammer, 2. Roy Cooper, 3. Kristin Griffith, 4. Fred Sadoff

Martha Swope Photos

Right Center: Amanda Plummer, Tammy Grimes in "A Month in the Country"

Boyd Gaines, Farley Granger, Tammy Grimes

157

ROUNDABOUT STAGE TWO
January 22–April 13, 1980 (98 performances)

THE BLOOD KNOT

By Athol Fugard; Director, Suzanne Shepherd; Scenery, Roger Mooney; Lighting, Norman Coates; Costumes, Shelly Friedman; Sound, Philip Campanella; Assistant to Director, Carol Katz; Production Assistants, Robin Karfo, Evan Shepherd, Brent Thompson, Thomas Clewell, Michael Gennaro, Laura Mosedale, Irwin Stern, Ron Taffel, Kate Shepherd; Stage Manager, Richard S. Viola; Press, Susan Bloch & Co.

CAST

Morris .... Cotter Smith
Zachariah............................ Danny L. Glover

A drama in 3 acts and 6 scenes. The action takes place in Korsten, South Africa.

Peter Krupenye Photo

Left: Danny L. Glover, Cotter Smith in "The Blood Knot"

ROUNDABOUT STAGE ONE
April 15–May 24, 1980 (48 performances)

HEARTBREAK HOUSE

By George Bernard Shaw; Director, George Keathley; Scenery, Roger Mooney; Costumes, Andrew B. Marlay; Lighting, Norman Coates; Sound, Philip Campanella; Production Assistants, T. J. Turgeon, Jim Robertson; Stage Manager, M. R. Jacobs; Press, Susan Bloch, Bill Rudman, Adrian Bryan-Brown

CAST

Rachel Gurney (Hesione Hushabye), Frank Hamilton (Capt. Shotover), Louise Troy (Lady Utterword), Michael Lipton (Hector Hushabye), David Sabin (Boss Mangan), Stephen Daley (Burglar), Barbara Lester (Nurse Guinness), Robert Moberly (Randall Utterword), Robert Nichols (Mazzini Dunn), Giulia Pagano (Ellie Dunn)

A comedy in three acts. The action takes place in a room in Captain Shotover's house in Sussex, England, and in the garden.

Peter Krupenye Photo

Right: Louise Troy, Frank Hamilton, Rachel Gurney in "Heartbreak House"

ROUNDABOUT STAGE TWO
April 22–July 20, 1980 (104 performances)

FALLEN ANGELS

By Noel Coward; Director, Stephen Hollis; Set, Roger Mooney; Costumes, Andrew B. Marlay; Lighting, Norman Coates; Sound, Philip Campanella; Assistant to Director, Mitzi Metzl-Pazer; Production Assistant, Victoria Grecki; Stage Manager, Michael S. Mantel; Press, Susan Bloch, Bill Rudman, Adrian Bryan-Brown

CAST

Julius Sterroll .... Jo Henderson[†1]
Fred Sterroll .... John Clarkson
Saunders .... Beulah Garrick
Willy Banbury .... Jim Osyter[†2]
Jane Banbury .... Carol Teitel
Maurice Duclos .... Stephen Schnetzer

A comedy in three acts. The action takes place during the 1920's in the dining-drawing room of the Sterrolls' flat in London.

† Succeeded by: 1. Valerie French, 2. Don Perkins

Susan Cook Photos

Valerie French, Stephen Schnetzer, Carol Teitel in "Fallen Angels"

SOHO REPERTORY THEATRE

Jerry Engelbach, Marlene Swartz, Directors

THE INSECT COMEDY by Josef and Karel Capek; Adapted and Directed by Trueman Kelley; Set, Mark Haack; Costumes, Veronica Curcione; Lighting, Steven Brant; Stage Manager, Brenda Ratliff. CAST: Margot Abbott, Rory Gerstle, Stephen Hamilton, Arthur Hanket, Beata Jachulski, Randy Knolle, Laura Livingston, Barbara Miller, Alex Mustelier, Charles Stafford (16 performances)

THE CANNIBALS by George Tabori; Director Carol Corwen; Music, Lois Britten; Set and Lights, Michael Gallagher; Costumes, Deborah Friedman; Assistant Director-Stage Manager, Lucy Hood. CAST: Lois Britten, Paul Michael Cassidy, Dustin Evans, Phil Garfinkel, Kevin Martin, Rick Montgomery, Burton Rosenburg, Fred Shanley, Victor Slezak, Daniel Snow, Jeff Ungerson (16 performances)

THE BARBER OF SEVILLE by Pierre-Augustin Caron de Beaumarchais; Translated by Albert Bermel; Director, Alison Mackenzie; Music, Jim Ragland; Costumes, Sally Lesser, Kathleen Smith; Set, Loy Arcenas; Lighting, Carol Corwen; Assistant Director, Virlana Tkacz; Stage Manager, Martin Smith. CAST: Jeff Avick, Roy Clyde Baldo, Richard DiPietra, Zivia Flomenhaft, Brooks McKay, Joe Polivy, George Weiss (16 performances)

WE HAVE ALWAYS LIVED IN THE CASTLE by Hugh Wheeler, from the novel by Shirley Jackson; Director, Gene Santarelli; Set, Rob Hamilton; Costumes, Deborah Friedman; Lighting, Stephen P. Edelstein; Stage Manager, Toby Mailman. CAST: Pamela Barone, Patrick Crea, Ginger Grace, Patrick Hazelwood, Paul Kazanoff, Elisa London, Mary Palmer (16 performances)

TWELFTH NIGHT by William Shakespeare; Director, Steven Brant; Set, Arthur Spero; Costumes, Veronica Curcione; Lighting, Karen Singleton; Assistant Director, Ann Egbert; Stage Manager, Andrea Christensen; Music, Gwyl O'Dell. CAST: Paul Michael Cassidy, Stephen DeStefano, Bill Doonan, Randy Knolle, Bert Kruse, Jorie Marlin, Barbara Miller, Julia C. Murray, Alan Nebelthau, Michael C. Patterson, Robert Toperzer (12 performances)

THE SECOND MAN by S. N. Behrman; Director, Jude Schanzer; Set, Ronald Placzek; Costumes, Amanda J. Klein; Lighting, Faith E. Baum; Assistant Director-Stage Manager, Marnie Powers. CAST: Jack L. Davis, Cassandra Lawyer, Aaron Lustig, Siri Wannamaker (12 performances)

FEATHERTOP by Nathaniel Hawthorne; Adapted by Trueman Kelley; and THE UGLY DUCKLING by A. A. Milne; Director, Trueman Kelley; Set, Rob Hamilton; Costumes, K. L. Fredericks; Lighting, Mark Weingartner; Sound, Kathleen King; Assistant Director, Erin Blackwell; Stage Manager, Lisa Kirsch. CAST: Mary Ewald, Joan Golomb, Ken Kessler, Michael Knight, John Miglietta, Barbara Miller, Nathan Tamarin (14 performances)

BREWSIE AND WILLIE by Gertrude Stein; Adapted by Ellen Violett, Lisabeth Blake; and HOME FRIES by John Guare; Director, Michael Bloom; Set, Rob Hamilton; Costumes, Gail Brassard; Lighting, Mark Weingartner; Sound, Kathleen King; Musical Arrangements, Jerry Engelbach; Assistant Director/Stage Manager, Marti Kovach. CAST: Jonathan Chappell, Jean Hackett, Kevin McGuire, Michael Quill, Alan Schack, James Scholfield, Eileen Schuyler, Charles Stramiello, Nancy Ward (13 performances)

THE GAMBLERS by Nikolai Gogol; Adapted by Penelope Hirsch; Director, Penelope Hirsch; and OLD POSSUM'S BOOK OF PRACTICAL CATS by T. S. Eliot; Adapted and Directed by Jonatha Foster; Music, Elyse Goodwin; Choreography, Selby Beebe, Peg Evans; Sets, Michael J. Gallagher; Lighting, Karen Singleton; Costumes, Esther M. Bialobroda; Musical Director, Michael Ward; Stage Managers, Martin Smith, Mitchell Haymes. CAST: Bill Bartlett, Jonathan Chappell, Gentry Clark, Martha Ferris, Bill Fitzgerald, Zivia Flomenhaft, John Goodwin, Chuck Hall, Pauline Kelly, Art Kempf, Bill Roice, Robert Sanders (14 performances)

THE PARTY by Slawomir Mrozek; Translated by Nicholas Bethell; and THE TRICYCLE by Fernando Arrabal; Translated by Barbara Wright; Director, Carol Corwen; Sets, Michael J. Gallagher; Costumes, Deborah Friedman; Lighting, Karen Singleton; Sound, Kathleen King; Assistant Director, Erin Blackwell; Stage Manager, Andrea Christensen. CAST: Ann Barrett, Daniel Holmberg, Alan Nebelthau, Michael Patterson, George Sand (13 performances)

THE LIFE AND DEATH OF TOM THUMB, THE GREAT, OR THE TRAGEDY OF TRAGEDIES by Henry Fielding; Director, Anthony Bowles; Music, Anthony Bowles; Set, Michael J. Gallagher; Costumes, David Bess; Lighting, Mary Jo Dondlinger; Assistant Director, Antoinette B. Nebel; Stage Manager, Dede Miller. CAST: Jackie Berger, Victor Caroli, Erick Devine, Daryl Hunt, Don Johanson, Cassandra Lawyer, Mark Raymond, Robert S. Ryan, Eileen Schuyler, Diane Seymour, Zeke Zaccaro (16 performances)

THE CARETAKER by Harold Pinter; Director, Marlene Swartz; Set, Peter Byrne; Costumes, Deborah Friedman; Lights, Mary Jo Dondlinger; Assistant Director, Peter Byrne; Stage Manager, Lisa Kirsch. CAST: Jonathan Chappell, Mark Keeler, Joe White (16 performances)

FAIRY TALES OF NEW YORK by J. P. Donleavy; Director, Jerry Engelbach; Set, Valerie Kuehn; Costumes, Jim Lowe; Lighting, Ronald M. Katz; Slides, Sally Sherwood, Jerry Engelbach; Assistant Director-Stage Manager, Joanna M. Smith. CAST: Jerry Engelbach, Pat Freni, Karen Jones, W. T. Martin, Peter Waldren (16 performances)

Top Right: Zivia Flomenhaft, Roy Clyde Baldo, Brooks McKay in "Barber of Seville" Below: Jerry Engelbach, Peter Waldren, Karen Jones in "Fairy Tales of New York" *(Sally Sherwood Photos)*

Above: Joe White, Jonathan Chappell, Mark Keeler in "The Caretaker"

SEPARATE THEATRE COMPANY
James Harter, Artistic Director

JAN HUS CHURCH
September 7–30, 1979 (12 performances)
ARMS AND THE MAN by George Bernard Shaw; Director, James Harter; Lighting, Karen Singleton; Technical Assistant, Sandra L. Burge; Stage Manager, Vida Cohen. CAST: Susan J. Baum (Raina), James Caulfield (Petkoff), Rory Lance (Officer), Susan C. Lloyd (Catherine), Timothy Minor (Bluntschli), Michael Nobel (Sergius), Rob Pherson (Nicola), Julie Ramaker (Louka)

October 12–November 4, 1979 (12 performances)
UNCLE VANYA by Anton Chekhov; Director, Anne Lucas; Costumes, Sydney Brooks; Lighting, Helen Anne Gatling; Set, Richard Singer; Stage Manager, Howard Kolins. CAST: Susan J. Baum (Sonya), Robert C. Brandt (Astrov), James Guido (Labourer), James Harter (Vanya), Betsy Johnson (Yelena), Rory Lance (Telyegin), Susan C. Lloyd (Marina), Lee Owens (Serebryakov), Julie Ramaker (Marya)

November 23–December 16, 1979 (12 performances)
TWELFTH NIGHT by William Shakespeare; Director, James Harter; Set, Richard Singer; Costumes, Richard Schurkamp; Lighting, Helen Anne Gatling; Original Music, E. Vicki Ellis; Stage Manager, Marty Kovach. CAST: Robert C. Brandt (Malvolio), James Caulfield (Sir Toby), Richard Costabile (Sebastian), Alph Edwards (Sea Captain/Priest), Larry Fishman (Sir Andrew), James Guido (Valentine/Officer), Bruce Kronenberg (Antonio), Erin Lamb (Servant), Rory Lance (Feste), Therese Land (Maria), Susan C. Lloyd (Viola), Anne Lucas (Curio), Lee Owens (Orsino), Julie Ramaker (Olivia), Victor Vead (Fabian)

January 4–27, 1980 (12 performances)
HEDDA GABLER by Henrik Ibsen; Director, Robert C. Brandt; Set, Richard Singer; Costumes, Sydney Brooks; Stage Manager, James Harter. CAST: Susan J. Baum (Miss Tesman), Eileen Desmond (Berte), Larry Fishman (Judge Brack), Susan C. Lloyd (Hedda), Anne Lucas (Thea), Lee Owens (Tesman), Victor Vead (Lovborg)

February 8–March 2, 1980 (12 performances)
THE SEA GULL by Anton Chekhov; Director, James Harter; Set, Leo Gambacorta; Costumes, Sydney Brooks; Lighting, Larry Johnson; Stage Manager, Liza Kercheval. CAST: Susan J. Baum (Nina), Robert C. Brandt (Treplev), James Caulfield (Trigorin), Vincent Christina (Yakov), Rory Lance (Medvedenko), Susan C. Lloyd (Irina), Timothy G. McInerney (Sorin), Lee Owens (Dorn), Julie Ramaker (Masha), Sandra Soehngen (Polina), Victor Vead (Shamraev)

March 14–30, 1980 (12 performances)
THE MISER by Moliere; Director, Howard J. Kolins; Sets and Lighting, Leo Gambacorta; Costumes, Richard Schurkamp; Stage Manager, Erin Lamb. CAST: Vincent Christian (Simon/La Merluche/Anselm), Larry Fishman (Harpagon), John Forte (Brindavoine/Officer), James Harter (Cleante), Erin Lamb (Dame Claude), Rory Lance (Jacques), Colleen Ledig (Elise), Lee Owens (Valere), Julie Ramaker (Mariane), Sandra Soehngen (Frosine), Victor Vead (La Fleche)

Betsy Johnson, Susan J. Baum, Julie Ramaker, Rory Lance, Susan Lloyd, Lee Owens, James Harter in "Uncle Vanya"

THEATRE-OFF-PARK
Patricia Flynn Peate, Executive Director
Jeffrey Solis, General Manager

THEATRE-OFF-PARK
October 27,–November 11, 1979 (12 performances)
PUCK AND THE MAGIC FLOWER adapted from Shakespeare's "A Midsummer Night's Dream"; Music, Leon Odenz; Lyrics, Nick DeNoia; Additional Lyrics, Anthony Calabrese; Adapted by Ken Berman, Leon Odenz; Director, Jamie Brown; Choreography, Laurie Brongo; Magic Consultant, Jack Neubeck; Lighting, Michael Newton-Brown; Stage Manager, Maria Petrera; Production Assistants, Tamara Block, Yvonne Nelson; Press, Anita Kroll. CAST: Laurie Brongo (Titania), Erick Devine (Bottom), Maria Ferrari (Allete), John Paul Moccia (Oberon), Michael Smit (Puck)

November 21–December 8, 1979 (13 performances)
GIVE MY REGARDS TO LEICESTER SQUARE conceived by Dean Burris, Clif Dowell; Musical Supervision and Arrangements, Dean Burris; Director, Clif Dowell; Narration, Bruce Vernon Bradley; Choreography, Helen Baldassare; Costumes, Lare Schultz, Bob Thompson; Set, Clif Dowell, Dean Burris; Lighting, Richard Dorfman; Costumes, Helen Baldassare; Set, Ronn Tonbaugh, Tamara Block, Yvonne Nelson; Stage Manager, Tamara Block. CAST: Neal Arluck, Helen Baldassare, Bruce Vernon Bradley, Dean Burris, Clif Dowell, Ernest Lehrer, Joanna Seaton, Richard Dorfman

January 25,–February 16, 1980 (14 performances)
RICOCHET by Paul S. Nathan; Director, Jay Stephens; Lighting, John Senter; Set, Terry Ariano; Costumes, Ann Sehrt; Stage Manager, Tamara Bock. CAST: Carla Charny, William Gibberson, Brian Kosnik, Ed Merullo, Adelle Reel, Robyn Reeves

February 22–23, 1980 (2 performances)
EDNA ST. VINCENT MILLAY through her poetry, letters and satiric writings; Director, Rod Clavery; Arranged, Written and Performed by Dolores McCullough; Costumes, Angeliki Varelakis; Set, Tamara Block; Lighting, Jeffrey Solis

February 28,–March 15, 1980 (12 performances)
OUT OF OUR MIMES with the New York Pantomime Theatre (Moni Yakim, Artistic Director); Lighting, Lisa Grossman; Costumes, Mina Menuha Yakim, Cheryl Blalock; Masks, Lois Bohovesky; Cards, Charlotte Davis Jambeck; Technical Director-Stage Manager, Larry Berman. CAST: Marilyn Galfin, Tony Lopresti, Lindanell Rivera, Joseph Zwerling

March 26,–April 19, 1980 (16 performances; Moved to Broadway May 25, 1980)
OF THE FIELDS, LATELY by David French; Director, Jamie Brown; Set, J. Robin Modereger; Lighting, Richard Dorfman; Costumes, Dolores Gamba; Stage Manager, Broooke Allen. CAST: Christopher W. Cooper, William B. Cain, Mary Fogarty, John Leighton

May 14,–June 7, 1980 (16 performances)
ERNEST IN LOVE based on Oscar Wilde's "The Importance of Being Earnest"; Book and Lyrics Anne Croswell; Music, Lee Pockriss; Director, Jay Stephens; Musical Direction, Deborah Lapidus; Stage Manager, Tamara Block, Lighting, David Crist. CAST: Dan Ahearn, Susan Bigelow, Virginia Downing, Kathleen Grennon, Alexander Korff, Jack Kyrieleison, Doreen Richardson, Barbara Surosky, Geri Winbarg, Ray Xifo

Dan Ahearn, Susan Bigelow in "Ernest in Love" *(Stanford Golob Photo)*

THE WRITERS THEATRE

Linda Laundra, Artistic Director

AMDA STUDIO ONE
June 1–17, 1979 (12 performances)
THE UNDERLINGS by Thomas M. Fontana; Director, John Valente; Sets, Duke Durfee; Costumes, Judith Fauvell; Press, Helene Davis. CAST: Dottie Dee, John Hammond, Doug James, Bram Lewis, P. A. Weber

NAMELESS THEATRE
April 3–20, 1980 (15 performances)
MY OWN STRANGER adapted from the writings of Anne Sexton by Linda Laundra and Marilyn Esper; Director, Linda Laundra; Costumes, R. C. Meyers; Lighting, David Laundra; Settings, Steve Westfield; Press, Keith Sherman. CAST: Marilyn Esper, Nancy-Elizabeth Kammer, Colby Willis

April 24–May 11, 1980 (15 performances)
MOVIN' MOUNTAINS by Thomas M. Fontana. Director, John P. Whitesell II; Setting and Lighting, Steve Westfield; Costumes, Judith Fauvell; Press, Keith Sherman. CAST: Sal Carollo, Jo Deodato Clark, Ralph De Lia, Marcia Magus.

David Laundra Photos

Marcia Magus, Sal Carollo, Jo Deodato Clark, Ralph DeLia in "Movin' Mountains"

YORK PLAYERS COMPANY

Janet Hayes Walker, Artistic Director

CHURCH OF THE HEAVENLY REST
November 16–December 2, 1979 (16 performances)
THE GRASS HARP based on the novel by Truman Capote; Book and Lyrics, Kenward Elmslie; Music, Claibe Richardson; Director, Janet Hayes Walker; Musical Director, Eileen LaGrange; Choreographer, Jon Engstrom; Scenery, James Morgan; Costumes, Robert W. Swasey; Lighting, Brian MacDevitt; Technical Directors, Sally Smith, James Bush; Stage Manager, Molly Grose, Martita DeWitt, Janet Stott. CAST: Geordie Austen (Bubber), Chris Blau (Burma Shave), I. Mary Carter (Verena), W. P. Dremak (Dr. Ritz), Dyllan McGee (Juicy Fruit), Gigi McHugh (Maude), Carolyn Miller (Catherine), Jeff Muldoon (Collin), Donna Pelc (Babylove), Jan Pessano (Dolly), Stuart Sclater-Booth (Dr. Pepper), Tristine Schmukler (Dixiecup), Ralph David Westfall (Amos), Don Woodman (Judge Cool)

January 11–27, 1980 (12 performances)
THE SUBJECT WAS ROSES by Frank D. Gilroy; Director, Joseph Stockdale; Set, James Morgan; Costumes, Robert W. Swasey; Lighting, Brian MacDevitt; Technical Director, Sally Smith; Stage Manager, Molly Grose. CAST: John Newton (John Cleary), Janet Hayes (Nettie Cleary), Tom Flagg (Timmy Cleary)

March 14–April 4, 1980 (19 performances)
ANYONE CAN WHISTLE with Book by Arthur Laurents; Music and Lyrics, Stephen Sondheim; Director, Fran Soeder; Musical Director, Eric Stern; Choreographer Cal del Pozo; Scenery, James Morgan; Lighting, David Gotwald; Costumes, Teri Rosario; Sound, Joseph D. Sukaskas; Technical Director, Sally Smith; Stage Manager, Molly Grose. CAST: Terry Baughan, David Berk (Magruder), Kermit Brown (Dr. Detmold), Gaylea Byrne (Cora), Catherine Caplin, Stephan DeGhelder (George), Carrie Drosnes (Baby Joan), Ileane Gudell (Mrs. Schroeder), Bill Hastings, Steve Heller, Stephen Hope (John), Suzie Jary, Gary Krawford (Hapgood), Diane Lam, Gail Lohla, Paul Mack, David E. Mallard, Mayla McKeehan, Rosemary McNamara (Fay), Kathy Morath (June), Dale Shields (Martin), Sam Stoneburner (Schub), Gail Titunik, Ralph David Westfall (Cooley)

May 23–31, 1980 (8 performances)
HADRIAN VII by Peter Luke; Director, Janet Hayes Walker; Set, James Morgan; Costumes, Robert W. Swasey; Lighting, David Gotwald; Sound, Joseph D. Sukaskas; Technical Director, Sally Smith; Stage Manager, Molly Grose. CAST: Mark Arnold (Cardinal-Archdeacon), Helen Lloyd Breed (Agnes), Kermit Brown (Jeremiah Sant), I. Mary Carter (Mrs. Crowe), John Cloke (St. Albans), Kenneth Garner (George Arthur Rose), Timothy Hall (Fr. William Rolfe), Edward Howes (French Cardinal/Swiss Guard), John Mawson (2nd Bailiff/Courtleigh), Silas W. Pickering (Rector), Douglas Stark (Berstein), Carl Williams (Ragna)

Tom Flagg, John Newton, Janet Hayes in "The Subject Was Roses" Above: Peter Saputo, Timothy Hall in "Hadrian VII"
J. K. Smith, David Gotwald Photos

Top Left: Gary Krawford, Gaylea Byrne in "Anyone Can Whistle"

161

SULLIVAN STREET PLAYHOUSE
Opened Tuesday, May 3, 1960.*
Lore Noto presents:

THE FANTASTICKS

Book and Lyrics, Tom Jones; Suggested by Edmond Rostand's "Les Romanesques"; Music, Harvey Schmidt; Director, Word Baker; Original Musical Direction and Arrangements, Julian Stein; Designed by Ed Wittstein; Associate Producers, Sheldon Baron, Dorothy Olim, Robert Alan Gold; Assistant Producers, Bill Mills, Thad Noto; Production Assistant, John Krug; Original Cast Album by MGM Records

CAST

The Narrator, El Gallo	Sal Provenza†1
The Girl	Carole-Ann Scott†2
The Boy	Christopher Seppe†3
The Boy's Father	Lore Noto†4
The Girl's Father	Sy Travers†5
The Old Actor	Bryan Hull†6
The Man Who Dies/The Indian	Robert R. Oliver†7
The Mute	Glenn Davish†8
At the piano	Jimmy Roberts
At the harp	Andre C. Tarantiles

UNDERSTUDIES: Glenn Davish (Narrator/Boy), Joan Wiest (The Girl), Sy Travers (The Boy's Father)
MUSICAL NUMBERS: Overture, Try to Remember, Much More, Metaphor, Never Say No, It Depends on What You Pay, Soon It's Gonna Rain, Rape Ballet, Happy Ending, This Plum Is Too Ripe, I Can See It, Plant a Radish, Round and Round, They Were You.

A musical in two acts.

Press: Anthony Noto
Stage Managers: Tom Brittingham, Glenn Davish

* Still playing May 31, 1980. For original production, see THEATRE WORLD Vol. 16.
† During its 20 year run, the following have appeared in the various parts: 1. Jerry Orbach, Gene Rupert, Bert Convy, John Cunningham, Don Stewart, David Cryer, Keith Charles, John Boni, Jack Metter, George Ogee, Tom Urich, Jack Crowder, Nils Hedrick, Robert Goss, Joe Bellomo, Michael Tartel, Donald Billett, Martin Vidnovic, David Rexroad, David Snell, Hal Robinson, Chapman Roberts, David Brummel, Roger Alan Brown, Joseph Galiano, Douglas Clark, Richard Muenz, Joseph Galiano, George Lee Andrews, 2. Rita Gardner, Carla Huston, Liza Stuart, Eileen Fulton, Alice Cannon, Royce Lenella, B. J. Ward, Leta Anderson, Carole Demas, Anne Kaye, Carolyn Mignini, Virginia Gregory, Marty Morris, Sharon Werner, Leilani Johnson, Sarah Rice, Cheryl Horne, Betsy Joslyn, Kathy Vestuto, Kathy Morath, Amy Niles, Debbi McLoed, Joan Wiest, Marty Morris, 3. Kenneth Nelson, Gino Conforti, Jack Blackton, Paul Giovanni, Ty McConnell, Richard Rothbard, Gary Krawford, Bob Spencer, Erik Howell, Steve Skiles, Craig Corneilla, Sam Ratcliffe, Jimmy Dodge, Geoffrey Taylor, Michael Glenn-Smith, Phil Killian, Richard Lincoln, Bruce Cryer, Ralph Bruneau, Jeff Knight, 4. William Larsen, Donald Babcock, George Riddle, Charles Blackburn, Richard A. Kennerson, David Sabin, Philip Baker Hall, Edward Garrabrandt, Lore Noto, Kenneth Kimmins, Tom Lacy, Jay Hampton, Dick Latassa, Richard Kinter, Ray Stewart, Hansford Rowe, Ed Penn, Charles Goff, Charles Welch, Lore Noto, 5. Hugh Thomas, David Vaughan, Charles Blackburn, Charles Goff, John High, Maurice Edwards, John J. Martin, Ray Stewart, Conzalo Madruga, Ken Parker, Jerry Russak, Arthur Anderson, David Vogal, John Martin, John High, Sy Travers, Jack Schmidt, Byron Grant, 6. Thomas Bruce (Tom Jones), Stanley Jay, Jay Hampton, John Heffernan, Ed Gall, Lowry Miller, Gary Nairns, Curt Williams, F. Murray Abraham, Hugh Alexander, Justin Gray, Ron Prather, Frano Geraci, Donald Babcock, Seamus O'Brien, Donald Babcock, George Riddle, Russell Lieb, Elliot Levine, Robert Molnar, 7. George Curley, Robert Worms, Don Pomes, Richard A. Kennerson, Jay Hampton, Curt Williams, Tom Lacy, Ed Garrabrandt, Richard Kuss, Peter Blaxill, Samuel As-said, William McIntyre, James Cook, Donald Babcock, James Cook, Bill Preston, James Cook, Liam O'Begley, James Cook, 8. Blair Stauffer, Richard Thayer, Jake Dengel, James Cook, Frano Geraci, Richard Barrie, Ron Prather, Les Shenkel, Robert Crest, Robert Brigham, Tom Flagg, John Thomas Waite, Douglas Clark, Alan Hemingway

Van Williams Photos

Sy Travers, Christopher Seppe, Carole-Anne Scott, Lore Noto
Above: 20th anniversary cast

PUBLIC/ANSPACHER THEATER
Opened Wednesday, June 14, 1978.*
(Moved December 16, 1978 to Circle in the Square)
Joseph Papp presents:

I'M GETTING MY ACT TOGETHER AND TAKING IT ON THE ROAD

Book and Lyrics, Gretchen Cryer; Music, Nancy Ford; Director, Word Baker; Costumes, Pearl Somner; Lighting, Martin Tudor; Associate Producer, Bernard Gersten; Choreography Assistant, Tina Johnson; Assistant to Director, Thomas Burke; Wardrobe, Barbara Rosenthal, Cynthia Deman; Sound, Gary Massey, Todd McEwen; Production Supervisor, Jason Steven Cohen; Original Cast Album by CSP

CAST

Heather	Gretchen Cryer†1
Joe	Joel Fabiani†2
Alice	Margot Rose†3
Cheryl	Betty Aberlin†4
Jake	Don Scardino†5
Piano	Scott Berry
Guitar	Lee Grayson
Drums	Bob George
Bass and Flute	Dean Swenson†6

UNDERSTUDIES: Nadine Connors, Ann Kaye (Alice/Cheryl), Gene Lindsey (Joe)†7, Michael Ayr (Jake)†8, Betty Aberlin, Anne Kay (Heather)
MUSICAL NUMBERS: Natural High, Smile, In a Simple Way I Love You, Miss America, Strong Woman Number, Dear Tom, Old Friend, Put in a Package and Sold, Feel the Love, Lonely Lady, Happy Birthday

A musical performed without intermission.
General Manager: Robert Kamlot
Company Managers: Noel Gilmore, Roger Gindi
Press: Merle Debuskey, William Schelble
Stage Managers: Marjorie Horne, Andy Lopata, Amy Schecter, Carol Horne

* Still playing May 31, 1980. For original production, see THEATRE WORLD Vol. 35.
† Succeeded by: 1. Virginia Vestoff, Betty Aberlin, Gretchen Cryer, Carol Hall, Betty Buckley, Carol Hall, 2. Steven Keats, George Hosmer, 3. Jackee Harry, Bonnie Strickman, 4. Anne Kaye, Betty Aberlin, 5. Michael Ayr, James Mellon, Mark Buchan, 6. Mark Zeray, 7. Peter Craig, George Hosmer, Greg Salata, Daniel Ziskie, Charles Tachovsky, 8. Mark Buchan, Richard Dunne, Eric Hansen

Susan Cook Photos

Gretchen Cryer, Lee Grayson (foreground), Betty Aberlin, Scott Berry, Bob George, Mark Zeray, Bonnie Strickman, Mark Buchan

CHELSEA WESTSIDE THEATER
Opened Monday, March 22, 1976.*
The Chelsea Theater Center presents the Lion Theatre Company/Playwrights Horizons production of:

VANITIES

By Jack Heifner; Director, Garland Wright; Scenery, John Arnone; Lighting, Patrika Brown; Costumes, David James; Wardrobe, Gertrude Sloan, Barbara Perkins; Associate Producer, James Hart; Presented by Milton Justice; Hairstylist, Patrik D. Moreton

CAST

Kathy	Jane Galloway†1
Mary	Susan Merson†2
Joanne	Kathy Bates†3
Standby: Robin Groves	

A comedy in three acts. The action takes place in 1963 in a gymnasium, 1968 in a sorority house, and in 1974 in the garden of an apartment.

General Manager: Albert Poland
Company Manager: Erik Murkoff
Press: Betty Lee Hunt, Maria Cristina Pucci, James Sapp
Stage Managers: Dan Early, Susana Meyer

* Closed May 27, 1979 and re-opened Tuesday, June 19, 1979. Closed Aug. 3, 1980 after 1785 performances. For original production, see THEATRE WORLD Vol. 32.
† Succeeded by: 1. Cordis Heard, Jane Dentinger, 2. Monica Merryman, Patricia Miller, 3. Sally Sockwell, Sharon Ullrick

Roger Greenawalt Photos

Sally Sockwell, Janet Dentinger, Patricia Miller in "Vanities"

OFF-BROADWAY PRODUCTIONS FROM PAST SEASONS THAT CLOSED THIS SEASON

The Passion of Dracula	9/27/77	7/22/79	718
Getting Out	5/15/79	12/9/79	237

(Failure to submit material necessitated several omissions)

AIN'T MISBEHAVIN'

Based on an idea by Murray Horwitz and Richard Maltby, Jr.; Music, Fats Waller; Conceived and Directed by Richard Maltby, Jr.; Musical Numbers Staged by Arthur Faria; Music Supervision, Luther Henderson; Conductor-Pianist, Shelton L. Becton; Associate Director, Murray Horwitz; Orchestrations and Arrangements, Luther Henderson; Vocal Direction and Arrangements, William Elliott; Set, John Lee Beatty; Costumes, Randy Barcelo; Lighting, Pat Collins; General Manager, Jose Vega; Company Manager, Stephanie S. Hughley; Associate Conductor, Neal Tate; Wardrobe, Martha Stanhope; Technical Coordinator, Arthur Siccardi; Stage Managers, Joel Tropper, Kenneth Hanson, Aurelio Padron; Press, Bill Evans, Harry Davies, Claudia McAllister; Presented by Emanuel Azenberg, Dasha Epstein, The Shubert Organization, Jane Gaynor and Ron Dante; Still playing May 31, 1980.

CAST

Teresa Bowers
Yvette Freeman
Ben Harney†1
Adriane Lenox†2
Ken Prymus†3

STANDBYS: Celeste Annette Holmes, Yvonne Talton Kersey, Leslie Barlow, Tim Parker, C. E. Smith For musical numbers, see Broadway Calendar, page 71.
† Succeeded by: 1. Lonnie McNeil, 2. Ms. Heaven, 3. Evan Bell. For original Broadway production, see THEATRE WORLD Vol. 34.

Teresa Bowers, Evan Bell, Ms. Heaven, Lonnie McNeil, Yvette Freeman

AIN'T MISBEHAVIN'

Conceived and Directed by Richard Maltby, Jr.; Based on an idea by Murray Horwitz and Richard Maltby, Jr.; Musical Numbers Staged by Arthur Faria; Music Supervision, Luther Henderson; Sets, John Lee Beatty; Costumes, Randy Barcelo; Lighting, Pat Collins; Associate Director, Murray Horwitz; Vocal Direction and Arrangement, William Elliott; Production Supervisor, Clint Spencer; General Manager, Jose Vega; Company Manager, Maria Anderson; Stage Managers, John Andrews, Richard Winnie; Press, Bill Evans, Judi Davidson, Daniel Kephart; Presented by Emanuel Azenberg, Dasha Epstein, The Shubert Organization, Jane Gaynor and Ron Dante; Opened Tuesday, Dec. 11, 1979 at the Aquarius Theatre in Hollywood, Ca., and still playing May 31, 1980.

CAST

Nell Carter
Andre DeShields
Armelia McQueen†1
Jackie Lowe
Ken Page†2

STANDBYS: Zoe Walker, E. G. Roberts, Debra Byrd, Jason Booker, Doug Eskew, Julia Lema For musical numbers, see Broadway Calendar, page 71.
† Succeeded by: 1. Debra Byrd, 2. Ken Prymus. For original Broadway production, see THEATRE WORLD Vol. 34.

Armelia McQueen, Ken Page

Ed Metzger as Einstein

ALBERT EINSTEIN:
The Practical Bohemian

Written by Ed Metzger, Laya Gelff; Director, Laya Gelff; Artistic Coordinator, Sully Boyar; Presented by MC Square Productions; Began tour during November 1979, and still touring May 31, 1980.

Ed Metzger
as
Albert Einstein

A solo performance portraying the character and ideas of Albert Einstein in two acts: The Years in Europe, The Years in America.

ANNIE

Book, Thomas Meehan; Based on "Little Orphan Annie" comic strip; Music, Charles Strouse; Lyrics, Martin Charnin; Director, Mr. Charnin; Choreography, Peter Gennaro; Sets, David Mitchell; Costumes, Theoni V. Aldredge; Lighting, Judy Rasmuson; Musical Direction, Glen Clugston; Dance Arrangements, Peter Howard; Orchestrations, Philip J. Lang; Production Supervisor, Janet Beroza; Assistant Conductor, Steve Hinnenkamp; Wardrobe, Linda Lee; Production Assistants, Mark Miller, Kathy Meehan; General Management, Gatchell & Neufeld; Hairstylist, Charles LaFrance, Ed de Orienzo; Producers, Irwin Meyer, Stephen R. Friedman, Lewis Allen, Peter Crane, Alvin Nederlander Associates, JFK Center, Icarus Productions; Presented by Mike Nichols; Company Managers, Mark Andrews, Morry Efron; Stage Managers, Brooks Fountain, Judith Binus, B. J. Allen, Edward Isser; Press, David Powers, Barbara Carroll; Opened Thursday, March 23, 1978 at O'Keefe Center, Toronto, Canada, and still touring May 31, 1980.

CAST

Annie	Kathy-Jo Kelly†1
Oliver Warbucks	Norwood Smith
Miss Hannigan	Ruth Kobart
Grace Farrell	Jan Pessano†2
Rooster Hannigan	Gary Beach†3
FDR	Sam Stoneburner†4
Lily	Lisa Raggio†5
July	Dara Brown†6
Tessie	April Lerman†7
Pepper	Shelle Monahan†8
Duffy	Alyson Mord†9
Kate	Dana Tapper
Molly	Kristin Williams†10
Sandy	Himself
Bundles McCloskey/Ickes	Gordon Stanley†11
Dog Catcher/Bert Healy/Hull	Stephen Everett†12
Dog Catcher/ Jimmy Johnson/Guard	Edmond Dante
Lt. Ward/Justice Brandeis	Charles Cagle
Sophie/Cecile/Ronnie Boylan	Linda Rios
Drake	John Anania
Mrs. Pugh/Connie Boylan	Linda Lauter†13
Mrs. Greer/Page/Perkins	Lynn Kearney†14
Annette/Bonnie Boylan	Penny Carroll†15
Fred McCracken/Howe	Michael Connolly†16

Alternates: G. Wayne Hoffman, Mimi Wallace

For musical numbers, see Broadway Calendar, page 72. For original production, see THEATRE WORLD Vol. 33.
† Succeeded by: 1. Mary K. Lombardi, 2. Ellen Martin, 3. Bob Morrisey, 4. Stephen Everett, 5. Jacalyn Switzer, 6. Laura Myers, 7. Rache Antill, 8. Courtney Stevens, 9. Melanie Martin, 10. Kristi Coombs, 11. Jim Brett, 12. Jimmy Todkill, 13. Laurel Cronin; !4. Kathleen Marsh, 15. Kerry Hill, 16. Randall Robbins

Martha Swope Photos

Reid Shelton, Marisa Morell

Ruth Kobart, Mary K. Lombardi

ANNIE

For credits, see preceding listing; Musical Direction, Milton Greene; Production Supervisor, Janet Beroza; Associate Conductor, Arthur Greene; Wardrobe, Adelaide Laurino, Robert Daily; Hairstylists, Ted Azar, Jack Mei Ling, Lily Pon; Stage Managers, Elizabeth Caldwell, Bryan Young, Ron Cummins, Lynda N. Lavin; Company Managers, John Corkill, Maria Anderson; Press, David Powers, Barbara Carroll, Stanley Kaminsky; Opened Thursday, June 22, 1978 at the Curran Theatre in San Francisco, Ca., and still touring May 31, 1980.

CAST

Molly	Michele DeCuir
Pepper	Jenny Cihi†1
Duffy	Paula Benedetti†2
July	Lori Kickliter†3
Tessie	Kirstan Sauter†4
Kate	Molly Ringwald†5
Annie	Patricia Ann Patta†6
Miss Hannigan	Jane Connell
Bundles McCloskey/Ickes	David Green
Dog Catcher/Fred McCracken/Guard	Chuck Bergman
Doc Catcher/Bert Healy/Hull	Frank O'Brien
Sandy	Himself
Lt. Ward/Morganthau/Brandies	John J. Fox
Sophie/Mrs. Pugh/Perkins	Toni Lamond
Grace Farrell	Kathryn Boulet†7
Drake	Jack Collins
Mrs. Greer/Connie Boylan	Lisa Robinson
Cecile/Star to Be/Bonnie Boylan	Carol Secretan
Annette/Ronnie Boylan	Frances Asher
Oliver Warbucks	Keene Curtis†8
Rooster Hannigan	Swen Swenson†9
Lily	Connie Danese†10
Jimmy Johnson/Howe	Walter Niehenke
FDR	Tom Hatten

† Succeeded by: 1. Molly Ringwald, Lork Kickliter, 2. Michele Graham, Stacey Morze, 3. Jilla Harrington, Stephanie Ann Levy, 4. Simone Francis, 5. Jessica Newell, Molly Copsey, Nicole Francis, 6. Louanne, Marisa Morell, 7. Lisa Robinson, 8. Reid Shelton, 9. Tom Offt, 10. Dorothy Holland, Linda Lauter
For musical numbers, see Broadway Calendar, page 72.

ANNIE

For credits, see preceding listing; Musical Director, Arthur Greene; Company Managers, Don Joslyn, Sandy Carlson; Stage Managers, Kathleen A. Sullivan, Moose Peting, Chip Neufeld, J. B. Adams; Assistant Conductor, Paul Ford; Wardrobe, Adelaide Laurino, H. Lee Huot, Alan Haller; Press, David Powers, Bruce D. Lynn; Opened Oct. 3, 1979 and still touring May 31, 1980.

CAST

Molly	Ellyn Gale
Pepper	Patti Gilbert
July	Theda Stemler
Tessie	Melissa Betancourt
Kate	Mollie Hall
Annie	Rosanne Sorrentino
Miss Hannigan	Patricia Drylie
Bundles McCloskey/Sound Effects Man/Kaltenborn's Voice/Ickes	Dick Decareau
Apple Seller/Jimmy Johnson/Howe	William McCalry
Dog Catcher/Bert Healy/Honor Guard	David Ardao
Sandy	Moose
Lt. Ward/Fred McCracken/Hull/Brandeis	Charles Rule
Sophie the Kettle/Annette/Star to Be/Ronnie Boylan/Perkins	Kim Creswell
Grace Farrell	Deborah Jean Templin
Drake/Morgenthau	David Wasson
Mrs. Pugh/NBC Page	Jill Harwood
Mrs. Greer/Connie Boylan	Sara Fidler
Cecile/Bonni Boylan	Jill Bosworth
Oliver Warbucks	Harve Presnell
Rooster Hannigan	Michael Leeds
Lily	Katharine Buffaloe
Duffy	Stephanie Wellings
FDR	Jack Denton

Ensemble Alternates: J. B. Adams, Gail Pearson

For musical numbers, see Broadway Calendar, page 72.

Top Right: Harve Presnell, Deborah Jean Templin, Rosanne Sorrentino (Annie), Nealey Gilbert

Harve Presnell, Rosanne Sorrentino, Sandy

Julie Harris as Emily Dickinson

THE BELLE OF AMHERST

By William Luce; Compiled by Timothy Helgeson from the life and works of Emily Dickinson; Director, Charles Nelson Reilly; Scenery and Lighting, H. R. Poindexter; Costume, Theoni V. Aldredge; Presented by Mike Merrick and Don Gregory; Opened Monday, September 24, 1979 in Storrs, Ct., and closed December 9, 1979 in Philadelphia, Pa. For original Broadway production, see THEATRE WORLD, Vol. 32.

CAST

JULIE HARRIS
as Emily Dickinson

A solo performance in two acts. The action takes place in the Dickinson home in Amherst, Massachusetts, from 1845 to 1886.

THE BEST LITTLE WHOREHOUSE IN TEXAS

Book, Larry L. King, Peter Masterson; Music and Lyrics, Carol Hall; Directors, Peter Masterson, Tommy Tune; Musical Numbers Staged by Tommy Tune; Sets, Marjorie Kellogg; Lighting, Beverly Emmons; Costumes, Gary Jones; Musical Supervision, Direction and Vocal Arrangements, Robert Billig; Hairstylist, Michael Gottfried; Sound, William Weingart; Assistant Choreographer, Jerry Yoder; Stage Managers, Jack Welles, Ric Barrett, Joe Gillie; Company Manager, Jo Rosner; Wardrobe, Ellen Anton; General Management, Jack Schlissel, Jay Kingwill; Presented by Universal Pictures; Press, Jeffrey Richards, Warren Knowlton, Marjorie Ornston, Diane Ornston; Opened Tuesday, October 2, 1979 at the Shubert Theatre in Boston, Ma., and still touring May 31, 1980. For original Broadway production, see THEATRE WORLD, Vol. 35.

CAST

Texas Tally Wackers .... Bradley Clayton King, Greg DeBelles, Mark Hummel, John Ciano, Gary Oleyar, Frank D. Wagner
Girls .... Valerie Leigh Bixler, Dolly Colby, Ruth Gottschall, Roxie Lucas, Amy Miller, Deborah Magid, Karen Tamburrelli, Mimi Bessette
Cowboys............ Don Bernhardt, Beau Allen, Davis Gaines
Narrator........................ Bradley Clayton King
Farmer....................................... Andy Parker
Shy Kid/Stage Manager/Cameraman.............. Jeff Calhoun
Miss Wulla Jean/Beatrice .... Roxie Lucas
Traveling Salesman/C. J. Scruggs/TV Announcer/Chip Brewster/-Governor .... Tom Avera
Slick Dude/Leroy Sliney .... Jeffry George
Choir .... Joe Hart, Ruth Gottschall, Robert R. Hendrickson, Deborah Magid, Robert Moyer
Angel .... Rebecca Ann Seay
Shy .... Valerie Austyn
Jewel .... Marilyn J. Johnson
Mona Stangley........................... Alexis Smith
The Girls at Miss Mona's:
    Linda Lou .... Valerie Leigh Bixler
    Dawn .... Mimi Bessette
    Ginger .... Ruth Gottschall
    Beatrice .... Roxie Lucas
    Taddy Jo .... Dolly Colby
    Ruby Rae .... Amy Miller
    Eloise .... Karen Tamburrelli
    Durla .... Deborah Magid
Dogettes.............. Davis Gaines, Andy Parker, Joe Hart, Robert R. Hendrickson
Melvin P. Thorpe .... Larry Hovis
Sheriff Ed Earl Dodd .... William Hardy
Mayor Rufus Poindexter/Senator Wingwoah .... Joseph Warren
Edsel Mackey .... Robert Moyer
Doatsey Mae .... Barbara Marineau
Aggies........ Beau Allen, Robert Hendrickson, Andy Parker, Don Bernhardt, Jeffry George, Davis Gaines, Jeff Calhoun, Joe Hart
Photographers .... Beau Allen, Joe Hart, Jeffry George, Davis Gaines
Reporters .... Barbara Marineau, Beau Allen, Jeff Calhoun
Governor's Aide .... Davis Gaines
    Alternates: Joe Gillie, Pamela Pilkenton,

UNDERSTUDIES: Barbara Marineau (Mona), Robert Moyer (Sheriff/Governor/Senator/Scruggs/Mayor/Announcer), Davis Gaines (Thorpe/Co-Dog), Roxie Lucas (Doatsey/Jewel), Andy Parker (Edsel/Narrator), Karen Tamburrelli (Dawn/Linda), Mimi Bessette (Angel), Dolly Colby (Shy), Amy Miller (Ginger)

For musical numbers, see Broadway Calendar, page 73.

Ilene Jones Photos

Top Right: (from top) Larry Hovis, Alexis Smith, William Hardy, Barbara Marineau, Marilyn J. Johnson in "Best Little Whorehouse in Texas" Below: Dawn Wells, Donald Gantry, David Faulkner, Kathleen Gaffney in "Chapter Two"

CHAPTER TWO

By Neil Simon; Original Direction, Herbert Ross; Re-Staged by Martin Herzer; Scenery, William Ritman; Costumes, Steve Atha; Lighting, Tharon Musser; Production Supervisors, Richard Martini, Jerry R. Moore; Company Manager, Don Joslyn; Stage Managers, Ron Rudolph, Rose Mary Taylor; Wardrobe, Lynn Rowe; Production Associate, David Kerley; General Manager, James Janek; Press, Max Eisen, Sandra Manley, Eileen McMahon; Presented by Tom Mallow in association with James Janek. Opened Sept. 14, 1979 in Norfolk, Va., and closed Apr. 6, 1980 in New Orleans, La. For original NY production, see THEATRE WORLD Vol. 34.

CAST

George Schneider .... David Faulkner
Leo Schneider .... Donald Gantry
Jennie Malone.............................. Dawn Wells
Faye Medwick............................. Kathleen Gaffney
    Understudies: Rose Mary Taylor, Michael Barry Greer

A comedy in two acts. The action takes place at the present time in Jennifer's apartment, and George's apartment, both in New York City.

Gerry Goldstein Photos

A CHORUS LINE

Conceived, Directed and Choreographed by Michael Bennett; Book, James Kirkwood, Nicholas Dante; Music, Marvin Hamlisch; Lyrics, Edward Kleban; Set, Robin Wagner; Costumes, Theoni V. Aldredge; Lighting, Tharon Musser; Sound, Abe Jacob; Co-Choreographer, Bob Avian; Musical Direction, Tom Hancock; Music Coordinator, Robert Thomas; General Manager, Laurel Ann Wilson, Robert Kamlot; Company Managers, Noel Gilmore, Mitzi Harder; Stage Managers, Martin Gold, Robert Kellogg, Tony Parise; Press, Merle Debuskey, Horace Greeley McNab, Ken Monzingo, Margot Duxler; Presented by Joseph Papp and the NY Shakespeare Festival in association with Plum Productions; Opened Tuesday, May 11, 1975 at the Curran Theatre, San Francisco, Ca., and still touring May 31, 1980. For original NY production, see THEATRE WORLD Vol. 31.

Anthony Teague (C)

CAST

Bobby	Michael Austin†1
Al	James Bontempo†2
Kristine	Kerry Casserly
Tom	Rick Conant
Lois	Catherine Cooper†3
Paul	Stephan Crenshaw†4
Greg	Mark Dovey†5
Mike	Rob Draper†6
Vickie	Susie Fenner†7
Butch	Glenn Ferrugiari†8
Don	Tom Fowler†9
Mark	Morris Freed†10
Claude	Ralph Glenmore†11
Richie	Rudy Lowe†12
Diana	Gay Marshall†13
Larry	Calvin McRae†14
Jarad	Stephen Moore
Frank	Brad Moranz†15
Sheila	Rita O'Connor†16
Roy	Tony Parise†17
Tricia	Karen Maris Pisani
Cassie	Wanda Richert†18
Bebe	Tracy Shayne†19
Connie	Sachi Shimizu
Zach	Anthony S. Teague†20
Maggie	Marcia Lynn Watkins†21
Val	Pamela Ann Wilson
Judy	Joanna Zercher†22
Todd	Marshall Hagins†23

† Succeeded by: 1. Matt West, 2. Jack Karcher, 3. Jan Horn Adams, 4. Sammy Williams, 5. Stephen Moore, John DeLuca, 6. Jamie Torcellini, 7. Terri Lombardozzi, 8. Daniel Dee, 9. Dennis Edenfield, Michael Danek, 10. Scott Plank, Brian Andrews, 11. Glenn Turner, 12. Ralph Glenmore, Eugene Fleming, 13. Alison Gertner, 14. Roy Smith, Marshall Hagins, 15. Conley Schnaterbeck, 16. Penelope Richards, 17. John Salvatore, 18. Catherine Cooper, 19. Kathleen Moore, 20. Alec Teague, 21. Stephanie Eley, 22. Jannet Horsley, Thia Fadel, 23. Jerry Mitchell

For musical numbers, see Broadway Calendar, page 74.

Martha Swope Photos

A CHORUS LINE

Conceived, Choreographed and Directed by Michael Bennett; Book, James Kirkwood, Nicholas Dante; Co-choreographer, Bob Avian; Lyrics, Edward Kleban; Music, Marvin Hamlisch; Setting, Robin Wagner; Costumes, Theoni V. Aldredge; Lighting, Tharon Musser; Musical Direction, Sherman Frank; General Manager, Laurel Ann Wilson; Company Manager, Manuel L. Levine; Press, Merle Debuskey, Susanna Rendon; Stage Managers, Tom Porter, Jeff Lee, Eric Horenstein; Assistant Conductor, Kim Bell; A NY Shakespeare Festival Production in association with Plum Productions; Presented by Joseph Papp; Opened Monday, May 3, 1976 at the Royal Alexandra Theatre, Toronto, Can., and still touring May 31, 1980. For original NY production, see THEATRE WORLD Vol. 31.

CAST

Iris	Kenya Benitez†1
Mark	Gregory Brock
Maggie	Pam Cecil†2
Sheila	Susan Danielle
Mike	Rob Draper†3
Kristine	Hilary Fields†4
Lisa	Karen Giombetti†5
Judy	Ganine Giorgione
Scott	Drew Geraci
Bobby	Michael Gorman
Vicki	Ann Heinricher†6
Val	Deborah Henry†7
Roy	Eric Horenstein
Rachel	Marlene Inden
Tom	Brian Kelly†8
Jenny	Kerry Kennedy†9
Al	Clifford Lipson
Richie	Reggie Mack†10
Jarad	Alex Mackay
Don	Tim Millett†11
Butch	Kevyn Morrow
Zach	Ed Nolfi†12
Lois	Peggy Parten†13
Jessica	Tina Paul
Larry	R. J. Peters
Bebe	Debra Pigliavento†14
Cassie	Alyson Reed†15
Diana	Rita Rehn
Paul	Phillip Riccobuono
Gordon	Timm Stetzner
Tricia	Zoe Vonder Haar†16
Greg	James Warren†17
Frank	Matt West†18
Connie	Lily-Lee Wong

† Succeeded by: 1. Thia Fadel, 2. Ann Heinricher, 3. Brian Kelly, 4. Peggy Parten, 5. Kimberly Dawn Smith, 6. Karen Giombetti, 7. Lisa Embs, Mitzi Hamilton, 8. Drew Geraci, 9. Mary C. Holton, 10. Gordon Owens, 11. Matt West, Cory Hawkins, 12. David Thome, 13. Kerry Kennedy, 14. Zoe Vonder Haar, 15. Tina Paul, 16. Marlene Inden, 17. Denny Martin Flinn, 18. Kevin Backstrom
For musical numbers, see Broadway Calendar, page 74.

Martha Swope Photos

"A Chorus Line"

DA

By Hugh Leonard; Director, Melvin Bernhardt; Set, Marjorie Kellogg; Costumes, Jennifer von Mayrhauser; Lighting, Arden Fingerhut; General Manager, Richard Horner; Company Manager, Stanley D. Silver; Stage Managers, Edward R. Fitzgerald, Dorothy French; Wardrobe, Barbara Hladsky; Technical Director, Mitch Miller; Press, Jeffrey Richards, Louis Sica, Ted Kilmer; Presented by Lester Osterman, Marilyn Strauss, Marc Howard; Opened Monday, Sept. 10, 1979 at the Royal Alexandra Theatre in Toronto, Can.; Closed June 28, 1980 at the Colonial Theatre, Boston, Ma.; For original NY production, see THEATRE WORLD Vol. 34.

CAST

Charlie Now	Tom Crawley
Oliver	Dennis McGovern
Da	Barnard Hughes
Mother	Helen Stenborg
Young Charlie	John Didrichsen
Drumm	John Wylie
Mary Tate	Laura Hughes
Mrs. Prynne	Victoria Boothby

STANDBYS: Robert Bridges (Charlie Now/Oliver), Edward McPhillips (Da/Drumm), Tom McCauley (Young Charlie), Alta McKay (Mother/Mrs. Prynne), Dorothy French (Mary Tate)

A comedy in two acts. The action takes place in a kitchen, and places remembered, in May of 1968, and later times remembered.

Ron Berlin Photos

Helen Stenborg, Tom Crawley, John Wylie, Barnard Hughes, John Didrichsen in "Da" Left Center: Jack Aranson, Cynthia Carle, Curtis J. Armstrong in "Da"

DA

By Hugh Leonard; Director, J Danelli; Scenery and Costumes, John Falabella; Lighting, Ken Billington; Production Supervisors, Richard Martini, Jerry R. Moore; General Manager, James Janek; Company Manager, Jay Brooks; Stage Managers, Mark S. Krause, Jan Birse; Wardrobe, Linda Berry; Production Associate, David Kerley; Press, Max Eisen, Irene Gandy; Presented by Tom Mallow in association with James Janek; Opened during September 1979 in Amherst, Ma., and closed in Providence, RI, during March 1980. For original NY production, see THEATRE WORLD Vol. 34.

CAST

Charlie Now	Ian Stuart
Oliver	George Feeney
Da	Jack Aranson
Mother	Virginia Mattis
Young Charlie	Curtis J. Armstrong
Drumm	Kevin O'Leary
Mary Tate	Cynthia Carle
Mrs. Prynne	Mavis Ray

Understudies: Richard Cottrell, Jan Birse

A comedy in two acts. The action takes place in a kitchen, and places remembered, in May of 1968, and later times remembered.

Gerry Goodstein Photo

DAISY MAYME

By George Kelly; Director, William Putch; Scenery, John Kavelin; Costumes, Joan Markert; Lighting, Martin Aronstein; General Manager, Victor Samrock; Company Manager, Robert H. Wallner; Wardrobe, Patricia Risser; Stage Managers, Joe Drummond, Channing Walker; Press, Louise Weiner Ment; Presented by Elliot Martin and Murbill, Inc.; Opened Monday, Oct. 15, 1979 in the Fox Theatre, San Diego, Ca., and closed March 16, 1980 in Birmingham, Al.

CAST

Ruth Fenner	Pamela Putch
Mrs. Laura Fenner	Polly Rowles
Mrs. Olly Kipax	Margaret Hill Ritter
Cliff Mettinger	Rex Robbins
May Phillips	Kristen Lowman
Daisy Mayme Plunkett	Jean Stapleton
Charlie Snyder	Doug Robinson
Mr. Filoon	Wil Love

UNDERSTUDIES: Carl Shurr (Cliff/Filoon), Linde Hayen, Laurie Klatscher (Ruth/May), Channing Walker (Charlie)

A comedy in 2 acts and 4 scenes. The action takes place in a room in the home of Cliff Mettinger in North Philadelphia, Pa., on a Saturday afternoon in early May of 1931.

Jay Thompson Photos

Jean Stapleton, Wil Love, Rex Robbins in "Daisy Mayme"

DANCIN'

A "Musical Entertainment" conceived, directed and choreographed by Bob Fosse; Production Supervisor, Gwen Verdon; Choreography re-created by Kathryn Doby, Christopher Chadman; Scenery, Peter Larkin; Costumes Willa Kim; Lighting/Executive Producer, Jules Fisher; Orchestrations, Ralph Burns; Music arranged and conducted by Gordon Lowry Harrell; Sound, Abe Jacob; Hairstylist, Romaine Green; Presented by Jules Fisher, The Shubert Organization and Columbia Pictures; General Manager, Marvin A. Krauss; Company Manager, Steven E. Goldstein; Wardrobe, Robert Strong Miller, Colleen Gieryn; Assistant Conductor, Don Rebic; Stage Managers, Phil Friedman, Charles Collins, Karen DeFrancis; Press, Merle Debuskey, Bill Wilson; Opened Thursday, Apr. 19, 1979 at the Shubert Theatre in Chicago, Il., and closed May 18, 1980 at the Saenger Center in New Orleans, La.; For original NY production, see THEATRE WORLD Vol. 34.

CAST

Hinton Battle, Sandahl Bergman, Stuart Carey, Gary Chapman, Anita Ehrler, Gary Flannery, Vicki Frederick, Bick Goss, Keith Keen, Frank Maatrocola, Valerie-Jean Miller, Cynthia Onrubia, Valarie Pettiford, Timothy Scott, Charles Ward, Allison Williams, Barbara Yeager, and alternates: Quin Baird, James Horvath, Manette La Chance, Katherine Meloche, Stanley Perryman, Lynn Rempalski Replacements during the tour were Russell Chambers, Andre De La Roche, Ron Dennis, Cecily Douglas, Lois Englund, Penny Fekany, Manette La Chance, Steve La Chance, Fred C. Mann III, Laurie Dawn Skinner, Rima Vetter, Gary Easterling, Lynne Savage, Zelda Pulliam

For musical numbers, see Broadway Calendar, page 75.

Martha Swope Photos

Right: Vicki Frederick, Sandahl Bergman, Valarie Pettiford Top: "I Wanna Be a Dancin' Man" number

DEATHTRAP

By Ira Levin; Director, Philip Cusack; Scenery, William Ritman; Costumes, Ruth Morley; Lighting, Marc B. Weiss; Sound, Christopher K. Bond; Production Supervisors, Richard Martini, Jerry R. Moore; Production Associate, Arthur Katz; General Manager, James Janek; Company Manager, Jay Brooks; Wardrobe, Linda Berry; Stage Managers, Mark S. Krause, Richard Stack; Press, Max Eisen, Barbara Glenn; Presented by Tom Mallow in association with James Janek; Opened during January 1980 in San Jose, Ca., and closed during June 1980 in Los Angeles, Ca. For original NY production, see THEATRE WORLD, Vol. 34.

CAST

Sidney Bruhl	Don Barton
Myra Bruhl	Patricia Guinan
Clifford Anderson	Michael McBride
Helga ten Dorp	Marian Baer
Porter Milgrim	Casper Roos

A "comedy thriller" in 2 acts and 6 scenes. The action takes place at the present time in Sidney Bruhl's study in the Bruhl home in Westport, Ct.

Martha Swope Photo

Donald Barton, Michael McBride in "Deathtrap"

THE ELEPHANT MAN

By Bernard Pomerance; Director, Jack Hofsiss; Setting, David Jenkins; Costumes, Julie Weiss; Lighting, Beverly Emmons; Associate Producers, Ray Larsen, Ted Snowdon; Production Supervisor, Roger Franklin; Company Manager, Paul Holland; Wardrobe, Byron Brice; Assistant to Director, Ethan Silverman; Production Assistant, Jean doPico; Production Coordinator, Scott Steele; Wigs, Paul Huntley; Musical Arrangements, David Heiss; Stage Managers, Robert Bruce Holley, Margaret Hatch; Press, Solters & Roskin, Joshua Ellis, Maurice Turet; Presented by Richmond Crinkley, Elizabeth I. McCann, Nelle Nugent; Opened Monday, Nov. 26, 1979 in the Mechanic Theatre, Baltimore, Md., and still touring May 31, 1980. For original NY production, see THEATRE WORLD, Vol. 35

CAST

Frederick Treves/Belgian Policeman	Ken Ruta
Carr Gomm/Conductor	Richard Neilson
Ross/Bishop How/Snork	Danny Sewell
John Merrick	Philip Anglim†1
Pinhead Manager/Policeman/Will/Lord John	Jeffrey Jones
Pinhead/Miss Sandwich/Princess Alexandra	Etain O'Malley
Mrs. Kendal/Pinhead	Penny Fuller
Orderly	Michael O. Smith†2
Cellist	Richard Sher

STANDBYS AND UNDERSTUDIES: Merrick (Jeff Hayenga), Jeffrey Jones (Policeman/Gomm/Conductor), Etain O'Malley (Mrs. Kendal), Michael O. Smith (Ross/Bishop/Snork/Will/Lord John), Margaret Hatch (Miss Sandwich/Pinhead/Princess), Robert Bruce Holley (Orderly)

A drama in 2 acts and 10 scenes. The action takes place in London between 1886 and 1890.

† Succeeded by: 1. David Bowie, 2. Kensyn Crouch

Philip Anglim, Ken Ruta Top: Anglim, Penny Fuller Left Center: David Bowie

EUBIE!

Conceived and Directed by Julianne Boyd; Music, Eubie Blake; Choreography, Henry LeTang; Musical Supervision and Arrangements, Danny Holgate; Set, Karl Eigsti; Costumes, Bernard Johnson; Lighting, William Mintzer; Musical Direction, William Gregg Hunter; Orchestrations, Neal Tate; Sound, Christopher K. Bond; Hairstylist, Breelun Daniels; Production Supervisors, Richard Martini, Jerry R. Moore; General Manager, James Janek; Press, Max Eisen, Barbara Glenn; Company Manager, Mary Card; Stage Managers, Chuck Linker, Roderick Spencer Sibert, Christopher K. Bond; Wardrobe, Al Costa; Production Assistants, Mary Trudeau, Allison L. Liddle; Production Associate, David Kerley; Presented by Tom Mallow in association with James Janek; Opened during August 1979 in Huntsville, AL, and closed during March 1980 in Providence, For original NY production, see THEATRE WORLD Vol. 35.

CAST

Susan Beaubian, Chris Calloway, Keith Alan Davis, Tony Franklin, Jackee Harry, Marva Hicks, Donna Patrice Ingram, Bernard Manners, Robert Melvin, Francine Claudia Moore, Keith Rozie, Deborah Lynn Sharpe, Roderick Spencer Silbert, Vernon Spencer

MUSICAL NUMBERS: Goodnight Angelin, Charleston Rag, In Honeysuckle Time, I'm Just Wild about Harry, Baltimore Buzz, Daddy, There's a Million Little Cupids in the Sky, I'm a Great Big Baby, My Handyman Ain't Handy No More, Low Down Blues, Gee I Wish I Had Someone to Rock Me in the Cradle of Love, Duet, I'm Just Simply Full of Jazz, High Steppin' Days, Dixie Moon, Weary, Roll Jordan Roll, Memories of You, If You've Never Been Vamped by a Brownskin, You've Got to Git the Gittin While the Gittin's Good, Oriental Blues, I'm Cravin' for That Kind of Love, Hot Feet, Finale

A musical in two acts.

Bert Andrews Photo

"Eubie!" company

EVITA

Lyrics, Tim Rice; Music, Andrew Lloyd Webber; Director, Harold Prince; Choreography, Larry Fuller; Sets, Costumes, Projections, Timothy O'Brien, Tazeena Firth; Lighting, David Hersey; Sound, Abe Jacob; Orchestrations, Hershy Kay, Andrew Lloyd Webber; Musical Supervisor, Rene Wiegert; Music Director, Arthur Rubinstein; Executive Producers, R. Tyler Gatchell, Jr., Peter Neufeld; Presented by Robert Stigwood in association with David Land; General Management, Howard Haines; Press, Mary Bryant, Judi Davidson, Barbara Desatnik; Company Manager, David Wyler; Assistant Musical Director, Seymour Rubenstein; Stage Managers, E. Bronson Platt, Jack Sims, Kenneth W. Urmston, Beverley Randolph; Wardrobe, Dorothy Priest; Hairstylist, Richard Allen, Bob Brophy; Production Assistant, Wilfy Hausam; Opened Sunday, January 13, 1980 at the Shubert Theatre in Los Angeles, and still playing May 31, 1980.

CAST

Eva	Loni Ackerman, Valerie Perri (matinees)
Che	Scott Holmes
Peron	Jon Cypher
Magaldi	Sal Mistretta
Peron's Mistress	Kelli James

PEOPLE OF ARGENTINA: Angela Maria Blasi, Tim Bowman, Mark Bradford, Richard Byron, Jenean Chandler, Harold W. Clousing, Sheri Cowart, Nikki D'Amico, Barbara Dobkin, Karen Elise-Brown, Barry Gorbar, David Gold, Julia Hannibal, Mark Harryman, Barbara Hartman, Mary Ann Hay, Robin-Ann Kay, Kathleen King, Larry Merritt, Sha Newman, Vincent Pirillo, Darlene Romano, David Romano, Michael Alan Ross, Wayne Scherzer, Sharon J. Scott, Jerry Scurlock, Bruce Senesac, Timothy Smith, Roger Spivy, James Stein, Dan Tullis, Jr., Kenneth W. Urmston, Brian Whitaker, Michel Woolworth, Karen Yarmat, and children: Dena Sue Gilmore, Melanie Hyatt, Danny Mortenson, Evan Richards

For MUSICAL NUMBERS see Broadway Calendar, page 17.

Top Right: Scott Holmes
Below: Loni Ackerman, Jon Cypher

Dick Van Dyke, Meg Bussert
in "The Music Man"

THE MUSIC MAN

Book, Music and Lyrics, Meredith Willson; Book in collaboration with Franklin Lacey; Direction and Choreography, Michael Kidd; Sets, Peter Wolf; Costumes, Stanley Simmons; Lighting, Marcia Madeira; Orchestrations, Don Walker; Assistant to Mr. Kidd, Bonnie Evans; Music and Vocal Direction, Milton Rosenstock; Presented by James M. Nederlander, Raymond Lussa, Fred Walker; General Managers, Jack Schlissel, James Walsh; Company Manager, David Hedges; Stage Managers, Conwell S. Worthington II, John M. Galo, Charles Reif; Associate Conductor, Alyce Billington; Wardrobe, Warren Morrill, Ursula Jones; Hairstylist, Dale Brownell; Production Assistant, Jay Binder; Assistant to Mr. Kidd, Randy Doney; Projections, Marcia Madeira; Press, Solters & Roskin, Milly Schoenbaum, Lisa Kasteler, Jack Abrams, Ellen Frey, Kevin Patterson; Opened Thursday, Oct. 18, 1979 at the Sahara in Reno, Nv., and closed May 25, 1980 in Chicago, Il. For original NY production, see THEATRE WORLD Vol. 14.

CAST

Dick Van Dyke (Harold Hill), Meg Bussert (Marian Paroo), Iggie Wolfington (Mayor Shinn), Carol Arthur (Mrs. Paroo), Richard Warren Pugh (Marcellus), Jen Jones (Eulalie MacKechnie Shinn), Jay Stuart (Charlie Cowell), Christina Saffran (Zaneeta Shinn), Calvin McRae (Tommy Djilas), Lara Jill Miller (Amaryllis), Christian Slater (Winthrop Paroo), Ralph Braun (Olin Britt), Marcia Brushingham (Alma Hix), Larry Cahn (Ewart Dunlop), Mary Gaebler (Maude Dunlop), Randy Morgan (Oliver Hix), P. J. Nelson (Ethel Toffelmeier), Mary Roche (Mrs. Squires), Lee Winston (Jacey Squires), Dennis Holland (Constable Locke), and Victoria Ally, Carol Ann Basch, Dennis Batutis, David Beckett, Mark A. Esposito, Tom Garrett, Lisa Gennaro, Andy Hostettler, Tony Jaeger, Wendy Kimball, Ara Marx, Darleigh Miller, Gail Pennington, Rosemary Rado, Michael J. Rockne, Coley Sohn, Peter Wandel, Swings: Alis-Elaine Anderson, J. J. Jepson

MUSICAL NUMBERS: Rock Island, Iowa Stubborn, Trouble, Piano Lesson, Goodnight My Someone, 76 Trombones, Sincere, Sadder-But-Wiser Girl, Pickalittle, Goodnight Ladies, Marian the Librarian, My White Knight, Wells Fargo Wagon, It's You, Shipoopi, Lida Rose, Will I Ever Tell You, Gary Indiana, Till There Was You, Goodnight My Someone, Finale

A musical in 2 acts and 17 scenes. The action takes place in 1912.

NATIONAL SHAKESPEARE CO.
Seventeenth Year

Artistic Director, Philip Meister; Administrative Director, Albert Schoemann; Production Designer, Terry Bennett; Tour Director, Michael Hirsch; Company Manager, Susanne Egli; Stage Managers, Anthony Ridley, Carole Roberts; Opened Oct. 1, 1979 in Poughkeepsie, NY, and closed May 1, 1980 in Kings Point, NY.

CAST

MUCH ADO ABOUT NOTHING by William Shakespeare; Director, Mario Siletti. CAST: Jim Harlan (Leonato), Kathleen Henderson (Hero), Susanne Egli (Beatrice), Carole Roberts (Margaret), Jerry Peters (Borachio), Michael Weddington (Don Pedro), Mitchell Sugarman (Don John), Michael Sigler (Claudio), Julian Bailey (Benedick), Joel Swetow (Seacol/Friar Francis), Erik Maaton (Dogberry), Anthony Ridley (Verges)

JULIUS CAESAR by William Shakespeare; Director, Jerome Guardino. CAST: Julian Bailey (Casca/Cinna), Michael Weddington (Julius Caesar), Susanne Egli (Portia), Jim Harlan (Trebonius/-Messala), Kathleen Henderson (Lucius/Soothsayer), Erik Maaton (Octavius Caesar/Artemidorus), Anthony Ridley (Decius Brutus/-Titinius), Carole Roberts (Calpurnia), Michael Sigler (Marcus Antonius), Mitchell Sugarman (Cinna/Marcus Aemilius Lepidus), Joel Swetow (Marcus Brutus), Jerry Peters (Cassius)

Top: "Much Ado about Nothing"
Right: "Julius Caesar"

ON THE 20th CENTURY

Book and Lyrics, Betty Comden, Adolph Green; Music, Cy Coleman; Director, Ruth Mitchell from the original by Harold Prince; Choreography, Larry Fuller; Assistant Choreographer, Gerald Teijelo; Scenery, Robin Wagner; Costumes, Florence Klotz; Lighting, Ken Billington; Musical Supervision, Paul Gemignani; Orchestrations, Hershy Kay; Musical Director, Jonathan Anderson; Production Associates, Nina Goodman, Edward Merkow, Rick Mandel; Furs, Ben Kahn; Associate Producers, Sam Crothers, Andre Pastoria; Based on plays by Ben Hecht, Charles MacArthur, Bruce Millholland; Presented by The Producers Cirlce 2 (Robert Fryer, Mary Lea Johnson, Martin Richards, James Cresson) in association with Joseph Harris and Ira Bernstein; Wardrobe, Helen McMahon; Hairstylist, Michael Kriston, Alan Schubert; Assistant Conductor, Arthur R. Wagner; Stage Managers, E. Bronson Platt, Jack Sims, Ken Urmston; Press, Faith Geer; Opened June 8, 1979 at the Fisher Theatre in Detroit, Mi., and closed in San Francisco, Ca., at the Orpheum Theatre on Nov. 24, 1979. For original NY production, see THEATRE WORLD Vol. 34.

CAST

Rock Hudson (Oscar Jaffee), Imogene Coca (Letitia Primrose), Judy Kaye (Lily Garland), Patrick Quinn (Bruce Granit), Lee Goodman (Owen O'Malley), Dean Dittman (Oliver Webb), Tom Batten (Conductor), Leslie Easterbrook (Agnes), Michael Connolly (Max Jacobs), Hal Norman (Lockwood), Stanley Simmonds (Train Secretary), Melvin Edmundson (Red Cap), Quitman Fludd III (Porter), Ray Stephens (Porter), Ted Williams (Redcap/Porter), Joseph Wise (Porter), Ken Hillard (Priest), Charles Rule (Bishop), Ray Gill (Stage Manager), Maris Clement (Joan), Emily Grinspan (Anita), Richard Cooper Bayne (Maxwell Finch), Michael Hayward-Jones (Otto von Bismark), Margarette Chisholm (Dr. Johnson), and Norma Jean Baker, Alyson Bristol, Christina Britton, Nancy Holcombe, Gary Holcombe, Robert Logan, Kenneth W. Urmston

MUSICAL NUMBERS: Stranded Again, On the 20th Century, I Rise Again, Indian Maiden's Lament, Veronique, I Have Written a Play, Together, Never, Our Private World, Repent, Mine, I've Got It All, Five Zeros, Sextet, She's a Nut, Max Jacobs, Babette, Lily Oscar.

A musical in two acts. The action takes place in the early 1930's, mainly on board the 20th Century Limited from Chicago to New York.

Imogene Coca, Rock Hudson, Stanley Simmonds, Lee Goodman Above: Judy Kaye, Rock Hudson

THEY'RE PLAYING OUR SONG

Book by Neil Simon; Music, Marvin Hamlisch; Lyrics, Carole Bayer Sager; Director, Robert Moore; Musical Numbers Staged by Patricia Birch; Scenery and Projections, Douglas W. Schmidt; Costumes, Ann Roth; Lighting, Tharon Musser; Music Director, Al Cavaliere; Orchestrations, Ralph Burns, Richard Hazard, Gene Page; Production Supervisor, Philip Cusack; Production Coordinator, Robert D. Currie; Company Managers, Mitchell Brower, Harold Sogard; Hairstylist, David Brown; Wardrobe, Chip Mulberger; Stage Managers, Craig Jacobs, James Bernardi, Judy Olsen; Press, Bill Evans, Harry Davies; Presented by Emanuel Azenberg; Opened Tuesday, December 11, 1979 at the Shubert, Chicago, Il., and still touring May 31, 1980. For original NY production, see THEATRE WORLD Vol. 35.

CAST

Vernon Gersch	Victor Garber
Sonia Walsk	Ellen Greene
Voices of Vernon	Kenneth Bryan, Clint Clifford, Bubba Rambo
Voices of Sonia	Ivy Austin, Andrea Green, Cheryl Howard
Voice of Phil, the engineer	Orrin Reiley

STANDBYS AND UNDERSTUDIES: Orrin Reiley (Vernon), Jean Elliott (Sonia), Clint Clifford (Vernon/Engineer's Voice), Andrea Green (Sonia)

For musical numbers, see Broadway Calendar, **page 81.**

Martha Swope Photos

**Victor Garber, Ellen Greene (foreground)
in "They're Playing Our Song"**

YOUR ARMS TOO SHORT TO BOX WITH GOD

Conceived from the Book of St. Matthew by Vinnette Carroll; Music and Lyrics, Alex Bradford; Additional Music and Lyrics, Micki Grant; Director, Vinnette Carroll; Choreography, Talley Beatty; Sets and Costumes, William Schroder; Lighting, Richard Winkler; Set Supervisor, Michael J. Hotopp; Orchestrations and Dance Music, H. B. Barnum; Musical Direction, Grenoldo Frazier; General Manager, James Janek; Production Supervisors, Jerry R. Moore, Richard Martini; Press, Max Eisen, Tom Brocato; Company Manager, Ken Krezel; Wardrobe, Donna Peck; Wardrobe, Dennis E. Wilson; Production Associate, David Kerley; Sound, Christopher Bond; Stage Managers, Carleton Scott Alsop, Gregory Nicholas, Ida M. Broughton; Opened during January 1979 in Hartford, Ct., and closed during March 1980 in Los Angeles, Ca. Presented by Tom Mallow in association with James Janek. For original NY production, see THEATRE WORLD Vol. 33.

CAST

Adrian Bailey, Ida M. Broughton, Julius Richard Brown (Preacher), Sheila Ellis, Ralph Farrington (Judas), Gwendolyn Fleming (Singing Mary), Thomas J. Fouse, Jr., Jamil K. Garland, Elijah Gill (Jesus), L. Michael Gray, Jennifer-Yvette Holliday, Garry Q. Lewis, Linda Morton, Rodney Saulsberry, Jai Oscar St. John, Leslie Hardesty Sisson, Kim L. Stroud, Quincella Swyningan (Dancing Mary), Darnell Williams, Linda E. Young
MUSICAL NUMBERS: Beatitudes, We're Gonna Have a Good Time, There's a Stranger in Town, Do You Know Jesus?, Just a Little Bit of Jesus Goes a Long Way, We Are the Priests and Elders, Something Is Wrong in Jerusalem, It Was Alone, Be Careful Whom You Kiss, Trial, It's Too Late, Judas' Dance, Your Arms Too Short to Box with God, Give Us Barabbas, See How They Done My Lord, Come on Down, Can't No Grave Hold My Body Down, Didn't I Tell You, When the Power Comes, Everybody Has His Own Way, Down by the Riverside, I Love You So Much Jesus, The Band

A musical in two acts.

Jay Thompson Photo

**"Your Arms Too Short
to Box with God"**

DADDY GOODNESS

Book, Ron Miller, Shauneille Perry; Based on play of same title by Richard Wright and Louis Sapin; Lyrics, Ron Miller; Music, Ken Hirsch; Director, Israel Hicks; Choreography and Musical Staging, Louis Johnson; Musical Supervision and Arrangements, Danny Holgate; Setting, Santo Loquasto; Lighting, Jennifer Tipton; Costumes, Bernard Johnson; Orchestrations, Robert M. Freedman; Musical Director, Lea Richardson; Choral Arrangements, Chapman Roberts; Sound, Joseph Donohue; Hairstylist, Breelun Daniels; Production Supervisor, Ron Abbott; General Management, Theatre Management Associates; Company Manager, Robert Ossenfort; Production Associate, Chesley Springer; Production Assistant, Maude Brickner; Assistant Choreographer, Mabel Robinson; Wardrobe, Olga Anderson; Props, Bob Anderson; Assistant Musical Director, Frank Anderson; Stage Managers, Steven Zweigbaum, Arturo E. Porazzi, Fred Tyson; Press, Jeffrey Richards, Warren Knowlton, Robert Ganshaw, Peter Filichia, Marjorie Ornston; Presented by Ashton Springer with Motown in association with Marty Markinson, Joseph Harris and Donald Tick; Opened Thursday, Aug. 16, 1979 in the Forrest Theatre, Philadelphia, Pa., and closed Oct. 7, 1979 at the National Theatre in Washington, DC.

CAST

Clifton Davis (Thomas), Freda Payne (Lottie), Ted Ross (Daddy Goodness), Rod Perry (Sam), Carol-Jean Lewis (Ethel), Arthur French (Jeremiah), Dan Strayhorn (Luke), Sandra Reaves-Phillips (Annie/Mary), Ann Duquesnay (Night Club Singer), Clebert Ford (Pastor Weeks), Stefanie Showell (Daughter), Clyde Williams (Willis), Roslyn Burrough (Mrs. Perkins), Brenda J. Davis (Mother), Vikki Baltimore (Singer/Dancer), Dwight Baxter (Dancer/Singer), Gary Easterling (Dancer/Singer), Brenda Garrett (Dancer/Singer), Charles "C.B." Murray (Dancer/Singer), Nancy-Suzanne (Dancer/Singer), Dwayne Phelps (Dancer/Singer), M. W. Reid (Dancer/Singer), Mabel Robinson (Singer/Dancer), Wynonna Smith (Dancer/Singer), Ned Wright, Understudies: Ann Duquesnay (Lottie), Ned Wright (Daddy Goodness/Jeremiah), M. W. Reid (Luke), Weyman Thompson (Sam/Weeks), Brenda J. Davis (Annie), Monique Brown (Daughter)
MUSICAL NUMBERS: Goodness Don't Come Easy When You're Bad, I Got Religion, Hungry, Spread Joy, Lottie's Purification, We'll Let the People Decide, One More Step, People Make Me Cry, I Don't Wanna Do It Alone No More, Daddy's Decision, Don't Touch That Dial, You're Home, Finale

A musical in 2 acts and 14 scenes. The action takes place in a country town in Louisiana during "Sweet Summer."

Bert Andrews Photos

Top Right: Dan Strayhorn, Clifton Davis in "Daddy Goodness"

SWING

Book, Conn Fleming; Music, Robert Waldman; Lyrics, Alfred Uhry; Director, Stuart Ostrow; Scenery, Robin Wagner; Costumes, Patricia Zipprodt; Lighting, Richard Pilbrow; Choreography, Kenneth Rinker; Orchestrations, Eddie Sauter; Musical Direction and Dance Arrangements, Peter Howard; Vocal Arrangements, Elise Bretton; Associate Producer-Music Consultant, George T. Simon; Hairstylist-Makeup, Patrik D. Moreton; Sound, Otts Munderloh; General Managers, Joseph Harris, Ira Bernstein, Peter T. Kulok; Company Manager, Steven E. Goldstein; Stage Managers, Phil Friedman, Perry Cline, David Rosenberg; Wardrobe, Helen McMahon; Press, John Springer, Meg Gordean, Suzanne Salter, Ann Todaro; Props, Paul Biega; Assistant Conductor, Dennis Anderson; Production Assistant, Emile Svitzer; Presented by Stuart Ostrow in association with Edgar M. Bronfman; Opened Monday, Feb. 25, 1980 at the Playhouse in Wilmington, De., and closed March 30, 1980 at the JFK Center, Washington, DC.

CAST

Raymond Baker (Henry), Paul Binotto (Tony Audino), Paul Bogaev (Elliot Pierce), Roy Brocksmith (Announcer), Jerry Colker (Dooley), Janet Eilber (Norma), Rebecca Gilchrist (Jane), John Hammil (Harry Donovan), Robert LuPone (Glenn), Pat Lysinger (Mildred), Ellen March (Eleanor), Adam Redfield (Claude), Debbie Shapiro (Ginny Hall), David Wilson (Little Joe), Mary Catherine Wright (Marilyn), Stephen Ferrera (Soldier), and Dancers: Beth Davis, Lisa Embs, Tim Flavin, Donna McCowen, Marty McDonough, Jeff Morring, Morgan Richardson, Teresa Rossomando
STANDBYS AND UNDERSTUDIES: Deborah Geffner (Norman/Ginny), Michael Rupert (Glenn/Tony), Paul Schiderhorn (Donovan/Announcer/Henry), Stephen Ferrera (Elliot Pierce), Tim Flavin (Claude), Beth Davis (Marilyn), Donna McCowen (Eleanor), Lisa Embs (Jane), Marty McDonough (Dooley)
MUSICAL NUMBERS: Swing, Good From Any Angle, Michigan Bound, The Real Thing, Marilyn, A Piece of Cake, Home, Miliaria Rubra, One Hundred Percent Cockeyed, All Clear, A Girl Can Go Wacky, Duet, The Doowah Diddy Blues, If You Can't Trot Don't Get Hot, Dream Time

Martha Swope Photos

Robert LuPone, Janet Eilber in "Swing"

ACT: A CONTEMPORARY THEATRE

Seattle, Washington
June 1, 1979–May 31, 1980
Fifteenth Season

Artistic Director, Gregory A. Falls; General Manager, Andrew M. Witt; Press, Louise Campion Cummings, Michael Eagan, Jr.; Company Manager, Karen Rotko; Music Director, Stan Keen; Resident Composer, Joseph Seserko; Technical Director, Phil Schermer; Costumer, Julie James; Sound, Mac Perkins; Production Assistants, Lora Shiner, Jim Blickensderfer, J. DeMers Connolly, Renee D. Reilly; Props, Shelley Henze Schermer; Assistant Lighting Director, Donna Grout; Stage Managers, Eileen MacRae Murphy, Michael Weholt; President, Mrs. E. L. Pierce Milholland

PRODUCTIONS

"For Colored Girls Who Have Considered Suicide ...," "Artichoke," "Wings," "Buried Child," "Starting Here, Starting Now," and *World Premiere* of "Catholics" by Brian Moore. (Casts not submitted)

Chris Bennion Photo

"For Colored Girls Who Have Considered Suicide ..."

ACTORS THEATRE OF LOUISVILLE

Louisville, Kentucky
October 11, 1979–May 18, 1980
Sixteenth Season

Producing Director, Jon Jory; Administrative Director, Alexander Speer; Associate Director, Trish Pugh; Press, Ronny J. McNulty, Gary Yawn; Assistant to Producing Director, L. Susan Rowland; Technical Director, Tom Rupp; Stage Managers, Frazier Marsh, Benita Hofstetter, Bob Hornung, Patricia Saphier; Directors, Larry Deckel, Radha Delamarter, Alan Duke, Ray Fry, Michael Hankins, Israel Hicks, Ken Jenkins, Walton Jones, Jon Jory, Pirie MacDonald, Peter Maloney, William McNulty; Musical Directors, Peter Ekstrom, J. Stephen Gottesman; Choreographers, Sherry Barnard, Lynne Gannaway, Michael Sokoloff; Sets, Paul Owen, David B. Hager, Grady Larkins, Hal Tine, Joseph A. Varga; Costumes, Kurt Wilhelm, Mary Lou Owen, Katharine E. Kraft; Lighting, Jeff Hill, David B. Hager, Paul Owen; Props, Sam Garst, Sandra Strawn

COMPANY

Kevin Bacon, Jean Barker, Billie Brenan, Kent Broadhurst, Shirley Bryan, Stephen Cowie, Bob Del Pazzo, Mia Dillon, Gloria Dorson, Alan Duke, Deanna Dunagan, Thom Edlun, Peter Ekstrom, Robert Ellenstein, Jeanne Even, Lee Anne Fahey, Laurie Franks, Arthur French, Ray Fry, Sue Anne Gershenson, Anneke Gough, Georgine Hall, Helen Harrelson, Anthony Heald, Benita Hofstetter, Gary Holcombe, Nancy Holcombe, Bob Horen, J. C. Hoyt, Ken Jenkins, Victor Jory, Robert Judd, Cynthia Judge, Susan Kaslow, Dolores Kenan, Michael Kevin, Susan Kingsley, Timothy Landfield, Richard Leighton, Pirie MacDonald, George Maguire, John Maynard, Michael McCarty, Jack McClure, Pat McNamara, William McNulty, Joan Miller, Mary Munder, Adale O'Brien, Gene O'Neill, Roxann Parker, Guy Paul, Polly Pen, David O. Petersen, John Pielmeier, Anne Pitoniak, George Riddle, Nada Rowand, J. Keith Ryan, P. Jay Sidney, Sam Singleton, Robertson Smith, Melodie Somers, William Swetland, Carol Teitel, Noreen Tobin, Dierk Toporzysek

PRODUCTIONS

Morning's at Seven, Childe Byron, Otherwise Engaged, A Christmas Carol, Animal Friends, Moose Tails, St. Mark's Gospel, Dylan Thomas Growing Up, A Christmas Carol in Prose, The Time of Your Life, Lone Star, In Fashion, and *PREMIERES* of The Slab Boys, Admissions, Today a Little Extra, Agnes of God, They're Coming to Make It Brighter, Sunset/Sunrise, Weekends Like Other People, Star Quality, Switching in the Afternoon or As the Screw Turns, Golden Accord, Vicki Madison Clocks Out, American Welcome, The Side of the Road, The Drummer, Tall Girls Have Everything, Hooray for Hollywood, San Salvador, Power Plays, Remington, Doctors and Diseases, The Incredible Murder of Cardinal Tosca, Tarantara! Tarantara!, Commencement

David S. Talbott Photos

Anneke Gough, Pirie MacDonald in "Sunset/Sunrise"

Left Center: Anne Pitoniak, Ray Fry in "Today A Little Extra"

ALASKA REPERTORY THEATRE

Anchorage/Fairbanks, Alaska
January 17–May 10, 1980
Fourth Season

Artistic Director, Robert J. Farley; Producing Director, Paul V. Brown; Director Statewide Services, Gary D. Anderson; Production Manager, Bennett E. Taber; Technical Director, Gary Field; Administrative Director, Mark Somers; Press, Bonnie Harris, Jack Lloyd, Nancy Campbell

PRODUCTIONS AND CASTS

DIAMOND STUDS by Jim Wann, Bland Simpson; Director, Robert J. Farley; Set and Costumes, Jamie Greenleaf; Lighting, James Sale; State Manager, Emil Holloway. CAST: Matthew Amson, Rose Barbee, Nicholas Cosco. Joan Gossett, Dana Hart, John Kelly, John Mason, Steve McKean, Gina McMather, Susan Mendel, Jim Morrison, Tim Morrissey, Ernie Norris, Dave Roth, Donn Ruddy, Luan Schooler
TOURING CAST: Brooks Almy, Mark Hardwick, Dana Hart, Sean Michael Kelly, Nancy Krebs, Joel Lockman, John Manson, Timothy McCusker, Scott Merrick, Tim Morrissey, Christine Ranck, Donn Ruddy
A CHRISTMAS CAROL by Charles Dickens; Adapted by Martin L. Platt; Director, Robert J. Farley; Set, Manie Greenleaf; Lighting, James Sale; Costumes, Nanrose Buchman; Sound, Michael Schweppe; Stage Manager, Dan Sedgwick. CAST: Charles Antalosky, Charles Berendt, Matt Brown, Natasha Ensign, Harry Frazier, Ed Gauss, Amy Hackett, Anker Hanson, Denyse Holm, Jim Holm, Tamara Holm, James Hotchkiss, Shirley Hughes, Peter Jack, Abbie Johnson, Shelly Johnson, Janet Kruse, Miller Lide, Jean Mackin, Joe Meek, Susan Mendel, Mark Minnerly, Susan Reilly, Ronan Short, Greg Stock, Joan Ulmer, Justin Vaughn, James Bell, Erik Kokborg
TALLEY'S FOLLY by Lanford Wilson; Director, Margaret Booker; Set, Jamie Greenleaf; Lighting, James Sale; Costumes, Nanrose Ruchman; Sound, Michael Schweppe; Stage Manager, Ann Mathews. CAST: Kirtan Coan, Jeff David
SOMETHING'S AFOOT by James McDonald, David Vos, Robert Gerlach; Director, Russell Treyz; Set, Jamie Greenleaf; Lighting, James Sale; Costumes, Nanrose Buchman; Sound, Michael Schweppe; Musical Director, John Clifton; Stage Manager, Ann Mathews. CAST: Kevin Daly, Robert Miller Driscoll, Ron Evans, Sarah Felcher, Sue Anne Gershenson, Frederick Major, Dick Sabol, Harold Shepard, Fran Stevens, Freyda Thomas, Susan Wingrove, Steve Wehmhoff, Paul Linford
SLY FOX by Larry Gelbart; Director; Gary D. Anderson; Set, Jamie Greenleaf; Lighting, James Sale; Costumes, Nanrose Buchman; Stage Manager, Vito Zingarelli. CAST: Charles Antalosky, Bill Arnold, Tom Bade, Charles Berendt, Marshall Borden, Dan Diggles, Ron Evans, Valerie Green, James Hotchkiss, Nancy Houfek, Max Howard, Richard C. Lavin, Gregory Murrell
LOOSE ENDS by Michael Weller; Director, Robert J. Farley; Set, Robert W. Zentis; Lighting, James Sale; Costumes, Nanrose Buchman; Sound, Michael Schweppe; Stage Manager, Ann Mathews. CAST: Bill Arnold, Tom Bade, Lissa Bell, Robert Browning, James Hotchkiss, Carole Lockwood, Gregory Murrell, Merritt Olsen, Freda Foh Shen, Douglas Simes, Eleanor Reissa

Jim Lavrakas Photos

**Robert Browning, Lissa Bell
in "Loose Ends" Top: Kirtan Coan,
Jeff David in "Talley's Folly"**

AMERICAN MIME THEATRE

New York, N.Y.
1952–1980

Director, Paul J. Curtis; Administrator, Jean Barbour; Counsel, Joel S. Charleston

COMPANY

Jean Barbour, Charles Barney, Paul Curtis, Dale Fuller, Jean Gennis, Kevin Kaloostian, Cesar Palma, Erica Sarzin, Mr. Bones

REPERTORY

The Lovers, The Scarecrow, Dreams, Hurly-Burly, Evolution, Sludge, Six, Abstraction

**Charles Barney, Paul Curtis, Kevin Kaloostian
in "Hurlyburly"**

ALLEY THEATRE
Houston, Texas
October 18, 1979–June 1, 1980

Executive Director, Nina Vance; Executive Producer, Herschell Wilkenfeld; Managing Director, Iris Siff; Business Manager, Bill Halbert; Press, Bob Feingold, John Eaton: Assistant to Ms. Vance, George Anderson; Staff Director, Beth Sanford; Production/Company Manager, Bettye Fitzpatrick; Stage Managers, Rutherford Cravens, Trent Jenkins, Janice Heidke; Assistant Production Manager, John Vreeke; Staff Designers, Ellen Ryba, James E. Stephens; Guest Designers, Michael Olich, Jerry Williams; Technical Director, William C. Lindstrom; Props, Mary Jo Goss; Mrs Chris Nickolas, President.

PRODUCTIONS AND CASTS

INDULGENCES IN THE LOUISVILLE HAREM by John Orlock; Director, Beth Sanford; Settings, Jerry Williams; Costumes, Ellen Ryba; Lighting, James E. Stephens; Sound, Stephen J. Houtz; Technical Director, William C. Lindstrom. CAST: Bella Jarrett (Florence Becker), Bettye Fitzpatrick (Viola Becker), Dale Helward (Amos Robbilet), David Wurst (Winfield Davis), Richard McWilliams (Understudy). A play in two acts. The action takes place during 1902 in Louisville, Ky.

BLACK COFFEE by Agatha Christie; Director, Robert Symonds; Assistant Director, John Vreeke; Set, Michael Olich; Costumes, Ellen Ryba; Lighting, James E. Stephens; Technical Director, William C. Lindstrom. CAST: Brandon Smith (Tredwell), Linda Thorson (Lucia Amory), Joan White (Caroline Amory), Michael Fletcher (Richard Amory), Margaret Bard (Barbara Amory), Daniel Szelag (Edward Raynor), Peter Messaline (Dr. Carelli), Frederick Clay (Claud Amory), Robert Symonds (Hercule Poirot), Rutherford Cravens (Capt. Hastings), Peter Sturgess (Dr. Graham), Jack Medley (Inspector), Blue Deckert (Constable)

THE WIZARD OF OZ by L. Frank Baum; Dramatized by Elizabeth F. Goodspeed; Director, Beth Sanford; Settings, John Bos, Jeff Seats; Costumes, Ellen Ryba; Original Music, Stephen Houtz; Lyrics, Jerry Williams; Stage Manager, Janice Heidke. CAST: Kathryn Paul (Dorothy), Monica Ward (Aunt Em), John Armstrong, Milton Blankenship, Melissa Kraft (Munchkins), Margaret Humphreys (Witch of the North), Gram Smith (Scarecrow), J. Shane McClure (Tin Man), David Williams (Lion), Blue Deckert (Guard), Philip Schuster (Oz), Therese Diekhans (Beautiful Lady), Lei Broadstone (Beast), Robin Moseley (Witch of the West), Elizabeth McGrath (Glinda, Witch of the South)

THE CHERRY ORCHARD by Anton Chekhov; Translated by Tyrone Guthrie and Leonid Kipnis; Director, Louis Criss; Assistant, Beth Sanford; Settings, Michael Olich; Costumes, Michael J. Cesario; Original Music, Stephen Houtz; Dances, John Jacobsen; Technical Director, William C. Lindstrom. CAST: Moya Fenwick (Mme. Ranevskaya), Robin Moseley (Anya), Gale Fury Childs (Varya), Jack Creley (Gaev), Robert Benson (Lopahin), Daniel Szelag (Trofimov), Jack Medley (Simeonoff-Pischchik), Lillian Evans (Charlotta Ivanovna), Michael Fletcher (Yepihodov), Margaret Bard (Dunyasha), Gillie Fenwick (Firs), Brandon Smith (Yasha), and Milton Blankenship, Blue Deckert, Margaret Humphreys, Deloris Lowman, J. Shane McClure, Elizabeth McGrath, Kathryn Paul

THE GOSPEL ACCORDING TO ST. MATTHEW with Robert Symonds; Co-Directors, Robery Symonds, John Vreeke; Setting, Jeff Seats; Costumes, Ellen Ryba; Lighting, James E. Stephens; Original Music, Stephen Houtz; Technical Director, William C. Lindstrom

OH, COWARD! with words and music by Noel Coward; Devised and Directed by Roderick Cook; Musical Arrangements, Rene Wiegert; Musical Direction, Sterling Tinsley; Settings, John Bos; Costumes, Ellen Ryba; Lighting, James E. Stephens; Technical Director, William C. Lindstrom. CAST: Christian Grey, Kimberly Gaisford, Gary Krawford

THE GOODBYE PEOPLE by Herb Gardner; Director, Pat Brown; Setting, Jeff Seats; Costumes, Ellen Ryba; Sound, John Vreeke; Technical Director, William C. Lindstrom. CAST: Max Silverman, Arthur Korman, Nancy Scott, Marcus Soloway, Michael Silverman, Eddie Bergson

Carl Davis, Bob Feingold Photos

Top Left: Bettye Fitzpatrick, David Wurst, Bella Jarrett, Dale Helward in "Indulgences in the Louisville Harem" Below: Gary Krawford, Kimberly Gaisford, Christian Grey in "Oh, Coward!" Left Center: Bettye Fitzpatrick, Gale Childs, Robin Moseley in "Sylvia Plath"

Robert Benson, Moya Fenwick, Jack Creley in "The Cherry Orchard"

ALLIANCE THEATRE COMPANY

Atlanta, Georgia
October 24, 1979–May 10, 1980

Managing Director, Bernard Havard; Artistic Director, Fred Chappell; Associate Director, Wallace Chappell; Guest Directors, Charles Abbott, Walter Dallas; Settings, Eldon Elder, Philipp Jung, Ming Cho Lee, Michael Stauffer, W. Joseph Stell, William B. Warfel; Lighting, Mark C. Cohen, Milton Duke, Michael Stauffer, W. Joseph Stell, William B. Warfel, Michael Orris Watson; Costumes, Thom Coates; Musical Director, Michael Fauss; Production Manager, Gully Stanford; Stage Managers, D. Wayne Hughes, Allen Wright, John J. Mulligan, Charlie Otte; Press, Mark Arnold

PRODUCTIONS AND CASTS

THE ROYAL FAMILY by George S. Kaufman, Edna Ferber. CAST: Sarah Anson, Don Bednarz, James C. Burge, Ron Culbreth, Stanton Cunningham, Tim Garret, Anne Haney, Ellen Heard, Clayton Landey, Anne Lynn, Donald Moore, Eleanor Phelps, Rob Roper, Lee Shepard, Judith Tillman, Christopher Wynkoop
OLIVER by Lionel Bart. CAST: Tommy Abernathy, Amy Bailey, Amanda Beason, Otho Tipton Bishop, Jr., Paul Diamond, Adrian Elder, Harlan Eplan, Lorna Erickson, Nancy Farrar, Travis Fine, Tim Garrett, Anne Gartlan, David Goss, Al Hamacher, Barbara Hancock, Anne Haney, Julien Havard, Ellen Heard, Jeff Higgins, Pat Hurley, Judy Langford, Cathy Larson, Robert Lund, Michael-John McGann, David Mermin, Chris Neiman, Anthony Pitillo, Philip Pleasants, Johnny Ragers, Rob Roper, Don Spalding, Tim Webber, Libby Whittemore
THE NIGHT OF THE IGUANA by Tennessee Williams. CAST: Nick Mancuso, Monique Mercure, Glenda Byars, Milton Chaikin, Ron Culbreth, Phil DiPietro, Sandra Dorsey, Tim Garrett, Anne Haney, Jim Kearny, Mary Kelly, Larry Larson, Philip Pleasants, Linda Stephens
FOR COLORED GIRLS WHO HAVE CONSIDERED SUICIDE WHEN THE RAINBOW IS ENUF by Ntozake Shange. CAST: Denise B. Mickelbury, Anne Mitchell, LaTanya Richardson, Iris Little-Roberts, Barbara Stokes, Barbara Sullivan
THE RIVALS by Richard Brinsley Sheridan. CAST: Paul Anthony, Elton Beckett, Jacqueline Bertrand, Rita Byrd, Arthur Lintion Clark III, Susan Connors, Al Garrison, Tom Key, Edward Lee, Bernardine Mitchell, Pyper Lynn Petty, Philip Pleasants, Ian Trigger, Richard Warwick, Willie Woods
MACBETH by William Shakespeare. CAST: Michael Zaslow, Carol Mayo Jenkins, Jim Ashley, Ron Barrymore, Terry Beaver, Jeffery Brocklin, Rita D. Byrd, James Caden, Ray Collins, Bill Crowe, Stanton Cunningham, Doug Dillingham, Travis Fine, Skip Foster, Al Hamacher, Anne Haney, Jeroy Hannah, David Head, Mary Ann Hearn, Roberta Illg, Edward Lee, James Loring, Eric Love, David McCann, Steven McCloskey, Ruth McRee, Gordon Paddison, Philip Pleasants, Tim Rutland, Tom Sasser, Randall Taylor, Robert Todd, Lee Toombs, Ian Trigger
VISIONS by Louis Nowra; Director, Wallace Chappell; *American Premiere*. CAST not submitted.

Charles Rafshoon Photos

**Kenneth Ryan, Carmen de Lavallade
in "A Midsummer Night's Dream"**

**Susan Connors, Richard Warwick in "The Rivals"
Top: Monique Mercure, Nick Mancuso
in "The Night of the Iguana"**

AMERICAN REPERTORY THEATRE

Cambridge, Massachusetts
First Season

Artistic Director, Robert Brustein; Managing Director, Robert J. Orchard; Production Manager, Jonathan Seth Miller; Press, Jan Geidt; Associate Manager, Patricia Quinn; Scenery, Andrew Jackness, Adrianne Lobel, Tony Straiges, Michael H. Yeargan; Costumes, Zack Brown, Nan Cibula, William Ivey Long, Dunya Ramicova; Lighting, William Armstrong, Paul Gallo; Technical Director, Donald Soule; Executive Assistant, Penelope Pigott; Stage Managers, Thomas DiMauro, Mary Hunter

PRODUCTIONS AND CASTS

A MIDSUMMER NIGHT'S DREAM by William Shakespeare; Director, Alvin Epstein; Music Director, Daniel Stepner. CAST: John Bottoms, Robert Brustein, Marilyn Caskey, Phillip Cates, Robertson Dean, Carmen de Lavallade, John Drabik, Eric Elice, Jennifer Geidt, Jeremy Geidt, Richard Grusin, Mark Linn-Baker, Jack Luceno, John McAndrew, Elizabeth Norment, Marianne Owen, Andrew Parker, Stephen Rowe, Kenneth Ryan, Robert Schaffer, Lisa Sloan, Peter Tamm, Walter van Dijk, Max Wright
HAPPY END with Lyrics by Bertolt Brecht; Music, Kurt Weill; Adaptation, Michael Feingold; Director, Walton Jones; Music Director, Gary Fagin. CAST: John Bottoms, Marilyn Caskey, Phillip Cates, Chris Glemenson, Carmen de Lavallade, John Drabik, Eric Elice, Margaret Fleming, Jeremy Geidt, Richard Grusin, John McAndrew, Nancy Mayans, Elizabeth Norment, Barbara Orson, Marianne Owen, Stephen Rowe, Kenneth Ryan, Grace Shohet, Peter Tamm, Maggie Topkis, Walter van Dijk, Max Wright
TERRY BY TERRY *(World Premiere)* by Mark Leib; Director, John Madden. CAST: John Bottoms, Marilyn Caskey, Phillip Cates, Robertson Dean, Carmen de Lavallade, Eric Elice, Richard Grusin, Mark Linn-Baker, Nancy Mayans, Elizabeth Norment, Marianne Owen, Stephen Rowe, Kenneth Ryan, Lisa Sloan, Ann Titolo
THE INSPECTOR GENERAL by Nikolai Vasilevich Gogol; Translated by Sam Guckenheimer, Peter Sellars; Director, Peter Sellars. CAST: Phillip Cates, Chris Clemenson, Robertson Dean, Eric Elice, Jeremy Geidt, Richard Grusin, Mark Linn-Baker, Elizabeth Norment, John McAndrew, Brian McCue, Nancy Mayans, Barbara Orson, Marianne Owen, Stephen Rowe, Grace Shohet, Lisa Sloan, Peter Tamm, Max Wright

Richard Feldman Photos

AMERICAN REVELS COMPANY

Richmond, Virginia
September 14, 1979–May 31, 1980
Artistic Director, Keith Fowler; Associate Director, M. Elizabeth Osborn; General Manager, J. Christie Cruger; Business Manager, Walter C. Swanson; Press, Karen Kevorkian; Assistant Executive Producer, Hazel Norris; Designers, Robert Franklin, Richard Carleton Hankins, Jeremy Conway, Fred Brumbach; Lighting Designers, Fred Brumbach, Ken White; Costumes, Joan Brumbach; Props, Nils Hanson; Stage Managers, Champe Leary, Hazel Norris, Doug Flinchum; Directors, Keith Fowler, M. Elizabeth Osborn, John Olon-Scrymgeour, Terri White, Larry Bland

COMPANY

Jay Lundy, Keith Fowler, Gilbert Shaw, Janet Bell, Walter Rhodes, Marie Goodman Hunter, Richard Lee, Jennie Brown, Russell P. Owen, Tania Myren, J.J. Quinn, Steve Beauchamp, Brian Parry, M. Elizabeth Osborn, Leigh Burch, Matthew Costello, Ron Burn, Cleo Holladay, Terri White, Mary Graham, Memrie Innerarity, Lisa McMillan, Cookie Harlin, Cameron Duncan, Ron Vigneault, Kevin Heelan, Jana Fontana, Deborah Hogg, Clayton Corbin, Edward Stevlingson, Henry K. Bal, Caryn West, Joann Swanson, Bev Appleton, Carl Blackwell Lester, Frances Parker Graham, Frank Howarth, Jessica Regelson, Kent Thompson, Marcia McReynolds, Donald Beck, Jody Smith, L'Retta Wooldridge
Claude Arthur, Al Bullock, Kelvin John Davis, Tommy L. Fleming, Patrice Hutchinson, Michael Gish, Jerry Winn, Chris Lucas, Robin McLeod, Peter Williamson, Amy Spain, Laura Null, Jeremy Fowler, Susan O'Conner, Jewel Sanford, Robert P. Smith, Terri Steele, Shauna Steele, Ted Ooghe, Leonard Anthony Brisendine, Robin Doran, Dale S. Hudson, Maripat Cronin Jiminez, Hoy Steele, Kevin Grantz, Marion Johnson, Jack Phillips, Mac Damron, D. Morgan Rice, Lelia Pendelton, Tom Maney, Susan Adams, Ed Collins, Clifford Smith, Patch Clark, Anne Storrs, Gayle Taylor, Coby Batty, Michael Guess, Tyrone Miller, Paul Martin, George Macklin, Tom Shelton, Andrew Turkington, Cliff Mirabella, Tony Cosby, Larry Bland, The Volunteer Choir, Steve Bassett, Robert Foreman, Laura Cruger, Michael Frith, Daniel Cruger, Peter Cruger, Soseh Kevorkian, Robert Burner, Bob Rollins, Reid Freeman, Sara Roderer, Rob Hall, Mary Fletcher Jones, Emily Skinner, Townes Coates, John W. Winn III, Emory Freeman, Sandra Ryan, Noah Scalin, Nancy Shocket, Kweli Leapart, Gretchen Jones, Jeffrey Fuquay, Derick Milford, Heidi Villiger

PRODUCTIONS

A Christman Carol, The Club, American Buffalo, Othello, El Grande de Coca Cola, I Have a Dream, Strutters Ball, Twelfth Night, Tales from the Vienna Woods, and *World Premieres* of Holy Ghosts by Romulus Linney, Hope I Hear It Again Sometime by Kevin Heelan, Ashes of Soldiers by Keith Fowler and M. Elizabeth Osborn, The Black and White Minstrel Show by Keith Fowler, Mac Calhoun and company.

Eric Dobbs Photos

Cameron Duncan, Ron Burn in "American Buffalo" Top: Ron Burn, Elizabeth Osborn, Gilbert Shaw, Russell Owen, Kent Thompson, Jessica Regelson, Keith Fowler, Claude Arthur in "Ashes of Soldiers"

AMERICAN THEATRE ARTS

Los Angeles, California
June 1, 1979–May 31, 1980
Artistic Director, Don Eitner; Managing Director, Jim Bennett; Production Director, Joseph Ruskin; Art Director, James J. Agazzi; Directors, Kip Niven, Don Eitner, Joseph Ruskin

PRODUCTIONS AND CASTS

THE PHYSICISTS by Friedrich Durrenmatt. CAST: John Terry Bell, A. Frank Bronson, Lisa Carole, Janice M. Christensen, Jim Dalesandro, Sara DeWitt, Robert Garrison, Harvey Gold, Daniel Grace, Bruce Mathews, Joseph Ruskin, Jayne Taini, Rebecca Westberg
BLUEWATER COTTAGE *(World Premiere)* by D. L. Coburn. CAST: Rolly Fanton, Nick Holt, Carol Locatell, Gregory Michaels, John Redman
THE CHALK GARDEN by Enid Bagnold. CAST: Rob Donohoe, Robert Garrison, Lynn Halley, Nancy Jeris, Kathy Perdue, Betty Ramey, Rebecca Westberg, Patti Whitten
DAYS IN THE DARK LIGHT *(World Premiere)* by James W. Kearns. CAST: Richard Bull, Barbara Collentine, Maureen McIlroy, Sara Shearer
NUDE WITH VIOLIN by Noel Coward. CAST: Howard Adler, Robert Garrison, Tanya George, Daniel Grace, Gary Graves, Nancy Jeris, Cathryn Perdue, Gary Spatz, Margo Speer, Kevin Spillane, Robbie Trombetta, Jeannie Van Dam

Carol Locatell, Rolly Fanton in "Bluewater Cottage"

180

ARENA STAGE

Washington, D.C.
October 5, 1979–June 22, 1980

Producing Director, Zelda Fichandler; Associate Producing Director, David Chambers; Executive Director, Thomas C. Fichandler; Production Coordinator, Nancy Quinn; Press, Richard Bryant; Stage Directors, David Chambers, Liviu Ciulei, Zelda Fichandler, Stephen Kanee, Michael Lessac, Gary Pearle, Douglas C. Wager; Sets, Karl Eigsti, David Gropman, Desmond Heeley, Paul King, Ming Cho Lee, Santo Loquasto, Tom Lynch, Tony Straiges; Costumes, Desmond Heeley, Carol Oditz, Mary Ann Powell, Marjorie Slaiman, Diane Schuster; Lighting, Arden Fingerhut, Allen Hughes, Hugh Lester, Roger Milliken, William Mintzer, Duane Schuler, Jennifer Tipton, Christopher Townsend; Composers, Nick Bicat, Robert Dennis, John Gray, Mel Marvin; Technical Director, Henry R. Gorfein; Stage Managers, Clinton Turner Davis, Suzanne Fry George Gracy, Stephen J. McCorkle, Stephen Nasuta.

COMPANY

F. Murray Abraham, Eunice Anderson, Stanley Anderson, Richard Bauer, Marshall Borden, Pandora Bronson, Blair Brown, Lynne Brown, Inga Bunsch, Leslie Cass, Caitlin Clarke, Juli Cooper, Peter Crombie, Terrence Currier, Brenda J. Davis, John Elko, Laura Esterman, Kurt Everhart, John Getz, John Glover, Ernest Graves, Mark Hammer, June Hansen, Joanne Hkrach, Christopher Hux, Marcia Hyde, Judith Ivey, Kent C. Jackson, Annalee Jeferies, James Jenner, Timothy Jerome, Linda Lee Johnson, John Christopher Jones, Kelly Kennedy, Will Kuluva, Jill Larson, Lee Lawson, Claire Kuang-Pi Lee, Mark Linn-Baker, Richard Lupino, Joan MacIntosh, Maeve McGuire, Tom Matsusaka, Anne Miyamoto, Debra Monk, Cristina Moore, Bruce Ed Morrow, W. Thomas Newman, Brad O'Hare, Michael O'Keefe, Joe Palmieri, Ron Perlman, Eric Peterson, Lorraine L. Pollack, Barry Primus, Robert Prosky, Kenneth Ryan, David P. Sampson, Barbara Sohmers, Cary Ann Spear, Jean-Pierre Stewart, Robert Thaler, David Toney, Stephen Weyte, Halo Wines

PRODUCTIONS

The Winter's Tale by William Shakespeare, Teibele and Her Demon by Isaac Bashevis Singer and Eve Friedman, Design for Living by Noel Coward, You Can't Take It with You by George S. Kaufman and Moss Hart, After the Fall by Arthur Miller, and *Premieres* of Plenty by David Hare (U.S.), Billy Bishop Goes to War (U.S.) by Eric Peterson and John Gray, An American Tragedy by Anthony Giardina (World)

Joe B. Mann Photos

Stanley Anderson, Richard Bauer, Mark Hammer in "After the Fall" Top: Ernest Graves, Michael O'Keefe, Marcia Hyde, Halo Wines, Joanne Hkrach in "An American Tragedy"

ARIZONA THEATRE COMPANY

Tuscon/Phoenix, Arizona
November 6, 1979–April 20 1980

Artistic Director, Sandy Rosenthal; Acting Artistic Director, Mark Lamos; Managing Director, David Hawkanson; Press, Mary Bensel, Christine Tamulaitis; Business Manager, Daphne L. Rudolph; Production Manager, Thomas Hall; Technical Director, John B. Forbes; Administrative Director, Sherilyn Forrester; Directors, Mark Lamos, Phil Killian, Harris Laskawy, George Keathley; Sets, Jim Newton, John Kavelin, Christina Haatainen, Ruth A. Wells; Costumes, Anna Belle Kaufman, Christina Haatainen, Ruth A. Wells, Merrily Ann Murray; Lighting, Dan T. Willoughby, John B. Forbes

COMPANY

Dan Butler, Carol Calkins, Christopher Carroll, Patricia Conolly, Robert Cornthwaite, Joe DeSalvio, Jerry Allan Jones, Sylvia Sage Lane, Harris Laskawy, Mary Layne, Dee Maaske, Ann-Sara Matthews, Anthony Mauro, Penny Metropulos, Barry Michlin, Dale Raoul, Jill Rogosheske, Benjamin Stewart, Rebecca Taylor, Jack van Natter, Peter Van Slyke
Howard T. Allen, Tony DeBruno, Harold Dixon, Tina Efron, Kathleen Gabel, Prindle Gorman, Johanna E. Grout, Charles F. Hartung, Charles Julian, Matthew A. Loney, Richard Muirr, Joe Orton, Barbara Robison, Susan Ronn, Lizette Tallon, Thom Wacker, William Thumser

PRODUCTIONS

A Flea in Her Ear, Twelfth Night, The Glass Menagerie, Father's Day, The Sea Gull, The Threepenny Opera

Joe DeSalvio, Mary Layne and company in "The Threepenny Opera"

ASOLO STATE THEATER

Sarasota, Florida
September 2, 1979–August 31, 1980
Executive Director, Richard G. Fallon; Artistic Director, Robert Strane; Managing Director, Howard J. Millman; Press, Edith N. Anson; Musical Director, John Franceschina; Choreographer, Jim Hoskins; Sets, Howard Bay, Bennet Averyt, David Emmons, Sandro La Ferla, Robert C. Barnes, Robert Darling; Costumes, Catherine King, Flozanne John, Sally A. Kos, Diane Berg; Lighting, Martin Petlock; Technical Director, Victor Meyrich; Stage Managers, Marian Wallace, Stephanie Moss, Dolly Meenan

COMPANY

Douglas H. Baker, Robert Beseda, Bill Blackwood, Pam Guest, David S. Howard, Max Howard, Monique Morgan, Robert Murch, Patricia Oetken, Bette Oliver, Chuch Patterson, William Pitts, Barbara Sohmers, Isa Thomas, Bradford Wallace, Bairbre Dowling, Patrick Egan, Robert Elliott, William Metzo, Clark Niederjohn, Dottie Dee, Fred Greene, Sharron Miller, Barbara Redmond, Robert Stallworth
Porter Anderson, Carolyn Blackinton, Dov Fahrer, Marilyn Foote, Christine Joelson, Jeff King, Michael L. Locklair, Carolyn Ann Meeley, Janet Nawrocki, Evan Parry, Ann Stafford, Susannah Berryman, Tara Buckley, Marnie Carmichael, James Clarke, James Daniels, Paula Dewey, Helen Halsey, Mark Hirschfield, Alan Kimberly, Clardy Malugen, Paul Singleton, Charles Bennison, Susan Esther Burnim, Charlie Cronk, Robert Ferguson, Barry Friedman, Jeanann Glassford, Marc H. Glick, Elizabeth Harrell, Michael Hodgson, Arthur Glen Hughes, Robert Kratky, Robin Llewellyn, Lowry Marshall, Peter Massey, Jonathan Michaelsen, Mark Rosenwinkel, Connie Rotunda, Elizabeth Streiff
GUEST ARTISTS: Stephen Rothman, Mark Epstein, John Reich, Alan Frenkel

PRODUCTIONS

Volpone, Let's Get a Divorce, Long Day's Journey into Night, A History of the American Film, Othello, Stag at Bay, The Cherry Orchard, Ah, Wilderness!, The Tempest, Da, Tintypes, and *World Premiere* of "Merlin!"

Gary W. Sweetman Photos

"A History of the American Film"
Top: "Ah, Wilderness!"

BARTER THEATRE

Abingdon, Virginia
Forty-seventh Season
Artistic Director/Producer, Rex Partington; Business Manager, Pearl Hayter; Press, Katherine Scoggins; Stage Directors, Larry Alford, John Going, Voigt Kempson, Jeff Meredith, John Olon-Scrymgeour, Owen Phillips, Kenneth Robbins; Musical Director, Byron Grant; Assistant Musical Director, Marvin Jones; Sets, Bennett Averyt, Gregory Buch, F. Leonard Darby, Parmalee Welles, T. Park Warne; Costumes, Georgia Baker, Judith Dolan, Carr Garnett, Sigrid Insull, Rachel Kurland, Anne Duff Parker; Lighting, Cindy Limauro; Stage Managers, Laura Burroughs, Champe Leary, Tony Partington, Steven Woolf

COMPANY

Sam Blackwell, James Carnelia, Edward Conery, Michael Guido, Terry Hinz, Cleo Holladay, Beverly Jensen, Michael Kolba, Robert McNamara, Tony Partington, Elizabeth Ann Reavey, Kimberly Ross, William Tost, Alan Zampese
GUEST ARTISTS: Gwen Arment, Jonathan Ball, Jeffery Burchfield, Gerald A. Burke, Gary Daniel, Mary Anne Dempsey, Adrienne Doucette, Dottie Dee, Henry Gardner, Larry Hansen, Anna McNeely, Tod Miller, Mary Neufield, Kevin O'Leary, Edward Prostak, George Riddle, Jane Ridley, Con Roche, Virginia Seidel, Tyson Stephenson, Ann Varley, Marsha Warner, Ruth Williamson

PRODUCTIONS

Hay Fever, I Do! I Do!, The Wonderful Ones, A Doll's House, Same Time Next Year, Misalliance, Dames at Sea, Absurd Person Singular, Side by Side by Sondheim, Luv, The Fantasticks, The Private Ear and the Public Eye

Greg Palmer Photos

Right Center: Terry Hinz, Sam Blackwell,
Michael Guido, Robert McNamara, William Tost
in "Misalliance"

Ruth Williamson, Tod Miller, Virginia
Seidel, Larry Hansen, Marsha Warner
in "Dames at Sea"

CENTER STAGE MAINSTAGE

Baltimore, Maryland
September 7, 1979–July 6, 1980
Artistic Director, Stan Wojewodski, Jr.; Managing Director, Peter W. Culman; Press, Sally Livingston; Stage Managers, Amanda Mengden, Jan Crean

PRODUCTIONS AND CASTS

MOTHER COURAGE AND HER CHILDREN by Bertolt Brecht; Director, Stan Wojewodski, Jr.; Set, Henry Millman; Lighting, Paul Gallo; Musical Director, Charles Brock; Costumes, Carrie Robbins; Additional Music, Don Scwartz. CAST: Thomas Kopache, Judd Jones, Trazana Beverley, Keith David, Keith Esau, Seret Scott, Michael McCarty, Robert Jackson, Scott Schofield, Brent Dickey, Beej Johnson, Daniel Corcoran, Gregory T. Daniel, Walter Pearthree, Rosemary Knower
PVT. WARS & LONE STAR by James McClure; Director, Stan Wojewodski, Jr.; Sets, Henry Millman, Barry Robison; Costumes, Barry Robison, Lighting, Annie Wrightson. CAST: Jamey Sheridan, Vasili Bogazianos, Daniel Ziskie, John Goodman, Steve Rankin, Billy Padgett
A CHRISTMAS CAROL: SCROOGE AND MARLEY: by Charles Dickens; Adapted by Israel Horowitz; Director, Jackson Phippin; Set, Hugh Landwehr; Costumes, Bob Wojewodski; Lighting, Judy Rasmuson; Sound, David Campbell; Movement, Elizabeth Walton; Film, Richard Chisolm. CAST: Louise Beachner, William Swetland, Terry O'Quinn, Gavin Reed, Walter Pearthree, Rosemary Knower, Vivienne Shub, Michele Luchs, Julian Fleisher, Daniel Corcoran, Jocelyn Wood, Timothy Green, Ray Dooley, Elizabeth Lanthram, Alice Adler, Denise Koch, Richard Dix, Chip Graham, Shirley Bryan, Kenny Peyton, Vickie Thomas, Reginald Vel Johnson, Renee Smith
WATCH ON THE RHINE by Lillian Hellman; Director, Irene Lewis; Set, Hugh Landwehr; Costume, Linda Fisher; Lighting, Arden Fingerhut; Sound, David Campbell. CAST: Vivienne Shub, Carmen Mathews, Everett Ensley, Terry O'Quinn, Keith Rubin, Sarah Hart, Richard Kavanaugh
A DAY IN THE DEATH OF JOE EGG by Peter Nichols; Director, Jackson Phippin; Set, John Kasarda; Costumes, Melissa F. Binder; Lighting, Bonnie Ann Brown. CAST: Richard Kavanaugh, Tana Hicken, Joan Shangold, Steven Sutherland, Carole Monferdini, Sheila Coonan
CRIMES OF THE HEART by Beth Henley; Director, J Ranelli; Set, Hugh Landwehr; Costumes Fred Voelpel; Lighting, John Gleason; Sound, Meredith Zydner. CAST: Barbara eda-Young, Jane Galloway, Terry O'Quinn, Ellen Parker, Sally Sockwell, Walter Pearthree, Justin Deas
CYRANO DE BERGERAC by Edmond Rostand; Translated and Adapted by Anthony Burgess; Director, Stan Wojewodski, Jr.; Set, Hugh Landwehr; Costumes, Dona Granata; Lighting, Judy Rasmuson. CAST: Mark Basile, David Hodge, Jason Moehring, Patti Kalember, Nels Hennum, Conal O'Brien, Ken Meseroll, Kenton Benedict, Ray Dooley, Daniel Szelag, Terry O'Quinn, Steve Rankin, Diana Stagmer, Karen Wadman, Cherie Weinert, Daniella DeFilippo, Paul Peeling, Mark Torres, J. S. Johnson, Anderson Matthews, Shaine Marinson, Vivienne Shub, Bob Burrus, Julian Fleisher, Brent Dickey, Walt MacPherson, F. Murray Abraham
SOPHIE & WILLIA by Michael Kassin; Director, Stan Wojewodski, Jr.; Set, Hugh Landwehr; Costumes, Lesley Skannal; Lighting, Bonnie Ann Brown. CAST: Deloris Gaskins, Ellis Williams, Estelle Gettleman
THE DUENNA by Lance Mulcahy; Director, Katherine Mendeloff; Set, Hugh Landwehr; Costumes, Lesley Skannal; Lighting, Bonnie Ann Brown. CAST: Gerrit DeBeer, Jay Lowman, Donalyn Petrucci, Liz Sheridan, Lance Davis, Ralph Bruneau, Sophie Schwab, Joel Kramer
THE WHALES OF AUGUST by David Berry; Director, Bill Ludel; Set, Hugh Landwehr; Costumes, Lesley Skannal; Lighting, Bonnie Ann Brown; Sound, David Campbell. CAST: Kate Wilkinson, Margaret Thomson, Vivienne Shub, Louis Beachner

Right Center: Vasili Bogazianos, Jamey Sheridan, Dan Ziskie in "Pvt. Wars"

BODY POLITIC

Chicago, Illinois
September 1979–May 1980
Managing Director, Sharon Phillips; Artistic Director, Dale McFadden; Press, Warner Crocker; Business Manager, Gretchen Althen

PRODUCTIONS AND CASTS

THE RUFFIAN ON THE STAIR by Joe Orton; Director, Dale McFadden; Set, Thomas Beall; Costumes, Maggie Bodwell; Lighting, John Rodriguez. CAST: Michael Tezla, Susan Dafoe, James McCance, with FUNERAL GAMES by Joe Orton with James Deuter, James McCance, Michael Tezla, Susan Dafoe, Keith Fort
THE KING'S CLOWN by David Vando; Director, Dale McFadden; Set and Lights, Lou Raimerez; Costumes, Sherry Ravitz. CAST: Patrick Brumbaugh, J. Neil Boyle, Tracy Callahan, Barrie Mason, Derrell Capes, Frank Farrell, Harry Caramanos, Julia Maish
THE DECLINE AND FALL OF THE ENTIRE WORLD AS SEEN THROUGH THE EYES OF COLE PORTER arranged by Ben Bagley; Director, Dean Button; Choreography, Dennis Grimaldi; Musical Direction, Sam Hill; Set and Lights, Thomas Beall; Costumes, Julie Nagel. CAST: Charles E. Gerber, Buddy King, Sally Benoit, Diane Hurley, Roberta Stack, Susanna Wells who was succeeded by Didi Hitt
MACBETH by William Shakespeare; Director, Dale McFadden; Set and Lights, John Rodriguez; Costumes, Sherry Ravitz. CAST: Barrie Mason, Julia Maish, Hollis Resnik, Stan Winiarski, Lawrence McCauley, Daniel Feldt, Victor Johnson, Richard Kuhlman, Jeffrey Adler, Frank Farrell, Michael Rider, Michael Lloyd, Pauline Brailsford, Hayden Jones, James McCance
RHYMING COUPLETS (U.S./Premiere) by Kevin Grattan; Director, Bruce Burgun; Lighting, Geri Kelly; Costumes, Carl Forsberg. CAST: Bruce Burgun, Martha Lavey, Moira McMahon, Charlotte Maier, Ann Woodworth, Byron Jones

Stuart Markson Photos

Top Left: Buddy King, Sally Benoit in "The Decline and Fall . . ."

Trazana Beverley, Seret Scott in "Mother Courage"

CENTER THEATRE GROUP
AHMANSON THEATRE

Los Angeles, California
October 12, 1979–May 31, 1980
Thirteenth Season
Managing Director, Robert Fryer; General Manager, Michael Grossman; Press, Rupert Allan, James H. Hansen; Michelle McGrath; Administrative Coordinator, Joyce Zaccaro; Associate, Tom Jordan; Chairman Emeritus, Mrs. Norman Chandler; Honorary Chairman of the Board, Lew R. Wasserman; Co-Chairman, Charlton Heston, Walter Mirisch.

PRODUCTIONS AND CASTS

CAUSE CELEBRE by Terence Rattigan; Director, George Keathley; Setting, David Emmons; Costumes, Noel Taylor; Lighting, Martin Aronstein; Music, Robert Prince; Production Associate, Robert Linden; Production Administrator, Ralph Beaumont; Stage Managers, William S. O'Brien, Patrick Watkins, John Sanderford, Woody Skaggs; Technical Supervisor, Robert Rourolo; Sound, William Young. CAST: Anne Baxter (Alma), Dorothy McGuire (Edith), William Roerick (O'Connor), Jack Gwillim (Judge), Jeanette Landis (Joan), Tom Covert-Nolan (George), John Eames (Francis), Ian Abercrombie (Coronore), Val Bettin (Croom-Johnson), Chad Christian Cowgill (Christopher), Joshua Daniel (Randolph), Kate Fitzmaurice (Irene), Patricia Fraser (Stella), James Charles-Garrett (Court Clerk), Daniel Grace (Sgt. Bagwell), Wiley Harker (Casswell), Charles Nicklin (Montagu), Eric Williams (Tony)
BEDROOM FARCE by Alan Ayckbourn; Director, Alan Ayckbourn, Peter Hall; Design, Timothy O'Brien, Tazeena Firth; Lighting, David H. Murdock; Associate Producer, Ron Abbott; Presented by Marshall T. Young, Gordon Crowe; Stage Managers, Don Lamb, John Stewart; Technical Supervisor, Robert Routolo; Hairstylist, Jean Rapollo. CAST: June Lockhart (Delia), Tom Elwell (Ernest), Jill Haworth (Jan), Barry Cullison (Malcolm), Jane House (Susannah), Ross Petty (Nick), Jill P. Rose (Kate), Malcolm Stewart (Trevor)
ON GOLDEN POND by Ernest Thompson; Director, George Schaefer; Setting, William Pitkin; Costumes, Noel Taylor; Lighting, Martin Aronstein; Production Associate, Robert Linden; Wardrobe, Eddie Dodds. CAST: Julie Harris (Ethel Thayer), Charles Durning (Norman Thayer), Marcia Rodd (Chelsea Thayer Wayne), William Lanteau (Charlie Martin), James Antonio (Bill Ray), Brad Savage (Billy Ray)
THE ELEPHANT MAN by Bernard Pomerance; Director, Jack Hofsiss. See National Touring Companies, page 171.

Jay Thompson Photos

**Ann Baxter, Dorothy Maguire
in "Cause Celebre"**

CENTER THEATRE GROUP
MARK TAPER FORUM

Los Angeles, California
August 23, 1979–July 27, 1980
Thirteenth Season
Artistic Director/Producer, Gordon Davidson; Managing Director, William P. Wingate; Associate Artistic Director, Kenneth Brecher; Improvisational Theatre Project Director, John Dennis; Press, Nancy Hereford, Anthony Sherwood, Karen Kruzich, Gail Browne; Designer, Tharon Musser; Technical Director, Robert Routolo; Stage Managers, Nikos Kafkalis, Mark Wright, Earl L. Frounfelter, Jonathan Barlow Lee, Frank Marino, James T. McDermott, Mary Michele Miner

PRODUCTIONS AND CASTS

TALLEY'S FOLLY by Lanford Wilson. See Broadway Calendar, Page 43, in repertory with 5th OF JULY by Lanford Wilson; Director, Marshall W. Mason; Set, John Lee Beatty; Costumes, Laura Crow; Lighting, Dennis Parichy; Sound, Chuck London; Presented in association with Circle Repertory Company (Marshall W. Mason, Artistic Director); Assistant Director, John Manulis. CAST: Christopher Allport (Kenneth Talley, Jr.), Amy Wright (Shirley Talley) or Karlene Crockett, Jeff Daniels (Jed Jenkins), Jonathan Hogan (John Landis), Susan Sullivan (Gwen Landis), Joyce Reehling (June Talley), Helen Stenborg (Sally Talley Friedman) or Mary Jackson, Danton Stone (Weston Hurley)
CHILDREN OF A LESSER GOD *(World Premiere)* by Mark Medoff; Director, Gordon Davidson; Set, Thomas A. Walsh; Costumes, Lilly Fenichel; Lighting, Tom Ruzika. CAST: Phyllis Frelich (Sarah), John Rubinstein (James), Lewis Merkin (Orin), William Frankfather (Franklin), Jo de Winter (Mrs. Norman), Julianne Gold (Lydia), Valerie Curtin (Edna). See Broadway Calendar, page 52.
I OUGHT TO BE IN PICTURES *(World Premiere)* by Neil Simon; Director, Herbert Ross; Set, David Jenkins; Costumes, Nancy Potts; Lighting, Tharon Musser. CAST: Joyce Van Patten (Steffy), Dinah Manoff (Libby), Tony Curtis (Herb). See Broadway Calendar, page 54.

SAYS I, SAYS HE by Ron Hutchinson; Director, Steven Robman; Set, David Jenkins; Costumes, Julie Weiss; Lighting, Martin Aronstein; Choreography, Tom Cashin; Musical Director, Mick Moloney. CAST: Alley Mills (Bella Phelan), Brian Dennehy (Pete Hannafin), John Pleshette (Jigger Hannafin), Mary Ann Chinn (Maeve McPherson), Paddy Edwards (Landlady/Old Biddy/Bridie), Sandy McCallum (Lodger/Carradine/Hughes/Sam), and The Irish Tradition: Billy McComiskey, Brendan Mulvihill, Andy O'Brien
DIVISION STREET *(World Premiere)* by Steve Tesich; Director, Tom Moore; Set, Ralph Funicello; Costumes, Robert Blackman; Lighting, Martin Aronstein. CAST: Andra Akers (Dianah), Didi Conn (Nadja), Keene Curtis (Yovan), Anthony Holland (Sal), Justin Lord (Betty), Tim Matheson (Chris), Joe Regalbuto (Roger), Madge Sinclair (Mrs. Bruchinski), Matthew Robin (Mr. Knight). A play in two acts. The action takes place at the present time in Chicago, Ill.

**Jane House, June Lockhart,
Tom Ewell in "Bedroom Farce"**

**Left Center: Charles Durning, Julie Harris,
Marcia Rodd, James Antonio, Brad Savage
in "On Golden Pond"**

Tony Papenfuss as Scrooge in "A Christmas Carol"

MARK TAPER FORUM
LABORATORY PRODUCTIONS

Staff Producer, Madeleine Puzo; Manager, Rebecca Blackwell; Production Manager, Joe Ward

PRODUCTIONS AND CASTS

CATHOLIC GIRLS by Doris Baizley; Director, Jeremy Blahnik; Music, Richard Weinstock; Lyrics, Doris Baizley, Richard Weinstock; Producer, Susan Albert Loewenberg; Set and Lighting, Barbara Ling; Costumes, Victoria de Kay; Associate Producer, Sara Maultsby; Technical Director, William David Carpenter; Stage Managers, Tami Toon, Sadie Boyd-Bodwell. CAST: Belita Moreno (Blackie), Lisa Jane Persky (Mary Clare), Sharon Barr (Anna), Darrell Fetty (Server/Skipper/Prince), Madge Sinclair (Mama)

A CHRISTMAS CAROL by Charles Dickens; Adapted by Doris Baizley; Director, John Dennis; Sets and Costumes, Charles Berliner; Lighting, Pamela Cooper; Music, Susan Seamans Harvey: Choreography, Lynn Dally. CAST: Tony Papenfuss (Scrooge), Andy Rivas (Tiny Tim), Paul Ainsley (Marley), Mark Herrier (Cratchit), Becky Gonzalez (Mrs. Crachtit), Michael McNilly (Ghost of Christmas Past), Roberto Covarrubias (Ghost of Christmas Present), Kim Conrad (Scavenger), R. Barry Moore (Charles Dickens), Rick Vartorella (Ghost of Christmas Present), Stephen Burks (Ghost of Christmas Present), Dan Gerrity (Fred), Nancy Lane Sheehy (Fred's Wife), Barry Cutler (Fezziwig), Donna Fuller (Mrs. Fezziwig)

DISABILITY: A COMEDY by Ronald Ranieri Whyte; Director, Frank Condon; Set, Gavin A. Holmes; Costumes, Deborah Dryden; Lighting, Cameron Harvey; Stage Managers, Dianne Lewis Hall, Victoria Fahn. CAST: Andrew Parks (Larry), Dorothy Chace (Mom), Bill Zuckert (Dad), Juanin Clay (Jayne)

FROM THE ORIGINAL ACCOUNTS OF THE LONE WOMAN OF SAN NICOLAS ISLAND collected and edited by Robert F. Herzer, Albert B. Elsasser; Adapted and Directed by Jeremy Blahnik; Stage Managers, Dianne Lewis Hall; Victoria Fahn; Sound, Paul Medaille. CAST: Will Hare (George Nidever), Scott Hylands (Carl Dittman), Pamela Dunlap (Emma Hardacre)

MUMFUKLE OR A SMALL GOAT IN CRETE by the Mum Family; Director, George Marchi; Set, Donald Kreiger; Costumes, The Family; Lighting, Karen Katz; Choreography, Kimberly Neubert; Stage Managers, Tami Toon, Sadie Boyd Bodwell. CAST: Laurel Steven (Harmoni Mum), Nathan Stein (Mini Mum), Judith Burnett (Platni Mum), Rob Sullivan (Opti Mum), Roy Johns (Maxi Mum), Elissa Negrim (Chrysantha Mum), Albie Selzniek (Pandemoni Mum), Marylou Vozza (Micro Mum)

CONCRETE DREAMS: A REHEARSAL FOR THE 80's by Doris Baizley; Director, John Dennis; Sets and Lighting, D. Martyn Bookwalter; Music, Susan Seamans Harvey; Choreography, Lynn Dally. CAST: Mark Herrier (J.D. Flagg), Michael McNeilly (Burt), Tony Papenfuss (Radio), Robert Covarrubias (Gato), Donna Fuller (Kay), Deborah Tilton (Bea), Stephen Burks (Green)

APEWATCH by Elaine Osio; Director, G. W. Bailey; Stage Manager, Dianne Lewis Hall; Production Assistant, Gregory Plotkin; Design, Keith Gonzales; Sound, Joe Ward. CAST: Caitlin O'Heaney (Lisa), Linda Carlson (Karen), Joan Crosby (Joan), Andy Wood (Christopher), Marty Ferrero (Alan)

Jay Thompson Photos

Left Center: Alley Mills, Brian Dennehy, John Pleshette in "Says I, Says He" Above: Dinah Manoff, Tony Curtis in "I Ought to Be in Pictures" Top: Andra Akers, Keene Curtis in "Division Street"

CALIFORNIA ACTORS THEATRE

Los Gatos/Redwood City, California
November 1, 1979–June 1, 1980

Producing Director, Sheldon Kleinman; General Manager, Francine E. Gordon; Artistic Director, Dakin Matthews; Business Manager, Emily Graham; Production Manager, Michael Jeffra; Press, Karolyn Raush, Karl R. Schuck; Stage Managers, Michael Jeffra, Ken Barton; Technical Director, Terry Cermak; Costumes, Diana Alexis Sonte, Janice Gartin, James F. Frank, Atkin Pace; Props, M. Levy Stelzer; Sets, Ron Krempetz, Atkin Pace, R. K. Richards, Ralph J. Ryan; Guest Directors, James Dunn, G. W. Bailey

COMPANY

Ken Barton, Catherine Butterfield, Kandis Chappell, Cab Covay, Michael Flynn, Nathan Haas, Christianne Hauber, Karl Hesser, Will Huddleston, Bob Kallus, Felicity LaFortune, Julian Lopez-Morillas, Dakin Matthews, Anne McNaughton, William Moreing, Tom Ramirez, Anne Swift

PRODUCTIONS

A Midsummer Night's Dream, A Life in the Theatre, Liberty Inn, Mrs. Warren's Profession, Who's Afraid of Virginia Woolf?, Absent Friends, The Rehearsal, Spokesong

TOURING COMPANY

Joe Conti, Bruce W. De Les Dernier, Shannon Orrock, Jeff Risk, P.D. Soinski, Annie Zeller

PRODUCTIONS

Androcles and the Lion, and *World Premieres* of Beauty and the Beast by Karl R. Schuck, Huckleberry Finn adapted from Mark Twain's novel by Rosine Weisbrod

Bruce Campbell Photos

**Anne Swift, Dakin Matthews
in "The Rehearsal"**

CINCINNATI PLAYHOUSE

Cincinnati, Ohio
October 23, 1979–June 8, 1980

Producing Director, Michael Murray; Managing Director, Robert W. Tolan; Directors, Michael Murray, Emily Mann, John Going, Martin Fried, Ernie Zulia; Musical Director, Don Mannon; Choreographer, David Holdgreiwe; Sets, Ursula Belden, Karl Eigsti, Neil Peter Jampolis, Duke Durfee; Costumes, Caley Summers, Ursula Belden, Ann Firestone, Jennifer von Mayrhauser, Jess Goldstein, William Schroder; Lighting, Spencer Mosse, Pat Collins, Neil Peter Jampolis, Duke Durfee, March B. Weiss; Press, Jerri Roberts; Stage Managers, Ed Oster, Patricia Ann Speelman; Business Manager, Kathy Mohylsky; Production Manager, Duke Durfee

PRODUCTIONS AND CASTS

MAGIC TO DO (*Professional Premiere*) Conceived by Ernie Zulia, Frank Bartolucci. CAST: Scott Bakula, C. J. Critt, Jill Hoel, Valerie Karasek, James Rich

THE DIARY OF ANNE FRANK with Susan Ball, Johann Carlo, Donald Christopher, Leslie Goldstein, John Hammond, Juergen Kuehn, Delphi Lawrence, Leslie Meeker, Nada Rowand, Robert Shrewsbury

TWELFTH NIGHT with Kenneth Bright, Learie Peter Callender, Johann Carlo, Donald Christopher, Bill Cobbs, Timothy de Zarn, Peter Francis-James, David A. Judson, Floyd King, Bram Lewis, Tom Nardirosian, Jay Patterson, Marc Sanders, Claude-Albert Saucier, Richard Scharer, Lynne Tallman, Vince Trani, Caryn West, Michele-Denise Woods

ASHES with Dan Hamilton, Marion Lines, Jane Murray, Michael Thompson

THE CHERRY ORCHARD (*World Premiere*) in a new translation by Michael Henry Heim. CAST: John Abajian, Paul Andor, Tony Aylward, Johann Carlo, Michael Graves, Jack Hollander, David A. Judson, Ralph C. Lewis, DeAnn Mears, Monica Merryman, Gun-Marie Nilsson, Addison Powell, Richard Schafer, Mary Shelley, Adrian Sparks, Jack Sweeney, Lynne Tallman, Derek Visser, Marcia Weiland, Bill Williamson

DYLAN THOMAS GROWING UP with Emlyn Williams

THE DOWNSTAIRS BOYS (*World Premiere* April 1, 1980) by Murray Schisgal. CAST: Paul Benedict, Fred Kareman, Marcia Jean Kurtz, Jane Murray, Allan Wasserman

THE BAKER'S WIFE (*World Premiere* of revised version on May 13, 1980) Music and Lyrics, Stephen Schwartz; Book, Joseph Stein. CAST: Kathryn Anne, Scott Bakula, Noah Bless, Donald Christopher, Michael Connolly, George Dash, Nazig Edwards, Iris Elliott, Jill Hoel, Tony Hoty, Juergen Kuehn, Vance Miselle, Krista Neumann, Alan North, Debby Watassek, Bill Williamson

Sandy Underwood Photos

**Krista Neumann, Alan North
in "The Baker's Wife"**

**Left Center: "The Diary
of Anne Frank"**

CLEVELAND PLAY HOUSE

Cleveland, Ohio
September 26, 1979–May 4, 1980
Sixty-fourth Season

Director, Richard Oberlin; Associate Director, Larry Tarrant; Business Manager, Nelson Isekeit; Scenic Design, Richard Gould, Technical Director, James Irwin; Press, Edwin P. Rapport, Cynthia G. Knapp; Administrative Assistant, Nadine Buchanan; Directors, Paul Lee, Evie McElroy, Richard Halverson, Richard Oberlin, William Rhys, Larry Tarrant, and Guests: Joseph J. Garry, Jr., Judith Haskell; Designers, Richard Gould, James Irwin, David Langston, Estefle Painter, David Smith, and Guests: Gary Eckhart, William Martin Jean; Costume Design, Estelle H. Painter; Stage Managers, Varney Knapp, Stanley R. Suchecki; Music Consultant, David Gooding; Props, David Smith

COMPANY

Mary Adams-Smith, Kenneth Albers, Norm Berman, Sharon Bicknell, Candice M. Cain, Sydney Erskine, Elisabeth Farwell, Jo Farwell, Paul A. Floriano, June Gibbons, Richard Halverson, James P. Kisicki, Joe D. Lauck, Kelly Lawrence, Allen Leatherman, Paul Lee, Harper Jane McAdoo, Evie McElroy, Richard Oberlin, Carolyn Reed, William Rhys, James Richards, Carol Schultz, Gary Smith, Wayne S. Turney GUEST ARTISTS: Catherine Albers, James Bartek, Cliff Bemis, Shirley Bryan, Catherine Cox, David O. Frazier, George Gould, Ralph Gunderman, Providence Hollander, Philip Kerr, Kelly C. Morgan, Judy Nevits, Si Osborne, Theresa Piteo, Peter Shawn, Dudley Swetland, William Swetland, Laura Waterbury

PRODUCTIONS

Images *(World Premiere)* with music of Serge Lama, A History of the American Film, Catsplay, A Mid-summer Night's Dream, Side by Side by Sondheim, A Lovely Sunday for Creve Coeur, Da, Custer, Wings, Wuthering Heights *(World Premiere)* by Paul Lee, Present Laughter, Peanuts and Cracker Jack

Michael Edwards Photos

Phillip Kerr, William Rhys in "Present Laughter" Top: "Custer"

DALLAS THEATER CENTER

Dallas, Texas
October 9, 1979–August 2, 1980

Managing Director, Paul Baker; Associate Director, Mary Sue Jones; Stage Directors, Robyn Flatt, Judith Davis, Mary Sue Jones, John Henson, Bryant J. Reynolds, C. P. Hendrie, Ryland Merkey, John Logan; Sets, Virgil Beavers, John Holloway, Peter Lynch, James Eddy, Robert Duffy, Yoichi Aoki; Costumes, Virgil Beavers, Tim Haynes, M. G. Johnston, Cheryl Denson, Sally Askins, Michael Krueger, Deborah Allen, Irene Corey, John Henson; Lighting, Randy Bonifay, Wayne Lambert, James Eddy Linda Blase, Don Thomas, Cliff Smith, Michael Scudday; Stage Managers, Philip Reeves, Michael Scudday, Candy Buckley, Ken Hudson, Dennis Vincent, Hanna Cusick, Joe Fioccola, Michael Kreuger, S. Carleton Guptill, Kenneth Hill

COMPANY

Yoichi Aoki, Virgil Beavers, Linda Blase, Randy Bonifay, Judith Davis, Cheryl Denson, Robert Duffy, John Figlmiller, Robyn Flatt, Martha Goodman, Tim Green, C. P. Hendrie, John Henson, Allen Hibbard, Mary Lou Hoyle, Mary Sue Jones, John Logan, Rebecca Logan, Ronni Lopez, Peter Lynch, Ryland Merkey, Norma Moore, Randy Moore, Bryant J. Reynolds, Synthia Rogers, Mary Rohde, Glenn Allen Smith, Louise Mosley Smith, John R. Stevens, Randolph Tallman, Jacque Thomas, Lynn Trammell, Lee Wheatley, Ronald Wilcox

PRODUCTIONS

To Kill a Mockingbird by Harper Lee, Remember by Preston Jones, A Man for All Seasons by Robert Bolt, A Christmas Carol adapted by John Figlmiller and Sally Netzel from Charles Dickens' novel, Ladybug Ladybug Fly Away Home by Mary Rohde, Sly Fox by Larry Gelbart, Holiday by Philip Barry, and *Premiere* of The Illusion by Randolph Tallman, Steven Mackenroth, John Henson and John Logan

Linda Blase, Jim Eddy Photos

John Figlmiller, Ryland Merkey, John Henson in "Remember"

Left Center: Deborah Allen, Randolph Tallman in "The Illusion"

DELAWARE THEATRE COMPANY

Wilmington, Delaware
December 7, 1979–May 30, 1980
First Season

Artistic Director, Cleveland Morris; Producing Director, Peter DeLaurier; Technical Director, Rick Harris; Designers Rick Harris, Ellen Dennis, Elizabeth Schweizer, Richard Johenning; Press, D'Arcy Webb

PRODUCTIONS AND CASTS

OVERRULES by George Bernard Shaw; Director, Cleveland Morris; with Peter DeLaurier, Ceal Phelan, Beverly Shatto, William Wright
PRIVATE LIVES by Noel Coward; Director, Cleveland Morris, with Sam Blackwell, Anne Eder, Marilynn Meyrick, Michael Petro, Ceal Phelan
THE GLASS MENAGERIE by Tennessee Williams; Director, Beverly Shatto, with Sam Blackwell, Michael Petro, Ceal Phelan, Elizabeth Phelan
PAGANO *(World Premiere)* by Drury Pifer; Director, Cleveland Morris, with David Baffone, Holly Cordes, Anne Eder, Marlene Hummel, Leo Irwin, Richard Mulrooney, Gary Pagano, Paris Peet, Drury Pifer, Michael Zalatoris

Left: Sam Blackwell, Ceal Phelan, Elizabeth Phelan in "The Glass Menagerie" Top: Marilynn Meyrick, Sam Blackwell, Ceal Phelan, Michael Petro in "Private Lives"

DENVER CENTER THEATRE COMPANY

Denver, Colorado
December 31, 1979–April 6, 1980
First Season

Artistic Director, Edward Payson Call; Managing Director, Peter B. England; Stage Directors, Edward Payson Call, Gene Lesser, William Woodman; Sets, Ralph Funicello, Marjorie Kellogg, Robert Mitchell, Bob Schmidt; Costumes, Nanzi Adzima, Deborah Bays, Lowell Detweiler, Kristina Watson; Lighting, Dirk Epperson, Duane Schuler; Composers, Benjamin James, Herb Pihofer, Steven Maurice Rydberg; Sound, Bruce Odland; Stage Managers, Dennis Bigelow, Peg Guilfoyle; Production Manager, Peter Davis; Press, Linda Kinsey

COMPANY

Gregg Almquist, Michael Lee Balch, Letitia Bartlett, Donnie Betts, Kay Casperson, John A. Coe, Maury Cooper, Tandy Cronyn, Tony Cummings, Sheila Dabney, Tyne Daly, Ted D'Arms, Margo Davis, Peggy Denious, Teddy Denious, Kevin Durkin, Karen Erickson, Donna Falcon, H. Mikel Feilen, John Galm, Chris Gauthier, Stanford Green, Lynnie Greene, Edward Hickok, Frank Jermance, Stephen Jimenez, David Johnson, Grace Keagy, Robert Keagy, Steve Eugene Klotz, Karen Landry, James Lawless, Darrie Lawrence, Ruth Margaret Lawyer, Damien Leake, Judy Leavell, Alice Lenicheck, Delroy Lindo, Mary Lopez, Allan Lurie, William Lyman, Stephen Markle, Cecelia Montoya, Loraine M. F. Masterson, John Napierala, James Newcome, Pamela O'Connor, Thomas S. Oleniacz, Daniel Onzo, Will Patton, Pippa Pearthree, Paul Perri, Lisa Jane Persky, Ian Phares, Schyleen Qualls, James Read, Ron Richardson, Richard Ross, Susan Ross, Robert Rutland, Kym Schwartz, David Seals, Brockman Seawell, Dutch Shindler, Dick Smith, Angel Vigil, Jerry Webb, Penelope Windust, Robin Wood, Michael Don Wymore.

PRODUCTIONS

The Caucasian Chalk Circle by Bertolt Brecht, Moby Dick—Rehearsed by Orson Welles, The Learned Ladies by Moliere (translated by Richard Wilbur), A Midsummer Night's Dream, Passing Game by Steve Tesich

Christopher Kirkland Photos

Right Center: Tandy Cronyn, Teddy Denious, Tyne Daly in "The Caucasian Chalk Circle"

William Lyman, Pippa Pearthree, Tandy Cronyn, Grace Keagy, Darrie Lawrence in "Learned Ladies"

DETROIT REPERTORY THEATRE

Detroit, Michigan
November 1, 1979–June 29, 1980
Artistic Director, Bruce E. Millan; Executive Director, Robert Williams; Production Coordinator, Marylynn Kacir; Production Assistant, Pat Ansuini; Lighting, Dick Smith; Sets, Bruce E. Millan; Costumes, Barbara Busby, Marianna Hoad, Bernadine Vida Darrell; Scenic Artist, John Knox; Stage Managers, Barbara Busby, Dee Andrus, William Boswell

PRODUCTIONS AND CASTS

A DELICATE BALANCE by Edward Albee with Barbara Busby, Robert Williams, Dee Andrus, Monika Ziegler, George Wilson, Juliette Gay

DECISION AT VALLEY FORGE (*World Premiere* January 10, 1980) by Muriel Andrew, with David Thomas, Michael W. Campbell, William Boswell, David Fox, Dennis Moore, Patrick Czeski, Richard Villaire, Robert Skrok, Ellis Foster, Roberta L. Rutherford, Ruth Allen Palmer, Sabrina Williams, Dee Andrus, Reginald McCloud, Luray Cooper, Pierre Chambers, Charlotte Nelson, Laura Hoskin, Janette Byrd, Initia Durley, Debbie Patrick, Timothy Roseborough, Sharon Douglas

DESIRE UNDER THE ELMS by Eugene O'Neill, with Robert Williams, Robert Skrok, Luray Cooper, David Fox, Barbara Busby, William Boswell, Michael W. Campbell, Celine Belanger, Phyllis Delois Clinkscales, Paula Davis, Laura Hoskins, Ilene McFadden, John Penallegon, Laurie M. Serwatowski

DESIGN FOR LIVING by Noel Coward, with Yolanda Williams, William Boswell, Dennis Moore, Council Cargle, Ruth Allen Palmer, Willie Hodge, Michael Wayne Campbell, Mattie Wolf, Sam Kirkland, Paula Davis, Jack E. Miller, Jr.

Roberta Rutherford, Ellis Foster, Dennis Moore, Robert Skrok in "Decision at Valley Forge"
Top: Barbara Busby, Robert Williams in "A Delicate Balance"

EAST WEST PLAYERS

Los Angeles, California
October 1979–September 1980
Artistic Director, Mako; Executive Producer, Rae Creevey; Administrator, Rick Momii; Assistant Artistic Director, Alberto Issac; Assistant Administrator, Dom Magwili; Sets, Rae Creevey, Woodward Romine, Jr., Ellen Wakamatsu; Musical Director, Glen Laurence Chin; Costumes, Shigeru Yaji, Terence Tam Soon; Lighting, Rae Creevey; Choreography, Shizuko Hoshi; Stage Directors, Mako, Michiko Tagawa, Alberto Issac, Saburo; Producers, Woodward Romine, Jr., Rae Creevey, Clyde Kusatsu; Stage Managers, Keone Young, Audrey Nash, Dave Jacobs, Irma Escamilla

PRODUCTIONS AND CASTS

PACIFIC OVERTURES with Ernest Harada, Alvin Ing, Mako, Soon Teck-Oh, Sab Shimono, Glen Laurence Chin, David Hirokane, Shizuko Hoshi, Richard Dana Lee, William Lee, John Lone, Dom Magwili, Robert Narita, Deb Nishimura, J. Maseras Pepito, Saachiko, Alberto Issac, Susan Ioka, Jim Ishida, Leigh Kim, Emily Kuroda, Clyde Kusatsu, Ellen Wakamatsu, Patti Yasutake, Keone Young, Kim Yumiko

TALES FROM EAST WEST with Glen Chin, Susan Haruye, Jim Ishida, Deb Nishimura, Ellen Wakamatsu, Keone Young, Dom Magwili

STORIES WITH STRINGS AND STICKS AND SHADOWS with Susan Haruye, Jim Ishida, Sala Iwamatsu, David Jacobs, Janet Mitsui, Deb Nishimura, J. Maseras Pepito, Michiko Tagawa, Ellen Wakamatsu, Patricia Yasutake

HAWAII NO KA OI with Keone Young, David Hirokane, Pat Li, Shizuko Hoshi, Jerry Tondo, Marilyn Tokuda, Marcus Mukai, Dave Jacobs, Lance Toyama, Ellen Wakamatsu, Tom L. Atha, Saachiko, Clyde Kusatsu

WHAT THE ENEMY LOOKS LIKE with Marilyn Tokuda, Emily Tokuda, Bill Lee, Patti Yasutake, Rob Narita, Jim Ishida, Tom L. Atha, Jason Nichols

DA KINE with David Hirokane, Jerry Tondo, Leigh Kim, Susan Haruye, Tom L. Atha, Herbert Victor, Dave Jacobs, Ellen Wakamatsu

(captions not submitted)

EAST WEST PLAYERS

FOLGER THEATRE GROUP

Washington, D. C.
September 25, 1979–July 27, 1980

Producer, Louis W. Scheeder; Associate Producer, Michael Sheehan; Production Manager, T. C. Behrens; Technical Director, Michael Foley; Business Manager, Mary Ann deBarbieri; Company Manager, Ruth Lancaster; Press, Paula Bond, Maris Newbold; Music Consultant, William Penn; Stage Directors, Mikel Lambert, Louis W. Scheeder, Leonard Peters, Kenneth Frankel, Roger Hendricks Simon; Sets, Hugh Lester, Russell Metheny, Kate Edmunds, Ursula Belden; Costumes, Hilary A. Sherred, Rosemary Ingham, Jess Goldstein, B. Allen Odom; Lighting, Hugh Lester, Richard Winkler; Choreography, Virginia Freeman, Erik Fredricksen; Stage Managers, Elizabeth Hamilton, Kevin Kinley, Peter Dowling, Jim Brady, Martha Knight

PRODUCTIONS AND CASTS

MACBETH by William Shakespeare, with Ray Aranha (Duncan/Siward/Murderer), Eric Zwemer (Malcolm), John Gilliss (Donalbain/Menteith/Witch), Sam Tsoutsouvas (Macbeth), Kenneth Gray (Banquo/Ghost), John Neville-Andrews (Macduff), Michael Gabel (Lennox), Ralph Cosham (Ross), Jim Beard (Angus/Murderer), Shepard Sobel (Caithness/Witch), Iliff McMahan (Fleance/Soldier), Marc Lee Adams (Young Siward/Witch), Mark Basile (Seyton/Servant/Messenger), Barbara Callander (Macduff's Son), Carlos Juan Gonzalez (Captain/Murderer), Bruce Ed Morrow (Doctor/Old Man), Leonardo Cimino (Porter), Glynis Bell (Lady Macbeth), Franchelle Stewart Dorn (Lady Macduff), Anne Stone (Gentlewoman), Nick Mathwick (Servant/Messenger), Karen Bayly (Maid), Robert Sacheli (Attendant/Soldier)

CUSTER by Robert E. Ingham, with Tom Blair (George Armstrong Custer), Sandy Faison (Elizabeth Bacon Custer), John McMartin (Frederick William Benteen), William Newman (Marcus A. Reno), Maggie Thatcher (First Woman), Ricki G. Ravitts (Second Woman), David Cromwell (Lt. Harrington), Robert Murch (Myles Moylan), John Mansfield (George Yates), Allan Carlsen (Man with carbine)

WILD OATS by John O'Keeffe, with Ralph Cosham (Sir George Thunder), John Neville-Andrews (Rover), Stephen Lang (Harry Thunder), Ray Aranha (Banks), Richard Mathews (Dory), Moultrie Patton (Gammon), Michael Gabel (Lamp), Kenneth Gray (Smooth), John Gilliss (Sim), Eric Zwemer (Zachariah), Iliff McMahan (Muz), Mark Basile (Trap), Jim Beard (Twitch), Henry Fonte (Waiter), Carlos Juan Gonzalez (Landlord), Marc Lee Adams (Ruffian), Lou Dickey (Ruffian), Cara Duff-MacCormick (Lady Amaranth), Mikel Lambert (Amelia), Glynis Bell (Jane), Karen Bayly (Maid)

LOVE LETTERS ON BLUE PAPER by Arnold Wesker, with William Myers (Victor Marsden), Tresa Hughes (Sonia Marsden), Ralph Cosham (Prof. Stapleton), John Neville-Andrews (Union Official)

CHARLIE AND ALGERNON (American Premiere) Book and Lyrics, David Rogers; Based on novel "Flowers for Algernon" by Daniel Keyes; Music, Charles Strouse; Musical Director-Conductor, Liza Redfield. CAST: Sandy Faison (Alice Kinnian), Chev Rodgers (Dr. Strauss), Robert Sevra (Dr. Nemur), P. J. Benjamin (Charlie), Nancy Franklin (Mrs. Donner), Loida Santos (Lita), Timothy Meyers (Frank), Julienne Marie (Charlie's Mother), John Edward Mueller or Anthony John-Carlo Paolillo (Little Charlie), Bruce Ed Morrow (Charlie's Father)

THE TAMING OF THE SHREW by William Shakespeare, with Chet Doherty (Lord/Vincentio), Floyd King (Christopher Sly/Pedant), Iliff McMahan (Bartholomew/Attendant), Mark Basile (Huntsman/Attendant), Brian Corrigan (Huntsman/Haberdasher), Henry Fonte (Huntsman/Attendant), Stuart Lerch (Huntsman/Tailor), Anne Stone (Hostess/Widow), Earle Edgerton (Baptista), Leonardo Cimino (Gremio), John Gillis (Lucentio), Count Stovall (Hortensio), John Neville-Andrews (Petruchio), David Cromwell (Servant), Jim Beard (Biondello), Brian Kale (Grumio), Wendy Hammond (Curtis), Ellen Newman (Katherina), Ricki G. Ravitts (Bianca), Mary Woods (Attendant)

TWELFTH NIGHT by William Shakespeare, with Ellen Newman (Viola), Count Stovall (Orsino), Glynis Bell (Olivia), Earle Edgerton (Sir Toby), Ralph Cosham (Sir Andrew), Mikel Lambert (Maria), David Cromwell (Malvolio), Floyd King (Feste), Leonardo Cimino (Fabian), Peter Jolly (Antonia), Eric Zwemer (Sebastian), Michael Gabel (Captain), Jim Beard (Valentine), Richard Cochrane (Curio), Irving Engleman (Priest), Mike Howell (First Officer), Henry Fonte (Second Officer), Mary Woods (Servant)

Joan Marcus Photos

Top Right: Stephen Lang, Cara Duff-Mac-Cormick in "Wild Oats"

P. J. Benjamin, Nancy Franklin in "Charlie and Algernon" Above: "Taming of the Shrew"

THE GOODMAN THEATRE
CHICAGO THEATRE GROUP

Chicago, Illinois
September 4, 1979–June 29, 1980

Artistic Director, Gregory Mosher; Managing Director, Janet Wade; Acting Managing Director, Roche Schulfer; Associate Artistic Director/Playwright-in-Residence, David Mamet; Press, Liz Skrodzki, Marie E. O'Conner; Business Manager, Barbara Janowitz; Production Manager, Philip Eickhoff; Stage Managers, Joseph Drummond, Chuck Henry, Cathryn Bulicek, Marsha Gitkind, Anne Claus, Thomas Giscotto; Props, James Swank; Sound, Uncle Tunes; Stage Directors, Wole Soyinka, Tony Mockus, Gregory Mosher, Marshall W. Mason, Michael Maggio, Burr Tillstrom, Samuel Beckett; Sets, Mary Rauscher, David Gropman, Joseph Nieminski, John Lee Beatty, Michael Merritt; Costumes, Christa Scholtz, James Edmund Brady, Jessica Hahn, Dunya Ramicova, Jennifer von Mayrhauser, Marsha Kowal; Lighting, Robert Christen, Pat Collins, Jennifer Tipton, Dennis Parichy, Duane Schuler, Rita Pietraszek

PRODUCTIONS AND CASTS

DEATH AND THE KING'S HORSEMAN *(American Premiere)* by Wole Soyinka, with Ben Halley, Jr., Norman Matlock, Masequa Myers, Celestine Heard, Faye Ternipsede-Bradbury, Alan Coates, Jill Shellabarger, Barry Reneau, Robert Jason, James R. Keith, Thomas Pool, Robert Scogin, Tod Wheeler, Terry Alexander, Harvy Blanks, Cheryl Bruce, Paul Butler, Patricia Cruz, Willie DeShong, Kimosha P. Murphy, Jody Naymik, Lenard Norris, Ernest Perry, Jr., Tonya Pinkins, Jackie Taylor, Lisa Ann Williamson, Babu Atiba, Eli Hoe Nai, Mosheh Milon, Betty Jean Jackson
A CHRISTMAS CAROL by Charles Dickens, with Robert Thompson, William J. Norris, Robert Scogin, Tim Halligan, Stewart Figa, Laurence Russo, Jack Hickey, Tony Lincoln, J. Pat Miller, Mark Christopher Maranto, Marcy Thompson, Peter Marks, Natalie Lee Anselmini, David Mink, Annabel Armour, William C. Renk, Dennis Kennedy, Sheila Keenan, Devorah Eizikovic, Michele Fitzsimmons, Richard G. Hill, Darryl Boehmer, Judy Barbosa, Jodean Culbert, Tricia Grennan, Philip Hoffman, Jeanine Morick, Del Close, Frank Howard, Fred Tumas, Geoff Herden
AN ENEMY OF THE PEOPLE by Henrik Ibsen, with Mike Genovese, Terry Kinney, Mary Cobb, William Marshall, Gregory Williams, Paul Winfield, Gregory C. Kramer, Mark Christopher Maranto, David Mink, Jeanine Morick, Roy K. Stevens, Dennis Kennedy, Bob Anderson, Harry Caramanos, George Grant, Marilyn Herrs, Gil Parker, Ernest Perry, Jr., Ed Rawson, William C. Renk, Mary Seibel, Charles Von Busch
BAL *(World Premiere)* by Richard Nelson, with Del Close, Michael Saad, John E. Mohrlein, Jim Belushi, Ellen Crawford, Dennis Kennedy, Patricia Hodges, Cosmo White, Leland Crooke, Belinda Bremner, Lora Staley, Daniel Cooney, Ron Dean, Caitlin Clarke
TALLEY'S FOLLY by Lanford Wilson, with Debra Mooney, Jordan Charney
CYRANO DE BERGERAC by Edmond Rostand, with Kenneth Welsh, Cara Duff-MacCormick, Larkin Malloy, Steven Sutherland, Mike Genovese, Eugene J. Anthony, Fern Persons, Greg Vinkler, Roger Mueller, Harry Caramanos, Laurence Russo, Frank Farrell, Jeanine Morick, Tracy Callahan, Molly Landgraf, Jack Hickey, Mark Voland, Stewart Figa, James D. Reynolds, Richard Kuhlman, Ed Meekin, David Kropp, Ross Lehman, Christopher McIntyre, Mitch Webb, Tod Wheeler, Dennis Kennedy, Megan McTavish, Sandra Lindberg, Hollis Resnik, Leland Crooke, Andrew Gorman, Bradley Mott
A LIFE IN THE THEATRE by David Mamet, with Mike Nussbaum, Cosmo White, and on tour with Cosmo White, Eugene Troobnick
KUKLA AND OLLIE LIVE! with Burr Tillstrom and the Kuklapolitans
BECKETT DIRECTS BECKETT: KRAPP'S LAST TAPE by Samuel Beckett who directed, with Rick Cluchey
THE FLYING KARAMAZOV BROTHERS with Timothy Daniel Furst, Randy Nelson, Paul David Magid, Howard Jay Patterson

Jim Clark Photos

Top Right: William Marshall, Paul Winfield in "Enemy of the People" Below: Michael Nussbaum, Cosmo White in "A Life in the Theatre"

Norman Matlock in "Death and the King's Horseman" Above: Jim Belushi, Del Close in "Bal"

GeVa THEATRE
Rochester, N. Y.
October 26, 1979–April 13, 1980
Managing Director, Jessica L. Andrews; Artistic Director, Gideon Y. Schein; Business Manager, Timothy C. Norland; Press, Bruce E. Rodgers; Technical Director, Tim Pickens; Props, Susan Weiss; Designer, Linda Joan Vigdor; Stage Managers, Marcy Gamzon, Jane Barish

PRODUCTIONS AND CASTS

WHO'S AFRAID OF VIRGINIA WOOLF? by Edward Albee, with Mary Louise Wilson, Cyril Mallett, Dale Hodges, Tony Pasqualini, Barry Robison, Paul Lyons, Lewis D. Rampino, Lee De-Lorme
BURIED CHILD by Sam Shepard, with Richard Humphrey, Phillip Jung, Paul Lyons, Linda Joan Vigdor, Lee DeLorme, Herman O. Arbeit, William Brenner, Barbara Bolton, Michael Longfield, Judith McIntyre, Patrick Turner, Cyril Mallett
WALTZ OF THE TOREADORS by Jean Anouilh, with Carol Gustafson, Owen S. Rachleff, Richard Loder, Barbara MacCameron, Susan Varon, Stephen Daley, Sonya Raimi, Linda Selman, I. Mary Carter, Morris Brown, Tricia Austin, Laurence Carr
FLIGHT TO THE FATHERLAND (World Premiere) by Michael Moriarty, with Janet Sarno, Herb Davis, David Chandler, Mary Jay, Leslie O'Hara, Cyril Mallett, Ben Levit, John Gisondi, Kristina Watson
SIDE BY SIDE BY SONDHEIM by Stephen Sondheim and Leonard Bernstein, Mary Rodgers, Richard Rodgers and Jules Styne, with Anna McNeely, Barbara Porteus, Mark Zimmerman, Michael Huffman, Michael Louis Grube, Henry Davis, Gretchen Glover
TWELFTH NIGHT by William Shakespeare, with William Brenner, George Hayden, Cheryl Giannini, Steven Barbash, Bob Ari, Lisa Evans, Peter Bartlett, Jacob Fruchtman, Lance Davis, Laura Copeland, Rogers Forbes, Dane Knell, Gilbert Cole, Lee Sloan, Pam Baker, Jane Barish, Ellen Jane Koch, Alan Richtmyer, Richard M. Isackes, Gerald Basserman, Paul Lyons, Linda Joan Vigdor

Steve Levinson Photos

Barbara MacCameron, Susan Varon, Mary Carter, Owen Rachleff in "Waltz of the Toreadors"
Top: Herman O. Arbeit, Judith McIntyre, Patrick Turner in "Buried Child"

HARTFORD STAGE COMPANY
Hartford, Connecticut
October 3, 1979–July 6, 1980
Producing Director, Paul Weidner; Managing Director, William Stewart; Associate Director, Irene Lewis; Business Manager, William W. Monroe; Press, Kathleen Cahill, Kathleen Johnston; Production Coordinator/Technical Director, Jack Conant; Stage Directors, Paul Weidner, Irene Lewis, Ron Lagomarsino; Sets, Lowell Detweiler, Santo Loquasto, John Conklin, Adrianne Lobel, John Jensen; Costumes, Linda Fisher, Jess Goldstein, Adrianne Lobel, Karen D. Miller; Lighting, Stephen Ross, Curt Ostermann, Peter Hunt, Steve Woodring, Paul Gallo; Choreography, Edmond Kresley; Stage Managers, Fred Hoskins, J. J. Jefferson

PRODUCTIONS AND CASTS

OLD WORLD by Aleksei Arbuzov, with Lori March, Alexander Scourby
DAMN YANKEES by George Abbott, Douglass Wallop; Music and Lyrics, Richard Adler, Jerry Ross. CAST: Bob Ari, Emery Battis, Elizabeth Bisberg, Josh Burton, Lenny Del Duca, Jr., Joel Frederickson, Petty O'Neill, Anthony Parker, David Rounds, Donn Ruddy, Michael Rupert, Stephen Rust, Sharon Friedman, Mary Fogarty, Erik Geier, Courtney George, Jason George, Lynnie Godfrey, Dolores Kenan, Robert Kellett, Matt Lombardo, Carole Monferdini, Fred Sanders, Kate Savchitz, Charlie Stavola, Swen Stengl, Dorothy Stinnette, Chris Sullivan, Alan Tibbet, Tom Toner, Pauline Weber, William Youmans
THE COCKTAIL PARTY by T. S. Elliott, with Barbara Caruso, Robertson Dean, Stefan Hartman, Rudy Hornish, Regina K. Mocey, Erika Petersen, Margaret Phillips, Stephen Rust, Richard Warwick
ARDELE by Jean Anouilh, with Barbara Caruso, Jerald Craig, Jeff Doctoroff, Elizabeth Goldberg, Richard Mathews, Kenneth Meseroll, Jack Murdock, John Newton, Margaret Phillips, Linda Scoullar, Lisabeth Shean
THE MEMBER OF THE WEDDING by Carson McCullers, with Dan Butler, Margaret Coughlin, Everett Ensley, Peter Francis-James, Sherri Kagan, David London, Nancy Madden, Theresa Merritt, Emily Norman, Amanda Plummer, Jerry Reid, Linda Scoullar, Robbie Stevenson, Christopher Sullivan
THE LADY FROM DUBUQUE by Edward Albee, with Elaine Bromka, Myra Carter, Frederick Coffin, Earle Hyman, Henry J. Jordan, Kate Kelly, Sharon Madden

Lanny Nagler Photos

Lori March, Alexander Scourby in "Old World"

Left Center: Amanda Plummer, Theresa Merritt, David London in "Member of the Wedding"

HARTMAN THEATRE COMPANY

Stamford, Connecticut
December 5, 1979–June 22, 1980
Fifth Season

Producing Directors, Del Tenney, Margot Tenney; Managing Director, Roger L. Meeker; Business Manager, Susan Schloemann; Production Manager, J. D. Ferrara; Press, Sally Christiansen; Stage Directors, Monroe Arnold, Louis Beachner, Austin Pendleton, Louis W. Scheeder, Terry Schreiber, Del Tenney, George C. White; Sets, Lowell Detweiler, John Falabella, Hugh Lester, Santo Loquasto, David Loveless, James F. Tilton; Costumes, Clifford Capone, Kathleen Egan, John Falabella, Linda Fisher, Rosemary Ingham, David Loveless, David Murin; Lighting, Frances Aronson, Rick Butler, Hugh Lester, John McLain, Jeffrey Schissler, James F. Tilton; Stage Managers, Hope Chillington, David N. Feight

PRODUCTIONS AND CASTS

MONSIEUR RIBADIER'S SYSTEM by Georges Feydeau *(U. S. Premiere)*, translated by Elizabeth Swain. CAST: Roderick Cook, Gwendolyn Lewis, George Morfogen, Mike Starr, Stephen Temperley, Margot Tenney
A VIEW FROM THE BRIDGE by Arthur Miller, with Jim Hale, Stafano LoVerso, Dan Mirro, Vic Polizos, Joseph Ragno, Bill Santoro, Judith Scarpone, Theodore Sorel, Mike Starr, Deborah Van Valkenburgh
CUSTER by Robert E. Ingham, with Glynis Bell, Tom Blair, Allan Carlsen, John Carroll, Richard Cochrane, David Cromwell, Sandy Faison, John Hertzler, John McMartin, William Newman, Ricki G. Ravitts, Maggie Thatcher
PRIVATE LIVES by Noel Coward, with Deborah Blair, Jacqueline Coslow, Terrence Markovich, Carrie Nye, Ian Sullivan
THE UNEXPECTED GUEST by Agatha Christie, with James C. Burge, Mark Diekmann, Timothy Doyle, Patrick Farrelly, Dan Hannafin, Celia Howard, Judith McGilligan, Dina Merrill, Jack Ryland, Stanley Sayer, Margot Tenney
UNCLE VANYA by Anton Chekhov; Adapted by Austin Pendleton; with Allan Arbus, Sara Botsford, Shirley Bryan, Katina Comings, Jacqueline Coslow, Joan Croydon, Miriam Lehmann-Haupt, Richard McKenzie, Bill Striglos, William Swetland
THE RESISTIBLE RISE OF ARTURO UI by Bertolt Brecht; Translated by George Tabori; Adapted by Monroe Arnold CAST: Frank Borgman, John C. Capodice, Gerrit de Beer, Dana Delaney, Pierre Epstein, Clarence Felder, Michael Galloway, John Gray, Marty Greene, Mel Haynes, Michael J. Hume, Lawrence C. Lott, Donna Mitchell, Julian Neil, Zack Norman, Moultrie Patten, Edward Penn, Seymour Penzner, Steve Pudenz, Peter Reznikoff, David Sage, Albert Sinkys, John D. Swain, John Terranova, Dianne Thompson, David Usdan, Ruis Woertendyke, Christopher Wynkoop

Kirsten Beck, Gerry Goodstein Photos

Joseph Ragno, Judith Scarpone, Deborah Van Valkenburgh in "A View from the Bridge"
Top: Ian Sullivan, Carrie Nye
in "Private Lives"

INDIANA REPERTORY THEATRE

Indianapolis, Indiana
October 19, 1979–March 29, 1980
Eighth Season

Producing Director, Benjamin Mordecai; Artistic Director, Edward Stern; Business Manager, Steven E. Ross; Press, Jimmy Seacat, Melissa Martin Goldsmith, Vicki Draper, Larry Zuber; Production Manager, Chris Armen; Production Assistant, Jim McBride; Assistant Artistic Director, Mary F. Monroe; Technical Director, J. T. Lacourse; Props, Deborah Woolford; Stage Managers, Joel Grynheim, James K. Tinsley; Stage Directors, Edward Stern, John Going, Harold Scott, Thomas Gruenewald, John Abajian; Sets, Bob Barnett, James Leonard Joy, John Arnone, David Potts, Ursula Belden, Elmon Webb, Virginia Dancy; Costumes, Shelley Steffens Joyce, Sigrid Insull, Kenneth M. Yount, James Berton Harris, Elizabeth Covey; Lighting, Joel Grynheim, Geoffrey T. Cunningham, Jeff Davis, Paul Gallo, Spencer Mosse

PRODUCTIONS AND CASTS

COLD STORAGE by Ronald Ribman, with Brian Hartigan, Susanne Peters, Bernard Kates
DESCENDANTS *(World Premiere)* by Jack Gilhooley; Director, Edward Stern. CAST: Roy Cooper (Peter Gavin), Steven Ryan (Dennis Gavin), Jacqueline Coslow (Noreen Gavin), Joan Shangold (Christine), Susanne Peters (Melinda Gavin), Dennis Bailey (Russell Gavin)
ABSURD PERSON SINGULAR by Alan Ayckbourn, with Allison Giglio, John Abajian, Bernard Kates, Sara Woods, Barbara Berge, John Bergstrom
TOYS IN THE ATTIC by Lillian Hellman, with Margaret Hilton, Patricia Englund, Hank Frazier, Patricia O'Connell, Judd Jones, Steve Simpson, Robin Groves, Tom Archer, Donald Christopher, Rockland Mers, Steve Punches
TWELFTH NIGHT by William Shakespeare, with Peter Burnell, Frank Lynn Csuti, Tom Archer, Nancy Boykin, Donald Christopher, Deem Bristow, Rockland Mers, Gerald Richards, Lois Foraker, Dennis Warning, Richard Peterson, Holly Cameron, Bernard Kates, John C. Capodice, Mark Hattan, Peter Thoemke, Lori Wolner, Amelia Zucker, Dorothy Williams
BORN YESTERDAY by Garson Kanin, with Ursula Ansback, Rudolph Willrich, Frank Lynn Csuti, Donald Christopher, Bernie Hall, Gerald Richards, Peter Thoemke, Susan Greenhill, Bernard Kates, Tom Archer, Mary F. Monroe, Rockland Mers, George Brengel, Mary Atkins, Deem Bristow
MUSICAL MIRAGE '80 by John Abajian, with Richard Allen, Don Bearden, Roy Cockrum, Virginia Etter, Ruth Didder, Teresa Metzger

Dan Francis Photos

Patricia Englund, Margaret Hilton
in "Toys in the Attic"

**Kevin Kuhlke, Joan Schulich
in "Blood Addiction"**

IOWA THEATER LAB

Catskills, N.Y.
August 6, 1979–June 15, 1980
COMPANY: Ric Zank (Director), Gillian Richards (Administrative Director), Martine Bellen, Mark Bronnenberg, Jim Cirilano, Kevin Kuhlke, Danny Meunier, Joan Schulich, Michelle Shulman
PRODUCTIONS: White Night, Blood Addiction (both *World Premieres*)

Ric Zank Photos

LONG WHARF THEATRE

New Haven, Connecticut
October 4, 1979–June 22, 1980
Fifteenth Season
Artistic Director, Arvin Brown; Executive Director, M. Edgar Rosenblum; Press, Rosalind Heinz, Patrick John Lombard; Stage Directors, Arvin Brown, Bill Glassco, Edward Gilbert, Mike Nichols, John Pasquin, Austin Pendleton, Tommy Tune; Sets, John Conklin, Karl Eigsti, Eldon Elder, David Jenkins, John Jensen, Steven Rubin, Tony Walton; Costumes, Whitney Blausen, John Conklin, Linda Fisher, Dona Granata, Rachel Kurland, Michael Stuart; Lighting, Jamie Gallagher, Judy Rasmuson, Jennifer Tipton, Ronald Wallace; Stage Managers, James Harker, Anne Keefe, Franklin Keysar, Fredric H. Orner, Nina Seely.

PRODUCTIONS AND CASTS

WATCH ON THE RHINE by Lillian Hellman: Joyce Ebert, Jill Eikenberry, Mary Fogarty, George Hearn, Robert Judd, Mark McLaughlin, Jan Miner, Bobby Scott, Monica Snowden, Joel Stedman, Harris Yulin
JITTERS by David French (*American Premiere*) William Carden, Sarah Chodoff, Josh Clark, Jane Galloway, Roland Hewgill, Jim Jansen, Charmion King, Joel Polis, George Sperdakos
DOUBLE FEATURE (*World Premiere*) with book, music and lyrics by Jeffry Moss: Pamela Blair, John Doolittle, Charles Kimbrough, Leland Palmer
THE BEACH HOUSE (*World Premiere*) by Nancy Donohue: Preston Brooks, Edward Herrmann, Swoosie Kurtz, Joanna Merlin
THE CARETAKER by Harold Pinter: Emery Battis, David Berman, Richard Council
MARY BARNES (*American Premiere)* by David Edgar: Eileen Atkins, Kevin Bacon, Veronica Castang, Peter Friedman, Michael Govans, Lois Markle, Tania Myren, Walter Niehenke, Susan Sharkey, David Spielberg, John Tillinger, J. T. Walsh, Kenneth Welsh
WHO'S AFRAID OF VIRGINIA WOOLF? by Edward Albee: Swoosie Kurtz, Elaine May, James Naughton, Mike Nichols
CYRANO DE BERGERAC by Edmond Rostand: Louis Beachner, Ian Blackman, John Carroll, Jack Davidson, Dawn Didawick, Tom Donaldson, Joyce Ebert, Joyce Fidor, James Harper, Gus Kaikkonen, Kurt Knudson, Harris Laskawy, Richard Mathews, Stephen Mendillo, William Newman, Walker Niehenke, Bruce Probst, Christopher Rich, Claude Saucier, Henry Stram, Michael Tylo, Anthony Zerbe

William Smith Photos

**Top Right: Elaine May, Mike Nichols, James Naughton in "Who's Afraid of Virginia Woolf?"
Below: Swoosie Kurtz, Preston Brooks, Edward Herrmann, Joanna Merlin in "Beach House"**

**Eileen Atkins, David Spielberg
in "Mary Barnes"**

LORETTO-HILTON REPERTORY THEATRE

St. Louis, Missouri
October 17, 1979–April 12, 1980
Producing Director, David Frank; Consulting Director, Davey Marlin-Jones; Administrative Director, Thomas K. Warner; Press, Sarah Beaman Jones, Noel F. Taylor; Associate Producer, Michael P. Pitek III; Production Manager, Steven Woolf; Technical Director, Drew McCoy; Company Manager, Joyce Volker Ruebel; Stage Managers, Glenn Dunn, Margaret Stuart-Ramsey, Mark Landis; Sets, Jim Bakkom, Tim Jozwick, Gary Barten; Costumes, Dorothy Marshall, Alison Todd; Lighting, Peter E. Sargent; Sound, Robert Wotawa; Resident Company: Brendan Burke, Alan Clarey, Robert Darnell, Stephen McKinley Henderson, Keith Jochim, Joneal Joplin, Robert Spencer, Susan Cash, Joe Patrick Gilday, Jonathan Gillard, Susan Maloy Wall, Bari K. Willerford

PRODUCTIONS AND CASTS

CRIMES OF THE HEART by Beth Henley; Director, R. Stuart White. CAST: Dawn Didawick, Kaiulani Lee, Pamela Lewis, Stephen Tobolowsky, Patricia Wettig
A CHRISTMAS CAROL by Charles Dickens; adapted by Addie Walsh. CAST; Eric Brooks, Linda Cook, Mickey Hartnett, Lance Valon Ashline' Phebe Bohart, Sherri Lynn Boonshaft, Gian Cavallini, Eric Fix, Scott Harris, Benjamin Chapman Hazelton, M. Neal Jones, Melinda McCrary, Michelle Morgan, Christopher Nickel, Megan R. Sargent, Helene Sayad, Kip Wahl
PUT THEM ALL TOGETHER by Anne Commire, with Janice Fuller, Mickey Hartnett, Caroline Kava, Shaine Marinson, Jack Reidelberger, Mary Beth Russo
A VIEW FROM THE BRIDGE by Arthur Miller: Eric Brooks, Mickey Hartnett, Robert Schenkkan, Kathleen Tolan, Johanna Ball, Haskell Schwartzberg, Joe Gargiulo, Scott Hanson, Peter C. Rybolt, John Starmer, Eugene J. Tierney
A SERVANT OF TWO MASTERS by Carlo Goldoni: Director, Geoffrey Sherman: Mickey Hartnett, Caroline Kava, Carol Kuykendall, Barry Signorelli, Brian Worley
MASQUERADE with Peter Lobdell, Jane Stein, Rebecca Bondor, Michael Wieben
SIZWE BANSI IS DEAD by Athol Fugard; Director, Jim O'Connor: John Cothran, Jr. Stephen McKinley Henderson
FATHER DREAMS by Mary Gallagher; Director, Michael P. Pitek III: David Cooper-Wall, Eda Seasongood, Addie Walsh, Jack Collard

(No photos submitted)

**Edward Power, David Groh
in "Drop Hammer"**

LOS ANGELES ACTORS THEATRE

Los Angeles, California
May 17, 1979–May 11, 1980
Fifth Season
Producing Director, William Bushnell, Jr.; Executive Director, Joseph B. Sax; Staff Producer, Diane White; Sets, D. Martyn Bookwalter; Lighting, Pauline Jenkins; Technical Director, Ted Carlsson; Press, Guy Giarrizzo; Assistant Producing Director, Adam Leipzig; Wardrobe, Naila Aladdin; Props, Jacqueline Crampton; Production Assistant, Aleta Chapelle; Stage Manager, Norman Simpler

PRODUCTIONS AND CASTS

OLD TIMES by Harold Pinter: Diana Douglas, Rita Gam, James Booth
THE TRICYCLE by Fernando Arrabal; Director, Jaime Jaimes: Hector Morales, Daniel Faraldo, Pete Leal, Marabina Davila, Ana Jimenez, Jose Edward Perez, George Reyes: Mario Martinez
SUNDAY by Joseph Scott Kierland (*World Premiere*); Director, Dan Mason; Lupe Ontiveros, Henry Darrow, Sheila Ochs, Christine Avila, Ismael (East) Carlo, Nicholas Cinardo, Panchito Gomez, Manuel Gallardo, John Salazar, George Reyes, Ric Montejano, Dorothy Feldman, Alexandra Melchi, Carmen Milito, Yvonne Regalado, Jerry Reynolds, Anne Gerety, Paul Dennis Martin
BURIED CHILD by Sam Shepard: Richard Hamilton, Edward Power, Eve McVeagh, Jack O'Leary, Charles Parks, Suzanna Peters, Daniel Zippi, Jim Nolan
THE NIGHT OF THE ASSASSINS by Jose Triana; Director, Jaime Jaimes: Pete Leal, Jose Armand, Marabina Davila, Ana Deavat, Roseanna Campos
DROP HAMMER by Emanuel Fried (*World Premiere*); Director, Al Rossi: Charles Hutchins, Carmen Filpi, David Groh, Antonie Becker, Frank McCarthy, Howard Goodwin, Judy Jean Berns, Edward Power, Duane Tucker, William Lodge, Roger Hampton, Duke Stroud, Herb Downer, Martin Beck, Dennis Dixie, Tim Cunningham, Don Starr, Al Allen, Frank Annese, Gregory Earl Binion, James Bowman, Stephen Bradbury, Norvell Carrere, Steven Jae Johnson, Tom Molitor, William Morgan, Dan Payne, Robert G. Reece, Niche Saboda, Curtis Stuart, Leonard Termo, David Young
THE TROJAN WOMEN by Euripides; Conceived and Directed by Rena Down; A Signed/Spoken production; Music by Michel Bolsey: Diana Douglas, Julianna Fjeld, Marc Jacobs, Richard Kendall, Regina Baff, Peggy O'Brien, Stephanie Feyne, Marion Perkins, David Ralphe, Peter Wolf, Rebecca Stanley, Elizabeth Quinn, Judy Kain, Anna Mindess, Brandyn Artiste, Teryn Jenkins, Alexandra Melchi, Shirley Neal, Suzanne Perkins, Veronica Redd, Margo Speer, Susan Tanner, Eileen T'Kaye, Judith Weston
WILD AIR by Tom Huey (*World Premiere*); Director, G. W. Bailey: Logan Ramsey, C. P. Robinson, Sharon Ernster
THE AL CHEMIST SHOW (*World Premiere*) Book by James Booth, with apologies to Ben Jonson; Music, Steve Allen; Lyrics, Steve Allen, James Booth. CAST James Booth, Derek Murcott, Al Mancini, Georgia Brown, Harry Frazier, Jeremy Lawrence, Scott Hylands, Sandy Kenyon, James Gleason, John Fleck, Francine Kessler, Lily Mariye, Philip Antora, Jonathan Brown, Denise Damico, Steven Jae Johnson, Andria Bedinger, Mark Miller, Robert O'Donnell, Eric Onstad

John Sanchez Photos

**Diana Douglas, James Booth, Rita Gam
in "Old Times" Above: Logan Ramsey,
C. P. Robinson in "Wild Air"**

MANITOBA THEATRE CENTRE

Winnipeg, Canada
October 12, 1979–May 17, 1980
Artistic Director, Arif Hasnain; General Manager, Joe Konrad:
Press, Pat Elsworth, Cheryl Griffin; Production Manager, Dwight
Griffin; Technical Director, Ron Kresky; Stage Director, Lewis Bau-
mander, Howard Dallin, Richard Digby-Day, Eddie Gilbert, Arif
Hasnain, Michael Mawson, Kurt Reis, Guy Sprung, Gregory Truck;
Sets and Costumes, Susan Benson, Debra Hanson, Neil Peter Jam-
polis, Mark Negin, Richard Roberts, Peter Wingate, Lighting, Clint
Duvall, Jeff Herd, Neil Peter Jampolis, Ron Kresky, Jane Reisman,
Monty Schneider, Michael Whitfield.

PRODUCTIONS AND CASTS

TRAVESTIES by Tom Stoppard: Diana Barrington, Mary Long,
Peter Millard, K. Lype O'Dell, Antony Parr, Allan Royal, Kathleen
Turner, Paxton Whitehead
AMERICAN BUFFALO by David Mamet: Walter Flanagan,
Frank Moore, Michael Zelniker
ARTICHOKE by Joanna M. Glass: Alexe Duncan, Walter Flana-
gan, Patricia Hamilton, John-Peter Linton, Walter Massey, Larry
Reynolds, Peter Rogan
CIRCUS GOTHIC written and performed by Jan Kudelka
WAITING FOR THE PARADE by John Murrell: Terri Cher-
niack, Rosemary Dunsmore, Deborah Grover, Maxine Miller, Mel-
ody Ryane
ABSURD PERSON SINGULAR by Alan Ayckbourn: Marcia
Bennett, Peter Dvorsky, Irene Hogan, Basil Hoskins, Peter Millard,
Judith Thompson
THE SEA GULL by Anton Chekhov: Tom Carson, Helen Maude
Dallas, Paul Gatchell, Laurence Hugo, Thomas Hulce, Andrew
Jarkowsky, Anthony Parr, Cynthia Parva, Blair Philpott, David
Sabin, Linda Thorson, Deborah Turnbull, Kathleen Turner
HILARY'S BIRTHDAY by Joe Wiesenfeld: Morison Bock, Jen-
nifer Nokes, Rebecca Toolan
THE DIARY OF ANNE FRANK by Frances Goodrich and Al-
bert Hackett: John W. Carroll, Ludi Claire, Lesleh Donaldson, Ar-
nie Hardt, Nancy Kerr, Julie Khaner, Diane Lasko, David
Opatoshu, Larry Reynolds, Thomas Waites
SPOKESONG by Stewart Parker: Jerry Franken, Paul Kelman,
Tom McBeath, Seana McKenna, Dixie Seatle, Joe Ziegler
DRACULA by Hamilton Deane, and John L. Balderston: Virginia
Brautigan, Alexe Duncan, Lisa Griffin, Sara Hickling, Nicholas Kil-
bertus, Robin Marshall, Tom McBeath, Frank Moore, K. Lype
O'Dell, Milton Selzer

Gerry Kopelow Photos

**Lesleh Donaldson, David Opatoshu in "Diary of
Anne Frank" Top: Paxton Whitehead, Allan
Royal in "Travesties"**

McCARTER THEATRE COMPANY

Princeton, N.J.
October, 2, 1979–April 20, 1980
Artistic Director, Nagle Jackson; Managing Director, Alison Harris;
Press, Kirby F. Smith; Technical Director, Rafe Scheinblum; Stage
Managers, Francis X. Kuhn, Trey Altemose, Kendall Crolius; Di-
rectors, Barry Boys, Kenneth Frankel, Nagle Jackson; Sets, Ralph
Funicello, John Jensen; Costumes, Michael J. Cesario, Elizabeth
Covey, Robert Morgan, Jennifer von Mayrhauser; Lighting, John
McLain

COMPANY

Francis P. Bilancio, Barry Boys, Sallie Brophy, Gideon Davis, Jay
Doyle, Herbert Foster, Leslie Geraci, Robert Lanchester, John
Mansfield, Stephen Mendillo, Portia Patterson, Michael Plunkett,
Anne Sheldon, Bruce Somerville, Stephen Stout, Jill Tanner, G
Wood

GUEST ARTISTS: Jonathan Arterton, Reathal Bean, Megan Cole,
Minerva Davenport, Dorothy Edwards, Ben Farrell, Sunni Farring-
ton, Harriet Hall, Seth Herzog, Celeste Holm, Amy Kopp, Karl
Light, Margo Martindale, Katherine McGrath, Josephine Nichols,
Douglas Parvin, Frances Peter, Penn Reynolds, Frank Romani,
Ellen Tobie, Shirin Trainor, Matthew Weinstein

PRODUCTIONS

The Visions of Simone Machard by Bertolt Brecht and Lion Feuch-
twanger, All the Way Home by Tad Mosel, Jumpers by Tom Stoppard, The Miser by Moliere, Hay Fever by Noel Coward, and
Premiere of 1959 Pink Thunderbird by James McLure

Cliff Moore Photos

**Celeste Holm, G Wood in "Hay Fever"
Above: "All the Way Home"**

MEADOW BROOK THEATRE

Rochester, Michigan
October 11, 1979–May 25, 1980

Artistic & General Director, Terence Kilburn; Tour Director/Assistant to General Director, Frank Bollinger; Press, Jane Mosher, Kevin Gilmartin; Stage Directors, Terence Kilburn, Charles Nolte, John Ulmer; Sets, Peter-William Hicks, Douglas Wright, C. Lance Brockman, Holly Ritchie, Glenna Handley; Lighting, Barry Griffith, Benjamin Levenberg, Larry Reed, Jean A. Montgomery; Production Manager, Peter-William Hicks; Stage Managers, Rachael Lindhart, Thomas Spence; Technical Director, Douglas Wright; Costume Coordinators, Mary L. Bonnell, Christa Gievers, Annette DiFilippo; Sound, Reid Johnson; Wardrobe, Linda Carpenter; Props, Charles Beal, Gail Fitzgibbons, Mary Ann Dailey

PRODUCTIONS AND CASTS

THE SCHOOL FOR SCANDAL: A. D. Cover, Donald W. Dailey, Robert Donley, Andrew Dunn, Deborah Eckols, Bruce Economou, Donald Ewer, Mariana Keros, David Kroll, Mark Halpin, Jillian Lindig, Tom Mahard, Ron Merkin, Marianne Muellerleile, Erika Petersen, Tom Spackman, William Wright
OF MICE AND MEN: Gail Bryson, A. D. Cover, Harry Ellerbe, David Graf, John W. Hardy, David Jeffrey, Michael Medeiros, Don Perkins, Tom Spackman, Eric Uhler
CHARLEY'S AUNT: Denise Bessette, A. D. Cover, Lori Donley, Deborah Eckols, George Gitto, Jillian Lindig, Terence Marinan, Don Perkins, Robert Moberly, Michael Tylo
A MOON FOR THE MISBEGOTTEN: Peter Brandon, Donald W. Dailey, Robert Donley, David Jeffrey, Lisa McMillan
A LIFE IN THE THEATRE: Tom Spackman, Eric Tavaris
A SUMMER REMEMBERED (*World Premiere*): Barbara Bissell, Gisela Caldwell, Booth Colman, Lori Donley, Peter Galman, Thom Haneline, Joseph Jamrog, Jane Lowry, George McCulloch, Marianne Muellerleile, Cyd Quilling, Steve Longmuir, Tine Turner
NIGHT MUST FALL: Barbara Berge, Dorothy Blackburn, Donald W. Dailey, Lori Donley, George Gitto, Mary Pat Gleason, Marianne Muellerleile, Helena Power, Tom Spackman
YOU CAN'T TAKE IT WITH YOU: Jeanne Arnold, Burniece Avery, Mary Benson, Marjorie Brown, A. D. Cover, J. L. Dahlmann, Andrew Dunn, Harry Ellerbe, Mary Pat Gleason, Thom Haneline, John Koch, Arthur Kohn, Kent Martin, Louise Martin, George McCulloch, Jack Prokop, Cyd Quilling, Albert H. Ratcliffe, Eric Tavaris

Dick Hunt Photos

Cast of "A Summer Remembered"
Top: "The School for Scandal"

MILWAUKEE REPERTORY THEATER

Milwaukee, Wisconsin
September 14, 1979–May 25, 1980

Artistic Director, John Dillon; Managing Director, Sara O'Connor; Business Manager, Peggy Rose; Press, Philip Orkin, Diane Nahabedian, Susan Medak; Stage Directors, John Dillon, Sharon Ott, Bill Ludel, Daniel Mooney, Sanford Robbins, Garland Wright; Sets, Laura Maurer, David Emmons, Hugh Landwehr, Michael Merritt, Joe Nieminski, Stuart Wurtzel; Lighting, Arden Fingerhut, Spencer Mosse, Rachel Budin, Toni Goldin; Costumes, Susan Tsu, Colleen Muscha, Patricia McGourty, Carol Oditz; Stage Manager, Robert Goodman; Production Manager, Gregory Murphy; Music, Mark Van Hecke, Peter Link, Alan Smallwood; Playwrights-in-Residence, Tom Cole, Amlin Gray, Daniel A. Stein, Larry Shue

COMPANY

Eugene J. Anthony, George Axler, Dana Barton, Lisa Brailoff, Ritch Brinkley, Maggie Burke, Terry Burrell, Cynthia Carle, David E. Chadderdon, John P. Connolly, Peggy Cowles, Mary Di Costanza, Bonnie Gallup, Julie Garfield, Douglas Jones, Patrick Jude, Marge Kotlisky, Ann Lange, Sonja Lanzener, William Leach, Don Austin Lowe, Lilene Mansell, Jack McLaughlin-Gray, Paul Meacham, James W. Monitor, Daniel Mooney, Natalie Mosco, Brenda Peyser, James Pickering, Rose Pickering, Rod Pilloud, Victor Raider-Wexler, Justin Ross, Larry Shue, Sam Singleton, Bruce Somerville, Henry Strozier, Sam Tsoutsouvas

PRODUCTIONS

The Recruiting Officer, The Dance of Death, Of Mice and Men, A Christmas Carol, Fighting Bob, Taming of the Shrew, An Independent Woman, and *Premieres* of Dead Souls (*English Language Premiere*), The Workroom (*American Premiere*), and *World Premieres* of On the Road to Babylon, Six Toes by Amlin Gray, Stark Mad in White Satin by Daniel A. Stein, Lakeboat by David Mamet, An American Chronicle by Paul Metcalf, and The Nerd by Larry Shune.

Mark Avery Photos

Rose Pickering, John Connolly, Henry Strozier
in "The Recruiting Officer" Above: "Dead Souls"

MISSOURI REPERTORY THEATRE

Kansas City, Missouri
July 5, 1979–March 16, 1980

Production Director, Patricia McIlrath; Directors, James Assad, Norman Ayrton, Francis J. Cullinan, Patricia McIlrath, Gerald Gutierrez, George Hamlin, George Keathley, Albert Marre, Ellis Rabb; Sets, John Ezell, James F. Gohl, James Leonard Joy, Carolyn Ross; Costumes, Michele Bechtold, Judith Dolan, Vincent Scassellati, Baker S. Smith; Lighting, Joseph Appelt, Michael D. Scott; Sound, Robert Neuhaus, Michael Schweppe, Steven W. Vrba; Technical Director, Douglas C. Taylor; Stage Managers, Terrence Dwyer, Joyce McBroom, Christine Michael, James K. Tinsley; Choreographer, Lynn Mahler-Shelton; Special Effects, Thomas D. Craner; Composer, Conrad Susa; Musical Director, Molly Jessup Alley; Production Manager, Ronald Schaeffer; Press, Patricia A. Moore; Dramaturg, Felicia Hardison Londre

COMPANY

Walter W. Atamaniuk, Peter Aylward, Daniel Barnett, Geoffrey Beauchamp, Jim Birdsall, Michael Anthony Blazina, Charlotte Booker, Julie Marie Boyd, Richard C. Brown, Robert Burke, W. Vosco Call, Jr., Liza Cole, John Cothran, Jr., Roy William Cox, David Coxwell, James M. Dawson, Cain De Vore, Judith Dorrell, Cynthia Dozier, Art Ellison, Steven Gefroh, Joanne Hamlin, Timothy S. Hancock, Michael Haney, Alan Heer, Rendall Himes, Walter Hook, Robin Humphrey, Gregory Johnston, Gregory Justice, Robert Lewis Karlin, Dewey Keener, Gerry Kinerk, John Kreipe, Michael LaGue, Sherry Lambert, Stephen Lee, James LeVaggi, Jess Lynn, Carol Mabbott, John Maddison, Dan Maddux, Gloria Mason, Peter Massey, Patti McGill, Jay Mitchell, Laura Susan Moore, Merle Moores, Jennifer L. Moudy, Phillip Officer, Wes Payne, Dan Putnam, Juliet Randall, Nancy Reardon, Mark Robbins, Scott Rowe, Elizabeth Rubino, Susan K. Selvey, Kathryn C. Sparer, Douglas Stewart, Todd Taylor, Ronetta Wallman, Marshall Watson, Ronald Wendschuh, Patricia A. Williams, Jennifer Winn, Elizabeth Zoole, Meg Wynn Owen

PRODUCTIONS

Hamlet, Rosencrantz and Guildenstern Are Dead, The New York Idea, The Chalk Garden, Oh Coward!, The Visit, Twelfth Night, Look Homeward Angel

Juliet Randall, Stephen Keener in "The New York Idea" Above: Joanne Hamlin, Meg Wynn Owen in "The Chalk Garden" Top: Robin Humphrey, Michael Haney in "Look Homeward, Angel"

NEW GLOBE THEATRE

Fairfield, Connecticut
September 1979–May 1980
First Season

Producing Director, Stuart Vaughan; Associate Producers, Anne Vaughan, Vincent Curcio; Production Stage Manager, William S. Taylor (Names of other staff members and of company not submitted)

PRODUCTIONS

Hedda Gabler, Candida, The Contrast, Macbeth, and *World Premiere* of The Royal Game by Stuart Vaughan

Don Perkins, Marlena Lustik, Stuart Vaughan in "Candida" Above: Sharon Laughlin, Stuart Vaughan in "Hedda Gabler"

NORTH LIGHT REPERTORY
Evanston, Illinois
October 21, 1979–May 17, 1980
Producing Director, Gregory Kandel; Business Manager, Susan Flahaven; Assistant Producing Director, Lisa Wilson; Press, Marilyn Liss, Bill Prenevost, Gretchen O'Neill; Designers, Maher Ahmad, Marsha Kowal; Administrative Assistant, Eileen Gill; Resident Playwright, Grace McKeaney; Stage Manager, John Kenny; Production Coordinator, Maher Ahmad; Production Assistants, Karen Markel, Ugo Imparato

PRODUCTIONS AND CASTS

CATSPLAY by Istvan Orkeny: Margrit Wyler, Fern Persons, Marge Kotlisky, Marji Bank, Megan McTavish, B. J. Jones, Douglas Mellor, Mary Best
BURIED CHILD by Sam Shepard: Nathan Davis, Mary Seibel, Bob Swan, Richard C. Lavin, Jonathan Fuller, Ina Jaffe, Jim Keith
ANGEL STREET by Patrick Hamilton: Jennifer Campbell, John Campbell, Anne Edwards, Kathleen Melvin, Robert Thompson, Greg Vinkler
WHO THEY ARE AND HOW IT IS WITH THEM (*World Premiere*) by Grace McKeaney: Nathan Davis, Ina Jaffe, Mark Milliken, Bob Swan, Peter Syvertsen
COLD STORAGE by Ronald Ribman: Nathan Davis, Robert Scogin, Candace Coor

Lisa Ebright Photos

**Left: Nathan Davis, Robert Scogin
in "Cold Storage" Top: Peter
Syvertsen, Ina Jaffe, Mark Millikén
in "Who They Are and How It Is With Them"**

PENNSYLVANIA STAGE COMPANY
Allentown, Pennsylvania
October 17, 1979–March 23, 1980
Third Season
Producing Director, Gregory S. Hurst; Managing Director, Jeff Gordon; Sets, Atkin Pace, Victor Capecce, Edward Cesaitis, Raymond Recht, Harry Darrow; Costumes, Andrew Marlay, Judith Grant Byrnes, Lewis Rampino, Elizabeth Palmer; Lighting, Todd Lichtenstein, Gregory Chabay, Robby Monk, Andrea Wilson, Harry Darrow; Stage Manager, Mimi Sherin; Technical Director, Marsha Hardy

PRODUCTIONS AND CASTS

THE PHILADELPHIA STORY by Philip Barry; Director, Gregory S. Hurst: Gwen Arment, Robert Rod Barry, Donna Davis, Mary Jay, Michael Martin, Theodore May, John MacKay, William R. Riker, Ron Siebert, Norma Jean True, Jane Uhler, Richard Director
VANITIES by Jack Heifner; Director, Ron Lagomarsino: Gwen Arment, Kathy Connell, Carole Lockwood
COUNT DRACULA by Ted Tiller; Director, Louis Rackoff: Allan Carlsen, Richard Director, Deborah Fezelle, Stanley Flood, Juergen Kuehn, Carole Lockwood, Craig MacDonald, Hunt Matthews, Peter D. Umbras
THE GLASS MENAGERIE by Tennessee Williams; Director, Jacques Levy: Katharine Houghton, Ken Jenkins, Eileen Letchworth, Ron Siebert
THE COMEDY OF ERRORS by William Shakespeare; Director, Gregory S. Hurst: Joe Birchak, Jeff Brooks, Deborah Fezelle, Bonnie Gallup, Jack Hoffman, Craig MacDonald, Judy Mayer, Donna Mavrides, James Maxwell, Todd Oleson, Marshall Shnider, Chris Simmons, Ronald Toczek, Norma Jean True, Keliher Walsh, Ray Xifo
DAMON'S SONG (*World Premiere*) with book by William F. Brown; Music and Lyrics, George Robertson; Director, Gregory S. Hurst; Choreographer, Jay Norman; Musical Director, Kevin Farrell: Susan Brandner, Cindy Converse, Michael Dantuano, Donna Drake, Gary Holcombe, Alexandra Korey, Elisa Lenhart, Cynthia Meryl, Keith Rice, George Riddle, William Schilling, Janice Solida, Debbie Williams, Robert Yacko

Mary Liz Colley, Gregory Fota Photos

**Right Center: Keith Rice, George Riddle,
Donna Drake, Gary Holcombe, Alex Korey
in "Damon's Song"**

**Katharine Houghton, Ron Siebert
in "The Glass Menagerie"**

PHILADELPHIA DRAMA GUILD

Philadelphia, Pennsylvania
October 19, 1979–April 6, 1980
Managing Director, Gregory Poggi; Artistic Director, Irene Lewis; Production Manager, Gerald Nobles; Press, Roy A. Snyder, Georgia Smith Ashby; Executive Assistant, Roberta T. Stern; Sets, John Kasarda; Costumes, David Murin; Lighting, Spencer Mosse; Sound, Chuck London

PRODUCTIONS AND CASTS

THE LAST FEW DAYS OF WILLIE CALLENDAR (*World Premiere*) by Val Coleman; Director, Thomas Bullard: Ira Hawkins, James Rebhorn, Susan Greenhill, Basil Wallace, Louise Troy, Brent Jennings, Gary Bolling, James Cahill, Osayande F. Johnson, Martin Gibson, Nathaniel Jones, Allyson Joyner, Dwight Mitchell, Connie Norwood, James Charles Roberts, Shelby Taylor, Geraldine White, Charles Young, Frederic Major

YOU NEVER CAN TELL by George Bernard Shaw; Director, Tony van Bridge: Mary Haney, James Valentine, Jona Huber, Christopher Gaze, Louise Troy, Judith Calder, John Scanlon, Peter Pagan, Douglas Seale, Marilyn Meyrick, Vaughn Patterson, David Sabin

SUMMER by Hugh Leonard; Director, Douglas Seale: David Sabin, John Leighton, John Washbrook, Annie Murray, Aideen O'Kelly, Ann MacMillan, Linda Martin, Lee Toombs

TWELFTH NIGHT by William Shakespeare; Director, Michael Montel: Nicholas Pennell, Osayande Baruti, David A. Simson, Domini Blythe, John Favorite, Clarence Felder, Aideen O'Kelly, Thomas A. Stewart, Normand Beauregard, Valerie von Volz, Paxton Whitehead, Eric Forsythe, Robert Fox, Douglas Wing, Dan Elia

THARK by Ben Travers; Director, Douglas Seale: William Preston, Carolyn Younger, Geraldine Sherman, Christopher Gaze, Anna Russell, Tony van Bridge, Paxton Whitehead, Lynne Griffin, James Valentine, Douglas Wing

Peter Lester Photos

Annie Murray, John Washbrook, David Sabin, Ann MacMillan in "Summer" Top: Anna Russell, Tony van Bridge, Paxton Whitehead in "Thark"

PHILADELPHIA REPERTORY COMPANY

Philadelphia, Pennsylvania
September 13, 1979–July 26, 1980
General Manager, Robin Dechert; Production Manager, Linda L. White; Artistic Direction Committee, Sarah Labov, David McCullough, P. J. Lyons, Chris Esser; Designers, Debra Rosenbaum, Valican Clark, David Williams; Stage Directors, David Williams, Bohden Senkow

COMPANY

Pat Carey, Chris Essler, Frank Lyons, David McCullough, Delia Mirarcili, Z. Toczek, Justin Douglas, Sarah Labov, Patrick Lyons, Marian Mazza, Ben Sweetwood, Linda White, and *Guest Artists:* Jude Ciccolella, Lin Kennedy, Barry Satiels, Dan Oreskes

PRODUCTIONS

The Lesson by Ionesco, Duck Variations by David Mamet, The Odd Couple by Neil Simon, The Lover by Harold Pinter, The Collection by Harold Pinter, Rosencrantz and Guildenstern Are Dead by Tom Stoppard, American Buffalo by David Man The Skin of Our Teeth by Thornton Wilder, The Chalk Garden by Enid Bagnold, Fallen Angels by Noel Coward

Ronn Gladis Photos

Ben Sweetwood, Justin Douglas in "The Odd Couple"

Left Center: David McCullough, Marian Mazza in "The Collection"

200

PITTSBURGH PLAYHOUSE THEATRE CENTER

Pittsburgh, Pennsylvania
September 20, 1979–June 1, 1980
General Director, Mark Lewis; Producer, James O. Prescott; Administration Director, Mary Turner; Production Manager, Alan Forino; Press; Maura Minteer; Technical Director, George Jaber: Assistants to General Director, Carole Berger, Joe McGoldrick; Assistant to Producer, Catherine Hischak; Lighting, Alan Forino, Jennifer Ford; Sets, Mary Burt, Eileen Garrigan; Costumes, Mary Turner, Don DiFonso, Julie Bohn; Stage Directors, Don Wadsworth, James Prescott, William Leech, Thomas Hischak, Raymond Laine

COMPANY

John Amplas, Nancy Chesney, Carol DePaul, James Prescott, Hugh A. Rose, Don Wadsworth, Jill Wadsworth, Raymond Laine, Maura Minteer, Kate Young, and *Guests:* Don Craig, Jeff Paul, Linda Warren, students from Point Park College, American Dance Machine, Pittsburgh Laboratory Theatre, Kathryn Posin Dance Company, Janet Gillespie Dance Company, American Dance Ensemble

PRODUCTIONS

Absent Friends by Alan Ayckbourn, Clarence Darrow by David Rintels, The Shadow Box by Michael Cristofer, A Life in the Theatre by David Mamet, A History of the American Film by Christopher Durang, Babes in Arms by Richard Rodgers and Lorenz Hart, A Comedy of Errors by William Shakespeare, The Effect of Gamma Rays on Man-in-the-Moon Marigolds by Paul Zindel, The Last Meeting of the Knights of the White Magnolia by Preston Jones

David Burt, Kelly Crawford Photos

Top Right: Robin Walsh, Doug Mertz, Eileen Seeley, John Hall in "Comedy of Errors"

Hugh A. Rose, John Amplas in "A Life in the Theatre"

ST. NICHOLAS THEATER COMPANY

Chicago, Illinos
October 1, 1979–August 29, 1980
Artistic Director, Steven Schachter; Managing Director, Peter Schneider; Business Manager, Nancy J. Cook; Assistant, Patrick Moloney; Assistant to Managing Director, Barbara Biederman; Production Manager, William Arnold; Press, Tom Thompson, Kevin Arnold: Technical Director, Walter Reinhardt; Props, Nancy McCarty; Design Coordinator, David Emmons; Musical Director, Alaric Jans; Stage Managers, Joanne Brocklebank, Pam Marsden
COMPANY: Names not submitted

PRODUCTIONS

The Primary English Class by Israel Horovitz, Character Lines by Larry Ketron, Celimare by Eugene LaBische, Shadow of Heroes by Robert Ardrey, and *World Premier* of The Enchanted Cottage adapted from Arthur Wing Pinero's play by Percy Grange with music by John McKinney

Dan Rest Photos

Left Center: Cristine Rose in "Primary English Class"

Martha Webster, John Martinuzzi, David Chadderdon in "Enchanted Cottage"

THE SECOND CITY

Chicago, Illinois
June 1, 1979–May 31, 1980

Producer, Bernard Sahlins; Associate Producer, Joyce Sloane; Director, Del Close; Stage Manager, Lawrence Perkins; Press, Joan McGrath
COMPANY: Danny Breen, Mary Gross, Bruce Jarchow, Tim Kazurinsky, Nancy McCabe-Kelly, Rob Riley
PRODUCTION: I Remember Dada, or Won' You Come Home, Saul Bellow?

Jay King Photo

Above: Members of The Second City

SEATTLE REPERTORY THEATRE

Seattle, Washington
October 24, 1979–May 18, 1980

Producing Director, Peter Donnelly; Consulting Artistic Director, John Hirsch; Resident Director, Daniel Sullivan; Associate Director, Richard Gershman; Technical Director, Robert Scales; Press, Shirley Dennis; Business Manager, Marene Wilkinson; Sets, Ming Cho Lee, Jim Newton, Robert Dahlstron, Robert Blackman; Costumes, Carrie F. Robbins, Tom Rasmussen, Laura Crow, Robert Dahlstrom, Robert Blackman; Lighting, David F. Segal, F. Mitchell Dana, Robert Dahlstrom, Robby Monk; Musical Director, Stan Keen, William Thomas, Jr.; Composer, Ken Benshoff; Choreography, David Nash, Bob Talmage; Stage Managers, Marc Rush, Milt Commons, James Verdery, Sandy Cruse

PRODUCTIONS AND CASTS

SAINT JOAN by Bernard Shaw: Paul C. Thomas (Beaudricourt), Lowry Miller (D'Estivet), Roberta Maxwell (Joan), John de Lancie (Poulengy/Ladvenu), Berry Kroeger (Archbishop of Rheims), Ted D'Arms (La Tremouille/Inquisitor), Paul Duke (Page/Court Member), Terrance Vorwald (Page/Court Member), Brian Thompson (Gilles De Rais/Decourcelles), John Aylward (La Hire/1920 Gentleman), Phillip Piro (Dauphin), Susan Ludlow (Duchess of Tremouille), Jack Ryland (Dunois), Stuart Wynn (Page), Biff McGuire (Earl of Warwick), Leon Pownall (De Stugumber), Charles Janasz (Page/Court Member), Louis Turenne (Peter Cauchon), Jim Dean (Executioner), Paul C. Thomas (English Soldier), and Jean Smart, Cheryl Whitener, Lachlan Macleahy, Daniel Noel, Bill Onteveiros, James Gordon, Michael Mancuso, Mark Perry, Daniel Noel, David Mong
A HISTORY OF THE AMERICAN FILM by Christopher Durang: Laurence Ballard (Jesus/Ferruchi/Pa Joad), Maureen Brennan (Loretta), Garret M. Brown (Hank/Minstrel Singer), Dorothy Lancaster (Blessed Mother/Ma O'Reilly), Jo Leffingwell (Prison Warden/Dolores Del Reego), Susan Ludlow (Allison/Ma Joad), Michael McCormick (Mickey/Newsboy/Abdhul), Lowry Miller (Fritz von Leffing/Victor Henreid), Bill Sadler (Jimmy), Jean Smart (Eve), Marcus Smythe (Policeman/Michael/Opera Singer), Jeannine Taylor (Clara), William Thomas, Jr. (Piano Man/Ethnic Roles), Anne Twomey (Bette), Paul Duke (Usher/Waiter/Telegram Boy), Daniel Noel (Usher/Santa Claus/Telegram Boy)
AN ENEMY OF THE PEOPLE by Henrik Ibsen; Adapted by Arthur Miller: Barney O'Sullivan (Morten), John Procaccino (Billing), Jeannie Carson (Catherine), David White (Peter), Laurence Ballard (Hofstad), Biff McGuire (Stockmann), Christopher Briggs (Morten), Jeff Covell (Ejlif), John Aylward (Horster), Marnie Mosiman (Petra), Clayton Corzatte (Aslaksen), Michael Santo (Drunk), and Susan Ludlow, Cheryl Whitener, Richard E. Arnold, Daniel Noel, Jonathan Simmons, Dean Melang, Bill DeYoung, Randy Schaub, John Smiley, Tony Amendola, Charles Janasz, James Gordon, Mark Perry, William Crossett
THE TAMING OF THE SHREW by William Shakespeare: Tony Amendola (Lord), John Aylward (Sly), Lori Larsen (Hostess/-Widow), Michael Santo (Page/Tailor), Paul C. Thomas (Baptista), Paul Milikin (Vincentio), John de Lancie (Lucentio), J. Kenneth Campbell (Petruchio), Clayton Corzatte (Gremio), John Procaccino (Hortensio), Laurence Ballard (Tranio), Charles Janasz (Biondello), R. Hamilton Wright (Grumio), Jonathan Simmons (Curtis), Katherine Ferrand (Katherina), Marnie Mosiman (Bianca), Corky Dexter (Haberdasher), and Gayle Bellows, Paul Duke, Daniel Noel, Mark Perry, Randy Schaub, Jonathan Simmons, Bill Bone, Lance Lu
SPOKESONG by Stewart Parker: Gannon McHale (Trick Cyclist), Bruce French (Frank), Elizabeth Lathram (Margaret), John Aylward (Francis), Linda Daugherty (Kitty), Andy Wood (Julian), Eleanor Wetzel (pianist)
PAL JOEY by Richard Rodgers, Lorenz Hart, John O'Hara: Scott Wentworth (Joey), Eve Roberts (Vera), Bob Basso (Mike), Nora McLellan (Gladys), Marnie Mosiman (Valerie), Pamela Cordova (Cordova), Alexis Hoff (Alice), Jeni Nudell (Jessie), Kristy Syverson (Krystal), Alan Manson (Ludlow), Ann Ungar (Melba), Michael Santo (Ernest), Laura Drake, Linda Hartzell (His Assistants), Jerry Harper (O'Brien), Gary Lakes (Louis), Jonathan Simmons (Doorman), Jerry Harper (Scholtz), Marc Pluf (Dancer), Susan Wands (Maid), Ron Ben Jarrett (Janitor), Michael Skubal (Bartender), Clint Pozzi (Waiter), Jim Etue (Newsboy), Clark Sandford (Escort), Scott Honeywell (Seift), Doug Smith (Gangster), Larry Bialock (The Horse), Gary Lakes (Santa Claus), Stan Keen (Jimmy)

Greg Gilbert Photos

Left Center: "The Taming of the Shrew"
Above: "An Enemy of the People"
Top: Roberta Maxwell as "Saint Joan"

SOUTH COAST REPERTORY THEATRE

Costa Mesa, California
October 2, 1979–May 25, 1980
Producing Artistic Director, David Emmes; Business Director, Tom Spray; Production Coordinator, Martin Benson: Press, John Mouledoux, Margaret McKay, Peg E. Davis; Technical Director, Leo Collin; Costume Coordinator, Dwight Richard Odle; Props, Terry Lieberstein, Michael Beech; Stage Managers, Bill Venom, Andrew Feigin, Linda L. Kimball, Mark Majarian; Stage Directors, Martin Benson, Frank Condon, David Emmes, John-David Keller, Barnet Kellman, Lee Shallat

COMPANY

George Archambeault, Ronald Boussom, Steve DeNaut, James E. dePriest, Richard Doyle, John Ellington, Wayne Grace, Noreen Hennessy, John-David Keller, Iris Korn, Art Koustik, Hal Landon, Jr., Carles Lanyer, Anni Long, Martha McFarland, Ron Michaelson, Richard Niles, Steve Patterson, Irene Roseen, Lee Shallat, Howard Shangra, Ann Siena-Schwartz, Don Tuche, Herb Voland, Candace Copeland, Ayre Gross, Kathryn Johnson
GUEST ARTISTS: Logan Ramsey, Roscoe Born, Nomi Mitty, Laura Campbell, Hal Bokar, Philip Baker Hall, James R. Winker, Teri Ralston, Gary Dontzig, Clarke Gordon, Frances Bay, Kenneth Tigar, William Needles, Megan Cole, Jonathan McMurtry, Wayne Alexander, Karen Henzel, Patti Johns, Karen Kondazian, Ann Greer, Mark Herrier

PRODUCTIONS

Wild Oats by John O'Keefe, Wings by Arthur Kopit, Side by Side by Sondheim by Stephen Sondheim, Right of Way by Richard Lees, Much Ado about Nothing by William Shakespeare, Ladyhouse Blues by Kevin O'Morrison, Life in the Theatre by David Mamet, Forever Yours Marie-Lou by Michel Tremblay, No Man's Land by Harold Pinter, and *World Premieres* of Points in Time by David Pollock and Elias Davis, Time Was by Shannon Keith Kelley

**Hal Landon, Jr., Herb Voland
in "Wild Oats"** *(Don Hamilton Photo)*
**Top: Richard Doyle, Teri Ralston, Gary
Dontzig, Martha McFarland in "Side by
Side by Sondheim"**

STAGE WEST

West Springfield, Massachusetts
November 1, 1979–April 20, 1980
Producing Director, Stephen E. Hays; General Manager, Robert A. Rosenbaum; Press, Sheldon Wolf, Michele Boudreau; Production Manager, Paul J. Horton; Technical Director, Joe Long; Stage Directors, Davey Marlin Jones, Harold Scott, Geoffrey Sherman, Ted Weiant, Timothy Near, Russell Treyz; Sets, Arthur Ridley, James Guenther, Thomas Cariello, Bennet Averyt, Tom Schwinn, Lawrence King; Costumes, Bill Walker, Joan Vick, Lewis D. Rampino, Anne Thaxter-Watson; Lighting, Paul J. Horton, Andrea Wilson, Bennet Averyt, Robby Monk; Stage Managers, Laura Burroughs, Gary Lamagna, Joseph DePauw, Ken Denison

PRODUCTIONS AND CASTS

THE NIGHT OF THE IGUANA by Tennessee Williams: Lou Ferguson, Carol Mayo Jenkins, Dan Manelin, Douglas Stender, Jay Cigna, Ross Cigna, Deborah Stenard, Terry Hinz, Judith Drake, Patrick Desmond, Lisa McMillan, Margaret Winn, Alice Brereton, Curt Williams, John Tormey
SIZWE BANSI IS DEAD by Athol Fugard, John Kani, Winston Ntshona: Lou Ferguson, Reuben Green
PEG O' MY HEART by J. Hartley Manners: Myra Carter, Francis Pichanick, Michelle LaMothe, Guy Siner, Gibby Brand, Beth Austin, Wyman Pendleton, Deborah Stenard, Richard Ryder
THE SEA HORSE by Edward J. Moore: Karen Shallo, John Henry Cox
OF MICE AND MEN by John Steinbeck: Christopher Rich, Michael Brennan Starr, Douglas Andros, Roger Patnode, Pope Brock, Diane Prusha, John Henry Cox, Ed O'Ross, Pete Edens, Hugh Hurd
RELATIVELY SPEAKING by Alan Ayckbourn: Marcus Smythe, Ellen Fiske, John Madden Towey, Joan Ulmer

Epstein & Armstrong Photos

**Right Center: Michelle LaMothe, Beth
Austin in "Peg o' My Heart"**

**John Towey, Marcus Smythe, Joan Ulmer
in "Relatively Speaking"** 203

STUDIO ARENA THEATRE

Buffalo, N.Y.
October 5, 1979–May 3, 1980
Fifteenth Season

Executive Producer, Neal DuBrock; Managing Director, Barry Hoffman; Associate Producer, Michael Healy; Press, Blossom Cohan, Eleanor Albertson; Business Manager, Mark W. Crotty; Assistant Managing Director, Patricia Brennan; Assistant to Producers, Rosemary Sheldon; Production Assistant, Lawrence Williams; Technical Director, John Baun; Stage Directors, Warren Enters, Stephen Porter, Lawrence Kornfeld, Tom O'Horgan, Neal Du Brock; Sets, Hal Tine, Zack Brown, John T. Baun, Bob Phillips, Bill Stabile; Costumes, Sauree N. Pinckard, Zack Brown, Randy Barcelo, Kristina Watson; Lighting, Marc B. Weiss, Peter Gill, John McLain, Robby Monk; Stage Managers, Beverly J. Andreozzi, Robert C. Mingus.

PRODUCTIONS AND CASTS

DA by Hugh Leonard: John G. Kellogg, Steven Sutherland, Stenja Lowe, Keith McDermott, Richard Frank, Eileen Letchworth, Catherine Bruno, Jack Bittner
MY HUSBAND'S WILD DESIRES ALMOST DROVE ME MAD by John Tobias: (*World Premiere*) MacIntyre Dixon (Burglar), Rosemary Prinz (Mrs. Griffin), Rex Everhart (Connelly), William Andrews (Griffin), Alice Drummond (Louise)
THE MOUSETRAP by Agatha Christie: Robert Burke, Joyce Fidor, Douglas Fisher, Kelsey Grammar, Franklin Kiser, Kathleen McKiernan, John Remme, Margaretta Warwick
ASHES by David Rudkin: Robin Chadwick, Don Allen Leslie, Gloria Maddox, Christine Von Dohln
I WON'T DANCE (*World Premiere*) by Oliver Hailey: Shirley Knight, David Selby, Arlene Golonka
THE GIN GAME by D. L. Coburn: William Prince, Pauline Flanagan
THE LETTER by W. Somerset Maugham: Carrie Nye, Dalton Dearborn, Paul Vincent, Douglas Stender, Glenn Cabrera, Shyrl Ryanharrt, Michael G. Chin, Marcie Stringer, Glenn Kubota

Phototech Studios Photos

Pauline Flanagan, William Prince in "The Gin Game" Top: (L) Carrie Nye in "The Letter" (R) Shirley Knight, David Selby in "I Won't Dance"

SYRACUSE STAGE

Syracuse, N.Y.
October 19, 1979–May 24, 1980

Producing Director, Arthur Storch; Managing Director, James A. Clark; Press, Charlaine Martin; Production Manager, Bob Davidson; Stage Managers, Cynthia Poulson, David Semonin; Sets, John Arnone, Hal Tine, Francois LaPlante, Tom Warren, John Doeppe; Costumes, Patricia McGourty, Lewis D. Rampino, Francois Laplante, James Berton Harris, Anne Shanto, Jania Szatanski; Lighting, Judy Rasmuson, Michael Newton-Brown, Robert Thompson, Jonathan K. Duff; Frances Aronson; Stage Directors, Arthur Storch, Larry Alford, Bill Glassco, John VanBurek, John Ulmer, Terry Schreiber, Lawrence Kornfeld

PRODUCTIONS AND CASTS

NAKED by Luigi Pirandello, translated by William Murray: John Ahlin, John LaGioia, Vera Visconti Lockwood, Scott McKay, Caitlin O'Heaney, Pamela Pascoe, Robert Thaler
SIDE BY SIDE BY SONDHEIM by Stephen Sondheim, Leonard Bernstein, Mary Rodgers, Richard Rodgers, Jule Styne, Ned Sherrin: Marianne Challis, Michael Davis, Anna McNeely
DAMNEE MANON, SACREE SANDRA by Michel Tremblay, translated by John VanBurek: Margot Dionne, Frank Moore
MAN AND SUPERMAN by George Bernard Shaw: Robert Baines, Beverly Bluem, Marjorie Lovett, Innes-Fergus McDade, Tom McDermott, Michael Medeiros, Ted Pejovich, Susanne Peters, Larry Pine, Karen Reichheld, Allan Stevens
WHO'S AFRAID OF VIRGINIA WOOLF? by Edward Albee: Christine Gavrile, Drew Keil, Alan Mixon, Meg Myles
OLD WORLD by Aleksei Arbuzov: Laurence Hugo, Shirin Devrim Trainer

Robert Lorenz, James VanPatten/Main Street Photos

Meg Miles, Alan Mixon in "Who's Afraid of Virginia Woolf?"

Left Center: Tom McDermott, Larry Pine in "Man and Superman"

THEATRE BY THE SEA

Portsmouth, N. H.
September 26, 1979–May 17, 1980
Producing Director, Jon Kimbell; Managing Director, William Michael Maher; Press, Amy Short Monninger, Sandi Bianco; Technical Directors, John Becker, Larry Markey: Stage Directors, Andrew Rohrer, Jon Kimbell, Ben Levit, Richard Harden, Tom Celli, Peter Thompson, Jack Allison; Sets, Fred Kolouch, Joan Brancale, Kathie Iannicelli, Larry Fulton, Bob Phillips, John Becker; Costumes, Kathie Iannicelli, Holly Urion, Linda Smith, Fred Kolouch; Lighting, Fred Kolouch, Tyrone Sanders, Mel Sturgio; Stage Managers, William Michael Maher, Carolyn Greer, Sam Aconfora; Musical Director, Bruce W. Coyle

PRODUCTIONS AND CASTS

GODSPELL by Stephen Schwartz: Elizabeth Bruzzese, Patrick D'Antonio, Paul F. Hewitt, Kyle Anne Kohler, Lorraine Robin Lazarus, Janna Morrison, Andrew Rohrer, Marlena Schroeder, Charlie Serrano, Scott Weintraub
A CHRISTMAS CAROL: SCROOGE AND MARLEY by Israel Horovitz from Charles Dickens' novel: Tom Celli, John H. Fields, Ginney Russell
STREAMERS by David Rabe: Scott Weintraub, Max Mayer, Basil A. Wallace, Ken Olin, James Craven, John H. Fields, Tom Celli, Paul F. Hewitt, Jim Burkholder, Michael Stacy
HOW THE OTHER HALF LOVES by Alan Ayckbourn: Joan Ulmer, Ginny Russell, Miller Lide, Bram Lewis, Paul F. Hewitt, Marlena Schroeder
OTHELLO by William Shakespeare: Maurice Woods, Ginny Russell, Bill Roberts, Stephanie Voss, Michael Stacy, Marlena Schroeder, Paul F. Hewitt, Tom Celli, John H. Fields, Gary Amagnac, Ted Mills, Larry Markey, Richard Bauer
THE GIN GAME by D. L. Coburn: Edward Seamon, Jane Cecil
BERLIN TO BROADWAY WITH KURT WEILL: Gary Barker, Claudine Cassan, Michael Davis, Karl Heist, Beverly Lambert

Andrew Edgar/North Light Photos

"Clark Street" Above: "Streamers"

**Bill Roberts, Maurice Woods
in "Othello"**

THEATER CENTER PHILADELPHIA

Philadelphia, Pennsylvania
October 10, 1979–June 28, 1980
Artistic Director, Albert Benzwie; Managing Director, Greg Maguire; Press, Sallie M. Gross; Production Assistants, Joseph Walker, George Black: Stage Directors, Tim Moyer, Michael Landenson, Albert Benzwie, Howard Zogott, Deborah Lundy, Walt Vail, Eric Forsythe, Donald O. Seidel; Sets, Tim Moyer, George Black, Philip Wysman, Herb Moskovitz, Judy Reingold, Dave Gordon; Costumes Valjean Clark, Kevin M. Boyle; Lighting, George Black, Barbara Post, Ted Silverman, Stephanie Drossin, Herbert Moskovitz, Henry Brann; Stage Managers, Michal Levin, Lisa Peachman, Philip Wysman, Bruce Robinson, Judith Panetta, Nancy Dale

PRODUCTIONS AND CASTS

MACBETH by William Shakespeare: Geoffrey Alnutt, Christopher Whelan, Michael Cory, Nicholas Bonanni, Joseph Pokorny, Peter Damian Palazzo, Dan Daly, Susan Cinoman, Bruce Robinson, Teri Sweeney, Toni Benjamin, Inga Baillystock
CAT ON A HOT TIN ROOF by Tennessee Williams: Eileen Grigg, Teri Sweeney, William Sarkees, Cara Marlowe, Lissa LeGrand, Keith Fox, William Sommerfield, Bruce Robinson, Bill McCardell, John Waldron, Starr Kristine

World Premieres:
WHAT DOES A BLIND LEOPARD SEE? by Lanie Robertson: Marcia Mahon, Jack Severyn, Ron Serlen, Craig Fols, Enid Reid, Jim Stanton, Walter Vail, John Houlihan
EXTREMITIES by William Mastrosimone: Patricia J. Moyer, Tom DiNardo, Barbara Driscoll, Barbara McElly
CLARK STREET by Jack Engelhard: Russell Reidinger, Sheilagh Weymouth, Tom DiNardo, Jeanne R. Fisher, Jesse C. Kennedy, Christopher Whelan
BEDTIME by Jay C Rehak and Lee Wright: Mitchell Balaban, Connie Majka, Sean Robins, Sandy Johnson, Neta Hodge, Lou DiPilla
OH, NO, NOT ME! by Jay C. Rehak and Lee Wright: Lou DiPilla, Louis Korff, Mitchell Balaban, Connie Majka, Neta Hodge
THE LAST SHOT by Susan Reinhardt: Lissa LeGrand, John Waldron, Benjamin Rubin, Michael Doran, Susan Jones, Susan Naidoff, Frank McGoon, Georgeann Catanella
TO DICK AND JANE by Bruce Feldman: Lynn Riccuti, Jerry Perna
JUST WHAT YOU EXPECT by Sydney Weinstone: Art Steinman, Helen McKenna
SILHOUETTE by Bill McCardell: William Sommerfield, Chris Ingaglio, Elizabeth Restuccia, Craig Riley, Bill McCardell
THE RISE AND FALL OF PHINEAS T. NOZZLE by Dennis Moritz: Evo Giomi, Karen Reichardt, Terry Sweeney, Andre Jones, Christine Melton, David Axler

Caryn J. Koffman Photo

**Georgia Clinton, Ralph M. Clift
in "The New York Idea"**

**Richard Kavanaugh, April Shawhan
in "Bosoms and Neglect" Above: "Waiting for
Godot" Top: "Buried Child"**

THEATRE THREE

Dallas, Texas
October 16, 1979–August 30, 1980
Producer-Director, Jac Alder; Associate Director, Charles Howard; Producer's Assistant, Nancy Akers: Press, Terri Taylor; Technical Director, Jim Haigler; Stage Directors, Larry O'Dwyer, Jac Alder, Charles Howard; Sets, Charles Howard, Harland Wright, Jac Alder; Costumes, Patty Greer McGarity, Leticia Guerra, Alan Nelson; Lighting, Shari Melde: Stage Managers, Shari Melde, Bick Ferguson; Musical Direction, Dean Crocker

PRODUCTIONS AND CASTS

CHICAGO by Fred Ebb, Bob Fosse, John Kander: David Benn, Alan Denny, Valerie Dowd, James Duff, B. Ferguson, Constance Hutchinson, David Lee Kistner, David Lamoureux, Beth Litherland, David May, Connie Nelson, Darlene O'Hara, Kaye Parriette, Joan Powers, Richard Roberts, Nancy Sherrard, Stephanie Stateson, Steve Tommey
THE NEW YORK IDEA by Langdon Mitchell: Ric Campo, Ralph M. Clift, Georgia Clinton, Dorothy Deavers, Ron Donigan, Pat Glass, Jo Haden, Mack Hays, Beverly Houston, Kelly Laughlin, Marsha Dianne Little, Steve Lovett, Larry O'Dwyer, Julie Oliver, Charles Rucker, Norma Young
FOR COLORED GIRLS WHO HAVE CONSIDERED SUICIDE WHEN THE RAINBOW IS ENUF by Ntozake Shange: Irma P. Hall, Shirley McFatter, Darlene O'Hara, Vickie Washington, Sharon Denise West, Joann M. Williams, Cynthia Dorn
THE TAKING AWAY OF LITTLE WILLIE by Tom Griffin: Robert Dracup, Sally Harris, Miles Mutchler, James Duff, Jo Livingston, Erin Jeanne Evans, Debra Stricklin
DRINKS BEFORE DINNER by E. L. Doctorow: Jenny Bourgeois, Gail Cronauer, Dorothy Deavers, Jo Livingston, Larry O'Dwyer, Erin Roy, Sean Roy, Carter Smith, Ann Stafford, Tim Steed, Peggy Townsley
HOW I GOT THAT STORY by Amlin Gray: Don Snell, Jac Alder
THE SEAGULL by Anton Chekhov: Jenny Bourgeois, Jack Curry, Dorothy Deavers, James Duff, Hugh Feagin, David A. Fenley, Sard Fleeker, Carolyn Gillespie, Kelly Laughlin, Annie Stafford, Billy Watson, Norma Young
PRESENT LAUGHTER by Noel Coward: Laurence O'Dwyer, Camilla Carr, Dorothy Deavers, Jo Haden, Connie Hearn, Brian Hinson, Jenna Jordan, Steve Lovett, Miles Mutchler, Eddie Thomas, Peggy Townsley

Andy Hanson Photos

TRINITY SQUARE REPERTORY COMPANY

Providence, Rhode Island
October 5, 1979–May 25, 1980
Director, Adrian Hall; Managing Director, E. Timothy Langan; General Manager, Arthur P. Bundey; Press, Scotti DiDonato; Marion Simon; Musical Director, Richard Cumming, Sets, Robert D. Soule; Lighting, John F. Custer; Costumes, William Lane; Choreography, Sharon Jenkins; Technical Director, David Ward; Props, Sandra Nathanson, Tom Walden, Cheryl Ottaviano; Stage Managers, Maureen F. Gibson, Joseph Kavanaugh, Franklin Keysar, Louis Scenti; Stage Directors, Adrian Hall, Larry Arrick, George Martin, Henry Velez, William Radka, Jonas Jurasas

COMPANY

Rob Anderson, Barbara Blossom, S. D. Brown, Edward Budz, Timothy Crowe, Barbara Damashek, William Damkoehler, Timothy Donoghue, Jeffrey Duarte, Monique Fowler, Elizabeth Franz, Peter Gerety, Bradford Gottlin, Tom Griffin, Ed Hall, Richard Jenkins, David C. Jones, Melanie Jones, Richard Kavanaugh, David Kennett, Richard Kneeland, Howard London, Mina Manente, George Martin, Ruth Maynard, Derek Meader, Barbara Meek, Barbara Orson, Lenka Peterson, Ford Rainey, Arthur H. Roberts, Dorothea Roberts, Anne Scurria, April Shawhan, Margo Skinner, Norman Smith, Amy Van Nostrand, Daniel Von Bargen, Diane Warren, Greg Young

PRODUCTIONS

Bosoms and Neglect, Sly Fox, Buried Child, Sea Marks, Born Yesterday, A Christmas Carol, The Night of the Iguana, Waiting for Godot, and *American Premiere* of The Suicide by Nikolai Erdman, translated by George Genereux, Jr. and Jacob Volkov

Constance Brown Photos

WESTCHESTER REGIONAL THEATRE
Harrision, New York
October 18, 1979–May 10, 1980
Fifth Season
Producing Director, Gay Goldman; Associate Producer, Sally C. B. Lee; Business Manager, Nora Stonehill; Press, Rena Abeles Margolis; Guest Directors, Geoffrey Sherman, Theodore Pappas, John Stix, Howard Ashman, Ronald Roston; Sets, Donato Moreno, John Lee Beatty, Karen Schulz, Ernest Allen Smith; Costumes, Donato Moreno, John David Ridge, Annette Beck, Ernest Allen Smith; Lighting, Susan White, Ruth Roberts, Todd Elmer, Robert Strohmeier; Stage Manager, Amy Chase

PRODUCTIONS AND CASTS

THE ECCENTRICITIES OF A NIGHTINGALE by Tennessee Williams: Catherine Burns, Frank Dent, Rosemary Foley, Megan Hunt, Justine Johnston, Michael Nobel, Wyman Pendleton, Robert Schenkkan, Prudence Wright Holmes
SOMETHING WONDERFUL (*World Premiere*) conceived and adapted by Alice Hammerstein Mathias: Harry Danner, Joy Franz, Randy Graff, Marti Rolph, Dean Russell
PUT THEM ALL TOGETHER by Anne Commire: Alma Cuervo, Jean DeBaer, Charlie Fields, Birdie M. Hale, Margo Martindale, J. J. Quinn, Richard Southern
A LIFE IN THE THEATRE by David Mamet: Larry Bryggman, Joel Polis

Ken Howard Photos

Left: Harry Danner, Randy Graff, Dean Russell, (front) Marti Rolph, Joy Franz in "Something Wonderful" Top: Catherine Burns, Robert Schenkkan in "Eccentricities of a Nightingale"

THE WHOLE THEATRE COMPANY
Montclair, New Jersey
October 9, 1979–May 25, 1980
Producing Director, Arnold Mittelman; Artistic Director, Olympia Dukakis; Managing Director, Sylvia Traeger; Production Coordinator, Paul Dorphley; Press, Barbara Benisch, Gerald Fierst; Business Manager, Tom Clark; Lighting, Marshall Spiller; Costumes, Sigrid Insull; Sets, Paul Dorphley, Patricia Woodbridge, Raymond C. Recht; Musical Director, Martin Silvestri; Stage Directors, Arnold Mittelman, Amy Saltz, Tony Tanner, Peter Kass

PRODUCTIONS AND CASTS

THE HOSTAGE by Brendan Behan: Bernard Frawley, Paddy Croft, Peter Murphy, Myra Turley, Marjorie Fierst, Joyce Slous, Kim Sullivan, Jason Bosseau, Apollo Dukakis, Marjorie Lovett, Eda Rothenberg, Quincy Long, Bill McIntyre, Gerald Cullity, James Campodonico, Dennis Bacigalupi
SPOON RIVER ANTHOLOGY by Edgar Lee Masters, adapted by Charles Aidman: W. B. Brydon, Maggie Abeckerly, Jessica Allen, Larry Pine, Kathrin King Segal, Roger Brown
WAITING FOR GODOT by Samuel Beckett: Judith Delgado, Olympia Dukakis, Maggie Abeckerly, Apollo Dukakis, Gregory Bendelius, Ralph Ellis
WORDS (*American Premiere*) by Tony Tanner and Martin Silvestri: Charles Ryan, Hal Davis, Susan Marchand, Mary Ann Robbins, and pianists Martin Silvestri, Grant Sturiale
A CAT IN THE GHETTO (*American Premiere*) by Shimon Wincelberg: Tom Costello, Apollo Dukakis, Raymond Barry, Rutanya Alda, Louis Zorich, Mordecai Lawner, Olympia Dukakis, Judith Delgado

Olympia Dukakis, Raymond Barry in "A Cat in the Ghetto"

YALE REPERTORY THEATRE

New Haven, Connecticut
October 5, 1979–May 24, 1980
Artistic Director, Lloyd Richards; Managing Director, Edward A. Martenson; Business Manager, Abigail P. Fearon; Press, Deborah J. Weiner; Production Coordinator, John Robert Hood; Technical Director, Bronislaw Joseph Sammler; Props, Hunter Nesbitt Spence; Stage Directors, Steven Robman, Carl Weber, John Madden, Tony Giordano, Andrei Belgrader, Athol Fugard, Lloyd Richards; Sets, Michael H. Yeargan, Charles McCarry, Lawrence Casey, Randy Drake, Loren Sherman; Costumes, Dunya Ramicova, Dean H. Reiter, Nan Cibula, Rita Ryack, Susan Hilferty, Judianna Makovsky; Lighting, Tom Skelton, William B. Warfel, Loren Sherman, William M. Armstrong, John I. Tissot, Rick Butler; Sound, Tom Voegeli; Music, Carman Moore; Choreography, Wesley Fata

PRODUCTIONS AND CASTS

BOSOMS AND NEGLECT by John Guare: Beverly May, James Sutorius, Jean DeBaer
THEY ARE DYING OUT (*American Premiere*) by Peter Handke: Richard M. Davidson, Soon-Teck Oh, Leonard Jackson, David Sabin, Jeffrey Jones, Dominic Chianese, Phyllis Somerville, Marianne Rossi
MEASURE FOR MEASURE by William Shakespeare: Gerry Bamman, Dominic Chianese, Christopher Walken, Jon Polito, John Gould Rubin, Dana B. Westberg, Kristine Nielsen, Geoffrey Pierson, Tom Klunis, Tony Shalhoub, Carol Ostrow, Roy Steinberg, Frances Conroy, Eve Gordon, Thomas Derrah, David Wiles, H. Lloyd Carbaugh, D. Benjamin Cameron, Dare Clubb, Polly Draper, David Alan Grier, Reg E. Cathey, Vytautas Ruginis
CURSE OF THE STARVING CLASS by Sam Shepard: Anne Gerety, Warren Manzi, Caris Corfman, Donald Linahan, William Andrews, Ron Faber, Clark Rogers, Andy Backer, David Wiles
UBU REX by Alfred Jarry, translated by David Copelin: Ron Faber, Ruth Jaroslow, Geoffrey Pierson, Jon Walker, Susan Blommaert, Thomas Derrah, Isabell Monk, H. S. Murphy, Kristine Nielsen, Carol Ostrow, Tony Shalhoub, Richard Spore, Charles Pistone
A LESSON FROM ALOES (*American Premiere*) written and directed by Athol Fugard: Harris Yulin, Maria Tucci, James Earl Jones
TIMON OF ATHENS by William Shakespeare: Leonard Jackson, John Gould Rubin, James Carruthers, Jeffrey Natter, Reg E. Cathey, Wyman Pendleton, John Lloyd, H. S. Murphy, Bill Nunnery, James Earl Jones, James Greene, David Prittie, Thomas Derrah, Michael Morgan, Andy Backer, Harris Yulin, Richard Greene, Michael Knight, Geoffrey Pierson, David Wiles, Scott Rickey Wheeler, Kristin Nielsen, Isabell Monk, Diana Lee Benson, Jance Kaczmarek, Angela J. Workman, Melissa Smith, Warren David Keith, David Alan Grier, Gordon Gray, Keith Grant, William Mesnick

Gerry Goodstein Photos

Right: James Earl Jones, Richard Greene in "Timon of Athens" Above: Leonard Jackson, Dominic Chianese in "They Are Dying Out" Top: Jean DeBaer, James Sutorius in "Bosoms and Neglect"

Frances Conroy, Christopher Walken in "Measure for Measure"

James Earl Jones, Maria Tucci, Harris Yulin in "A Lesson from Aloes"

GLOBE PLAYHOUSE

Los Angeles, California
June 1, 1979–May 31, 1980

Founder-Executive Producer, R. Thad Taylor; General Manager, Edward E. Milder; Business Manager, Susan P. Marrone; Press, Harriet Held; Stage Directors, Mark Majarian, Walter Scholz, Shannon Eubanks, Jack Manning, David Coombs, R. Thad Taylor; Costumes, Shannon Eubanks, Lane Davies, Sue Ellen Rohrer, Terry Troutt, Yvonne James Johnson, Blaine Smith, Pam Grossman; Lighting, Alan Feldman, Ilya Mindlin, Leslie Jordan, Michael M. Bergfeld; Stage Manager, John Davis, Evan Cole, Carolee Schumaker, Paul McEvoy, Miranda Smith, Anthony DiNovi, Leslie Jordan, Ernie Cordova, Leslie Quinn, Janet Callahan, Victoria Fahn, Lauren Goldman; Artistic Coordinator, Walter Scholz

PRODUCTIONS AND CASTS

HENRY VIII: Lloyd Hollar, William Utay, Rob Evan Collins, Melvin F. Allen, Mack Dugger, Marcia Moran, Art Goldman, Patrick Rowe, Victoria Tucker, Kathy Bell-Denton, Dan Covey, Robert Vernon-Gould, Neale Harper, William Nye, Mark Ringer, Lauren Goldman, Annette McCarthy, Matthew Laidlau

THE TWO NOBLE KINSMEN (American Premiere) by John Fletcher and William Shakespeare: Eugene Brezany, Patrick Depew, Richard Blood, Toni Macdonald, Louie Gutierrez, Ellyn Stern, Cam-Lelsie Wilder, Jane Burch, Maureen O'Connell, Lee Taylor, Douglas Blair, Nocona Aranda, Michele Hart, Michael Richards, David Hunt Stafford, Suzanna Peters, Barbara Downs, Paul McEvoy, Adrian Suarez, David Gutierrez, Gilbert Lawrence Kaan, George Ceres, Victoria Hartman

HENRY V: Woody Eney, Lane Davies, Bob Boyd, Seamus McGraw, William Wright, Steven J. Paull, Kael Blackwood, Al Strobel, Robert Budaska, J. D. Mackay, John Garrick, Richard Lebed, Dale Swann, John P. Flynn, John Megna, Walter Scholz, Guy BonGiovanni, Bert Hinchman, Rozsika Horvath, Kate Zentall, Dorene Ludwig, Maggie Hepburn, Nay K. Dorsey, Kim Eney, Teaka Allyn

THE MERRY WIVES OF WINDSOR: Gloria Grahame, Leon Charles, Valerie Seelie-Snyder, Dixie Neyland Tymitz, Joel Asher, Philip Persons, Eugene Brezany, Richard Cordery, Lee Fishel, Lanny Broyles, Paul Aron Scott, Lisa Barnes, Addison Randall, Lucinda Dooling, William Nye, Lyle Stephen, Bert Hinchman, Renee Mandel, Stephanie Seebold, David Brooks, Matt W. Wills, David Stifel, Brian Sullivan, Keith Blackmer, Richie Levene, Havre Von Lambach

RICHARD II: Michael Baseleon, Eugene Brezany, Gardner Hayes, Stephen Johnson, Steve Osborn, John Stuart West, Zenius Muleckis, Larry Barnes, David Gautreaux, Mark Ringer, Larry Barnes, Carl Moebus, Roger Jones, Steven J. Paull, Carl Walsh, Patrick D. McGuire, Don Higdon, Fred G. Smith, Aviva Goldkorn, Mary Thomas Barry, June Claman, Lynn Capri, Pamela Vandervalk, Michael Calder, Larry Barnes

CORIOLANUS: Michael Richards, Lloyd Hollar, Edgar Weinstock, Steven J. Paull, Joan Crosby, Mary-Kate Edmonston, Maggie McOmie, Tristan Peach, Nocona Aranda, Melodee M. Spevack, Richard Blood, Douglas Blair, Ev Jasper, Gil Alvarez, Amina Lee, Michele Hart, David Stifel, Paul McEvoy, Barbara Downs, Renette Zimmerly, Mitzi Meyers, Charles Kruger, Peter Martyniuk, Max Mulder, Tracey Weddle, Janine Cousins, Archie H. Waugh III, Stuart Greif, Michael J. Dias, Mitchell Gibney, Ana Maria Gutierrez

THE TEMPEST: Jeffrey G. Forward, Michael Stephen Peru, Richmond F. Johnson, Carl Moebus, Carl Walsh, Walt Dodge, David Kondo, Kavi Raz, Mark Del Castillo-Morante, Gordon D. Pinkney, Michael Morrison, Danny Dayan, Nick Demos, Nay K. Dorsey, Erik Wolfe, Yvonne Regalado, Valerie Niccore, Judith Bridges, Paunita Nichols, Ree Ra, Michelle Banks, Barbara Gutheridge, May-Brith Nilsen, Gwendolyn Rogers-Hanks, Kathleen Shoaf

SHAKESPEARE'S SONNETS: Sally Kirkland, Jared Martin, John Barrymore III, Valerie Niccore, Jeffrey G. Forward, William Galligan, Seamus McGraw, Kasi Lemmons, Evelyn Levings, Ursaline Bryant-King, Howard Stearn, Larry Barret, Nick Edmett, Rita Zohar, Pamela McKernan, Michelle Mindlin, Wendy Robbins, William Galligan

Photos by Sealy

Top Right: Valerie Seelie-Snyder, Leon Charles, Gloria Grahame in "Merry Wives of Windsor" Below: Suzanna Peters, Michael Richards in "Two Noble Kinsmen"

Sally Kirkland, John Barrymore III in "Shakespeare's Sonnets"

COLORADO SHAKESPEARE FESTIVAL

Boulder, Colorado
July 20 through August 18, 1979
Twenty-second Season

Producing Director, Daniel S. P. Yang; Stage Directors, Ronald Mitchell, William Glover, Tom Markus; Sets, Dan Dryden, Norvid Roos; Costumes, David A. Busse, Deborah Dryden; Lighting, Richard Riddell; State Manager, Jane Page; Vocal Coach, Bonnie Raphael; Press, Beverly Shaw

COMPANY

Kip Baker, Tim Batson, Shirley Carnahan, Casey Childs, David Cleveland, Patrick Crea, Julius Dahne, Maggie Donaghy, James Finnegan, Larry Friedlander, Scott Harper, Annette Helde, Todd Jamieson, Kjeld Lyth, Michael McKenzie, Ursula Meyer, Mary Olson, Tom Rowan, Dan Sanders, Sam Sandoe, Margie Shaw, Philip Sneed, Thomas G. Thomas, Allan Trautman, David Wells, Charles Wilcox, Denis Williams, Will York, and *Guest Artist* Gordon Wickstrom
PRODUCTIONS: A Midsummer Night's Dream, King Lear, Henry IV Part II

Jerry Stowall Photos

Ursula Meyer, Annette Helde, Todd Jamieson, David Cleveland in "A Midsummer Night's Dream"

Katherine McGrath, Jonathan McMurtry in "Julius Caesar" Above: Jeffrey Combs, William Ian Gamble in "Comedy of Errors"

NATIONAL SHAKESPEARE FESTIVAL

San Diego, California
June 12,–September 23, 1979
Thirtieth Season

Producing Director, Craig Noel; General Manager, Bob McGlade; Company Manager, Thomas Hall; Press, William B. Eaton; Technical Director, Ron Keller; Stage Directors, Jerome Kilty, Ken Ruta, Nagle Jackson; Dramaturge, Diana Maddox; Sets, Cliff Faulkner; Costumes, Peggy Kellner, Deborah Dryden, Lewis Brown; Lighting, John McLain; Sound, Dan Dugan, Roger Gans; Fight Director David L. Boushey; Choreographer, Bonni Johnston; Music, Ken Benshoof; Stage Managers, Thomas Hall, Betsy Kincaid, Anne Salazar

COMPANY

Don Bilotti, Jeffrey Combs, William Ian Gamble, Tom Henschel, Jerry Allan Jones, Sandy McCallum, Katherine McGrath, Jonathan McMurtry, John H. Napierala, Thomas S. Oleniacz, Michael Parish, Jenifer Parker, William Roesch, G Wood, Michael Byers, Kandis Chappell, Jody Horowitz, Don Sparks, George Noe, Lindy Nisbet, Chava Burgueno, Arnie D. Burton, Dennis Dal Covey, Timothy Flanagan, Robin Good, Thomas P. Harrison, Karl W. Hesser, Mark Kincaid, Fritz Lennon, J. T. Loudenback, Maria Mayenzet, Mary Mendoza, Miki Outland, Thomas Reiter, Janis Stevens, Darrold Lee Strubbe, Valeda Turner, Michael Winston, Derrick Harrison Hurd, Steve Parvin, Raymond Wohl, Roger Smith, Rob Bacon, Pat Crawford, Victor Salazar

PRODUCTIONS

Julius Caesar, The Comedy of Errors, Macbeth, The Norman Conquests by Alan Ayckbourn

Above: Jody Horowitz, Lindy Nisbet, Don Sparks, Buzz Noe in "Norman Conquests"

NEW JERSEY SHAKESPEARE FESTIVAL

Madison, New Jersey
June 26,–December 2, 1979
Fifteenth Season

Artistic Director, Paul Barry; Associate Director/Press, Ellen Barry; Managing Director, Ed Cimbala; Sets/Props, Peter B. Harrison; Costumes, Ann Emonts, Kathleen Blake, Alice S. Hughes; Lighting, Gary C. Porto; Company Manager, Susan Socolowski; Musical Director, Stewart W. Turner; Guest Director, John Ulmer; Stage Managers, Joseph DePauw, Dianna M. Paradis, Gary C. Porto

COMPANY

Ellen Barry, Paul Barry, Denise Bessette, Tom Brennan, Gwendolyn Brown, Martha J. Brown, Brendan Burke, Clarence Felder, George Gitto, Richard Graham, David Howard, Vivien Landau, Ronald Martell, Timothy Meyers, Sharon Morrison, Phillip Pruneau, Steven Ryan, Albert Sanders, Margery Shaw, Eric Tavaris, Zeke Zaccaro Robynne Archia-Williams, Marc Aronoff, William E. Benson, E. A. Boerner III, Anthony Catalani, Robert Chambers, Charlotte Cheatham, Peter Clayton, Bob Collins, Katherine Collins, Frank Collison, Elaine Conner, Christine Contreras, Lee Crogham, Jamie DeLorenzo, Robert DiCerbo, Peggy Eisenhaver, Amy Elizabeth Epstein, Dominic Fico, Tom Fortmuller, Anne Terease Fox, Olivia Gans, Lisa Gluck, Allison Gobac, Michael Linden Greene, Lee Grober, Joe Gross, Julie Hackett, David Heisey, Frieda E. Henry, Jennifer Hiers, Lynne A. Holley, Ann Jamison, Joan Keyes, Ken Kirschenbaum, Alfred Kirschman, Andrea Jenya Klein, Julie Krasnow, Frank G. Lamb, Peter Lund, Louise Manske, Jane Mohr, Mimi Monaco, Joseph Montalvo, Walter Morrison, June Anne Murphy, John Nichols, John O'Hara, Alene Paone, Gail Pepper, Peggy Pharr, Dolly Reisman, Daniel Riordan, Lyle Sandler, Patricia C. Sanftner, Melinda Schodt, Joel Selzer, Mary Elizabeth Sheridan, Eric W. Shute, Deborah Ann Smith, Sandra Soehngen, Sheila Spencer, Joseph Lawrence Spiegel, Mary E. Stewart, Amy Stoller, Sue Sullivan, James Swartz, Teresa Tan, Gregg Thomas, Meg VanZyl, Candace Warner, Wayne Wieser, Gary L. Wissman

PRODUCTIONS

King Lear, A Midsummer Night's Dream, A Streetcar Named Desire by Tennessee Williams,.The Importance of Being Earnest by Oscar Wilde, Travesties by Tom Stoppard, Two for the Seesaw by William Gibson, Luv by Murray Schisgal

Blair Holley, Jerry Dalia Photos

Right: Ellen Barry, Margery Shaw, Steven Ryan in "Streetcar Named Desire" Top: Eric Tavaris, Martha Brown, Gregory Bendelius, Timothy Meyers in "Midsummer Night's Dream"

**Richard Graham, Margery Shaw
in "King Lear"**

**Tom Brennan, David Howard,
Vivien Landau in "Luv"**

NEW YORK SHAKESPEARE FESTIVAL

Delacorte Theater/Central Park, NYC
June 22,–August 26, 1979
Twenty-third Season

Producer, Joseph Papp; General Manager, Robert Kamlot; Production Supervisor, Jason Steven Cohen; Direction and Scenery, Wilford Leach; Associate Set Designer, Paul Eads; Costumes, Patricia McGourty; Lighting, Jennifer Tipton; Fight Sequences, Erik Fredricksen, B. H. Barry; Music, Stanley Silverman (Coriolanus), William Elliott (Othello); Press, Merle Debuskey, Bob Ullman, Richard Kornberg; Production Manager, Andrew Mihok; Technical Director, Mervyn Haines, Jr., Darrel Ziegler; Sound, Bill Dreisbach; Props, Joe Toland; Company Manager, Roger Gindi; Stage Managers, Sherman Warner, Ron Nguvu, Zane Weiner, Patricia Morinelli

PRODUCTIONS AND CASTS

CORIOLANUS: Maurice Woods (Agrippa), Clark Morgan (Senator), Bimbo (Patrician), J. J. Johnson (Patrician), Earle Hyman (Cominius), Morgan Freeman (Coriolanus), Jay Fernandez (Officer), Gloria Foster (Volumnia), Michele Shay (Virginia), Khayyam Kain (Young Martius), C. C. H. Pounder (Valeria), Clebert Ford (Velutus), Frank Adu (Brutus), Denzel Washington, Keith Williams (Aediles), Count Stovall (1st Citizen), Jose Santana (2nd Citizen), Robbie McCauley, Cynthia McPherson (Aides), Castulo Guerra (Senator/Nicanor), Thomas Martell Brimm, David Toney (Senators), Robert Christian (Aufidius), Keith Esau (His Lieutenant), Thomas Martell Brimm (Adrian), and Wayne Anthony, Christine Campbell, Peter Francis-James, Jose Maldonado, Clark Morgan, Francisco Prado, Catherine E. Slade, Dennis Tate

OTHELLO: James Rebhorn (Roderigo), Richard Dreyfuss (Iago), James Greene (Brabantio), Raul Julia (Othello), Mark Linn Baker (Orderly), John Heard (Cassio), Castulo Guerra (Officer), James Cahill (Duke of Venice), Ric Lavin (Gratiano), Tom Costello (Senator), Bruce McGill (Lodonico), Michael Gross (Montano), Frances Conroy (Desdemona), Kaiulani Lee (Emilia), Margaret Whitton (Bianca), Douglas Broyles, John Ferraro, Matthew Ransom, Thomas A. Stewart, Caitlin Clarke, Keith David, Margaret Warncke

MOBILE THEATER: THE MIGHTY GENTS by Richard Wesley; Director, Ntozake Shange; Set, Edward Burbridge; Costumes, Beverly Parks; Lighting, Victor En Yu Tan; Music, Baikida Carroll; Choreography, Avery Brooks; Technical Director, Art Muhleisen; Stage Managers, Elizabeth Holloway, Bill McComb; Production Assistant, Paul Armand Brasuell. CAST: Richard Lawson (Frankie), C. C. H. Pounder (Rita), Bill Cobbs (Zeke), Gary Bolling (Eldridge), Samuel L. Jackson (Lucky), Otis Young-Smith (Tiny), Tucker Smallwood (Braxton), Frank Adu (Father)

George E. Joseph, Martha Swope Photos

**Right: Morgan Freeman, Earle Hyman
Top: Morgan Freeman, Gloria Foster
in "Coriolanus"**

**Richard Dreyfuss, Raul Julia, Frances Conroy,
Bruce McGill in "Othello"**

**Richard Lawson, Gary Bolling, Sam Jackson,
Otis Young-Smith in "The Mighty Gents"**

OREGON SHAKESPEARE FESTIVAL

Ashland, Oregon
February 27,–October 27, 1979
Forty-fourth Season

President Board of Directors, Robert C. Bernard; General Manager, William W. Patton; Producing Director, Jerry Turner; Directors, Dennis Bigelow, Elizabeth Huddle, Michael Kevin, Michael Leibert, James Moll, Judd Parkin, Pat Patton, Audrey Stanley, Jerry Turner; Designers, Robert Blackman, William Bloodgood, Michael Chapman, Jeannie Davidson, Deborah M. Dryden, Dirk Epperson, Richard L. Hay, Merrily Ann Murray, Robert Peterson; Composer, Todd Barton; Choreographers, Angene Feves, Judith Kennedy; Fight Director, David L. Boushey; Production Manager, Pat Patton; Technical Directors, R. Duncan MacKenzie, Jeff Robbins; Props,, Paul-James Martin; Stage Managers, Peter W. Allen, Dennis Bigelow, Lee Alan Byron, Michael B. Paul, David F. Riley; Press, Margaret Rubin

COMPANY

Rex E. Allen, Tony Amendola, Robert L. Burns, Kerry Calkins, Jack Wellington Cantwell, Mimi Carr, Susan Chapman, Philip Davidson, Leonardo DeFilippis, Patrick DeSantis, Cameron Dokey, Stuart Duckworth, James Edmondson, Michael T. Folie, Danny Frishman, Craig R. Gardner, Peter D. Giffin, Stephen J. Godwin, Bruce T. Gooch, Rick Hamilton, Malcolm Hillgartner, Robert Hirschboeck, Michael Kevin, Maureen Kilmurry, Dan Kremer, Philip Lombardo, Lawrence C. Lott, John Norwalk, Brigit Olson, Eric Olson, Fredi Olster, Joann Johnson Patton, Shirley Patton, Rex Rabold, Robert M. Reid, Randy Schaub, John Shepard, Gary Sloan, Sally Smythe, Anya Springer, Joan Stuart-Morris, Bill Terkuile, Kirk Thornton, Mary Turner, Tom Weiner, Time Winters, Ronald Edmundson Woods, Evan Davidson, Cooper A. Lewis, Courtney Lewis

PRODUCTIONS

A Midsummer Night's Dream, As You Like It, Macbeth, The Play's the Thing by Ferenc Molnar, Born Yesterday by Garson Kanin, The Tragical History of Doctor Faustus by Christopher Marlowe, Miss Julie by August Strindberg, Who's Happy Now? by Oliver Hailey, Root of the Mandrake by Niccolo Machiavelli adapted by Robert Symonds, The Wild Duck by Henrik Ibsen translated by Jerry Turner, Indulgences by John Orlock

Hank Kranzler Photos

**Right: Michael Kevin, James Edmondson
in "Dr. Faustus" Top: Anya Springer,
Maureen Kilmurry in "As You Like It"**

**Stuart Duckworth, Joan Stuart-Morris
in "Midsummer Night's Dream"**

**Lawrence C. Lott
as Macbeth**

213

STRATFORD FESTIVAL OF CANADA

Stratford, Ontario, Canada
June 4,–November 4, 1979
Twenty-seventh Season

Artistic Director, Robin Phillips; Executive Producer, John Hayes; Director-Festival Stage, William Hutt; Director of Production, Thomas Hooker; Director-Third Stage, Peter Moss; Press, Anne Selby, Leonard McHardy, Bryan Grimes, Betty Ross; Company Manager, Barry MacGregor; Head of Design, Daphne Dare; Production Manager, Peter Roberts; Technical Director, Kent McKay; Audio-Visual Technical Director, Richard Clarke; Assistant to Artistic Director, Margaret Ryerson; Director of Music, Berthold Carriere; Stage Managers, Nora Polley, Martin Bragg, Colleen Stephenson, Tomas Montvila, John Tiggeloven, John Wilbur, Vincent Berns, Michael Benoit, Laurie Freeman, Ann Stuart, Ron Davies, Jane Needles, Simon Reeve, Michael Shamata; Wardrobe, Gail Homersham Robertson, Pauline Harrison, Karen Matthews; Production Assistants, Valerie Holland, Tamsin Brown, Jane Norman; Stage Directors, Robin Phillips, Urjo Kareda, Zoe Caldwell, Peter Moss, Buster Davis, Frances Hyland, Pamela Hawthorn, Kathryn Shaw, Pam Brighton, Donald Saddler

COMPANY

Stewart Arnott, Karen Austin, Rodger Barton, Paul Batten, Rod Beattie, Leigh Beery, Christopher Blake, Mervyn Blake, Ingrid Blekys, John Bluethner, Domini Blythe, Jessica Booker, Barbara Budd, Graeme Campbell, Patrick Christopher, William Copeland, Clare Coulter, Philip J. Craig, Richard Curnock, John Cutts, Diane D'Aguila, Margot Dionne, Peter Donaldson, Eric Donkin, Wilfrid Dube, Craig Dudley, David Dunbar, Kirsten Ebsen, Edward Evanko, Ted Follows, Carol Forte, Edda Gaborek, Sophie Gascon, Richard Gira, Maurice Good, Donna Goodhand, Lewis Gordon, Jeffrey Guyton, Amelia Hall, Richard Hardacre, Dean Hawes, Max Helpmann, Martha Henry, David Holmes, William Hutt, Gerald Isaac, Keith James, Alicia Jeffery, Geordie Johnson, Lorne Kennedy, Joel Kenyon, Francois-Regis Klanfer, John Lambert, Barry MacGregor, Barbara Maczka, William Merton Malmo,, Frank Maraden, Marti Maraden, F. Braun McAsh, Robert McClure, Dion McHugh, Richard McMillan, Jim McQueen, Wally Michaels, Richard Monette, Marylu Moyer, William Needles, Robert Ouellette, Stephen Ouimette, Angelo Pedari, Nicholas Pennell, Jennifer Phipps, John Pollard, Douglas Rain, Paul Rapsey, Pamela Redfern, Maida Rogerson, Stephen Russell, Alan Scarfe, LeRoy Schulz, Cedric Smith, Victoria Snow, Rex Southgate, David Stein, Barbara Stewart, Hank Stinson, Heather Summerhays, Winston Sutton, Michael Totzke, Peter Ustinov, Barry Van Elen, Gregory Wanless, William Webster, Ian White, John Wojda, Barrie Wood, Tom Wood

PRODUCTIONS

Love's Labour's Lost, Richard II, Henry IV Part I, The Importance of Being Earnest by Oscar Wilde, Henry IV Part II, Ned and Jack by Sheldon Rosen, Happy New Year by Burt Shevelove from Philip Barry's play Holiday with music by Cole Porter, Othello, The Woman by Edward Bond, The Taming of the Shrew, Victoria by Steve Petch, Yerma by Federico Garcia Lorca, King Lear

Photos by Zoe Dominic, Robert Ragsdale, Hockings

**Left Center: Craig Dudley, Martha Henry
in "The Woman" Above: Domini Blythe,
William Needles, Alan Scarfe in "Othello"
Top: Craig Dudley (seated foreground)
in "Richard II"**

**Leigh Berry, Edward Evanko
in "Happy New Year"**

214

OAK PARK FESTIVAL THEATRE COMPANY
Oak Park, Illinois
July 10,–August 5, 1979
Artistic Director-Producer, Marion Karczmar; Press, Robert Trezevant, Randall Kryn; Business Manager, Phyllis Cormack; Stage Director, Joseph Bell; Scenery and Lighting, John Rodriguez; Costumes, Kate Bergh; Stage Manager, Monica Fox

PRODUCTION AND CAST

THE TAMING OF THE SHREW by William Shakespeare: Michael Rider (Petruchio), Arlene Schulfer (Katherina), John Pankow (Lucentio), Thomas William Miller (Tranio), Harry Caramanos (Baptista), Pamela Peterson (Bianca), John Ostrander (Gremio), Daniel Frick (Grumio), Lawrence McCauley (Hortensio), Sam Heller (Biondello), Henry Sadowski (Messenger), Charles Shallenberg (Curtis), Paul Thompson (Tailor), Allan McClure (Pedant), William Hammack (Vincentio), Anita Eisenstein (Widow), Servants: Angela Kier, Leonard Lloyd, Henry Sadowski

Diane Klotz Photos

**Below: Michael Rider, Arlene Schulfer
in "Taming of the Shrew" (Oak Park)**

Mervyn Blake, Alan Scarfe, Richard McMillan, Gregory Wanless, Paul Batten, Richard Monette in "Love's Labour's Lost" Top: Richard Monette, Lewis Gordon, Tom Wood in "Henry IV Part I" (Stratford Festival)

THEATREVENTURE '80
Beverly, Massachusetts
May 5–24, 1980
Manager, Theda Taylor; Assistant Managers, Joyce Smith, Duane Fletcher; Promotion Director, Kenneth Goldsmith; Sets, Eve Lyon; Lighting, Theda Taylor; Costumes, Deborah Shaw; Directors, DeVeren Bookwalter (The Tempest), Mesrop Kesdekian (The Glass Menagerie); Stage Manager, David George; Technical Director, Christian Kuhlthau; Production Assistant, Tommy Louie; Sound, Buddy Richardson; Props, Frank Jackson; Wardrobe, Beverley Gordon

PRODUCTIONS AND CASTS

THE TEMPEST by William Shakespeare: Robert Aberdeen (Ariel), Evan Thompson (Prospero), Kathy Connell (Miranda), Mike Herter (Boatswain), David Scott (Adrian), John Stobaeus (Francisco), Keith Jochim (Alonso), Gary Garth (Antonio), Max Gulack (Gonzalo), Larry Kent Bramble (Sebastian), George T. Crowley, Jr. (Ferdinand), DeVeren Bookwalter (Caliban), John Guerrasio (Trinculo), Richard Kinter (Stephano), Dori Arnold (Iris), Marilyn Byrd (Ceres), Georgette Fleischer (Juno)
THE GLASS MENAGERIE by Tennessee Williams: Christopher McCann (Tom), Constance Dix (Amanda), Sharon Morrison (Laura), George T. Crowley, Jr. (Gentleman Caller)

Robert Beauvais Photos

**"The Tempest"
TheatreVenture '80**

PULITZER PRIZE PRODUCTIONS

1918–Why Marry?, 1919– No award, 1920–Beyond the Horizon, 1921–Miss Lulu Bett, 1922–Anna Christie, 1923–Icebound, 1924–Hell-Bent fer Heaven, 1925–They Knew What They Wanted, 1926–Craig's Wife, 1927–In Abraham's Bosom, 1928–Strange Interlude, 1929–Street Scene, 1930–The Green Pastures, 1931–Alison's House, 1932–Of Thee I Sing, 1933–Both Your Houses, 1934–Men in White, 1935–The Old Maid, 1936–Idiot's Delight, 1937–You Can't Take It with You, 1938–Our Town, 1939–Abe Lincoln in Illinois, 1940–The Time of Your Life, 1941–There Shall Be No Night, 1942–No award, 1943–The Skin of Our Teeth, 1944–No award, 1945–Harvey, 1946–State of the Union, 1947–No award, 1948–A Streetcar Named Desire, 1949–Death of a Salesman, 1950–South Pacific, 1951–No award, 1952–The Shrike, 1953–Picnic, 1954–The Teahouse of the August Moon, 1955–Cat on a Hot Tin Roof, 1956–The Diary of Anne Frank, 1957–Long Day's Journey into Night, 1958–Look Homeward, Angel, 1959–J. B., 1960–Fiorello!, 1961–All the Way Home, 1962–How to Succeed in Business without Really Trying, 1963–No award, 1964–No award, 1965–The Subject Was Roses, 1966–No award, 1967–A Delicate Balance, 1968–No award, 1969–The Great White Hope, 1970–No Place to Be Somebody, 1971–The Effect of Gamma Rays on Man-in-the-Moon Marigolds, 1972–No award, 1973–That Championship Season, 1974–No award, 1975–Seascape, 1976–A Chorus Line, 1977–The Shadow Box, 1978–The Gin Game, 1979–Buried Child, 1980–Talley's Folly.

NEW YORK DRAMA CRITICS CIRCLE AWARDS

1936–Winterset, 1937–High Tor, 1938–Of Mice and Men, Shadow and Substance, 1939–The White Steed, 1940–The Time of Your Life, 1941–Watch on the Rhine, The Corn is Green, 1942–Blithe Spirit, 1943–The Patriots, 1944–Jacobowsky and the Colonel, 1945–The Glass Menagerie, 1946–Carousel, 1947–All My Sons, No Exit, Brigadoon, 1948–A Streetcar Named Desire, The Winslow Boy, 1949–Death of a Salesman, The Madwoman of Chaillot, South Pacific, 1950–The Member of the Wedding, The Cocktail Party, The Consul, 1951–Darkness at Noon, The Lady's Not for Burning, Guys and Dolls, 1952–I Am a Camera, Venus Observed, Pal Joey, 1953–Picnic, The Love of Four Colonels, Wonderful Town, 1954–Teahouse of the August Moon, Ondine, The Golden Apple, 1955–Cat on a Hot Tin Roof, Witness for the Prosecution, The Saint of Bleecker Street, 1956–The Diary of Anne Frank, Tiger at the Gates, My Fair Lady, 1957–Long Day's Journey into Night, The Waltz of the Toreadors, The Most Happy Fella, 1958–Look Homeward Angel, Look Back in Anger, The Music Man, 1959–A Raisin in the Sun, The Visit, La Plume de Ma Tante, 1960–Toys in the Attic, Five Finger Exercise, Fiorello!, 1961–All the Way Home, A Taste of Honey, Carnival, 1962–Night of the Iguana, A Man for All Seasons, How to Succeed in Business without Really Trying, 1963–Who's Afraid of Virginia Woolf?, 1964–Luther, Hello, Dolly!, 1965–The Subject Was Roses, Fiddler on the Roof, 1966–The Persecution and Assassination of Marat as Performed by the Inmates of the Asylum of Charenton under the Direction of the Marquis de Sade, Man of La Mancha, 1967–The Homecoming, Cabaret, 1968–Rosencrantz and Guildenstern Are Dead, Your Own Thing, 1969–The Great White Hope, 1776, 1970–The Effect of Gamma Rays on Man-in-the-Moon Marigolds, Borstal Boy, Company, 1971–Home, Follies, The House of Blue Leaves, 1972–That Championship Season, Two Gentlemen of Verona, 1973–The Hot l Baltimore, The Changing Room, A Little Night Music, 1974–The Contractor, Short Eyes, Candide, 1975–Equus, The Taking of Miss Janie, A Chorus Line, 1976–Travesties, Streamers, Pacific Overtures, 1977–Otherwise Engaged, American Buffalo, Annie, 1978–Da, Ain't Misbehavin', 1979–The Elephant Man, Sweeney Todd, 1980–Talley's Folly, Evita, Betrayal

AMERICAN THEATRE WING
ANTOINETTE PERRY (TONY) AWARD PRODUCTIONS

1948–Mister Roberts, 1949–Death of a Salesman, Kiss Me, Kate, 1950–The Cocktail Party, South Pacific, 1951–The Rose Tattoo, Guys and Dolls, 1952–The Fourposter, The King and I, 1953–The Crucible, Wonderful Town, 1954–The Teahouse of the August Moon, Kismet, 1955–The Desperate Hours, The Pajama Game, 1956–The Diary of Anne Frank, Damn Yankees, 1957–Long Day's Journey into Night, My Fair Lady, 1958–Sunrise at Campobello, The Music Man, 1959–J. B., Redhead, 1960–The Miracle Worker, Fiorello! tied with The Sound of Music, 1961–Becket, Bye Bye Birdie, 1962–A Man for All Seasons, How to Succeed in Business without Really Trying, 1963–Who's Afraid of Virginia Woolf?, A Funny Thing Happened on the Way to the Forum, 1964–Luther, Hello, Dolly!, 1965–The Subject Was Roses, Fiddler on the Roof, 1966–The Persecution and Assassination of Marat as Performed by the Inmates of the Asylum of Charenton under the Direction of the Marquis de Sade, Man of La Mancha, 1967–The Homecoming, Cabaret, 1968–Rosencrantz and Guildenstern Are Dead, Hallelujah Baby!, 1969–The Great White Hope, 1776, 1970–Borstal Boy, Applause, 1971–Sleuth, Company, 1972–Sticks and Bones, Two Gentlemen of Verona, 1973–That Championship Season, A Little Night Music, 1974–The River Niger, Raisin, 1975–Equus, The Wiz, 1976–Travesties, A Chorus Line, 1977–The Shadow Box, Annie, 1978–Da, Ain't Misbehavin', Dracula, 1979–The Elephant Man, Sweeney Todd, 1980–Children of a Lesser God, Evita, Morning's at Seven.

MAXWELL CAULFIELD
of "Class Enemy"

LESLIE DENNISTON
of "Happy New Year"

SUSAN KELLERMANN
of "Last Licks"

BOYD GAINES
of "A Month in the Country"

RICHARD GERE
of "Bent"

DINAH MANOFF
of "I Ought to Be in Pictures"

MARIANNE TATUM
of "Barnum"

HARRY GROENER
of "Oklahoma!"

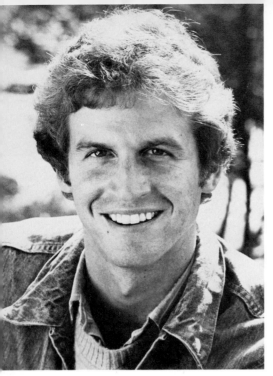

STEPHEN JAMES
of "The 1940's Radio Show"

ANNE TWOMEY
of "Nuts"

DIANNE WIEST
of "The Art of Dining"

LONNY PRICE
of "Class Enemy"

THEATRE WORLD AWARDS PARTY: Thursday, May 22, 1980. Top: Sandy Duncan, Eileen Brennan, John Cullum, Maureen Stapleton, Cliff Robertson, Dinah Manoff, Elizabeth Ashley; Anthony Perkins, Elizabeth Ashley; David Rounds, Elizabeth Ashley, Gregory Hines, Patricia Elliott, Kristoffer Tabori, Carol Lynley; **Below:** Leslie Denniston, Gregory Hines; Harry Groener, Eileen Brennan; Julie Garfield (for Dianne Wiest); **Second Row from Bottom:** Lonny Price, Marianne Tatum, Stephen James, Susan Kellermann, David Rounds; **Bottom:** Boyd Gaines, Anne Twomey, Richard Gere, Anthony Perkins, Ann Miller, Mickey Rooney, Berry Berenson Perkins

Evan Romero, Michael Viade, Van Williams Photos

Top: **Eileen Brennan, John Cullum, John Willis, Maureen Stapleton, Cliff Robertson, Marianne Tatum; Mickey Rooney, Ann Miller; Maxwell Caulfield, Maureen Stapleton, Elizabeth Ashley, Gregory Hines, Patricia Elliott, Kristoffer Tabori; Below: Maureen Stapleton, Clive Barnes, Tammy Grimes, Walter Willison; John Raitt, Anita Gillette; Glenn Close, Len Cariou, (seated) Marianne Tatum, Charles Glennon; Second Row from Bottom: John Rubinstein, John Raitt; Beatrice Straight, Paula Laurence; David Dukes, Jay Harnick, Barbara Barrie; Florence Lacey, Radie Harris; Bottom: Manhattan Rhythm Kings, Joan Fontaine**
Evan Romero, Michael Viade, Van Williams Photos

Barbara Bel Geddes   **Alan Alda**   **Anita Gillette**   **Jack Lord**   **Bernadette Peters**

PREVIOUS THEATRE WORLD AWARD WINNERS

1944–45: Betty Comden, Richard Davis, Richard Hart, Judy Holliday, Charles Lang, Bambi Linn, John Lund, Donald Murphy, Nancy Noland, Margaret Phillips, John Raitt
1945–46: Barbara Bel Geddes, Marlon Brando, Bill Callahan, Wendell Corey, Paul Douglas, Mary James, Burt Lancaster, Patricia Marshall, Beatrice Pearson
1946–47: Keith Andes, Marion Bell, Peter Cookson, Ann Crowley, Ellen Hanley, John Jordan, George Keane, Dorothea MacFarland, James Mitchell, Patricia Neal, David Wayne
1947–48: Valerie Bettis, Edward Bryce, Whitfield Connor, Mark Dawson, June Lockhart, Estelle Loring, Peggy Maley, Ralph Meeker, Meg Mundy, Douglass Watson, James Whitmore, Patrice Wymore
1948–49: Tod Andrews, Doe Avedon, Jean Carson, Carol Channing, Richard Derr, Julie Harris, Mary McCarty, Allyn Ann McLerie, Cameron Mitchell, Gene Nelson, Byron Palmer, Bob Scheerer
1949–50: Nancy Andrews, Phil Arthur, Barbara Brady, Lydia Clarke, Priscilla Gillette, Don Hanmer, Marcia Henderson, Charlton Heston, Rick Jason, Grace Kelly, Charles Nolte, Roger Price
1950–51: Barbara Ashley, Isabel Bigley, Martin Brooks, Richard Burton, James Daly, Cloris Leachman, Russell Nype, Jack Palance, William Smothers, Maureen Stapleton, Marcia Van Dyke, Eli Wallach
1951–52: Tony Bavaar, Patricia Benoit, Peter Conlow, Virginia de Luce, Ronny Graham, Audrey Hepburn, Diana Herbert, Conrad Janis, Dick Kallman, Charles Proctor, Eric Sinclair, Kim Stanley, Marian Winters, Helen Wood
1952–53: Edie Adams, Rosemary Harris, Eileen Heckart, Peter Kelley, John Kerr, Richard Kiley, Gloria Marlowe, Penelope Munday, Paul Newman, Sheree North, Geraldine Page, John Stewart, Ray Stricklyn, Gwen Verdon
1953–54: Orson Bean, Harry Belafonte, James Dean, Joan Diener, Ben Gazzara, Carol Haney, Jonathan Lucas, Kay Medford, Scott Merrill, Elizabeth Montgomery, Leo Penn, Eva Marie Saint
1954–55: Julie Andrews, Jacqueline Brookes, Shirl Conway, Barbara Cook, David Daniels, Mary Fickett, Page Johnson, Loretta Leversee, Jack Lord, Dennis Patrick, Anthony Perkins, Christopher Plummer
1955–56: Diane Cilento, Dick Davalos, Anthony Franciosa, Andy Griffith, Laurence Harvey, David Hedison, Earle Hyman, Susan Johnson, John Michael King, Jayne Mansfield, Sarah Marshall, Gaby Rodgers, Susan Strasberg, Fritz Weaver
1956–57: Peggy Cass, Sydney Chaplin, Sylvia Daneel, Bradford Dillman, Peter Donat, George Grizzard, Carol Lynley, Peter Palmer, Jason Robards, Cliff Robertson, Pippa Scott, Inga Swenson
1957–58: Anne Bancroft, Warren Berlinger, Colleen Dewhurst, Richard Easton, Tim Everett, Eddie Hodges, Joan Hovis, Carol Lawrence, Jacqueline McKeever, Wynne Miller, Robert Morse, George C. Scott
1958–59: Lou Antonio, Ina Balin, Richard Cross, Tammy Grimes, Larry Hagman, Dolores Hart, Roger Mollien, France Nuyen, Susan Oliver, Ben Piazza, Paul Roebling, William Shatner, Pat Suzuki, Rip Torn
1959–60: Warren Beatty, Eileen Brennan, Carol Burnett, Patty Duke, Jane Fonda, Anita Gillette, Elisa Loti, Donald Madden, George Maharis, John McMartin, Lauri Peters, Dick Van Dyke
1960–61: Joyce Bulifant, Dennis Cooney, Sandy Dennis, Nancy Dussault, Robert Goulet, Joan Hackett, June Harding, Ron Husmann, James MacArthur, Bruce Yarnell
1961–62: Elizabeth Ashley, Keith Baxter, Peter Fonda, Don Galloway, Sean Garrison, Barbara Harris, James Earl Jones, Janet Margolin, Karen Morrow, Robert Redford, John Stride, Brenda Vaccaro
1962–63: Alan Arkin, Stuart Damon, Melinda Dillon, Robert Drivas, Bob Gentry, Dorothy Loudon, Brandon Maggart, Julienne Marie, Liza Minnelli, Estelle Parsons, Diana Sands, Swen Swenson

1963–64: Alan Alda, Gloria Bleezarde, Imelda De Martin, Claude Giraud, Ketty Lester, Barbara Loden, Lawrence Pressman, Gilbert Price, Philip Proctor, John Tracy, Jennifer West
1964–65: Carolyn Coates, Joyce Jillson, Linda Lavin, Luba Lisa, Michael O'Sullivan, Joanna Pettet, Beah Richards, Jaime Sanchez, Victor Spinetti, Nicolas Surovy, Robert Walker, Clarence Williams III
1965–66: Zoe Caldwell, David Carradine, John Cullum, John Davidson, Faye Dunaway, Gloria Foster, Robert Hooks, Jerry Lanning, Richard Mulligan, April Shawhan, Sandra Smith, Lesley Ann Warren
1966–67: Bonnie Bedelia, Richard Benjamin, Dustin Hoffman, Terry Kiser, Reva Rose, Robert Salvio, Sheila Smith, Connie Stevens, Pamela Tiffin, Leslie Uggams, Jon Voight, Christopher Walken
1967–68: David Birney, Pamela Burrell, Jordan Christopher, Jack Crowder (Thalmus Rasulala), Sandy Duncan, Julie Gregg, Stephen Joyce, Bernadette Peters, Alice Playten, Michael Rupert, Brenda Smiley, Russ Thacker
1968–69: Jane Alexander, David Cryer, Blythe Danner, Ed Evanko, Ken Howard, Lauren Jones, Ron Leibman, Marian Mercer, Jill O'Hara, Ron O'Neal, Al Pacino, Marlene Warfield
1969–70: Susan Browning, Donny Burks, Catherine Burns, Len Cariou, Bonnie Franklin, David Holliday, Katharine Houghton, Melba Moore, David Rounds, Lewis J. Stadlen, Kristoffer Tabori, Fredricka Weber
1970–71: Clifton Davis, Michael Douglas, Julie Garfield, Martha Henry, James Naughton, Tricia O'Neil, Kipp Osborne, Roger Rathburn, Ayn Ruymen, Jennifer Salt, Joan Van Ark, Walter Willison
1971–72: Jonelle Allen, Maureen Anderman, William Atherton, Richard Backus, Adrienne Barbeau, Cara Duff-MacCormick, Robert Foxworth, Elaine Joyce, Jess Richards, Ben Vereen, Beatrice Winde, James Woods
1972–73: D'Jamin Bartlett, Patricia Elliott, James Farentino, Brian Farrell, Victor Garber, Kelly Garrett, Mari Gorman, Laurence Guittard, Trish Hawkins, Monte Markham, John Rubinstein, Jennifer Warren, Alexander H. Cohen (Special Award)
1973–74: Mark Baker, Maureen Brennan, Ralph Carter, Thom Christopher, John Driver, Conchata Ferrell, Ernestine Jackson, Michael Moriarty, Joe Morton, Ann Reinking, Janie Sell, Mary Woronov, Sammy Cahn (Special Award)
1974–75: Peter Burnell, Zan Charisse, Lola Falana, Peter Firth, Dorian Harewood, Joel Higgins, Marcia McClain, Linda Miller, Marti Rolph, John Sheridan, Scott Stevensen, Donna Theodore, Equity Library Theatre (Special Award)
1975–76: Danny Aiello, Christine Andreas, Dixie Carter, Tovah Feldshuh, Chip Garnett, Richard Kelton, Vivian Reed, Charles Repole, Virginia Seidel, Daniel Seltzer, John V. Shea, Meryl Streep, A Chorus Line (Special Award)
1976–77: Trazana Beverley, Michael Cristofer, Joe Fields, Joanna Gleason, Cecilia Hart, John Heard, Gloria Hodes, Juliette Koka, Andrea McArdle, Ken Page, Jonathan Pryce, Chick Vennera, Eva LeGallienne (Special Award)
1977–78: Vasili Bogazianos, Nell Carter, Carlin Glynn, Christopher Goutman, William Hurt, Judy Kaye, Florence Lacy, Armelia McQueen, Gordana Rashovich, Bo Rucker, Richard Seer, Colin Stinton, Joseph Papp (Special Award)
1978–79: Philip Anglim, Lucie Arnaz, Gregory Hines, Ken Jennings, Michael Jeter, Laurie Kennedy, Susan Kingsley, Christine Lahti, Edward James Olmos, Kathleen Quinlan, Sarah Rice, Max Wright, Marshall W. Mason (Special Award)
1979–80: Maxwell Caulfield, Leslie Denniston, Boyd Gaines, Richard Gere, Harry Groener, Stephen James, Susan Kellermann, Dinah Manoff, Lonny Price, Marianne Tatum, Anne Twomey, Dianne Wiest, Mickey Rooney (Special Award)

Gregory Abels   **Jill Andre**   **Beau Allen**   **Kathy Andrini**   **Herman Arbeit**

BIOGRAPHIES OF THIS SEASON'S CAST

ABBOTT, JOSEPH. Born Feb. 9, 1968 in Philadelphia, PA. Bdwy debut 1979 in "Peter Pan."

ABELS, GREGORY. Born Nov. 6, 1941 in Jersey City, NJ. Studied with Stella Adler. Debut 1970 OB in "War of the Roses," followed by "Macbeth," "Phoebus," "Oedipus at Colonus," "I Love Thee Freely," "Veil of Infamy," "The Boss," "The Violano Virtuoso," Bdwy 1980 in "Nuts."

ABERLIN, BETTY. Born Dec. 30, 1942 in NYC. Graduate Bennington College. Debut OB 1954 in "Sandhog," followed by "Upstairs at the Downstairs," "I'm Getting My Act Together," Bdwy 1964 in "Cafe Crown."

ABRAHAM, F. MURRAY. Born Oct. 24, 1939 in Pittsburgh, PA. Attended UTex. OB bow 1967 in "The Fantasticks," followed by "An Opening in the Trees," "Fourteenth Dictator," "Young Abe Lincoln," "Tonight in Living Color," "Adaptation," "Survival of St. Joan," "The Dog Ran Away," "Fables," "Richard III," "Little Murders," "Scuba Duba," "Where Has Tommy Flowers Gone?," "Miracle Play," "Blessing," "Sexual Perversity in Chicago," "Landscape of the Body," "The Master and Margarita," "Biting the Apple," Bdwy in "The Man in the Glass Booth" (1968), "6 Rms Riv Vu," "Bad Habits," "The Ritz," "Legend," "Teibele and Her Demon."

ABUBA, ERNEST. Born Aug. 25, 1947 in Honolulu, HI. Attended Southwestern Col. Bdwy debut 1976 in "Pacific Overtures," followed by "Loose Ends," OB in "Sunrise."

ACKROYD, DAVID. Born May 30, 1940 in Orange, NJ. Graduate Bucknell, Yale. Bdwy debut 1971 in "Unlikely Heroes," followed by "Full Circle," "Hamlet," "Hide and Seek," OB in "Isadora Duncan Sleeps with the Russian Navy."

ADAMS, BROOKE. Born in NYC in 1949. Attended Dalton Sch. Debut OB 1974 in "The Petrified Forest," followed by "Split."

ADAMS, J. B. (formerly Jon-Alan Adams) Born Sept. 29, 1954 in Oklahoma City, OK. Graduate OklaCityU. Debut OB 1980 in ELT's "Plain and Fancy."

ADAMS, JOSEPH. Born Feb. 4, 1956 in Concord, CA. Debut 1980 in ELT's "Romeo and Juliet."

ADAMS, MOLLY. Born in Portchester, NY. Graduate Smith Col. Debut OB 1973 in "Older People," followed by "Hot l Baltimore," "The Unicorn in Captivity," Bdwy 1979 in "Bedroom Farce."

ADAMS, SHEILA K. Born June 24, 1950 in Omaha, NE. Attended AADA. Bdwy debut 1973 in "A Little Night Music," followed by "Summer Brave," OB in "M. Amilcar."

ADAMSON, DAVID. Born Nov. 30, 1944 in Winona, MN. Graduate UNI and UNC. Debut 1980 OB in "Kohlhass."

ADLER, BRUCE. Born Nov. 27, 1944 in NYC. Attended NYU. Debut 1957 OB in "It's a Funny World," followed by "Hard to Be a Jew," "Big Winner," Bdwy 1971 in "A Teaspoon Every 4 Hours," followed by "Oklahoma!" (1979).

ALBANESE, JAMES VINCENT. Born Jan. 6, 1955 in Brooklyn, NY. Graduate Bklyn Col. Debut 1979 OB in "Chinchilla," followed by "Frankie and Anne."

ALDREDGE, TOM. Born Feb. 28, 1928 in Dayton, OH. Attended Dayton U., Goodman Theatre. Bdwy bow 1959 in "The Nervous Set," followed by "UTBU," Slapstick Tragedy," "Everything in the Garden," "Indians," "Engagement Baby," "How the Other Half Loves," "Sticks and Bones," "Where's Charley?," "Leaf People," "Rex," "Vieux Carre," "St. Joan," "Stages," "On Green Pond," OB in "The Tempest," "Between Two Thieves," "Henry V," "The Premise," "Love's Labour's Lost," "Troilus and Cressida," "Butter and Egg Man," "Ergo," "Boys in the Band," "Twelfth Night," "Colette," "Hamlet," "The Orphan," "King Lear," "Iceman Cometh."

ALEXANDER, JANE. Born Oct. 28, 1939 in Boston, MA. Attended Sarah Lawrence Col., UEdinburgh. Bdwy debut 1968 in "The Great White Hope" for which she received a Theatre World Award, followed by "6 Rms Riv Vu," "Find Your Way Home," LC's "Hamlet," "The Heiress," "First Monday in October," OB in "Losing Time," "Goodbye Fidel."

ALEX-COLE, STEVEN. Born Jan. 6, 1949 in Baltimore, MD. Graduate Union Col., UStockholm. Debut 1975 OB in "Let My People Come," Bdwy in "Treemonisha," "Porgy and Bess," "Most Happy Fella."

ALEXIS, ALVIN. Born July 5 in NYC. Debut 1976 OB in "In the Wine Time," followed by "Rear Column," "Class Enemy."

ALICE, MARY. Born Dec. 3, 1941 in Indianola, MS. Debut OB 1967 in "Trials of Brother Jero," followed by "The Strong Breed," "Duplex," "Thoughts," "Miss Julie," "House Party," "Terraces," "Heaven and Hell's Agreement," "In the Deepest Part of Sleep," "Cockfight," "Julius Caesar," "Nongogo," "Second Thoughts," "Spell #7." Bdwy 1971 in "No Place to Be Somebody."

ALLEN, BEAU. Born Mar. 2, 1950 in Wilmington, DE. Graduate Tufts U. Bdwy debut 1972 in "Jesus Christ Superstar," followed by "Two Gentlemen of Verona," "Best Little Whorehouse in Texas."

ALLEN, DEBBIE (a.k.a. Deborah) Born Jan 16, 1950 in Houston, TX. Graduate Howard U. Debut OB 1972 in "Ti-Jean and His Brothers," followed by "Anna Lucasta," Bdwy in "Raisin" (1973), "Ain't Misbehavin'," "West Side Story."

ALLEN, SETH. Born July 13, 1941 in Brooklyn, NY. Attended Musical Theatre Acad. OB in "Viet Rock," "Futz," "Hair," "Candaules Commissioner," "Mary Stuart," "Narrow Road to the Deep North," "More Than You Deserve," "Split Lip," "The Misanthrope," "Hard Sell," Bdwy 1972 in "Jesus Christ Superstar."

ALLEN, SHEILA. Born Oct. 22, 1932 in Chard, Somerset, Eng. RADA graduate. Debut with Royal Shakespeare Co.'s 1975 season at BAM. With BAM Theatre Co. in "Winter's Tale," "The Barbarians" and "The Wedding."

ALLMON, CLINTON. Born June 13, 1941 in Monahans, TX. Graduate Okla. State U. Bdwy debut 1969 in "Indians," followed by "The Best Little Whorehouse in Texas," OB in "The Bluebird," "Khaki Blue," "One Sunday Afternoon."

ANDERMAN, MAUREEN. Born Oct. 26, 1946 in Detroit, MI. Graduate UMich. Bdwy debut 1970 in "Moonchildren" for which she received a Theatre World Award, "An Evening with Richard Nixon . . . ," "The Last of Mrs. Lincoln," "Seascape," "Who's Afraid of Virginia Woolf?" "A History of the American Film," "The Lady from Dubuque," OB in "Hamlet," "Elusive Angel," "Out of Our Father's House," "Sunday Runners."

ANDERSON, C. B. Born June 18, 1939 in Nashville, TN. Attended UGa. Debut 1980 with BAM Theatre Co. in "The Winter's Tale," "Johnny on a Spot."

ANDERSON, PAUL. Born in Boston, MA. Attended Middlebury Col., Fordham U., AADA. Bdwy debut 1944 in "Decision," followed by "Mary Rose," "Playboy of the Western World," "Minnie and Mrs. Williams," CC's "The Devil's Disciple," "She Stoops to Conquer," "The Corn Is Green" and "The Heiress," OB in "Les Blancs!"

ANDRE, JILL. Born Feb. 16, 1935 in NYC. Attended CCNY, Columbia U. Debut 1952 OB in "Madwoman of Chaillot," followed by "Dark of the Moon," "Last Analysis," "Horseman Pass By," "From Here Inside My Head," "Kennedy's Children," "Stop the Parade," "Monkey, Monkey," "Battle of Angels," "Four Friends," "Augusta," "Wayside Motor Inn," Bdwy in "Sunrise at Campobello," "The Great White Hope," "An Evening with Richard Nixon . . . ," "The Trip Back Down," "Devour the Snow."

ANDREAS, CHRISTINE. Born Oct. 1, 1951 in Camden, NJ. Bdwy debut 1975 in "Angel Street," followed by "My Fair Lady" for which she received a Theatre World Award, "Oklahoma" (1979), OB in "Disgustingly Rich."

ANDRES, BARBARA. Born Feb. 11, 1939 in NYC. Catholic U. graduate. Bdwy debut 1969 in "Jimmy," followed by "The Boy Friend," "Rodgers and Hart," "Rex," "On Golden Pond."

ANDREWS, GEORGE LEE. Born Oct. 13, 1942 in Milwaukee, WI. Debut OB 1970 in "Jacques Brel Is Alive," followed by "Starting Here Starting Now," Bdwy in "A Little Night Music" (1973), "On the 20th Century."

ANDRINI, KATHY. Born May 17, 1958 in San Francisco, CA. Bdwy debut 1979 in "The 1940's Radio Hour."

ANGLIM, PHILIP. Born Feb. 11, 1953 in San Francisco, CA. Yale graduate. Debut OB and Bdwy 1979 in "The Elephant Man" for which he received a Theatre World Award.

ARBEIT, HERMAN O. Born Apr. 19, 1925 in Brooklyn, NY. Attended CCNY, HB Studio, Neighborhood Playhouse. Debut 1939 OB in "The Golem," followed by "Awake and Sing," "A Delicate Balance," "Yentl the Yeshiva Boy," "A Yank in Beverly Hills," "Second Avenue Rag," Bdwy 1975 in "Yentl."

ARLT, LEWIS. Born Dec. 5, 1949 in Kingston, NY. Graduate Carnegie Tech. Bdwy debut 1975 in "Murder Among Friends," OB in "War and Peace," "The Interview."

ARI, BOB. Born July 1, 1949 in NYC. Graduate Carnegie-Mellon U. Debut OB in "Boys from Syracuse" (1976), followed by "Gay Divorce," "Devour the Snow."

ARNAZ, LUCIE. Born July 17, 1951 in Los Angeles, CA. Bdwy debut 1979 in "They're Playing Our Song" for which she received a Theatre World Award.

ARNOLD, VICTOR. Born July 1, 1936 in Herkimer, NY. Graduate NYU. OB in "Shadows of Heroes," "Merchant of Venice," "3 X 3," "Lovey," "Fortune and Men's Eyes," "Time for Bed, Take Me to Bed," "Emperor of Late Night Radio," "Macbeth" (LC), "The Sign in Sidney Brustein's Window," "Cacciatore," Bdwy in "The Deputy," "Malcolm," "We Bombed in New Haven," "Fun City."

ARONIN, MICHAEL J. Born Nov. 5, 1944 in NYC. Bdwy debut 1979 in "Knockout," OB in "Marlon Brando Sat Here."

ARONSON, JONATHAN. Born June 17, 1953 in Miami, FL. Attended Dade Col. AMDA. Bdwy debut 1979 in "Whoopee!" followed by "Sugar Babies," OB in "Tip-Toes."

ARTHUR, KEN. Born June 18, 1951 in Indiana. Graduate Haverford Col. Debut 1980 OB in "Fourtune."

ARTHUR, PERRY. Born July 23, 1956 in Spirit Lake, LA. Attended Mansfield State Col., Drew U, AMDA. Bdwy debut 1977 in "Hair," OB in "Dementos."

ASBURY, CLEVE. Born Dec. 29, 1958 in Houston, TX. Attended L.A. Valley Col. Bdwy debut 1979 in "Peter Pan," followed by "West Side Story."

ASHER, DAVID. Born June 3, 1953 in Cleveland, OH. Graduate Stanford, Yale. Debut 1979 OB and 1980 Bdwy in "Canterbury Tales."

ASHER, LAWRENCE. Born July 30, 1948 in Palisades Park, NJ. Ithaca Col. graduate. Debut OB 1974 in "The Proposition," Bdwy 1979 in "Most Happy Fella."

ASHLEY, ELIZABETH. Born Aug. 30, 1939 in Ocala, FL. Attended Neighborhood Playhouse. Bdwy debut 1959 in "The Highest Tree," followed by "Take Her, She's Mine" for which she received a Theatre World Award, "Barefoot in the Park," "Ring Round the Bathtub," "Cat on a Hot Tin Roof," "The Skin of Our Teeth," "Legend," "Caesar and Cleopatra," "Hide and Seek."

ASTREDO, HUMBERT ALLEN. Born in San Francisco, CA. Attended SFU. Debut 1967 OB in "Arms and the Man," followed by "Fragments," "Murderous Angels," "Beach Children," "End of Summer," "Knuckle," "Grand Magic," "Big and Little," "The Jail Diary of Albie Sachs," Bdwy in "Les Blancs," "An Evening with Richard Nixon. . . ."

ATHERTON, WILLIAM. Born July 30, 1947 in Orange, CT. Graduate Carnegie Tech. Debut 1971 OB in "House of Blue Leaves," followed by "The Basic Training of Pavlo Hummel," "Suggs," for which he received a Theatre World Award, "Rich and Famous," "The Passing Game," Bdwy in "The Sign in Sidney Brustein's Window" (1972), "Happy New Year."

AUBERJONOIS, RENE. Born June 1, 1940 in NYC. Graduate Carnegie Inst. With LCRep in "A Cry of Players," "King Lear," and "Twelfth Night," Bdwy in "Fire," "Coco," "Tricks," "The Good Doctor," "Break A Leg," "Every Good Boy Deserves Favor," BAM Co. in "The New York Idea," "Three Sisters," "The Play's the Thing," and "Julius Caesar,"

AVALOS, LUIS. Born Sept. 2, 1946 in Havana, Cuba. Debut OB in "Never Jam Today," followed by "Rules for Running of Trains," LC's "Camino Real," "Beggar on Horseback," "Good Woman of Setzuan" and "Kool Aid," "The Architect and the Emperor," "As You Like It," "El Grande de Coca Cola," "Zoo Story," "Payment as Pledged," "Armenians," "Marco Polo," "Save Grand Central."

AYR, MICHAEL. Born Sept. 8, 1953 in Great Falls, MT. Graduate SMU. Debut 1976 OB in "Mrs. Murray's Farm," followed by "The Farm," "Ulysses in Traction," "Lulu" "Cabin 12," "Stargazing," "The Deserter," "Hamlet," "Mary Stuart," "Save Grand Central," Bdwy 1980 in "Hide and Seek."

BABATUNDE, OBBA. Born in Jamaica, NY. Attended Brooklyn Col. Debut OB 1970 in "The Secret Place," followed by "Guys and Dolls," "On Toby Time," "The Breakout," "Scottsbourogh Boys," "Showdown Time," "Dream on Monkey Mt.," "Sheba," Bdwy in "Timbuktu," "Reggae."

BACKUS, RICHARD. Born Mar 28, 1945 in Goffstown, NH. Harvard graduate. Bdwy debut 1971 in "Butterflies Are Free," followed by "Promenade, All" for which he received a Theatre World Award, "Ah, Wilderness!," OB in "Studs Edsel," "Gimme Shelter," "Sorrows of Stephen."

BADOLATO, DEAN. Born June 6, 1952 in Chicago, IL. Attended UIll. Bdwy debut 1978 in "A Chorus Line."

BAILEY, DENNIS. Born Apr. 12, 1953 in Grosse Pointe Woods, MI. UDetroit graduate. Debut 1977 OB in "House of Blue Leaves," Bdwy 1978 in "Gemini."

BAKER, MARK. Born Oct. 2, 1946 in Cumberland, MD. Attended Wittenberg U., Carnegie-Mellon U., Neighborhood Playhouse, AADA. Bdwy debut 1972 in "Via Galactica," followed by "Candide" for which he received a Theatre World Award, "Habeas Corpus," OB in "Love Me, Love My Children," "A Midsummer Night's Dream."

BAKER, SCOTT. Born May 30, 1948 in Tulsa, OK. Graduate UTulsa, Northwestern U. Debut 1973 OB in "Christmas Rappings," followed by "Love's Labour's Lost," "East Lynne," Bdwy 1978 in "Oh! Calcutta!"

BALABAN, ROBERT. Born Aug. 16, 1945 in Chicago, IL. Attended Colgate, NYU. Debut 1967 OB in "You're a Good Man, Charlie Brown," followed by "Up Eden," "White House Murder Case," "Basic Training of Pavlo Hummel," "The Children," "Marie and Bruce," Bdwy in "Plaza Suite" (1968), "Some of My Best Friends," "The Inspector General."

BALLINGER, JUNE. Born Nov. 15, 1949 in Camden, NJ. Attended Briarcliff Col. Debut 1980 OB in "Mr. Wilson's Peace of Mind," followed by "Dona Rosita."

BARANSKI, CHRISTINE. Born May 2, 1952 in Buffalo, NY. Graduate Juilliard Sch. Debut OB 1978 in "One Crack Out," followed by "Says I Says He," "The Trouble with Europe," Bdwy 1980 in "Hide and Seek."

BARBOUR, THOMAS. Born July 25, 1921 in NYC. Graduate Princeton, Harvard. Bdwy debut 1968 in "Portrait of a Queen," followed by "The Great White Hope," "Scratch," "The Lincoln Mask," OB in "Twelfth Night," "Merchant of Venice," "The Admirable Bashville," "The Lady's Not for Burning," "The Enchanted," "Antony and Cleopatra," "The Saintliness of Margery Kemp," "Dr. Willy Nilly," "Under the Sycamore Tree," "Epitaph for George Dillon," "The Thracian Horses," "Old Glory," "Sjt. Musgrave's Dance," "A Nestless Bird," "The Seagull," "Wayside Motor Inn," "Arthur," "The Grinding Machine," "Mr. Simian," "The Sorrows of Frederick," "The Terrorists," "Dark Ages."

BARCROFT, JUDITH. Born July 6 in Washington, DC. Attended Northwestern, Stephens Col. Bdwy debut 1965 in "Mating Dance," followed by "Plaza Suite," "Dinner at 8," "The Elephant Man," OB in "M. Amilcar."

BARKER, MARGARET. Born Oct. 10, 1908 in Baltimore, MD. Attended Bryn Mawr. Bdwy debut 1928 in "The Age of Innocence," followed by, among others, "The Barretts of Wimpole Street," "House of Connelly," "Men in White," "Gold Eagle Guy," "Leading Lady," "Member of the Wedding," "Autumn Garden," "See the Jaguar," "Ladies of the Corridor," "The Master Builder," OB in "Wayside Motor Inn," "The Loves of Cass McGuire."

BARNES, VERONA. Born June 2, 1940 in Wilson, NC. Graduate Winston-Salem State Col. Bdwy debut 1968 in "The Great White Hope," followed by OB's "Sleep," "The Cherry Orchard," "House Party," "All God's Chillun," "Divine Comedy," "Milk of Paradise."

BARNEY, JAY. Born Mar. 14, 1918 in Chicago, IL. Attended Chicago U., Theatre Wing, Actors Studio. Bdwy debut 1948 in "Hope's the Thing with Feathers" and "The Respectful Prostitute," followed by "Detective Story," "The Number," "The Grass Harp," "Richard III," "Stockade," "The Immoralist," "The Trial," "Young and Beautiful," "Eugenia," "Fig Leaves Are Falling." "All the Girls Come-Out to Play," "Harold and Maude," OB in "A Certain Young Man," "Beyond Desire," "Goa," "The David Show," "Man with a Flower in His Mouth," "Mary."

BARON, EVALYN. Born Apr 21, 1948 in Atlanta, GA. Graduate Northwestern, UMinn. Debut OB 1979 in "Scrambled Feet."

BARON, JOANNE. Born Feb. 3, 1953 in New Haven, CT. Attended UConn., Neighborhood Playhouse. Has appeared OB in "Pops!," "Bah Humbug," "Baal."

BARRETT, BRENT. Born Feb. 28, 1957 in Quinter, KS. Graduate Carnegie-Mellon U. Bdwy debut 1980 in "West Side Story."

BARRETT, JOHN PETER. Born Aug. 3, 1937 in Lebanon, IL. Attended Goodman Theatre. Debut OB 1967 in "Jonah," followed by "Bread," "Victims of Duty," "The Trial," "Heart of Darkness," Bdwy in "Trick."

BARRETT, LESLIE. Born Oct. 30, 1919 in NYC. Bdwy debut 1936 in "But for the Grace of God," followed by "Enemy of the People," "Dead End," "Sundown," "There's Always a Breeze," "Primrose Path," "Stroke of 8," "Horse Fever," "Good Neighbor," "All in Favor," "Counsellor-at-law," "Deadfall," "Rhinoceros," "The Investigation," "Slapstick Tragedy," "What Did We Do Wrong," OB in "Hamp," "The Contractor," "Play Me, Zoltan," "Savages," "The Dragon," "Trial of Dmitri Karamatzov," "Purple Dust," "My Old Friends," "Romeo and Juliet."

BARRON, DAVID. Born May 11, 1938 in Pilot Point, TX. Graduate Baylor U., Yale, UIll. Debut 1976 OB in "The Fantasticks," followed by "Trouble in Tahiti," "Sound of Music" (ELT).

BARRON, HOLLY. Born Feb. 1, 1947 in Oakland, CA. Graduate UCBerkeley. Debut 1977 OB in "Cracks," followed by "Mecca."

BARROWS, DIANA. Born Jan. 23, 1966 in NYC. Bdwy debut 1975 in "Cat on a Hot Tin Roof," followed by "Panama Hattie" (ELT), "Annie."

BARRY, B CONSTANCE. Born Apr. 29, 1913 in NYC. Attended Hofstra, New School. Debut 1974 OB in "Blue Heaven," followed by "Dark of the Moon," "Native Son," "Passing Time," "All the Way Home" (ELT).

BARTENIEFF, GEORGE. Born Jan. 24, 1933 in Berlin, Ger. Bdwy bow 1947 in "The Whole World Over," followed by "Venus Is," "All's Well That Ends Well," "Quotations from Chairman Mao Tse-Tung," "The Death of Bessie Smith," "Cop-Out," "Room Service," "Unlikely Heroes," OB in "Walking to Waldheim," "Memorandum," "The Increased Difficulty of Concentration," "Trelawny of the Wells," "Charley Chestnut Rides the IRT," "Radio (Wisdom): Sophia Part I," "Images of the Dead."

BARTON, DANIEL. Born Jan. 23, 1949 in Buffalo, NY. Attended Buffalo State, Albany State. Bdwy debut 1976 in "The Poison Tree," followed by "Timbuktu."

BARTON, DONALD. Born May 2, 1928 in Eastland, TX. Attended UTex. Credits include "Design for a Stained Glass Window," "Paint Your Wagon," "Wonderful Town," "Goldilocks," "Much Ado About Nothing," "The Royal Family," "Deathtrap."

Richard Backus   **Harolyn Blackwell**   **James Bartz**   **Francine Beers**   **Robert Black**

BARTZ, JAMES. Born Apr. 23, 1948 in Racine, WI. Graduate UWisc. Bdwy debut 1976 in "Wheelbarrow Closers," followed by "Salome," "Mandragola," "Antigone," "You Are What You Are," "Woman of Iron," "Innocent Thoughts," "Tom Tom," "War and Peace."

BASSETT, STEVE. Born June 25, 1952 in Escondido, CA. Graduate Juilliard. Bdwy debut 1979 in "Deathtrap," OB in "Spring Awakening."

BATES, KATHY. Born June 28, 1948 in Memphis, TN. Graduate Southern Methodist U. Debut 1976 in "Vanities," followed by "The Art of Dining," Bdwy 1980 in "Goodbye Fidel."

BATTISTA, LLOYD. Born May 14, 1937 in Cleveland, OH. Graduate Carnegie Tech. Bdwy Debut 1966 in "Those That Play the Clowns," followed by "The Homecoming," "The Flame and the Rose," "Murder in the Cathedral," "The Miser," "Gorky," "Sexual Perversity in Chicago," "King of Schnorrers."

BAUGHAN, TERRY. Born Feb. 21, 1951 in Lincoln, NE. Graduate UNeb. Debut 1979 OB in "The Sound of Music" (ELT), followed by "Anyone Can Whistle."

BAUM, SUSAN J. Born July 12, 1950 in Miami, FL. Graduate UFla. Has appeared OB in "The Children's Hour," "Holy Ghosts," "Hay Fever," "Doctor in the House," "Trifles," "Arms and the Man," "Uncle Vanya," "Hedda Gabler."

BAVAN, YOLANDE. Born June 1, 1942 in Ceylon. Attended UColombo. Debut 1964 OB in "A Midsummer Night's Dream," followed by "Jonah," "House of Flowers," "Salvation," "Tarot," "Back Bog Beast Bait," "Leaves of Grass," Bdwy in "Heathen," "Snow White."

BAXTER, KEITH. Born Apr. 29, 1935 in Newport, Wales. Graduate RADA. Bdwy debut 1961 in "A Man for All Seasons" for which he received a Theatre World Award, followed by "The Affair," "Avanti," "Sleuth," "A Meeting by the River," OB in "The Penultimate Problem of Sherlock Holmes."

BAYER, GARY. Born June 25, 1944 in Los Angeles, CA. Graduate UEvansville, NYU. Bdwy debut 1978 in "A History of the American Film," followed by "Richard III," with BAM Theatre Co. in "Winter's Tale," "Johnny on a Spot," "The Barbarians."

BEALS, FREDERICK. Born July 3, 1916 in Mt. Vernon, NY. Graduate Williams Col. Debut 1978 OB in "Desire under the Elms," followed by "Peace in Our Time," "The Importance of Being Earnest," "Dark of the Moon," "The Old Woman Broods," "Caligula," "All the Way Home" (ELT).

BEAN, ORSON. Born July 22, 1928 in Burlington, VT. Bdwy bow 1953 in "Men of Distinction," followed by "John Murray Anderson's Almanac" for which he received a Theatre World Award, "Will Success Spoil Rock Hunter?," "Nature's Way," "Mister Roberts" (CC), "Subways Are for Sleeping," "Say, Darling" (CC), "Never Too Late," "I Was Dancing," "Ilya Darling," OB in "Home Movies," "A Round with Ring," "Make Someone Happy."

BEERS, FRANCINE. Born Nov. 26 in NYC. Attended Hunter Col., CCNY, HB Studio. Debut 1962 OB in "King of the Whole Damned World," followed by "Kiss Mama," "Monopoly," "Cakes with Wine," "The American Clock," Bdwy in "Cafe Crown," "6 Rms Riv Vu."

BEHREN, RICHARD. Born Mar. 18, 1952 in St. Louis, MO. Graduate Southeast Mo. U. Debut 1980 OB in "War Play."

BELACK, DORIS. Born Feb. 26 in NYC. Attended AADA. Debut OB 1956 in "World of Sholom Aleichem," followed by "P.S. 193," "Letters Home," Bdwy in "Middle of the Night," "The Owl and the Pussycat," "The Heroine," "You Know I Can't Hear You . . . ," "90 Day Mistress," "Last of the Red Hot Lovers," "Bad Habits," "The Trip Back Down."

BELANGER, JOANNE. Born Feb. 26, 1945 in Chicago, IL. Graduate Wayne State U., UIowa. Debut 1971 OB in "Dowager's Hump," followed by "The Red Hat," "Crystal and Fox," "Night Must Fall," "Falling Apart," "Love's Labour's Lost."

BELGRAVE, CYNTHIA. Born in NYC. Graduate Boston U. Bdwy debut 1959 in "Raisin in the Sun," followed by "The Amen Corner," OB in "Take a Giant Step," "The Blacks," "Funny-house of a Negro," "Trials of Brother Jero," "Citizen Bezique," "Emma," "Making Peace," "Remembrance," "Jam."

BELL, BRIAN. Born Apr. 18, 1945 in NYC. Graduate UDenver. Debut 1977 OB in "The Passion of Dracula."

BELLOMO, JOE. Born Apr. 12, 1938 in NYC. Attended Manhattan Sch. of Music. Bdwy bow 1960 in "New Girl in Town," followed by CC's "South Pacific" and "Guys and Dolls," OB in "Cindy," "Fantasticks."

BENECKE, MARC. Born Oct. 30, 1956 in Brooklyn, NY. Attended Albany State, Hunter Col. Bdwy debut 1979 in "Got Tu Go Disco."

BENDO, MARK. Born Jan. 28, 1964 in NYC. Studied with Lee Strasberg. Debut 1977 OB in "The Dream Watcher," followed by "All the Way Home," Bdwy 1979 in "On Golden Pond."

BENJAMIN, P. J. Born Sept. 2, 1951 in Chicago, IL. Attended Loyola U., Columbia. Bdwy debut 1973 in "Pajama Game," followed by "Pippin," "Sarava."

BENTLEY, JOHN. Born Jan. 31, 1940 in Jackson Heights, NY. Graduate AADA, attended USyracuse. Debut 1961 OB in "King of the Dark Chamber," Bdwy in "Mike Downstairs," "Lysistrata," "The Selling of the President," "A Funny Thing Happened on the Way to the Forum" (1972), "West Side Story" (1980).

BERDGER, GREGORY. Born Oct. 25, 1953 in Arlington, VA. Debut 1980 OB in "Come Back to the 5 and Dime, Jimmy Dean."

BEREZIN, TANYA. Born Mar. 25, 1941 in Philadelphia, PA. Attended Boston U. Debut 1967 in "The Sandcastle," followed by "Three Sisters," "Great Nebula in Orion," "him," "Amazing Activity of Charlie Contrare," "Battle of Angels," "Mound Builders," "Serenading Louie," "My Life," "Brontosaurus," "Glorious Morning," "Mary Stuart."

BERK, DAVID. Born July 20, 1932 in NYC. Graduate Manhattan School of Music. Debut OB 1958 in "Eloise," followed by "Carnival" (CC), "So Long 174th Street," "Wonderful Town" (ELT), "Anyone Can Whistle."

BERMAN, DONALD F. Born Jan. 23, 1954 in NYC. Graduate USyracuse. Debut 1977 OB in "Savages," followed by "Dona Rosita."

BERMAN, NORMAN L. Born Mar. 19, 1949 in Detroit, MI. Attended NYU, Pace U. Has appeared in, and/or composed for OB productions of "Design for Living," "Him," "Battle of Angels," "Hamlet," "By Bernstein," "Unsung Cole," "King of Schnorrers," and Bdwy debut 1979 in "Strider."

BERNER, GARY. Born in Mt. Kisco, NY. Attended Hampshire Col., Brandeis U. Debut 1979 OB in "Minnesota Moon" followed by "The Runner Stumbles," "Hamlet," "Mary Stuart."

BESSETTE, DENISE. Born Aug. 25, 1954 in Midland, MI. Graduate Marymount Manhattan Col., RADA. Debut 1977 OB in "Freshwater/Evening at Bloomsbury," followed by "La Ronde," "Admirable Crichton," "War and Peace."

BEVERLEY, TRAZANA. Born Aug. 9, 1945 in Baltimore, MD. Graduate NYU. Debut 1969 OB in "Rules for Running Trains," followed by "Les Femmes Noires," "Geronimo," "Antigone," Bdwy in "My Sister, My Sister," "For Colored Girls Who Have Considered Suicide When the Rainbow Is Enuf" for which she received a Theatre World Award.

BEY, RICHARD. Born July 22, 1951 in Far Rockaway, NY. Graduate UCal., Yale. Debut 1979 OB in "The Vienna Notes," followed by "Table Settings," "Second Avenue Rag."

BIGELOW, SUSAN. Born Apr. 11, 1952 in Abington, PA. Attended UMd. Bdwy debut 1978 in "Working," followed by "Oklahoma!"

BILLINGTON, LEE. Born July 15, 1932 in Madison, WI. Attended UWisc. Bdwy debut 1969 in "But Seriously," OB in "Dance of Death," "3 by O'Neill," "Our Town," "Capt. Brasbound's Conversion," "Henry VIII," "Boy with a Cart," "Epicoene," "The Homecoming," "Paterson."

BISHOP, KELLY (formerly Carole). Born Feb. 28, 1944 in Colorado Springs, CO. Bdwy debut 1967 in "Golden Rainbow," followed by "Promises, Promises," "On the Town," "Rachel Lily Rosenbloom," "A Chorus Line," OB in "Piano Bar," "Changes."

BITTNER, JACK. Born in Omaha, NE. Graduate UNeb. Has appeared OB in "Nathan the Wise," "Land of Fame," "Beggar's Holiday," "Rip Van Winkle," "Dear Oscar," "What Every Woman Knows," "By Bernstein," "The Philanderer," Bdwy 1980 in "Harold and Maude."

BLACK, ROBERT. Born July 6, 1947 in Cedar Rapids, IA. Graduate UTx. Bdwy debut 1970 in "Wilson in the Promise Land," followed by "Clothes for a Summer Hotel."

BLACKTON, JACK. Born Mar. 16, 1938 in Colorado Springs, CO. OB in "The Fantasticks," "Put It in Writing," "Jacques Brel Is Alive . . . ," "Hark," "Kaboom," Bdwy in "Mame" (1966), "Side by Side by Sondheim," "Rockette Spectacular."

BLACKWELL, HAROLYN M. Born Nov. 23, 1955 in Washington, DC. Graduate Catholic U. Bdwy debut 1980 in "West Side Story."

BLACKWELL, THOMMIE. Born Sept. 11, 1945 in Brooklyn, NY. Graduate Boston U. Debut 1972 OB in "Black Visions," followed by "The Last Chord," "Going-a-Buffalo," "The Sign in Sidney Brustein's Window."

BLAIR, PAMELA. Born Dec. 5, 1949 in Arlington, VT. Attended Ntl. Acad. of Ballet. Made Bdwy debut in 1972 in "Promises, Promises," followed by "Sugar," "Seesaw," "Of Mice and Men," "Wild and Wonderful," "A Chorus Line," "The Best Little Whorehouse in Texas," "King of Hearts," OB in "Ballad of Boris K.," "Split."

BLAISDELL, NESBITT. Born Dec. 6, 1928 in NYC. Graduate Amherst, Columbia U. Debut 1978 OB in "Old Man Joseph and His Family," followed by "Moliere in spite of Himself," "Guests of the Nation."

BLAKE, HOBAN (Formerly Leslie Blake). Born Aug. 4 in Brooklyn, NY. Graduate NYU. Has appeared OB in "Electra," "Journey," "Hamlet," "The Constant Wife," "Romeo and Juliet" (ELT).

BLAXILL, PETER. Born Sept. 27, 1931 in Cambridge, MA. Graduate Bard Col. Debut 1967 OB in "Scuba Duba," followed by "The Fantasticks," "The Passion of Antigona Perez," "Oh, Boy!," Bdwy in "Marat/deSade," "The Littlest Circus," "The Innocents."

BLAYMORE, ENID. Born Nov. 13, 1929 in NYC. Graduate USyracuse. Bdwy debut 1980 in "Musical Chairs."

BLAZER, JUDITH. Born Oct. 22, 1956 in Dover, NJ. Graduate Manhattan School of Music. Debut 1979 OB in "Oh, Boy!"

BLOCH, SCOTTY. Born Jan. 28 in New Rochelle, NY. Attended AADA. Debut 1945 OB in "Craig's Wife," followed by "Lemon Sky," "Battering Ram," "Richard III," "In Celebration," "An Act of Kindness," "The Price," Bdwy in "Children of a Lesser God."

BLOOM, VERNA. Born Aug. 7 in Lynn, MA. Graduate Boston U. Bdwy debut 1967 in "Marat/deSade," followed by OB in "Kool Aid," "The Cherry Orchard," "Bits and Pieces."

BLOUNT, HELON. Born Jan. 15 in Big Spring, TX. Graduate UTx. Bdwy debut 1956 in "Most Happy Fella," followed by "How to Succeed in Business . . .," "Do I Hear a Waltz?" "Fig Leaves Are Falling," "Follies," "Very Good Eddie," "Musical Chairs," OB in "Fly Blackbird," "Riverwind," "My Wife and I," "Curley McDimple," "A Quarter for the Ladies Room," "Snapshot."

BLUM, MARK. Born May 14, 1950 in Newark, NJ. Graduate UPa., UMinn. Debut 1976 OB in "The Cherry Orchard," followed by "Green Julia," "Say Goodnight, Gracie," "Table Settings."

BODIN, DUANE. Born Dec. 31, 1932 in Duluth, MN. Bdwy debut 1961 in "Bye Bye Birdie," followed by "La Plume de Ma Tante," "Here's Love," "Fiddler on the Roof," "1776," "Sweeney Todd."

BOGARDUS, STEPHEN. Born Mar. 11, 1954 in Norfolk, VA. Princeton graduate. Bdwy debut 1980 in "West Side Story."

BOGAZIANOS, VASILI. Born Feb. 1, 1949 in NYC. Graduated San Francisco State Col. Debut 1978 OB in "P. S. Your Cat Is Dead" for which he received a Theatre World Award, followed by "Loney's 66."

BOND, SUDIE. Born July 13, 1928 in Louisville, KY. Attended Rollins Col. OB in "Summer and Smoke," "Tovarich," "American Dream," "Sandbox," "Endgame," "Theatre of the Absurd," "Home Movies," "Softly Consider the Nearness," "Memorandum," "Local Stigmatic," "Billy," "New York! New York!," "Cherry Orchard," "Albee Directs Albee," "Dance for Me Simeon," Bdwy in "Waltz of the Toreadors," "Auntie Mame," "The Egg," "Harold," "My Mother, My Father and Me," "The Impossible Years," "Keep It in the Family," "Quotations from Chrmn. Mao Tse-Tung," "American Dream," "Forty Carats," "Hay Fever," "Grease."

BONELLE, DICK. Born Apr. 11, 1936 in Houston, TX. Graduate UHouston. Debut 1970 OB in "Lyle," followed by "Carousel," "Call Me Madam," "Bus Stop," Bdwy in "Sugar" (1973).

BOOTH, ERIC. Born Oct. 18, 1950 in NYC. Graduate Emerson Col., Stanford U. Bdwy debut 1977 in "Caesar and Cleopatra," followed by "Golda," "Whose Life Is It Anyway?," OB in "The Taming of the Shrew."

BOOTHE, POWERS. Born June 1, 1948 in Snyder, TX. Graduate SMU. Debut 1974 in "Richard III" (LC), followed by "Othello," "Lone Star/Private Wars."

BOSCO, PHILIP. Born Sept. 26, 1930 in Jersey City, NJ. Graduate Catholic U. Credits: "Auntie Mame," "Rape of the Belt," "Ticket of Leave Man" (OB), "Donnybrook," "Man for All Seasons," "Mrs. Warren's Profession," with LCRep in "The Alchemist," "East Wind," "Galileo," "St. Joan," "Tiger at the Gate," "Cyrano," "King Lear," "A Great Career," "In the Matter of J. Robert Oppenheimer," "The Miser," "The Time of Your Life," "Camino Real," "Operation Sidewinder," "Amphitryon," "Enemy of the People," "Playboy of the Western World," "Good Woman of Setzuan," "Antigone," "Mary Stuart," "Narrow Road to the Deep North," "The Crucible," "Twelfth Night," "Enemies," "Plough and the Stars," "Merchant of Venice," and "A Streetcar Named Desire," "Henry V," "Threepenny Opera," "Streamers," "Stages," "St. Joan," "The Biko Inquest," "Man and Superman," "Whose Life Is It Anyway," "Major Barbara," "A Month in the Country."

BOUTSIKARIS, DENNIS. Born Dec. 21, 1952 in Newark, NJ. Graduate Hampshire Col. Debut 1975 OB in "Another Language," followed by "Funeral March for a One-Man Band," "All's Well That Ends Well." Bdwy in "Filumena," "Bent."

BOYD, TOM. Born Oct. 1 in Hamilton, Ont., Can. Bdwy debut 1962 in "How to Succeed in Business . . .," followed by "Walking Happy," "Irene," "Sugar Babies."

BOYDEN, PETER. Born July 19, 1945 in Leominster, MA. Graduate St. Anselm's Col., Smith Col. Debut OB in "One Flew Over the Cuckoo's Nest," followed by "Nice Girls," "Claw," "Berkeley Square," "Pericles," "Pig!," "Smart Aleck," Bdwy in "Whoopee!" (1979).

BOYLE, ROBERT. Born Mar. 28, 1950 in Patton, PA. Graduate Carnegie-Mellon U. Debut 1980 OB in "Merton of the Movies."

BOZYK, REIZI (ROSE). Born May 13, 1914 in Poland. Star of many Yiddish productions before 1966 Bdwy debut in "Let's Sing Yiddish," followed by "Sing, Israel, Sing," "Mirele Efros," OB in "Light, Lively and Yiddish," "Rebecca, the Rabbi's Daughter."

BRAND, GIBBEY. Born May 20, 1946 in NYC. Ithaca Col. graduate. Debut 1977 OB in "The Castaways," followed by "The Music Man" (JB)

BRASINGTON, ALAN. Born in Monticello, NY. Attended RADA. Bdwy debut 1968 in "Pantagleize," followed by "The Misanthrope," "Cock-a-Doodle Dandy" and "Hamlet" with APA, "A Patriot for Me," OB in "Sterling Silver," "Shakespeare's Cabaret."

BRENNAN, EILEEN. Born Sept. 3, 1935 in Los Angeles, CA. Attended AADA. Debut 1959 OB in "Little Mary Sunshine" for which she received a Theatre World Award, followed by "The King and I" (CC), "A Coupla White Chicks Sitting Around Talking," Bdwy in "The Student Gypsy," "Hello, Dolly!"

BRENNAN, MAUREEN. Born Oct. 11, 1952 in Washington, DC. Attended UCincinnati. Bdwy debut 1974 in "Candide" for which she received a Theatre World Award, followed by "Going Up," "Knickerbocker Holiday," OB in "Shakespeare's Cabaret."

BRENNAN, MIKE. Born Feb. 4, 1948 in NYC. Fordham U. Graduate. Debut 1973 OB in "Arms and the Man," followed by "Gay Divorce," "Blues for Mr. Charlie."

BRENNAN, TOM. Born Apr. 16, 1926 in Cleveland, OH. Graduate Oberlin, Western Reserve. Debut 1958 OB in "Synge Trilogy," followed by "Between Two Thieves," "Easter," "All in Love," "Under Milkwood," "An Evening with James Purdy," "Golden Six," "Pullman Car Hiawatha," "Are You Now or Have You . . . ," "Diary of Anne Frank," "Milk of Paradise."

BRESLIN, TOMMY. Born Mar. 24, 1946 in Norwich, CT. Graduate Iona Col. OB in "For Love or Money," "Freedom Is a Two-Edged Sword," "Who's Who, Baby?," "Beggar on Horseback" (LC), "Moon Walk," "Dear Oscar," Bdwy bow 1971 in "70 Girls 70," followed by "Good News," "Musical Chairs."

BRETT, JEREMY. Born Nov. 3, 1933 in Berkswell, Eng. Attended Eaton. Bdwy debut 1956–57 with Old Vic's "Troilus and Cressida," "Macbeth," "Richard II," and "Romeo and Juliet," followed by "The Deputy," "Dracula."

BRIDGES, RAND. Born Jan 10 in Chicago, IL. Attended Pfeiffer Col., Trinity U. Bdwy debut 1979 in "Dracula," followed by "Major Barbara."

BRIGHT, RICHARD. Born June 28, 1937 in Brooklyn, NY. OB in "The Balcony," "Does a Tiger Wear a Necktie?," "The Beard," "Survival of St. Joan," "Kool Aid," "Gogol," Bdwy in "The Basic Training of Pavlo Hummel," "Richard III."

BRIGULIO, ELIZABETH. Born Oct. 31, 1949 in NYC. Graduate C. W. Post Col. Debut 1980 OB in "The Cocktail Party."

BROCK, POPE. Born July 21, 1949 in Atlanta, GA. Graduate Harvard, NYU. Debut 1980 OB in "Class Enemy."

BROCKSMITH, ROY. Born Sept. 15, 1945 in Quincy, IL. Debut OB 1971 in "Whip Lady," followed by "The Workout," "Beggar's Opera," "Polly," "Threepenny Opera," "The Master and Margarita," "Jungle of Cities," Bdwy in "The Leaf People" (1975), "Stages," "Tartuffe."

BRODERICK, DIANA. Born July 15, in NYC. Attended NYU. Bdwy debut 1979 in "The Best Little Whorehouse in Texas."

BROMKA, ELAINE. Born Jan. 6 in Rochester, NY. Smith Col. graduate. Debut 1975 OB in "The Dybbuk," followed by "Naked," "Museum," "The Son."

BROOK, PAMELA. Born Jan. 21, 1947 in London, Ont., Can. Graduate UToronto, UMinn. Debut 1976 OB in "The Philanderer," Bdwy 1980 in "Goodbye Fidel."

BROOKES, JACQUELINE. Born July 24, 1930 in Montclair, NJ. Graduate UIowa, RADA. Bdwy debut 1955 in "Tiger at the Gates," followed by "Watercolor," "Abelard and Heloise," OB in "The Cretan Woman" for which she received a Theatre World Award, "The Clandestine Marriage," "Measure for Measure," "Duchess of Malfi," "Ivanov," "Six Characters in Search of an Author," "An Evening's Frost," "Come Slowly, Eden," "The Increased Difficulty of Concentration," "The Persians," "Sunday Dinner," "House of Blue Leaves," "A Meeting by the River," "Owners," "Hallelujah," "Dream of a Blacklisted Actor," "Knuckle," "Mama Sang the Blues," "Buried Child," "On Mt. Chimorazo," "Winter Dancers," "Hamlet," "Old Flames."

BROWN, GRAHAM. Born Oct. 24 in NYC. Graduate Howard U. OB in "Widower's Houses," "The Emperor's Clothes," "Time of Storm," "Major Barbara," "Land Beyond the River," "The Blacks," "Firebugs," "God Is a (Guess What?)," "An Evening of One Acts," "Man Better Man," "Behold! Cometh the Vanderkellans," "Ride a Black Horse," "Great MacDaddy," "Eden," "Nevis Mountain Dew," "Season Unravel," "The Devil's Tear," Bdwy in "Weekend," "Man in the Glass Booth," "River Niger," "Pericles," "Black Picture Show," "Kings."

BROWN, KATHERINE-MARY. Born Jan. 4, 1948 in Lubbock, TX. Graduate Mary Washington Col., UVa. Debut 1978 OB in "Eccentricities of a Nightingale," followed by "Biography: A Game," Bdwy 1979 in "Strider."

Thommie Blackwell   **Pamela Brook**   **Stephen Bogardus**   **Edye Byrde**   **Jay Bursky**

BROWN, KERMIT. Born Feb. 3, 1937 in Asheville, NC. Graduate Duke U. With APA in "War and Peace," "Judith," "Man and Superman," "The Show-Off," "Pantagleize," "The Cherry Orchard," OB in "The Millionairess," "Things," "Lulu," "Heartbreak House," "Glad Tidings," "Anyone Can Whistle."

BROWN, SHIRLEY. Born Oct. 5, 1953 in Cincinnati, OH. Attended UCin. Debut 1976 OB in "Eden," followed by "What Would You Do?"

BROWNLEE, BRIAN. Born July 6 in Virginia. Attended UNC, AADA. Debut 1972 OB in "We Bombed in New Haven," followed by "A Streetcar Named Desire" (LC), "The Rapists," "Give My Regards to Broadway," Bdwy 1980 in "Harold and Maude."

BROWNLEE, JOHN. Born Sept. 25, 1952 in Hutchinson, KS. Graduate UAriz. Bdwy debut 1979 in "Strider."

BRUCE, SHELLEY. Born May 5, 1965 in Passaic, NJ. Debut OB 1973 in "The Children's Mass," Bdwy 1977 in "Annie."

BRUMMEL, DAVID. Born Nov. 1, 1942 in Brooklyn, NY. Bdwy debut 1973 in "The Pajama Game," followed by "Music Is," "Oklahoma!," OB in "Cole Porter," "The Fantasticks."

BRUNEAU, RALPH. Born Sept. 22, 1952 in Phoenix, AZ. Graduate UNotre Dame. Debut 1974 OB in "The Fantasticks," followed by "Saints," "Suddenly the Music Starts," "On a Clear Day You Can See Forever," "King of the Schnorrers."

BRUNS, PHILIP. Born May 2, 1931 in Pipestone, MN. Graduate Augustana Col., Yale. Bdwy bow 1964 in "The Deputy," followed by "Lysistrata," OB in "Mr. Simian," "The Cradle Will Rock," "He Who Gets Slapped," "Dr. Willy Nilly," "Come Play With Me," "Listen to the Mocking Bird," "Bald Soprano," "Jack of the Submission," "Endgame," "Servant of Two Masters," "Pantomania," "Square in the Eye," "Butter and Egg Man," "Spitting Image," "Henry V," "A Dream Out of Time," "Two."

BRYAN, WAYNE. Born Aug. 13, 1947 in Compton, CA. Graduate UCal. Bdwy debut 1974 in "Good News," followed by "Rodgers and Hart," OB in "Tintypes."

BRYGGMAN, LARRY. Born Dec. 21, 1938 in Concord, CA. Attended CCSF, AmThWing. Debut 1962 OB in "A Pair of Pairs," followed by "Live Like Pigs," "Stop, You're Killing Me," "Mod Donna," "Waiting for Godot," "Ballymurphy," "Marco Polo Sings a Solo," "Brownsville Raid," "Two Small Bodies," "Museum," "Winter Dancers," Bdwy in "Ulysses in Nighttown," "Checking Out," "Basic Training of Pavlo Hummel," "Richard III."

BUBBLES, JOHN. Born Feb. 19, 1902 in Louisville, KY. Appeared in minstrels, carnivals, circuses, nightclubs, and Bdwy in "Ziegfeld Follies," "Porgy and Bess," "Carmen Jones," "George White's Varieties," "Show Time," "Laugh Time," "Curtain Time," "At Home at the Palace," "Black Broadway."

BUCHAN, MARK. Born Sept. 28, 1950 in Regina, Sas., Can. Graduate USaskatchewan, UWash. Debut 1979 OB in "I'm Getting My Act Together and Taking It on the Road."

BUCKLEY, BETTY. Born July 3, 1947 in Big Spring, TX. Graduate TCU. Bdwy debut 1969 in "1776," followed by "Pippin," OB in "Ballad of Johnny Pot," "What's a Nice Country Like You . . . ," "Circle of Sound," "I'm Getting My Act Together. . . ."

BUELL, BILL. Born Sept. 21, 1952 in Paipai, Taiwan. Attended Portland State. Debut 1972 OB in "Crazy Now," Bdwy 1979 in "Once a Catholic."

BUKA, DONALD. Born Dec. 18, 1921 in Cleveland, OH. Attended Carnegie Tech. Has appeared in "Twelfth Night," "The Corn Is Green," "Bright Boy," "Helen Goes to Troy," "Sophie," "Live Life Again," "Those That Play the Clowns," "Heritage" (OB), "Major Barbara."

BULOFF, JOSEPH. Born Dec. 6, 1907 in Wilno, Lith. Bdwy debut 1936 in "Don't Look Now," followed by "Call Me Ziggy," "To Quito and Back," "The Man from Cairo," "Morning Star," "Spring Again," "My Sister Eileen," "Oklahoma!," "The Whole World Over," "Once More with Feeling," "Fifth Season," "Moonbirds," "The Wall," OB in "Yoshke Musikant," "The Price."

BULOS, YUSEF. Born Sept. 14, 1940 in Jerusalem. Attended Beirut AmU, AADA. Debut 1965 OB with American Savoyards in repertory, followed by "Saints," "The Trouble with Europe," "The Penultimate Problem of Sherlock Holmes," Bdwy in "Indians," "Capt. Brassbound's Conversion."

BURCH, PETER. Born Nov. 30, 1955 in Albany, NY. Debut OB 1979 in "The Dark at the Top of the Stairs."

BURGE, JAMES. Born Dec. 3, 1943 in Miami, FL. Graduate UOk., Wayne State U. Bdwy bow 1970 in "Grin and Bare It," followed by "The Royal Family," OB in "Happy Hunter."

BURKE, MICHAEL. Born Jan. 4, 1936 in Richmond, VA. Attended Randolph-Macon, Johns Hopkins U. Debut 1977 OB in "The Crucible," followed by "Who Wants To Be the Lone Ranger?"

BURKHARDT, GERRY. Born June 14, 1946 in Houston, TX. Attended Lon Morris Col. Bdwy debut 1968 in "Her First Roman," followed by "The Best Little Whorehouse in Texas."

BURNELL, PETER. Born Apr. 29, 1950 in Johnstown, NY. OB in "Henry IV," "Antony and Cleopatra," "The Tempest," "Macbeth," "Olathe Response," "Ubu Roi/Ubu Bound," "Dancing for the Kaiser," "The Prince of Homburg," "Flying Blind," Bdwy 1974 in "In Praise of Love" for which he received a Theatre World Award.

BURNS, CATHERINE. Born Sept. 25, 1945 in NYC. Attended AADA. Bdwy debut 1968 in "The Prime of Miss Jean Brodie," OB in "Dream of a Blacklisted Actor," "Disintegration of James Cherry," "Operation Sidewinder," "Dear Janet Rosenberg, Dear Mr. Kooning" for which she received a Theatre World Award, "Two Small Bodies," "Voices," "Jungle of Cities," "One Wedding," "Metamorphosis."

BURR, ROBERT. Born in Jersey City, NJ. Attended Colgate U. Has appeared in "The Cradle Will Rock," "Mr. Roberts," "Romeo and Juliet," "Picnic," "The Lovers," "Anniversary Waltz," "Top Man," "Remains to Be Seen," "The Wall," "Andersonville Trial," "A Shot in the Dark," "Man for All Seasons," "Luther," "Hamlet," "Bajour," "White Devil," "Royal Hunt of the Sun," "Dinner at 8," "King John," "Henry VI," "Love-Suicide at Schofield Barracks," "Wild and Wonderful," "Look Back in Anger" (OB).

BURRELL, PAMELA. Born Aug. 4, 1945 in Tacoma, WA. Bdwy debut 1966 in "Funny Girl," followed by "Where's Charley?" "Strider," OB in "Arms and the Man" for which she received a Theatre World Award, "Berkeley Square," "The Boss," "Biography: A Game," "Strider: Story of a Horse."

BURSKY, JAY. Born Mar. 27, 1954 in Cleveland, OH. Graduated Indiana U. OB and Bdwy debut 1978 in "The Best Little Whorehouse in Texas."

BUSTAMANTE, MAURICIO. Born Jan. 14, 1948 in Mexico City, MX. Attended Loretto Heights Col., Strasberg Inst. Debut 1980 OB in "Annie Get Your Gun" (ELT).

BUTTRAM, JAN. Born June 19, 1946 in Clarkesville, TX. Graduate NTexState. Debut 1974 OB in "Fashion," followed by "Startup," Bdwy 1978 in "The Best Little Whorehouse in Texas."

BYRDE, EDYE. Born Jan. 19, 1929 in NYC. Bdwy debut 1975 in "The Wiz," OB in "Jam."

BYRNE, GAYLEA. Born in Baltimore, MD. Graduate Peabody Consv. Debut 1961 OB in "All in Love," followed by "The Music Man" (CC), "Man of LaMancha," "Anyone Can Whistle" (OB).

CAHILL, JAMES. Born May 31, 1940 in Brooklyn, NY. Bdwy debut 1967 in "Marat/deSade," followed by "Break a Leg," OB in "The Hostage," "The Alchemist," "Johnny Johnson," "Peer Gynt," "Timon of Athens," "An Evening for Merlin Finch," "The Disintegration of James Cherry," "Crimes of Passion," "Rain," "Screens," "Total Eclipse," "Entertaining Mr. Sloane," "Hamlet," "Othello," "The Trouble with Europe."

CAIN, WILLIAM B. Born May 27, 1931 in Tuscaloosa, AL. Graduate George Washington U, Catholic U. Debut 1962 OB in "Red Roses for Me," followed by "Jericho Jim Crow," "Henry V," "Antigone," Bdwy in "Wilson in the Promise Land," "Of the Fields, Lately."

CALL, ANTHONY D. Born Aug. 31, 1940 in Los Angeles, CA. Attended UPa. Debut 1969 OB in "The David Show," followed by "Frequency," Bdwy in "Crown Matrimonial," "The Trip Back Down," "Suspenders."

CALLMAN, NANCY. Born Apr. 12, 1949 in Buffalo, NY. Graduate SUNY/-Binghamton, Manhattan School of Music. Bdwy debut 1976 in "1600 Pennsylvania Ave.," followed by "Sweeney Todd," OB in "Circa 1900," "Broadway a la Carte," "Hit Tunes from Flop Shows."

227

CALLOWAY, TERRY. Born Mar. 21, 1954 in London, Eng. Has appeared on Bdwy in "Pippin," "Rockabye Hamlet," "Once a Catholic."

CANARY, DAVID H. Born Aug. 25 in Elwood, IN. Graduate UCin., Cincinnati Consv. Debut 1960 OB in "Kittywake Island," followed by "The Fantasticks," "The Father," "Hi, Paisano," Bdwy in "Great Day in the Morning," "Happiest Girl in the World," "Clothes for a Summer Hotel."

CAPES, MICHAEL. Born Sept. 18, 1952 in Lawrence, KS. Graduate Eastern New Mx. U. Bdwy debut 1979 in "The Most Happy Fella."

CARDEN, WILLIAM. Born Feb. 2, 1947 in NYC. Attended Lawrence U, Brandeis U. Debut 1974 OB in "Short Eyes," followed by "Leaving Home," "Back in the Race."

CAREY, DAVID. Born Nov. 16, 1945 in Brookline, MA. Graduate Boston U, Ohio U. Debut 1969 OB in "Oh, What a Wedding," followed by "Let's Sing Yiddish," "Dad, Get Married," "Light, Lively and Yiddish," "Wedding in Shtetl," "Big Winna," "Rebecca, the Rabbi's Daughter."

CARIOU, LEN. Born Sept. 30, 1939 in Winnipeg, Can. Bdwy debut 1968 in "House of Atreus," followed by "Henry V" and "Applause" for which he received a Theatre World Award, "Night Watch," "A Little Night Music," "Cold Storage," "Nero" Bdwy in "A Sorrow Beyond Dreams."

CARLIN, PAUL. Born Nov. 26, 1956 in The Bronx, NY. Graduate Allentown Col. Debut 1980 OB in "Milk of Paradise."

CARLING, P. L. Born March 31. Graduate Stanford, UCLA. Debut 1955 OB in "The Chairs," followed by "In Good King Charles' Golden Days," "Magistrate," "Picture of Dorian Gray," "The Vise," "Lady from the Sea," "Booth Is Back in Town," "Ring Round the Moon," "Philadelphia, Here I Come," "Sorrows of Frederick," "Biography," Bdwy in "The Devils" (1965), "Scratch," "Shenandoah."

CARLSEN, ALLAN. Born Feb. 7 in Chicago, IL. Attended UPa. Bdwy debut 1974 in "The Freedom of the City," OB in "The Morning after Optimism," "Iphigenia in Aulis," "Peg O' My Heart," "Star Treatment."

CARNEGIE, ROBERT. Born Mar. 11, 1951 in Berryville, VA. Attended Neighborhood Playhouse. OB in "Saints Alive!," "Breakers," "Survivors," "The Sign in Sidney Brustein's Window," "My Great Dead Sister."

CARR, CATHERINE. Born May 25, 1956 in Ironton, MO. Graduate Oberlin Col., NYU. Bdwy debut 1980 in "Barnum."

CARRUTHERS, JAMES. Born May 26, 1931 in Morristown, NJ. Attended Lafayette Col., HB Studio. Debut 1959 OB in "Our Town," followed by "Under the Sycamore Tree," "Misalliance," "The Hostage," "Telemachus Clay," "Shadow of a Gunman," "Masks," "Biography: A Game," "Lulu," "Salt Lake City Skyline," Bdwy in "Poor Murderer."

CARTER, DIXIE. Born May 25, 1939 in McLemoresville, TN. Graduate Memphis State U. Debut 1963 OB in "The Winter's Tale," followed by "Carousel," "The Merry Widow," "The King and I," at LC, "Sextet," "Jesse and the Bandit Queen" for which she received a Theatre World Award, "Fathers and Sons," "A Coupla White Chicks . . . ," "Taken in Marriage," Bdwy in "Pal Joey" (1976).

CARTER, NELL. Born Sept. 13 in Birmingham, AL. Bdwy debut 1971 in "Soon," followed by "Jesus Christ Superstar," "Dude," "Don't Bother Me, I Can't Cope," "Ain't Misbehavin' " for which she received a Theatre World Award, OB in "Iphigenia in Taurus," "Bury the Dead," "Fire in the Mindhouse," "The Dirtiest Show in Town," "Black Broadway."

CASS, PEGGY. Born May 21, 1926 in Boston, MA. Attended Wyndham Sch. Credits include "Touch and Go," "Live Wire," "Bernardine," "Othello," "Henry V," "Auntie Mame" for which she received a Theatre World Award, "A Thurber Carnival," "Children from Their Games," "Don't Drink the Water," "Front Page" (69), "Plaza Suite," "Once a Catholic," OB in "Phoenix '55," "Are You Now or Have You Ever Been."

CASSIDY, TIM. Born Mar. 22, 1952 in Alliance, OH. Attended UCincinnati. Bdwy debut 1974 in "Good News," followed by "A Chorus Line."

CASTANG, VERONICA. Born Apr. 22, 1938 in London, Eng. Attended Sorbonne. Bdwy debut 1966 in "How's the World Treating You?," followed by "The National Health," "Whose Life Is It Anyway?," OB in "The Trigon," "Sjt. Musgrave's Dance," "Saved," "Water Hens," "Self-Accusation," "Kaspar," "Ionescapade," "Statements after and Arrest under the Immorality Act," "Ride a Cock Horse," "Banana Box."

CASTILLO, HELEN. Born Feb. 5, 1955 in Santurce, PR. Graduate UPR, Juilliard. Bdwy debut 1979 in "They're Playing Our Song."

CASTLE, ELOWYN. Born Nov. 26, 1940 in New Haven, CT. Attended Conservatoire de Geneve. Debut 1980 OB in "Romeo and Juliet" (ELT).

CAULFIELD, MAXWELL. Born Nov. 23, 1959 in Glasgow, Scot. Debut OB 1979 in "Class Enemy" for which he received a Theatre World Award, followed by "Crimes and Dreams."

CELLARIO, MARIA. Born June 19, 1948 in Buenos Aires, Arg. Graduate Ithaca Col. Bdwy debut 1975 in "The Royal Family," OB in "Fugue in a Nursery."

CHAIKIN, SHAMI. Born Apr. 21, 1931 in NYC. Debut 1966 OB in "America Hurrah," followed by "Serpent," "Terminal," "Mutation Show," "Viet Rock," "Mystery Play," "Electra," "The Dybbuk," "Endgame," "Bag Lady," "The Haggadah."

CHANNING, STOCKARD. Born in 1944 in NYC. Attended Radcliffe Col. Debut 1970 OB in "Adaptation/Next," Bdwy in "Two Gentlemen of Verona," "They're Playing Our Song."

CHAPIN, MILES. Born Dec. 6, 1954 in NYC. Studied at HB Studio. Debut 1974 OB in "Joan of Lorraine," followed by "Two Rooms," Bdwy in "Summer Brave."

CHAPMAN, ROGER. Born Jan. 1, 1947 in Cheverly, MD. Graduate Rollins, Col. Debut 1976 OB in "Who Killed Richard Cory?," followed by "My Life," "Hamlet," "Innocent Thoughts, Harmless Intentions."

CHARLES, WALTER. Born Apr. 4, 1945 in East Stroudsburg, PA. Graduate Boston U. Bdwy debut 1973 in "Grease," followed by "1600 Pennsylvania Avenue," "Knickerbocker Holiday," "Sweeney Todd."

CHARNEY, DEBORAH (aka Didi). Born Aug. 1, 1951 in NYC. Graduate Carleton Col. Debut 1976 OB in "Heartbreak House," followed by "Twelfth Night" (ELT), "My Life," "Romeo and Juliet" (ELT), "The Chronicle of Jane."

CHARNEY, EVA. Born June 7 in Brooklyn, NY. Graduate Douglass Col., Boston U. Debut 1977 OB in "NYC Street Show," followed by "The Wanderers," "Caligula," "I Can't Keep Running," Bdwy in "Hair" (1977).

CHARNEY, JORDAN. Born in NYC; graduate Brooklyn Col. OB in "Harry, Noon and Night," "A Place for Chance," "Hang Down Your Head and Die," "The Pinter Plays," "Telemachus Clay," "Zoo Story," "Viet Rock," "MacBird," "Red Cross," "Glorious Ruler," "Waiting for Godot," "Slow Memories," "One Flew Over the Cuckoo's Nest," "Boy Who Came to Leave," "Cretan Bull," "Naomi Court," Bdwy in "Slapstick Tragedy," "The Birthday Party," "Talley's Folly."

CHATINOVER, MARVIN A. Born Apr. 24, 1927 in Los Angeles, CA. Graduate Yale, NYU. OB in "The Crucible," "Shay," "God Bless You, Mr. Rosewater," "Yank in Beverly Hills," "Archy and Mehitabel."

CHELSI, LARRO. Born July 2, 1932 in Portland, OR. Graduate UOre., Columbia U. Bdwy debut 1946 in "Of Thee I Sing," followed by "Baker Street," OB in "Golden Apple," "Family Portrait," "Housewives' Cantata," "She Shall Have Music," "Oh, Boy!"

CHEN, KITTY. Born in Shanghai, China. Graduate Brown U. Debut 1972 OB in "A Maid's Tragedy," followed by "The King and I," "Rashomon," "And the Soul Shall Dance," "Peking Man."

CHIANESE, DOMINIC. Born Feb. 24, 1932 in NYC. Graduate Brooklyn Col. Debut 1952 OB with American Savoyards, followed by "Winterset," "Jacques Brel Is Alive . . . ," "Ballad for a Firing Squad," "City Scene," "End of the War," "Passione," Bdwy in "Oliver!," "Scratch," "The Water Engine," "Richard III."

CHINN, LORI. Born July 7 in Seattle, WA. Bdwy debut 1970 in "Lovely Ladies, Kind Gentlemen," OB in "Coffins for Butterflies," "Hough in Blazes," "Peer Gynt," "King and I," "Children," "Secret Life of Walter Mitty," "Bayou Legend," "Primary English Class," "G. R. Point," "Peking Man."

CHOATE, TIM. Born Oct. 11, 1954 in Dallas, TX. Graduate UTx. Bdwy debut 1979 in "Da."

CHRISTIAN, ROBERT. Born Dec. 27, 1939 in Los Angeles. Attended UCLA. OB in "The Happening," "Hornblend," "Fortune and Men's Eyes," "Boys in the Band," "Behold! Cometh the Vanderkellans," "Mary Stuart," "Narrow Road to the Deep North," "Twelfth Night," "The Past Is the Past," "Going Through Changes," "Black Sunlight," "Terraces," "Blood Knot," "Boesman and Lena," "Statements after and Arrest under the Immorality Act," "Julius Caesar," "Coriolanus," "Mother Courage," Bdwy in "We Bombed in New Haven," "Does a Tiger Wear a Necktie?," "An Evening with Richard Nixon," "All God's Chillun."

CHRISTMAS, DAVID. Born May 2, 1942 in Pasadena, CA. Attended Pasadena City Col., HB Studio. Bdwy debut 1970 in "Grin and Bare It," followed by "Very Good Eddie," OB in "Butter and Egg Man," "Dames at Sea," "Give My Regards to Broadway," "Bird With Silver Feathers," "God Bless You, Mr. Rosewater."

CHRISTOPHER, RICHARD. Born Nov. 1, 1948 in Ft. Knox, KY. Graduate SWLaU. Bdwy debut 1973 in "Seesaw," followed by "King of Hearts, "Happy New Year," OB in "Three Musketeers."

CHRISTOPHERSON, INDIRA STEFANIANNE. Born Dec. 6 in San Fr... cisco, CA. Attended San Francisco State Col/San Mateo. Debut 1979 OB in "The Umbrellas of Cherbourg."

CHRYST, GARY. Born in LaJolla, CA. Joined Joffrey Ballet in 1968. Bdwy debut 1979 in "Dancin'."

CIANO, OCTAVIO. Born Nov. 26, 1954 in San Juan, PR. Attended UPR, NYU. Debut 1979 OB in "Altar Boys."

CIESLA, DIANE. Born May 20, 1952 in Chicago, IL. Graduate Clarke Col. Debut 1980 OB in "Uncle Money."

CLARK, BRYAN E. Born Apr. 5, 1929 in Louisville, KY. Graduate Fordham U. Bdwy debut 1978 in "A History of the American Film," followed by "Bent," OB in "Winning Isn't Everything."

CLARK, CHERYL. Born Dec. 7, 1950 in Boston, MA. Attended Ind. U., NYU. Bdwy debut 1972 in "Pippin," followed by "Chicago," "A Chorus Line."

CLARK, MARILYN. Born Sept. 28 in Spokane WA. Attended UCLA, Pasadena Playhouse. Bdwy debut 1957 in "Middle of the Night," followed by "Dinner at 8," "Romantic Comedy."

CLARKE, RICHARD. Born Jan. 31, 1933 in England. Graduate U Reading. With LCRep In "St. Joan," "Tiger at the Gates," "Cyrano de Bergerac," followed by Bdwy in "Conduct Unbecoming," "Elephant Man," OB in "Old Glory."

CLARKSON, JOHN. Born Jan. 19, 1932 in London, Eng. Graduate Oxford U. Debut OB 1971 in "Murderous Angels," followed by "An Evening with Ma Bell," "Staircase," "Just a Little Bit Less Than Normal," "The Jail Diary of Albie Sachs," "Fallen Angels," Bdwy in "No Sex Please. We're British," "My Fair Lady," (1977), "Travesties."

Catherine Carr   **Larro Chelsi**   **Indira Christopherson**   **Kevin Conway**   **Jacqueline Coslow**

CLAUSON, WILLIAM. Born Dec. 30, 1948 in Newton, KS. Graduate Rutgers U. Debut 1977 OB in "The Private Ear," followed by "Knitters in the Sun."

CLEIN, ED. Born Oct. 1944 in Atlanta, GA. Graduate Emory U. Debut 1968 OB in "The Cannibals," followed by "Archy and Mehitabel."

CLOSE, GLENN. Born May 19, 1947 in Greenwich, CT. Graduate William & Mary Col. Bdwy debut 1974 with Phoenix Co. in "Love for Love," "Member of the Wedding," and "Rules of the Game," followed by "Rex," "Crucifer of Blood," "Barnum," OB in "The Crazy Locomotive," "Uncommon Women and Others," "Wine Untouched," "The Winter Dancers."

COCA, IMOGENE, Born Nov. 18, 1908 in Philadelphia, PA. Bdwy debut 1925 in "When You Smile," followed by "Garrick Gaieties," "Flying Colors," "New Faces," "Fools Rush In," "Who's Who," "Folies Bergere," "Straw Hat Revue," "All in Fun," "Concert Varieties," "Janus," "Girls in 509," "On the 20th Century."

COFFIN, FREDERICK. Born Jan. 16, 1943 in Detroit, MI. Graduate UMich. Debut 1971 OB in "Basic Training of Pavlo Hummel," followed by "Much Ado About Nothing," "King Lear," "As You Like It," "Boom Boom Room," "Merry Wives of Windsor," "Secret Service," "Boy Meets Girl," "Hot Grog," "God Bless You, Mr. Rosewater," Bdwy in "We Interrupt This Program" (1975).

COHEN, JOYCE. Born Nov. 25, 1948 in West Hartford, CT. Graduate UNC. Debut 1975 OB in "Diamond Studs," followed by "It's Called the Sugar Plum," "Of Men and Angels," "Living at Home," Bdwy 1979 in "Once a Catholic."

COHEN, MARGERY. Born June 24, 1947 in Chicago, IL. Attended UWisc, UChicago. Bdwy debut 1968 in "Fiddler on the Roof," followed by "Jacques Brel is Alive . . . .," OB in "Berlin to Broadway," "By Bernstein," "Starting Here, Starting Now," "Unsung Cole," "Paris Lights."

COLBY, CHRISTINE. Born Feb. 27 in Cincinnati, OH. Attended UCincinnati. Bdwy debut 1978 in "Dancin'."

COLE, GILBERT. Born July 13, 1955 in Geneva, IL. Graduate Juilliard. Debut 1976 OB in "Henry V," followed by "Midsummer Night's Dream," "Dark at the Top of the Stairs," Bdwy 1979 in "A Meeting at the River."

COLE, KAY. Born Jan. 13, 1948 in Miami, FL. Bdwy debut 1961 in "Bye Bye Birdie," followed by "Stop the World I Want to Get Off," "Roar of the Greasepaint . . . .," "Hair," "Jesus Christ Superstar," "Words and Music," "Chorus Line," OB in "The Cradle Will Rock," "Two if By Sea," "Rainbow," "White Nights," "Sgt. Pepper's Lonely Hearts Club Band."

COLES, CHARLES HONI. Born Apr. 2, 1911 in Philadelphia, PA. Debut 1933 OB in "Humming Sam," Bdwy 1949 in "Gentlemen Prefer Blondes," followed by "Black Broadway."

COLL, IVONNE. Born Nov. 4, in Fajardo, PR. Attended UPR, LACC, HB Studio. Debut 1980 OB in "Spain 1980," followed by "Animals," Bdwy 1980 in "Goodbye Fidel."

COLLAMORE, JEROME. Born Sept. 25, 1891 in Boston, MA. Debut 1918 with Washington Square Players in "Salome," and subsequently in, among others, "Christopher Bean," "Hamlet," "Romeo and Juliet," "Kind Lady," "Androcles and the Lion," "George Washington Slept Here," "The Would-Be Gentleman," "Cheri," "Abraham Cochran," "That Hat," Bam Co.'s "New York Idea," "Trouping Since 1912."

COLLINS, BILL. Born Mar. 27, 1935 in Santa Monica, CA. UCLA graduate. Debut 1961 OB in "King of the Dark Chamber," followed by "Lost in the Stars," "Days of the Dancing," "Tenth Man," Bdwy in "Desert Song" (1973).

COLLINS, PAUL. Born July 25, 1937 in London, Eng. Attended Los Angeles City & State Col. OB in "Say Nothing," "Cambridge Circus," "The Devils," "Rear Column," "The Jail Diary of Albie Sachs," Bdwy in "Royal Hunt of the Sun," "A Minor Adjustment," "A Meeting at the River."

COLLINS, STEPHEN. Born Oct. 1, 1947 in Des Moines, IO. Graduate Amherst Col. Bdwy debut 1972 in "Moonchildren," followed by "No Sex, Please, We're British," "The Ritz," "Censored Scenes from King Kong," OB in "Twelfth Night," "More Than You Deserve," "Macbeth"(LC), "Last Days of British Honduras," BAM's "New York Idea," "Three Sisters" and "The Play's the Thing."

COLLINS, SUZANNE. Born in San Francisco, CA. Graduate USan Francisco. Debut 1975 OB in "Trelawny of the Wells," followed by "The Cherry Orchard," "The Art of Dining."

COLODNER, JOEL. Born May 1, 1946 in Brooklyn, NY. Graduate Cornell, SMU. Bdwy debut 1973 with CCActing Co. in "Three Sisters," "Beggar's Opera," "Measure for Measure," OB in "Do I Hear a Waltz?," "A Memory of Two Mondays," "They Knew What They Wanted," "Daisy," "Dona Rosita."

COLON, MIRIAM. Born in 1945 in Ponce, PR. Attended UPR, Actors Studio. Bdwy debut 1953 in "In the Summer House," OB in "Me, Candido," "The Ox Cart," "Passion of Antigona Perez," "Julius Caesar," "Fanlights."

COLSON, C. DAVID. Born Dec. 23, 1941 in Detroit, MI. Debut 1970 OB in "The Last Sweet Days of Isaac," followed by "Masquerade," "Ballet Behind the Bridge," "Mother Courage," Bdwy 1970 in "Purlie."

COLTON, CHEVI. Born Dec. 21 in NYC. Attended Hunter Col. OB in "Time of Storm," "Insect Comedy," "The Adding Machine," "O Marry Me," "Penny Change," "The Mad Show," "Jacques Brel is Alive," "Bits and Pieces," "Spelling Bee," "Uncle Money," Bdwy in "Cabaret," "Grand Tour."

CONNOLLY, MICHAEL. Born Sept. 22, 1947 in Boston, MA. Graduate Fordham U. Bdwy debut 1977 in "Otherwise Engaged," followed by "Break a Leg," "Clothes for a Summer Hotel."

CONROY, FRANCES. Born in 1953 in Monroe, GA. Attended Dickinson Col., Juilliard, Neighborhood Playhouse. Debut 1978 OB with the Acting Co. in "Mother Courage," "King Lear," "The Other Half," followed by "All's Well That Ends Well," "Othello," "Sorrows of Stephen," Bdwy 1980 in "The Lady from Dubuque."

CONROY, JARLATH. Born Sept. 30, 1944 in Galway, IR. Attended RADA. Bdwy debut 1976 in "Comedians," followed by "The Elephant Man."

CONRY, KATHLEEN. Born Nov. 15, 1947 in Cleveland, OH. Bdwy debut 1968 in "George M!," followed by "No, No, Nanette," OB in "Merton of the Movies" (ELT).

CONVERY, ANN. Born Apr. 4 in Trenton, NJ. Graduate Trinity Col., U. Wash. Debut 1980 OB in "The Sign in Sidney Brustein's Window."

CONWAY, KEVIN. Born May 29, 1942 in NYC. Debut 1968 OB in "Muzeeka," followed by "Saved," "The Plough and the Stars," "One Flew over the Cuckoo's Nest," "When You Comin' Back, Red Ryder?," "Long Day's Journey into Night," Bdwy in "Indians," "Moonchildren," "Of Mice and Men," "The Elephant Man."

COOK, JAMES. Born Mar. 7, 1937 in NYC. Attended AADA. OB in "The Fantasticks," "Goa," "Cyrano," "A Cry of Players," "King Lear," "Playboy of the Western World," "Good Woman of Setzuan," "Enemy of the People," "In the Matter of J. Robert Oppenheimer," "The Architect and the Emperor," "Arsenic and Old Lace," Bdwy in "The Great White Hope," "Wrong Way Light Bulb," "Peter Pan."

COOK, JILL. Born Feb. 25, 1954 in Plainfield, NJ. Bdwy debut 1971 in "On the Town," followed by "So Long, 174th Street," "Dancin'," "Best Little Whorehouse in Texas," OB in "Carnival," "Potholes."

COOPER, CHRISTOPHER W. Born July 9, 1951 in Kansas City, MO. Attended UMo. Bdwy debut 1980 in "Of the Fields, Lately."

COOPER, ROY. Born Jan. 22, 1930 in London, Eng. Bdwy debut 1968 in "The Prime of Miss Jean Brodie," followed by "Canterbury Tales," "St. Joan," OB in "A Month in the Country."

COPELAND, JOAN. Born June 1, 1922 in NYC. Attended Brooklyn Col., AADA. Debut 1945 OB in "Romeo and Juliet," followed by "Othello," "Conversation Piece," "Delightful Season," "End of Summer," "The American Clock," Bdwy in "Sundown Beach," "Detective Story," "Not for Children," "Hatful of Fire," "Something More," "The Price," "Two by Two," "Pal Joey," "Checking Out."

COPELAND, MAURICE. Born June 13, 1911 in Rector, AR. Pasadena Playhouse graduate. Bdwy debut 1974 in "The Freedom of the City," followed by "The First Monday in October," "Morning's at 7," OB in "Henry V."

COPPOLA, SAM J. Born July 31, 1935 in NJ. Attended Actors Studio. Debut 1968 OB in "A Present from Your Old Man," followed by "Things That Almost Happen," "Detective Story," "Jungle of Cities."

CORTEZ, KATHERINE. Born Sept. 28, 1950 in Detroit, MI. Graduate UNC. Debut 1979 OB in "The Dark at the Top of the Stairs," followed by "Corners."

COSGRAVE, PEGGY. Born June 23, 1946 in San Mateo, CA. Graduate San Jose State, Catholic U. Debut 1980 OB in "Come Back to the 5 and Dime, Jimmy Dean."

COSLOW, JACQUELINE. Born Feb. 19, 1943 in Hollywood, CA. Attended Mills Col., ULondon, RADA. Debut 1960 OB in "Borak," followed by "Androcles and the Lion," "Arms and the Man," "Shadow of a Gunman," "Trial of the Catonsville 9."

COSTABILE, RICHARD. Born July 16, 1947 in The Bronx, NY. Graduate Fordham U., Neighborhood Playhouse. Debut 1979 OB in "The Electra Myth" (ELT), followed by "Twelfth Night."

COSTIGAN, KEN. Born Apr. 1, 1934 in NYC. Graduate Fordham U., Yale U. Debut 1960 OB in "Borak," followed by "King of the Dark Chamber," "The Hostage," "Next Time I'll Sing to You," "Curley McDimple," "The Runner Stumbles," "Peg o' My Heart," "The Show-Off," "Midsummer Night's Dream," "Diary of Anne Frank," "Knuckle Sandwich," "Seminary Murder," Bdwy 1962 in "Gideon."

COTTRELL, RICHARD. Born Sept. 4, 1944 in Springfield, IL. Graduate UArk. Bdwy debut 1968 with Minn. Theatre Co. in "Arturo Ui" and "House of Atreus," followed by OB "Guests of the Nation."

COUNCIL, RICHARD. Born Oct. 1, 1947 in Tampa, FL. Graduate UFla. Debut 1973 OB in "Merchant of Venice," followed by "Ghost Dance," "Look, We've Come Through," "Arms and the Man," "Isadora Duncan Sleeps with the Russian Navy," "Arthur," "The Winter Dancers," Bdwy in "The Royal Family" (1975).

COURTNEY, DENNIS. Born Apr. 30, 1958 in Detroit, MI. Attended Col. Conservatory of Music. Debut 1978 OB in "Coolest Cat in Town," Bdwy 1979 in "Peter Pan."

COWAN, EDIE. Born Apr. 14 in NYC. Graduate Butler U. Bdwy debut 1964 in "Funny Girl," followed by "Sherry," "Annie."

COWLES, MATTHEW. Born Sept. 28, 1944 in NYC. Attended Neighborhood Playhouse. Bdwy bow 1966 in "Malcolm," followed by "Sweet Bird of Youth," OB in "King John," "The Indian Wants the Bronx," "Triple Play," "Stop, You're Killing Me!," "The Time of Your Life," "Foursome," "Kid Champion," "End of the War," "Tennessee."

COX, CATHERINE. Born Dec. 13, 1950 in Toledo, OH. Wittenberg U. graduate. Bdwy debut 1976 in "Music Is," followed by "Whoopee!," "Oklahoma!," OB in "By Strouse."

CRABTREE, DON. Born Aug. 21, 1928 in Borger, TX. Attended Actors Studio. Bdwy bow 1959 in "Destry Rides Again," followed by "Happiest Girl in the World," "Family Affair," "Unsinkable Molly Brown," "Sophie," "110 in the Shade," "Golden Boy," "Pousse Cafe," "Mahagonny" (OB), "The Best Little Whorehouse in Texas."

CRAIG, DONALD. Born Aug. 14, 1941 in Abilene, TX. Graduate Hardin-Simmons Col., UTex. Debut 1975 OB in "Do I Hear a Waltz?"(ELT). Bdwy 1977 in "Annie."

CRAIG, JOEL. Born Apr. 26 in NYC. Attended Brandeis U. Bdwy debut 1961 in "Subways Are for Sleeping," followed by "Nowhere to Go but Up," "Hello, Dolly!," "Follies," "Cyrano," "Very Good Eddie," OB in "Out of this World," "Carnival," "Speakeasy."

CRAIN, STEPHEN. Born Oct. 3, 1952 in Tokyo, Japan. Graduate MIT, Boston U. Bdwy debut 1979 in "Oklahoma!"

CRAWFORD, SCOTT. Born Dec. 25, 1949 in Chicago, IL. Graduate UIll. Bdwy debut 1977 in "Caesar and Cleopatra," OB in "The Mischief You Foresee."

CRISCUOLO, LOU. Born Jan 23, 1934 in NYC. Attended Actors Studio. Debut 1964 OB in "Matty, the Moron and the Madonna," followed by "Hooray! It's a Glorious Day," "Smith," "Rubbers," "Yanks 3, Detroit 0," "The Derby," Bdwy in "Man of La Mancha," "Hurry Harry."

CROFOOT, LEONARD JOHN. Born Sept. 20, 1948 in Utica, NY. Bdwy debut 1968 in "The Happy Time," followed by "Come Summer," "Gigi," "Barnum," OB in "Circus," "Joseph and the Amazing Technicolor Dreamcoat."

CROFT, PADDY. Born in Worthing, Eng. Attended Avondale Col. Debut 1961 OB in "The Hostage," followed by "Billy Liar," "Live Like Pigs," "Hogan's Goat," "Long Day's Journey Into Night," "Shadow of a Gunman," "Pygmalion," "The Plough and the Stars"(LC), Bdwy in "Killing of Sister George," "The Prime of Miss Jean Brodie," "Crown Matrimonial," "Major Barbara."

CRONIN, JANE. Born Apr. 4, 1936 in Boston, MA. Attended Boston U. Bdwy debut 1965 in "Postmark Zero," OB in "Bald Soprano," "One Flew over the Cuckoo's Nest," "Hot 1 Baltimore," "The Gathering," "Catsplay," "The Violano Virtuoso," "Afternoons in Vegas," "The Frequency," "A Month in the Country."

CROTHERS, JOEL. Born Jan. 28, 1941 in Cincinnati, OH. Harvard graduate. Bdwy debut 1953 in "The Remarkable Mr. Pennypacker," followed by "A Case of Libel," "Barefoot in the Park," "The Jockey Club Stakes," OB in "Easter," "The Office Murders."

CROUSE, LINDSAY ANN. Born May 12, 1948 in NYC. Radcliffe graduate. Bdwy debut 1972 in "Much Ado About Nothing." OB in "The Foursome," "Fishing," "Long Day's Journey into Night," "Total Recall," "Father's Day," "Hamlet," "Reunion."

CROYDON, JOAN. Born May 15, 1908 in NYC. Bdwy debut 1923 in "Romeo and Juliet," and subsequently in, among others, "The Miracle," "Mima," "First Crocus," "The Bad Seed," "Major Barbara."

CRYER, GRETCHEN. Born Oct. 17, 1935 in Indianapolis, IN. Graduate DePauw U. Bdwy U. in "Little Me," "110 in the Shade," OB in "Now Is the Time for All Good Men," "Gallery," "Circle of Sound," "I'm Getting My Act Together . . ."

CUERVO, ALMA. Born Aug. 13, in Tampa, FL. Graduated Tulane U., Yale U. Debut 1977 OB in "Uncommon Women and Others," followed by "A Foot in the Door," Bdwy in "Once in a Lifetime," "Bedroom Farce," "Censored Scenes from King Kong."

CULLUM, JOHN. Born Mar. 2, 1930 in Knoxville, TN. Graduate U. Tenn. Bdwy bow 1960 in "Camelot," followed by "Infidel Caesar," "The Rehearsal," "Hamlet," "On a Clear Day You Can See Forever" for which he received a Theatre World Award," "Man of LaMancha," "1776," "Vivat! Vivat Regina!," "Shenandoah," "Kings," "The Trip Back Down," "On the 20 Century," "Deathtrap," OB in "Three Hand Reel," "The Elizabethans," "Carousel," "In the Voodoo Parlor of Marie Leveau," "The King and I" (JB).

CUNNINGHAM, JOHN. Born June 22, 1932 in Auburn, NY. Graduate of Yale and Dartmouth. OB in "Love Me Little," "Pimpernel," "The Fantasticks," "Love and Let Love," "The Bone Room," "Dancing in the Dark," "Father's Day," "Snapshot," Bdwy in "Hot Spot," "Zorba," "Company," "1776."

CURRY, CHRISTOPHER. Born Oct. 22, 1948 in Grand Rapids, MI. Graduated UMich. Debut 1974 OB in "When You Comin' Back, Red Ryder?" followed by "The Cherry Orchard," "Spelling Bee," "Ballymurphy," "Isadora Duncan Sleeps with the Russian Navy," "The Promise," "Mecca," Bdwy in "The Crucifer of Blood."

CURTIS, KEENE. Born Feb. 15, 1925 in Salt Lake City, UT. Graduate UUtah. Bdwy bow 1949 in "Shop at Sly Corner," with APA in "School for Scandal," "The Tavern," "Anatole," "Scapin," "Right You Are," "Importance of Being Earnest," "Twelfth Night," "King Lear," "Seagull," "Lower Depths," "Man and Superman," "Judith," "War and Peace," "You Can't Take It With You." "Pantagleize," "Cherry Orchard," "Misanthrope," "Cocktail Party," "Cock-a-Doodle Dandy" and "Hamlet," "A Patriot for Me," "The Rothchilds," "Night Watch," "Via Galactica," "Annie," OB in "Colette," "Ride across Lake Constance."

CUSACK, PHILIP. Born May 10, 1934 in Boston, MA. Attended Emerson Col. Bdwy bow 1966 in "3 Bags Full," followed by "God's Favorite," "The Good Doctor," "The Gingerbread Lady," "Children, Children," "Let Me Hear You Smile," "California Suite," "They're Playing Our Song," OB in "Boys in the Band."

CUSHMAN, NANCY. Born Apr. 26, 1913 in Brooklyn, NY. Graduate Rollins Col. Bdwy in "White Man," "Storm Over Patsy," "Gloriana," "Janie," "Be Your Age," "J.B.," "Little Me," "Skyscraper," "Harold," OB in "American Dream," "Child Buyer," "Sondra," "Dear Oscar," "Poets from the Inside."

CYPKIN, DIANE. Born Sept. 10, 1948 in Munich, Ger. Attended Brooklyn Col. Bdwy debut 1966 in "Let's Sing Yiddish," followed by "Papa Get Married," "Light, Lively and Yiddish," OB in "Yoshke Musikant," "Stempenyu," "Big Winner," "A Millionaire in Trouble."

DAILEY, IRENE. Born Sept. 12, 1920 in NYC. Bdwy debut 1943 in "Nine Girls," followed by "Truckline Cafe," "Idiot's Delight" (CC), "Miss Lonelyhearts," "Andorra," "The Subject Was Roses," "You Know I Can't Hear You When . . . ," OB in "Good Woman of Setzuan," "Rooms," "The Loves of Cass McGuire."

DALE, JIM. Born in 1936 in Rothwell, Eng. Debut 1974 OB with Young Vic Co. in "Taming of the Shrew," followed by "Scapino" that moved to Bdwy, "Barnum."

DANA, LEORA. Born Apr. 1, 1923 in NYC. Attended Barnard Col., RADA. Bdwy debut 1947 in "Madwoman of Chaillot," followed by "Happy Time," "Point of No Return," "Sabrina Fair," "Best Man," "Beekman Place," "The Last of Mrs. Lincoln," "The Women," "Mourning Pictures," OB in "In the Summer House," "Wilder's Triple Bill," "Collision Course," "Bird of Dawning," "The Increased Difficulty of Concentration," "Place without Mornings," "Rebel Women," "The Tennis Game," "The Loves of Cass McGuire," "Time steps."

DANIEL, GARY. Born Sept. 22, 1948 in San Angelo, TX. Graduate USColo. Bdwy debut 1979 in "Peter Pan."

DANNER, BLYTHE. Born in Philadelphia, PA. Graduate Bard Col. Debut 1966 OB in "The Infantry," followed by "Collision Course," "Summertree," "Up Eden," "Someone's Comin' Hungry," LCRep's "Cyrano" and "The Miser" for which she received a Theatre World Award, "Twelfth Night," Bdwy in "Butterflies Are Free" (1969), BAM'S "New York Idea," "Betrayal."

DANSON, RANDY. Born Apr. 30, 1950 in Plainfield, NJ. Graduate Carnegie Mellon. Debut 1978 OB in "Gimme Shelter," followed by "Big and Little," "The Winter Dancers," "Time Steps."

DANZIGER, MAIA. Born Apr. 12, 1950. Attended NYU. Debut 1973 in "Waltz of the Toreadors," OB in "Total Eclipse," "Milk of Paradise."

DaPRATO, WILLIAM. Born Sept. 22, 1924 in The Bronx, NY. Attended TSDA. Debut 1963 OB in "The Burning," followed by "Holy Ghosts," "Awake and Sing," "Not Like Him," "Kohlhass," Bdwy in "Mike Downstairs," "Shenandoah."

D'ARCY, MARY. Born in 1956 in Yardville, NJ. Graduate Glassboro State Col. Bdwy debut 1980 in "The Music Man."

DARNAY, TONI. Born Aug. 11 in Chicago, IL. Attended Northwestern U. Debut OB 1942 in "Name Your Poison," followed by "When the Bough Breaks," "Nocturne in Daylight," "The Gold Watch," "Possibilities," "The Music Man" (JB), Bdwy in "Sadie Thompson" (1944), "Affair of Honor," "Life with Father"(CC), "The Women," "Molly," "The Heiress," "Vieux Carre."

DARWICK, BETH. Born June 7, 1933 in NYC. Attended School of Social Research, HB Studio. Debut 1973 OB in "A Memory of Childhood," followed by "Lady of the Larkspur Lotion," "Lovely Rita," "Yank in Beverly Hills."

DAVID, CLIFFORD. Born June 30, 1932 in Toledo, OH. Attended UToledo, Actos Studio. Bdwy debut 1960 in "Caligula," followed by "Wildcat," "Aspern Papers," "On a Clear Day You Can See Forever," "A Joyful Noise," "1776," OB in "Boys from Syracuse," "Camino Real," "Museum," "Holy Places."

DAVIDSON, JACK. Born July 17, 1936 in Worcester, MA. Graduate Boston U. Debut 1968 OB in "Moon for the Misbegotten," followed by "Big and Little," "The Battle of Angels," "Midsummer Night's Dream," "Hot l Baltimore," "A Tribute to Lili Lamont," "Ulysses in Traction," "Lulu," "Hey, Rube," "In the Recovery Lounge," "The Runner Stumbles," "Winter Signs," "Hamlet," "Mary Stuart," "Ruby Ruby Sam Sam," Bdwy in "Capt. Brassbound's Conversion" (1972), "Anna Christie."

DAVIES, DAVID. (A.K.A. David Davis). Born Feb. 5, 1941 in Washington, DC. Graduate Wake Forest, UMd., Wayne State U. Debut 1971 OB in "Hamlet," followed by "A Flea in Her Ear," "Warbeck," "Economic Necessity," Bdwy 1979 in "Bent."

DAVIS, ANDREW. Born Aug. 9, 1950 in San Antonio, TX. Graduate UNew Orleans, Yale. Bdwy debut 1978 in "Crucifer of Blood," OB in "Word of Mouth," "Says I Says He," "Dreck/Vile," "Justice."

DAVIS, BRUCE ANTHONY. Born Mar. 4, 1959 in Dayton, OH. Attended Juilliard. Bdwy debut 1979 in "Dancin'."

DAVIS, CLAYTON. Born May 18, 1948 in Pensacola, FL. Graduate Princeton, U., FlaStateU. Debut 1978 OB in "Oklahoma!"

DAVIS, DONNA. Born June 28, 1949 in Elkin, NC. Graduate UNC. Bdwy debut 1978 in "Angel," followed by "Filumena," OB in "Getting Out, "Radical Solutions," "The Mousetrap."

DAVISON, BRUCE. Born June 28, 1946 in Philadelphia, PA. Graduate Penn State, NYU. Debut 1969 OB in "A Home Away From," followed by LCRep's "Tiger at the Gates," "A Cry of Players," "King Lear," Bdwy 1980 in "The Elephant Man."

DAWSON, ANN-MAXINE. Born Mar. 30 in NYC. Attended Carnegie-Mellon U., NYU. Debut 1980 OB in "Annie Get Your Gun" (ELT).

DAWSON, CURT. Born Dec. 5, 1941 in Kansas. Graduate RADA. Debut 1968 OB in "Futz," followed by "Boys in the Band," "Not Now, Darling," "White Nights," "Enter a Free Man," "You Never Can Tell," "Dona Rosita," "The Penultimate Problem of Sherlock Holmes," Bdwy 1975 in "Absurd Person Singular."

DEAN, JACQUE. Born Jan. 21 in Washington, DC. Attended UMd., HB Studio. Debut 1961 OB in "Little Mary Sunshine," followed by "Gorky, "Mata Hari," "Ruby Ruby Sam Sam," Bdwy in "The Student Gypsy," "Lolita My Love," "Coco," "Dear World," "I'm Solomon," "Drat! The Cat!," "I Had a Ball."

de BANZIE, LOIS. Born May 4 in Glasgow, Scot. Bdwy debut 1966 in "Elizabeth the Queen," followed by "Da," "Morning's at 7," OB in "Little Murders," "Mary Stuart," "People Are Living There," "Ride Across Lake Constance," "The Divorce of Judy and Jane," "What the Butler Saw," "Man and Superman," "The Judas Applause."

DeFABEES, RICHARD. Born Apr. 4, 1947 in Englewood, NJ. Graduate Georgetown U. Debut 1973 OB in "Creeps," followed by "Monsters (Sideshow)," Bdwy in "The Skin of Our Teeth," "Whose Life Is It Anyway?"

DeFRANK, ROBERT. Born Nov. 29, 1945 in Baltimore, MD. Graduate Towson State, Essex Community Col. Debut 1977 OB in "The Crazy Locomotive," followed by "The Taming of the Shrew," "The Madman and the Nun," "The Good Parts."

DeGHELDER, STEPHAN. Born Oct. 6, 1945 in Independence, MO. Attended UMo. Debut 1959 OB in "Once upon a Mattress," followed by "It's a Mod Mod World," "Sancocho," "Anyone Can Whistle," Bdwy in "Hello, Dolly!" (1967), "Celebration."

DEITCH, DAN. Born Oct. 26, 1945 in San Francisco, CA. Graduate Princeton, Yale, LAMDA. Bdwy debut 1972 in "Grease," OB in "Troilus and Cressida," "Verdict."

DeKOVEN, ROGER. Born Oct. 22, 1907 in Chicago, IL. Attended UChicago, Northwestern, Columbia. Bdwy bow 1926 in "Juarez and Maximilian," followed by "Mystery Man," "Once in a Lifetime," "Counselor-at-Law," "Murder in the Cathedral," "Eternal Road," "Brooklyn U.S.A.," "The Assassin," "Joan of Lorraine," "Abie's Irish Rose," "The Lark," "Hidden River," "Compulsion," "Miracle Worker," "Fighting Cock," "Herzl," "Strider," OB in "Deadly Game," "Steal the Old Man's Bundle," "St. Joan," "Tiger at the Gates," "Walking to Waldheim," "Cyrano de Bergerac," "An Enemy of the People," "Ice Age," "Prince of Homburg," "Biography: A Game," "Strider."

DEL REGNO, JOHN. Born Apr. 27, 1947 in NYC. Attended HB Studio. Debut 1979 OB in "Sorrows of Stephen."

DeMAIO, PETER. Born in Hartford, CT. Attended New School, Juilliard. Debut 1961 OB in "Threepenny Opera," followed by "Secret Life of Walter Mitty," "Dark of the Moon," "Welcome to Black River," "Last Breeze of Summer," "After the Rise," Bdwy in "Billy," "Indians," "The Changing Room."

DEMPSEY, JEROME. Born Mar. 1, 1929 in St. Paul, MN. Toledo U graduate. Bdwy bow 1959 in "West Side Story," followed by "The Deputy," "Spofford," "Room Service," "Love Suicide at Schofield Barracks," "Dracula," OB in "Cry of Players," "Year Boston Won the Pennant," "The Crucible," "Justice Box," "Trelawny of the Wells," "The Old Glory," "Six Characters in Search of an Author," "Threepenny Opera," BAM's "Johnny on the Spot," "The Barbarians," "He and She."

DeMUNN, JEFFREY P. Born Apr. 25, 1947 in Buffalo, NY. Graduate Union Col. Debut 1975 OB in "Augusta," followed by "A Prayer for My Daughter," "Modigliani," Bdwy in "Comedians," "Bent."

DENNISTON, LESLIE. Born May 19, 1950 in San Francisco, CA. Attended HB Studio. Bdwy debut 1976 in "Shenandoah" followed by "Happy New Year" for which she received a Theatre World Award.

DENTINGER, JANE. Born Sept. 9, 1951 in Rochester, NY. Ithaca Col. graduate. Debut 1974 OB in "All My Sons," followed by "Pericles," "Vanities."

DeRAEY, DANIEL. Born Apr. 2, 1946 in NYC. Graduate Fordham U. Debut 1979 OB in "Class Enemy."

DESAI, SHELLY. Born Dec. 3, 1935 in Bombay, India. Graduate Okla. State U. Debut 1968 OB in "The Indian Wants the Bronx," followed by "Babu," "Wonderful Year," "Jungle of Cities," "Gandhi," "Savages," "Cuchulain."

DeSALVO, ANNE. Born Apr. 3 in Philadelphia, PA. OB in "Iphigenia in Aulis," "Lovers and Other Strangers," "The First Warning," "Warringham Roof," "God Bless You, Mr. Rosewater," Bdwy 1977 in "Gemini."

DeSANTIS, JOE. Born June 16, 1909 in NYC. Attended CCNY, Beaux Arts Inst. Bdwy debut 1931 in "Sirena," followed by "Saul," "Cyrano de Bergerac," "Count of Monte Cristo," "Othello," "Les Miserables," "Camille," "St. Helena," "Journey to Jerusalem," "Walk into My Parlor," "Arsenic and Old Lace," "Men in Shadow," "Storm Operation," "The Searching Wind," "Front Page," "Golden Boy," "In Any Language," "The Highest Tree," "Daughter of Silence," "Horowitz and Mrs. Washington."

DeSHIELDS, ANDRE. Born Jan. 12, 1946 in Baltimore, MD. Graduate UWisc. Bdwy debut 1973 in "Warp," followed by "Rachel Lily Rosenbloom," "The Wiz," "Ain't Misbehavin," OB in "2008½."

DESMOND, EILEEN. Born Dec. 26, 1950 in Kohler, WI. Attended Ripon Col., Wisc. State. Debut 1976 OB in "Master Psychologist," followed by "Footworks," "Hedda Gabler."

DeVRIES, JON. Born Mar. 26, 1947 in NYC. Graduate Bennington Col., Padasena Playhouse. Debut 1977 OB in "The Cherry Orchard," followed by "Agamemnon," Bdwy in "The Inspector General," "Devour the Snow," "Major Barbara."

DIAKUN, ALEX. Born Feb. 8, 1946 in Rycroft, Alb., Can. Graduate UAlberta. Debut 1979 OB in "The Winter Dancers."

DILLEHAY, KAYLYN. Born Dec. 1, 1954 in Oklahoma City, OK. Attended TCU, OkCityU. Debut 1976 OB in "Follies," followed by "Carnival," "Beowulf," Bdwy 1980 in "Canterbury Tales."

DILLON, DENNY. Born May 18, 1951 in Cleveland, OH. Graduate Syracuse U. Bdwy debut 1974 in "Gypsy," followed by "The Skin of Our Teeth," "Harold and Maude."

DILLON, MIA. Born July 9, 1955 in Colorado Springs, CO. Graduate Penn State U. Bdwy debut 1977 in "Equus," followed by "Da," "Once a Catholic," OB in "The Crucible."

DIXON, ED. Born Sept. 2, 1948 in Oklahoma. Attended OklaU. Bdwy in "The Student Prince," followed by "No, No Nanette," OB in "By Bernstein," "King of the Schnorrers."

DOLINER, ROY. Born June 27, 1954 in Boston, MA. Attended Tufts U., HB Studio. Debut 1977 OB in "Don't Cry, Child, Your Father's 'an American," followed by "Zwi Kanar Show," "Big Bad Burlesque."

DONEGAN, MARTIN. Born Nov. 11, 1931 in County Longford, Ire. Debut 1959 OB in "The Shy and Lonely," followed by "The Plough and the Stars," "A Village Wooing," "Before I Wake," "Broadway," "Marlon Brando Sat Right Here."

DONNELLY, DONAL. Born July 6, 1931 in Bradford, Eng. Bdwy debut 1966 in "Philadelphia, Here I Come," followed by "A Day in the Death of Joe Egg," "Sleuth," "The Faith Healer," "The Elephant Man," OB in "My Astonishing Self."

DONNET, MARY. Born July 18, 1953 in Englewood, NJ. Graduate Sarah Lawrence Col. Debut OB in "La Ronde," followed by "Come Back to the 5 & Dime, Jimmy Dean."

DOOLITTLE, JOHN. Born Oct. 9, 1947 in Chicago, IL. Graduate US Naval Acad., Yale. Bdwy debut 1979 in "1940's Radio Hour."

DORFMAN, ROBERT. Born Oct. 8, 1950 in Brooklyn, NY. Attended CUNY, HB Studio. Debut 1979 OB in "Say Goodnight, Gracie."

DOTRICE, ROY. Born May 26, 1925 in Guernsey, Channel Islands. Bdwy debut 1967 in "Brief Lives," a return engagement in 1974, "Mr. Lincoln" (1980).

DOVA, NINA. Born Jan. 15, 1926 in London, Eng. Attended Neighborhood Playhouse. Debut 1954 OB in "I Feel Wonderful," followed by "A Delicate Balance," "Naked," "Strider," Bdwy in "Zorba," "The Rothschilds," "Saturday Sunday Monday," "Strider."

DOW, RICHARD A. Born Aug. 30, 1941 in Cambridge, MA. Graduate UPa. Debut 1970 OB in "The Dirtiest Show in Town," followed by "Baba Goya," "Nourish the Beast," "Hothouse," "Action," "International Stud," "Bird with Silver Feathers," "Lenz."

DOWNING, VIRGINIA. Born Mar. 7 in Washington, DC. Attended Bryn Mawr. OB in "Juno and the Paycock," "Man with the Golden Arm," "Palm Tree in a Rose Garden," "Play with a Tiger," "The Wives," "The Idiot," "Medea," "Mrs. Warren's Profession," "Mercy Street," "Thunder Rock," "Pygmalion," "First Week in Bogota," "Rimers of Eldritch," "Les Blancs," "Shadow of a Gunman," "All the Way Home" (ELT), Bdwy in "Father Malachy's Miracle," "Forward the Heart," "The Cradle Will Rock, "A Gift of Time," "We Have Always Lived in the Castle."

DRAKE, JUDITH. Born Feb. 9 in Tulsa, OK. Graduate UTulsa. Bdwy debut 1968 in "Hello, Dolly!," followed by "Lysistrata," OB in "The Guardsman," "My Great Dead Sister."

DREYFUSS, RICHARD. Born in 1948 in Brooklyn, NY. Bdwy debut 1969 in "But Seriously," OB in "Line," "Julius Caesar," "Othello."

DRIVER, JOHN. Born Jan. 16, 1947 in Erie, PA. Graduate Smith Col., Northwestern U. Debut OB 1972 in "One Flew over the Cuckoo's Nest," followed by "Scrambled Feet," Bdwy in "Grease" (1973), "Over Here" for which he received a Theatre World Award.

DRUM, LEONARD. Born Feb. 21 in Pittsfield, MA. Graduate UNMex., Columbia. OB in "Kaleidoscope," "The Golden Six," "On the Town," "O Marry Me!," "The Giants' Dance," "Gay Divorce," "An Evening of Theatre Comedy," Bdwy 1967 in "Marat/deSade." (1967), "Whoopee!"

DUDLEY, CRAIG. Born Jan. 22, 1945 in Sheepshead Bay, NY. Graduate AADA, AmThWing. Debut 1970 OB in "Macbeth," followed by "Zou," "Othello," "War and Peace."

DUELL, WILLIAM. Born Aug. 30, in Corinth, NY Attended Ill. Wesleyan, Yale. OB in "Portrait of the Artist . . .," "Barroom Monks," "Midsummer Night's Dream," "Henry IV," "Taming of the Shrew," "The Memorandum," "Threepenny Opera," "Loves of Cass McGuire," Bdwy in "A Cook for Mr. General," "Ballad of the Sad Cafe," "Ilya, Darling," "1776," "Kings," "Stages," "The Inspector General."

DUKES, DAVID. Born June 6, 1945 in San Francisco, CA. Attended Mann Col. Bdwy debut 1971 in "School for Wives," followed by "Don Juan," "The Play's the Thing," "The Visit," "Chemin de Fer," "Holiday," "Rules of the Game," "Love for Love," "Travesties," "Dracula," "Bent," OB in "Rebel Women."

DUNCAN, SANDY. Born Feb. 20, 1946 in Henderson TX. Attended Len Morris Col. NY debut 1965 in CC's revivals of "The Music Man," "Carousel," "Finian's Rainbow," "Sound of Music," "Wonderful Town," and "Life with Father," OB in "Ceremony of Innocence" for which she received a Theatre World Award, "Your Own Thing," Bdwy in "Canterbury Tales" (1969), "Love Is a Time of Day," "The Boy Friend" (1970), "Peter Pan" (1979).

DUNNE, GRIFFIN. Born June 8, 1955 in NYC. Attended Neighborhood Playhouse. Debut 1980 OB in "Marie and Bruce."

EARLE, EDWARD. Born Dec. 20, 1929 in Santa Barbara, CA. Graduate USC. Bdwy debut 1959 in "The Dark at the Top of the Stairs," followed by "Viva Madison Avenue," "Show Me Where the Good Times Are," "Roar of the Greasepaint," "Musical Chairs."

EBERT, JOYCE. Born June 26, 1933 in Homestead, PA. Carnegie Tech graduate. Debut 1956 OB in "Liliom," followed by "Sign of Winter," "Asmodee," "King Lear," "Hamlet," "Under Milkwood," "Trojan Women," "White Devil," "Tartuffe," Bdwy in "Solitaire/Double Solitaire" (1971), "The Shadow Box," "Watch on the Rhine" (1980).

eda-YOUNG, BARBARA. Born Jan. 30, 1945 in Detroit, MI. Bdwy debut 1968 in "Lovers and Other Strangers," OB in "The Hawk," LCRep's "The Time of Your Life," "Camino Real," "Operation Sidewinder," "Kool Aid" and "A Streetcar Named Desire," "The Gathering," "The Terrorists," "Drinks before Dinner," "Shout Across the River."

EDE, GEORGE. Born Dec. 22, 1931 in San Francisco, CA. Bdwy debut 1969 in "A Flea in Her Ear," followed by "Three Sisters," "The Changing Room," "The Visit," "Chemin de Fer," "Holiday," "Love for Love," "Rules of the Game," "Member of the Wedding," "Lady from the Sea," "A Touch of the Poet," OB in "The Philanderer," "The American Clock."

EDMONDS, LOUIS. Born Sept. 24, 1923 in Baton Rouge, LA. Attended Carnegie Tech. OB in "Life in Louisiana," "Way of the World," "The Cherry Orchard," "Uncle Vanya," "Duchess of Malfi," "Ernest in Love," "The Rapists," "Amoureuse," "The Interview," Bdwy in "Candide," "Maybe Tuesday," "The Killer," "Passage to India," "Fire!," "Otherwise Engaged."

EDWARDS, BRANDT. Born Mar. 22, 1947 in Holly Springs, MS. Graduate UMiss. NY debut off and on Bdwy 1975 in "A Chorus Line."

EDWARDS, SUSAN. Born Aug. 24, 1950 in Levittown, NY. Graduate Hofstra U. Bdwy debut 1976 in "Bubbling Brown Sugar," OB in "Jazz Babies," "The Boys from Syracuse"(ELT), "Scrambled Feet."

EISENBERG, NED. Born Jan. 13, 1957 in NYC. Attended Cal. Inst. of Arts, HB Studio. Debut 1980 OB in "The Time of the Cuckoo"(ELT).

ELIC, JOSEP. Born Mar. 21, 1921 in Butte, MT. Attended UWisc. Debut OB in "Threepenny Opera," followed by "Don Juan in Hell," "Leave It to Jane," "Comic Strip," "Coriolanus," "Too Much Johnson," "Stag Movie," "Rise and Fall of Burlesque Humor," "Big Bad Burlesque," Bdwy in "Hamlet," "Baptiste," "West Side Story," "Sign in Sidney Brustein's Window," "Kelly."

ELLIN, DAVID. Born Jan. 10, 1925 in Montreal, Can. Attended AADA. Bdwy in "Swan Song," "West Side Story," "Education of Hyman Kaplan," "Light, Lively and Yiddish," OB in "Trees Die Standing," "Mirele Efros," "End of All Things Natural," "Yoshe Kalb," "Fiddler on the Roof"(JB), "Rebecca, the Rabbi's Daughter."

ELLINGTON, MERCEDES. Born Feb. 9, 1949 in NYC. Juilliard graduate. Bdwy debut 1970 in "No, No, Nanette," followed by "The Grand Tour," "Happy New Year," "Black Broadway," OB in "Around the World"(JB), "An Evening of Jerome Kern."

ELLIOTT, ALICE. Born Aug. 22, 1950 in Durham, NC. Graduate Carnegie-Mellon U, Goodman Theatre. Debut 1972 OB in "In the Time of Harry Harass," followed by "American Gothics," "Bus Stop," "As You Like It."

ELLIOTT, PATRICIA. Born July 21, 1942 in Gunnison, CO. Graduate U. Colo., London Academy. Debut with LCRep 1968 in "King Lear," and "A Cry of Players," followed OB in "Henry V," "The Persians," "A Doll's House," "Hedda Gabler," "In case of Accident," "Water Hen," "Folly," "But Not for Me," "By Bernstein," "Prince of Homburg," "Artichokes," "Wine Untouched," Bdwy bow 1973 in "A Little Night Music" for which she received a Theatre World Award, followed by "The Shadow Box," "Tartuffe," "13 Rue de L'Amour," "The Elephant Man."

ELLIS, SCOTT. Born Apr. 19, 1957 in Washington, DC. Attended Goodman Theatre. Bdwy debut in "Grease," followed by "Musical Chairs," OB in "Mrs. Dally Has a Lover."

ELSTON, ROBERT. Born May 29, 1934 in NYC. Graduate Hunter Col., CCNY. Bdwy debut 1958 in "Maybe Tuesday," followed by "Tall Story," "Golden Fleecing," "Spoon River Anthology," "You Know I Can't Hear You When . . . ," "Vivat! Vivat Regina!," OB in "Undercover Man," "Conditioned Reflex," "Archy and Mehitabel," "Notes from the Underground."

EMERSON, JONATHAN. Born Apr. 22, 1955 in Huntington, WVA. Harvard graduate. Debut 1979 OB in "Dawn," followed by "Romeo and Juliet"(ELT).

ENSLEY, EVERETT. Born June 21, 1931 in NYC. Debut 1964 OB in "Automation," followed by "Mummers Play," "My Sister, My Sister," "One Last Look," "Yank in Beverly Hills."

EPSTEIN, ALVIN. Born May 14, 1925 in NYC. Attended Queens Col., Decroux School of Mime. Appeared on Bdwy with Marcel Marceau, and in "King Lear," "Waiting for Godot," "From A to Z," "No Strings," "The Passion of Josef D.," "Postmark Zero," "A Kurt Weill Cabaret," OB in "Purple Dust," "Pictures in a Hallway," "Clerambard," "Endgame," "Whores, Wares and Tin Pan Alley," "A Place Without Doors."

EPSTEIN, PIERRE. Born July 27, 1930 in Toulouse, France. Graduate UParis, Columbia. Bdwy bow 1962 in "A Shot in the Dark," followed by "Enter Laughing," "Bajour," "Black Comedy," "Thieves," "Fun City," "Filumena," OB in "Incident at Vichy," "Threepenny Opera," "Too Much Johnson," "Second City," "People vs. Ranchman," "Promenade," "Cakes with Wine," "Little Black Sheep," "Comedy of Errors," "A Memory of Two Mondays," "They Knew What They Wanted," "Museum," "The Bright and Golden Land," "Manny," "God Bless You, Mr. Rosewater."

ESTERMAN, LAURA. Born Apr. 12, in NYC. Attended Radcliffe, LAMDA. Debut 1969 OB in "The Time of Your Life," (LCR), followed by "Pig Pen," "The Carpenters," "Ghosts, "Waltz of the Toreadors," "Macbeth" (LC), "The Seagull," "Rubbers," "Yanks 3, Detroit 0", "Golden Boy," "Out of Our Father's House," "The Master and Margarita," "Chinchilla," "Dusa, Fish, Stas and Vi," Bdwy 1974 "God's Favorite," "Teibele and Her Demon."

ESTES, MICHAEL P. Born July 10, 1955 in St. Louis, MO. Attended Butler U. Debut 1978 OB in "Can-Can," followed by "Mary," Bdwy 1979 "Peter Pan."

ESTEY, SUELLEN. Born Nov. 21 in Mason City, IA. Graduate Stephens Col., Northwestern U. Debut 1970 OB in "Some Other Time," followed by "June Moon," "Buy Bonds Buster," "Smile, Smile, Smile," "Carousel," "The Lullaby of Broadway," "I Can't Keep Running," Bdwy 1972 in "The Selling of the President."

EVANS, PETER. Born May 27, 1950 in Englewood, NJ. Graduate Yale, London Central School of Speech. Debut OB 1975 in "Life Class," followed by "Streamers," "A Life in the Theatre," "Don Juan Comes Back from the War," "The American Clock," Bdwy in "Night and Day" (1979).

EVERETT, TOM. Born Oct. 21, 1948 in Oregon. Graduate NYU, LAMDA. Debut 1972 OB in "Elizabeth I," followed by "Boccaccio," "Hosanna," "A Midsummer Night's Dream," "A Life in the Theatre," "Winning Isn't Everything," "Rockaway Boulevard," "Dance for Me Simeon," Bdwy in "Habeas Corpus."

FABER, RON. Born Feb. 16, 1933 in Milwaukee, WI. Graduate Marquette U. Debut OB 1959 in "An Enemy of the People," followed by "The Exception and the Rule," "America, Hurrah," "Ubu Cocu," "Terminal," "They Put Handcuffs on Flowers," "Dr. Selavy's Magic Theatre," "Troilus and Cressida," "The Beauty Part," "Woyzeck," "St. Joan of the Stockyards," "Jungle of Cities," Bdwy in "Medea" (1973), "First Monday in October."

FABIANI, JOEL. Born Sept. 28, 1936 in Watsonville, CA. Attended LaSierra, Actors Workshop. Debut 1963 OB in "Dark Corners," followed by "Ashes," "I'm Getting My Act Together . . . ," Bdwy in "Love for Love," "Beyond the Fringe," "Rules of the Game."

FAIRBANK, SPRING. Born Mar. 15, 1941 in Chicago, IL. Attended New Eng. Consv. Debut 1968 in "My Fair Lady"(CC), followed by OB "Oh, Lady, Lady"(ELT), "Ludlow Ladd," Bdwy in "Very Good Eddie" (1975).

FAIRFAX, SARAH. Born July 12, 1954 in Evanston, IL. Juilliard graduate. Has appeared OB in "Stage Door," "Trade-Offs," "Alcestis," "Oedipus Rex," with Potter's Field Co.

FALKENHAIN, PATRICIA. Born Dec. 3, 1926 in Atlanta, GA. Graduate Carnegie-Mellon, NYU. Debut 1946 OB in "Juno and the Paycock," followed by "Hamlet," "She Stoops to Conquer," "Peer Gynt," "Henry IV," "The Plough and the Stars," "Lysistrata," "Beaux Stratagem," "The Power and the Glory," "M. Amilcar," Bdwy in "Waltz of the Toreadors," "The Utter Glory of Morrissey Hall," "Once a Catholic."

FARER, RHONDA. Born Oct. 19, 1951 in Colonia, NJ. Graduate Rider Col. Debut 1973 in "Rachel Lily Rosenbloom," followed by "They're Playing Our Song," OB in "The Dog Beneath the Skin."

FARIN, PAUL. Born July 1, 1947 in NYC. Graduate St. Michaels, Catholic U. Debut 1980 OB in "Elizabeth and Essex."

FARR, KIMBERLY. Born Oct. 16, 1948 in Chicago, IL. Graduate UCLA. Bdwy debut 1972 in "Mother Earth," followed by "The Lady from the Sea," "Going Up," "Happy New Year," OB in "More Than You Deserve," "The S. S. Benchley," "At Sea with Benchley."

FARRINGTON, RALPH. Born Nov. 8, 1954 in Brooklyn, NY. Graduate SUNY/Purchase. Debut 1968 OB in "Finian's Rainbow," Bdwy in "Your Arms Too Short to Box with God," "The Wiz."

| Craig Dudley | Mercedes Ellington | Tom Everett | Joy Franz | Clebert Ford |

FAWCETT, ROGER. Born Apr. 28, 1943 in Brooklyn, NY. Attended AmTh-Wing. Debut 1962 OB in "Murder in the Cathedral," followed by "The Infernal Machine," "Oldest Trick in the World," "Hollow Crown," "The Skin of Our Teeth," "I Can't Go On Without You, Minna Mandelbaum," "Three Musketeers," "Loves of Cass McGuire."

FEAGAN, LESLIE. Born Jan. 9, 1951 in Hinckley, OH. Graduate Ohio U. Debut 1978 OB in "Can-Can," followed by "Merton of the Movies" (ELU).

FEARL, CLIFFORD. Born in NYC; graduate Columbia U. Bdwy debut 1950 in "Flahooley," followed by "Three Wishes for Jamie," "Two's Company," "Kismet," "Happy Hunting," "Oh, Captain," "Redhead," "Let It Ride," "110 in the Shade," "Ben Franklin in Paris," "Mame," "La Plume de Ma Tante," "Dear World," "Jimmy," "My Fair Lady," "The Music Man"(JB).

FELDER, CLARENCE. Born Sept 2, 1938 in St. Matthews, SC. Debut 1964 OB in "The Room," followed by "Are You Now or Have You Ever Been?," "Claw," "Henry V," "The Winter Dancers," Bdwy in "Red, White and Maddox," "Love for Love," "Rules of the Game," "Golden Boy," "A Memory of Two Mondays," "They Knew What They Wanted."

FELDON, BARBARA. Born Mar. 12, 1941 in Pittsburgh, PA. Attended Carnegie Tech. Bdwy debut 1960 in "Caligula," followed by "Past Tense."

FERRELL, ANDY. Born Sept. 9, 1950 in Wilson, NC. Graduate NCStateU. Debut 1976 OB in "The Boys from Syracuse," Bdwy 1980 in "Canterbury Tales."

FERRONE, FRAN. Born Feb. 29, 1948 in Chicago, IL. Graduate Catholic U. Debut 1980 OB in "Elizabeth and Essex."

FIELDS, ROBERT. Born July 10, 1938 in Boston, MA. Graduate Carnegie Tech, Neighborhood Playhouse. Bdwy debut 1967 in "Marat/deSade," OB in "The Good Parts," "Sunday Runners," "Bits and Pieces."

FIELDS, THOR. Born Sept. 19, 1968 in NYC. Bdwy debut 1978 in "The King and I," followed by OB's "Yo Yo," "A Month in the Country," "Camelot" (1980).

FISHER, DOUGLAS. Born July 9, 1934 in Brooklyn, NY. Attended St. John's U, AADA. Debut 1963 OB in "Best Foot Forward," followed by "Frere Jacques," "Devil's Disciple," "Accent on Youth," "Lost in the Stars," "Say, Darling," "Shoestring Revue," "Penthouse Legend," "Call Me Madam," "Marjorie Daw," "God Bless You, Mr. Rosewater."

FITZGERALD, FERN. Born Jan. 7, 1947 in Valley Stream, NY. Bdwy debut 1976 in "Chicago," followed by "A Chorus Line."

FITZGERALD, GERALDINE. Born Nov. 24, 1914 in Dublin, Ire. Bdwy debut 1938 in "Heartbreak House," followed by "Sons and Soldiers," "Doctor's Dilemma," "King Lear," "Hide and Seek," "Ah, Wilderness," "The Shadow Box," "A Touch of the Poet," OB in "Cave Dwellers," "Pigeons," "Long Day's Journey into Night," "Everyman and Roach," "Streetsongs."

FITZPATRICK, JIM. Born Nov. 26, 1950 in Omaha, NE. Attended UNeb. Debut 1977 OB in "Arsenic and Old Lace"(ELT), followed by "Merton of the Movies"(ELT), "Oh, Boy!"

FITZPATRICK, KELLY. Born Dec. 31, 1937 in MT. Kisco, NY. Graduate Hobart Col. Bdwy debut 1971 in "Abelard and Heloise," followed by OB in "The Trial of Denmark Vesey," "Oakville," "Mississippi Moonshine," "Trees in the Wind," "Hothouse," "True History of Squire Jonathan . . . ," "Knitters in the Sun."

FLAGG, FANNIE. Born Sept. 21, 1944 in Birmingham, AL. Attended Pittsburgh Playhouse. Debut 1963 OB in "Just for Opening," followed by "Patio/-Porch," "Come Back to the 5 & Dime, Jimmy Dean," Bdwy 1980 in "The Best Little Whorehouse in Texas."

FLAGG, TOM. Born Mar. 30, 1949 in Canton, OH. Attended Kent State U., AADA. Debut 1975 OB in "The Fantasticks," followed by "Give Me Liberty," "The Subject Was Roses," Bdwy in "Legend," "Shenandoah," "Players."

FLANDERS, ED. Born in 1934 in Minnesota. Bdwy debut 1967 in "The Birthday Party," followed by "A Man for All Seasons," "The Crucible," "Trial of the Catonsville 9," "Moon for the Misbegotten," "Last Licks."

FLANIGAM, LOUISA. Born May 5, 1945 in Chester, SC. Graduate UMd. Debut 1971 OB in "The Shrinking Bride," Bdwy 1976 in "Magic Show," followed by "Most Happy Fella" (1979).

FLETCHER, JACK. Born Apr. 21, 1921 in Forest Hills, NY. Attended Yale. Bdwy debut 1947 in "Trial Honeymoon," followed by "She Stoops to Conquer," "Romeo and Juliet," "Ben Franklin in Paris," "Drat! The Cat!," "Lysistrata," "Lorelei," "Sugar Babies," CC's "Can-Can," "Cyrano," and "Wonderful Town," OB in "Comic Strip," "Way of the World," "Thieves' Carnival," "The Amorous Flea," "American Hamburger League," "The Time of Your Life," "Music Man"(JB).

FLOREK, DAVE. Born May 19, 1953 in Dearborn, MI. Graduate Eastern MiU. Debut 1976 OB in "The Collection," followed by "Richard III," "Much Ado about Nothing," Bdwy 1980 in "Nuts."

FOGARTY, MARY. Born in Manchester, NH. Debut 1959 OB in "The Well of Saints," followed by "Shadow and Substance," "Nathan, the Wise," Bdwy in "The National Health," "Watch on the Rhine" (1980), "Of the Fields Lately."

FOGT, JULIE ANN. Born Apr. 4, 1953 in Galion, OH. Attended UCincinnati. Debut 1979 OB in "On a Clear Day You Can See Forever," "The Sound of Music"(ELT).

FORD, CLEBERT. Born. Jan. 29, 1932 in Brooklyn, NY. Graduate CCNY, Boston U. Bdwy debut 1960 in "The Cool World," followed by "Les Blancs," "Ain't Supposed to Die a Natural Death," "Via Galactica," "Bubbling Brown Sugar," "The Last Minstrel Show," OB in "Romeo and Juliet," "Antony and Cleopatra," "Ti-Jean and His Brothers," "The Blacks," "Ballad for Bimshire," "Daddy," "Gilbeau," "Coriolanus," "Before the Flood."

FORD, RUTH. Born July 7, 1915 in Hazelhurst, MS. Bdwy debut 1938 in "Shoemaker's Holiday," followed by "Danton's Death," "Swingin' the Dream," "No Exit," "This Time Tomorrow," "Clutterbuck," "House of Bernarda Alba," "Island of Goats," "Requiem for a Nun," "The Milk Train Doesn't Stop Here Anymore," "Grass Harp," "Harold and Maude," OB in "Glass Slipper," "Miss Julie," "Madame de Sade," "A Breeze from the Gulf."

FORSYTHE, HENDERSON. Born Sept. 11, 1917 in Macon, MO. Attended UIowa. Debut 1956 OB in "The Iceman Cometh," "The Collection," "The Room," "A Slight Ache," "Happiness Cage," "Waiting for Godot," "In Case of Accident," "Not I" (LC), "An Evening with the Poet-Senator," "Museum," "How Far Is It to Babylon?," Bdwy in "The Cellar and the Well," "Miss Lonelyhearts," "Who's Afraid of Virginia Woolf?," "Malcolm," "Right Honourable Gentleman," "Delicate Balance," "Birthday Party," "Harvey," "Engagement Baby," "Freedom of the City," "Texas Trilogy," "The Best Little Whorehouse in Texas."

FOSTER, FRANCES. Born June 11 in Yonkers, NY. Bdwy debut 1955 in "The Western Trees," followed by "Nobody Loves an Albatross," "Raisin in the Sun," "The River Niger," "First Breeze of Summer," OB in "Take a Giant Step," "Edge of the City," "Tammy and the Doctor," "The Crucible," "Happy Ending," "Day of Absence," "An Evening of One Acts," "Man Better Man," "Brotherhood," "Akokawe," "Rosalee Pritchett," "Sty of the Blind Pig," "Ballet Behind the Bridge," "Good Woman of Setzuan" (LC), "Behold! Cometh the Vanderkellans," "Orrin," "Boesman and Lena," "Do Lord Remember Me," "Nevis Mountain Dew," "Daughters of the Mock," "Big City Blues."

FOSTER, GLORIA. Born Nov. 15, 1936 in Chicago, IL. Attended IllStateU. Goodman Th. Debut 1963 OB in "In White America," followed by "Medea" for which she received a Theatre World Award, "Yerma," "A Hand Is on the Gate," "Black Visions," "The Cherry Orchard," "Agamemnon," "Coriolanus," "Mother Courage."

FRANCINE, ANNE. Born Aug. 8, 1917 in Philadelphia, PA. Bdwy debut 1945 in "Marriage to Single People," followed by "By the Beautiful Sea," "Great Sebastians," "Tenderloin," "Mame," "A Broadway Musical," "Snow White," OB in "Guitar," "Valmouth," "Asylum," "Are you Now or Have you . . . "

FRANK, RICHARD. Born Jan. 4, 1954 in Boston, MA. Graduate UMich. Debut 1978 OB in "Spring Awakening," followed by "Salt Lake City Skyline."

FRANKFATHER, WILLIAM. Born Aug. 4, 1944 in Kermit, TX. Graduate NMexStateU, Stanford U. Bdwy debut 1980 in "Children of a Lesser God."

FRANKLIN, NANCY. Born in NYC. Debut 1959 OB in "Buffalo Skinner," followed by "Power of Darkness," "Oh, Dad, Poor Dad. . . . " "Theatre of Peretz," "Seven Days of Mourning," "Here Be Dragons," "Beach Children," "Safe Place," "Innocent Pleasures," "The Loves of Cass McGuire," Bdwy in "Never Live over a Pretzel Factory," "Happily Never After," "The White House."

FRANZ, JOY. Born in 1944 in Modesto, CA. Graduate UMo. Debut 1969 OB in "Of Thee I Sing," followed by "Jacques Brel Is Alive . . . ," "Out of This World," Bdwy in "Sweet Charity," "Lysistrata," "A Little Night Music," "Pippin," "Musical Chairs."

FRASER, BRYANT. Born Feb. 10, 1955 in Newark, NJ. Attended ForhamU. Bdwy debut 1962 in "Oliver," followed by "Poor Bitos," "Child's Play," "The Yearling," "Our Town" (1969), OB in "Vestigial Parts," "Love's Labour's Lost."

FRAZER, ALISON. Born May 21, 1948 in England. Attended Guildhall School of Drama. Bdwy debut 1979 in "Dogg's Hamlet, Cahoot's Macbeth."

FREEMAN, ANN. Born in Portsmouth, Eng. Bdwy debut 1967 in "Life with Father," followed by OB's "Present Laughter," "The Home," "The Crucible."

FREEMAN, ARNY. Born Aug. 28, 1908 in Chicago, IL. Bdwy bow 1949 in "A Streetcar Named Desire," followed by "The Great Sebastians," "Tall Story," "Hot Spot," "What Makes Sammy Run?" "Cactus Flower," "Minnie's Boys," "Much Ado about Nothing," "Sunshine Boys," "Working," "The 1940's Radio Show," "The Roast," OB in Gay Divorce," "Dream Girl," "The Shrike," "Gun Play."

FREEMAN, MORGAN. Born June 1, 1937 in Memphis, TN. Attended LACC. Bdwy bow 1967 in "Hello, Dolly!" followed by "The Mighty Gents," OB in "Ostrich Feathers," "Niggerlovers," "Exhibition," "Black Visions," "Cockfight," "White Pelicans," "Julius Caesar," "Coriolanus," "Mother Courage."

FREEMAN, YVETTE. Born Oct. 1, 1950 in Chester, PA. Graduate UDel. Debut 1976 OB in "Let My People Come," Bdwy 1979 in "Ain't Misbehavin'."

FRELICH, PHYLLIS. Born Feb. 29, 1944 in NDakota. Graduate Gallaudet Col. Bdwy debut 1970 in Ntl. Theatre of the Deaf's "Songs from Milkwood," followed by "Children of a Lesser God," OB in "Poets from the Inside."

FRENCH, ARTHUR. Born in NYC. Attended Brooklyn Col. Debut 1962 OB in "Raisin' Hell in the Sun," followed by "Ballad of Bimshire," "Day of Absence," "Happy Ending," "Jonah," "Black Girl," "Ceremonies in Dark Old Men," "An Evening of One Acts," "Man Better Man," "Brotherhood," "Perry's Mission," "Rosalee Pritchett," "Moonlight Arms," "Dark Tower," "Brownsville Raid," "Nevis Mt. Dew," "Julius Caesar," "Friends," Bdwy in "Ain't Supposed to Die a Natural Death," "The Iceman Cometh," "All God's Chillun Got Wings."

FRENCH, VALERIE. Born in London, Eng. Bdwy debut 1965 in "Inadmissible Evidence," followed by "Help Stamp Out Marriage," "Mother Lover," "Children, Children," OB in "Tea Party," "Trelawny of the Wells," "Studs Edsel," "Henry V," "John Gabriel Borkman," "Fallen Angels."

FREY LEONARD. Born Sept. 4, 1938 in Brooklyn, NY. Attended Cooper Union, Neighborhood Playhouse. OB in "Little Mary Sunshine," "Funny House of a Negro," "Coach with Six Insides," "Boys in the Band," "The Time of Your Life," "Beggar on Horseback," "People Are Living There," "Twelfth Night," "Troilus and Cressida," Bdwy in "Fiddler on the Roof," "The National Health," "Knock Knock," "Kurt Weill Cabaret."

FROMEWICK, STEVEN. Born Oct. 29, 1954 in The Bronx, NY. Graduate Lehman Col., HB Studio. Debut 1980 OB in "Say Goodnight, Gracie."

GABLE, JUNE. Born June 5, 1945 in NYC. Carnegie Tech graduate. OB in "Macbird," "Jacques Brel Is Alive and Well . . . ," "A Day in the Life of Just About Everyone," "Mod Donna," "Wanted," "Lady Audley's Secret," "Comedy of Errors," "Chinchilla," "Star Treatment," Bdwy in "Candide" (1974).

GAFFIGAN, CATHERINE. Born Dec. 25 in NYC. Graduate Catholic U. Debut 1966 OB in "Journey of the Fifth Horse," followed by Bdwy 1979 in "Whose Life Is It Anyway?"

GAINES, BOYD. Born May 11, 1953 in Atlanta, GA. Juilliard graduate. Debut 1978 OB in "Spring Awakening," followed by "A Month in the Country" for which he received a Theatre World Award, BAM Theatre Co.'s "Winter's Tale," "The Barbarians," and "Johnny On a Spot."

GALIANO, JOSEPH. Born Mar. 26, 1944 in Beaumont, TX. Graduate SMU. Debut 1976 OB in "The Fantasticks."

GALE, DAVID. Born Oct. 2, 1936 in England. Debut 1958 OB in "Elizabeth the Queen," followed by "Othello," "White Devil," "Baal," "What Do They Know About Love Uptown?," "Joe Egg," "The Trial," "Dumbwaiter," "The Dodge Boys," "The Biko Inquest," "Buy the Bi and Bye," Bdwy in "Of Mice and Men" (1974), "Sweet Bird of Youth."

GARBER, VICTOR. Born Mar. 16, 1949 in London, Can. Debut 1973 OB in "Ghosts" for which he received a Theatre World Award, followed by "Joe's Opera," "Cracks," Bdwy in "Tartuffe," "Deathtrap," "Sweeney Todd."

GARDNER, LAURA. Born Mar. 17, 1951 in Flushing, NY. Graduate Boston U., Rutgers U. Debut 1979 OB in "The Office Murders."

GARNETT, GALE. Born July 23, 1946 in Auckland, NZ. Debut 1959 OB in "Jack," followed by "Sisters of Mercy," "Greatest Fairy Story Ever Told," "Cracks," "Ladyhouse Blues," "My Sister's Keeper," Bdwy in "The World of Suzie Wong," "Ulysses in Nighttown."

GARREY, COLIN. Born in Norwich, NY. Graduate AADA, RADA. Debut 1971 OB in "Ballad of Johnny Pot," followed by "As You Like It," "The Youth Hostel," "Love's Labour's Lost," Bdwy 1977 in "Miss Margarida's Way."

GARRICK, BEULAH. Born June 12, 1921 in Nottingham, Eng. Bdwy debut 1959 in "Shadow and Substance," followed by "Auntie Mame," "Juno," "Little Moon of Alban," "High Spirits," "The Hostage," "Funny Girl," "Lovers," "Abelard and Heloise," "Ulysses in Nighttown," OB in "Little Boxes," "Berkeley Square," "Fallen Angels."

GARRISON, DAVID. Born June 30, 1952 in Long Branch, NJ. Graduate Boston U. Debut 1977 OB in "Joseph and the Amazing Technicolor Dreamcoat," followed by "Living at Home," Bdwy in "A History of the American Film," "A Day in Hollywood/A Night in the Ukraine."

GASCO, ERNESTO. Born July 10, 1937 in Bagnasco, Italy. Graduate Inst. del Teatro Colon. Bdwy debut 1980 in "Betrayal."

GAVON, IGORS. Born Nov. 14, 1937 in Latvia. Bdwy bow 1961 in "Carnival," followed by "Hello, Dolly!" "Marat/deSade," "Billy," "Sugar," "Mack and Mabel," "Musical Jubilee," "Strider," OB in "Your Own Thing," "Promenade," "Exchange," "Nevertheless They Laugh," "Polly," "The Boss," "Biography: A Game," "Strider."

GAYNOR, JANET. Born Oct. 6, 1906 in Philadelphia, PA. Bdwy debut 1980 in "Harold and Maude."

GEFFNER, DEBORAH. Born Aug. 26, 1952 in Pittsburgh, PA. Attended Juilliard, HB Studio. Debut 1978 OB in "Tenderloin," Bdwy in "Pal Joey," "A Chorus Line."

GELKE, BECKY. Born Feb. 17, 1953 in Ft. Knox, KY. Graduate Western Ky.U. Debut 1978 OB and Bdwy in "The Best Little Whorehouse in Texas."

GENEST, EDMOND. Born Oct. 27, 1943 in Boston, MA. Attended Suffolk U. Debut 1972 OB in "The Real Inspector Hound," Bdwy in "Dirty Linen/New-Found Land," "Whose Life Is It Anyway?"

GENTILE, LYNNE. Born Nov. 12, 1955 in Perth Amboy, NJ. Graduate Ithaca Col. Debut 1980 OB in "The Mischief You Foresee."

GENTLES, AVRIL. Born Apr. 2, 1929 in Upper Montclair, NJ. Graduate UNC. Bdwy debut 1955 in "The Great Sebastians," followed by "Nude With Violin," "Present Laughter," "My Mother, My Father and Me," "Jimmy Shine," "Grin and Bare It," "Lysistrata," "Texas Trilogy," OB in "Dinny and the Witches," "The Wives," "Now Is the Time," "Man With a Load of Mischief," "Shay," BAM's "Winter's Tale," "Johnny on a Spot," "The Barbarians," "The Wedding."

GERBER, KATHY K. Born July 18, 1946 in Baltimore, MD. Attended UMd. AADA. Debut 1975 OB in "The Zykovs," followed by "Starstruck."

GERDES, HEATHER LEA. Born Jan. 15, 1959 in Sunset Beach, CA. Attended USFl. Bdwy debut 1980 in "West Side Story."

GERE, RICHARD. Born Aug. 29, 1949 in Philadelphia, PA. Attended UMa. Debut 1971 OB in "Soon," followed by "Taming of the Shrew," "A Midsummer Night's Dream"(LC), "Killer's Head," Bdwy in "Grease" (1973), "Habeas Corpus," "Bent" for which he received a Theatre World Award.

GHOSTLEY, ALICE. Born Aug. 14, 1926 in Eve, MO. Attended UOkla. Bdwy debut in "New Faces of 1952," followed by "Sandhog," "Livin' the Life," "Trouble in Tahiti," "Shangri-La," "Maybe Tuesday," "Thurber Carnival," "The Beauty Part," "The Sign in Sidney Brustein's Window," "Love Is a Ball," "Annie."

GIBBS, SHEILA. Born Feb. 16, 1947 in NYC. Graduate NYU. Bdwy debut 1971 in "Two Gentlemen of Verona," OB in "Last Days of British Honduras," "Poets From the Inside."

GIERASCH, STEFAN. Born Feb. 5, 1926 in NYC. On Bdwy in "Kiss and Tell," "Snafu," "Billion Dollar Baby," "Montserrat," "Night Music," "Hatful of Rain," "Compulsion," "Shadow of a Gunman," "War and Peace," "Of Mice and Men," "Tartuffe," OB in "7 Days of Mourning," "AC/DC," "Owners," "Nellie Toole & Co." "The Iceman Cometh," "Man With a Flower in His Mouth," "Old Tune," "Bella Figura."

GILBERT, BARBARA. Born July 20 in Brooklyn, NY. Attended AADA, HB Studio. Bdwy debut 1956 in "Pajama Game," followed by "Fiorello!," "Cop-Out," OB in "Threepenny Opera," "Spoon River Anthology," "Archy and Mehitabel."

GILBORN, STEVEN. Born in New Rochelle, NY. Graduate Swarthmore Col., Stanford U. Bdwy debut 1973 in "Creeps," followed by "Basic Training of Pavlo Hummel," "Tartuffe," OB in "Rosmersholm," "Henry V," "Measure for Measure," "Ashes," "The Dybbuk," "Museum," "Shadow of a Gunman."

GILL, TERI. Born July 16, 1954 in Long Island City, NY. Graduate USIU. Bdwy debut 1976 in "Going Up," followed by "Evita," OB in "Allegro."

GIOMBETTI, KAREN. Born May 24, 1955 in Scranton, PA. Graduate NYU. Debut 1978 in "Stop the World, I Want to Get Off," Bdwy 1979 in "The Most Happy Fella."

GIRARDEAU, FRANK. Born Oct. 19, 1942 in Beaumont, TX. Attended Rider Col., HB Studio. Debut 1972 OB in "22 Years," followed by "The Soldier," "Hughie."

GLENN-SMITH, MICHAEL. Born July 2, 1945 in Abilene, TX. Attended NTexStateU. Bdwy debut 1969 in "Celebration," OB in "The Fantasticks," "Once I Saw a Boy Laughing," "Philemon," "Patch Patch."

GLYNN, CARLIN. Born Feb. 19, 1940 in Cleveland, OH. Attended Sophie Newcomb Col., Actors Studio. Debut 1959 OB in "Waltz of the Toreadors," Bdwy debut 1978 in "The Best Little Whorehouse in Texas" for which she received a Theatre World Award.

GODFREY, LYNNIE. Born Sept. 11, 1952 in NYC. Hunter Col. graduate. Debut 1976 OB in "I Paid My Dues," Bdwy 1978 in "Eubie!"

GOLD, JULIANNE. Born June 18, 1960 in Rochester, MN. Attended CalStateU. Bdwy debut 1980 in "Children of a Lesser God!"

GOLDSMITH, MERWIN. Born Aug. 7, 1937 in Detroit MI. Graduate UCLA, Old Vic. Bdwy debut 1970 in "Minnie's Boys," followed by "The Visit," "Chemin de Fer," "Rex," "Dirty Linen," "The 1940's Radio Show," OB in "Hamlet as a Happening," "Chickencoop Chinaman," "Wanted," "Comedy," "Rubbers," "Yankees 3, Detroit 0," "Trelawny of the Wells," "Chinchilla."

GOLDSTEIN, LESLIE. Born Jan. 22, 1940 in Newark, NJ. Graduate Newark Col. Debut 1976 OB in "Men in White," followed by "Native Bird," "Antigone," "The Lover," "Middle of the Night," "Second Avenue Rag," Bdwy 1979 in "Meeting by the River."

GOODMAN, ROBYN. Born Aug. 24, 1947 in NYC. Graduate Brandeis U. Debut 1973 OB in "When You Comin' Back, Red Ryder?," followed by "Richard III," "Museum," "Bits and Pieces."

GOOTENBERG, AMY. Born Feb. 29, 1952 in Boston, MA. Graduate Middlebury Col., Catholic U. Debut 1980 OB in "The Time of the Cuckoo"(ELT).

GORBEA, CARLOS. Born July 3, 1938 in Santurce, PR. Graduate Fordham U. Bdwy debut 1964 in "West Side Story," followed by "Fiddler on the Roof," "Cabaret," "Candide," "Evita," OB in "Time of Storm," "Theatre in the Street."

GORDON, CHARLES. Born in 1925 in Cleveland, OH. Has appeared OB in "The Blacks," "No Place to Be Somebody," "Crazy Horse," "Liliom."

GORDON, KEITH. Born Feb. 3, 1961 in NYC. Debut 1976 OB in "Secrets of the Rich," followed by "A Traveling Companion," "Suckers," "Gimme Shelter," "Sunday Runners."

GORRILL, MAGGY. Born Feb. 19, 1952 in Long Island City, NY. Attended Barnard Col. Debut 1975 OB in "Diamond Studs," followed by Bdwy in "Dr. Jazz," "A Broadway Musical," "Peter Pan."

GOTLIEB, BEN. Born June 27, 1954 in Kfar Saba, Israel. Attended RADA, CUNY/Brooklyn Col. Bdwy debut 1979 in "Dogg's Hamlet and Cahoot's MacBeth," OB in "Kohlhass."

GOULD, GORDON. Born May 4, 1930 in Chicago, IL. Yale graduate. With APA in "Man and Superman," "War and Peace," "Judith," "Lower Depths," "Right You Are," "Scapin," "Impromptu at Versailles," "You Can't Take It With You," "The Hostage," "The Tavern," "A Midsummer Night's Dream," "Merchant of Venice," "Richard II," "Much Ado About Nothing," "Wild Duck," "The Show-Off," and "Pantagleize," "Strider," Bdwy in "Freedom of the City,"

GRABENSTEIN, CHRIS. Born Sept. 2, 1955 in Buffalo, NY. Graduate UTn. Debut 1980 OB in "Merton of the Movies."

GRAHAM, DONNA. Born Sept. 28, 1964 in Philadelphia, PA. Bdwy debut 1977 in "Annie."

GRAMMIS, ADAM. Born Dec. 8, 1947 in Allentown, PA. Graduate Kutztown State Col. Bdwy debut 1971 in "Wild and Wonderful," followed by "Shirley MacLaine Show," "A Chorus Line," OB in "Dance Continuum," "Joseph and the Amazing Technicolor Dreamcoat."

GRANGER, FARLEY. Born July 1, 1928 in San Jose, CA. Bdwy debut 1959 in "First Impressions," followed by "The Warm Peninsula," "Advise and Consent," CC's "The King and I" and "Brigadoon," "The Seagull," "The Crucible," OB in "The Carefree Tree," "A Month in the Country."

GRANGER, MICHAEL. Born May 14, 1923 in Kansas City, MO. Debut 1963 OB in "A Man's a Man," followed by "Joan of Lorraine," "Danton's Death," "The Alchemist," "Eastwind," "Caucasian Chalk Circle," "Country Wife," "A Doll's House," Bdwy 1980 in "Clothes for a Summer Hotel."

GRANT, DAVID MARSHALL. Born June 21, 1955 in New Haven, CT. Attended ConnCol., Yale. Debut OB 1978 in "Sganarelle," followed by "Table Settings," Bdwy 1979 in "Bent."

GRANT, KATIE. Born Jan. 5, 1955 in Philadelphia, PA. Juilliard graduate. Debut 1978 OB in "Spring Awakening," followed by "A Month in the Country."

GRAVES, RUTHANNA. Born Sept. 14, 1957 in Philadelphia, PA. Attended NYU. Debut 1980 OB in "Mother Courage and Her Children."

GRAY, BRUCE. Born Sept. 7, 1936 in San Juan, PR. Graduate UToronto. Debut 1976 OB in "Who Killed Richard Cory?," followed by "Richard II," "Total Recall," "Winter Signs," "Hamlet."

GREEN, DEL. Born July 8, 1938 in Pocatello, ID. Bdwy debut 1967 in "Illya, Darling," followed by "Love-Suicide at Schofield Barracks," OB in "Archy and Mehitabel."

GREEN, HOWARD. Born March 9 in Detroit, MI. OB in "Darkness at Noon," "Cyrano de Bergerac," "Ceremony of Innocence," "Henry VI," "Richard III," "Anna K," "12 Angry Men," "The Lover."

GREEN, MARY-PAT. Born Sept. 24, 1951 in Kansas City, MO. Attended UKan. Bdwy debut 1974 in "Candide," followed by "Sweeney Todd."

GREENBERG, MITCHELL. Born Sept. 19, 1950 in Brooklyn, NY. Graduate Harpur Col., Neighborhood Playhouse. Debut 1979 OB in "Two Grown Men," followed by "Scrambled Feet," Bdwy 1980 in "A Day in Hollywood, A Night in the Ukraine."

GREENE, ELLEN. Born Feb. 22 in NYC. Attended Ryder Col. Debut 1973 in "Rachel Lily Rosenbloom," followed OB by "In the Boom Boom Room," "Threepenny Opera," "The Nature and Purpose of the Universe," "Teeth 'n' Smiles," "The Sorrows of Stephen."

GREENE, JAMES. Born Dec. 1, 1926 in Lawrence, MA. Graduate Emerson Col. OB in "The Iceman Cometh," "American Gothic," "The King and the Duke," "The Hostage," "Plays for Bleecker Street," "Moon in the Yellow River," "Misalliance," "Government Inspector," "Baba Goya," LCRep 2 years, "You Can't Take It With You," "School for Scandal," "Wild Duck," "Right You Are," "The Show-Off," "Pantagleize," "Festival of Short Plays," "Nourish the Beast," "One Crack Out," "Artichoke," "Othello," "Salt Lake City Skyline," Bdwy in "Romeo and Juliet," "Girl on the Via Flaminia," "Compulsion," "Inherit the Wind," "Shadow of a Gunman," "Andersonville Trial," "Night Life," "School for Wives," "Ring Round the Bathtub," "Great God Brown," "Don Juan."

GREENAN, DAVID. Born Sept. 21 in Burlington, VT. Graduate Boston U., UCLA. Debut 1979 OB in "Plain and Fancy"(ELT), followed by "Twelfth Night," "Murder in the Cathedral."

GRIFFITH, KRISTIN. Born Sept. 7, 1953 in Odessa, TX. Juilliard graduate. Bdwy debut 1976 in "A Texas Trilogy," OB in "Rib Cage," "Character Lines," "3 Friends/2 Rooms," "A Month in the Country."

GRIMES, TAMMY. Born Jan. 30, 1934 in Lynn, MA. Attended Stephens Col., Neighborhood Playhouse. Debut 1956 OB in "The Littlest Revue," followed by "Clerambard," "Molly," "Trick," "Are You Now or Have You Ever Been," "Father's Day," "A Month in the Country," Bdwy in "Look After Lulu" (1959) for which she received a Theatre World Award, "The Unsinkable Molly Brown," "Rattle of a Simple Man," "High Spirits," "The Only Game in Town," "Private Lives," "Musical Jubilee," "California Suite," "Tartuffe."

GROENENDAAL, CRIS. Born Feb. 17, 1948 in Erie, PA. Attended Allegheny Col., Exeter (Eng) U, HB Studio. Bdwy debut 1979 in "Sweeney Todd."

GROENER, HARRY. Born Sept. 10, 1951 in Augsburg, Ger. Graduate UWash. Bdwy debut 1979 in "Oklahoma!" for which he received a Theatre World Award.

GROSS, MICHAEL. Born in 1947 in Chicago, IL. UIll and Yale graduate. Debut 1978 OB in "Sganarelle," followed by "Othello," "Endgame," Bdwy 1979 in "Bent."

GROVE, GREGORY. Born Dec. 15, 1949 in Ada, OK. Graduate SMU, HB Studio. Debut 1977 OB in "K: Impressions of Kafka's Trial," Bdwy 1979 in "Lone Star/Private Wars."

GUERRASIO, JOHN. Born Feb. 18, 1950 in Brooklyn, NY. Attended Bklyn Col. Boston U. Debut 1971 OB in "Hamlet," followed by "And They Put Handcuffs on Flowers," "Eros and Psyche," "The Marriage Proposal," "Macbeth," "K," "Sunday Promenade," "Family Business," "Knuckle Sandwich."

GUIDALL, GEORGE. Born June 7, 1938 in Plainfield, NJ. Attended UBuffalo, AADA. Bdwy debut 1969 in "Wrong Way Light Bulb," followed by "Cold Storage," OB in "Counsellor-at-Law," "Taming of the Shrew," "All's Well That Ends Well," "The Art of Dining," "Biography."

GUITTARD, LAWRENCE. Born July 16, 1939 in San Francisco, CA. Stanford U. graduate. Bdwy debut 1965 in "Baker Street," followed by "Anya," "Man of La Mancha," "A Little Night Music" for which he received a Theatre World Award, "Rodgers and Hart," "She Loves Me," "Oklahoma!" (1979), OB in "Umbrellas of Cherbourg."

GUNTON, BOB. Born Nov. 15, 1945 in Santa Monica, CA. Attended UCal. Debut 1971 OB in "Who Am I?," followed by "The Kid," "Desperate Hours," "Tip-Toes," Bdwy in "Happy End" (1977), "Working," "King of Hearts," "Evita."

GURNEY, RACHEL. Born March 5 in England. Debut 1977 OB in "You Never Can Tell," followed by "Heartbreak House," Bdwy 1980 in "Major Barbara."

GURRY, ERIC. Born Dec. 14, 1966 in NYC. Debut 1980 OB in "Table Settings."

GUSKIN, HAROLD. Born May 25, 1941 in Brooklyn, NY. Graduate Rutgers U, Ind.U. Debut 1980 OB in "Second Avenue Rag."

GUSKIN, PAUL. Born Sept. 12, 1939 in Brooklyn, NY. Attended Pratt Inst., HB Studio. Debut 1979 OB in "Manny."

GWYNNE, FRED. Born July 10, 1926 in NYC. Harvard graduate. Bdwy debut 1952 in "Mrs. McThing," followed by "Love's Labour's Lost," "Frogs of Spring," "Irma La Douce," "Here's Love," "The Lincoln Mask," "Cat on a Hot Tin Roof," "A Texas Trilogy," "Angel," "Players," OB in "More Than You Deserve," "Fair Game," "Grand Magic," "Salt Lake City Skyline."

HADARY, JONATHAN. Born Oct. 11, 1948 in Chicago, IL. Attended Tufts U. Debut 1974 OB in "White Nights," followed by "El Grande de Coca-Cola," "Songs from Pins and Needles," "God Bless You, Mr. Rosewater," "Pushing 30," "Scrambled Feet," Bdwy 1977 in "Gemini" (also OB).

HADDOW, JEFFREY. Born Oct. 8, 1947 in NYC. Northwestern U. graduate. Debut 1979 OB in "Scrambled Feet."

HAGAN, PETER. Born Oct. 3, 1954 in Alexandria, VA. Graduate UVa. Debut 1980 OB in "Class Enemy."

HAGEN, UTA. Born June 11, 1919 in Goettingen, Ger. Bdwy debut 1938 in "The Seagull," followed by "The Happiest Years," "Key Largo," "Vickie," "Othello," "A Streetcar Named Desire," "Country Girl," "St. Joan," "The Whole World Over," "In Any Language," "The Magic and the Loss," CC's "Angel Street," and "Tovarich," "Who's Afraid of Virginia Woolf?," "The Cherry Orchard," "Charlotte," OB in "A Month in the Country," "Good Woman of Setzuan."

HAIGH, KENNETH. Born Mar. 25, 1930 in Yorkshire, Eng. Attended Central School. Bdwy debut 1957 in "Look Back in Anger," followed by "Caligula," "California Suite," "Clothes for a Summer Hotel," OB in "Endecott and the Red Cross."

HALL, CHARLES. Born Nov. 12, 1951 in Frankfort, KY. Graduate Murray State U. Debut 1977 OB in "Molly's Dream," followed by "Sheridan Square," "The Doctor in Spite of Himself," Bdwy 1979 in "Snow White."

HALL, DAVIS. Born Apr. 10, 1946 in Atlanta, GA. Graduate Northwestern U. Bdwy debut 1973 in "Butley," followed by "Dogg's Hamlet and Cahoot's MacBeth," OB in "The Promise."

HALL, GEORGE. Born Nov. 19, 1916 in Toronto, Can. Attended Neighborhood Playhouse. Bdwy bow 1946 in "Call Me Mister," followed by "Lend an Ear," "Touch and Go," "Live Wire," "The Boy Friend," "There's a Girl in My Soup," "An Evening with Richard Nixon . . . ," "We Interrupt This Program," "Man and Superman," "Bent," OB in "The Balcony," "Ernest in Love," "A Round with Ring," "Family Pieces," "Carousel," "The Case Against Roberta Guardino," "Marry Me! Marry Me!," "Arms and the Man," "The Old Glory," "Dancing for the Kaiser."

HALLETT, JACK. Born Nov. 7, 1948 in Philadelphia, PA. Attended AADA. Debut 1972 OB in "Servant of Two Masters" (ELT), Bdwy 1979 in "The 1940's Radio Show."

HAMILTON, ROGER. Born May 2, 1928 in San Diego, CA. Attended San Diego Col., RADA. OB in "Merchant of Venice," "Hamlet," "Live Like Pigs," "Hotel Passionato," "Sjt. Musgrave's Dance," Bdwy in "Someone Waiting," "Separate Tables," "Little Moon of Alban," "Luther," "The Deputy," "Rosencrantz and Guildenstern Are Dead," "The Rothschilds," "Pippin," "Happy New Year."

HAMMIL, JOHN. Born May 9, 1948 in NYC. Attended UCLA. Bdwy debut 1972 in "Purlie," followed by "Oh! Calcutta!," "Platinum," "They're Playing Our Song," OB in "El Grande de Coca-Cola," "Songs from the City Streets."

HAMMOND, MICHAEL. Born Apr. 30, 1951 in Clinton, IA. Graduate UIowa, LAMDA. Debut 1974 OB in "Pericles," followed by "The Merry Wives of Windsor," BAM Theatre Co.'s "A Winter's Tale," "Barbarians," "The Purging."

HANKS, BARBARA. Born Sept. 1, 1951 in Salt Lake City, UT. Debut 1978 OB in "Gay Divorce," Bdwy 1979 in "Sugar Babies."

HANNUM, KRISTIE. Born June 12, 1955 in Memphis, TN. Graduate Principia Col., Young Vic. Debut 1979 OB in "On a Clear Day You Can See Forever," "Annie Get Your Gun" (JB).

HARA, MARY. Born in Nebraska. Bdwy debut 1968 in "Rosencrantz and Guildenstern Are Dead," followed by "Waltz of the Toreadors," OB in "The Kitchen," "Glorious Ruler," "Dona Rosita."

HARAN, MARY-CLEERE. Born May 13, 1952 in San Francisco, CA. Attended San Francisco State. Bdwy debut 1979 in "The 1940's Radio Hour."

HARDY, WADE L. III. Born Oct. 13, 1954 in St. Louis, MO. Graduate IndU. Debut 1980 OB in "Elizabeth and Essex."

HARNEY, BEN. Born Aug. 29, 1952 in Brooklyn, NY. Bdwy debut 1971 in "Purlie," followed by "Pajama Game," "Treemonisha," "Pippin," OB in "Don't Bother Me, I Can't Cope," "The Derby," "The More You Get."

HARPER, CHARLES THOMAS. Born Mar. 29, 1949 in Carthage, NY. Graduate Webster Col. Debut 1975 OB in "Down by the River . . . ," followed by "Holy Ghosts," "Hamlet," "Mary Stuart."

HARRELSON, HELEN. Born in Missouri; graduate Goodman Theatre. Bdwy debut 1950 in "The Cellar and the Well," followed by "Death of a Salesman," "Days in the Trees," "Romeo and Juliet," OB in "Our Town," "His and Hers," "House of Atreus," BAM's "He and She."

HARRINGTON, DELPHI. Born Aug. 26 in Chicago, IL. Northwestern U. graduate. Debut 1960 OB in "Country Scandal," followed by "Moon for the Misbegotten," "Baker's Dozen," "The Zykovs," "Character Lines," Bdwy in "Thieves," "Everything in the Garden," "Romeo and Juliet," "Chapter 2."

HARRIS, BAXTER. Born Nov. 18, 1940 in Columbus, KS. Attended U Kan. Debut 1967 OB in "America Hurrah," followed by "The Reckoning," "Wicked Women Revue," "More Than You Deserve," "Pericles," "him," "Battle of Angels," "Down by the River . . . ," Bdwy in "A Texas Trilogy" (1976), "Dracula," "The Lady from Dubuque."

HARRIS, CYNTHIA. Born in NYC. Graduate Smith Col. Bdwy debut 1963 in "Natural Affection," followed by "Any Wednesday," "Best Laid Plans," "Company," OB in "The Premise," "3 by Wilder," "America Hurrah," "White House Murder Case," "Mystery Play," "Bad Habits," "Merry Wives of Windsor," "Beauty Part," "Jules Feiffer's Hold Me," "Second Avenue Rag."

HARRIS, NIKI. Born July 20, 1948 in Pittsburgh, PA. Graduate Duquesne U. Bdwy debut 1980 in "A Day in Hollywood/A Night in the Ukraine."

HARRIS, SKIP. Born Oct. 27, 1952 in Hempsted, NY. Graduate UCinn. Bdwy debut 1979 in "Sweeney Todd."

HART, ROXANNE. Born in 1952 in Trenton, NJ. Attended Skidmore and Princeton U. Bdwy debut 1977 in "Equus," followed by "Loose Ends," BAM Theatre Co.'s "Winter's Tale," "Johnny On a Spot," and "The Purging."

HARTMAN, ELEK. Born Apr. 26, 1922 in Canton, OH. Graduate Carnegie Tech, OB in "Where People Gather," "Goa," "Loyalties," "The Matchmaker," "Mirandolina," Bdwy in "We Bombed in New Haven" (1968), "Angel."

HASTINGS, BILL. Born July 30, 1952 in Vinita, OK. Graduate LSU. Bdwy debut 1979 in "The Most Happy Fella," followed by OB in "Anyone Can Whistle."

HAWKINS, TRISH. Born Oct. 30, 1945 in Hartford, CT. Attended Radcliffe, Neighborhood Playhouse. Debut 1970 in "Oh! Calcutta!" followed by "Iphigenia," "The Hot l Baltimore" for which she received a Theatre World Award, "him," "Come Back, Little Sheba," "Battle of Angels," "Mound Builders," "The Farm," "Ulysses in Traction," "Lulu," "Hogan's Folly," Bdwy 1977 in "Some of My Best Friends," "Talley's Folly" (1979).

HAYES, EVERY. Born Sept. 1, 1949 in Montclair, NJ. OB in "Step Lively, Boys," "Croesus and the Witch," "The Flies," "Ups and Downs of Theophilus Maitland," "Jam," Bdwy in "Purlie," "Don't Bother Me, I Can't Cope," "All Over Town."

HAYES, JANET. Born June 11 in Shanghai, China. Graduate NEConsv. of Music, Hunter Col. Bdwy debut 1954 in "The Golden Apple," followed by "Anyone Can Whistle," "Camelot," "Music Man," "Damn Yankees," OB in "Boys from Syracuse," "A Touch of the Poet," "Plain and Fancy," "Candide," "Rain," "The Subject Was Roses."

HAYNES, TIGER. Born Dec. 13, 1907 in St. Croix, VI. Bdwy bow 1956 in "New Faces," followed by "Finian's Rainbow," "Fade Out—Fade In," "The Pajama Game," "The Wiz," "A Broadway Musical," "Comin' Uptown."

HAYS, REX DAVID. Born June 17, 1946 in Hollywood, CA. Graduate San Jose State U., Brandeis U. Bdwy debut 1975 in "Dance With Me," followed by "Angel," "King of Hearts," "Evita."

HEARD, CORDIS. Born July 27, 1944 in Washington, DC. Graduate Chatham Col. Bdwy debut 1973 in "Warp," followed by "The Elephant Man," OB in "Vanities," "City Junket."

HEARD, JOHN. Born Mar. 7, 1946 in Washington, DC. Graduate Clark U. Debut 1974 OB in "The Wager," followed by "Macbeth," "Hamlet," "Fishing," "G. R. Point" for which he received a Theatre World Award, "Creditors," "The Promise," "Othello," "Split," Bdwy 1973 in "Warp."

HEARN, GEORGE. Born June 18, 1934 in St. Louis, MO. Graduate Southwestern Col. OB in "Macbeth," "Antony and Cleopatra," "As You Like It," "Richard III," "Merry Wives of Windsor," "Midsummer Night's Dream," "Hamlet," "Horseman, Pass By," Bdwy in "A Time for Singing," "The Changing Room," "An Almost Perfect Person," "I Remember Mama," "Watch on the Rhine," "Sweeney Todd."

HEATH, GORDON. Born Sept. 20, 1918 in NYC. Attended CCNY. Bdwy debut 1945 in "Deep Are the Roots," OB in "Oedipus," "Endgame," "Sounds of a Triangle," "Kohlhass."

HEBERT, GAIL. Born May 20, 1951 in Seattle, WA. Debut 1980 OB in "Fortune."

HECHT, PAUL. Born Aug. 16, 1941 in London, Eng. Attended McGill U. OB in "Sjt. Musgrave's Dance," "MacBird," Bdwy in "Rosencrantz and Guildenstern Are Dead," "1776," "The Rothschilds," "The Ride Across Lake Constance" (LC), "The Great God Brown," "Don Juan," "Emperor Henry IV," "Herzl," "Caesar and Cleopatra," "Night and Day."

HEFFERNAN, JOHN. Born May 30, 1934 in NYC. Attended CCNY, Columbia, Boston U. Bdwy debut 1963 in "Luther," followed by "Tiny Alice," "Postmark Zero," "Woman Is My Idea," "Morning, Noon and Night," "Purlie," "Bad Habits," "Lady from the Sea," "Knock Knock," "Sly Fox," OB in "The Judge," "Julius Caesar," "Great God Brown," "Lysistrata," "Peer Gynt," "Henry IV," "Taming of the Shrew," "She Stoops to Conquer," "The Plough and the Stars," "Octoroon," "Hamlet," "Androcles and the Lion," "A Man's a Man," "Winter's Tale," "Arms and the Man," "St. Joan" (LC), "Memorandum," "Invitation to a Beheading," "The Sea," "Shadow of a Gunman," BAM's "A Winter's Tale," "Johnny On a Spot" and "Barbarians."

HEIST, KARL. Born June 14, 1950 in West Reading, PA. Graduate McMurry Col. Debut 1976 OB in "Fiorello," followed by "Silk Stockings," "Winterville."

HELLER, STEVE. Born Nov. 22, 1951 in Philadelphia, PA. Graduate Dickinson Col. Debut 1980 OB in "Anyone Can Whistle."

HELLMAN, BONNIE. Born Jan. 10, 1950 in San Francisco, CA. Graduate Cal. State U. Bdwy debut 1979 in "The Utter Glory of Morrissey Hall," followed by "Once a Catholic," OB in "The Derby."

HELTON, MELANIE. Born Feb. 19, 1956 in Cincinnati, OH. Graduate IndU. Debut 1978 OB in "One for My Baby," Bdwy 1979 in "The Most Happy Fella."

HEMSLEY, WINSTON DeWITT. Born May 21, 1947 in Brooklyn, NY. Bdwy debut 1965 in "Golden Boy," followed by "A Joyful Noise," "Hallelujah, Baby," "Hello, Dolly!" Rockabye Hamlet," "A Chorus Line," "Eubie!," OB in "Buy Bonds Buster."

HENDERSON, JO. Born in Buffalo, NY. Attended WMiU. OB in "Camille," "Little Foxes," "An Evening with Merlin Finch," "20th Century Tar," "A Scent of Flowers," "Revival," "Dandelion Wine," "My Life," "Ladyhouse Blues," "Fallen Angels."

HENDERSON, MELANIE. Born Sept. 20, 1957 in NYC. Debut 1970 OB in "The Me Nobody Knows," followed by "Sidewalkin'."

HENRITZE, BETTE. Born May 3 in Betsy Layne, KY. Graduate UTenn. OB in "Lion in Love," "Abe Lincoln in Illinois," "Othello," "Baal," "Long Christmas Dinner," "Queens of France," "Rimers of Eldritch," "Displaced Person," "Acquisition," "Crime of Passion," "Happiness Cage," "Henry VI," "Richard III," "Older People," "Lotta," "Catsplay," "A Month in the Country," Bdwy in "Jenny Kissed Me" (1948), "Pictures in the Hallway," "Giants, Sons of Giants," "Ballad of the Sad Cafe," "The White House," "Dr. Cook's Garden," "Here's Where I Belong," "Much Ado About Nothing," "Over Here," "Angel Street," "Man and Superman."

HEUCHLING, PETER. Born May 26, 1953 in Evanston, IL. Graduate UMiami. Debut 1974 OB in "Oh Lady, Lady!" (ELT), Bdwy 1980 in "The Best Little Whorehouse in Texas."

HEWETT, CHRISTOPHER. Born Apr. 5 in England, attended Beaumont Col. Bdwy debut 1957 in "My Fair Lady," followed by "First Impressions," "Unsinkable Molly Brown," "Kean," "The Affair," "Hadrian VII," "Music Is," "Peter Pan" (1980), OB in "Tobias and the Angel," "Trelawny of the Wells," "Finian's Rainbow (JB), "New Jerusalem."

HICKEY, WILLIAM. Born in 1928 in Brooklyn, NY. Studied at HB Studio. Bdwy bow 1951 in "St. Joan," followed by "Tovarich," "Miss Lonelyhearts," "Body Beautiful," "Make a Million," "Not Enough Rope," "Moonbirds," "Step on a Crack," "Thieves," OB in "On the Town," "Next," "Happy Birthday, Wanda June," "Small Craft Warnings," "Mourning Becomes Electra," "Siamese Connections," "Troilus and Cressida," "Sunday Runners."

HICKS, LOIS DIANE. Born Sept. 3, 1940 in Brooklyn, NY. Graduate NYCCC, AADA. Debut 1979 OB in "On A Clear Day You Can See Forever," "Yank in Beverly Hills."

HIGGINS, JAMES. Born June 1, 1932 in Worksop, Eng. Graduate Cambridge U., Yale. Debut 1963 OB in "The Magistrate," followed by "Stevie," Bdwy in "The Zulu and the Zayda," "Whose Life Is It Anyway?"

HIGGINS, JOEL. Born Sept. 28, 1943 in Bloomington, IL. Graduate MichStateU. Bdwy debut 1975 in "Shenandoah" for which he received a Theatre World Award, followed by "Music Is," "Angel," "Oklahoma!" (1980), OB in "Camp Meeting."

| **Kristie Hannum** | **Gordon Heath** | **Gloria Hoye** | **George Hosmer** | **Annette Hunt** |

HIGGINS, MICHAEL. Born Jan. 20, 1926 in Bklyn. Attended Theatre Wing. Bdwy bow 1946 in "Antigone," followed by "Our Lan'," "Romeo and Juliet," "The Crucible," "The Lark," "Equus," "Whose Life Is It Anyway?," OB in "White Devil," "Carefree Tree," "Easter," "The Queen and the Rebels," "Sally, George and Martha," "L'Ete," "Uncle Vanya," "The Iceman Cometh," "Molly," "Artichoke," "Reunion," "Chieftans."

HIGGINS, ROBERT. Born Feb. 6, 1932 in Fall River, MA. Bdwy debut 1956 in "Auntie Mame," OB in "Teeth 'n' Smiles."

HIKEN, GERALD. Born May 23, 1927 in Milwaukee, WI. Attended UWis. OB in "Cherry Orchard," "Seagull," "Good Woman of Setzuan," "The Misanthrope," "The Iceman Cometh," "The New Theatre," "Strider," Bdwy in "Lovers," "Cave Dwellers," "Nervous Set," "Fighting Cock," "49th Cousin," "Gideon," "Foxy," "Three Sisters," "Golda," "Strider."

HILLNER, JOHN. Born Nov. 5, 1952 in Evanston, IL. Graduate Denison U. Debut 1977 OB in "Essential Shepard," followed by Bdwy 1979 in "They're Playing Our Song."

HINES, GREGORY. Born Feb. 14, 1946 in NYC. Bdwy debut 1954 in "The Girl in Pink Tights," followed by "Eubie!" for which he received a Theatre World Award, "Comin' Uptown," "Black Broadway."

HINES, PATRICK. Born Mar. 17, 1930 in Burkesville, TX. Graduate TexU. Debut OB in "Duchess of Malfi," followed by "Lysistrata," "Peer Gynt," "Henry IV," "Richard III," "Hot Grog," BAM's "A Winter's Tale," "Johnny on a Spot," "Barbarians," "The Wedding," Bdwy in "The Great God Brown," "Passage to India," "The Devils," "Cyrano," "The Iceman Cometh," "A Texas Trilogy," "Caesar and Cleopatra."

HINNANT, SKIP. Born Sept. 12, 1940 in Chincoteague Island, VA. Yale graduate. Debut 1964 OB in "The Knack," followed by "You're a Good Man, Charlie Brown," "Two."

HIRSCH, JUDD. Born Mar. 15, 1935 in NYC. Attended AADA. Bdwy debut 1966 in "Barefoot in the Park," followed by "Chapter Two," "Talley's Folly," OB in "On the Necessity of Being Polygamous," "Scuba Duba," "Mystery Play," "Hot l Baltimore," "Prodigal," "Knock Knock," "Life and/or Death," "Talley's Folly."

HOFFMAN, JANE. Born July 24, in Seattle, WA. Graduate UCal. Bdwy debut 1940 in "Tis of Thee," followed by "Crazy with the Heat," "Something for the Boys," "One Touch of Venus," "Calico Wedding," "Mermaids Singing," "Temporary Island," "Story for Strangers," "Two Blind Mice," "Rose Tattoo," "The Crucible," "Witness for the Prosecution," "Third Best Sport," "Rhinoceros," "Mother Courage and Her Children," "Fair Game for Lovers," "A Murderer Among Us," "Murder Among Friends," OB in "American Dream," "Sandbox," "Picnic on the Battlefield," "Theatre of the Absurd," "Child Buyer," "A Corner of the Bed," "Someone's Comin' Hungry," "Increased Difficulty of Concentration," "American Hamburger League," "Slow Memories," "Last Analysis," "Dear Oscar," "Hocus-Pocus," "Lessons," "The Art of Dining," "Second Avenue Rag."

HOGAN, JONATHAN. Born June 13, 1951 in Chicago, IL. Graduate Goodman Theatre. Debut OB 1972 in "The Hot l Baltimore," followed by "Mound Builders," "Harry Outside," "Cabin 12," "5th of July," "Glorious Morning," "Innocent Thoughts, Harmless Intentions," "Sunday Runners," Bdwy in "Comedians" (1976). "Otherwise Engaged."

HOLBROOK, RUBY. Born Aug. 28, 1930 in St. John's Nfld. Attended Denison U. Debut 1963 OB in "Abe Lincoln in Illinois," followed by "Hamlet," "James Joyce's Dubliners," "Measure for Measure," "The Farm," Bdwy 1979 in "Da."

HOLGATE, RONALD. Born May 26, 1937 in Aberdeen, SD. Attended Northwestern U., New Eng. Cons. Debut 1961 OB in "Hobo," followed by "Hooray, It's a Glorious Day," Bdwy in "A Funny Thing Happened on the Way . . .," "Milk and Honey," "1776," "Saturday Sunday Monday," "The Grand Tour," "Musical Chairs."

HOLM, CELESTE. Born Apr. 29, 1919 in NYC. Attended UCLA, UChicago. Bdwy debut 1938 in "Gloriana," followed by "The Time of Your Life," "Another Sun," "Return of the Vagabond," "8 O'Clock Tuesday," "My Fair Ladies," "Papa Is All," "All the Comforts of Home," "Damask Cheek," "Oklahoma!," "Bloomer Girl," "She Stoops to Conquer," "Affairs of State," "Anna Christie," "The King and I," "His and Hers," "Interlock," "Third Best Sport," "Invitation to a March," "Mame," "Candida," "Habeas Corpus," "The Utter Glory of Morrissey Hall," OB in "A Month in the Country," "Paris Was Yesterday."

HOLMAN, BRYCE. Born Jan. 3, 1934 in Trenton, NJ. Attended Yale. Debut 1964 OB in "The Amorous Flea," followed by "The Secret Affairs of Mildred Wild," "Deli's Fable," "Merton of the Movies" (ELT).

HOLMES, PRUDENCE WRIGHT. Born in Boston, MA. Attended Carnegie Tech. Debut 1971 OB in "Godspell," followed by "Polly," "The Crazy Locomotive," "Dona Rosita," Bdwy 1977 in "Happy End."

HOMYAK, LOUIS F. Born Nov. 7, 1947 in Newark, NJ. Graduate Montclair State Col. Bdwy 1976 in "Marat/deSade," OB in "Exit the King," "Cenci," "Saints and Sinners," "Young Wolves," "Takeover," "Moon of the Caribees," "Teeth 'n' Smiles," "Love's Labour's Lost."

HOROWITZ, JEFFREY. Born Mar. 29, 1949 in NYC. Graduate UCLA. Bdwy debut 1977 in "The Merchant," OB in "Youth Hostel," "The Enchanted," "The Persians," "Love's Labour's Lost."

HORWITZ, MURRAY. Born Sept. 28, 1949 in Dayton, OH. Graduate Kenyon Col. Debut 1976 OB in "An Evening of Sholom Aleichem," followed by "Hard Sell."

HOSBEIN, JAMES. Born Sept. 24, 1946 in Benton Harbor, MI. Graduate UMich. Debut 1972 OB in "Dear Oscar," followed by "Darrel and Carol and Kenny and Jenny," Bdwy 1977 in "Annie."

HOSMER, GEORGE. Born Sept. 4, 1941 in Essex, NY. Attended USC, UMd, UHeidelberg, HB Studio. Debut 1979 OB in "I'm Getting My Act Together and Taking It On the Road."

HOSTETTER, CURTIS. Born Dec. 16, 1953 in Harrisburg, PA. Graduate Messiah Col. Debut 1977 OB in "My Life," followed by "Romeo and Juliet" (ELT).

HOWES, LINDA. Born Aug. 20 in Flint, MI. Graduate UMich. Bdwy debut 1980 in "Nuts."

HOXIE, RICHMOND. Born July 21, 1946 in NYC. Graduate Dartmouth Col., LAMDA. Debut 1975 OB in "Shaw for an Evening," followed by "The Family," "Justice."

HOYE, GLORIA. Born July 24, 1932 in NYC. Attended Actors Studio. Bdwy debut 1959 in "The Highest Tree," followed by "Isle of Children," "Face of a Hero," OB in "The Dark at the Top of the Stairs."

HUBBARD, ELIZABETH. Born Dec. 22 in NYC. Graduate Radcliffe Col. RADA. Bdwy debut 1960 in "The Affair," followed by "The Physicists," "A Time for Singing," "A Day in the Death of Joe Egg," "Children, Children," "I Remember Mama" (1979), OB in "The Threepenny Opera," "Boys from Syracuse," "War and Peace."

HUGHES, BARNARD. Born July 16, 1915 in Bedford Hills, NY. Attended Manhattan Col. OB in "Rosmersholm," "A Doll's House," "Hogan's Goat," "Lime," "Older People," "Hamlet," "Merry Wives of Windsor," "Pericles," BAM Co.'s "Three Sisters," Bdwy in "The Ivy Green," "Dinosaur Wharf," "Teahouse of the August Moon" (CC), "A Majority of One," "Advise and Consent," "The Advocate," "Hamlet," "I Was Dancing," "Generation," "How Now, Dow Jones?," "Wrong Way Light Bulb," "Sheep On the Runway," "Abelard and Heloise," "Much Ado About Nothing," "Uncle Vanya," "The Good Doctor," "All Over Town," "Da."

HUGHES, TRESA. Born Sept. 17, 1929 in Washington, DC. Attended Wayne U. OB in "Electra," "The Crucible," "Hogan's Goat," "Party on Greenwich Avenue," "Fragments," "Passing through from Exotic Places," "Beggar on Horseback," (LC), "Early Morning," "The Old Ones," "Holy Places," Bdwy in "Miracle Worker," "The Devil's Advocate," "Dear Me, the Sky Is Falling," "Last Analysis," "Spofford," "Man in the Glass Booth," "Prisoner of Second Avenue," "Tribute."

HULL BRYAN. Born Sept. 12, 1937 in Amarillo, TX. Attended UNMex., Wayne State U. Bdwy debut 1976 in "Something's Afoot," OB in "The Fantasticks."

HUNT, ANNETTE. Born Jan. 31, 1938 in Hampton, VA. Graduate Va. Intermont Col. Debut 1957 OB in "Nine by Six," followed by "The Taming of the Shrew," "Medea," "The Anatomist," "The Misanthrope," "The Cherry Orchard," "Electra," "Last Resort," "The Seducers," "A Sound of Silence," "Charades," "Dona Rosita," Bdwy 1972 in "All the Girls Came Out to Play."

HUNT, RUTH. Born Dec. 26 in Kansas City, MO. Graduate Yale, Stanford. Bdwy debut 1973 in "Crown Matrimonial," followed by "Emperor Henry IV," "Dogg's Hamlet, Cahoot's MacBeth," OB in "Ice Age."

HURT, WILLIAM. Born Mar. 20, 1950 in Washington, DC. Graduate Tufts U., Juilliard. Debut 1976 OB in "Henry V," followed by "My Life," "Ulysses in Traction," "Lulu," "5th of July," "The Runner Stumbles," He received a 1978 Theatre World Award for his performances with Circle Repertory Theatre, followed by "Hamlet," "Mary Stuart."

HYMAN, EARLE. Born Oct. 11, 1926 in Rocky Mount, NC. Attended New School, Theatre Wing. Bdwy debut 1943 in "Run, Little Chillun," followed by "Anna Lucasta," "Climate of Eden," "Merchant of Venice," "Othello," "Julius Caesar," "The Tempest," "No Time for Sergeants," "Mr. Johnson" for which he received a Theatre World Award, "St. Joan," "Hamlet," "Waiting for Godot," "Duchess of Malfi," "Les Blancs," "The Lady from Dubuque," OB in "The White Rose and the Red," "Worlds of Shakespeare," "Jonah," "Life and Times of J. Walter Smintheus," "Orrin," "Cherry Orchard," "House Party," "Carnival Dreams," "Agamemnon," "Othello," "Julius Caesar," "Coriolanus," "Remembrance."

IACANGELO, PETER. Born Aug. 13, 1948 in Brooklyn, NY. Attended Hofstra U. Bdwy debut 1968 in "Jimmy Shine," followed by "Filumena," OB in "One Flew over the Cuckoo's Nest," "Moonchildren," "Comedy of Errors."

INGRAM, TAD. Born Sept. 11, 1948 in Pittsburgh, PA. Graduate TempleU, LAMDA. Debut 1979 in "Biography: A Game," Bdwy 1979 in "Strider."

INTROCASO, JOHN C. Born June 3, 1947 in Rutherford, NJ. Graduate St. Peter's Col. Debut 1979 OB in "The Sound of Music."

IVEY, JUDITH. Born Sept. 4, 1951 in El Paso, TX. Graduate IllStateU. Bdwy debut 1979 in "Bedroom Farce," followed OB in "Dusa, Fish, Stas and Vi," "Sunday Runners."

JABLONS, KAREN. Born July 19, 1951 in Trenton, NJ. Juilliard graduate. Debut 1969 OB in "The Student Prince," followed by "Sound of Music," "Funny Girl," "Boys from Syracuse," "Sterling Silver," "People In Show Business Make Long Goodbyes," Bdwy in "Ari," "Two Gentlemen of Verona," "Lorelei," "Where's Charley?," "A Chorus Line."

JACOBS, MARC RUSTY,. Born July 10, 1967 in NYC. Debut OB 1979 in "Tripletale," Bdwy 1979 in "Peter Pan."

JAMES, ELMORE. Born May 3, 1954 in NYC. Graduate SUNY/Purchase. Debut 1970 OB in "Moon on a Rainbow Shawl," followed by "The Ups and Downs of Theopholus Maitland," "Carnival," Bdwy 1979 in "But Never Jam Today."

JAMES, JESSICA. Born Oct. 31, 1933 in Los Angeles, CA. Attended USC. Bdwy debut 1970 in "Company," followed by "Gemini," OB in "Nourish the Beast," "Hothouse," "Loss of Innocence," "Rebirth Celebration of the Human Race," "Silver Bee," "Gemini."

JAMES, STEPHEN. Born Feb. 2, 1952 in Mt. Vernon, OH. Princeton graduate. Debut 1977 OB in "Castaways," followed by "Green Pond," Bdwy in "The 1940's Radio Hour" for which he received a Theatre World Award, "A Day in Hollywood, A Night in the Ukraine."

JAMES, WILLIAM. Born Apr. 29 in Jersey City, NJ. Graduate NJ State Teachers Col. Bdwy bow 1962 in "Camelot," followed by "Maggie Flynn," "Coco," "My Fair Lady" (CC & 1976), "Where's Charley?" (CC), "She Loves Me," OB in "Anything Goes," "Smith," "The Music Man" (JB).

JAMISON, BETSY. Born Apr. 23, 1952 in Princeton, NJ. Graduate Lindenwood Col. Debut 1980 OB in "It's Wilde!"

JASPER, ZINA. Born Jan 29, 1939 in The Bronx, NY. Attended CCNY. Bdwy debut 1967 in "Something Different," followed by "Paris Is Out," OB in "Saturday's Children," "Moondreamers," "A Dream out of Time," "Quail Southwest," "On Green Pond," "Artichoke," "My Mother, My Father and Me."

JAY, MARY. Born Dec. 23, 1939 in Brooklyn, NY. Graduate UMaine, AmThWing. Debut 1962 OB in "Little Mary Sunshine," followed by "Toys in the Attic," "Telecast," "Sananda Sez," Bdwy in "The Student Gypsy."

JAY-ALEXANDER, RICHARD. Born May 24, 1953 in Syracuse, NY. Graduate S.IllU. Debut 1975 OB in "Boys Meets Boy," Bdwy 1979 in "Zoot Suit."

JENKINS, CAROL MAYO. Born Nov. 24 in Knoxville, TN. Attended Vanderbilt U., UTn., London Central Sch. of Speech. Bdwy debut 1969 in "The Three Sisters," followed by "There's One in Every Marriage," "Kings," "First Monday in October," OB in "Zinnia."

JENNINGS, KEN. Born Oct. 10, 1947 in Jersey City, NJ. Graduate St. Peter's Col. Bdwy Debut 1975 in "All God's Chillun Got Wings," followed by "Sweeney Todd" for which he received a Theatre World Award.

JETER, MICHAEL. Born Aug. 26, 1952 in Lawrenceburg, TN. Graduate Memphis State U. Bdwy debut 1978 in "Once in a Lifetime," OB in "The Master and Margarita," "G. R. Point" for which he received a Theatre World Award.

JILLIAN, ANN. Born Jan. 29, 1950 in Cambridge, MA. Graduate CCLA. Bdwy debut 1979 in "Sugar Babies."

JOHNSON, ARCH. Born Mar. 14, 1931 in Minneapolis, MN. Attended UPa., Neighborhood Playhouse. Debut 1952 OB in "Down in the Valley," followed by "St. Joan," "Purple Dust," Bdwy in "Mrs. McThing," "Bus Stop," "The Happiest Millionaire," "West Side Story" (1957 & 1980).

JOHNSON, KURT. Born Oct. 5, 1952 in Pasadena, CA. Attended LACC, Occidental Col. Debut 1976 OB in "Follies," followed by "Walking Papers," "A Touch of Marble," Bdwy in "Rockaby Hamlet," "A Chorus Line."

JOHNSON, LORNA. Born Oct. 19, 1943 in PA. Graduate West Chester State Col. Debut 1979 OB in "The Last Days at the Dixie Girl Cafe," followed by "The Chronicle of Jane."

JOHNSON, MEL JR. Born Apr. 16, 1949 in NYC. Graduate Hofstra U. Debut 1972 OB in "Hamlet," followed by "Love! Love! Love!" "Shakespeare's Cabaret," Bdwy in "On the 20th Century," "Eubie!"

JOHNSON, ONNI. Born Mar. 16, 1949 in NYC. Graduate Brandeis U. Debut 1964 in "Unfinished Business," followed by "She Stoops to Conquer," "22 Years," "The Master and Margarita," Bdwy in "Oh, Calcutta!"

JOHNSON, PAGE. Born Aug. 25, 1930 in Welch, WV. Graduate Ithaca Col. Bdwy bow 1951 in "Romeo and Juliet," followed by "Electra," "Oedipus," "Camino Real," "In April Once" for which he received a Theatre World Award, "Red Roses for Me," "The Lovers," "Equus," OB in "The Enchanted," "Guitar," "4 in 1," "Journey of the Fifth Horse," APA's "School for Scandal," "The Tavern," and "The Seagull," "Odd Couple," "Boys In The Band," "Medea," "Deathtrap."

JOHNSON, TINA. Born Oct. 27, 1951 in Wharton, TX. Graduate North Tx. State U. Debut 1979 OB in "Festival," Bdwy in "The Best Little Whorehouse in Texas."

JOLLEY, NICK. Born Feb. 17, 1948 in Hindsboro, IL. Gradaute. S.Ill.U. Bdwy debut 1979 in "Oklahoma!"

JONES, BAMBI. Born Apr. 14, 1961 in NYC. Debut 1969 OB in "An Evening of One Acts," followed by "Forty-Deuce!"

JONES, CHARLOTTE. Born Jan. 1 in Chicago, IL. Attended DePaul, Loyola U. Bdwy debut 1953 in "Camino Real," followed by "Buttrio Square," "Mame," "How Now Dow Jones," "Skin of Our Teeth," "A Matter of Gravity," OB in "False Confessions," "Sign of Jonah," "Girl on the Via Flaminia," "Red Roses for Me," "Night in Black Bottles," "Camino Real," "Plays for Bleecker St.," "Pigeons," "Great Scot!," "Sjt. Musgrave's Dance," "Papers," "Johnny Johnson," "Beggar's Opera," "200 Years of American Furniture," "Belle Femme."

JONES, EDDIE. Born in Washington, PA. Debut 1960 OB in "Dead End," followed by "Curse of the Starving Class," "The Ruffian on the Stair," Bdwy 1974 in "That Championship Season," "Devour the Snow."

JONES, REED. Born June 30, 1953 in Portland, OR. Graduate USIU. Bdwy debut 1979 in "Peter Pan," followed by "West Side Story."

JORDAN, MARC. Born Jan. 14, 1931 in New Haven, CT. Graduate UConn. Debut 1960 OB in "Leave It to Jane," followed by "To Be Young, Gifted and Black," "Saturday Night," "Get Thee to Canterbury," Bdwy in "Do Re Mi," "Little Me," "Funny Girl," "The Apple Tree," "Darling of the Day," "Her First Roman," "Pajama Game" (1973), "Something's Afoot," "Music Is," "Spotlight," "Carmelina," "Harold and Maude."

JOSEPH, ALLEN. Born May 29, 1919 in Minneapolis, MN. Graduate UMinn. Bdwy debut 1954 in "Anastasia," OB in "The Mousetrap," "Time of Vengeance," "Krapp's Last Tape," "The Buskers," "Taming of the Shrew," "Second Avenue Rag."

JOSEPH, STEPHEN. Born Aug. 27, 1952 in Shaker Heights, OH. Graduate Carnegie-Mellon, Fla. State U. Debut 1978 OB in "Oklahoma!"

JOSLYN, BETSY. Born Apr. 19, 1954 in Staten Island, NY. Graduate Wagner Col. Debut 1976 OB in "The Fantasticks," Bdwy 1979 in "Sweeney Todd."

JOYCE, KIYA ANN. Born Aug. 9, 1953 in Tachikawa, Japan. Attended Dade Jr. Col. Debut 1980 OB in "Innocent Thoughts, Harmless Intentions."

JOYCE, STEPHEN. Born Mar. 7, 1933 in NYC. Attended Fordham U. Bdwy bow 1966 in "Those That Play the Clowns," followed by "The Exercise," "The Runner Stumbles," "Devour the Snow," OB in "Three Hand Reel," "Galileo," "St. Joan," "Stephen D" for which he received a Theatre World Award, "Fireworks," "School for Wives," "Savages," "Scribes," "Daisy."

JUDD, ROBERT. Born Aug. 3, 1927 in NYC. Debut 1972 OB in "Don't Let It Go to Your Head," followed by "Black Visions," "Sweet Enemy," "The Lion Is a Soul Brother," "Welfare," Bdwy 1980 in "Watch on the Rhine."

JUDE, PATRICK. Feb. 25, 1951 in Jersey City, NJ. Bdwy debut 1972 in "Jesus Christ Superstar," followed by 1977 revival, "Got Tu Go Disco," OB in "The Haggadah."

JULIA, RAUL. Born Mar. 9, 1940 in San Juan, PR. Graduate UPR. OB in "Macbeth," "Titus Andronicus" (CP), "Theatre in the Streets," "Life Is a Dream," "Blood Wedding," "Ox Cart," "No Exit," "Memorandum," "Frank Gagliano's City Scene," "Your Own Thing," "Persians," "Castro Complex," "Pinkville," "Hamlet," "King Lear," "As You Like It," "Emperor of Late Night Radio," "Threepenny Opera," "The Cherry Orchard," "Taming of the Shrew," "Othello," Bdwy bow 1968 in "The Cuban Thing," followed by "Indians," "Two Gentlemen of Verona," "Via Galactia," "Where's Charley?," "Dracula," "Betrayal."

KANDEL, PAUL. Born Feb. 15, 1951 in Queens, NYC. Graduate Harpur Col. Debut 1977 OB in "Nightclub Cantata," followed by "Two Grown Men."

KANSAS, JERI. Born Mar. 10, 1955 in Jersey City, NJ. Debut 1978 OB in "Gay Divorce," Bdwy 1979 in "Sugar Babies."

KAPEN, BEN. Born July 2, 1928 in NYC. Graduate NYU. Bdwy debut 1968 in "The Happy Time," followed by "The Man in the Glass Booth," "Penny Wars," OB in "No Trifling with Love," "Good News," "A Memory of Two Mondays," "They Knew What They Wanted," "Deli's Fable."

KAREMAN, FRED. Born June 24, 1934 in Asbury Park, NJ. Attended Rutgers U., Neighborhood Playhouse. Debut 1955 OB in "Salvage," followed by "Taming of the Shrew," "Days and Nights of Beebee Fenstermaker," "Pushcart Peddlers," Bdwy in "The Skin of Our Teeth," "The Time of Your Life" (CC), "The Re-education of Horse Johnson," "A Cook for Mr. General."

KARIBALIS, CURT. Born Feb. 24, 1947 in Superior, WI. Graduate UWis. Debut 1971 OB in "Woyzeck," Bdwy in "The Great God Brown," "Don Juan," "The Visit," "Chemin de Fer," "Holiday," "Goodbye Fidel."

KARIN, RITA. Born Oct. 24, 1919 in Warsaw, Poland. Bdwy debut 1960 in "The Wall," followed by "A Call on Kuprin," "Penny Wars," "Yentl," OB in "Pocket Watch," "Scuba Duba," "House of Blue Leaves," "Yentl the Yeshiva Boy," "Poets from the Inside," "Sharon Shashanovah."

KARLIN, KRISTINA. Born July 8, 1943 in Wichita, KS. Graduate Wichita State U. Bdwy debut 1976 in "1600 Pennsylvania Avenue," followed by "My Fair Lady," OB in "The Sound of Music" (ELT).

KARNOVSKY, BILL. Born Mar. 21, 1951 in Rensselaer, IN. Graduate Northwestern U. Bdwy debut 1980 in "Filumena," OB in "The Passion of Dracula."

KARPEN, PAT. Born Feb. 21, 1951 in Washington, DC. Graduate Catholic U. Debut 1980 OB in "The Marriage."

KARR, PATTI. Born July 10 in St. Paul, MN. Attended TCU. Bdwy debut 1953 in "Maggie," followed by "Carnival in Flanders," "Pipe Dream," "Bells Are Ringing," "New Girl in Town," "Body Beautiful," "Bye Bye Birdie," "New Faces of 1962," "Come on Strong," "Look to the Lilies," "Different Times," "Lysistrata," "Seesaw," "Irene," "Pippin," "A Broadway Musical," "Got Tu Go Disco," "Musical Chairs," OB in "A Month of Sundays," "Up Eden," "Snapshot," "Housewives Cantata."

KATCHER, HOPE. Born June 22, 1951 in Brooklyn, NY. Graduate Boston U. Bdwy debut 1976 in "Fiddler on the Roof," OB in "King David and His Wives."

KAVANAUGH, RICHARD. Born in 1943 in NYC. Bdwy debut 1977 in "Dracula."

KAWALEK, NANCY. Born Feb. 25, 1956 in Brooklyn, NY. Graduate Northwestern U. Bdwy debut 1979 in "Strider."

KAYE, JUDY. Born Oct. 11, 1948 in Phoenix, AZ. Attended UCLA, Ariz. State U. Bdwy debut 1977 in "Grease," followed by "On the 20th Century" for which she received a Theatre World Award.

KAYE, TONI. Born Aug. 26, 1946 in Chicago, IL. Bdwy debut 1979 in "Sugar Babies."

KEACH, STACY. Born June 2, 1941 in Savannah, GA. Graduate UCal., Yale, LAMDA. Debut 1967 OB in "MacBird," followed by "Niggerlovers," "Henry IV," "Country Wife," "Hamlet," Bdwy in "Indians," "Deathtrap."

KEAGY, GRACE. Born Dec. 16 in Youngstown, OH. Attended New Eng. Consv. Debut 1974 OB in "Call Me Madam," Bdwy in "Goodtime Charley," "The Grand Tour," "Carmelina," "I Remember Mama," "Musical Chairs."

KEARNEY, LYNN. Born Apr. 9, 1951 in Chicago, IL. Graduate NYU. Bdwy debut 1978 in "Annie."

KEITH, BRIAN. (a.k.a. Robert, Jr.) Born Nov. 14, 1921 in Bayonne, NJ. Bdwy in "Mister Roberts," "Darkness at Noon," "Da."

KEITH, LAWRENCE (LARRY). Born Mar. 4, 1931 in Brooklyn, NY. Graduate Bklyn Col. Indiana U. Bdwy debut 1960 in "My Fair Lady," followed by "High Spirits," "I Had a Ball," "Best Laid Plans," "Mother Lover," OB in "The Homecoming," "Conflict of Interest," "Brownsville Raid," "M. Amilcar."

KELL, MICHAEL. Born Jan. 18, 1944 in Jersey City, NJ. Attended HB Studio. Debut 1972 OB in "One Flew Over The Cuckoo's Nest," followed by "Boom Boom Room," "Golden Boy," "Streamers," "Awake and Sing," "Mr. Shandy," "Sunday Runners," Bdwy 1979 in "Loose Ends."

KELLER, JEFF. Born Sept. 8, 1947 in Brooklyn, NY. Graduate Monmouth Col. Bdwy debut 1974 in "Candide," followed by "Fiddler on the Roof," "On the 20th Century," "The 1940's Radio Show."

KELLERMANN, SUSAN. Born July 4. Attended Neighborhood Playhouse. Bdwy debut 1979 in "Last Licks," for which she received a Theatre World Award, followed by "Whose Life Is It Anyway?", OB in "Wine Untouched," "Crab Quadrille," "Country Club," "Cinque and the Jones Man."

KELLY, K. C. Born Dec. 12, 1952 in Baraboo, WI. Attended UWisc. Debut 1976 OB in "The Chicken Ranch," followed by Bdwy in "Romeo and Juliet," (1977), "The Best Little Whorehouse in Texas."

KENNEDY, LAURIE. Born Feb. 14, 1948 in Hollywood, CA. Graduate Sarah Lawrence Col. Debut 1974 OB in "End of Summer," followed by "A Day in the Death of Joe Egg," "Ladyhouse Blues," BAM's "He and She," Bdwy in "Man and Superman," (1978) for which she received a Theatre World Award, "Major Barbara."

KENYON, LAURA. Born Nov. 23, 1948 in Chicago, IL. Attended USCal. Debut 1970 OB in "Peace," followed by "Carnival," "Dementos," Bdwy in "Man of LaMancha" (1971), "On the Town."

KERNER, NORBERTO. Born July 19, 1929 in Valparaiso, Chile. Attended Piscator Workshop, Goodman Theatre. Debut 1971 OB in "Yerma," followed by "I Took Panama," "The F. M. Safe," "My Old Friends," "Sharon Shashanovah," "Blood Wedding."

KERR, PHILIP. Born Apr. 9, 1940 in NYC. Attended Harvard, LAMDA. Bdwy debut 1969 in "Tiny Alice," followed by "A Flea in Her Ear," "Three Sisters" "Jockey Club Stakes," OB in "Hamlet" "The Rehearsal," "Cuchlain."

KERT, LARRY. Born Dec. 5, 1934 in Los Angeles, CA. Attended LACC. Bdwy bow 1953 in "John Murray Anderson's Almanac," followed by "Ziegfeld Follies," "Mr. Wonderful," "Walk Tall," "Look, Ma, I'm Dancin'," "Tickets Please," "West Side Story," "A Family Affair," "Breakfast at Tiffany's," "Cabaret," "La Strada," "Company," "Two Gentlemen of Verona," "Music! Music!," "Musical Jubilee," "Side by Side by Sondheim," OB in "Changes."

KEYLOUN, MARK. Born Oct. 20, 1955 in Brooklyn, NY. Attended Georgetown U. Debut 1980 in "M. Amilcar."

KHEEL, LEE. Born Oct. 24, 1918 in Springfield, MA. Graduate Ithaca Col., URochester. Debut 1980 OB in "The Time of the Cuckoo" (ELT).

KHOUTIEFF, JEANNINE. Born Nov. 6, 1956 in Michigan. Graduate SUNY. Debut 1979 OB in "Biography: A Game," followed by "Strider," (also Bdwy).

KILLMER, NANCY. Born Dec. 16, 1936 in Homewood, IL. Graduate Northwestern U. Bdwy debut 1969 in "Coco," followed by "Goodtime Charley," "So Long, 174th Street," OB in "Exiles," "A Little Night Music," "Sweeney Todd," OB in "Exiles," "Mrs. Murray's Farm."

KILTY, JEROME. Born June 24, 1922 in Pala Ind. Reservation, CA. Attended London's Guildhall Sch. Bdwy debut 1950 in "The Relapse," followed by "Love's Labour's Lost" (CC), "Misalliance," "A Pin to See the Peepshow," "Frogs of Spring," "Quadrille," "Othello," "Henry IV," OB in "Dear Liar," "A Month in the Country."

KING, MICHAEL E. Born June 28, 1956 in Winter Haven, FL. Graduate Ringling Bros. Clown Col. Bdwy debut 1979 in "Snow White."

KING, PERRY. Born Apr. 30 in Alliance, OH. Yale graduate. Debut 1972 OB in "Jesse James," followed by "Knuckle," "The Trouble with Europe."

KIRSCH, CAROLYN. Born May 24, 1942 in Shreveport, LA. Bdwy debut 1963 in "How to Succeed . . . ," followed by "Folies Bergere," "La Grosse Valise," "Skyscraper," "Breakfast at Tiffany's," "Sweet Charity," "Hallelujah, Baby!," "Dear World," "Promises, Promises," "Coco," "Ulysses in Nighttown," "A Chorus Line," OB in "Silk Stockings," "Telecast."

KLEIN, ROBERT. Born Feb. 8, 1942 in NYC. Graduate Alfred U., Yale. OB in "Six Characters in Search of an Author," "Second City Returns," "Upstairs at the Downstairs," Bdwy in "The Apple Tree," "New Faces of 1968," "Morning, Noon and Night," "They're Playing Our Song."

KLINE, KEVIN. Born Oct. 24, 1947 in St. Louis, MO. Graduate Ind. U., Juilliard. Debut 1970 OB in "Wars of Roses," followed by "School for Scandal," "Lower Depths," "The Hostage," "Women Beware Women," "Robber Bridegroom," "Edward II," "The Time of Your Life," "Beware the Jubjub Bird," "Dance on a Country Grave," Bdwy in "Three Sisters," "Measure for Measure," "Beggar's Opera," "Scapin," "On the 20th Century," "Loose Ends."

KLING, IRENE FRANCES. Born Mar. 25, 1947 in Brooklyn, NY. Graduate NYU, AADA. Debut 1966 OB in "Miss Julie," followed by "The Stronger," "Death of Bessie Smith," "Don Juan in Hell," "Hands of God," "Beggar's Opera," "Bees."

KLUNIS, TOM. Born in San Francisco, CA. Bdwy debut 1961 in "Gideon," followed by "The Devils," "Henry V," "Romeo and Juliet," "St. Joan," "Hide and Seek," OB in "The Immoralist," "Hamlet," "Arms and the Man," "Potting Shed," "Measure for Measure," "Romeo and Juliet," "The Balcony," "Our Town," "Man Who Never Died," "God is My Ram," "Rise, Marlowe," "Iphigenia in Aulis," "Still Life," "The Master and Margarita," "As You Like It," "The Winter Dancers."

KNIGHT, SHIRLEY. Born July 5, in Goessel, KS. Attended Phillips U., Wichita U. Bdwy debut 1964 in "The Three Sisters," followed by "We Have Always Lived in a Castle," "The Watering Place," "Kennedy's Children," OB in "Journey to the Day," "Rooms," "Happy End," "Landscape of the Body," "A Lovely Sunday for Creve Coeur,' "Losing Time."

KNIGHT, WAYNE. Born Aug. 7, 1955 in NYC. Graduate UGa. Bdwy debut 1979 in "Gemini."

KOBLICK, MELINDA. Born Dec. 20, 1959 in St. Louis, MO. Debut 1980 OB in "Plain and Fancy" (ELT).

KOPYC, FRANK. Born Aug. 6, 1948 in Troy, NY. Graduate Yankton Col. Debut 1973 OB in "Pop," followed by "Fiorello!," Bdwy in "Sweeney Todd."

KOREY, ALEXANDRA. Born May 14 in Brooklyn, NY. Graduate Columbia U. Debut 1976 OB in "Fiorello!" (ELT), followed by "Annie Get Your Gun," Bdwy 1978 in "Hello, Dolly!"

KORZEN, ANNE. Born Nov. 8, 1938 in NYC. Graduate Bard Col. Debut 1976 OB in "Fiorello, (ELT), followed by "Intermission," "I Can't Keep Running."

KRAMER, MARSHA. Born June 19, 1945 in Chicago, IL. Graduate UCLA. Debut 1973 OB in "Out of This World" (ELT), Bdwy 1979 in "Peter Pan."

KRAUS, PHILIP. Born May 10, 1949 in Springville, NY. Graduate Carnegie Tech. Bdwy debut 1973 in "Shelter," followed by "Equus," "Bent," OB in "Julius Caesar."

KRAWFORD, GARY. Born Mar. 23, 1941 in Kitchener, Can. Debut 1968 OB in "The Fantasticks," followed by "Manhattan Apartment," "Dear Oscar," "Anyone Can Whistle," Bdwy in "Pousse Cafe," "Education of Hyman Kaplan," "Company."

KREMPEL, JOYCE. Born Feb. 15 in NYC. Attended Brooklyn Col. Debut 1980 OB in "Dona Rosita."

KRISCH, MICHAEL DAVID. Born Dec. 21, 1965 in NYC. Debut 1979 OB in "Oliver!," followed by "The Music Man" (JB), "The Sound of Music" (ELT).

KURTZ, SWOOSIE. Born Sept. 6 in Omaha, NE. Attended USCal., LAMDA. Debut 1968 OB in "The Firebugs," followed by "The Effect of Gamma Rays . . . ," "Enter a Free Man," "Children," "Museum," "Uncommon Women and Others," "Wine Untouched," Bdwy in "Ah, Wilderness" (1975), "Tartuffe," "A History of the American Film."

KUSS, RICHARD. Born July 17, 1927 in Astoria, NY. Attended Ithaca Col. Debut 1951 OB in "Mother Said No," followed by "A Maid's Tragedy," "Winning Isn't Everything," Bdwy in "J.B.," "Wait Until Dark," "Solitaire/Double Solitaire," "Golda," "Loves of Cass Mcguire."

KYRIELEISON, JACK. Born May 6, 1950 in Washington, DC. Attended Clemson U., UMd. Debut 1979 OB in "The Sound of Music."

LACEY, FLORENCE. Born July 22, 1948 in McKeesport, PA. Graduate Pittsburgh Playhouse. Bdwy debut 1978 in "Hello, Dolly!" for which she received a Theatre World Award, followed by "The Grand Tour," OB in "Elizabeth and Essex."

LACY, TOM. Born Aug. 30, 1933 in NYC. Debut 1965 OB in "The Fourth Pig," followed by "The Fantasticks," "Shoemaker's Holiday," "Love and Let Love," "The Millionairess," "Crimes of Passion," "The Real Inspector Hound," "Enemies," "Flying Blind," Bdwy in "Last of the Red Hot Lovers."

LACHOW, STAN. Born Dec. 20, 1931 in Brooklyn, NY. Graduate Roger Williams U. Debut 1977 OB in "Come Back, Little Sheba," followed by "Diary of Anne Frank," "Time of the Cuckoo" (ELT), Bdwy in "On Golden Pond."

LAGERFELT, CAROLYN. Born Sept. 23 in Paris. Graduate AADA. Bdwy debut 1971 in "The Philanthropist," followed by "4 on a Garden," "Jockey Club Stakes," "The Constant Wife," "Otherwise Engaged," "Betrayal," OB in "Look Back in Anger."

LAGERWALL, BERIT. Born May 8, 1945 in Sweden. Debut 1977 OB in "A Servant of Two Masters," followed by "Old Man Joseph and His Family," "Moliere in spite of Himself," "Devour the Snow," Bdwy 1980 in "Harold and Maude."

LAHTI, CHRISTINE. Born Apr. 4, 1950 in Detroit, MI. Graduate UMich., HB Studio. Debut 1979 OB in "The Woods" for which she received a Theatre World Award, Bdwy 1980 in "Loose Ends."

LAM, DIANE. Born Mar. 6, 1945 in Honolulu, HI., SMU. Bdwy debut 1976 in "Pacific Overtures," followed by "The King and I," OB in "Anyone Can Whistle."

LAMBERT, BEVERLY. Born May 20, 1956 in Stamford, CT. Graduate UNH. Debut 1980 OB in "Plain and Fancy" (ELT).

LANCE, RORY. Born Apr. 10, 1954 in Brooklyn, NY. Graduate Bklyn Col. Debut 1978 OB in "She Stoops to Conquer," followed by "Bartleby the Scrivener," "Arms and the Man," "Twelfth Night."

LANG, STEPHEN. Born July 11, 1952 in NYC. Graduate Swarthmore Col. Debut 1975 OB in "Hamlet," followed by "Henry V," "Shadow of a Gunman," Bdwy in "St. Joan" (1977), BAM's "A Winter's Tale," "Johnny on a Spot," "Barbarians."

LANG, CHARLEY. Born Oct. 24, 1955 in Passaic, NJ. Graduate Catholic U. Bdwy debut 1978 in "Da," followed by "Once a Catholic."

LANSBURY, ANGELA. Born Oct. 16, 1925 in London, Eng. Bdwy debut 1957 in "Hotel Paradiso," followed by "A Taste of Honey," "Anyone Can Whistle," "Mame," "Dear World," "Gypsy," "The King and I" (1978), "Sweeney Todd."

LASKY, ZANE. Born Apr. 23, 1953 in NYC. Attended Manhattan Com.Col., HB Studio. Debut 1973 OB in "The Hot 1 Baltimore," followed by "The Prodigal," "Innocent Thoughts, Harmless Intentions," Bdwy 1974 in "All Over Town."

LASSER, LOUISE. Born in NYC. Attended Brandeis U. Bdwy debut 1962 in "I Can Get It for You Wholesale," followed by "Henry, Sweet Henry," "The Chinese and Dr. Fish," "Thieves," OB in "The Third Ear," "Are You Now or Have You Ever Been," "Marie and Bruce."

LATHAN, BOBBI JO. Born Oct. 5, 1951 in Dallas, TX. Graduate NTexStateU. Bdwy debut 1979 in "The Best Little Whorehouse in Texas."

LAURIA, DAN. Born Apr. 12, 1947 in Brooklyn, NY. Graduate SConnState, UConn. Debut 1978 OB in "Game Plan," followed by "All My Sons," "Marlon Brando Sat Here."

LAURIE, PIPER. Born Jan. 22, 1932 in Detroit, MI. Attended Neighborhood Playhouse. Debut 1958 OB in "Rosemary and the Alligators," followed by "Biography," Bdwy 1965 in "The Glass Menagerie."

LAWRENCE, CAROL. Born Sept. 5, 1935 in Melrose Park, IL. Bdwy debut in "New Faces of 1952," followed by "Plain and Fancy," "South Pacific" (CC), "Shangri-La," "Ziegfeld Follies" (1957), "West Side Story," for which she received a Theatre World Award, "Saratoga," "Subways Are for Sleeping," "Night Life," "Rockette Spectacular."

LAWSON, LEE. Born Oct. 14, 1941 in NYC. Attended Boston U., Columbia. OB in "The Firebugs," "The Knack," LC's "Birthday Party," "Scenes from American Life," "Suggs" and "The Plough and the Stars," Bdwy in "Agatha Sue, I Love You," "Cactus Flower," "My Daughter, Your Son," "An American Millionaire," "Teibele and Her Demon."

LEAGUE, JANET. Born Oct. 13 in Chicago, IL. Attended Goodman Theatre. Debut 1969 OB in "To Be Young, Gifted and Black," followed by "Tiger at the Gates," "The Screens," "Mrs. Snow," "Please Don't Cry and Say No," "Banana Box," Bdwy in "The First Breeze of Summer," (1975), "For Colored Girls Who Have Considered . . ."

LEARY, DAVID. Born Aug. 8, 1939 in Brooklyn, NY. Attended CCNY. Debut 1969 OB in "Shoot Anything That Moves," followed by "Macbeth," "The Plough and the Stars," Bdwy in "The National Health," "Da," "The Lady from Dubuque."

LeCLERC, JEAN. Born July 7, 1945 in Montreal, Can. Graduate Quebec U. Bdwy debut 1979 in "Dracula."

LEE, ANDREA. Born Apr. 6, 1957 in Ohio. Attended Interlochen Arts Acad. Debut 1980 OB in "Oh, Boy!"

LEE, IRVING. Born Nov. 21, 1948 in NYC. Boston U. graduate. Debut 1969 OB in "Kiss Now," followed by "Ride the Winds," "A Visit with Death," "Changes," Bdwy in "Pippin" (1973), "Rockabye Hamlet," " A Broadway Musical."

LEE, KAIULANI. Born Feb. 28, 1950 in Princeton, NJ. Attended American U. Bdwy debut 1975 in "Kennedy's Children," OB in "Ballad of the Sad Cafe," "Museum," "Safe House," "Othello."

LEEDS, LYDIA. Born May 22, 1955 in NYC. Graduate Hofstra U. Debut 1980 OB in "Romeo and Juliet," followed by "The Tenth Man."

LEIBMAN, RON. Born Oct. 11, 1937 in NYC. Attended Ohio Wesleyan, Actors Studio. Bdwy debut 1963 in "Dear Me, the Sky Is Falling," followed by "Bicycle Ride to Nevada," "The Deputy," "We Bombed in New Haven," for which he received a Theatre World Award, "Cop-Out," "I Ought to Be in Pictures," OB in "The Academy," "John Brown's Body," "Scapin," Legend of Lovers," "Dead End," "Poker Session," "The Premise," "Transfers," "Room Service," "Love Two," "Rich and Famous."

LEIGHTON, John. Born Dec. 30 on Staten Island, NY. Attended NYU, Columbia. Debut 1954 OB in "In Splendid Error," followed by "Juno and the Paycock," "A Christmas Carol," "Quare Fellow," "Brothers Karamazov," "Montserrat," "Othello," "Merchant of Venice," "Enter a Free Man," Bdwy 1980 in "Of the Fields Lately."

LeMASSENA, WILLIAM. Born May 23, 1916 in Glen Ridge, NJ. Attended NYU. Bdwy bow 1940 in "Taming of the Shrew," followed by "There Shall Be No Night," "The Pirate," "Hamlet," "Call Me Mister," "Inside U.S.A.," "I Know My Love," "Dream Girl," "Nina," "Ondine," "Fallen Angels," "Redhead," "Conquering Hero," "Beauty Part," "Come Summer," "Grin and Bare It," "All over Town," "A Texas Trilogy," "Deathtrap," OB in "The Coop," "Brigadoon," "Life with Father," "F. Jasmine Addams," "The Dodge Boys."

LENZ, THOMAS. Born Jan. 29, 1951 in Madison, WI. Graduate St. Mary's Col. Debut 1975 OB in "Running of the Deer," followed by Wild Cats," "Richard II," "Henry IV," "Marquis of Keith," "Madwoman of Chaillot," "Love's Labour's Lost."

LEO, TOM. Born Nov. 28, 1936 in Teaneck, NJ. Graduate UToronto. Debut 1974 OB in "More Than You Deserve," followed by "Beethoven/Karl," "A Little Wine with Lunch," "The Matchmaker."

LEON, JOSEPH. Born June 8, 1923 in NYC. Attended NYU, UCLA. Bdwy debut 1950 in "Bell, Book and Candle," followed by "Seven Year Itch," "Pipe Dream," "Fair Game," "Gazebo," "Julia, Jake and Uncle Joe," "Beauty Part," "Merry Widow," "Henry, Sweet Henry," "Jimmy Shine," "All over Town," "California Suite," "The Merchant," "Break a Leg," "Once a Catholic," OB in "Come Share My House," "Dark Corners," "Interrogation of Havana," "Are You Now or Have You Ever Been." "Second Ave. Rag."

LeROUX, MADELEINE. Born May 28, 1946 in Laramie, WY. Graduate UCapetown. Debut 1969 OB in "Moondreamers," followed by "Dirtiest Show in Town," "Rain," "Troilus and Cressida," "2008½," "Glamour, Glory, Gold," "Lisping Judas," "Why Hanna's Skirt Won't Stay Down," "Women Behind Bars," Bdwy in "Lysistrata," (1972), "Clothes for a Summer Hotel."

LESTER, BARBARA. Born Dec. 27, 1928 in London, Eng. Graduate Columbia U. Bdwy Debut 1956 in "Protective Custody," followed by "Legend of Lizzie," "Luther," "Inadmissible Evidence," "Johnny-no-Trump," "Grin and Bare It," "Abelard and Heloise," "One in Every Marriage," "Butley," "Man and Superman," "The Faith Healer," OB in "Electra," "Queen after Death," "Summer of the 17th Doll," "Richard II," "Much Ado about Nothing," "One Way Pendulum" "Biography," "Heartbreak House."

LEVENE, SAM. Born Aug. 28, 1905 in NYC. Graduate AADA. Bdwy debut 1927 in "Wall Street," followed by "3 Men on a Horse," "Dinner at 8," "Room Service," "Margin for Error," "Sound of Hunting," "Light Up the Sky," "Guys and Dolls," "Hot Corner," "Fair Game," "Make A Million," "Heartbreak House," "Good Soup," "Devil's Advocate," "Let It Ride," "Seidman & Son," "Cafe Crown," "Last Analysis," "Nathan Weinstein, Mystic, Conn.," "Impossible Years," "Paris Is Out," "Sunshine Boys," "Dreyfus in Rehearsal," "The Royal Family," "Horowitz and Mrs. Washington," OB in "A Dream Out of Time."

LEVINE, ANNA KLUGER. Born Sept. 18, 1955 in NYC. Attended Actors Studio. Debut 1975 OB in "Kid Champion," followed by "Uncommon Women and Others," "City Sugar," BAM's "A Winter's Tale," "Johnny on a Spot," "The Wedding."

LEWIS, ABBY. Born Jan. 21, 1910 in Mesilla Park, NMX. Graduate NMxU. Bdwy debut 1934 in "Richard III," followed by "You Can't Take It with You," "Macbeth," "The Willow and I," "The Chase," "Four Winds," "Howie," "Riot Act," "Life with Father," "70 Girls 70," "We Interrupt This Program," OB in "All My Sons."

LEWIS, DAVID. Born Oct. 19, 1916 in Pittsburgh, PA. Bdwy debut 1943 in "Goodbye Again," followed by "The Streets Are Guarded," "Little Women" (1944), "Taming of the Shrew," "The Wild Duck," "King of Hearts," OB in "Star Treatment."

LEWIS, GILBERT. Born Apr. 6, 1941 in Philadelphia, PA. Attended Morgan State Col. Bdwy bow 1969 in "The Great White Hope." OB in "Who's Got His Own," "Transfers," "Ballet behind the Bridge," "Coriolanus."

LEWIS, JENIFER. Born Jan. 25, 1957 in St. Louis, MO. Graduate Webster College. Bdwy debut 1979 in "Eubie," followed by "Comin' Uptown."

LIEBERMAN, RICK. Born May 10, 1950 in NYC. Graduate CornellU. Debut 1979 OB in "Justice," followed by "Split."

LINDO, DELROY. Born Nov. 18, 1952 in London, Eng. Debut 1979 OB in "Spell #7," followed by "Les Blancs."

LINDSAY, PHILLIP. Born July 31, 1924 in Cairo, IL. Attended UChicago, Goodman Theatre. OB in "Clandestine on the Morning Line," "Orpheus Descending," "3 by Wilder," "Mamba's Daughters," "The Blacks," "Crazy Horse," Bdwy in "Member of the Wedding," "The Great White Hope," "God's Favorite," "The Skin of Our Teeth," "Sweet Bird of Youth."

LINN, BAMBI. Born Apr. 26, 1926 in Brooklyn, NY. Bdwy debut 1943 in "Oklahoma!" followed by "Carousel" for which she received a Theatre World Award, "Alice in Wonderland," "Sally," "Great to Be Alive," "I Can Get It for You Wholesale," OB in "Women of Ireland."

LIPTON, MICHAEL. Born Apr. 27, 1925 in NYC. Attended Queens Col. Credits include "Caesar and Cleopatra," "The Moon is Blue," "Sing Me No Lullaby," "Wake Up, Darling," "Tenth Man," "Separate Tables," "Inquest," "Loose Ends," OB in "Lover," "Trigon," "Long Christmas Dinner," "Hamp," "Boys in the Band," "Justice Box," "Cold Storage," "Heartbreak House."

Caroline Lagerfelt   **Irving Lee**   **Diane Lam**   **Donald Madden**   **Michele Mais**

LITHGOW, JOHN. Born Oct. 19, 1945 in Rochester, NY. Graduate Harvard U. Bdwy debut 1973 in "The Changing Room," followed by "My Fat Friend," "Comedians," "Anna Christie," "Once in a Lifetime," "Spokesong," "Bedroom Farce," OB in "Hamlet," "Trelawny of the Wells," "A Memory of Two Mondays," "Secret Service," "Boy Meets Girl," "Salt Lake City Skyline."

LITTLE, ALAN DAVID. Born June 8, 1954 in Atlanta, GA. Debut 1979 OB in "God Bless You, Mr. Rosewater."

LITTLE, DAVID. Born Mar. 21, 1937 in Wadesboro, NC. Graduate Wm. & Mary Col., Catholic U. Debut 1967 OB in "MacBird," followed by "Iphigenia in Aulis," "Antony and Cleopatra," "Antigone," "An Enemy of the People," "Three Sons," "God Bless You, Mr. Rosewater," "Les Blancs," Bdwy in "Thieves," "Zalmen, or the Madness of God."

LLOYD SUSAN C. Born Sept. 28, 1950 in Long Island City, NY. Attended Villanova U. Debut 1973 OB in "Tonight We Improvise," followed by "The Incognita," "The Real Inspector Hound," "The Trojan Women," "Arms and the Man," "Uncle Vanya," "Twelfth Night," "Hedda Gabler."

LOCANTE, SAM. Born Sept. 12, 1918 in Kenosha, WI. Graduate UWis., Goodman Sch. Bdwy bow 1955 in "Anniversary Waltz," followed by "Hidden Stranger," "Moonbirds," OB in "The Beaver Coat," "The Soldier," "Virgin Producers," "Game Plan," "The Time of Your Life," "Stone Killers," "Happy Anniversary," "Middle of the Night," "The Wrong Man," "The Relics."

LODEN, BARBARA. Born July 8 in Marion, NC. Bdwy debut 1957 in "Compulsion," followed by "Look after Lulu," "The Long Dream," "After the Fall," for which she received a Theatre World Award, OB in "Winter Journey,"Come Back to the 5 & Dime, Jimmy Dean."

LONG, JODI. Born In NYC; graduate SUNY/Purchase. Bdwy debut 1963 in "Nowhere to Go but Up," followed by "Loose Ends," OB in "Fathers and Sons."

LOPEZ, PRISCILLA. Born Feb. 26, 1948 in The Bronx, NY. Bdwy debut 1966 in "Breakfast at Tiffany's," followed by "Henry Sweet Henry," "Lysistrata," "Company," "Her First Roman," "The Boy Friend," "Pippin," "A Chorus Line," "A Day in Hollywood/A Night in the Ukraine," OB in "What's a Nice Country Like You . . . "

LOUDON, DOROTHY. Born Sept. 17, 1933 in Boston, MA. Attended Emerson Col., Syracuse U. Debut 1961 OB in "World of Jules Feiffer," Bdwy 1963 in "Nowhere to Go but Up," for which she received a Theatre World Award, followed by "Noel Coward's Sweet Potato," "Fig Leaves Are Falling," "Three Men on a Horse," "The Women," "Annie," "Ballroom.'

LOVE, EDWARD. Born June 29, 1952 in Toledo, OH. Graduate Ohio U, NYU. Debut 1972 OB in "Ti-Jean and His Brothers," followed by "Spell #7," Bdwy in "Raisin," "A Chorus Line," "Dancin'," "Censored Scenes from King Kong."

LUCAS, CRAIG. Born Apr. 30, 1951 in Atlanta, GA. Graduate Boston U. Debut 1974 OB in "Carousel" (ELT), Bdwy in "Shenandoah" (1975), "Rex," "On the 20th Century," "Sweeney Todd."

LUCAS, J. FRANK. Born in Houston, TX. Graduate TCU. Debut 1943 OB in "A Man's House," followed by "Coriolanus," "Edward II," "Long Gallery," "Trip to Bountiful," "Orpheus Descending," "Guitar," "Marcus in the High Grass," "Chocolates," "To Bury a Cousin," "One World at a Time," Bdwy in "Bad Habits," "The Best Little Whorehouse in Texas."

LUCKINBILL, LAURENCE. Born Nov. 21, 1938 in Ft. Smith, AR. Graduate UArk., Catholic U. Bdwy debut in "A Man for All Seasons," followed by "Beekman Place," "Poor Murderers," "The Shadow Box," "Chapter 2," "Past Tense," OB in "Oedipus Rex," "There's a Play Tonight," "Fantasticks," "Tartuffe," "Boys in the Band," "Horseman, Pass By," "Memory Bank," "What the Butler Saw," "A Meeting by the River," "Alpha Beta," "A Prayer for My Daughter," "Life of Galileo."

LUDD, PATRICIA. Born Oct. 27, 1956 in Elizabeth, NJ. Graduate Hartt Col. Debut 1980 in "It's Spring."

LUDWIG, KAREN. Born Oct. 9, 1942 in San Francisco, CA. Bdwy debut 1964 in "The Deputy," followed by "The Devils," OB in "Trojan Women," "Red Cross," "Muzeeka," "Huui, Huui," "Our Late Night," "The Seagull," "Museum," "Nasty Rumors," "Daisy."

LUDWIG, SALEM. Born July 31, 1915 in Brooklyn, NY. Attended Bklyn Col. Bdwy bow 1946 in "Miracle in the Mountains," followed by "Camino Real," "Enemy of the People," "All You Need Is One Good Break," "Inherit the Wind," "Disenchanted," "Rhinoceros," "Three Sisters," "The Zulu and the Zayda," "Moonchildren," OB in "Brothers Karamazov," "Victim," "Troublemaker," "Man of Destiny," "Night of the Dunce," "Corner of the Bed," "Awake and Sing," "Prodigal," "Babylon," "The Burnt Flowerbed," "The American Clock."

LUGENBEAL, CAROL. Born July 14, 1952 in Detroit, MI. Graduate U.S. International U. Bdwy debut 1974 in "Where's Charley?" followed by "On the 20th Century," "Evita."

LUNA, BARBARA. Born Mar. 2 in NYC. Bdwy debut 1951 in "The King and I," followed by "West Side Story" (LC), "A Chorus Line."

LUNDWALL, SANDY. Born Sept. 19 in San Francisco, CA. Graduate SFStateU. Debut 1980 OB in "Plain and Fancy" (ELT).

LuPONE, PATTI. Born Apr. 21, 1949 in Northport, NY. Juilliard graduate. Debut 1972 OB in "School for Scandal," followed by "Women Beware Women," "Next Time I'll Sing to You," "Beggar's Opera," "Scapin," "Robber Bridegroom," "Edward II," Bdwy in "The Water Engine" (1978), "Working," "Evita."

LUTE, DENISE. Born Aug. 2, 1954 in NYC. Attended HB Studio. Debut 1975 OB in "Harry Outside," followed by "Green Fields."

LYNDECK, EDMUND. Born Oct 4, 1925 in Baton Rouge, LA. Graduate Montclair State Col., Fordham U. Bdwy debut 1969 in "1776," followed by "Sweeney Todd," OB in "The King and I" (JB), "Mandragola," "A Safe Place." "Amoureuse," "Piaf: A Remembrance."

LYDIARD, ROBERT. Born Apr. 28, 1944 in Glen Ridge, NJ. Graduate Fla-Atlantic U. Debut 1968 OB in "You're a Good Man, Charlie Brown," followed by Johnny Johnson," "Dear Oscar," "Oh, Lady! Lady!," "Winterville," Bdwy in "Hello, Dolly!" (1978).

MacINTOSH, JOAN E. Born Nov. 25, 1945 in NJ. Graduate Beaver Col., NYU. Debut OB 1969 in "Dionysus in '69," followed by "Makbeth," "The Beard," "Tooth of Crime," "Mother Courage," "Marilyn Project," "Seneca's Oedipus," "St. Joan of the Stockyards," "Wonderland in Concert," "Dispatches," "Endgame."

MADDEN, DONALD. Born Nov. 5, 1933 in NYC. Attended CCNY. Bdwy debut 1958 in "Look Back in Anger," followed by "First Impressions," "Step on a Crack," "One by One," "White Lies," "Black Comedy," OB in "Julius Caesar" for which he received a Theatre World Award, "Lysistrata," "Pictures in a Hallway," "Henry IV," "She Stoops to Conquer," "Octoroon," "Hamlet," "Ceremony of Innocence," "Henry VI," "Richard III," "A Doll's House," "Hedda Gabler," "The Philanderer," "Scribes," "Trick," "Jungle of Cities."

MADDUX, JACKLYN. Born Apr. 8, 1951 in San Francisco, CA. Attended S.F.StateU. Debut 1979 OB in "The Art of Dining."

MAGGART, BRANDON. Born Dec. 12, 1933 in Carthage, TN. Graduate UTn. OB in "Sing Muse!" "Like Other People," "Put It in Writing" for which he received a Theatre World Award, "Wedding Band," "But Not For Me," "Romance," "Potholes," Bdwy in "Kelly," "New Faces of 1968," "Applause," "Lorelei," "We Interrupt This Program," "Musical Chairs."

MAGUIRE, GEORGE. Born Dec. 4, 1946 in Wilmington, DE. Graduate UPa. Debut 1975 OB in "Polly," followed by "Follies," "Antigone," Bdwy 1980 in "Canterbury Tales."

MAHER, JOSEPH. Born Dec. 29, 1933 in Westport, Ire. Bdwy bow 1964 in "The Chinese Prime Minister," followed by "The Prime of Miss Jean Brodie," "Henry V," "There's One in Every Marriage," "Who's Who in Hell," "Days in the Trees," "Spokesong," "Night and Day," OB in "The Hostage," "Live Like Pigs," "Importance of Being Earnest," "Eh?" "Local Stigmatic," "Mary Stuart," "The Contractor," "Savages."

MAHONE, JUANITA M. Born Sept. 12, 1952 in Boston, MA. Graduate Boston U. Debut 1975 OB in "Don't Bother Me, I Can't Cope," followed by "Birdland," "The Verandah," "Face of Love," "The Sun Always Shines for the Cool," "Antigone."

MAILLARD, CAROL LYNN. Born Mar. 4, 1951 in Philadelphia, PA. Graduate Catholic U. Debut 1977 OB in "The Great MacDaddy," followed by "It's So Nice to Be Civilized," "A Photograph," Bdwy 1979 in "Eubie!"

MAIS, MICHELE. Born July 30, 1954 in NYC. Graduate CCNY. Debut 1975 OB in "Godspell," followed by "Othello," "Superspy," "Yesterday Continued," "We'll Be Right Back," "Que Ubo?," Bdwy 1979 in "Zoot Suit."

MANN, PJ. Born Apr. 9, 1953 in Pasadena, CA. Bdwy debut 1976 in "Home Sweet Homer," followed by "A Chorus Line," "Dancin'."

MANNING, KATHARINE. Born Oct. 12, 1950 in Columbia, SC. Graduate Salem Col., Wake Forest U. Debut 1976 OB in "Visions of Kerouac," followed by "Kohlhass."

MANOFF, DINAH. Born Jan. 25, 1958 in NYC. Attended CalArts. Bdwy debut 1980 in "I Ought to Be in Pictures" for which she received a Theatre World Award.

MANSON, ALLISON R. Born July 21, 1958 in NYC. Attended Queens Col. Bdwy debut 1979 in "Comin' Uptown."

MARADEN, FRANK. Born Aug. 9, 1944 in Norfolk, VA. Graduate UMn., MichStateU. Debut 1980 OB with BAM Theatre Co. in "A Winter's Tale," "Johnny on a Spot," "Barbarians" and "The Wedding."

MARADEN, MARTI. Born June 22, 1945 in El Centro, CA. Attended UMn., MichStateU. Debut 1980 OB in BAM Theatre Co.'s "A Winter's Tale," "Barbarians," and "He and She."

MARCHAND, NANCY. Born June 19, 1928 in Buffalo, NY. Carnegie Tech graduate. Debut 1951 in "Taming of the Shrew" (CC), followed by "Merchant of Venice," "Much Ado about Nothing," "Three Bags Full," "After the Rain." LCRep's "The Alchemist," "Yerma," "Cyrano de Bergerac," "Mary Stuart." "Enemies" and "The Plough and the Stars," "40 Carats," "And Miss Reardon Drinks a Little," "Veronica's Room," OB in "The Balcony," "Children." "Taken in Marriage." "Morning's at 7,"

MARDIROSIAN, TOM. Born Dec 14, 1947 in Buffalo, NY. Graduate UBuffalo. Debut 1976 OB in "Gemini," followed by "Grand Magic," "Losing Time," "Passione," Bdwy in "Happy End," "Magic Show."

MARGOLIS, MARK. Born Nov. 26, 1939 in Malta. Attended Temple U. Bdwy debut 1962 in "Infidel Caesar," OB in "Second Avenue Rag."

MARINOS, PETER. Born Oct. 2, 1951 in Pontiac, MI. Graduate MiStateU. Bdwy debut 1976 in "Chicago," followed by "Evita."

MARSHALL, LARRY. Born Apr. 3, 1944 in Spartanburg, SC. Attended Fordham U., New Eng. Cons. Bdwy debut in "Hair," followed by "Two Gentlemen of Verona," "A Midsummer Night's Dream," "Rockabye Hamlet," "Porgy and Bess," "A Broadway Musical," "Comin' Uptown," OB in "Spell #7," "Jus' Like Livin'."

MARTELLA, DIANE. Born Dec. 10, 1943 in Pueblo, CO. Attended USCo. Debut 1979 OB in "Wine Untouched," followed by "The Time of the Cuckoo"-(ELT).

MARTIN, ANDREA. Born Jan. 15, 1947 in Portland, ME. Graduate Emerson Col. Debut 1980 OB in "Hard Sell," followed by "The Sorrows of Stephen"

MARTIN, ANNE HAMILTON. Born Nov. 3, 1944 in South Carolina. Graduate Immaculate Heart Col. Debut 1979 OB in "Love's Labour's Lost," followed by "War and Peace."

MARTIN, LUCY. Born Feb. 8, 1942 in NYC. Graduate Sweet Briar Col. Debut 1962 OB in "Electra," followed by "Happy as Larry," "The Trojan Women," "Iphigenia in Aulis," Bdwy in "Shelter" (1973), "Children of a Lesser God."

MARTIN, SANDY. Born Mar. 3, 1949 in Philadelphia, PA. Debut 1980 OB in "What's So Beautiful about a Sunset over Prairie Avenue?," followed by "Killings on the Last Line."

MASTERS, ANDREA. Born Nov. 16, 1949 in Chicago, IL. Attended Mills Col, Columbia U. Debut 1975 OB in "The Long Valley," followed by "Justice," Bdwy in "The Basic Training of Pavlo Hummel" (1977).

MATTHIESSEN, JOAN. Born Feb. 27, 1930 in Orange, NJ. Graduate Allegheny Co. Debut 1979 OB in "The Art of Dining," followed by "The Cocktail Party."

MATTSON, WAYNE. Born July 13, 1952 in Rochester, MN. Attended Allan Hancock Col., Pacific Cons. Bdwy debut 1974 in "Lorelei," followed by "Music Is," "They're Playing Our Song."

MAURICE, MICHAEL. Born Feb. 17, 1952 in Detroit, MI. Attended MiStateU, Actors Studio. Debut 1975 OB in "The Three Musketeers," followed by "Twelfth Night," "Joyful Noises."

MAY, BEVERLY. Born Aug. 11, 1927 in East Wellington, BD, Can. Graduate Yale U. Debut 1976 OB in "Female Transport," Bdwy 1977 in "Equus," followed by "Once in a Lifetime," "Whose Life Is It Anyway?"

MAY, DEBORAH S. Born Sept. 28, 1948 in Lafayette, IN. Attended IndU. Am. Consv. Theatre. Bdwy debut 1978 in "Once in a Lifetime," followed by "Romantic Comedy."

MAY, THEODORE. Born Dec. 27, 1954 in Northampton, MA. Juilliard graduate. Debut 1980 OB in "Biography."

MAY, WINSTON. Born Feb. 3, 1937 in Mammoth Spring, AR. Graduate ArkStateU., AmThWing. Debut OB 1967 in "The Man Who Washed His Hands," followed by "King Lear," "Candida," "Trumpets and Drums," "Otho the Great," "Uncle Vanya," "Servant of Two Masters," "The Play's the Thing," "Autumn Garden," "Madmen."

MAYER, JERRY. Born May 12, 1941 in NYC. Graduate NYU. Debut 1968 OB in "Alice in Wonderland," followed by "L'Ete," "Marouf," "Trelawny of the Wells," "King of the Schnorrers," "Mother Courage," Bdwy in "Much Ado about Nothing"(1972).

McCABE, EILEEN. Born Feb. 4, 1931 in Toledo, OH. Attended Wayne State, Hunter Col. Bdwy debut in 1948 in "Park Avenue," followed by "The Chocolate Soldier," "Oklahoma!" (1951), "Musical Chairs."

McCANN, CHRISTOPHER. Born Sept. 29, 1952 in NYC. Graduate NYU. Debut 1975 OB in "The Measures Taken," followed by "Ghosts," "Woyzzeck." "St. Joan of the Stockyards," "Buried Child," "The Consoling Virgin."

McCAREN, JOSEPH. Born Sept. 2, 1945 in Los Angeles, CA. UCLA graduate. Bdwy debut 1980 in "Whose Life Is It Anyway?"

McCARREN, PAUL. Born Jan. 19, 1943 in Yonkers, NY. Graduate Fordham U. Debut 1979 OB in "Second Thoughts," followed by "Love's Labour's Lost."

McCARROLL, EARL. Born Aug. 20, 1939 in Memphis, TN. Graduate Duke U, UArk. Bdwy debut 1980 in "Canterbury Tales."

McCARTY, CONAN. Born Sept. 16, 1955 in Lubbock, TX. Attended USCal., AADA/West. Debut 1980 OB in "Star Treatment."

McCLAIN, MARCIA. Born Sept. 30, 1949 in San Antonio, TX. Graduate Trinity U. Debut 1972 OB in "Rainbow," followed by "A Bistro Car on the CNR," "The Derby," Bdwy 1974 in "Where's Charley?" for which she received a Theatre World Award.

McCLARNON, KEVIN. Born Aug. 25, 1952 in Greenfield, IN. Graduate Butler U, LAMDA. Debut 1977 OB in "The Homecoming," followed by "Heaven's Gate," BAM Theatre Co.'s "A Winter's Tale," "Johnny on a Spot," and "The Wedding."

McCLURE, DOUG. Born May 11, 1935 in Glendale, CA. Attended UCLA. Bdwy debut 1980 in "The Roast"

McCORMICK, PARKER. Born Dec. 29, in NYC. Attended Wheaton Col., Irvine Studio. Bdwy debut 1947 in "Harvey," followed by "The Tender Trap," "Third Best Sport," "One Eye Closed," "Three Bags Full," OB in "The Seagull," "Dr. Willy-Nilly," "Marcus in the High Grass," "Play That on Your Old Piano," "Little Boxes," "The Divorce of Judy and Jane," "Medea," "Marco Polo Sings a Solo," "Stage Door," "Marie and Bruce," "Time Steps."

McCOY, BASIA. Born Dec. 15, 1916 in Plains, PA. Graduate Carnegie-Mellon U. Debut 1948 OB in "The Fifth Horseman," followed by "Mary Stuart," "The Crucible," "Knitters in the Sun."

McCRANE, PAUL. Born Jan. 19, 1961 in Philadelphia, PA. Debut 1977 OB in "Landscape of the Body," followed by "Dispatches," "Split," Bdwy 1978 in "Runaways."

McDERMOTT, KEITH. Born in Houston, TX. Attended LAMDA. Bdwy debut 1976 in "Equus," followed by "A Meeting by the River," "Harold and Maude."

McDONALD, ROBERT. (a.k.a. Bob) Born Feb. 10 1944 in Waterbury, CT. Graduate Marlboro Col. Debut 1979 OB in "The Office Murders."

McDONALD, TANNY. Born Feb. 13, 1939 in Princeton, IN. Graduate Vassar Col. Debut OB with Am. Savoyards, followed by "All in Love," "To Broadway with Love," "Carricknabauna," "Beggar's Opera," "Brand," "Goodbye, Dan Bailey." "Total Eclipse," "Gorky," "Don Juan Comes Back from the War." Bdwy in "Fiddler on the Roof," "Come Summer," "The Lincoln Mask," "Clothes for a Summer Hotel."

McDONNELL, MARY. Born in 1952 in Ithaca, NY. Graduate SUNY Fredonia. Debut OB 1978 in "Buried Child," followed by "Letters Home."

McELHINEY, RICK. Born Apr. 4, 1940 in Waltham, MA. Graduate Lowell State Col., Rutgers U. Debut 1979 OB in "King of Schnorrers."

McFARLAND, ROBERT. Born May 7, 1931 in Omaha, NE. Graduate UMich, Columbia U. Debut 1978 OB in "The Taming of the Shrew," followed by "When the War Was Over."

McGANN, MICHAELJOHN. Born Feb. 2, 1952 in Cleveland, OH. Graduate OhioU. Debut 1975 OB in "The Three Musketeers," followed by "Panama Hattie," BAM Theatre Co.'s "A Winter's Tale," "Johnny on a Spot," "Barbarians."

McGILL, EVERETT. Born Oct. 21, 1945 in Miami Beach, FL. Graduate UMo., RADA. Debut OB 1971 in "Brothers," followed by "The Father," "Enemies," Bdwy in "Equus" (1974), "A Texas Trilogy," "The Merchant," "Dracula," "Whose Life Is It Anyway?"

McGREEVEY, ANNIE. Born in Brooklyn, NY. Graduate AADA. Bdwy debut 1971 in "Company," followed by "The Magic Show," "Annie," OB in "Booth Is Back in Town."

McGUIRE, MAEVE. Born in Cleveland, OH. Graduate Sarah Lawrence Col., Cleveland Playhouse. Debut 1968 with LCRep in "Cyrano de Bergerac," followed by "The Miser," "Charades."

McHATTIE, STEPHEN. Born Feb. 3 in Antigonish, NS. Graduate Acadia U, AADA. Bdwy debut 1968 in "The American Dream," OB in "Henry IV," "Richard III," "The Persians," "Pictures in the Hallway," "Now There's Just the Three of Us," "Anna K.," "Twelfth Night" "Mourning Becomes Electra," "Alive and Well in Argentina," "The Iceman Cometh," "The Winter Dancers."

McINERNEY, BERNIE. Born Dec. 4, 1936 in Wilmington, DE. Graduate UDel., Catholic U. Bdwy debut 1972 in "That Championship Season," followed by OB in "Life of Galileo." "Losing Time," "3 Friends," "The American Clock."

McINTYRE, BILL. Born Sept. 2, 1935 in Rochester, NY. Debut OB 1970 in "The Fantasticks." followed by "City Junket," Bdwy in "Secret Affairs of Mildred Wild," "Legend," "The Inspector General."

McINTYRE, MARILYN. Born May 23, 1949 in Erie, PA. Graduate Penn-State, NCSch. of Arts. Debut 1977 OB in "The Perfect Mollusc," followed by "Measure for Measure," "The Promise," "Action," Bdwy 1980 in "Gemini."

McKECHNIE, DONNA. Born in Nov. 1944 in Detroit, MI. Bdwy debut 1961 in "How to Succeed in Business ....," followed by "Promises, Promises," "Company," "On the Town," "Music! Music!" (CC), "A Chorus Line," OB in "Wine Untouched."

McKEEHAN, MAYLA. Born Dec. 8 in Barbourville, KY. Graduate FlaStateU. Debut 1979 OB in "Big Bad Burlesque," followed by "God Bless You, Mr. Rosewater," "Anyone Can Whistle."

McKINZIE, VIRGINIA. Born Feb. 9 in Midland City, AL. Graduate Hunter Col., NYU. Debut 1963 OB in "So Wonderful in White," Bdwy 1979 in "Comin' Uptown."

McKITTERICK, TOM. Born Jan. 23 in Cleveland, OH. Amherst graduate. Debut 1978 OB in "Fathers and Sons," followed by "Say Goodnight, Gracie," "Salt Lake City Skyline."

McLAREN, CONRAD. Born Nov. 13 in Greenfield, IL. Graduate IllWesleyanU, StateUIowa. Debut 1973 OB in "Medea," followed by "Shay," "The Show-Off," "Company," "Time Steps," "Crimes and Dreams."

McLAUGHLIN, MARK. Born Apr. 25, 1963 in Bridgeport, CT. Bdwy debut 1980 in "Watch on the Rhine."

McLERNON, PAMELA. Born March 1 in Lynn, MA. Lowell State Col. graduate. Debut 1975 OB in "Tenderloin," Bdwy in "Sweeney Todd."

McMARTIN, JOHN. Born in Warsaw, IN. Attended Columbia U. Debut 1959 OB in "Little Mary Sunshine" for which he received a Theatre World Award, followed by "Too Much Johnson," "The Misanthrope," Bdwy in "The Conquering Hero," "Blood, Sweat and Stanley Poole," "Children from Their Games," "A Rainy Day in Newark," "Sweet Charity," "Follies," "Great God Brown," "Don Juan," "The Visit," "Chemin de Fer," "Love for Love," "Rules of the Game," "Happy New Year."

McNAMARA, ROSEMARY. Born Jan. 7, 1943 in Summit, NJ. Attended Newark Col. OB in "The Master Builder," "Carricknabauna," "Rocket to the Moon," "The Most Happy Fella" (CC). "The Matchmaker," "Anyone Can Whistle," Bdwy in "The Student Gypsy."

McNAUGHTON, STEPHEN. Formerly Steve Scott. Born Oct. 11, 1949 in Denver, CO. Graduate UDenver. Debut 1971 OB in "The Drunkard," followed by "Summer Brave," "Monsters," "Chase a Rainbow," Bdwy in "The Ritz" (1976), "Shenandoah."

McQUEEN, ARMELIA. Born Jan. 6, 1952 in North Carolina. Attended HB Studio, Bklyn. Consv. Bdwy debut 1978 in "Ain't Misbehavin'" for which she received a Theatre World Award.

McROBBIE, PETER. Born Jan. 31, 1943 in Hawick, Scot. Yale graduate. Debut 1976 OB in "The Wobblies," Bdwy 1979 in "Whose Life It It Anyway?"

MEDEIROS, JOHN. Born June 5, 1944 in Winston-Salem, NC. Attended IndU, Boston Consv. Bdwy debut 1968 in "Fig Leaves Are Falling," OB in "Que Ubo?/Loney's 66."

MELLIN, MARA. Born Jan. 16, 1963 on Long Island, NY. Attended AADA. Debut 1974 OB in "Zorba the Greek," followed by "Annie Get Your Gun" (ELT).

MERCADO, HECTOR JAIME. Born in NYC in 1949. Graduate H. S. Performing Arts. Attended Harkness Ballet Sch., HB Studio, Bdwy debut 1960 in "West Side Story," followed by "Mass," "Dr. Jazz," "1600 Pennsylvania Ave.," "Your Arms Too Short to Box with God," "West Side Story" (1980), OB in "Sancocho," "People in Show Business Make Long Goodbyes."

MEREDITH, LEE. Born Oct. 22, 1947 in River Edge, NJ. Graduate AADA. Bdwy debut 1969 in "A Teaspoon Every Four Hours," followed by "The Sunshine Boys," "Once in a Lifetime," "Musical Chairs."

MERKIN, LEWIS. Born Dec. 18, 1955 in Philadelphia PA. Attended CalStateU. Bdwy debut 1980 in "Children of a Lesser God."

MERRILL, GARY. Born Aug. 2, 1915 in Hartford, CT. Attended Trinity Col. Bdwy debut 1937 in "Brother Rat," followed by "See My Lawyer," "This Is the Army," "Winged Victory," "Born Yesterday," "At War with the Army," "Step on a Crack," "The World of Carl Sandburg," "Morning's at 7."

MERSON, SUSAN. Born Apr. 25, 1950 in Detroit, MI. Graduate Boston U. Bdwy debut 1974 in "Saturday Sunday Monday," followed by OB "Vanities."

METCALF, MARK. Born Mar. 11 in Findlay, OH. Attended UMich. Debut 1973 OB in "Creeps," followed by "The Tempest," "Beach Children," "Hamlet," "Patrick Henry Lake Liquors," "Streamers," "Salt Lake City Skyline."

MEYERS, MAIDA. Born May 2, 1954 in Philadelphia, PA. Graduate Temple U. Bdwy debut 1977 in "Knickerbocker Holiday," OB in "Come Back to the 5 & Dime, Jimmy Dean."

MICHAEL, STEVEN. Born Aug. 31, 1957 in Fall River, MA. Attended Pasadena City Col. Attended Ringling Bros. Clown Col. Bdwy debut 1980 in "Barnum."

MICHAELS, GUY. Born Oct. 30, 1968 in NYC. Debut 1979 OB in "All the Way Home," followed by BAM Theatre Co.'s "A Winter's Tale" and "The Purging."

MICHELE, LINDA. (a.k.a. Linda Lee Agee) Born June 2 in Oakland, CA. Graduate UPacific. Bdwy debut 1979 in "The Most Happy Fella."

MILES, ROSS. Born in Poughkeepsie, NY. Bdwy debut 1962 in "Little Me," followed by "Baker Street," "Pickwick," "Darling of the Day," "Mame," "Jumpers," "Goodtime Charley," "Chicago," "Dancin'."

MILGRIM, LYNN. Born Mar. 17, 1944 in Philadelphia, PA. Graduate Swarthmore Col., Harvard U. Debut 1969 OB in "Frank Gagliano's City Scene," followed by "Crimes of Passion," "Macbeth," "Charley's Aunt," "The Real Inspector Hound," "Rib Cage," "Museum," "Bits and Pieces," Bdwy in "Otherwise Engaged," "Bedroom Farce."

MILLER, ANN. Born Apr. 12, 1923 in Chireno, TX. Bdwy debut 1940 in "George White's Scandals," followed by "Mame," "Sugar Babies."

MILLER, COURT. Born Jan. 29, 1952 in Norwalk, CT. Debut 1980 in "Elizabeth and Essex."

MILLER, MICHAEL. Born Sept. 1, 1931 in Los Angeles, CA. Attended Bard Col. Debut 1961 OB in "Under Milk Wood," followed by "The Lesson," "A Memory of Two Mondays," "Little Murders," "Tom Paine," "Morning, Noon and Night," "Enemy of the People," "Whitsuntide," "Say When," "Case Against Roberta Guardino," "Dandelion Wine," "Museum," Bdwy in "Ivanov," "Black Comedy," "Trial of Lee Harvey Oswald," "Past Tense."

MILLER, PATRICIA. Born Dec. 1, 1950 in Seattle, WA. Graduate UGa. Debut 1978 OB in "Vanities."

MILLER, VALERIE-JEAN. Born Aug. 22, 1950 in Miami Beach, FL. Bdwy debut 1978 in "Dancin'."

MINER, JAN. Born Oct. 15, 1917 in Boston, MA. Debut 1958 OB in "Obligato," followed by "Decameron." "Dumbbell People," "Autograph Hound," "A Lovely Sunday for Creve Coeur," Bdwy in "Viva Madison Avenue," "Lady of the Camelias," "Freaking Out of Stephanie Blake," "Othello," "The Milk Train Doesn't Stop Here Anymore," "Butterflies Are Free," "The Women," "Pajama Game," "Saturday Sunday Monday," "The Heiress," "Romeo and Juliet," "Watch on the Rhine."

MISTRETTA, SAL. Born Jan. 9, 1945 in Brooklyn, NY. Ithaca Col. graduate Bdwy debut 1976 in "Something's Afoot," followed by "On the 20th Century," "Evita."

MITCHELL, CHIP. Born Nov. 20, 1954 in Carthage, TX. Graduate SMU. Debut 1980 OB in "Plain and Fancy"(ELT).

MIZELLE, VANCE. Born Aug. 6, 1934 in Atlanta, GA. Graduate Davidson Col, UGa. Debut 1975 OB in "Hamlet," followed by "On a Clear Day You Can See Forever," "Love's Labour's Lost," Bdwy 1980 in "Canterbury Tales."

MOBERLY, ROBERT. Born Apr. 15, 1939 in Excelsior Springs, MO. Graduate UKan. Debut 1967 OB in "Arms and the Man," followed by "The Millionairess," "A Gun Play," "Shadow of a Gunman," "Heartbreak House," Bdwy in "A Place for Polly," "A Matter of Gravity."

MODELL, FRANK. Born Sept. 6, 1917 in Philadelphia, PA. Attended Phila. Col. of Art. Debut 1980 OB in "Marie and Bruce."

MOONEY, DEBRA. Born in Aberdeen, SD. Graduate Auburn, UMinn. Debut 1975 OB in "Battle of Angels," followed by "The Farm," "Summer and Smoke," "Stargazing," Bdwy 1978 in "Chapter 2," followed by "Talley's Folly."

MOOR, BILL. Born July 13, 1931 in Toledo, OH. Attended Northwestern U., Dennison U. Bdwy debut 1964 in "Blues for Mr. Charlie," followed by "Great God Brown," "Don Juan," "The Visit," "Chemin de Fer," "Holiday," "P.S. Your Cat Is Dead," "Night of the Tribades," "The Water Engine," OB in "Dandy Dick," "Love Nest," "Days and Nights of Beebee Fenstermaker," "The Collection," "The Owl Answers," "Long Christmas Dinner," "Fortune and Men's Eyes," "King Lear," "Cry of Players," "Boys in the Band," "Alive and Well in Argentina," "Rosmersholm," "The Biko Inquest," "BAM Theatre Co.'s "Winter's Tale," "Johnny on a Spot," "Barbarians," "The Purging."

MOORE, MARY TYLER. Born Dec. 29, 1936 in Brooklyn, NY. Bdwy debut 1980 in "Whose Life It It Anyway?"

MORALES, MARK. Born Nov. 9, 1954 in NYC. Attended Trenton State, SUNY/Purchase. Debut 1978 OB in "Coolest Cat in Town," Bdwy 1980 in "West Side Story."

MORALES, SANTOS. Born June 1, 1935 in NYC. Attended AmThWing, HB Studio. Bdwy debut 1973 in "A Streetcar Named Desire," OB in "Operation Sidewinder," "The Sun Always Shines for the Cool."

MOREA, GABOR. Born Apr. 27 in Cambridge, MA. Debut 1970 OB in "Steambath," followed by "Grand Magic," "Trials of Oz," "Where Has Tommy Flowers Gone?," Bdwy in "Filumena" (1980).

MORENZIE, LEON. Born in Trinidad, WI. Graduate Sir George William U. Debut 1972 OB in "Ti-Jean and His Brothers," followed by "The Cherry Orchard," "Cockeyed Tiger," "Twilight Dinner," "Rum and Coca Cola," "Old Phantoms," "Season Unravel," "The Devil's Tear," Bdwy in "The Leaf People."

MORGAN, ELISA. Born May 28. Graduate UWisc., Columbia U, HB Studio. Debut 1979 OB in "Deli's Fable."

MORIARTY, MICHAEL. Born Apr. 5, 1941 in Detroit, MI. Graduate Dartmouth, LAMBDA. Debut OB 1963 in "Antony and Cleopatra," followed by "Peanut Butter and Jelly," "Long Day's Journey into Night," "Henry V," "Alfred the Great," "Our Father's Failing," "G. R. Point," "Love's Labour's Lost," Bdwy in "Trial Of the Catonsville 9," "Find Your Way Home" for which he received a Theatre World Award, "Richard III" (LC).

MORRIS, ABBIE. Born Nov. 1, 1951 in Bement, IL. Graduate Webster Col. Debut 1979 OB in "Love's Labour's Lost."

MORRIS, DUANE. Born Apr. 10, 1935 in Racine, WI. Graduate St. Olaf Col. Debut 1965 OB in "The Cat and the Canary," followed by "Out of Control," Bdwy in "Sherry" (1967), "Sweeney Todd."

MORRIS, NAT. Born Mar. 13, 1951 in Richmond, VA. Attended Howard U. Bdwy debut 1972 in "Hair," followed by "Jesus Christ Superstar," "Dude," OB in "The More You Get."

MORTON, JOE. Born Oct. 18, 1947 in NYC. Attended Hofstra U. Debut 1968 OB in "A Month of Sundays," followed by "Salvation," "Charlie Was Here and Now He's Gone," "G. R. Point," "Crazy Horse," BAM Theatre Co.'s "A Winter's Tale" and "Johnny on a Spot," Bdwy in "Hair," "Two Gentlemen of Verona," "Tricks," "Raisin" for which he received a Theatre World Award.

MUENZ, RICHARD. Born in Hartford, CT., in 1948. Attended Eastern Baptist College. Bdwy debut 1976 in "1600 Pennsylvania Avenue," followed by "The Most Happy Fella," "Camelot."

MULLAVEY, GREG. Born in 1943 in Buffalo, NY. Bdwy debut 1979 in "Romantic Comedy."

MULLER, FRANK. Born May 5, 1951 in Beverwijk, The Netherlands. Attended UMinn, NCSchool of Arts. Bdwy debut 1980 in "Salt Lake City Skyline."

MUNDELL, MICHELE. Born May 4, 1950 in Washington, DC. Graduate UMd. Debut 1979 OB in "The Sound of Music" (ELT).

MURNEY, CHRISTOPHER. Born July 20, 1943 in Narragansett, RI. Graduate URI, UNH, Penn State U. Bdwy debut 1973 in "Tricks" followed by "Mack and Mabel," OB in "As You Like It," "Holeville."

MURRAY, BRIAN. Born Oct. 9, 1939 in Johannesburg, S.A. Debut 1964 OB in "The Knack," followed by "King Lear," "Ashes," "The Jail Diary of Albie Sachs," BAM Theatre Co.'s "A Winter's Tale," "Barbarians," "The Purging," Bdwy in "All in Good Time," "Rosencrantz and Guildenstern Are Dead," "Sleuth," "Da."

MURRAY, CHRISTOPHER. Born Mar. 19, 1957 in Hollywood, CA. Attended Carleton Col. Debut 1980 OB in "Paris Lights."

MUSANTE, TONY. Born June 30, 1936 in Bridgeport, CT. Graduate Oberlin Col. Debut 1960 OB in "Borak," followed by "The Balcony," "Theatre of the Absurd," "Half-Past Wednesday," "The Collection," "Tender Heel," "Kiss Mama," "Mme. Mousse," "Zoo Story," "Match-Play," "Night of the Dunce," "Gun Play," "A Memory of Two Mondays," "27 Wagons Full of Cotton," "Grand Magic," Bdwy in "P.S. Your Cat is Dead" (1975), "The Lady from Dubuque."

MUSNICK, STEPHANIE. Born Apr. 12, 1950 in Philadelphia. PA. Graduate Villanova U. Bdwy debut 1977 in "Gemini."

NADEL, BARBARA. Born Dec. 18, 1947 in New Haven, CT. Graduate Simmons Col. Bdwy debut 1980 in "Barnum."

NASTASI, FRANK. Born Jan. 7, 1923 in Detroit, MI. Graduate Wayne U, NYU. Bdwy debut 1963 in "Lorenzo," followed by "Avanti," OB in "Bonds of Interest," "One Day More," "Nathan the Wise," "The Chief Things," "Cindy," "Escurial," "The Shrinking Bride," "Macbird," "Cakes with the Wine," "Metropolitan Madness," "Rockaway Boulevard."

NAUGHTON, JAMES. Born Dec. 6, 1945 in Middletown, CT. Graduate Brown, Yale U. Debut 1971 OB in "Long Day's Journey Into Night" for which he received a Theatre World Award, followed by "Drinks Before Dinner," "Losing Time," Bdwy in "I Love My Wife," "Whose Life Is It Anyway?"

NEGRO, MARY JOAN. Born Nov. 9, 1948 in Brooklyn, NY. Debut 1972 OB in "The Hostage," followed by "Lower Depths," "Women Beware Women." "Ladyhouse Blues." "The Promise," Bdwy in "Three Sisters," "Measure for Measure," "Beggar's Opera," "Wings," "Modigliani,"

NEIL, ROGER. Born Nov. 19, 1948 in Galesburg, IL. Graduate Northwestern U. Debut 1974 OB in "The Boy Friend"(ELT), followed by "Scrambled Feet."

NELSON, GAIL. Born Mar. 29 in Durham, NC. Graduate Oberlin Col. Bdwy debut 1968 in "Hello, Dolly!," followed by "Applause," "On The Town," "Music! Music!" (CC), "Eubie!," "Rockette Spectacular," OB in "Six," "By Strouse."

NELSON, MARK. Born Sept. 26, 1955 in Hackensack, NJ. Graduate Princeton U. Debut 1977 OB in "The Dybbuk," followed by "Green Fields."

NEVILLE-ANDREWS, JOHN. Born Aug. 23, 1948 in Woking Surrey, Eng. Attended Westminister Tech. Col. Debut 1973 OB in "El Grande de Coca-Cola," followed by "Bullshot Drummond," Bdwy in "The Elephant Man."

NEWMAN, ELLEN. Born Sept. 5, 1950 in NYC. Attended San Diego State U., Central Sch. London. Debut 1972 OB in "Right You Are," followed by LCRep's "Merchant of Venice" and "Streetcar Named Desire," "The Importance of Being Earnest," "A Midsummer Night's Dream," "Benya the King."

NEWMAN, PHYLLIS. Born Mar. 19, 1935 in Jersey City, NJ. Attended Western Reserve U. Bdwy debut 1953 in "Wish You Were Here," followed by "Bells Are Ringing," "First Impressions," "Subways Are for Sleeping," "The Apple Tree," "On the Town," "Prisoner of Second Avenue," "Madwoman of Central Park West," OB in "I Feel Wonderful," "Make Someone Happy."

NEWMAN, STEPHEN D. Born Jan. 20, 1943 in Seattle, WA. Graduate Stanford U. Debut 1971 OB in "Hamlet," followed by "School for Wives," "Beggar's Opera," "Pygmalion," "In the Voodoo Parlor," "Richard III," "Santa Anita '42," "Polly," Bdwy in "An Evening with Richard Nixon . . . ," "Emperor Henry IV," "Habeas Corpus," "Rex," "Dirty Linen," "Dogg's Hamlet, Cahoot's Macbeth."

NEWTON, JOHN. Born Nov. 2, 1925 in Grand Junction, CO. UWash. graduate. Debut 1951 OB in "Othello," followed by "As You Like It," "Candida," "Candaules Commissioner," "Sextet," LCReps, "The Crucible" and "A Streetcar Named Desire," "The Rivals," "The Subject Was Roses," "The Brass Ring," "Hadrian VII," "The Best Little Whorehouse in Texas." Bdwy in "Weekend," "First Monday in October."

NICHOLS, JOSEPHINE. Born Nov. 11, 1913 in Lawrenceville, IL. Graduate UOkla., Columbia U. Debut 1960 in "The Prodigal," followed by "Roots," "The Golden Six," "The Adding Machine," "The Storm," "Uncommon Women and Others," "The Grinding Machine," Bdwy in "On an Open Roof." "The Skin of Our Teeth," "Clothes for a Summer Hotel."

NICHOLS, ROBERT. Born July 20, 1924 in Oakland, CA. Attended Coll. of Pacific, RADA. Debut 1978 OB in "Are You Now or Have You Ever Been," followed by "Heartbreak House," Bdwy in "Man and Superman."

NILES, MARY ANN. Born May 2, 1933 in NYC. Attended Miss Finchley's Ballet Acad. Bdwy debut in "Girl from Nantucket," followed by "Dance Me a Song," "Call Me Mister," "Make Mine Manhattan," "La Plume de Ma Tante," "Carnival," "Flora the Red Menace," "Sweet Charity," "George M!," "No, No, Nanette," "Irene," "Ballroom," OB in "The Boys from Syracuse," CC's "Wonderful Town" and "Carnival."

NOONAN, TOM. Born Apr. 12, 1951 in Greenwich, CT. Yale graduate. Debut 1978 OB in "Buried Child," followed by "The Invitational."

NORCIA, PATRIZIA. Born Apr. 6, 1954 in Rome, Italy. Graduate Hofstra U, Yale. Debut 1978 OB in "Sganarelle," followed by "The Master and Margarita," "The Loves of Cass McGuire."

NORTH, ALAN. Born Dec. 23, 1927 in NYC. Attended Columbia U. Bdwy bow 1955 in "Plain and Fancy," followed by "South Pacific," "Summer of the 17th Doll," "Requiem for a Nun," "Never Live over a Pretzel Factory," "Dylan," "Spofford," "Finian's Rainbow" (JB), "Music Man" (JB), "Annie Get Your Gun" (JB).

NOVA, CAROLINE. Born Jan. 15, 1950 in Flushing, NY. Debut 1978 OB in "Oklahoma!"

NOVY, NITA. Born June 13, 1950 in Wilkes-Barre, PA. Duke U. graduate. Bdwy debut 1960 in "Gypsy," followed by "Sound of Music," "Harold and Maude," OB in "How to Succeed . . . ," "Maggie Flynn," "Too Much Johnson."

NURENBERG, LORY. Born Apr. 12, 1954 in Cleveland, OH. Graduate UILL. Debut 1979 OB in "The Dark at the Top of the Stairs."

NUTE, DON. Born Mar. 13, in Connellsville, PA. Attended Denver U. Debut OB 1965 in "The Trojan Women," followed by "Boys in the Band," "Mad Theatre for Madmen," "The Eleventh Dynasty," "About Time," "The Urban Crisis," "Christmas Rappings," "The Life of a Man," "A Look at the Fifties."

NYE, GENE. Born Feb. 23, 1939 in Brooklyn, NY. Graduate Hofstra U. OB in "Too Much Johnson," "Elizabeth the Queen," "Trelawny of the Wells," "Seminary Murder."

O'BRIEN, MARCIA. Born Mar. 17, 1934 in Indiana. Graduate IndU. Bdwy debut 1970 in "Man of La Mancha," followed by "Evita," OB in "Now Is the Time for All Good Men," "House Party."

O'BRIEN, SYLVIA. Born May 4, 1924 in Dublin, Ire. Debut OB 1961 in "O Marry Me," followed by "Red Roses for Me," "Every Other Evil," "3 by O'Casey," "Essence of Woman," "Dear Oscar," "Dona Rosita," Bdwy in "Passion of Josef D.," "Right Honourable Gentleman," "Loves of Cass McGuire," "Hadrian VII," "Conduct Unbecoming," "My Fair Lady," "Da."

O'CONNOR, KEVIN. Born May 7 in Honolulu, HI. Attended UHi., Neighborhood Playhouse. Debut 1964 OB in "Up to Thursday," followed by "Six from LaMama," "Rimers of Eldritch," "Tom Paine," "Boy on the Straightback Chair," "Dear Janet Rosenberg," "Eyes of Chalk," "Alive and Well in Argentina," "Duet," "Trio," "The Contractor," "Kool Aid," "The Frequency," Bdwy in "Gloria and Esperanza," "The Morning after Optimism," "Figures in the Sand," "Devour the Snow," "The Lady from Dubuque."

O'DELL, K. LYPE. Born Feb. 2, 1939 in Claremore, OK. Graduate Los Angeles State Col. Debut 1972 OB in "Sunset," followed by "Our Father," "Ice Age," "Prince of Homburg," "Passion of Dracula," "M. Amilcar."

OEHLER, GRETCHEN. Born in Chicago, IL. Attended Goodman Theatre Sch. Debut 1971 OB in "The Homecoming," Bdwy 1977 in "Dracula."

O'KARMA, ALEXANDRA. Born Sept. 28, 1948 in Cincinnati, OH. Graduate Swarthmore Col. Debut 1976 OB in "A Month in the Country," followed by "Warbeck," "A Flea in Her Ear," "Knitters in the Sun."

OLIVER-NORMAN, PETER. Born July 14, 1944 in Philadelphia, PA. Attended PennStateU, UPa. Bdwy debut 1967 in "Hello, Dolly!," followed by "Beggar on Horseback," "Maggie Flynn," "Two Gentlemen of Verona," "1600 Pennsylvania Ave.," "The Wiz," OB in "Mother Courage."

O'NEILL, GENE. Born Apr. 7, 1951 in Philadelphia, PA. Graduate Loyola U. Bdwy debut 1976 in "Poison Tree," followed by "Best Little Worehouse in Texas," OB in "Afternoons in Vegas."

OREM, SUSAN. Born June 15, 1949 in Elizabeth, NJ. Graduate NYU. Debut 1979 OB in "Big Bad Burlesque."

ORMAN, ROSCOE. Born June 11, 1944 in NYC. Debut 1962 OB in "If We Grow Up," followed by "Electronic Nigger," "The Great McDaddy," "The Sirens," "Every Night When the Sun Goes Down," "Last Street Play," "Julius Caesar," "Coriolanus."

O'SHEA, MILO. Born June 2, 1926 in Dublin, Ire. Bdwy debut 1968 in "Staircase," followed by "Dear World," "Mrs. Warren's Profession" (LC), "Comedians," "A Touch of the Poet," OB in "Waiting for Godot," "Mass Appeal."

O'SULLIVAN, MAUREEN. Born May 17, 1911 in Roscommon, Ire. Bdwy debut 1962 in "Never Too Late," followed by "The Subject was Roses," "Keep It in the Family," "Front Page," "Charley's Aunt," "No Sex Please, We're British," "Morning's at 7."

OSUNA, JESS. Born May 28, 1933 in Oakland, CA. OB in "Blood Wedding," "Come Share My House," "This Side of Paradise," "Bugs and Veronica," "Monopoly," "The Infantry," "Hamp," "The Biko Inquest," "The American Clock," Bdwy in "The Goodbye People."

OTTO, LIZ. Born in Coral Gables, FL. Graduate UFL. Debut 1963 OB in "The Plot against the Chase Manhattan Bank," followed by "I Dreamt I Dwelt in Bloomingdale's," "One for the Money," "Two."

OUSLEY, ROBERT. Born July 21, 1946 in Waco, TX. Graduate Baylor U. Debut 1975 OB in "Give Me Liberty," followed by Bdwy 1979 in "Sweeney Todd."

OWEN, KATE. Born Mar. 5, 1936 in Lansing, MI. Graduate MiStateU, NYU. Debut 1975 OB in "Home Is the Hero," followed by "The Night Thoreau Spent in Jail," "The Seagull," "Romeo and Juliet," "The Sound of Music" (ELT).

OWENS, ELIZABETH. Born Feb 26. 1938 in NYC. Attended New School, Neighborhood Playhouse. Debut 1955 OB in "Dr. Faustus Lights the Lights," followed by "Chit Chat on a Rat," "The Miser," "The Father," "Importance of Being Earnest," "Candida," "Trumpets and Drums," "Oedipus," "Macbeth," "Uncle Vanya," "Misalliance," "Master Builder," "American Gothics," "The Play's the Thing" "The Rivals," "Death Story," "The Rehearsal," "Dance on a Country Grave" "Othello," "Candida," "Little Eyolf," Bdwy in "The Lovers," "Not Now Darling," "The Play's the Thing."

Don Nute	Mary Ann Niles	Roscoe Orman	Paula Parker	Ron Perlman

OYSTER, JIM. Born May 3, 1930 in Washington, DC. OB in "Coriolanus," "The Cretan Woman," "Man and Superman," "Fallen Angels," Bdwy in "Cool World," "Hostile Winners," "The Sound of Music," "The Prime of Miss Jean Brodie," "Who's Who in Hell."

PACINO, AL. Born Apr. 25, 1940 in NYC. Attended Actors Studio. Bdwy bow 1969 in "Does a Tiger Wear a Necktie?" for which he received a Theatre World Award followed by "The Basic Training of Pavlo Hummel," "Richard III," OB in "Why Is a Crooked Letter?," "Peace Creeps," "The Indian Wants the Bronx," "Local Stigmatic," "Camino Real" (LC), "Jungle of Cities."

PAGANO, GIULIA. Born July 8, 1948 in NYC. Attended AADA. Debut 1977 OB in "The Passion of Dracula," followed by "Heartbreak House"

PAGE, GERALDINE. Born Nov. 22, 1924 in Kirksville, MO. Attended Goodman Theatre. Debut 1945 OB in "Seven Mirrors," followed by "Yerma," "Summer and Smoke," "Macbeth," "Look Away," "The Stronger," Bdwy in "Midsummer" (1953) for which she received a Theatre World Award, "The Immoralist," "The Rainmaker," "Innkeepers," "Separate Tables," "Sweet Bird of Youth," "Strange Interlude," "Three Sisters," "P.S. I Love you," "The Great Indoors," "White Lies," "Black Comedy," "The Little Foxes," "Angela," "Absurd Person Singular," "Clothes for a Summer Hotel."

PAGE, KEN. Born Jan 20, 1954 in St. Louis, MO. Attended Fontbonne Col. Bdwy debut 1976 in "Guys and Dolls" for which he received a Theatre World Award followed by "The Wiz," "Ain't Misbehavin."

PAISNER, DINA. Born in Brooklyn, NY. Bdwy debut 1963 in "Andorra," OB in "The Cretan Woman," "Pullman Car Hiawatha," "Lysistrata," "If 5 Years Pass," "Troubled Waters," "Sap of Life," "Cave at Machpelah," "Threepenny Opera," "Montserrat," "Gandhi," "Medea," "Blood Wedding."

PALMER, SCOTT. Born Jan. 25, 1953 in San Francisco, CA. Attended MonStateU. Bdwy debut 1976 in "Caesar and Cleopatra," followed by "Clothes for a Summer Hotel."

PAPE, JOAN. Born Jan. 23, in Detroit, MI. Graduate Purdue U., Yale. Debut 1972 OB in "Suggs," followed by "Bloomers," "Museum," "Funeral Games," "Getting out," BAM Theatre Co.'s "Barbarians, "He and She," Bdwy in "The Secret Affairs of Mildred Wild," "Cat on a Hot Tin Roof," "A History of the American Film."

PARKER, ELLEN. Born Sept. 30, 1949 in Paris, FR. Graduate Bard Col. Debut 1971 OB in "James Joyce Liquid Memorial Theatre," followed by "Uncommon Women and Others," "Dusa, Fish, Stas and Vi," "Justice," Bdwy in "Equus," "Strangers."

PARKER, PAULA. Born Aug. 14, 1950 in Chicago, IL. Graduate S.Ill.U. Debut 1971 OB in "The Debate," followed by "Maggie Flynn," "Metropolitan Madness."

PARKS, TRINA. Born Dec. 26 in Brooklyn, NY. Debut 1964 OB in "Prodigal Son," followed by "House of Flowers," "Never Jam Today," "Changes," Bdwy in "Her First Roman" (1968), "The Selling of the President."

PARRIS, STEVE. Born in Athens, Greece. Graduate CCNY. Debut 1964 OB in "The Comforter," followed by "Consider the Lilies," "A Christmas Carol," "The Man with the Flower in His Mouth," "King David and His Wives."

PARRY, WILLIAM. Born Oct. 7, 1947 in Steubenville, OH. Graduate Mt. Union Col. Bdwy debut 1971 in "Jesus Christ Superstar," followed by "Rockabye Hamlet," "The Leaf People," OB in "Sgt. Pepper's Lonely Hearts Club Band," "The Conjuror," "Noah," "The Misanthrope," "Joseph and the Amazing Technicolor Dreamcoat," "Agamemnon," "The Coolest Cat in Town," "Dispatches," "The Derby."

PARSONS, ESTELLE. Born Nov. 20, 1927 in Lynn, MA. Attended Boston U, Actors Studio. Bdwy debut 1956 in "Happy Hunting," followed by "Whoop-Up!," "Beg, Borrow or Steal," "Mother Courage," "Ready When You Are, C.B.," "Malcolm," "The 7 Descents of Myrtle," "And Miss Reardon Drinks a Little," "The Norman Conquests," "Ladies at the Alamo," "Miss Margarida's Way," OB in "Demi-Dozen," "Pieces of 8," "ThreePenny Opera," "Automobile Graveyard," "Mrs. Dally Has a Lover" for which she received a Theatre World Award, "Next Time I'll Sing to You," "Come to the Palace of Sin," "In the Summer house," "Monopoly," "The East Wind," Galileo," "Peer Gynt," "Mahagonny," "People Are Living There," "Barbary Shore," "Oh Glorious Tintinnabulation," "Mert and Paul," "Elizabeth and Essex."

PARVA, CYNTHIA. Born Nov. 6 in San Antonio, TX. Attended HB Studio. Bdwy debut 1979 1n "The Utter Glory of Morrissey Hall," OB in "Potholes."

PASSERO, LISA. Born July 29, 1952 in Norwalk, CT. Graduate Emerson Col. Bdwy debut 1980 in "Filumena."

PATTERSON, NEVA. Born Feb. 10, 1922 in Nevada, IA. Bdwy debut 1947 in "The Druid Circle," Followed by "The Ivy Green," "Ring Round the Moon," "The Long Days," "Lace on Her Petticoat," "Seven Year Itch," "Speaking of Murder," "Double in Hearts," "Make a Million," "Romantic Comedy."

PAUL, DON. Born Oct. 22, 1951 in Chattanooga, TN. Graduate UTn. Debut 1975 OB in "A New Breed," followed by "Streamers," "Bojangles."

PEARSON, SCOTT. Born Dec. 13, 1941 in Milwaukee, WI. Attended Valparaiso U, UWisc. Bdwy debut 1966 in "A Joyful Noise," followed by "Promises, Promises," "A Chorus Line."

PEARTHREE, PIPPA. Born Sept. 23, 1956 in Baltimore, MD. Attended NYU. Bdwy debut 1977 in "Grease," followed by "Whose Life Is It Anyway?"

PEDEN, CAROL. Born Dec. 1, 1948 in St. Louis, MO. Graduate Duke U, Washington U. Debut 1979 OB in "The Sound of Music" (ELT).

PEISNER, MARVIN. Born Apr. 24 in Detroit, MI. Graduate Wayne State U. Debut 1960 OB in "A Country Scandal," followed by "Way of the World," "The Exception and the Rule," "The Balcony," "3000 Red Ants," "Pantagleize," "Line," "Dona Rosita."

PELIKAN, LISA. Born July 12 in Paris, France. Attended Juilliard. Debut 1975 OB in "Spring's Awakening," followed by "An Elephant in the House," "The American Clock," Bdwy in "Romeo and Juliet" (1977).

PENDLETON, AUSTIN. Born Mar. 27, 1940 in Warren, OH. Attended Yale. Appeared with LCRep 1962–63, and OB in "O, Dad, Poor Dad . . . ," "The Last Sweet Days of Isaac," BAM's "Three Sisters," "Say Goodnight, Gracie," "The Office Murders," Bdwy in "Fiddler on the Roof," "Hail Scrawdyke," "The Little Foxes," "An American Millionaire," "The Runner Stumbles."

PENDLETON, WYMAN. Born Apr. 18, 1916 in Providence, RI. Graduate Brown U. Bdwy in "Tiny Alice," "Malcolm," "Quotations from Chairman Mao Tse-Tung," "Happy Days," "Henry V," "Othello," "There's One in Every Marriage," "Cat on a Hot Tin Roof," OB in "Gallows Humor," "American Dream," "Zoo Story," "Corruption in the Palace of Justice," "Giant's Dance," "Child Buyer," "Happy Days," "Butter and Egg Man," "Othello," "Albee Directs Albee," "Dance for Me Simeon."

PENN, EDWARD. Born in Washington, DC. Studied at HB studio. Debut 1965 OB in "The Queen and the Rebels," followed by "My Wife and I," "Invitation to a March," "Of Thee I Sing," "Fantasticks," "Greenwillow," "One for the Money," "Dear Oscar," "Speed Gets the Poppys," "Man with a Load of Mischief," "Company," "The Constant Wife," "Tune the Grand Up!," "Reflected Glory," Bdwy bow 1975 in "Shenandoah."

PENZNER, SEYMOUR. Born July 29, 1915 in Yonkers, NY. Attended CCNY. OB in "Crystal Heart," "Guitar," "Paterson," Bdwy in "Oklahoma!," "Finian's Rainbow," "Call Me Madam," "Paint Your Wagon," "Can-Can," "Kean," "Baker Street," "Man of La Mancha."

PERKINS, ANTHONY. Born Apr. 4, 1932 in NYC. Attended Rollins Col., Columbia U. Bdwy debut 1954 in "Tea and Sympathy" for which he received a Theatre World Award," followed by "Look Homeward, Angel," "Greenwillow," "Harold," "Star Spangled Girl," "Equus," "Romantic Comedy," OB in "Steambath."

PERKINS, DON. Born Oct. 23, 1928 in Boston, MA. Graduate Emerson Col. OB in "Drums under the Window," "Henry VI," "Richard III," "The Dubliners," "The Rehearsal," "Fallen Angels," Bdwy in "Borstal Boy" (1970).

PERKINS, PATTI. Born July 9 in New Haven, CT. Attended AMDA. Debut 1972 OB in "The Contrast," followed by "Fashion," "Tuscaloosa's Calling Me . . . ," "Patch Patch," "Shakespeare's Cabaret," Bdwy in "All Over Town" (1974).

PERLEY, WILLIAM. Born Nov. 24, 1942 in NYC. Graduate UFla. Debut 1975 OB in "Tenderloin," followed by "Housewives' Cantata," Bdwy 1977 in "Vieux Carre."

PERLMAN, RON. Born Apr. 13, 1950 in NYC. Graduate Lehman Col., UMin. Debut 1976 OB in "The Architect and the Emperor of Assyria," followed by "Tartuffe," "School for Bufoons," "Measure for Measure," "Hedda Gabler," Bdwy 1979 in "Teibele and Her Demon."

245

PERRY, ELIZABETH. Born Oct. 15, 1937 in Pawtuxet, RI. Attended RISU, AmThWing. Bdwy debut 1956 in "Inherit the Wind," followed by "The Women," with APA in "The Misanthrope," "Hamlet," "Exit the King," "Beckett" and "Macbeth," OB in "Royal Gambit," "Here Be Dragons," "Lady from the Sea," "Heartbreak House," "Him," "All the Way Home," "The Frequency," "Fefu and Her Friends," "Out of the Broomcloset," "Ruby Ruby Sam Sam."

PESATURO, GEORGE. Born July 29, 1949 in Winthrop, MA. Graduate Manhattan Col. Bdwy debut 1976 in "A Chorus Line," OB in "The Music Man" (JB).

PETERS, GEORGE J. Born Mar. 23, 1923. Bdwy in "Medea," "Caesar and Cleopatra," OB in "Climate of Eden," "Independence Day," "Streamers."

PETERSON, LENKA. Born Oct. 16, 1925 in Omaha, NE. Attended UIowa. Bdwy debut 1946 in "Bathsheba," followed by "Harvest of Years," "Sundown Beach," "Young and Fair," "The Grass Harp," "The Girls of Summer," "The Time of Your Life," "Look Homeward, Angel," "All the Way Home," "Nuts," OB in "Mrs. Minter," "American Night Cry," "Leaving Home," "The Brass Ring."

PETTY, ROSS. Born Aug. 29, 1946 in Winnipeg, Can. Graduate U Manitoba Debut 1975 OB in "Happy Time," followed by "Maggie Flynn," "Carnival," "Little Eyolf," "It's Wilde!," Bdwy in "Wings."

PFISTER, DENNIS. Born Sept. 27, 1951 in Detroit, MI. Bdwy debut 1980 in "Romeo and Juliet."

PHERSON, ROB. Born Nov. 9, 1950 in Phoenix AZ. Graduate UAz. Debut 1976 OB in "The Mousetrap," followed by "Arms and the Man."

PHILLIPS, ETHAN. Born Feb. 8, 1950 in Rockville Center, NY. Graduate Boston U, Cornell U. Debut 1979 OB in "Modigliani."

PHILLIPS, GARRISON. Born Oct. 8, 1929 in Tallahassee, FL. Graduate UWVa. Debut 1956 OB in "Eastward in Eden," followed by "Romeo and Juliet," "Time of the Cuckoo," "Triptych," Bdwy 1980 in "Clothes for a Summer Hotel."

PHILLIPS, MARY BRACKEN. Born Aug. 15, 1946 in Kansas City, MO. Attended KanU. Debut 1969 OB in "Perfect Party," followed by "Look Where I'm At," "Hot Grog," Bdwy in "1776," "Different Times," "Hurry Harry," "Annie."

PHILLIPS, MIRIAM. Born May 28, 1899 in Philadelphia, PA. Graduate UPenn. Bdwy debut 1926 in "Spring Song," followed by "Half a Widow," "Waltz of the Toreadors," "Legend of Lizzie," "Filumena," OB in "A House Remembered," "Evenings with Chekhov," "Lion in Love," "Hamlet of Stepney Green," among others.

PHILLIPS, PETER. Born Dec. 7, 1949 in Darby, PA. Graduate Dartmouth Col., RADA. Debut 1976 OB in "Henry V," followed by "The Cherry Orchard," "Total Eclipse," "Catsplay," "Warriors from a Long Childhood," BAM's "A Winter's Tale," "Johnny on a Spot," and "Barbarians," Bdwy in "Equus" (1977)

PIAZZA, FRANK. Born Aug. 31, 1945 in Bridgeport, CT. Graduate Quinnipiac Col. Bdwy debut 1977 in "Unexpected Guests," OB in "Rockaway Boulevard."

PICON, MOLLY. Born Feb. 28, 1898 in NYC. Star of Yiddish theatre has appeared on Bdwy in "Morning Star," "For Heaven's Sake, Mother," "Milk and Honey," "How to Be a Jewish Mother," "Front Page," "Paris Is Out," "Something Old, Something New," OB in "Abi Gezunt."

PIERCE, HARVEY. Born June 24, 1917 in NYC. Graduate NYU. OB credits include "The Gentle People," "Native Son," "The Country Girl," "Men in White," "To Bury a Cousin," "Time of the Cuckoo" (ELT).

PIERRE, CHRISTOPHE. Born Dec. 25, 1949 in New Orleans, LA. Attended Theological Seminary. Bdwy debut 1973 in "Don't Bother Me, I Can't Cope," followed by "The Wiz," "Guys and Dolls," OB in "Miss Truth."

PIETROPINTO, ANGELA. Born Feb. 5 in NYC. Graduate NYU. OB credits include "Henry IV," "Alice in Wonderland," "Endgame," "Our Late Night," "The Sea Gull," "Jinxs Bridge," "The Mandrake," "Marie and Bruce."

PINERO, JOHN. Born Jan. 31, 1945 in Brooklyn, NY. Attended HB Studio. Deubt 1976 OB in "Where Is My Little Gloria," followed by "The Web," "Yank in Beverly Hills."

PLOWRIGHT, JOAN. Born Oct. 28, 1929 in Scunthorpe, Brigg, Lincolnshire, Eng. Attended Old Vic School. Debut 1958 OB in "The Chairs" and "The Lesson," Bdwy in "The Entertainer" (1958), followed by "A Taste of Honey," "Filumena."

PLUMLEY, DON. Born Feb. 11, 1934 in Los Angeles, CA. Graduate Pepperdine Col. Debut 1961 OB in "The Cage," followed by "Midsummer Night's Dream," "Richard II," "Cymbeline," "Much Ado About Nothing," "Henry V," "Saving Grace," "A Whistle in the Dark," "Operation Sidewinder" (LC), "Enemy of the People" (LC), "Back Bog Beast Bait," "The Kid," "Salt Lake City Skyline," Bdwy 1975 in "Equus."

PLUMMER, AMANDA MICHAEL. Born Mar. 23, 1957 in NYC. Attended Middlebury Col., Neighborhood Playhouse. Debut 1979 OB in "Artichoke," followed by "A Month in the Country."

PLUMMER, AMY. Born Apr. 24, 1953 in Forest City, AR. Graduate Elmira Col. Debut 1979 OB in "Love's Labour's Lost."

POGEE, MARIA. Born Apr. 7 in Buenos Aires, Argentina. Bdwy debut 1979 in "Peter Pan."

POLAK, MARGRIT. Born Nov. 17, 1955 in Bronxville, NY. Graduate Kenyon Col. Debut 1979 OB in "The Mischief You Forsee," followed by "Uncommon Women and Others."

POLENZ, ROBERT. Born June 9, 1953 in Trenton, NJ. Graduate Muskingam Col. Bdwy debut 1974 in "Over Here," followed by "Candide," OB in "Apple Pie," "Children of Adam," "Snapshot".

POLITO, JON. Born Dec. 29, 1950 in Philadelphia, PA. Graduate Villanova U. Debut 1976 OB in "The Transfiguration of Benno Blimpie," followed by "Gemini," "New Jerusalem," BAM Theatre Co.'s "Emigres," "A Winter's Tale," "Johnny on a Spot," "Barbarians," and "The Wedding," Bdwy 1977 in "American Buffalo."

POLLOCK, WENDE. Born May 2, 1950 in Buffalo, NY. Attended UWisc. Debut 1977 OB in "Carnival," followed by "Merton of the Movies" (ELT).

PONAZECKI, JOE. Born Jan. 7, 1934 in Rochester, NY. Attended Rochester U, Columbia U. Bdwy debut 1959 in "Much Ado about Nothing," followed by "Send Me No Flowers," "A Call on Kuprin," "Take Her, She's Mine," "Fiddler on the Roof," "Xmas in Las Vegas," "3 Bags Full," "Love in E-Flat," "90 Day Mistress," "Harvey," "Trial of the Catonsville 9," "The Country Girl," "Freedom of the City," "Summer Brave," "Music Is," OB in "The Dragon," "Muzeeka," "Witness," "All Is Bright," "The Dog Ran Away," "Dream of a Blacklisted Actor," "Innocent Pleasures," "The Dark at the Top of the Stairs."

POOLE, ROY. Born Mar. 31, 1924 in San Bernardino, CA. Graduate Stanford U. Bdwy debut 1950 in "Now I Lay Me Down To Sleep," followed by "St. Joan," "The Bad Seed," "I Knock at the Door," "Long Day's Journey into Night," "Face of a Hero," "Moby Dick," "Poor Bitos," "1776," "Scratch," "Once a Catholic," OB in "27 Wagons Full of Cotton," "A Memory of Two Mondays," "Secret Service," "Boy Meets Girl."

POTTER, DON. Born Aug. 15, 1932 in Philadelphia, PA. Debut 1961 OB in "What a Killing," followed by "Sunset," "You're a Good Man Charlie Brown," "One Cent Plain," "Annie Get Your Gun" (JB), Bdwy in "Gypsy" (1974), "Snow White."

POWELL, BUDDY. (Formerly Randy.) Born Aug. 18, 1952 in Chicago, IL. Graduate Murray State U. Bdwy debut 1978 in "Grease."

POWERS, NEVA RAE. Born in Oakland City, IN. Graduate Cincinnati Consv. Debut 1974 OB in "The Boy Friend," followed by "Love! Love! Love!," Bdwy 1979 in "Peter Pan."

PRADO, FRANCISCO. Born Nov. 3, 1941 in San Juan, PR. Graduate UPR. Debut 1977 OB in "G. R. Point," followed by "Julius Caesar," "Coriolanus," "Antony and Cleopatra," "Lewlulu," "Puerto Rican Obituary."

PREECE, K. K. Born Nov. 14, 1949 in Anna, IL. Graduate Brenau Col. Debut 1976 OB in "Panama Hattie," Bdwy 1980 in "Canterbury Tales."

PRESS, GWYNN. Born July 28 in NYC. Attended Queens Col. Debut 1975 OB in "The Wild Duck," followed by "Out of Sight," "Romeo and Juliet," "Greenfields," "A New England Legend," "Richard II," "Bird with Silver Feathers."

PRICE, GILBERT. Born Sept. 10, 1942 in NYC. Attended AmThWing. Debut 1962 OB in "Fly Blackbird," followed by "Jerico-Jim Crow" for which he received a Theatre World Award, "Promenade," "Slow Dance on the Killing Ground," "Six," "Melodrama Play," "The Crucifixion," Bdwy in "Roar of the Greasepaint . . .,(1965)," "Lost in the Stars," "The Night That Made America Famous," "1600 Pennsylvania Ave.," "Timbuktu!"

PRICE, LONNY. Born Mar. 9, 1959 in NYC. Attended Juilliard. Debut 1979 OB in "Class Enemy" for which he received a Theatre World Award.

PRICE, SHERILL. Born Nov. 7 in Pierre, SD. Graduate SD State U. Bdwy debut 1964 in "Oliver!," followed by "Man of La Mancha," OB in "The Penny Friend," "Memphis Store-Bought Teeth," "Romeo and Juliet."

PRIMONT, MARIAN. Born Oct. 2, 1913 in NYC. Graduate NYU. Debut 1957 OB in "Richard III," followed by "The Anatomist," "Come Share My House," "Dona Rosita," Bdwy 1961 in "All the Way Home."

PRIMUS, BARRY. Born Feb. 16, 1938 in NYC. Attended CCNY. Bdwy debut 1960 in "The Nervous Set," followed by "Oh, Dad, Poor Dad . . . ," "Creation of the World and Other Business," "Teibele and Her Demon," OB in "Henry IV," "Huui, Huui," "The Criminals," "Diary of a Scoundrel," "Jesse and the Bandit Queen."

PROVENZA, SAL. Born Sept. 21, 1946 in Brooklyn, NY. Attended Brooklyn Col., Juilliard. Debut 1980 OB in "The Fantasticks."

PRUETT, EDDIE. Born July 21, 1951 in Terre Haute, IN. Attended Austin Peay Col. Bdwy debut 1979 in "Sugar Babies."

PUDENZ, STEVE. Born Sept. 25, 1947 in Carroll, IA. Graduate UIowa. Debut 1980 OB in "Dona Rosita."

PULLIAM, ZELDA. Born Oct. 18 in Chicago, IL. Attended Roosevelt U. Bdwy debut 1969 in "Hello, Dolly!," followed by "Purlie," "Raisin," "Pippin," "Dancin'," OB in 'Croesus and the Witch."

PURSLEY, DAVID. Born July 13, 1938 in Lewisburg, PA. Graduate Harvard, Baylor U. Debut 1969 OB in "Peace," followed by "The Faggott," "Wings," "The Three Musketeers," Bdwy in "Happy End" (1977), "Snow White."

QUINN, HENRY J. Born Aug. 6, 1928 in Boston, MA. Graduate Catholic U. Debut 1979 OB in "The Sound of Music" (ELT).

QUINN, TOM. Born Oct. 6, 1934 in NYC. Attended IndU., CCNY. Debut 1974 OB In "Moonchildren," followed by "Boom Boom Room," "Oklahoma!"

RACHELLE, BERNIE. Born Oct. 7, 1939 in NYC. Graduate Yeshiva U, Hunter Col. OB in "Winterset," "Golden Boy," "Street Scene," "World of Sholom Aleichem," "The Diary of Anne Frank," "Electra," "Nighthawks," "House Party," "Dancing in NY," "Metropolitan Madness."

RADIGAN, MICHAEL. Born May 2, 1949 in Springfield, IL. Graduate Springfield Col., Goodman Theatre. Bdwy debut 1974 in "Music! Music!" (CC), followed by "Sugar Babies," OB in "Broadway Dandies," "Beowulf."

RADNER, GILDA. Born June 28 in Detroit, MI. Debut 1975 OB in "The National Lampoon Show," Bdwy 1979 in "Gilda Radner—Live from NY."

RAE, AUDREE. Born Feb. 12, 1942 in North Shields, Eng. Debut 1962 OB in "One Way Pendulum," Bdwy 1980 in "Clothes for a Summer Hotel."

RAGGIO, LISA. Born May 12 in NYC. Graduate NYU. Bdwy debut 1975 in "The Magic Show," followed by "Grease," "Got Tu Go Disco."

RALPH, SHERYL LEE. Born Dec. 30, 1957 in NYC. Graduate Rutgers U. Debut 1977 OB in "Eden," followed by "One Night Only," Bdwy 1980 in "Reggae."

RAMAKER, JULIANNE. (a.k.a. Julie) Born Aug. 16, 1952 in LaCross, WI. Graduate Drake U. OB in "The Real Inspector Hound," "Doctor in the House," "Hay Fever," "Shakespeare Pastiche," "Arms and the Man," "Uncle Vanya," "Twelfth Night."

RAMIREZ, RAMIRO (RAY). Born Feb. 1, 1939 in NYC. Attended CCNY. OB in "Down in the Valley," "Shakespeare in Harlem," "Harold Arlen Songbook," "Sancocho," "The Sun Always Shines for the Cool."

RAMSAY, REMAK. Born Feb. 2, 1937 in Baltimore, MD. Graduate Princeton U. Debut 1964 OB in "Hang Down Your Head and Die," followed by "The Real Inspector Hound," "Landscape of the Body," "All's Well That Ends Well" (CP), "Rear Column," Bdwy in "Half a Sixpence," "Sheep on the Runway," "Lovely Ladies, Kind Gentlemen," "On the Town," "Jumpers," "Private Lives," "Dirty Linen," "Every Good Boy Deserves Favor" (LC), "Save Grand Central."

RAMSEL, GENA. Born Feb. 19, 1950 in El Reno, OK. Graduate SMU. Bdwy debut 1974 in "Lorelei," followed by "The Best Little Whorehouse in Texas," OB in "Joe Masiell Not at the Palace."

RAMSEY, MARION. Born May 10, 1947 in Philadelphia, PA. Bdwy bow 1969 in "Hello, Dolly!," followed by "The Me Nobody Knows," "Rachel Lily Rosenbloom," "Eubie!," OB in "Soon," "Do It Again," "Wedding of Iphigenia." "2008½."

REYNOLDS, JEFFREY. Born Dec. 7, 1955 on Long Island, NY. Graduate Ind.U. Bdwy debut 1980 in "West Side Story."

RAND, SUZANNE. Born Sept. 8, 1949 in Chicago, IL. Graduate Stephens Coll. Debut OB 1973 in "The Proposition," Bdwy 1979 in "Monteith and Rand."

RANDALL, CHARLES. Born Mar. 15, 1923 in Chicago, IL. Attended Columbia U. Bdwy bow 1953 in "Anastasia," followed by "Enter Laughing," "Trial of Lee Harvey Oswald," OB in "The Adding Machine," "The Cherry Orchard," "Brothers Karamazov," "Susan Slept Here," "Two for Fun," "Timon of Athens," "Endgame," "Yank in Beverly Hills."

RANDELL, RON. Born Oct. 8, 1920 in Sydney, Aust. Attended St. Mary's Col. Bdwy debut 1949 in "The Browning Version," followed by "A Harlequinade," "Candida," "World of Suzie Wong," "Sherlock Holmes," "Mrs. Warren's Profession" (LC), "Measure for Measure" (CP), "Bent," OB in "The Grinding Machine."

RANDOLPH, BILL. Born Oct. 11, 1953 in Detroit, MI. Attended Allen Hancock Col., SUNY Purchase. Bdwy debut 1978 in "Gemini," OB in "Holy Places."

RANDOLPH, JOHN. Born June 1, 1915 in the Bronx, NY. Attended CCNY, Actors Studio. Bdwy debut 1937 in "Revolt of the Beavers," followed by "The Emperor's New Clothes," "Capt. Jinks," "Nor More Peace," "Coriolanus," "Medicine Show," "Hold on to Your Hats," "Native Son," "Command Decision," "Come Back, Little Sheba," "Golden State," "Peer Gynt," "Paint Your Wagon," "Seagulls over Sorrento," "Grey-Eyed People," "Room Service," "All Summer Long," "House of Flowers," "The Visit," "Mother Courage," "Sound of Music," "Case of Libel," "Conversation at Midnight," "My Sweet Charlie," OB in "An Evening's Frost," "The Peddler and the Dodo Bird," "Our Town," "Line," "Baba Goya," "Nourish the Beast," "Back in the Race," "The American Clock."

RASCHE, DAVID. Born Aug. 7, 1944 in St. Louis, MO. Graduate Elmhurst Col., U Chicago. Debut 1976 OB in "John," followed by "Snow White," "Isadora Duncan Sleeps with the Russian Navy," "End of the War," Bdwy in "Shadow Box" (1977), "Loose Ends."

RAWLINS, LESTER. Born Sept. 24, 1924 in Farrell, PA. Attended Carnegie Tech. Bdwy in "Othello," "King Lear," "The Lovers," "A Man for All Seasons," "Herzl," "Romeo and Juliet," "Da," OB in "Endgame," "Quare Fellow," "Camino Real," "Hedda Gabler," "Old Glory," "Child Buyer," "Winterset," "In the Bar of a Tokyo Hotel," "The Reckoning," "Nightride."

RAWLS, EUGENIA. Born Sept. 11, 1916 in Macon, GA. Attended UNC. Bdwy debut 1934 in "The Children's Hour," followed by "To Quito and Back," "Journeyman," "Little Foxes," "Guest in the House," "Man Who Had All the Luck," "Strange Fruit," "The Shrike," "The Great Sebastians," "First Love," "Case of Libel," "Sweet Bird of Youth," OB in "Poker Session," "Just the Immediate Family," "Tallulah, A Memory."

REAMS, LEE ROY. Born Aug. 23, 1942 in Covington, KY. Graduate U. Cinn. Cons. Bdwy debut 1966 in "Sweet Charity," followed by "Oklahoma!" (LC). "Applause," "Lorelei," "Show Boat" (JB), "Hello Dolly!" (1978)., OB in "Sterling Silver," "Potholes."

REAUX, ANGELINA. Born Jan. 23, 1954 in Houston, TX. Graduate Northwestern U. Debut 1979 OB in "King of Schnorrers."

REDFIELD, MARILYN. Born May 2, 1940 in Chicago, IL. Graduate Vassar, Harvard, HB Studio. Debut 1973 OB in "Monologia," "Mod Madonna," "King of the U.S.," "Too Much Johnson," Bdwy in "Chapter 2" (1979).

REED, ALAINA. Born Nov. 10, 1946 in Springfield, OH. Attended Kent State U. Bdwy debut in "Hair" (original and 1977), followed by "Eubie!," OB in "Sgt. Pepper's Lonely Hearts Club Band."

REED, PAMELA. Born Apr. 2, 1949 in Tacoma, WA. Graduate U Wash. Bdwy debut 1978 in "The November People," OB in "The Curse of the Starving Class.," "All's Well That Ends Well" (CP), "Seduced," "Getting Out," "The Sorrows of Stephen."

REEHLING, JOYCE. Born Mar. 5, 1949 in Baltimore, MD. Graduate NC Sch. of Arts. Debut 1976 OB in "Hot l Baltimore," followed by "Who Killed Richard Cory?," "Lulu," "5th of July," "The Runner Stumbles," "Life and/or Death," "Back in the Race."

REESE, ROXANNE. Born June 6, 1952 in Washington, DC. Graduate Howard U. Debut 1974 OB in "Freedom Train," followed by "Feeling Good," "No Place to Be Somebody," "Spell #7" "Shakespeare's Cabaret," Bdwy 1976 in "For Colored Girls Who Have Considered Suicide . . . "

REGAN, MOLLY. Born Oct. 8 in Mankato, MN. Graduate Northwestern U. Debut 1979 OB in "Say Goodnight, Gracie."

REICHER, STEVE. Born June 5, 1944 in NYC. Graduate Columbia U. Debut 1979 OB in "Blues for Mr. Charlie."

REILLY, CHARLES NELSON. Born Jan. 13, 1931 in NYC. Attended ConnU. Debut 1956 OB in "Best Foot Forward," followed by "Saintliness of Marjory Kemp," "Fall Out," "Lend an Ear," "Parade," "Inspector General," Bdwy in "Bye Bye Birdie" (1960), "How to Succeed in Business . . . ," "Hello, Dolly!," "Skyscraper," "God's Favorite," "Charlotte."

REINHARDSEN, DAVID. Born Jan. 13, 1949 in NYC. Graduate Westminster Col. Bdwy debut 1976 in "Zalmen, or the Madness of God," followed by OB's "Altar Boys."

REINKING, ANN. Born Nov. 10, 1949 in Seattle, WA. Attended Joffrey Sch., HB Studio. Bdwy debut 1969 in "Cabaret," followed by "Coco," "Pippin," "Over Here" for which she received a Theatre World Award, "Goodtime Charley," "A Chorus Line," "Chicago," "Dancin'."

REISNER, CHRIS. Born Aug. 31, 1951 in NYC. Attended HB Studio. Debut 1978 OB in "Can-Can," after four years with Nikolais Dance Theatre, followed by "The More You Get."

REPOLE, CHARLES. Born May 24, 1945 in Brooklyn, NY. Graduate Hofstra U. Bdwy debut 1975 in "Very Good Eddie" for which he received a Theatre World Award, followed by "Finian's Rainbow" (JB)., "Whoopee!," OB in "Make Someone Happy."

REY, ANTONIA. Born Oct. 12, 1927 in Havana, Cuba. Graduate Havana U. Bdwy debut 1964 in "Bajour," followed by "Mike Downstairs," "Engagement Baby," "The Ritz," OB in "Yerma," "Fiesta in Madrid," "Camino Real" (LC), "Back Bog Beast Bait," "Rain," "42 Seconds from Broadway," "Streetcar Named Desire" (LC), "Poets from the Inside," "Blood Wedding."

RICE, SARAH. Born Mar. 5, 1955 in Okinawa, attended Ariz State U. Debut 1974 OB in "The Fantasticks," Bdwy 1979 in "Sweeney Todd" for which she received a Theatre World Award.

RICH, TONY. Born Jan. 21, 1952 in Baltimore, MD. Graduate Morgan State, Coppin State. Debut 1979 OB in "All Night Strut!"

RICHARDS, JESS. Born Jan. 23, 1943 in Seattle, WA. Attended UWash. Bdwy debut 1966 in "Walking Happy," followed by "South Pacific" (LC), "Blood Red Roses," "Two by Two," "On the Town" for which he received a Theatre World Award, "Mack and Mabel," "Musical Chairs," OB in "One for the Money," "Lovesong," "A Musical Evening with Josh Logan," "The Lullaby of Broadway," "All Night Strut!"

RICHARDS, PAUL-DAVID. Born Aug. 31, 1935 in Bedford, IN. Graduate IndU. Bdwy debut 1959 in "Once upon a Mattress," followed by "Camelot," "It's Superman!," "A Joyful Noise," "1776," "Devour the Snow," OB in "Black Picture Show," "Devour the Snow."

RICHARDSON, BARBARA. Born July 21, 1951 in Durham, NC. Graduate East Carolina U. Debut 1980 OB in "Fourtune."

RICHARDSON, PATRICIA. Born Feb 23 in Bethesda, MD. Graduate Southern Methodist U. Bdwy debut 1974 in "Gypsy," followed by "Loose Ends," OB in "Coroner's Plot," "Vanities," "Hooters," "The Frequency."

RIEGERT, PETER. Born Apr. 11, 1947 in NYC. Graduate UBuffalo. Debut 1975 OB in "Dance with Me," followed by "Sexual Perversity in Chicago," "Sunday Runners," Bdwy 1980 in "Censored Scenes from King Kong."

RIFKIN, RON. Born OCT. 31, 1939 In NYC. NYU graduate. Bdwy debut 1960 in "Come Blow Your Horn." followed by "The Goodbye People," OB in "Rosebloom," "The Art of Dining."

RILEY, LARRY. Born June 21, 1952 in Memphis, TN. Graduate Memphis State U. Bdwy debut 1978 in "A Broadway Musical," followed by "I Love My Wife," "Night and Day," OB in "Street Songs," "Amerika," "Plane Down," "Sidewalkin'."

RINEHART, ELAINE. Born Aug. 16, 1952 in San Santonio, TX, Graduate NC Sch of Arts. Debut 1975 OB in "Tenderloin," Bdwy in "The Best Little Whorehouse in Texas."

ROBBINS, JANA. Born Apr. 18, 1947 in Johnstown, PA. Graduate Stephens Col. Bdwy debut 1974 in "Good News," followed by "I Love My Wife," OB in "Tickles by Tucholsky," "Tip-Toes," "All Night Strut!"

ROBBINS, REX. Born in Pierre, SD. Bdwy debut 1964 in "One Flew over the Cuckoo's Nest," followed by "Scratch," "The Changing Room," "Gypsy," "Comedians," "An Almost Perfect Person," "Richard III," OB in "Servant of Two Masters," "The Alchemist," "Arms and the Man," "Boys in the Band," "A Memory of Two Mondays," "They Knew What They Wanted," "Secret Service," "Boy Meets Girl," BAM's "Three Sisters," "The Play's the Thing," and "Julius Caesar."

ROBERTS, ERIC. Born Apr. 18, 1956 in Biloxi, MS. Attended RADA, AADA. Debut 1976 OB in "Rebel Women," followed by "Mass Appeal."

ROBERTS, RACHEL. Born Sept. 30, 1927 in Llanelly, Wales. Attended RADA. Bdwy debut 1973 in "The Visit," followed by "Chemin de Fer," "Habeas Corpus," "Once a Catholic."

ROBERTS, TONY. Born Oct. 22, 1939 in NYC. Graduate Northwestern U. Bdwy bow 1962 in "Something about a Soldier," followed by "Take Her, She's Mine," "Last Analysis," "Never Too Late," "Barefoot in the Park," "Don't Drink the Water," "How Now, Dow Jones," "Play It Again, Sam," "Promises, Promises," "Sugar," "Absurd Person Singular," "Murder at the Howard Johnson's." "They're Playing Our Song," OB in "The Cradle Will Rock," "Losing Time."

ROCCO, MARY. Born Sept. 12, 1933 in Brooklyn, NY. Graduate Queens Col., CCNY. Debut 1976 OB in "Fiorello!," followed by "The Constant Wife," "Archy and Mehitabel."

ROCKAFELLOW, MARILYN. Born Jan. 22, 1939 in Middletown, NJ. Graduate Rutgers U. Debut 1976 OB in "La Ronde," followed by "The Art of Dining," Bdwy 1980 in "Clothes for a Summer Hotel."

ROE, PATRICIA. Born Sept. 18, 1932 in NYC. Attended Columbia U, Actors Studio. Bdwy debut 1951 in "Romeo and Juliet," followed by "Cat on a Hot Tin Roof," "Compulsion," "By the Beautiful Sea," "Night Circus," "A Distant Bell," "Look after Lulu," "Night of the Iguana," "A Texas Trilogy," "Horowitz and Mrs. Washington," OB in "The Collection," "After the Fall," "But For Whom Charlie," "The Homecoming," "Bananas," "Transfers," "Milk of Paradise."

ROERICK, WILLIAM. Born Dec. 17, 1912 in NYC. Bdwy bow 1935 in "Romeo and Juliet," followed by "St. Joan," "Hamlet," "Our Town," "The Importance of Being Earnest," "The Land Is Bright," "Autumn Hill," "This Is the Army," "The Magnificent Yankee," "Tonight at 8:30," "The Heiress," "Medea," "Macbeth," "The Burning Glass," "The Right Honourable Gentleman," "Marat/deSade," . "Homecoming," "We Bombed in New Haven," "Elizabeth the Queen" (CC), "Waltz of the Toreadors," "Night of the Iguana," "The Merchant," "Happy New Year," OB in "Madam, Will You Walk," "The Cherry Orchard," "Come Slowly, Eden," "A Passage to E. M. Forster," "Trials of Oz."

ROFFMAN, ROSE. Has appeared OB in "La Madre," "Harold Pinter Plays," "Arthur Miller Double Bill," "Happy Hypocrite," "Under Gaslight," "Beaux Strategem," "Tea Party," "The Boy Friend," "Marlon Brando Sat Here."

ROGERS, CANDACE. Born Oct. 21, 1957 in Hollywood, CA. Graduate L. A. Valley Col. Bdwy debut 1979 in "Most Happy Fella," followed by "Sweeney Todd."

ROGERS, ENID. Born Apr. 29, 1924 in London, Eng. Attended Royal Col. Debut 1969 OB in "Sourball," followed by "Getting Married" (ELT), "Bird with Silver Feathers," Bdwy in "Jockey Club Stakes" (1973), "Crown Matrimonial."

ROGERS, GIL. Born Feb. 4, 1934 in Lexington, KY. Attended Harvard. OB in "The Ivory Branch," "Vanity of Nothing," "Warrior's Husband," "Hell Bent fer Heaven," "Gods of Lightning," "Pictures in the Hallway," "Rose," "Memory Bank," "A Recent Killing," "Birth," "Come Back, Little Sheba," "Life of Galileo," "Remembrance," "Mecca," Bdwy in "The Great White Hope," "The Best Little Whorehouse in Texas."

ROGERS, HARRIET. Born Dec. 25, 1910 in St. Regis Falls, NY. Graduate Emerson Col. Debut 1965 OB in "Live Like Pigs," followed by "Richard II," Bdwy in "Richard III" (1979).

ROLLE, ESTHER. Born Nov. 8 in Pompano Beach, FL. Attended Hunter Col. Bdwy debut 1964 in "Blues for Mr. Charlie," followed by "Purlie Victorious," "Amen Corner," "Don't Play Us Cheap," "Horowitz and Mrs. Washington," OB in "The Blacks" (1961), "Happy Ending," "Day of Absence," "Evening of One Acts," "Man Better Man," "Brotherhood," "Okakawe," "Rosalee Pritchett," "Dream on Monkey Mountain," "Ride a Black Horse," "Ballet behind the Bridge."

ROMAGUERA, JOAQUIN. (a.k.a. Fidel Romann) Born Sept. 5, 1932 in Key West, FL. Graduate Fla. Southern Col. Debut 1961 OB in "All in Love," followed by Bdwy 1979 in "Sweeney Todd."

ROMILLY, CHRIS. Born Oct. 19, 1950 in NYC. Graduate Cornell U. Debut 1974 OB in "The Desperate Hours," followed by "I Am a Camera."

ROONEY, MICKEY. Born Sept. 23, 1920 in Brooklyn, NY. As a child, appeared in vaudeville with his parents Joe Yule and Nell Brown. Bdwy debut 1979 in "Sugar Babies," for which he received a Special Theatre World Award.

ROSE, GEORGE. Born Feb. 19, 1920 in Bicester, Eng. Bdwy debut with Old Vic 1946 in "Henry IV," followed by "Much Ado about Nothing," "A Man for All Seasons," "Hamlet," "Royal Hunt of the Sun," "Walking Happy," "Loot," "My Fair Lady," (CC '68), "Canterbury Tales," "Coco," "Wise Child," "Sleuth," "My Fat Friend," "My Fair Lady," "She Loves Me," "Peter Pan," BAM's "The Play's the Thing," "The Devil's Disciple," and "Julius Caesar," "The Kingfisher."

ROSE, MARGOT. Born July 17, 1951 in Pittsburgh, PA. Attended Yale. NC School of Arts. Debut 1978 OB in "I'm Getting My Act Together and Taking It on the Road."

ROSENBAUM, DAVID. Born in NYC. Debut OB 1968 in "America Hurrah," followed by "The Cavedwellers," "Evenings with Chekhov," "Out of the Death Cart," "After Miriam," "The Indian Wants the Bronx," "Allergy," "Family Business," Bdwy in "Oh! Calcutta!"

ROSIN, JAMES. Born Oct. 20, 1946 in Philadelphia, PA. Attended Temple U. Debut 1979 OB in "A Yank in Beverly Hills."

ROSKAM, CATHRYN. Born May 30, 1943 in Hempstead, NY. Graduate Middlebury Col. Debut 1970 OB in "Gandhi," followed by "Autumn Garden," "Maggie Flynn," "Reflected Glory," "Mothers and Daughters."

ROSLER, LARRY. Born Apr. 19, 1951 in Newark, NJ. Graduate Seton Hall U. Debut 1978 OB in "Who Killed Richard Cory?," followed by "All the Way Home" (ELT).

ROSS, JUSTIN. Born Dec. 15, 1954 in Brooklyn, NY. Debut 1974 OB in "More Than you Deserve," Bdwy 1975 in "Pippin," followed by "A Chorus Line," "Got Tu Go Disco," OB in "Fourtune."

ROTH, ANDY. Born Jan. 5, 1952 in NYC. Graduate Brown U., Juilliard. Bdwy debut 1979 in "They're Playing Our Song."

ROUNDS, DAVID. Born Oct. 9, 1930 in Bronxville, NY. Attended Denison U. Bdwy debut 1965 in "Foxy," followed by "Child's Play" for which he received a Theatre World Award, "The Rothschilds," "The Last of Mrs. Lincoln," "Chicago," "Romeo and Juliet," "Morning's at 7," OB in "You Never Can Tell," "Money," "The Real Inspector Hound," "Epic of Buster Friend," "Enter a Free Man."

ROWE, DEE ETTA. Born Jan. 29, 1953 in Lewiston, ME. Graduate UHartford. Bdwy debut 1979 in "The Most Happy Fella."

ROWE, HANSFORD. Born May 12, 1924 in Richmond, VA. Graduate URichmond. Bdwy debut 1968 in "We Bombed in New Haven," followed by "Porgy and Bess," "Nuts," OB in "Curley McDimple," "The Fantasticks," "Last Analysis," "God Says There Is No Peter Ott." "Mourning Becomes Electra," "Bus Stop," "Secret Service," "Boy Meets Girl," "Getting Out."

RUANE, JANINE. Born Dec. 17, 1963 in Philadelphia, PA. Bdwy debut 1977 in "Annie."

RUBINSTEIN, JOHN. Born Dec. 8, 1946 in Los Angeles, CA. Attended UCLA. Bdwy debut 1972 in "Pippin" for which he received a Theatre World Award, followed by "Children of a Lesser God."

RUBIO, YOLANDA. Born Nov. 10, 1954 in Los Angeles, CA. Attended UCLA. Debut 1979 OB in "On a Clear Day You Can See Forever," followed by "The More You Get."

RUCKER, BO. Born Aug. 17, 1948 in Tampa, FL. Studied with Stella Adler, Lee Strasburg. Debut 1978 OB in "Native Son" for which he received a Theatre World Award, followed by "Blues for Mr. Charlie," "Streamers."

RUISINGER, THOMAS. Born May 13, 1930 in Omaha, NE. Graduate SMU, Neighborhood Playhouse. Bdwy debut 1959 in "Warm Peninsula," followed by "The Captain and the Kings," "A Shot in the Dark," "Frank Merriwell," "The Importance of Being Earnest," "Snow White," OB in "The Balcony," "Thracian Horses," "Under Milk Wood," "Six Characters in Search of an Author," "Papers."

RUPERT, MICHAEL. Born Oct. 23, 1951 in Denver, CO. Attended Pasadena Playhouse. Bdwy debut 1968 in "The Happy Time" for which he received a Theatre World Award, followed by "Pippin," OB in "Festival."

RUSSOM, LEON. Born Dec. 6, 1941 in Little Rock, AR. Attended Southwestern U. Debut 1968 OB in "Futz," followed by "Cyrano," "Boys in the Band," "Oh! Calcutta!," "Trial of the Catonsville 9," "Henry VI," "Richard III," "Shadow of a Gunman," BAM's "New York Idea" and "Three Sisters," "Old Flames."

RYALL, WILLIAM. Born Sept. 18, 1954 in Binghamton, NY. Graduate AADA. Bdwy debut 1980 in "Canterbury Tales," OB in "Elizabeth and Essex."

RYAN, J. KEITH. Born Dec. 3, 1956 in Roanoke, VA. Debut 1979 OB in "Potholes."

RYAN, MICHAEL. Born Mar. 19, 1929 in Wichita, KS. Attended St. Benedict's Col, Georgetown U. Bdwy debut 1960 in "Advise and Consent," followed by "Complaisant Lover," OB in "Richard III," "King Lear," "Hedda Gabler," "Barroom Monks," "Portrait of the Artist as a Young Man," "Autumn Garden," "Naomi Court," "Caveat Emptor," "Deli's Fable.

SACKS, DAVIA. Born July 10 in Flushing, NY. Attended Dade Jr. Col. Debut 1973 OB in "Swiss Family Robinson," followed by "Zorba," Bdwy in "Fiddler on the Roof" (1976), "Evita."

SADUSK, MAUREEN. Born Sept. 8, 1948 in Brooklyn, NY. Attended AADA. Debut 1969 OB in "We'd Rather Switch," followed by "O Glorious Tintinnabulation," "New Girl in Town," Bdwy in "Fiddler on the Roof" (1976), Canterbury Tales."

SAFFRAN, CHRISTINA. Born Oct. 21, 1958 in Quincy, IL. Attended Webster Col. Bdwy debut 1978 in "A Chorus Line," followed by "A New York Summer."

SAINT, DAVID. Born June 20, 1957 in Boston, MA. Graduate Holy Cross Col. Debut 1979 OB in "South across the River," followed by "The Loves of Cass McGuire."

Marilyn Rockafellow **Joaquin Romaguera** **Yolanda Rubio** **Charlie Serrano** **Janie Sell**

SALATA, GREGORY. Born July 21, 1949 in NYC. Graduate Queens Col. Bdwy debut 1975 in "Dance with Me," followed by "Equus," "Bent," OB in "Piaf, A Remembrance."

SANABRIA, IZZY. Born June 30, 1939 in Puerto Rico. Debut 1979 OB in "The Sun Always Shines for the Cool."

SANCHEZ, JAIME. Born Dec. 19, 1938 in Rincon, PR. Attended Actors Studio. Bdwy bow 1957 in "West Side Story," followed by "Oh, Dad, Poor Dad ...," "Midsummer Night's Dream," "Richard III," OB in "The Toilet" "Conerico Was Here to Stay" for which he received a Theatre World Award, "The Ox Cart," "The Tempest," "Merry Wives of Windsor," "Julius Caesar," "Coriolanus."

SANDERS, JAY O. Born Apr. 16, 1953 in Austin, TX. Graduate SUNY Purchase. Debut 1976 OB in "Henry V," followed by "Measure for Measure," "Scooping," "Buried Child," Bdwy 1979 in "Loose Ends."

SARANDON, CHRIS. Born July 24, 1942 in Beckley, WVA. Graduate UWVa, Catholic U. Bdwy debut 1970 in "The Rothschilds," followed by "Two Gentlemen of Verona," "Censored Scenes from King Kong," OB in "Marco Polo Sings a Solo," "The Devil's Disciple," "The Woods."

SARANDON, SUSAN. Born Oct. 4, 1946 in NYC. Graduate Catholic U. Bdwy debut 1972 in "An Evening with Richard Nixon and ...," OB in "A Coupla White Chicks Sitting around Talking."

SARNO, JANET. Born Nov. 18, 1933 in Bridgeport, CT. Graduate SCTC, Yale U. Bdwy debut 1963 in "Dylan," followed by "Equus," "Knockout," OB in "6 Characters in Search of an Author," "Who's Happy Now," "Closing Green," "Fisher," "Survival of St. Joan," "The Orphan," "Mamma's Little Angels," "Knuckle Sandwich," "Marlon Brando Sat Right Here."

SARRACINO, ERNEST. Born Feb. 12 in Valdez, CO. Graduate LACC. Bdwy debut 1946 in "He Who Gets Slapped," followed by "Girl of the Golden West," "At War with the Army," "Filumena!"

SAUNDERS, NICHOLAS. Born June 2, 1914 in Kiev, Russia. Bdwy debut 1942 in "Lady in the Dark" followed by "A New Life," "Highland Fling," "Happily Ever After," "The Magnificent Yankee," "Anastasia," "Take Her, She's Mine," "A Call on Kuprin," "Passion of Josef D.," OB in "An Enemy of the People," "End of All Things Natural," "The Unicorn in Captivity," "After the Rise," "All My Sons."

SCARDINO, DON. Born in Feb. 1949 in NYC. Attended CCNY. On Bdwy in "Loves of Cass McGuire," "Johnny No-Trump," "My Daughter, Your Son," "Godspell," "Angel," "King of Hearts," OB in "Shout from the Rooftops," "Rimers of Eldrich," "The Unknown Soldier and His Wife," "Godspell," "Moonchildren," "Kid Champion," "Comedy of Errors," "Secret Service," "Boy Meets Girl," "Scribes," "I'm Getting My Act Together ...," "As You Like It," "Holeville," "Sorrows of Stephen."

SCHACT, SAM. Born Apr. 19, 1936 in The Bronx, NY. Graduate CCNY. OB in "Fortune and Men's Eyes," "Cannibals," "I Met a Man," "The Increased Difficulty of Concentration" (LCR), "One Night Stands of a Noisy Passenger," "Owners," "Jack Gelber's New Play," "The Master and Margarita," "Was It Good for You?," Bdwy in "The Magic Show," "Golda."

SCHECHTER, DAVID. Born Apr. 12, 1956 in NYC. Bard Col. Neighborhood Playhouse graduate. Debut 1976 OB in "Nightclub Cantata," followed by "Dispatches," "The Haggadah," Bdwy in "Runaways" (1978).

SCHEIDER, ROY. Born Nov. 10, 1935 in Orange, NJ. Graduate Franklin-Marshall Col. Bdwy debut 1965 in "The Chinese Prime Minister," followed by "Betrayal," OB in "The Alchemist" (LC), "Sjt. Musgrave's Dance," "Stephen D.," "The Year Boston Won the Pennant" (LC), "The Nuns."

SCHEINE, RAYNOR. Born Nov. 10 in Emporia, VA. Graduate Va. Commonwealth U. Debut 1978 OB in "Curse of the Starving Class," followed by "Blues for Mr. Charlie," "Salt Lake City Skyline."

SCHENKKAN, ROBERT. Born Mar. 19, 1953. Graduate Cornell U., UTex. Debut 1978 OB in "The Taming of the Shrew.," followed by "Last Day at the Dixie Girl Cafe," "The Passion of Dracula."

SCHILKE, MICHAEL. Born Dec. 10, 1953 in Sulphur, OK. Graduate Dennison U., UCincinnati. Debut 1978 OB in "Tribute to Women," followed by "On a Clear Day You Can See Forever," "Plain and Fancy" (ELT).

SCHLAMME, MARTHA. Born Sept. 25 in Vienna, Austria. Debut 1963 OB in "The World of Kurt Weill," followed by "A Month of Sundays," "Mata Hari," "Beethoven and Karl," "Aspirations," "God of Vengeance," Bdwy in "Fiddler on the Roof," "Threepenny Opera" (CC), "Solitaire/Double Solitaire," "A Kurt Weill Cabaret."

SCHMUKLER, TRISTINE. Born July 27, 1971 in NYC. Debut 1979 OB in "The Sound of Music" (ELT).

SCHNABEL, STEFAN. Born Feb. 2, 1912 in Berlin, Ger. Attended UBonn. Old Vic. Bdwy bow 1937 in "Julius Caesar," followed by "Shoemaker's Holiday," "Glamour Preferred," "Land of Fame," "Cherry Orchard," "Around the World in 80 Days," "Now I Lay Me Down to Sleep," "Idiot's Delight," "Love of Four Colonels," "Plain and Fancy," "Small War on Murray Hill," "A Very Rich Woman," "A Patriot for Me," "Teibele and Her Demon," OB in "Tango," "In the Matter of J. Robert Oppenheimer," "Older People," "Enemies," "Little Black Sheep," "Rosmersholm," "Passion of Dracula," "Biography."

SCHNETZER, STEPHEN. Born June 11, 1948 in Boston, MA. Graduate UMa. Bdwy debut 1971 in "The Incomparable Max," followed by "Filumena," OB in "Timon of Athens," "Antony and Cleopatra," "Julius Caesar," "Fallen Angels."

SCHRAMM, DAVID. Born Aug. 14, 1946 in Louisville, KY. Attended Western Ky. U., Juilliard. Debut 1972 OB in "School for Scandal," followed by "Lower Depths," "Women Beware Women," "Mother Courage," "King Lear," "Duck Variations," Bdwy in "Three Sisters," "Next Time I'll Sing to You," "Edward II," "Measure for Measure," "The Robber Bridegroom," "Bedroom Farce," "Goodbye Fidel."

SCHULTZ, CATHERINE. Born Jan. 11, 1954 in Pittsburgh, PA. Graduate Chatham Col. Debut 1978 OB in "Arturo Ui," followed by "Refrigerators," "Mopealong," "Love's Labour's Lost."

SCHWAB, SOPHIE. Born Feb. 23, 1954 in Miami, FL. Graduate Northwestern U. Debut 1976 OB in "Fiorello!," followed by "King of Schnorrers," Bdwy 1980 in "Barnum."

SCOTT, BOBBY. Born Aug. 6, 1964 in Detroit, MI. Debut 1979 in "Every Good Boy Deserves Favor" (LC), followed by Bdwy in "Watch on the Rhine."

SCOTT, ERNIE. Born March 20 in New Brunswick, NJ. Attended Fisk, Rutgers, Kean, Trenton State. Debut 1980 OB in "Jam."

SCOTT, LORETTA. Born June 13, 1953 in The Bronx, NY. Graduate UCLA. Bdwy debut 1979 in "Once a Catholic."

SCOTT, MICHAEL. Born Jan. 24, 1954 in Santa Monica, CA. Attended Cal. State U. Debut 1978 (OB and Bdwy) in "The Best Little Whorehouse in Texas," followed by "Happy New Year."

SCOTT, T.J. Born Sept. 24, 1967 in Detroit, MI. Bdwy debut 1979 in "Night and Day."

SEAMON, EDWARD. Born Apr. 15, 1937 in San Diego, CA. Attended San Diego State Col. Debut 1971 OB in "The Life and Times of J. Walter Sminthecous," followed by "The Contractor," "The Family," "Fishing," "Feedlot," "Cabin 12," "Rear Column," "Devour the Snow," "Buried Child," "Friends," Bdwy in "The Trip Back Down," "Devour the Snow."

SEER, RICHARD. Born Oct. 13, 1949 in Anchorage, AK. Graduate Cal. State U. Debut 1972 OB in "Hey Day," followed by "Joseph and the Amazing Technicolor Dreamcoat," Bdwy in "Da" for which he received a 1978 Theatre World Award.

SEFF, RICHARD. Born Sept. 23, 1927 in NYC. Attended NYU. Bdwy debut 1951 in "Darkness at Noon," followed by "Herzl," OB in "Big Fish, Little Fish," "Modigliani."

SELDES, MARIAN. Born Aug. 23, 1928 in NYC. Attended Neighborhood Playhouse. Bdwy debut 1947 in "Medea," followed by "Crime and Punishment," "That Lady," "Tower Beyond Tragedy," "Ondine," "On High Ground," "Come of Age," "Chalk Garden," "The Milk Train Doesn't Stop Here Anymore," "The Wall," "A Gift of Time," "A Delicate Balance," "Before You Go," "Father's Day," "Equus," "The Merchant," "Deathtrap," OB in "Different," "Ginger Man," "Mercy Street," "Candle in the Wind," "Isadora Duncan Sleeps with the Russian Navy."

SELL, JANIE. Born Oct. 1, 1941 in Detroit, MI. Attended UDetroit. Debut 1966 OB in "Mixed Doubles," followed by "Dark Horses," "Dames at Sea," "By Bernstein," "God Bless You, Mr. Rosewater," "Sidewalkin'," Bdwy in "George M!," "Irene," "Over Here" for which she received a Theatre World Award, "Pal Joey," "Happy End.," "I Love My Wife."

SELMAN, LINDA. Born Sept. 14 in NYC. Graduate CCNY. Bdwy debut 1968 in "You Know I Can't Hear You When The Water's Running," followed by "Richard III," OB in "The Criminals."

SERRANO, CHARLIE. Born Dec. 4, 1952 in Rio Piedras, PR. Attended Brooklyn Col. Debut 1978 OB in "Allegro" (ELT), Bdwy 1979 in "Got Tu Go Disco."

SERRECCHIA, MICHAEL. Born Mar. 26, 1951 In Brooklyn, NY. Attended Brockport State U. Teachers Col. Bdwy debut 1972 in "The Selling of the President," followed by "Heathen!," "Seesaw," "A Chorus Line," OB in "Lady Audley's Secret."

SETRAKIAN, ED. Born Oct. 1, 1928 in Jenkintown. WV. Graduate Concord Col., NYU. Debut 1966 OB in "Drums in the Night," followed by "Othello," "Coriolanus," "Macbeth," "Hamlet," "Baal," "Old Glory," "Futz," "Hey Rube," "Seduced," "Shout across the River," Bdwy in "Days in the Trees," "St. Joan," "The Best Little Whorehouse in Texas."

SEUBERT, EVELYN MARY. Born Jan. 1, 1949 in San Francisco, CA. Graduate S.F. State Col. Debut 1979 OB in "Love's Labour's Lost."

SHANE, HAL. Born Mar. 17, 1948 in Rockaway, NY. Graduate Hofstra U. Bdwy debut 1975 in "Very Good Eddie," followed by "They're Playing Our Song."

SHAPIRO, DEBBIE. Born Sept. 29, 1954 in Los Angeles, CA. Graduate LACC. Bdwy debut 1979 in "They're Playing Our Song."

SHARKEY, SUSAN. Born Dec. 12 in NYC. Graduate UAz. Debut 1968 OB in "Guns of Carrar," followed by "Cuba Si," "Playboy of the Western World," "Good Woman of Setzuan," "Enemy of the People," "People Are Living There," "Narrow Road to the Deep North," "Enemies," "The Plough and the Stars," "The Sea," "The Sykovs," "Catsplay," "Ice."

SHEA, JOHN V. Born Apr. 14 in North Conway, NH. Graduate Bates Col., Yale. Debut OB 1974 in "Yentl, the Yeshiva Boy," followed by "Gorky," "Battering Ram," "Safe House," "The Master and Margarita," "Sorrows of Stephen," Bdwy in "Yentl" (1975) for which he received a Theatre World Award, "Romeo and Juliet."

SHEARA, NICOLA. Born May 23 in NYC. Graduate USyracuse. Debut 1975 OB in "Another Language" (ELT), followed by "Sananda Sez," "All the Way Home" (ELT).

SHELLEY, CAROLE. Born Aug. 16, 1939 in London, Eng. Bdwy debut 1965 in "The Odd Couple," followed by "Astrakhan Coat," "Loot," "Noel Coward's Sweet Potato," "Hay Fever," "Absurd Person Singular," "The Norman Conquests," "The Elephant Man," OB in "Little Murders," "The Devil's Disciple," "The Play's the Thing."

SHELTON, REID, Born Oct. 7, 1924 in Salem, OR. Graduate U. Mich. Bdwy bow 1952 in "Wish You Were Here," Followed by "Wonderful Town," "By The Beautiful Sea," "Saint of Bleecker Street," "My Fair Lady," "Oh! What a Lovely War!," "Carousel" (CC), "Canterbury Tales," "Rothschilds," "1600 Pennsylvania Avenue," "Annie," OB in "Phedre," "Butterfly Dream," "Man with a Load of Mischief," "Beggars Opera," "The Contractor," "Cast Aways."

SHELTON, SLOANE. Born Mar. 17, 1934 in Asheville, NC. Attended Berea Col., RADA. Bdwy debut 1967 in "The Imaginary Invalid," followed by "A Touch of the Poet," "Tonight at 8:30," "I Never Sang for My Father," "Sticks and Bones," "The Runner Stumbles," "Shadow Box," OB in "Androcles and the Lion," "The Maids," "Basic Training of Pavlo Hummel," "Play and Other Plays," "Julius Caesar," "Chieftains," "Passione."

SHERMAN, BRUCE. Born June 20, 1953 in Philadelphia, PA. Graduate UFL., Neighborhood Playhouse. Debut 1976 OB in "The Boys from Syracuse," followed by "The Music Man" (JB), Bdwy 1979 in "Snow White."

SHERWIN, MIMI. Born in NYC. Graduate UMich. Bdwy debut 1980 in "Canterbury Tales."

SHIELDS, DALE. Born Nov. 4, 1952 in Cleveland, OH. Graduate Ohio U. Debut 1976 OB in "Sing America," followed by "Fashion" "Contributions," "Anyone Can Whistle."

SHIMERMAN, ARMIN. Born Nov. 5, 1949 in Lakewood, NJ. Graduate UCLA. Debut 1976 in "Threepenny Opera" (LC), followed by "Silk Stockings" (ELT), "When the War Was Over," Bdwy in "St. Joan," (1977). "I Remember Mama." (1979)

SHIMIZU, KEENAN. Born Oct. 22, 1956 in NYC. Graduate HS of Performing Arts. Bdwy 1965 in CC's "South Pacific" and "The King and I," OB in "Rashomon," "The Year of the Dragon," "The Catch," "Peking Man."

SHORT, BOBBY. Born Sept. 15, 1924 in Danville, IL. Debut 1956 in "Kiss Me, Kate" (CC), followed by "Nightlife," "Black Broadway."

SHORT, SYLVIA. Born Oct. 22, 1927 in Concord, MA. Attended Smith Col., Old Vic. Debut 1954 OB in "The Clandestine Marriage," followed by "Golden Apple," "Passion of Gross," "Desire Caught by the Tail," "City Love Story," "Family Reunion," "Beaux Stratagem," "Just a Little Bit Less Than Normal," "Nasty Rumors," "Says I, Says He," "Milk of Paradise," Bdwy in "King Lear" (1956), "Hide and Seek."

SHROPSHIRE, NOBLE. Born Mar. 2, 1946 in Cartersville, GA. Graduate LaGrange Col., RADA. Debut 1976 OB in "Hound of the Baskervilles," followed by "The Misanthrope," "The Guardsman."

SHULTZ, TONY. Born Aug. 8, 1947 in Los Angeles, CA. Graduate UCal. Berkeley. Bdwy debut 1974 in "Grease," followed by "Platinum," OB in "Seminary Murder."

SIEGLER, BEN. Born Apr. 9, 1958 in Queens, NY. Attended HB Studio. Debut 1980 OB in "Innocent Thoughts, Harmless Intentions."

SIFF, IRA. Born Feb. 15, 1946 in NYC. Graduate Cooper Union. Debut 1972 in "Joan," followed by "The Faggot," "The Haggadah."

SILLIMAN, MAUREEN. Born Dec. 3 in NYC. Attended Hofstra U. Bdwy debut 1975 in "Senandoah," followed by "I Remember Mama," OB in "Umbrellas of Cherbourg," "Two Rooms."

SILVER, ALAN. Born Dec. 23, 1952 in Philadelphia, PA. Graduate Temple U, Goodman School. Debut 1980 OB in "Class Enemy."

SILVER, JOE. Born Sept. 28, 1922 in Chicago, IL. Attended UIll., AmThWing. Bdwy bow 1942 in "Tobacco Road," followed by "Doughgirls," "Heads or Tails," "Nature's Way," "Gypsy," "Heroine," "Zulu and the Zayda," "You Know I Can't Hear You When . . .," "Lenny," "The Roast," OB in "Blood Wedding," "Lamp at Midnight," "Joseph and His Brethern," "Victors," "Shrinking Bride," "Family Pieces," "Cakes with the Wine."

SIMON, MARK. Born Sept. 11, 1948 in NYC. Attended NYU. Debut OB 1974 in "Naked Lunch," followed by "Henry V," "Measure for Measure," "Hagar's Children," "All the Way Home" (ELT).

SIMON, ROGER HENDRICKS. Born Oct. 21, 1942 in NYC. Graduate Middlebury Col., Yale. Debut 1967 OB in "Volpone," followed by "Shadow of a Gunman," "Benya the King," "Uncle Money."

SINCLAIR, THOMAS LEE. Born Aug. 26, 1941 in Vernon, TX. Debut 1968 OB in "Get Thee to Canterbury," followed by "Little Mary Sunshine" (ELT), "Carousel" (ELT), "King of Schnorrers."

SKINNER, LAURIE DAWN. Born June 23, 1952 in Ft. Campbell, KY. Debut 1975 OB in "The Three Sisters," followed by "Panama Hattie," "Brigadoon," Bdwy in "The Act" (1977), "Got Tu Go Disco."

SLACK, BEN. Born July 23, 1937 in Baltimore, MD. Graduate Catholic U. Debut 1971 OB in "Oedipus at Colonus" followed by "Interrogation of Havana," "Rain," "Thunder Rock," "Trelawny of the Wells," "Heartbreak House," "The Dodge Boys," Bdwy in "Legend," "On Golden Pond."

SLAVIN, SUSAN. Born Nov. 21 in Chicago, IL. Attended HB Studio. Debut 1968 OB in "The Mad Show," followed by "Dark of the Moon," "Sidnee Poet Heroical," "Wine Untouched," "Motherlove."

SLOAN, LISA. Born Sept. 30, 1952 in Lexington, KY. Graduate Mary Baldwin Col., Catholic U. Bdwy debut 1979 in "Gemini," OB in "Angel City," "Living at Home," "Ladyhouse Blues."

SLOMAN, JOHN. Born June 23, 1954 in Rochester, NY. Graduate SUNY/-Genesco. Debut 1977 OB in "Unsung Cole," Bdwy in "Whoopee!," "The 1940's Radio Show."

SMALL, LARRY. Born Oct. 6, 1947 in Kansas City, MO. Attended Manhattan School of Music. Bdwy debut 1971 in "1776," followed by "La Strada," "Wild and Wonderful," OB in "Plain and Fancy" (ELT).

SMITH, ANNA DEAVERE. Born Sept. 18, 1950 in Baltimore, MD. Graduate Beaver Col., AmConsvTheatre. Debut 1980 OB in "Mother Courage."

SMITH, COTTER. Born May 29, 1949 in Washington, DC. Graduate Trinity Col. Debut 1980 OB in "The Blood Knot."

SMITH, EBBE ROE. Born June 25, 1949 in San Diego, CA. Graduate San Francisco State U. Debut 1978 OB in "Curse of the Starving Class," followed by "New Jerusalem," "Shout across the River," "Sunday Runners."

SMITH, ERIKA. Born July 30 in NYC. Graduate Ricker Col, LIU. Debut 1979 OB in "Blues for Mr. Charlie."

SMITH, J. THOMAS. Born Apr. 13, 1956 in Worcester, MA. Bdwy debut 1980 in "Happy New Year."

SMITH, LOIS. Born Nov. 3, 1930 in Topeka, KS. Attended UWash. Bdwy debut 1952 in "Time Out for Ginger," followed by "The Young and Beautiful." "Wisteria Tress," "Glass Menagerie," "Orpheus Descending," "Stages," OB in "Sunday Dinner," "Present Tense." "The Iceman Cometh," "Harry Outside." "Hillbilly Women," "Touching Bottom," "Tennessee."

SMITH, SAMMY. Born Mar. 3, 1904 in Brooklyn, NY. Graduate Drake School. Bdwy credits include "Buckaroo," "Wish You Were Here," "Plain and Fancy," "Li'l Abner, "How to Succeed in Business . . . ," "Oklahoma!" "The Goodbye People," "Wrong Way Light Bulb," "West Side Story" (1979).

SNOW, NORMAN. Born Mar. 29, 1950 in Little Rock, AR. Juilliard graduate. Debut 1972 OB in "School for Scandal," followed by "Lower Depths," "Hostage," "Timon of Athens," "Cymbeline," "U.S.A.," "Women Beware Women," "One Crack Out," BAM Theatre Co.'s "A Winter's Tale," "Johnny on a Spot," "The Wedding," Bdwy in "Three Sisters," "Measure for Measure," "Beggar's Opera," "Next Time I'll Sing to You."

SOCKWELL, SALLY. Born June 14 in Little Rock, AR. Debut 1976 OB in "Vanities."

SOMMER, JOSEF. Born June 26, 1934 in Greifswald, Ger. Carnegie-Tech graduate. Bdwy bow 1970 in "Othello," followed by "Children, Children," "Trial of the Catonsville 9," "Full Circle," "Who's Who in Hell," "The Shadow Box," "Spokesong," "The 1940's Radio Show," "Whose Life Is It Anyway?," OB in "Enemies," "Merchant of Venice," "The Dog Ran Away," "Drinks Before Dinner."

SONDERGAARD, GALE. Born Feb. 15, 1899 in Litchfield, MN. Graduate UMn. Bdwy debut 1923 in "What's Your Wife Doing?," followed by "Faust," "Major Barbara," "Strange Interlude," "Karl and Anna," "Red Dust," "Alison's House," "American Dream," "Dr. Monica," "Invitation to a Murder," "Cue for Passion," "Goodbye Fidel," OB in "Woman," "Kicking the Castle Down," "John Gabriel Borkman."

SONTAG, DONNA. Born Dec. 15, 1952 in Cincinnati, OH. Graduate Cinn-Consv. of Music. Debut 1979 OB in "Big Bad Burlesque."

SOREL, ANITA. Born Oct. 25, in Hollywood, CA. Graduate UUtah, Cal-State/Long Beach. Debut 1980 OB in "The Time of the Cuckoo" (ELT).

SOREL, THEODORE. Born Nov. 14, 1936 in San Francisco, CA. Graduate Col. of the Pacific. Bdwy debut 1977 in "Sly Fox," followed by "Horowitz and Mrs. Washington," OB in "Arms and the Man," "Moon Mysteries."

SPIEGEL, BARBARA. Born Mar. 12 in NYC. Debut 1969 in LCRep's "Camino Real," "Operation Sidewinder," and "Beggar on Horseback," OB in "Feast for Flies," "Museum," "Powder," "The Bleachers," "Nightshift."

SPOTO, FRANCO. Born Aug. 12, 1945 in Lincoln, NE. Graduate Oberlin Col. Bdwy debut 1979 in "The Most Happy Fella."

SQUIRE, KATHERINE. Born Mar. 9, 1903 in Defiance, OH. Attended Ohio Wesleyan, Cleveland Playhouse. Bdwy debut 1932 in "Black Tower," followed by "Goodbye Again," "High Tor," "Hipper's Holiday," "What a Life," "Liberty Jones," "The Family," "Shadow of a Gunman," "Traveling Lady," OB in "Roots," "This Here Nice Place," "Boy on a Straight-Back Chair," "Catsplay," "Hillbilly Women."

STANLEY, GORDON. Born Dec. 20, 1951 in Boston, MA. Graduate Brown U., Temple U. Debut 1977 OB in "Lyrical and Satirical," followed by "Allegro," "Elizabeth and Essex."

STARK, MOLLY. Born in NYC. Graduate Hunter Col. Debut 1969 OB in "Sacco-Vanzetti," followed by "Riders to the Sea," "Medea," "One Cent Plain," "Elizabeth and Essex," Bdwy 1973 in "Molly."

STATTEL, ROBERT. Born Nov. 20, 1937 in Floral Park, NY. Graduate Manhattan Col. Debut 1958 OB in "Heloise," followed by "When I Was a Child," "Man and Superman," "The Storm," "Don Carlos," "Taming of the Shrew," "Titus Andronicus," "Henry IV," "Peer Gynt," "Hamlet," LCRep's "Danton's Death," "Country Wife," "Caucasian Chalk Circle," and "King Lear," "Iphigenia in Aulis," "Ergo," "The Persians," "Blue Boys," "The Minister's Black Veil," "Four Friends," "Two Character Play," "The Merchant of Venice," "Cuchulain."

STEDMAN, JOEL. Born Feb. 23, 1945 in Minneapolis, MN. Attended UMinn, Goodman Theatre. Bdwy debut 1980 in "Watch on the Rhine."

STEELE, VERNON. Born Apr. 18, 1954 in Rehoboth Beach, DE. Graduate UDel. Debut 1980 OB in "Plain and Fancy" (ELT).

STEINBERG, ROY. Born Mar. 24, 1951 in NYC. Graduate Tufts U., Yale. Debut 1974 OB in "A Midsummer Night's Dream," followed by "Firebugs," "The Doctor in spite of Himself," "Romeo and Juliet," "After the Rise," Bdwy in "Wings."

STEINER, SHERRY. Born Sept. 29, 1948 in NYC. Graduate Chatham Col. Debut 1978 OB in "Catsplay," followed by "Safe House," "Frankie and Annie," "The Sorrows of Stephen," BAM Theatre Co.'s "A Winter's Tale," "Barbarians," and "The Purging."

STENBORG, HELEN. Born Jan. 24, 1925 in Minneapolis, MN. Attended Hunter Col. OB in "A Doll's House," "A Month in the Country," "Say Nothing," "Rosmersholm," "Rimers of Eldrich," "Trial of the Catonsville 9," "Hot l Baltimore," "Pericles," "Elephant in the House," "A Tribute to Lili Lamont," "Museum," "5th of July," "In the Recovery Lounge," Bdwy in "Sheep on the Runway." "Da."

STENNETT, MYRA. Born Sept. 28 in Brooklyn, NY. Graduate Brandeis U, NYU. Debut 1972 OB in "Poems of Sylvia Plath," followed by "42 Seconds from Broadway," "Because I Said So," "The Big Knife," "Hard Up," "Plays for Living," "Dona Rosita," "Crimes and Dreams."

STEPHENSON, ALBERT. Born Aug. 23, 1947 in Miami, FL. Attended Boston Consv. Bdwy debut 1973 in "Irene," followed by "Debbie Reynolds Show," "The Act," "A Broadway Musical," "A Day in Hollywood/A Night in the Ukraine."

STERNHAGEN, FRANCES. Born Jan. 13, 1932 in Washington, DC. Vassar graduate, OB in "Admirable Bashful," "Thieves' Carnival," "Country Wife," "Ulysses in Nighttown." "Saintliness of Margery Kemp," "The Room," "A Slight Ache," "Displaced Person," "Playboy of the Western World" (LC), Bdway in "Great Day in the Morning," "Right Honourable Gentleman," with APA in "Cocktail Party," and "Cock-a-doodle Dandy," "The Sign in Sidney Brustein's Window," "Enemies" (LC), "The Good Doctor," "Equus," "Angel," "On Golden Pond."

STEVENS, ALLAN. Born Nov. 30, 1949 in Los Angeles, CA. Attended LAMDA. Bdwy debut 1975 in "Shenandoah," followed by "Kings," OB in "It's Wilde!"

STEWART, DON. Born Nov. 14, 1935 in Staten Island, NY. Attended Wichita U. Bdwy debut 1960 in "Camelot," followed by "The Student Gypsy," OB in "The Fantasticks," "Jo," "Babes in the Woods," "The Music Man" (JB).

STEWART, SCOT. Born June 3, 1941 in Tylertown, MS. Graduate UMiss. Debut 1975 OB in "New Girl in Town," Bdwy 1979 in "Sugar Babies."

STILLER, JERRY. Born June 8, 1931 in NYC. Graduate USyracuse. Debut 1953 OB in "Coriolanus," followed by "The Power and the Glory," "Golden Apple," "Measure for Measure," "Taming of the Shrew," "Carefree Tree," "Diary of a Scoundrel," "Romeo and Juliet," "As You Like It," "Two Gentlemen of Verona," "Passione," Bdwy in "The Ritz," "Unexpected Guests."

STILLMAN, RICHARD. Born Nov. 24, 1954 in Midland, MI. Graduate Dartmouth Col. Debut 1979 OB in "Hamlet," Bdwy 1980 in "Canterbury Tales."

ST. JAMES, DAVID. Born Sept. 4, 1947 in Honolulu, HI. Graduate UGa. Debut 1977 OB in "Silk Stockings" (ELT), followed by "Intermission."

STOECKLE, ROBERT. Born Sept. 21, 1947 in Port Chester, NY. Graduate Hartt Col. Bdwy debut 1980 in "Canterbury Tales."

STOLARSKY, PAUL. Born Feb. 18, 1933 in Detroit, MI. Graduate Wayne State U, UMich. Debut 1972 OB in "Bluebird," followed by "Let Yourself Go," "Rocket to the Moon," "D.," "My Mother, My Father and Me," Bdwy 1980 in "Nuts."

STONE, MAX. Born Oct. 23, 1954 in Greenville, TX. Attended Tx Christian U., SMU. Bdwy debut 1979 in "They're Playing Our Song."

STONEBURNER, SAM. Born Feb. 24, 1934 in Fairfax, VA. Graduate Georgetown U, AADA. Debut 1960 OB in "Ernest in Love," followed by "Foreplay," "Anyone Can Whistle," Bdwy in "Different Times" (1972), "Bent."

STOUT, MARY. Born Apr. 8, 1952 in Huntington, WV. Graduate Marshall U. Debut 1980 OB in "Plain and Fancy" (ELT).

STOVALL, COUNT. Born Jan. 15, 1946 in Los Angeles, CA. Graduate UCal. Debut 1973 OB in "He's Got a Jones," followed by "In White America," "Rashomon," "Sidnee Poet Heroical," "A Photo," "Julius Caesar," "Coriolanus," "Spell #7," "The Jail Diary of Albie Sachs."

STRAIGHT, BEATRICE. Born Aug. 2, 1916 in Old Westbury, NY. Attended Dartington Hall. Bdwy debut 1934 in "Bitter Oleander," followed by "Twelfth Night," "Land of Fame," "Wanhope Building," "Eastward in Eden," "Macbeth," "The Heiress," "The Innocents," "Grand Tour," "The Crucible," "Everything in the Garden," OB in "Sing Me No Lullaby," "River Line," "Ghosts," "All My Sons," "Hamlet."

STRANGE, CLAYTON. Born Nov. 24, 1956 in Philadelphia, PA. Bdwy debut 1976 in "1600 Pennsylvania Avenue," OB in "But Never Jam Today."

STRICKLER, DAN. Born Feb. 4, 1949 in Los Angeles, CA. Graduate CalStateU, Temple U. Debut 1977 OB in "Jules Feiffer's Hold Me!," followed by "Flying Blind."

STRIMPELL, STEPHEN. Born Jan. 17, 1937 in NYC. Graduate Columbia U. Bdwy bow 1964 in "The Sunday Man," OB in "A School for Scandal," "Henry IV," "Dumbbell People in a Barbell World," "To Be Young, Gifted and Black," "The Disintegration of James Cherry" (LC), "The Good Parts."

STROMAN, GUY. Born Sept. 11, 1951 in Terrell, TX. Graduate Tx. Christian U. Bdwy debut 1979 in "Peter Pan."

SULLIVAN, ELIZABETH. Born June 25, 1949 in NYC. Debut 1975 OB in "A Bedtime Story," followed by "Love's Labour's Lost."

SUMMER, LAURA. Born Nov. 5, 1956 in NYC. Attended UMiami. Debut 1979 OB in "Antony and Cleopatra," followed by "The Sun Always Shines for the Cool," "Merton of the Movies" (ELT).

SUNDSTEN, LANI. Born Feb. 27, 1949 in NYC. Attended Am. Col. in Paris. Bdwy debut 1970 in "The Rothschilds," followed by "Tricks," "California Suite," "Scapino," "They're Playing Our Song," OB in "Carousel," "In the Boom Boom Room."

SUROVY, NICOLAS. Born June 30, 1944 in Los Angeles, CA. Attended Northwestern U., Neighborhood Playhouse. Debut 1964 OB in "Helen" for which he received a Theatre World Award, followed by "Sisters of Mercy," Bdwy in "Merchant," "Crucifer of Blood," "Major Barbara."

SWANN, ELAINE. Born May 9 in Baltimore, MD. Attended UNC. Bdwy debut 1957 in "The Music Man," followed by "Greenwillow," "A Thurber Carnival," "My Mother, My Father and Me," "Jennie," OB in "Miss Stanwyck Is Still in Hiding," "Oh, Boy!"

SWENSON, SWEN. Born Jan. 23, 1932 in Inwood, IA. Bdwy debut 1950 in "Great to be Alive," followed by "Bless You All," "As I Lay Dying," "Destry Rides Again," "Wildcat," "Golden Apple," "Little Me" for which he received a Theatre World Award, "Molly," "Ulysses in Nighttown."

SWITKES, WILLY. Born Nov. 12, 1929 in New Haven, CT. Graduate Catholic U. Debut 1960 OB in "A Country Scandal," followed by "The Firebugs," "Conerico Was Here to Stay," "Benya the King," Bdwy in "Sly Fox" (1976).

SYERS, MARK. Born Oct. 25, 1952 in Trenton, NJ. Graduate Emerson Col. Bdwy debut 1976 in "Pacific Overtures," followed by "Jesus Christ Superstar" (1977), "Evita."

TABORI, KRISTOFFER. Born Aug. 4, 1952 in Calif. Bdwy debut 1969 in "The Penny Wars," followed by "Henry V," "Habeas Corpus," OB in "Emile and the Detectives," "Guns of Carrar," "A Cry of Players," "Dream of Blacklisted Actor," "How Much, How Much?" for which he received a Theatre World Award, "The Wager," "Scribes," "The Trouble with Europe."

TALBOT, SHARON. Born Mar. 12, 1949 in Denver, CO. Graduate Denver U. Bdwy debut 1975 in "Musical Jubilee," OB in "The Housewives' Cantata."

TANNER, MELINDA. Born Oct. 5, 1946 in Calif. CA. Attended LACC. Debut 1975 OB in "The Sea," followed by "Godspell," "I Can't Keep Running," Bdwy in "The Robber Bridegroom" (1976).

TARLETON, DIANE. Born Oct. 25 in Baltimore, MD. Graduate UMd. Bdwy debut 1965 in "Anya," followed by "A Joyful Noise," "Elmer Gantry," "Yentl," OB in "A Time for the Gentle People," "Spoon River Anthology," "International Stud," "Too Much Johnson," "To Bury a Cousin."

TASK, MAGGIE, Born July 4 in Marion, OH. Attended Wright Col. Bdwy debut 1960 in "Greenwillow," followed by "A Family Affair," "Tovarich," CC's "Most Happy Fella" and "Carousel," "Funny Girl," "Kelly," "Anya," "A Time for Singing," "Darling of the Day," "Education of Hyman Kaplan," "Sound of Music," "CoCo," "Sweeney Todd," OB in "Sing Melancholy Baby."

TATE, DENNIS. Born Aug. 31, 1938 in Iowa City, IA. Attended UIowa. Bdwy debut 1970 in "Les Blancs," followed by "The Poison Tree," OB in "Black Monday," "The Blacks," "The Hostage," "Bohikee Creek," "Happy Bar," "Trials of Brother Jero," "Strong Breed," "Goa," "Electronic Nigger," "Black Quartet," "Life and Times of J. Walter Smintheus," "Jazznite ," "Cherry Orchard," "Phantasmagoria Historia . . . ," "Merry Wives of Windsor," "Coriolanus."

TATUM, BILL. Born May 6, 1947 in Philadelphia, PA. Graduate Catawba Col. Bdwy debut 1971 in "Man of La Mancha," OB in ELT's "Missouri Legend" and "Time of the Cuckoo."

TATUM, MARIANNE. Born Feb. 18, 1951 in Houston, TX. Attended Manhattan School of Music. Debut 1971 OB in "Ruddigore," followed by "The Sound of Music" (ELT), Bdwy 1980 in "Barnum" for which she received a Theatre World Award.

TAVARIS, ERIC. Born Apr. 8, 1939 in Fall River, MA. Debut 1959 OB in "An Enemy of the People," followed by "The Prodigal," "In White America," "Butterfly Dream," "Macbeth," "Mummers and Men," "Androcles and the Lion," "The Guardsman," Bdwy in "The Lincoln Mask" (1972).

TAYLOR, GEORGE. Born Sept. 18, 1930 in London, Eng. Attended AADA. Debut 1972 OB in "Hamlet," followed by "Enemies" (LC), "The Contractor," "Scribes," "Says I, Says He," "Teeth 'n' Smiles," "Viaduct," Bdwy in "Emperor Henry IV," "The National Health."

TEITEL, CAROL. Born Aug. 1, 1929 in NYC. Attended AmTh Wing. Bdwy debut 1957 in "The Country Wife," followed by "The Entertainer," "Hamlet," "Marat/deSade," "A Flea in Her Ear," "Crown Matrimonial," "All Over Town," OB in "Way of the World," "Juana La Loca," "An Evening with Ring Lardner," "Misanthrope," "Shaw Festival," "Country Scandal," "The Bench," "Colombe," "Under Milk Wood," "7 Days of Mourning," "Long Day's Journey into Night," "The Old Ones," "Figures in the Sand," "World of Sholom Aleichem," "Big and Little," "Duet," "Trio," "Every Good Boy Deserves Favor" (LC), "Fallen Angels."

TETIRICK, ROBERT. Born Dec. 2, 1952 in Columbus, OH. Graduate Northwestern U. Bdwy debut 1980 in "Canterbury Tales."

THOMAS, PHILIP MICHAEL. Born May 26, 1949 in Columbus, OH. Attended UCal. Bdwy debut 1971 in "No Place to Be Somebody," followed by "The Selling of the President," "Reggae."

THOME, DAVID. Born July 24, 1951 in Salt Lake City, UT. Bdwy debut 1971 in "No, No, Nanette," followed by "Different Times," "Good News," "Rodgers and Hart," "A Chorus Line."

THOMPSON, EVAN. Born Sept. 3, 1931 in NYC. Graduate UCal. Bdwy bow 1969 in "Jimmy," OB in "Mahagonny," "Treasure Island," "Knitters in the Sun."

THOMPSON, TAZEWELL. Born May 27, 1950 in NYC. Attended Actors Co. School. Debut 1968 OB in "Goa," followed by "Graven Image," Bdwy in "The National Health" (1974), "Checking Out."

THOMPSON, WEYMAN. Born Dec. 11, 1950 in Detroit, MI. Graduate Wayne State U, UDetroit. Bdwy debut 1980 in "Clothes for a Summer Hotel."

THORNE, RAYMOND. Born Nov. 27, 1934 in Lackawanna, NY. Graduate UConn. Debut 1966 OB in "Man with a Load of Mischief," followed by "Rose," "Dames at Sea," "Love Course," "Blue Boys" Bdwy 1977 in "Annie."

TIRELLI, JAIME. Born Mar. 4, 1945 in NYC. Attended UMundial, AADA. Debut 1975 OB in "Rubbers," followed by "Yanks 3, Detroit 0," "The Sun Always Shines on the Cool."

TOMEI, CONCETTA. Born Dec. 30, 1945 in Kenosha, WI. Graduate UWisc, Goodman School. Debut 1979 OB in "Little Eyolf," Bdwy 1979 in "The Elephant Man."

TOMPKINS, TOBY. Born Sept. 8, 1942 in NYC. Yale graduate. Bdwy debut 1968 in "Man of La Mancha," OB in "Hail Scrawdyke," "The Cherry Orchard," "In White America," "Mirandolina."

TORAN, PETER. Born July 16, 1955 in McLean, VA. Graduate Tufts U. Debut 1980 OB in "Romeo and Juliet," followed by "It's Wilde!"

TOREN, SUZANNE. Born Mar. 15, 1947 in NYC. Graduate CCNY, UWisc. Bdwy debut 1980 in "Goodbye Fidel."

TOWERS, CONSTANCE. Born May 20, 1933 in Whitefish, MT. Attended Juilliard, AADA, Bdwy debut 1965 in "Anya," followed by "Show Boat" (LC), "Carousel" (CC), "Sound of Music" (CC '67, JB '70, '71, '80), "Engagement Baby," "The King and I" (CC '68, JB '72, Bdwy '77).

TRAMON, CARL. Born May 7, 1968 in NJ. Bdwy debut 1979 in "Peter Pan."

TRAVERSE, MARTHA. Born Feb. 13, 1954 in Grand Forks, ND. Graduate S.Ill.U. Bdwy debut 1979 in "Oklahoma!"

TRIBBLE, DARRYL. Born Mar. 20, 1960 in Brooklyn, NY. Attended Purchase Col. Bdwy debut 1980 in "West Side Story."

TRINK, LEE. Born Jan. 1, 1968 in Queens, NY. Debut 1980 OB in "Plain and Fancy" (ELT).

TROY, LOUISE. Born Nov. 9 in NYC. Attended AADA. Debut 1955 OB in "The Infernal Machine," followed by "Merchant of Venice," "Conversation Piece," "Salad Days," "O, Oysters!," "A Doll's House," "The Last Analysis," "Judy and Jane," "Heartbreak House," Bdwy in "Pipe Dream" (1955), "A Shot in the Dark," "Tovarich," "High Spirits," "Walking Happy," "Equus."

TURNER, JAKE. Born May 6, 1953 in Pittsburgh, PA. Graduate Carnegie Tech. Bdwy debut 1980 in "West Side Story."

TURNER, KATHLEEN. Born June 19, 1954 in Springfield, MO. Graduate Southwest Mo. State. Bdwy debut 1978 in "Gemini."

TURQUE, MIMI. Born Sept. 30, 1939 in Brooklyn, NY. Graduate Brooklyn Col. Bdwy bow 1945 in "Carousel," followed by "Seeds in the Wind," "The Enchanted," "Cry of the Peacock," "Anniversary Waltz," "Carnival," "Man of La Mancha," OB in "Johnny Summit," "The Dybbuk," "Romeo and Juliet," "The Happy Journey," "God Bless You, Mr. Rosewater."

TWOMEY, ANNE. Born June 7, 1951 in Boston, MA. Graduate Temple U. Debut 1975 OB in "Overruled," followed by "The Passion of Dracula," Bdwy 1980 in "Nuts" for which she received a Theatre World Award.

TYLER, JUANITA GRACE. Born Mar. 9, 1956 in Brooklyn, NY. Attended Kingsborough CC. Bdwy debut 1980 in "Reggae."

TYNES, BILL. Born Nov. 9, 1956 in Placentia, CA. Attended AzState U, Cal-State U. Debut 1977 OB in "The Three Sisters," followed by "Can-Can," "Strider," Bdwy in "Strider" (1979).

TYRRELL, SUSAN. Born in 1946 in San Francisco, CA. Bdwy debut 1952 in "Time Out for Ginger," OB in "The Knack," "Futz," "A Cry of Players," "The Time of Your Life," "Camino Real," "Father's Day."

UHLER, ERIC. Born Feb. 25, 1949 in Youngstown, OH. Graduate Ohio U. Bdwy debut 1978 in "Once in a Lifetime," OB in "Show Me a Hero," "Love and Junk."

URICH, TOM. Born Mar. 26 in Toronto, OH. Attended Cincinnati Cons. Bdwy debut 1970 in "Applause," followed by "Musical Chairs," OB in "Streets of NY," "The Fantasticks," "Shoemaker's Holiday."

URMSTON, KENNETH. Born Aug. 6, 1929 in Cincinnati, OH. Attended Xavier U. Bdwy debut 1950 in "Make a Wish," followed by "Top Banana," "Guys and Dolls," "John Murray Anderson's Almanac," "Can-Can," "Silk Stockings," "Oh Captain!," "Bells Are Ringing," "Redhead," "Madison Avenue," "Tenderloin," "We Take the Town," "Lovely Ladies, Kind Gentlemen," "Follies," "Pippin," "Ballroom."

VAN HUNTER, WILLIAM. Born Feb. 1, 1947 in Worcester, MA. Graduate Nassau Col., USyracuse. Debut 1975 OB in "The Three Musketeers," followed by "Lenz."

VAN NORDEN, PETER, Born Dec. 16, 1950 in NYC. Graduate Colgate U., Neighborhood Playhouse. Debut 1975 OB in "Hamlet," followed by "Henry V," "Measure for Measure," "A Country Scandal," "Hound of the Baskervilles," "Tartuffe," "Antigone," "Bingo," "Taming of the Shrew," "The Balcony," "Shadow of a Gunman," "Jungle of Cities," "Shakespeare's Cabaret," Bdwy in "Romeo and Juliet" (1977), "St. Joan," "Inspector General."

VANNUYS, ED. Born Dec. 28, 1930 in Lebanon, IN. Attended Ind. U. Debut 1969 OB in "No Place to Be Somebody," followed by "Conflict of Interest," "The Taming of the Shrew," "God Bless You, Mr. Rosewater," Bdwy in "Black Terror," "Nuts."

VAN PATTEN, JOYCE. Born Mar. 9 in Kew Gardens, NY. Bdwy bow 1941 in "Popsy," followed by "This Rock," "Tomorrow the World," "The Perfect Marriage," "The Wind is 90," "Desk Set," "A Hole in the Head," "Murder at the Howard Johnson's," "I Ought to Be in Pictures," OB in "Between Two Thieves," "Spoon River Anthology."

VAN SCOTT, GLORY. Born in Chicago, IL. Graduate Goddard Col., Antioch-Union. Debut 1962 OB in "Fly Blackbird," followed by "Billy Noname," "Don't Bother Me, I Can't Cope," "Love! Love! Love!," "Miss Truth," Bdwy in "The Great White Hope" (1968), "Kwamina," "Show Boat," "Porgy and Bess."

VARRONE, GENE. Born Oct. 30, 1929 in Brooklyn, NY. Graduate LIU. Bdwy in "Damn Yankees," "Take Me Along," "Ziegfeld Follies," "Goldilocks," "Wildcat," "Tovarich," "Subways Are for Sleeping," "Bravo Giovanni," "Drat! The Cat," "Fade Out–Fade In," "Don't Drink the Water," "Dear World," "Coco," "A Little Night Music," "So Long 174th St.," "Knickerbocker Holiday," "The Grand Tour," "The Most Happy Fella" (1979), OB in "Promenade."

VAUGHN, DONA D. Born Aug. 13 in Waynesboro, PA. Graduate Wesleyan Col., Hunter Col. Bdwy debut 1970 in "Company," followed by "Seesaw," "Jesus Christ Superstar," OB in "She Stoops to Conquer," "Les Blancs."

VEAZEY, JEFF. Born Dec. 6 in New Orleans, LA. Bdwy debut 1975 in "Dr. Jazz," followed by "The Grand Tour," "Sugar Babies," OB in "Speakeasy."

VEGA, ROBERT. Born Feb. 21, 1949 in Denning, NMX. Graduate Adam State Col., UNMx. Bdwy debut 1978 in "The King and I."

VESTOFF, VIRGINIA. Born Dec. 9, 1940 in NYC. Bdwy debut 1960 in "From A to Z," followed by "Irma La Douce," "Baker Street," "1776," "Via Galactica," "Nash at 9," "Boccacio," "Spokesong," OB in "The Boy Friend," "Crystal Heart," "Fall Out," "New Cole Porter Revue," "Man with a Load of Mischief," "Love and Let Love," "Short-Changed Review," "The Misanthrope," "Drinks Before Dinner," "I'm Getting My Act Together . . ."

VIDNOVIC, MARTIN. Born Jan. 4, 1948 in Falls Church, VA. Attended Cincinnati Consv. of Music. Debut 1972 OB in "The Fantasticks," followed by Bdwy in "Home Sweet Homer" (1976), "The King and I" (1977), "Oklahoma!" (1979).

VIGARD, KRISTEN. Born May 15, 1963 in St. Paul, MN. Debut 1970 OB in "A Cheap Trick," followed by "100 Miles from Nowhere," "Wedding Band," Bdwy in "Annie," "Hair" (1978), "I Remember Mama."

VILLAIRE, HOLLY. Born Apr. 11, 1944 in Yonkers, NY. Graduate UDetroit, UMich. Debut 1971 OB in "Arms and the Man," followed by "Purity," "Eyes of Chalk," "Anna-Luse," "Village Wooing," "The Fall and Redemption of Man," BAM Co.'s "New York Idea," "Three Sisters," "Devil's Disciple," "The Play's the Thing," and "Julius Caesar," "God Bless You, Mr. Rosewater," Bdwy in "Scapino" (1974), "Habeas Corpus."

VINOVICH, STEVE. Born Jan. 22, 1945 in Peoria, IL. Graduate UIll., UCLA, Juilliard. Debut 1974 OB in "The Robber Bridegroom," followed by "King John," "Father Uxbridge Wants to Marry," "Hard Sell," Bdwy in "Robber Bridegroom" (1976), "The Magic Show," "The Grand Tour," "Loose Ends."

Weyman Thompson   **Kristen Vigard**   **Eric Uhler**   **Diane Warren**   **William Whitener**

VIPOND, NEIL. Born Dec. 24, 1929 in Toronto, Can. Bdwy debut 1956 in "Tamburlaine the Great," OB in "Three Friends," "Sunday Runners," "Hamlet" (ELT).

VITA, MICHAEL. Born in NYC. Studied at HB Studio. Bdwy debut 1967 in "Sweet Charity," followed by "Golden Rainbow," "Promises, Promises," "Cyrano," "Chicago," "Ballroom," OB in "Sensations," "That's Entertainment," "Rocket to the Moon."

VON BERG, PETER. Born Nov. 7, 1947 in Germany. Graduate Fordham U. Debut 1979 OB in "Love's Labour's Lost," followed by "The Mischief You Foresee."

VON SCHERLER, SASHA. Born Dec. 12, in NYC. Bdwy debut 1959 in "Look after Lulu," followed by "Rape of the Belt," "The Good Soup," "Great God Brown," "First Love," "Alfie," "Harold," "Bad Habits," OB in "Admirable Bashville," "The Comedian," "Conversation Piece," "Good King Charles' Golden Days," "Under Milk Wood," "Plays for Bleecker Street," "Ludlow Fair," "Twelfth Night," "Sondra," "Cyrano de Bergerac," "Crimes of Passion," "Henry VI," "Trelawny of the Wells," "Screens," "Soon Jack November," "Pericles," "Kid Champion," "Henry V," "Comanche Cafe," "Museum," "Grand Magic," "The Penultimate Problem of Sherlock Holmes."

VOSBURGH, DAVID. Born Mar. 14, 1938 in Coventry, RI. Attended Boston U. Bdwy debut 1968 in "Maggie Flynn," followed by "1776," "A Little Night Music," "Evita," OB in "Smith."

WALDROP, MARK. Born July 30, 1954 in Washington, DC. Graduate Cincinnati Consv. Debut 1977 OB in "Movie Buff," Bdwy in "The Grand Tour," "Evita."

WALKER, NICHOLAS. Born July 26, 1953 in Bogota, Col. Graduate Providence Col., UCal., LAMDA. Bdwy debut 1980 in "Major Barbara."

WALL, BRUCE. Born July 14, 1956 in Bath, Eng. Graduate Cambridge, UToronto, RADA. Debut 1979 OB in "Class Enemy."

WALLACH, ELI. Born Dec. 7, 1915 in Brooklyn, NY. Graduate UTx, CCNY. Bdwy bow 1945 in "Skydrift," followed by "Henry VIII," "Androcles and the Lion," "Alice in Wonderland," "Yellow Jack," "What Every Woman Knows," "Antony and Cleopatra," "Mr. Roberts," "Lady from the Sea," "The Rose Tatoo," for which he received a Theatre World Award, "Mlle. Colombe," "Teahouse of the August Moon," "Major Barbara," "The Cold Wind and the Warm," "Rhinoceros," "Luv," "Staircase," "Promenade, All!," "Waltz of the Toreadors," "Saturday, Sunday, Monday," OB in "The Diary of Anne Frank," "Every Good Boy Deserves Favor" (LC).

WALLACH, KATHERINE. Born July 13, 1958 in NYC. Attended Sarah Lawrence Col., Neighborhood Playhouse. Debut 1978 OB in "The Diary of Anne Frank," followed by "Kid Champion."

WALSH, MARTIN J. Born June 5, 1947 in Worcester, MA. Graduate Assumption Col. Debut 1970 OB in "The Lark," followed by "Interview with God," Bdwy in "Shenandoah" (1977), "Canterbury Tales."

WALTERS, KELLY. Born May 28, 1950 in Amarillo, TX. Graduate UWash. Debut 1973 OB in "Look, We've Come Through" (ELT), Bdwy in "Candide" (1975), "Canterbury Tales," "Barnum."

WARD, CHARLES. Born Oct. 24, 1952 in Los Angeles, CA. Soloist with American Ballet Theatre before 1978 Bdwy debut in "Dancin'."

WARD, DOUGLAS TURNER. Born May 5, 1930 in Burnside, LA. Attended UMich. Bdwy bow 1959 in "A Raisin in the Sun," followed by "One Flew Over the Cuckoo's Nest," "Last Breeze of Summer," OB in "The Iceman Cometh," "The Blacks," "Pullman Car Hiawatha," "Bloodknot," "Happy Ending," "Day of Absence," "Kongi's Harvest," "Ceremonies in Dark Old Men," "The Harangues," "The Reckoning," "Frederick Douglass through His Own Words," "River Niger," "The Brownsville Raid," "The Offering," "Old Phantoms," "The Michigan."

WARD, JANET. Born Feb. 19 in NYC. Attended Actors Studio. Bdwy debut 1945 in "Dream Girl," followed by "Anne of a Thousand Days," "Detective Story," "King of Friday's Men," "Middle of the Night," "Miss Lonelyhearts," "J.B.," "Cheri," "The Egg," "Impossible Years," "Of Love Remembered," OB in "Chapparal," "The Typists," "The Tiger," "Summertree," "Dream of a Blacklisted Actor," "Cruising Speed 600 MPH," "One Flew over the Cuckoo's Nest," "Love Gotta Come by Saturday Night," "Home Is the Hero," "Love Death Plays," "Olympic Park," "Hillbilly Women."

WARNING, DENNIS. Born June 18, 1951 in East St. Louis, IL. Graduate Southwest Mo. State U. Bdwy debut 1976 in "The Robber Bridegroom," followed by "The Most Happy Fella" (1979), OB in "Jimmy and Billy."

WARREN, DIANE. Born Apr. 6 in Fall River, MA. Graduate RICol. Debut 1980 OB in "Biography."

WATKINS, DANIEL. Born Oct. 12, 1950 in Lynchburg, VA. Attended NCSchool of Arts. Debut 1979 OB in "The Wait," followed by "Come Back to the 5 & Dime, Jimmy Dean."

WATSON, BRIAN. Born Feb. 17, 1937 in NYC. Debut 1979 OB in "Reunion," followed by "Streamers," "Uncle Money."

WATSON, DOUGLASS. Born Feb. 24, 1921 in Jackson, GA. Graduate UNC. Bdwy bow 1947 in "The Iceman Cometh," followed by "Antony and Cleopatra" for which he received a Theatre World Award, "Leading Lady," "Richard III," "The Happiest Years," "That Lady," "Wisteria Trees," "Romeo and Juliet," "Desire under the Elms," "Sunday Breakfast," "Cyrano de Bergerac," "Confidential Clerk," "Portrait of a Lady," "The Miser," "The Young and Beautiful," "Little Glass Clock," "Country Wife," "Man for All Seasons," "Chinese Prime Minister," "Marat/deSade," "Prime of Miss Jean Brodie," "Pirates of Penzance," "Over Here," OB in NYSF's "Much Ado about Nothing," "King Lear" and "As You Like It," "The Hunger," "Dancing for the Kaiser," "Money," "My Life," "Sightlines," "Glorious Morning," "Hamlet."

WEATHERHEAD, CHRIS. Born Jan. 11, 1948 in Glendale, CA. Attended UCal/Santa Barbara. Debut 1979 OB in "Table Settings."

WEAVER, FRITZ. Born Jan. 19, 1926 in Pittsburgh, PA. Graduate UChicago. Bdwy debut 1955 in "Chalk Garden" for which he received a Theatre World Award, followed by "Protective Custody," "Miss Lonelyhearts," "All American," "Lorenzo," "The White House," "Baker Street," "Child's Play," "Absurd Person Singular," OB in "The Way of the World," "White Devil," "Doctor's Dilemma," "Family Reunion," "The Power and the Glory," "The Great God Brown," "Peer Gynt," "Henry IV," "My Fair Lady" (CC), "Lincoln," "The Biko Inquest," "The Price."

WEBER, FREDRICKA. Born Dec. 22, 1940 in Beardstown, IL. Attended Northwestern U. Bdwy debut 1965 in "Those That Play the Clowns," OB in "Upstairs at the Downstairs," "The Last Sweet Days of Isaac" for which she received a Theatre World Award, "Two."

WEEKS, JAMES RAY. Born Mar. 21, 1942 in Seattle, WA. Graduate UOre., AADA. Debut 1972 in LCR's "Enemies," "Merchant of Venice" and "A Streetcar Named Desire," followed by OB's "49 West 87th," "Feedlot," "The Runner Stumbles," "Glorious Morning," "Just the Immediate Family," "The Deserter," "Life and/or Death," "Devour the Snow," "Innocent Thoughts, Harmless Intentions," Bdwy in "My Fat Friend," "We Interrupt This Program," "Devour the Snow."

WELCH, CHARLES C. Born Feb. 2, 1921 in New Britain, CT. Attended AmThWing. Bdwy debut 1958 in "Cloud 7," followed by "Donnybrook," "Golden Boy," "Little Murders," "Holly Go Lightly," "Darling of the Day," "Dear World," "Follies," "Status Quo Vadis," "Shenandoah," OB in "Half-Past Wednesday," "Oh Lady! Lady!," "God Bless You, Mr. Rosewater."

WELLER, PETER. Born June 24, 1947 in Stevens Point, WI. Graduate AADA. Bdwy bow 1972 in "Sticks and Bones," followed by "Full Circle," "Summer Brave," OB in "Children," "Merchant of Venice," "Macbeth," "Rebel Women," "Streamers," "The Woolgatherer."

WESTFALL, RALPH DAVID. Born July 2, 1934 in North Lewisburg, OH. Graduate Ohio Wesleyan U., SUNY New Paltz. Debut 1977 OB in "Richard III," followed by "The Importance of Being Earnest," "Anyone Can Whistle."

WESTON, CELIA. Born in South Carolina. Attended Salem Col., NCSchool of the Arts. Bdwy debut 1979 in "Loose Ends."

WETHERALL, JACK. Born Aug. 5, 1950 in Sault Ste. Marie, Can. Graduate Glendon Col., York U. Bdwy debut 1979 in "The Elephant Man."

WETTIG, PATRICIA. Born Dec. 4 in Cincinnati, OH. Graduate Temple U. Debut 1980 OB in "Innocent Thoughts, Harmless Intentions," followed by "The Woolgatherer."

WETZEL, PETER. Born July 3, 1953 in Potsdam, NY. Graduate New England Col. Debut 1979 OB in "Deli's Fable."

WHITE, RICHARD. Born Aug. 4, 1953 in Oak Ridge, TN. Graduate Oberlin Col. Bdwy debut 1979 in "The Most Happy Fella," OB in "Elizabeth and Essex."

WHITE, TERRI. Born Jan. 24, 1953 in Palo Alto, CA. Attended USIU. Debut 1976 OB in "The Club," followed by Bdwy in "Barnum" (1980).

WHITENER, WILLIAM. Born Aug. 17, 1951 in Seattle, WA. With Joffrey Ballet before Bdwy debut 1978 in "Dancin'."

WHITTON, MARGARET. (formerly Peggy). Born Nov. 30 in Philadelphia, PA. Debut 1973 OB in "Baba Goya," followed by "Arthur," "The Wager," "Nourish the Beast," "Another Language," "Chinchilla," "Othello," "The Art of Dining."

WICKES, MARY. Born June 13 in St. Louis, MO. Attended Wash. U. Bdwy debut 1934 in "The Farmer Takes a Wife," followed by "One Good Year," "Spring Dance," "Stage Door," "Swing Your Lady," "Father Malachy's Miracle," "Hitch Your Wagon," "Too Much Johnson," "Danton's Death," "The Man Who Came to Dinner," "George Washington Slept Here," "Jackpot," "Dark Hammock," "Hollywood Pinafore," "Apple of His Eye," "Park Avenue," "Town House," "Oklahoma!" (1979).

WIEST, DIANE. Born Mar. 28, 1948 in Kansas City, MO. Attended UMd. Debut 1976 OB in "Ashes," followed by "Leave It to Beaver Is Dead," "The Art of Dining," for which she received a Theatre World Award.

WILEY, BILL. Born Nov. 1, 1928 in Gainesville, FL. Graduate Wm & Mary Col. Debut 1967 OB in "The Hostage" (ELT), followed by "Missouri Legend," "Buried Child," "Merton of the Movies," Bdwy 1969 in "Hadrian VII."

WILLIAMS, BARBARA. Born May 24 in Milwaukee, WI. Attended Northwestern U. Bdwy in "Damn Yankees," "Music Man," "Different Times," OB in "Streets of NY," "Horse Opera," "All's Well That Ends Well," "The Sorrows of Stephen."

WILLIAMS, CHARLES LaVONT. Born Sept. 10, 1956 in Chicago, IL. Attended Kennedy-King Col. Bdwy debut 1977 in "The Wiz," OB in "The More You Get," "Miss Truth."

WILLIAMS, CLARENCE III. Born Aug. 21, 1939 in NYC. Bdwy bow 1960 in "The Long Dream," followed by "Slow Dance on the Killing Ground" for which he received a Theatre World Award, "Night and Day," "The Great Indoors," OB in "The Egg and I," "Walk in Darkness," "Double Talk," "Sarah and the Sax," "Party on Greenwich Ave.," "King John," "Suspenders."

WILLIAMS, JACK ERIC. Born Mar. 28, 1944 in Odessa, TX. Attended Tx. Tech. U. Debut 1975 OB in "The Homecoming," followed by "Threepenny Opera," "Where's the Beer, Fritz?" "The Tempest," Bdwy 1979 in "Sweeney Todd."

WILLIAMS, L. B. Born May 7, 1949 in Richmond, VA. Graduate Albion Col. Bdwy debut 1976 in "Equus," OB in "Spa," "Voices," "5 on the Blackhand Side," "Chameleon."

WILLIS, SUSAN. Born in Tiffin, OH. Attended Carnegie Tech. Cleveland Play House. Debut 1953 OB in "The Little Clay Cart," followed by "Love and Let Love," "The Glorious Age," "The Guardsman," Bdwy in "Take Me Along" (1959), "Gypsy," "Dylan," "Come Live With Me," "Cabaret."

WILSON, DOLORES. Born Aug. 9 in Philadelphia, PA. Bdwy debut 1965 in "The Yearling," followed by "Fiddler on the Roof," "Cry for Us All," "I Remember Mama," "Annie."

WILSON, ELIZABETH. Born Apr. 4, 1925 in Grand Rapids, MI. Attended Neighborhood Playhouse. Bdwy debut 1953 in "Picnic," followed by "Desk Set," "Tunnel of Love," "Big Fish, Little Fish," "Sheep on the Runway," "Sticks and Bones," "Secret Affairs of Mildred Wild," "The Importance of Being Earnest," "Morning's at 7," OB in "Plaza 9," "Eh?," "Little Murders," "Good Woman of Setzuan," "Uncle Vanya," "Threepenny Opera," "All's Well That Ends Well," "Taken in Marriage."

WILSON, KEVIN. Born May 26, 1950 in Indianapolis, IN. Graduate UMd., HB Studio. Bdwy debut 1977 in "Shenandoah," followed by "Carmelina," "The Most Happy Fella."

WILSON, MARY LOUISE. Born Nov. 12, 1936 in New Haven, CT. Graduate Northwestern U. OB in "Our Town," "Upstairs at the Downstairs," "Threepenny Opera," "A Great Career," "Whispers on the Wind," "Beggar's Opera," "Buried Child," Bdwy in "Hot Spot," "Flora, the Red Menace," "Criss-Crossing," "Promises, Promises," "The Women," "Gypsy," "The Royal Family," "The Importance of Being Earnest."

WINDE, BEATRICE. Born Jan. 6 in Chicago, IL. Debut 1966 OB in "In White America," followed by "June Bug Graduates Tonight," "Strike Heaven on the Face," "Divine Comedy," "Crazy Horse," "My Mother, My Father and Me," Bdwy 1971 in "Ain't Supposed to Die a Natural Death" for which she received a Theatre World Award.

WINSTON, HATTIE. Born Mar. 3, 1945 in Greenville, MS. Attended Howard U. OB in "Prodigal Son," "Day of Absence," "Pins and Needles," "Weary Blues," "Man Better Man," "Billy Noname," "Sambo," "The Great MacDaddy," "A Photo," "Oklahoma!," "The Michigan," Bdwy in "The Me Nobody Knows," "Two Gentlemen of Verona," "I Love My Wife."

WINTER, ALEXANDER. Born July 17, 1965 in London, Eng. Bdwy debut 1978 in "The King and I," followed by "Peter Pan."

WINTERS, WARRINGTON. Born July 28, 1909 in Bigstone Country, MN. Graduate UMinn. Debut 1975 OB in "Another Language" (ELT), followed by "A Night at the Black Pig," "Uncle Vanya," "Richard III."

WISNET, CHARLES. Born Sept. 23, 1956 in Buffalo, NY. Attended NYU, SUNY/Buffalo. Bdwy debut 1980 in "Reggae."

WITTER, WILLIAM C. Born Mar. 15, 1950 in Portland, OR. Graduate UWash. Bdwy debut 1980 in "Barnum."

WOLF, CATHERINE. Born In Philadelphia, PA. Attended Neighborhood Playhouse. Bdwy debut 1976 in "The Innocents," OB in "After the Rise," "I Can't Keep Running."

WOLFE, ELISSA. Born Mar. 17, 1963 in New Rochelle, NY. Attended AADA. Bdwy debut 1979 in "I Remember Mama," OB in "Snapshot."

WONG, JANET. Born Aug. 30, 1951 in Berkeley, CA. Attended UCal. Bdwy debut 1977 in "A Chorus Line."

WOODARD, CHARLAINE. Born Dec. 29 in Albany, NY. Graduate Goodman Sch. of Drama, SUNY. Debut 1975 OB in "Don't Bother Me, I Can't Cope," Bdwy in "Hair" (1977), "Ain't Misbehavin'."

WOODESON, NICHOLAS. Born in England. Graduate USussex, RADA. Debut 1978 OB in "Strawberry Fields," followed by "The Taming of the Shrew," Bdwy 1978 in "Man and Superman."

WOODS, RICHARD. Born May 9, 1921 in Buffalo, NY. Graduate Ithaca Col. Bdwy in "Beg Borrow or Steal," "Capt. Brassbound's Conversion," "Sail Away," "Coco," "Last of Mrs. Lincoln," "Gigi," "Sherlock Holmes," "Murder among Friends," "The Royal Family," "Deathtrap," "Man and Superman," OB in "The Crucible," "Summer and Smoke," "American Gothic," "Four-in-one," "My Heart's in the Highlands," "Eastward in Eden," "The Long Gallery," "The Year Boston Won the Pennant," "In the Matter of J. Robert Oppenheimer" (LC), with APA in "You Can't Take It with You," "War and Peace," "School for Scandal," "Right You Are," "The Wild Duck," "Pantagleize," "Exit the King," "The Cherry Orchard," "Cock-a-doodle Dandy," and "Hamlet," "Crimes and Dreams."

WORTH, IRENE. Born June 23, 1916 in Nebraska. Graduate UCLA. Bdwy debut 1943 in "The Two Mrs. Carrolls," followed by "The Cocktail Party," "Mary Stuart," "Toys in the Attic," "King Lear," "Tiny Alice," "Sweet Bird of Youth," "The Cherry Orchard" (LC), "The Lady from Dubuque," OB in "Happy Days," "Letters of Love and Affection."

WORTH, PENNY. Born Mar. 2, 1950 in London, Eng. Attended Sorbonne, Paris. Bdwy debut 1970 in "Coco," followed by "Irene," "Annie."

WRIGHT, MARY CATHERINE. Born Mar. 19, 1948 in San Francisco, CA. Attended CCSF, SFState Col. Bdwy debut 1970 in "Othello," followed by "A History of the American Film," OB in "East Lynne," "Mimi Lights the Candle," "Marvin's Gardens," "The Tempest," "The Doctor in spite of Himself," "Love's Labour's Lost," "Pushcart Peddlers."

WRIGHT, MAX. Born Aug. 2, 1943 in Detroit, MI. Attended Wayne State U. Bdwy debut 1968 in "The Great White Hope," followed by "The Cherry Orchard," "Basic Training of Pavlo Hummel," "Stages," "Once in a Lifetime" for which he received a Theatre World Award, "The Inspector General," "Richard III."

WRIGHT, TERESA. Born Oct. 27, 1918 in NYC. Bdwy debut 1938 in "Our Town," followed by "Life with Father," "The Dark at the Top of the Stairs," "Mary, Mary," "I Never Sang for My Father," "Death of a Salesman," "Ah, Wilderness," "Morning's at 7," OB in "Who's Happy Now," "A Passage to E. M. Forster."

WRIGHT, WILLIAM. Born Jan. 21, 1943 in Los Angeles, CA. Graduate UUtah, Bristol Old Vic. Debut 1973 OB in "Merchant of Venice" (LC), "The Way of the World," "The Constant Wife," Bdwy 1976 in "Equus," followed by "Oh! Calcutta!"

WYMAN, NICHOLAS. Born May 18, 1950 in Portland, ME. Graduate Harvard U. Bdwy debut 1975 in "Very Good Eddie," followed by "Grease," "The Magic Show," "On the 20th Century," "Whoopee!," OB in "Paris Lights."

YODER, JERRY. Born in Columbus, OH. Graduate Ohio State U. Bdwy debut 1973 in "Seesaw," followed by "Goodtime Charley," "Chicago," "Best Little Whorehouse in Texas," OB in "Boys from Syracuse."

YORK, MICHAEL. Born Mar. 27, 1942 in Fulmer, Eng. Attended UCollege/Oxford. Bdwy debut 1973 in "Outcry," followed by "Bent" (1980).

YOSHIDA, PETER. Born May 28, 1945 in Chicago, IL. Graduate UIll., Princeton U., AADA. Debut 1965 OB in "Coriolanus," followed by "Troilus and Cressida," "Santa Anita '42," "Pursuit of Happiness," "Servant of Two Masters," "The Peking Man."

YOST, JOHN. Born Jan. 30 in NYC. Graduate CCNY. Bdwy debut 1979 in "Evita."

YUHASZ, STEVEN. Born Mar. 14, 1953 in Perth Amboy, NJ. Graduate Maryville Col., Trinity U. Bdwy debut 1979 in "Peter Pan."

YULIN, HARRIS. Born Nov. 5, 1937 in Calif. Attended USCal. Debut 1963 OB in "Next Time I'll Sing to You," followed by "A Midsummer Night's Dream," "Troubled Waters," "Richard III," "King John," "The Cannibals," Bdwy 1980 in "Watch on the Rhine."

ZAKS, JERRY. Born Sept. 7, 1946 in Germany. Graduate Dartmouth, Smith Col. Bdwy debut 1973 in "Grease," followed by "Once in a Lifetime," OB in "Death Story," "Dream of a Blacklisted Actor," "Kid Champion," "Golden Boy," "Marco Polo," "One Crack Out," "Tintypes."

ZALKIND, DEBRA. Born Mar. 30, 1953 in NYC. Graduate Juilliard. Appeared with several dance companies before Bdwy debut 1978 in "The Best Little Whorehouse in Texas."

ZANG, EDWARD. Born Aug. 19, 1934 in NYC. Graduate Boston U. OB in "Good Soldier Schweik," "St. Joan," "Boys in the Band," "The Reliquary of Mr. and Mrs. Potterfield," "Last Analysis," "As You Like It," "More than You Deserve," "Polly," "Threepenny Opera," BAM Co.'s "New York Idea," "The Misanthrope," "Banana Box," "The Penultimate Problem of Sherlock Holmes," Bdwy in "Crucifer of Blood."

ZENOBIA. Born July 19, 1952 in Los Angeles, CA. Bdwy debut 1970 in "Hair," OB in "The Karl Marx Play," "I Paid My Dues," "Dementos."

ZIEN, CHIP. Born in 1947 in Milwaukee, WI. Attended UPa. OB in "You're a Good Man, Charlie Brown," followed by "Kadish," "How to Succeed in Business . . ." (ELT), "Dear Mr G.," "Tuscaloosa's Calling . . . ," "Hot l Baltimore," "El Grande de Coca Cola," "Split," Bdwy 1974 in "All Over Town."

OBITUARIES

FELIX AYLMER, 90, one of Britian's most admired stage, film and TV character actors, died Sept. 2, 1979 in Sussex, Eng. His career began in 1911 and he continued acting until the mid-1970's. His Broadway debut was in 1922 in "Loyalties," followed by "The Last of Mrs. Cheyney," "The Flashing Stream," and "The Prescott Proposals." He was knighted in 1965 for his services to the theatre. A daughter, Jennifer, survives.

CECIL BEATON, 76, London-born designer, painter, writer and photographer, died in his sleep Jan. 18, 1980 in his home in Broadchalke, Eng. For Broadway in 1946 he designed the sets for "Lady Windermere's Fan" (in which he also appeared), followed by "Cry of the Peacock," "The Grass Harp," Quadrille," "Portrait of a Lady," "The Chalk Garden," "My Fair Lady," "Vanessa," "La Traviata" and "Turandot" at the Metropolitan Opera, "Saratoga." He won Academy Awards for his costumes in the films "Gigi" and "My Fair Lady." For many years he was the favorite photographer for the royal family, as well as leading figures in films, theatre and literature. He was knighted in 1972. After a stroke, he lived in semi-retirement and learned to paint and photograph with his left hand. He was never married.

ISADORA BENNETT, 79, a theatrical publicity agent who was among the first to champion American dance, died Feb. 8, 1980 in her NYC home. She was born in Missouri, attended the Univ. of Chicago, and became a city reporter for the Chicago Daily News. During the 1930's she devoted herself to theatrical publicity, and in 1939 began a long association with the Martha Graham company. She was the widow of actor Daniel Reed, and is survived by their daughter, folk singer Susan Reed.

RITA ROMILLY BENSON, 79, teacher and former actress, died Apr. 4, 1980 in NYC. After studying at the American Academy of Dramatic Arts, she was invited to be a teacher there, and later became a director of the school. She had appeared in "Bird of Paradise," "The Unchastened Woman," "A Man's Man" and "The Living Corpse." Her husband, Martin Benson, died in 1971. No immediate survivors.

JOAN BLONDELL, 73, NYC-born stage, film and tv actress, died of leukemia Dec. 25, 1979 in Santa Monica, CA. After several years in vaudeville with her parents, she made her Broadway debut in 1927 in "The Trial of Mary Dugan," followed by "Maggie the Magnificent," "Penny Arcade" that took her to Hollywood and films, "The Naked Genius," "A Tree Grows in Brooklyn," "Call Me Madam," "Come Back, Little Sheba," "The Time of the Cuckoo," "Happy Birthday," "New Girl in Town," "Watch the Birdie," "Copper and Brass," "The Rope Dancers," "Crazy October," "A Palm Tree in a Rose Garden," and her last stage role in 1970 "The Effect of Gamma Rays on Man in-the-Moon Marigolds" (Off-Bdwy). She was divorced from cameraman George Barnes, actor Dick Powell, and producer Mike Todd. Surviving are her son Norman Powell, a tv producer, a daughter Ellen, and her sister, actress Gloria Blondell.

GUY BOLTON, 96, English-born author or co-author of many Broadway plays and musicals, died Sept. 5, 1979 in London. Considered one of the originators of the Broadway musical, he collaborated with P. G. Wodehouse, Jerome Kern, Ira Gershwin and Cole Porter, among others. He had written over 100 plays and musicals, including "The Drone," "Rule of Three," "Sally," "Lady Be Good," "Tip-Toes," "Oh, Kay!," "Five O'Clock Girl," "Rosalie," "Girl Crazy," "Simple Simon," "Anything Goes," "Leave It to Jane," "Very Good Eddie," "Follow the Girls," "Ankles Aweigh," "Anastasia," and the musical "Anya" based on the last named play. He was married four times and had two sons and two daughters.

HELEN CAREW, age unreported, Illinois-born stage and screen actress, died Mar. 7, 1980. After her Broadway debut in 1916 in "The Flame" she appeared in many productions, including "Kempy," "The Wooden Kimona," "Big Hearted Herbert," "Harriet," "Our Town," "Papa Is All," "January Thaw," "Hope for a Harvest," "Mrs. January and Mr. X," and "The Traveling Lady." No reported survivors.

CLAIRE CARLTON, 66, NYC-born stage and film actress, died of cancer Dec. 11, 1979 at her home in North Ridge, CA. Her Broadway credits include "The Body Beautiful," "The Great Magoo," "Come Easy," "20th Century," "The Women," "I Must Love Someone," "Kill That Story" and 'Clutterbuck." No reported survivors.

LEWIS CHARLES, 63, character actor on stage, film and tv, died of cancer Nov. 9, 1979 in Los Angeles, CA. He appeared in 22 Broadway productions, including "Summer Night," "Good Neighbor," "What Big Ears!," "Talking to You," "Across the Board on Tomorrow Morning," "Sun Field," "Apology," "The Milky Way," "Boy Meets Girl," "The Streets Are Guarded," "Star Spangled Family," and for two years acted in the tv series "Feather and Father Gang." He is survived by his wife and three step-daughters.

JOHN CROMWELL, 65, NY-born actor and playwright, died Sept. 1, 1979 after a lengthy illness in London. He made his Broadway debut in 1935 in "The Old Maid," followed by "Romeo and Juliet" with Evans and Cornell. "St. Joan," "Hamlet" with Gielgud and Anderson, "Bright Rebel," "Candida," "Outward Bound," "Macbeth," and "Pygmalion." His plays include "Opening Night," "Banquet for the Moon," "A Matter of Like Life and Death," "Split Lip," "The Mystery of Perry Clews" and "Jardie's Roommate." There are no immediate survivors.

JOHN CROMWELL, 91, Ohio-born actor, director and producer on stage and film, died of a pulmonary embolism Sept. 26, 1979 in Santa Barbara, CA. After several tours, he made his NY stage debut in 1910 in "Baby Mine," and subsequently in "Immodest Violet," "Personality," "Marie Antoinette," "The Lawbreaker," "Lucky Sam McCarver," "Fanny," "The Racket," "Gentlemen of the Press," "Grey Farm," "Yankee Point," "Point of No Return" for which he received a "Tony" Award, "Climate of Eden," "Sabrina Fair," "What Every Woman Knows," "Mary, Mary," "Hamlet," "Death of a Salesman," "Henry V," "Richard III," "Country People," and "Don Juan." He directed "Bewitched," "She Had to Know," "Devils," "Kitty's Kisses," "The Silver Cord," "What the Doctor Ordered," "Women Go on Forever," "The Queen's Husband," "Ghost of Yankee Doodle," "Yr. Obedient Husband," "Yankee Point," and "Moon Vine." Surviving are his fourth wife, actress Ruth Nelson, and son, actor James Cromwell.

Cecil Beaton

Joan Blondell (1971)

John Cromwell (1953)

Jimmy Durante (1962)

Luella Gear (1953)

Hugh Griffith (1963)

DON DE LEO, 74, stage, screen and tv actor, after a stroke Aug. 14, 1979 in NYC. Made his Broadway debut in 1927 in "Good News," with subsequent credits including "Burlesque," "Common Ground," "Catherine Was Great," "Billion Dollar Baby," "Single Man at a Party," "Don't Drink the Water" and "Hello, Dolly!" on tour. He is survived by his wife, agent Roseanne Kirk, and a son Michael.

FREDERIC de WILDE, 66, popular Broadway stage manager for 30 years, died Apr. 3, 1980 in his native NYC. He was on leave of absence from "Betrayal." Among his many credits are "Mrs. McThing," "The Emperor's Clothes," "The Remarkable Mr. Pennypacker," "Flowering Peach," "Bus Stop," "Separate Tables," "Waltz of the Toreadors," "The Visit," "Goldilocks," "Come Blow Your Horn," "A Man for All Seasons," "Bedroom Farce," "Poor Murderer," and "Finishing Touches." His actor son, Brandon, was killed in a 1972 accident. His widow survives.

AMY DOUGLASS, 77, Ohio-born stage and screen actress, died March 5, 1980 in her home in Los Angeles, Ca. Her Broadway credits include "Kiss Them for Me," "Crime and Punishment," "Life with Mother," "Mr. Barry's Etchings" and "Anniversary Waltz." A daughter survives.

JESSICA DRAGONETTE, age unreported, died of a heart attack March 18, 1980 in her NYC home. She was born in India and began her professional singing career in 1924 in "The Miracle," followed by "The Student Prince," "Earl Carroll's Vanities," and "The Grand Street Follies." Her greatest fame and success came from her 22 consecutive years of singing on radio's "Cities Service Concerts," "The Coca-Cola Girl" serial, "The Philco Hour," "Ford Summer Show" and "Saturday Night Serenade." Her husband, Nicholas M. Turner survives.

JIMMY DURANTE, 86, NYC-born actor, comedian and singer, died of pneumonitis Jan. 29, 1980 in Santa Monica, Ca. As one of America's most loved entertainers for 60 years, he had appeared on stage film, radio, tv, and in night clubs with his prominent nose, raspy voice, piano and crushed hat to the delight of millions. He never resorted to vulgarity, but trusted his good will and energy, and jokes about himself, "Schnozzola." He was a genuine artist. After playing and singing in saloons, he made his Broadway debut in 1929 in the revue "Show Girl," followed by "The New Yorkers," "Strike Me Pink," "Jumbo," "Red, Hot and Blue!," "Stars in Your Eyes," "Keep Off the Grass." He is survived by his second wife, and their adopted daughter Cecelia. Burial was in Holy Cross Cemetery.

KATHERINE EMERY, 73, Alabama-born stage and screen actress, died of pulmonary illnesses Feb. 7, 1980 in Portland, Me. After her 1932 Broadway debut in "Carry Nation," she appeared in "Strangers at Home," "The Children's Hour," "Roosty," "Everywhere I Roam," "Three Sisters," "Proof Through the Night" and "The Cherry Orchard." After her 1944 marriage to Paul Eaton, she moved to California and appeared in films. She is survived by a son and a daughter.

ALLAN FRANK, 64, stage, screen and tv actor, died in his native NYC Aug. 9, 1979 after a short illness. He had appeared in "Pinocchio," "Revolt of the Beavers," "Steel," "Skipper Next to God," "Angel Street," "A Flag Is Born," "Daughter of Silence" and "I Never Sang for My Father." He co-produced "A Whitman Portrait" and toured as Walt Whitman. Surviving are his widow and three children.

LOU FRIZZELL, 59, stage, film and tv actor, died June 17, 1979 after a lengthy illness in his Los Angeles home. In NYC he was seen in "Oklahoma!," "The Balcony," "Desire under the Elms," "Great Day in the Morning," "Quare Fellow," "Red Roses for Me," "Pullman Car Hiawatha," "After the Fall," "Marco Millions," "Once Upon a Tailor" and "The Andersonville Trial." He is survived by his father.

JANE FROMAN, 72, Missouri-born actress singer, died Apr. 22, 1980 at her home in Columbia, Mo. After singing on radio and with bands, she made her Broadway debut in 1934 in "Ziegfeld Follies," followed by "Keep Off the Grass," "Laugh, Clown, Laugh!," and "Artists and Models." Her Heroic recovery from injuries in a plane crash during WW2 was portrayed in the film "With a Song in My Heart." Her second husband survives.

FRANK GABRIELSON, 69, film and tv writer, playwright, and former actor and stage manager, died Jan 24, 1980 in Calabasas, Ca. He appeared in "Stevedore," "Whatever Goes Up" and "But for the Grace of God." His plays include "Parade," "The Illustrator's Show," "The More the Merrier," and "The Days of Our Youth." He also adapted the novel "Mama's Bank Account" for the tv series "Mama" that ran for 7 years. A daughter survives.

LUELLA GEAR, 80, comedienne-actress, died Apr. 3, 1980 after a long illness in her native NYC. After her 1917 Broadway debut in "Love O' Mike," she appeared in "The Gold Diggers," "A Bachelor's Night," "Elsie," "Poppy," "Queen High," "The Optimists," "Ups-a-Daisy," "Gay Divorcee," "Life Begins at 8:40," "On Your Toes," "Love in My Fashion," "Streets of Paris," "Crazy with the Heat," "Pie in the Sky," "Count Me In," "That Old Devil," "My Romance," "To Be Continued," "Sabrina Fair," and "Four Winds." Each of her three marriages ended in divorce. No immediate survivors.

STANLEY GILKEY, 79, Delaware-born retired producer, died Nov. 3, 1979 in Pacifica, Ca. For 35 years he was exutive producer for Guthrie McClintic-Katharine Cornell productions. He co-produced "One for the Money," "The Deep Mrs. Sykes," "Three to Make Ready," "John Murray Anderson's Almanac," "A Roomful of Roses," "The Day the Money Stopped." He was general manager and later acting administrator of the Repertory Theatre of Lincoln Center. No reported survivors.

JOYCE GRENFELL, 69, British stage and film actress-comedienne, died Nov. 30, 1979 in London. Her sketches and impersonations of slightly daffy British upper-class ladies delighted audiences in both London and NYC. In 1955 she appeared on Broadway in "Joyce Grenfell Requests the Pleasure," and in 1958 in "Joyce Grenfell." Her husband, Reginald Grenfell, survives.

HUGH GRIFFITH, 67, Welsh stage and film character actor, died May 14, 1980 after a long illness in his London home. He made his Broadway debut in 1951 in "Legend of Lovers," followed by "Richard II," "Waltz of the Toreadors," "Look Homeward, Angel" and "Andorra." His widow survives.

JACK HALEY, 79, Boston-born stage and film comedian and actor, died June 6, 1979 after a heart attack in his home in Beverly Hills, Ca. After appearing in vaudeville, he made his Broadway debut in 1924 in "Around the Town," subsequently appearing in "Gay Paree," "Good News," "Follow Thru," "Take a Chance," "Show Time" and "Inside U.S.A." Surviving are his wife of 52 years, a former Ziegfeld dancer, a son, producer Jack, Jr., and a daughter.

JED HARRIS, 79, one of Broadway's most successful producer-directors, died Nov. 15, 1979 after a long illness in NYC. He was born Jacob Horowitz in Vienna, Austria, and came to the U.S. in 1901. He dropped out of Yale and worked as a theatrical reporter and press agent before producing his first play "Weak Sisters" in 1925, followed by "Love 'Em and Leave 'Em," "Broadway," "Spread Eagle," "Coquette," "The Royal Family," "The Front Page," "Serena Blandish," "Uncle Vanya," "Mr. Gilhooley," "Inspector General," "The Wiser They Are," "Wonder Boy," "Fatal Alibi," "The Green Bay Tree," "The Lake," "Life's Too Short," "Spring Dance," "A Doll's House," "Our Town," "Dark Eyes," "The World's Full of Girls," "One-Man Show," "Apple of His Eye," "Loco," "The Heiress," "The Traitor," "Red Gloves," "The Crucible," and "Child of Fortune," many of which he also directed. Surviving are a son, Jones Harris, and a daughter.

KENNETH HARVEY, 60, stage and tv actor-writer, died of cancer June 6, 1979 in Norwalk, Ct. On Broadway he appeared in "Pipe Dream," "Calculated Risk," "The Sound of Music," and "The Old Glory." He was starred in the tv series "Search for Tomorrow" for 7 years, and was a writer for the series "All My Children." He had served as president of AFTRA's NYC local, and as the national president. He is survived by his widow, actress Rita Morley.

JUNE HELMERS, 38, Ohio-born actress singer, died Apr. 9, 1980 in NYC. After her Broadway debut in 1967 in "Hello, Dolly!," she appeared in "Oklahoma!" (Lincoln Center), "The Beggar's Opera," "Johnny Johnson," and "Tricks." For the last three years she had been teaching at SUNY Purchase. No reported survivors.

BERN HOFFMAN, 66, stage, film and tv character actor, died after a long illness on Dec. 15, 1979 in North Hollywood, Ca. On Broadway he had appeared in "The 19th Hole of Europe," "Guys and Dolls," "The Hot Corner," and "Li'l Abner." He was on the tv series "Ironside," "Streets of San Francisco" and "General Hospital." No reported survivors.

JANE HOUSTON, 88, stage and radio actress, died Sept. 27, 1979 in Edna, TX. Among her Broadway credits are "Call the Doctor," "Open House," "Springboard," "A Free Soul," and "Back Here." She played Mrs. Grosvenor in the "Stella Dallas" radio serial, and appeared often with Fred Allen and Jack Benny. No reported survivors.

ARTHUR HUNNICUTT, 69, Arkansas-born character actor on stage, film and tv, died of cancer Sept. 26, 1979 in Woodlawn Hills, Ca. His Broadway appearances include "Love's Old Sweet Song," "The Time of Your Life," "Lower North," "Dark Hammock," "Too Hot for Maneuvers," "Beggars Are Coming to Town," "Apple of His Eye" and "Mr. Peebles and Mr. Hooker." His widow survives.

JULES IRVING, 54, former artistic director of the Lincoln Center Repertory Theater, died July 28, 1979 of a heart attack while vacationing in Reno, NV. He had been an actor and teacher, and with Herbert Blau formed the successful San Francisco Actors Workshop from which they were chosen to be co-artistic directors of the Repertory Theater. After Mr. Blau resigned, he remained as director until his resignation in 1972-73 season. He went to Hollywood where he made tv films. Surviving are his wife, actress Priscilla Pointer, two daughters, Katie and actress Amy, and a son David, a film producer.

PRESTON JONES, 43, New Mexico-born actor and playwright, died Sept. 19, 1979 following surgery for ulcers in Dallas, TX. For several years he had been an actor with the Dallas Theater Center company, and was in rehearsal at the time of his illness. In 1976, his "Texas Trilogy": "Lu Ann Hampton Laverty Oberlander," "The Last Meeting of the Knights of the White Magnolia," and "The Oldest Living Graduate" were presented in rotating repertory on Broadway, but lasted for only 6 previews and 63 performances at the Broadhurst Theatre, artistically, but not commercially successful. However, they have been well received in many regional theatres. In addition to the trilogy, he wrote "A Place on the Magnolia Flats" and "Remember." He is survived by his second wife, and a daughter by his first wife.

JAMES RICHARD JONES, 67, Pennsylvania-born stage, radio and tv actor, died Apr. 3, 1980 in East Orange, NJ. His Broadway appearances include "Brother Rat," "Charley's Aunt," "John Loves Mary," "The Glass Menagerie" and "Tunnel of Love." After WW2 he became a radio and tv actor. No reported survivors.

RICHARD "DICK" KALLMAN, 46, antiques dealer and former stage, film and tv actor, and clothing designer, was found shot to death in his NYC home on Feb. 22, 1980. For his 1951 Broadway debut in "Seventeen," he received a Theatre World Award, and subsequently appeared in "The Fifth Season," "Come Blow Your Horn," "How to Succeed in Business . . .," and "Half a Sixpence." He starred in the 1965 tv series "Hank." No reported survivors.

IDA KAMINSKA, 80, Russian-born stage and film actress, director and producer, died of a heart ailment May 21, 1980 in NYC. For many years she was the outstanding star of Yiddish classical theatre, and for 21 years headed the Jewish State Theatre of Poland, until she left in 1968. She had appeared in NYC in "Mirele Efros," "Mother Courage," "The Trees Die Standing" and "The Investigation." Her greatest recognition outside the Yiddish theatre was for her role in the 1966 Czechoslovak film "The Shop on Main Street." She is survived by her daughter, actress Ruth Turkow Kaminska, and a son, Victor Melman.

KURT KASZNAR, (nee Serwicher), 65, Vienna-born character actor on stage, screen and tv, died of cancer Aug. 6, 1979 in Santa Monica, Ca. He came to the U. S. in 1936 and appeared on Broadway in "The Eternal Road," "The Army Play by Play," "Joy to the World," "Make Way for Lucia," "The 19th Hole of Europe," "Montserrat," "The Happy Time," "Waiting for Godot," "Seventh Heaven," "Look after Lulu," "The Sound of Music," "Barefoot in the Park," and Off Broadway in "Six Characters in Search of an Author" and "The Play's the Thing." He produced and directed "Crazy with the Heat," and wrote "First Cousins." He was divorced from his second wife, actress Leora Dana.

Richard Kallman (1967)

Ida Kaminska (1968)

Kurt Kasznar (1967)

257

LOUIS KRONENBERGER, 75, Cincinnati-born critic, teacher and author, died of Alzheimer's disease on Apr. 30, 1980 in Brookline, Ma. He served as drama critic for *Time* from 1938 to 1961 and for PM from 1940-48. He did an idiomatic adaption of Anouilh's play "Mlle. Colombe" that was performed on Broadway in 1954. Surviving are his widow, a son and a daughter.

JUDSON LAIRE, 76, NYC-born actor on stage film and tv, died July 5, 1979 in Rhinebeck, NY. He abandoned a career as stockbroker and appeared in "Technique," "The Nude in Washington Square," "The Constant Wife," "Stardust," "The Play's the Thing," "First Lady," "Honor Bright," "All That Glitters," "Best Foot Forward," "Mr. Big," "The Patriots," "Doctors Disagree," "Signature," "Candida," "Third Best Sport" and "Advise and Consent." He was Papa in the 1950's tv series "I Remember Mama," and acted in "Young Dr. Malone," "The Nurses" and "The Edge of Night." A sister survives.

LOUIS A. LOTITO, 79, theatrical executive, producer and investor, died Feb. 12, 1980 after a heart attack in his home in Spring Lake, NJ. He started as an usher and retired 50 years later as president of a group of Broadway theatres. He produced "Another Love Story," "Goldilocks," "The Cold Wind and the Warm," "The Visit" and "Much Ado about Nothing." After retiring, he served as president of the Actors Fund of America. He also served as president of the League of NY Theatres. Surviving are his widow, a son and a daughter.

HALE MATTHEWS, 49, Pittsburgh-born Broadway producer, died of a heart attack May 22, 1980 in Key West, Fl. He was associated with the productions "The Niggerlovers," "Collision Course," "The Dozens," "The Love Suicide at Schofield Barracks," "Freedom of the City," "The Mother of Us All," "Gorey Stories," "The Lady from Dubuque" and "Happy New Year." A brother survives.

MARGERY MAUDE, 90, English-born actress, died Aug. 7, 1979 in Cleveland, Oh. Daughter of celebrated actor Cyril Maude, she made her NYC debut with his company in 1913 in "The Second in Command," and "Grumpy," subsequently she appeared in "Lady Windermere's Fan," "Paganini," "The Old Foolishness," "Plan M," "The Two Mrs. Carrolls," "O Mistress Mine," "The High Ground," "First Lady," "The Rivals," "Anne of England," "Escapade" and "My Fair Lady." She is survived by two daughters.

MARY McCARTY, 56, Kansas-born singer-actress on stage, screen and tv, died of a heart attack Apr. 3, 1980 in her home in Westwood, Ca. She was appearing as Nurse Starch on the tv series "Trapper John, M.D." After singing in clubs, she made her Broadway debut in 1948 in "Sleepy Hollow" for which she received a Theatre World Award, and subsequently appeared in "Small Wonder," "Miss Liberty," "Bless You All," "A Rainy Day in Newark," "Follies," "Chicago" and "Anna Christie" for which she received a "Tony." No reported survivors.

LARRY McMILLIAN, 31, Alabama-born actor-dancer-choreographer, died after a lengthy illness on Jan. 24, 1980 in NYC. He appeared on Broadway in the 1975 revival of "Very Good Eddie." He had been a performer and assistant director at the Goodspeed Opera House, East Haddam, Ct., for several productions. He is survived by his parents and three brothers.

JOHN McQUADE, 63, Pittsburgh-born actor-singer on stage, screen and tv, died Sept. 21, 1979 in NYC. A protege of George M. Cohan, he began his career in the 1939 Maurice Evans' "Hamlet," followed by "Richard II," "The Trojan Women," "Henry IV," "Twelfth Night," "Macbeth," "Elizabeth the Queen," "Counsellor-at-Law," "The Petrified Forest," "A Highland Fling," "Arsenic and Old Lace," "Meet a Body," "Ghosts," "The Hostage" and "Calculated Risk." His tv roles were in the "Jethro Adams" and "Charlie Wild" series. No reported survivors.

KAY MEDFORD, 59, nee Maggie O'Regin, comedienne on stage, film and tv, died of cancer Apr. 10, 1980 in her native NYC. After many movies, she made her Broadway debut in 1951 in "Paint Your Wagon," followed by "Lullaby" for which she received a Theatre World Award, "Two's Company," "John Murray Anderson's Almanac," "Black-Eyed Susan," "Maya," "Little Clay Cart," "Almost Crazy," "Wake Up, Darling," "Mr. Wonderful," "A Hole in the Head," "Carousel," "Pal Joey," "A Handful of Fire," "Bye Bye Birdie," "In the Counting House," "The Heroine," "Funny Girl," "Don't Drink the Water," "Where Memories Are Magic." She was a familiar face on tv's "Dean Martin Show," "Barney Miller" and "Starsky and Hutch." A sister survives.

BYRON MITCHELL, age unreported, actor and dance instructor, died Oct. 8, 1979 in NYC. He had appeared in "Quadrille," "Copper and Brass," "The Crystal Heart," "Irma La Duoce" and "Tovarich." He is survived by his parents and two sisters.

ALBERT M. OTTENHEIMER, 75, Washington-born character actor on stage screen, radio and tv, died Jan. 25, 1980 in Cincinnati, Oh. After his 1946 NYC debut in "Affair of Honor," he appeared in "West Side Story," "Deputy," "Yentl," and Off Broadway in "Monday's Heroes," "Tiger," "Mother Riba," "A Christmas Carol," "Juno and the Paycock," "Italian Straw Hat," "The Iceman Cometh," "Call It Virtue," "The Immoralist," "The Cat and the Canary," "The Exhaustion of Our Son's Love," "Deadly Game," "Brother Gorski," "The Kid," "Holy Ghosts," "Yentl the Yeshiva Boy." His widow survives.

S. J. PERELMAN, 75, Brooklyn-born humorist, playwright, screenwriter, and author, died Oct. 17, 1979 in NYC. For Broadway, he wrote or co-wrote or contributed sketches to "The Third Little Show," "Walk a Little Faster," "All Good Americans," "Two Weeks with Pay," "The Night before Christmas," "One Touch of Venus," "Sweet Bye and Bye" and "The Beauty Part." A son and daughter survive.

NANCY POLLOCK, nee Reiben, 77, stage and screen actress, died following a stroke on June 2, 1979 in her native NYC. She had appeared in many stock and regional companies before making her 1950 Broadway debut in "Diamond Lil," followed by "One Bright Day," "In the Summer House," "Middle of the Night," "Period of Adjustment," "Come Blow Your Horn," "In the Counting House," "Have I Got a Girl for You," "Ceremony of Innocence," "A Day in the Death of Joe Egg," "Wrong Way Light Bulb." She had also performed on radio and tv. Surviving are her husband, Herbert Pollock, and a daughter.

Kay Medford (1967)

Albert Ottenheimer

Nancy R. Pollock

EVA PUCK, 86, former star of vaudeville and Broadway musicals, died Oct. 25, 1979 in Granada Hills, Ca. After performing with her brother in vaudeville, she married entertainer Sammy White and they became vaudeville headliners. She became a musical comedy star in "The Greenwich Village Follies of 1923," followed by "Melody Man," "The Girl Friend" that Rodgers and Hart wrote for her, and she created the role of Ellie in "Show Boat." She was active in the 1919 actors strike that was instrumental in the establishment of Actors Equity. No reported survivors.

MARITA REID, 83, Gibraltar-born actress and pioneer of Spanish theatre in NYC, died of apoplexy July 18, 1979 in NYC. She had appeared in "Passion Flower," "Malvaloca," "In the Summer House" and "Come Share My House." She was the widow of bullfighter Jose Tavira. A brother survives.

WILLIAM ROBERTSON, 71, Virginia-born character actor on stage, screen and tv, died of a heart attack March 16, 1980 in NYC. After his 1936 Braodway debut in "Tapestry in Grey," he appeared in "Cup of Trembling," "Liliom," "Our Town," "Caesar and Cleopatra," and Off Broadway in "Uncle Harry," "The Shining Hour," "The Aspern Papers," "Madame Is Served," "Tragedian in spite of Himself," "Kibosh," "Sun-up," "The Last Pad," "Hamlet," "Girls Most Likely to Succeed," "The Petrified Forest," "The Minister's Black Veil," "Santa Anita," "Babylon," "Midsummer Night's Dream," "A Touch of the Poet," "The Zykovs," "Rimers of Eldritch," "The Crucible" and "Lulu." His sister survives.

ELEANOR ROBSON, 100, English-born patron of the arts, and former actress, died in her sleep on Oct. 24, 1979 in her home in NYC. With her actor parents, she moved to the U.S., and at 17 became the ingenue with their company in San Francisco and was an immediate success. She made her NYC debut four years later in "Arizona" and a star was born. She subsequently appeared in "Romeo and Juliet," "Nurse Marjorie," "She Stoops to Conquer," "Merely Mary Ann," "Salomy Jane," "In a Balcony" and "The Dawn of a Tomorrow," her last vehicle before retirement and her marriage to banker-turfman August Belmont. George Bernard Shaw wrote "Major Barbara" for her but a conflicting contract prevented her playing the role. She collaborated with Harriet Ford on the play "In the Next Room" that became a 1923 Broadway success. She worked tirelessly for the opera and organized the Metropolitan Opera Guild, and devoted much time to the Red Cross and other charitable organizations. She was widowed in 1924, and there are no immediate survivors.

RICHARD RODGERS, 77, world renowned composer, died Dec. 30, 1979 in his native NYC. For 55 years he contributed music to 42 Broadway productions, and received two Pulitzer Prizes (for "Oklahoma!" and "South Pacific"), seven "Tony" Awards, the Lawrence Langner Award for a "lifetime of distinguished achievement in the American theater," and a 1946 "Oscar" Award for "It Might as Well Be Spring" from "State Fair." Most of his work was done with lyricists Lorenz Hart (1918–1943) and Oscar Hammerstein 2nd (1942–1960). He wrote over 1500 songs, nearly 100 of them considered popular classics. His first song was composed at 14, his first musical at 17, and he had his first hit show "Garrick Gaities" at 23. Other musicals include "The Girl Friend," "A Connecticut Yankee," "Present Arms," "Heads Up!," "Jumbo," "On Your Toes," "Babes in Arms," "I'd Rather Be Right," "I Married an Angel," "Boys from Syracuse," "Too Many Girls," "Pal Joey," "By Jupiter," "Oklahoma!," "Carousel," "Allegro," "South Pacific," "The King and I," "Me and Juliet," "Pipe Dream," "Flower Drum Song," "The Sound of Music," "No Strings," "Do I Hear a Waltz?," "Two by Two," "Rex," and his last in 1979 "I Remember Mama." He is survived by his widow, Dorothy, and two daughters, Linda, and composer Mary Rodgers.

JANE ROSE, 67, Washington-born character actress on stage, screen and tv, died of cancer June 29, 1979 in her home in Studio City, Ca. She had appeared on the NY stage in "The Women," "Jennie," "The Time of the Cuckoo," "Wooden Dish," "Orpheus Descending," "The Gazebo," "Heartbreak House," "All's Well That Ends Well," "Measure for Measure," "Richard III," "Arms and the Man" and "Enemies." She had been in the tv serials "Somerset," "The Secret Storm," and as the mother-in-law in "Phyllis." For 11 years she taught acting and was director of recreation at the NY Association for the Blind. She leaves no immediate survivors.

LILLIAM ROTH, 69, Boston-born singer and actress, died after a long illness on May 12, 1980 in NYC. After beginning her career at 6 in vaudeville, she became Broadway's youngest star at 8 in "Shavings," subsequently appearing in "Artists and Models," "Padlocks of 1927," "Vanities," "Midnight Frolics," "I Can Get It for You Wholesale," "Funny Girl," "70, Girls, 70." She also appeared on tv and in films, and was a popular night club singer. Her autobiography, "I'll Cry Tomorrow," was made into a 1956 film with Susan Hayward. No immediate survivors.

FAY SAPPINGTON, nee Harriet Richardson, 83, Texas-born character actress on stage and tv, died June 16, 1980 in Englewood, NJ. After her 1950 Broadway debut in "Southern Exposure," she appeared in "The Cellar and the Well," "Glad Tidings," "J.B.," "The Yearling," "Golden Rainbow," "Campbells of Boston," "In Case of Accident" and "Pippin." A son and two daughters survive.

JEAN-PAUL SARTRE, 74, philosopher, playwright and writer, died of edema of the lung Apr. 15, 1980 in his native Paris. His existentialist philosophy influenced two generations throughout the world. His plays include "Les Mouches" (The Flies), "No Exit," "The Respecful Prostitute," "Men without Shadows," "The Red Gloves," "Kean," "The Condemned of Altona" and an adaptation of Euripides' "The Trojan Women." He was awarded, but refused, the Nobel Prize for Literature. Surviving are his almost life-long companion Simone de Beauboir, and an adopted daughter, Arlette el Kaim. After cremation, his ashes were returned to Montparnasse Cemetery.

DANIEL SELTZER, 47, actor and professor of English at Princeton, died of a heart attack on March 1, 1980 in NYC. At the time of his death, he was on leave of absence from teaching and was in rehearsal for Chekhov's "Three Sisters." He had appeared Off and on Broadway in "Knock Knock"for which he received a Theatre World Award, and in "Endgame." He had a role in the film "An Unmarried Woman." He had taught at Harvard for 14 years before becoming director of Princeton's Theatre and Dance Program.

Richard Rodgers

Fay Sappington (1972)

Daniel Seltzer (1980)

HERMAN SHUMLIN, 80, Colorado-born producer director, died of heart failure June 14, 1979 in NYC. His productions include "Celebrity," "Command Performance," "Tonight at 12," "Wine of Choice," "Button, Button, Button," "The Last Mile," "Grand Hotel," "Clear All Wires," "Bride of Torozko," "The Children's Hour," "Sweet Mystery of Life," "Days to Come," "The Merchant of Yonkers," "The Little Foxes," "The Male Animal," "The Corn Is Green," "Watch on the Rhine," "Great Big Doorstep," "The Searching Wind," "The Visitor," "Kiss Them for me," "The Biggest Thief in Town," "Daphne Laureola," "The High Ground," "Lace on Her Petticoat," "To Dorothy, a Son," "Gertie," "Candida," "The Gambler," "Regina" (CC), "Wedding Breakfast," "Inherit the Wind," "Tall Story," "Little Moon of Alban," "Dear Me, the Sky Is Falling," "Bicycle Ride to Nevada," "The Deputy," "Spofford" which he also wrote, "Soldiers" and "Transfers." His third wife survives.

CORNELIA OTIS SKINNER, 78, Chicago-born actress, monologist playwright and author, died of a cerebral hemorrhage July 9, 1979 in her NYC home. She made her first professional appearance in 1921 with her celebrated father, Otis Skinner, in "Blood and Sand." Later she appeared in "Will Shakespeare," "Tweedles," "The Wild Westcotts," "In His Arms," "White Collars," "Love for Love," "Candida," "Theatre," "The Searching Wind," "Lady Windermere's Fan," "Major Barbara," "Fun and Magic," "The Pleasure of His Company," and her one-woman presentations "The Wives of Henry VIII," "The Empress Eugenie," "The Loves of Charles II," "Mansion on the Hudson," "Edna, His Wife," and "Paris '90." She is survived by a son, Otis Skinner Blodget, and two stepchildren.

ARNOLD SOBOLOFF, 48, NYC-born actor-singer, died Oct. 28, 1979 of a heart attack backstage during a performance of "Peter Pan" in which he was appearing at the Lunt-Fontanne Theatre. He had been seen previously in "Mandingo," "The Egg," "Beauty Part," "One Flew Over the Cuckoo's Nest," "Anyone Can Whistle," "Bravo Giovanni," "Sweet Charity," "Mike Downstairs," "Cyrano," "The Act," "The Inspector General," and Off Broadway in "Threepenny Opera," "Career," "Brothers Karamazov," "Vincent," "Bananas," "Papp," "Camino Real," "Are You Now . . .," "Music! Music!" and "The Sea." His widow survives.

GUY SPAULL, 76, Baltimore-born stage and tv actor, died Jan. 6, 1980 in Englewood, NJ. After his 1938 Broadway debut in "Good Hunting," he appeared in 40 productions, including "The Importance of Being Earnest," "Family Portrait," "Leave Her to Heaven," "Innocent Voyage," "Around the World," "Duchess of Malfi," "The Vigil," "Leading Lady," "Lost in the Stars," "Billy Budd," "Music in the Air," "Getting Married," "First Lady," "Witness for the Prosecution," "The Apple Cart," "The First Gentleman," "Under Milk Wood," "The Entertainer," "The Lion in Love," and "Smith." Surviving are his widow, actress Joan Croydon, and a son, Malcolm.

GEORGE TOBIAS, 78, NYC-born character actor on stage, film and tv, died of cancer Feb. 27, 1980 in Hollywooed, Ca. After his 1920 debut in "The Mob," he appeared in "The Fool," "What Price Glory?," "Road to Rome," "The Gray Fox," "S. S. Glencairn," "Fiesta," "Elizabeth the Queen," "Sailors of Cattaro," "Hell Freezes Over," "Star Spangled," "You Can't Take It with You," "Good Hunting," "Stalag 17" and "Silk Stockings." He was probably best known for Abner Kravitz on the tv series "Betwiched." A brother survives.

IVAN TRIESAULT, 80, Estonia-born tv, stage and film character actor and former ballet dancer, died of heart failure Jan. 3, 1980 in Los Angeles, Ca. In NYC he had appeared in "The Jeweled Tree," "Marathon," "Divine Drudge," "Star Spangled," "Hamlet," Foreigners," "The Burning Deck" and "The Walrus and the Carpenter." He is survived by his widow and a son.

NINA VANCE, nee Nina Whittington, 65, founder and producing director of Houston's Alley Theatre, died of cancer Feb. 18, 1980 in Houston, Tx. Her original 87-seat theatre established in 1947 in an alley developed into one of the nation's foremost professional resident repertory theatres, providing space, not only for classical works, but also for works by new playwrights. She was divorced from Houston lawyer Milton Vance.

VIVIAN VANCE, nee Jones, 66, Kansas-born actress on stage and tv, died of cancer Aug. 17, 1979 in her home in Belvedere, Ca. After singing in nightclubs, she made her Broadway debut in 1934 in "Anything Goes," followed by "Red, Hot and Blue!," "Hooray for What!," "Skylark," "Out from Under," "Let's Face It," "It Takes Two," "The Cradle Will Rock" and "My Daughter, Your Son." She was best known as Ethel Mertz in the "I Love Lucy" tv series. Surviving is her husband, a publishing executive, John Dodds, a brother and four sisters.

RICHARD WARD, 64, Philadelphia-born stage and tv actor, died of a heart ailment July 1 1979 in his home in Coxsackie, NY. After his Broadway debut in "St. Louis Woman," he had appeared in "Jeb," "Shuffling Along," "Our Lan'," "Blues for Mr. Charlie," and Off-Broadway in "Anna Lucasta," "Nat Turner," "Christopher Columbus Brown," "The Cellar," "Land Beyond the River," "Midnight Caller," "My Heart's in the Highlands," "Ballad of Jazz Street," "The Man Who Never Died," "Walk in Darkness," "Sweet Enemy," "Banners of Steel," "Firebugs," and "Penance." He had roles in several tv series, including Granpa Evans on "Good Times." He is survived by his widow and step-son.

ETHEL WILSON, 88, Baltimore-born stage and radio actress, died April 19, 1980 in St. Petersburg, FL. After her stage debut in 1914, she subsequently appeared in "Tyranny of Love," "Magnolia," "Gypsy Jim," "Spooks," "The Monkey Talks," "Just Life," "Her First Affair," "Spring Song," "So This Is Paris," "Hello Paris," "Rain," "Meet the Prince," "The Bishop Misbehaves," "Life's Too Short," "First Lady," "The Happiest Days," "The Doughgirls," "You Can't Take It with You" and "My Sister Eileen." On radio she was heard on "Henry Aldrich," "Backstage Wife," "Our Gal Sunday," "Ma Perkins" and "The Goldbergs." A sister survives.

ANATOL WINOGRADOFF, 89, Russian-born character actor on stage, screen and tv, died Apr. 27, 1980 in Canoga Park, Ca. He began his career at 16 before coming to the U.S. In 1935 he made his Broadway debut in "Winterset," subsequently appearing in "Othello," "Major Noah," "Riverside Drive," "Revolt," "Josephus," "They Knew What They Wanted," "The Water Carrier," "Day of Judgment," "A Family Affair," "Shylock and His Daughter," "Voice of Israel," "Hershel, the Jester," "The Number," "The Grass Is Always Greener" and "Build with One Hand." His last tv appearance was in "The Trial of Julius and Ethel Rosenberg." No reported survivors.

Cornelia Otis Skinner

Guy Spaull (1973)

Richard Ward (1976)

INDEX

262

265